Research on Spanish in the United States

Linguistic Issues and Challenges

edited by Ana Roca

Cascadilla Press Somerville 2000

ISBN 1-57473-013-4 paperback
ISBN 1-57473-113-0 library binding

The cover drawing of the Mission of San Jose is from
Spanish Institutions of the Southwest, by Frank W. Blackmar,
published 1891 in Baltimore by The Johns Hopkins Press.

Library of Congress Cataloging-in-Publication Data

Research on Spanish in the United States : linguistic issues and
challenges / edited by Ana Roca.
p. cm.
English and Spanish
Includes bibliographical references and index.
ISBN 1-57473-113-0 (lib. bdg.) -- ISBN 1-57473-013-4 (pbk.)
1. Spanish language--United States. 2. Languages in contact--United
States. I. Roca, Ana.
PC4826 .A36 2000
460'.973--dc21

00-065741
CIP

To order a copy of this book or to request a current catalog, contact:

Cascadilla Press
P.O. Box 440355
Somerville, MA 02144, USA

phone: 1-617-776-2370
fax: 1-617-776-2271
e-mail: sales@cascadilla.com
http://www.cascadilla.com

Contents

4. Borrowings

5. Codeswitching, Narratives, and Discourse

6. Sociolinguistics and Pragmatics

Acknowledgments

Most of the papers in this volume were selected from among those presented at the 17th National Conference on Spanish in the United States. I would like to take this opportunity to thank all of the participants who helped make that conference a success. My warmest gratitude and thanks go to Dr. Eduardo Gamarra, Director of the Latin American and Caribbean Center (LACC) at Florida International University, for his continuous support of faculty initiatives and efforts in the areas of research and professional development. Without the steady support from LACC and from colleagues like Douglas Kincaid, Lidia Tuttle, and the rest of its competent and courteous staff, the conference would not have been possible. My gratitude is also warmly extended to my department chairperson, Dr. Isabel Castellanos, who was extremely supportive and enthusiastic from the moment I asked for authorization to organize a national conference.

I would like to offer a word of very special thanks to the two keynote speakers, Drs. Guadalupe Valdés and John M. Lipski. Their work in the area of Spanish–English bilingualism and Spanish in the United States has been pioneering, consistent, and continuous, making its mark in the research literature and in the profession at large. An understanding of research and sociolinguistic issues in Spanish in the United States would be incomplete without their incisive contributions. I am most grateful for their participation in the conference and for their important chapters in this book.

Last but not least, I would like to express my sincerest gratitude and appreciation to each of the contributing authors to this volume and a most special thanks to Michael Bernstein at Cascadilla Press, with whom it has been both a professional and personal pleasure to interact throughout the publication process.

I also wish to warmly acknowledge the continuous support and encouragement of my partner, Helena, and my colleagues and friends.

Introduction

Ana Roca
Florida International University

This collection brings together thoughtful academic essays on a variety of linguistic topics related to the analysis of the Spanish language and its dynamic societal role in contact with English in the United States. The volume also aims to raise awareness of linguistic contact phenomena, as well as socio-political and ideological research issues underlying the complexities of Spanish in the United States. The volume should both advance our understanding and stimulate further in-depth discussion and research about theoretical and practical issues concerning languages in contact, public and educational policy, the nature of different types of bilingualism, and language maintenance, change, and loss.

Most of the contributions here are revised and developed papers selected from those that were originally presented at the 17th National Conference on Spanish in the United States. The conference was held at the Biltmore Hotel in Coral Gables, Miami–Dade County, in March 1999, and was sponsored by the Latin American and Caribbean Center and the Department of Modern Languages at Florida International University. One of the objectives of this conference has always been to allow scholars to present their original research in a forum that stimulates discussion among experts in the field. The conference brought together a healthy mix of numerous established scholars as well as newer Ph.D.'s and graduate students from around the nation.

Papers were selected for this volume through a refereed process involving myself as editor, the general editor and publisher, and his designated anonymous reviewers in the field. Several chapters were also specially commissioned for this volume to round out coverage of important topics. Scholars in linguistics and related areas who are concerned with research issues related to Spanish in the United States will find valuable and compelling insights here. This collection contributes to our understanding of the complexities of the Spanish language, spoken by over 400 million people in the world today.

1. Español y "Spanglish" por todas partes: The Hispanic population in the United States is here to stay

One of the greatest challenges facing the United States in the 21st century is to deal with the new "in your face" and "in your ear" dimensions of the demographic changes that are happening at a lightning pace. Although the Spanish language and its speakers have long played a key role in our history, it is only as we approached the end of the 20th century that the country finally appeared to wake up and take notice of the fact that, not just south of the border, but here in the United States, we have one of the largest Spanish-speaking populations in the hemisphere, one that is growing at a pace nearly five times faster than the general population. Denial of the tremendous growth and impact of the U.S. Hispanic population in the last thirty years is neither healthy nor wise.

Immigration from Latin America and Spain has contributed significantly to the continued growth and variety of the U.S. Hispanic population. Today the Hispanic presence seems to be almost everywhere we look, even in areas where one would least expect it, such as small cities and towns in North Carolina, Minnesota, or Iowa. It is no longer only in New York, California, Texas, and South Florida where we see signage in Spanish, community papers in Spanish, flourishing Hispanic food markets, and where we hear Spanish more and more in public and in the media. Enclaves of Spanish speakers are developing in different regions. We see how public relations and marketing firms have taken giant steps forward in Spanish- and English-language advertising geared to the Latino market, which now represents well over $350 billion in purchasing power. Hispanics form the largest U.S. linguistic minority group, and this group is literally changing the face of America today. It is also this ethnic group which is making its cultural and linguistic presence most felt because of its growing economic power and its political impact, particularly notable in the 2000 presidential campaigns.

In the area of language education, the United States is starting to pay more attention to the needs of its heritage language learners and to Spanish speakers in particular (AATSP 2000). While the Spanish teaching profession at large and the foreign language teaching profession in general had not been supportive of heritage language learners in the past, now the profession is starting to make scattered progress via grants and national projects through language associations and organizations like the American Association of Teachers of Spanish and Portuguese, the National Foreign Language Center, and the American Council on the Teaching of Foreign Languages. One national project that has started to make a difference in the area of education and teacher training is the Funds for the Improvement of Secondary Education project of the American Council for the Teaching of Foreign Languages (ACTFL), Hunter College, and Hunter High School. In the summer of 2000 they completed a three-year teacher training project involving a selected group of teachers of Spanish and of Haitian Creole from New York City's public secondary schools. Their goal was to develop a model teacher training program in heritage language instruction. Through this project, Hunter College aims to be the first college to require such formal training as part of a graduation requirement for language teacher candidates; the next step, which we may be witnessing in the coming years, will be the struggle to implement these requirements for state teacher certification too. Why would we want Spanish teachers in particular to take such courses? Because in schools and colleges throughout the nation, we are facing more and more students who are home speakers of Spanish and wish to take Spanish classes in order to maintain and develop their Spanish language abilities and expand their knowledge about their own Hispanic heritage.

According to the 1990 census, the total population of the United States was 248,709,873. Out of this total, 22,354,059 (or 9%) were classified as being of Hispanic origin – figures which do not include undocumented Hispanics. Based on the census, 61% of Hispanics in the United States are of Mexican origin, 12% are from Puerto Rico, 11% from Central and South America, about 5% from Cuba, and 11% from elsewhere. California, New York, Texas, and Florida have the greatest number of Hispanics. Ten years later, in 2000, the Hispanic population has risen substantially. It is calculated that there are currently well over 32 million Hispanics in the United States. Projections based on the updates of the census data suggest that Hispanics may surpass African-Americans as the largest ethnic minority in the United States by the year 2005 or sooner, and will be approximately 50 million strong before 2050. The constant flow of immigrants arriving every year from Latin America and Spain is not likely to stop, and the population trends for both Latin American and the United States point toward major increases in population. If the Latin American population triples periodically as predicted, more immigrants, legally or illegally, will continue to make the move to *el Norte* in search of a better and more stable life.

Although many U.S. Latinos have lost some or all of their fluency in Spanish, the language remains a strong and unifying factor among the population. According to Carrasquillo (1991: 60), "the principle characteristic that is widely shared by Hispanics is the Spanish language: it is the single most unifying element of Hispanics in the United States. The retention of Spanish in varying degrees of proficiency or even a form of 'Spanglish' has become one of the most obvious and palpable signs of retained Hispanic cultural characteristics." Contrary to popular stereotypes, however, most Latinos who speak Spanish – 74%, according to the 1990 census – also report that they speak English "well" or "very well."

2. Flourishing of the field: Research on Spanish in the U.S.

The topic of Spanish in the United States is not a new area of professional discussion, research, or public debate. Early in the 20th century, Aurelio Espinosa was already conducting his pioneering studies in dialectology in New Mexico (Espinosa 1909). What is new is the rapid growth and maturing of this field of research within Spanish linguistics in the last thirty years. (Please see the references at the end of this introduction.) It parallels the growth of the U.S. Hispanic population itself and the increasing empowerment of sectors of the Latino population. Interested academics or students of linguistics only have to conduct a simple electronic search to find that we can now take advantage of a large body of scholarly works on Spanish in the United States and related areas in academic journals in linguistics, sociology, cognitive science, psychology, bilingual education, and foreign language education; and in edited book collections, conference proceedings, and authored monographs and books. (For example, see Amastae and Elías-Olivares 1982, Elías-Olivares 1983, Sánchez 1983, Elías-Olivares et al. 1985, Wherritt and García 1989, Bergen 1990, Coulmas 1990, Roca and Lipski 1993, and more.)

Much more has been written about the Spanish of Mexican-American and Puerto Rican communities than the Spanish of Cuban-Americans and Central Americans in the U.S. However, in recent years, we have seen a few sporadic publications and dissertations on these more recent immigrants (cf. Resnick 1988, Castellanos 1990, Roca 1991, Varela 1992, and Lynch 2000 on Cuban Americans, and Lipski 2000 on Central Americans).

While scholarly articles deal with a variety of themes connected to the Spanish language in the United States and Hispanics as a diverse group, newspapers and popular magazines offer news and human interest stories as well as special features on the need for bilingualism for purposes of trade and commerce, codeswitching, bilingual literature, award-winning Latin American literature in translation, English-Only vs. English Plus debates, immigration and assimilation stories, and issues of interpreting and translation in public life, such as in courts and hospitals. Media coverage has explored issues of bilingual competencies, "Spanglish," the Spanish language as it relates to cultural and demographic factors, ethnicity, mother-tongue loss and maintenance, home language literacy development, tolerance and discrimination questions related to attitudes, language policies, and national questions pertaining to language planning and group and individual identity, and issues in bilingual acquisition. All of these and more are research topics treated or touched upon in this book.

The chapters in this book reflect current research trends. Organizing a large collection of papers such as this can be difficult. Rather than following a geographical orientation, we have divided the papers into eight parts consisting of different linguistic themes or research topics. Readers should keep in mind that some papers could have easily fit into other sections as well.

Part 1, **U.S. Spanish: An Overview of the Issues**, consists of John Lipski's valuable and comprehensive essay "Back to Zero or Ahead to 2001? Issues and Challenges in U.S. Spanish Research." This chapter provides a clear overview and historical analysis of linguistic research on U.S. Spanish.

Part 2, **Bilingualism and Interpreting**, contains three very different papers. Guadalupe Valdés and her co-authors will open many eyes concerning the exceptional abilities of young interpreters from immigrant communities. This chapter is followed by a paper on interpreting issues with adults and the court system. Virginia Benmaman, who teaches court interpreting, brings to the forefront compelling and disturbing questions regarding the lack of equal access in terms of what is recorded, in what language, and what the defendant needs to have available in the record for a fair case. To complete this section, Erik Camayd-Freixas categorizes the types of false cognates that court interpreters must be aware of.

Part 3, **Historical Perspectives**, provides readers with three chapters focusing on the development of Spanish in California, the Southwest, and New Mexico in particular. Rebeca Acevedo offers a detailed historical account of verb usage in California Spanish. Ysaura Bernal-Enríquez examines socio-historical factors in the loss of Spanish in the Southwest while looking at the implications of its revitalization. Garland Bills, well known for his work on mapping the use of Spanish in New Mexico and parts of Colorado and for his many publications on Spanish in the Southwest, looks at Nahuatlisms in New Mexican Spanish.

Part 4 deals with the topic of **Borrowings** through very different perspectives. J. Halvor Clegg analyzes morphological adaptations of Anglicisms into Spanish in the Southwest, while Robert N. Smead asks whether phrasal calques in Chicano Spanish are linguistic or cultural in nature. Beatriz Varela, who just a few years ago wrote a full-length book on Cuban-American Spanish (Varela 1994), provides a brief summary and description of selected borrowings in the Cuban-American speech community. The final paper of the section, by Mónica Cantero, discusses morphopragmatics and the types of adaptations made when words enter Spanish.

Part 5, **Codeswitching, Narratives, and Discourse**, brings together five research papers on a subject not often well understood by the public at large. Almeida Jacqueline Toribio examines Spanish–English codeswitching in narratives of fairy tales. Florencia Riegelhaupt looks at codeswitching in the classroom, while Cecilia Montes-Alcalá analyzes attitudes toward both oral and written codeswitching among bilingual youths. Liliana Paredes and Vicky Nova-Dancausse deal with how bilingual children acquire and use the past tense in narratives, and Barbara I. Ávila-Shah writes about discourse connectedness in the speech of Puerto Rican and Cuban Spanish speakers.

Part 6, **Sociolinguistics and Pragmatics**, contains six chapters. Little has been written previously about the language situation and issues of identity in the case of Dominicans in the U.S.; Almeida Jacqueline Toribio examines just this topic of language and self-definition. Andrew Lynch, a recent Ph.D. from the University of Minnesota, presents a study based on his dissertation work looking at Spanish use and language maintenance among the Cuban-American population in Miami. Arnulfo Ramírez, author of a 1992 book in Spanish titled *El español de los Estados Unidos*, offers a look at attitudes toward Spanish among youths from various Hispanic groups. Cecilia Colombi, known for her work in the area of discourse, writing, and theory and practice in teaching Spanish as a heritage language, offers an outstanding contribution to the field of literacy with her chapter about Spanish academic language development among native speakers of Spanish in the U.S. The last two papers in the section explore issues of forms of address and politeness. Diane Ringer Uber looks at when *tú* and *usted* are used in different business situations in Puerto Rico. Silvia Arellano examines strategies for politeness in requests among Spanish speakers in California.

Part 7 encompasses essays on **Phonology, Morphology, and Syntax**. Robert M. Hammond's work deals with an aspect of phonology in U.S. Spanish: the multiple vibrant liquid. MaryEllen Garcia and Michael Tallon's co-authored paper on the use of *estar* in Mexican-American Spanish looks into questions of both phonological and morphological variability. Francisco Zabaleta analyzes morphosyntactic aspects of the Spanish spoken as a mother tongue among university students from California.

Part 8, **Language Ideologies: Attitudes, Planning, and Policy Issues**, closes out the volume. The section opens with Susana Rivera-Mills' interesting examination of intraethnic attitudes among Hispanics in Northern California. Luis A. Ortiz-López's chapter provides a historical overview of language politics surrounding Spanish in Puerto Rico. Thomas D. Boswell, a social geographer who has been interested in language issues for many years, offers a cogent analysis of the recent demographic changes happening in Florida and their significance for educational policy. Finally, Stephen Krashen, well known for his many contributions in theoretical and applied linguistics as well as for his commitment to and activism in the areas of bilingualism and bilingual education, provides an incisive invited essay on bilingual education in the U.S. and how it impacts both the acquisition of English and the retention of Spanish.

3. Concluding remarks

An important stimulus for this book has been my desire to help better inform scholars and students interested in Spanish in the United States. The papers in this book shed light on current research as well as on the directions which future research ought to take. Two directions which should be explored in the coming years are more substantial linkages between Spanish linguistics and other disciplines (such as psychology, sociology, politics, economics, education, business, public relations and marketing, health, translation and interpretation, international studies, and Latin American studies) and language issues in more spheres of public life (such as telecommunications and the Internet, international commerce, Spanish media, popular culture, entertainment, the legal world, and more). In our times, we have seen the deportation of illegal immigrants, the rise and fall of bilingual education funding, the language rights and anti-immigrant backlash, and red-hot public debates on language politics, the merits of bilingual education and foreign language study, and the English Only movement, all while falling in love with new Latino Pop Culture icons like Ricky Martin and his *vida loca*, taco-touting chihuahuas, and more established figures such as Gloria Estefan and Carlos Santana. To study Spanish in the United States is also to study culture, language contact, and bilingualism. In order to do justice to this endeavor, we need to look at Spanish in the U.S. from multiple and interdisciplinary perspectives. We must not forget to place our studies in historical perspective and to address issues of empowerment, societal attitudes, politics, economics, literacy, and education. We must bear in mind that a purely linguistic perspective in isolation from other fields can only offer a partial view of Spanish in the United States.

References

Amastae, John and Lucía Elías-Olivares, eds. 1982. *Spanish in the United States: Sociolinguistic aspects*. Cambridge: Cambridge University Press.

American Association of Teachers of Spanish and Portuguese (AATSP). 2000. *Spanish for native speakers*. AATSP National Committee on Spanish for Native Speakers. Professional Development Series Handbook for Teachers K–16. Vol. I. Fort Worth: Harcourt College.

Azevedo, Milton. 1992. El español en los Estados Unidos. In *Introducción a la lingüística española*, 371–398. Englewood Cliffs, NJ: Prentice Hall.

Bergen, John, ed. 1990. *Spanish in the United States: Sociolinguistic issues*. Washington, D.C.: Georgetown University Press.

Carrasquillo, Angela. 1991. *Hispanic children and youth in the United States: A resource guide*. New York: Garland Publishing.

Castellanos, Isabel. 1990. The use of English and Spanish among Cubans in Miami. *Cuban Studies* 20: 49–63.

Coulmas, Florian, ed. 1990. Spanish in the USA: New quandaries and prospects. *International Journal of the Sociology of Language* 84.

Crawford, James. 1993. *Hold your tongue: Bilingualism and the politics of 'English Only.'* Reading, MA: Addison-Wesley.

Del Valle, Manuel. 1990. Developing a national-based origin discrimination modality. *Journal of Hispanic Policy* 1989–1990: 54–56.

Elías-Olivares, Lucía, ed. 1983. *Spanish in the U.S. setting: Beyond the Southwest.* Rosslyn, VA: National Clearinghouse for Bilingual Education.

Elías-Olivares, Lucía, Elizabeth Leone, René Cisneros, and John Gutiérrez, eds. 1985. *Spanish language use and public life in the USA*. The Hague: Mouton.

Espinosa, Aurelio. 1909. Studies in New Mexico Spanish, Part 1: Phonology. *Bulletin of the University of New Mexico* 1: 47–162. Translated and printed as "Estudios sobre el español de Nuevo Méjico" in *Biblioteca de Dialectología Hispanoamericana* 1 (1930): 19–313.

García, Ofelia and Ricardo Otheguy. 1988. The language situation of Cuban Americans. In *Language diversity: Problem or resource?*, ed. Sandra McKay and Sau-ling Cynthia Wong, 166–192. Cambridge and New York: Newbury House.

Hernández-Chávez, Eduardo. 1993. Native language loss and its implications for the revitalization of Spanish in Chicano communities. In *Language and culture in learning: Teaching Spanish to native speakers of Spanish*, ed. Barbara J. Merino, Henry T. Trueba, and Fabián A. Samaniego, 58–74. London: The Falmer Press.

Klee, Carol and Luis Ramos-García, eds. *Sociolinguistics of the Spanish-speaking world: Iberia, Latin America, United States*. Tempe: Bilingual Press/Editorial Bilingüe.

Lipski, John. 1989. Salvadorans in the United States: Patterns of sociolinguistic integration. *National Journal of Sociology* 3.1: 97–119.

Lipski, John. 2000. The linguistic situation of Central Americans. In *New immigrants in the United States*, ed. Sandra McKay and Sau-ling Cynthia Wong, 189–214. Cambridge: Cambridge University Press.

Lope Blanch, Juan. 1990. El español hablado en el suroeste de los Estados Unidos. Mexico: Universidad Nacional Autónoma de México.

Lynch, Andrew. 1999. The subjunctive in Miami Cuban Spanish: Bilingualism, contact, and language variability. Ph.D. dissertation, University of Minnesota, Minneapolis.

McKay, Sandra and Sau-ling Cynthia Wong, eds. 2000. *New immigrants in the United States*. Cambridge: Cambridge University Press.

Otheguy, Ricardo, Ofelia García, and Ana Roca. 2000. In *New immigrants in the United States*, ed. Sandra McKay and Sau-ling Cynthia Wong, 165–188. Cambridge: Cambridge University Press.

Ramírez, Arnulfo. 1992. *El español de los Estados Unidos: El lenguaje de los hispanos*. Madrid: MAPFRE.

Resnick, Melvyn. 1988. Beyond the ethnic community: Spanish language roles and maintenance in Miami. *International Journal of the Sociology of Language* 69: 89–104.

Roca, Ana. 1991. Language maintenance and language shift in the Cuban American community of Miami: The 1990s and beyond. In *Language planning: Focusschrift in honor of Joshua A. Fishman*, ed. David F. Marshall, 245–257. Amsterdam: John Benjamins.

Roca, Ana. 1999. Foreign language policy and planning in higher education: The case of the State of Florida. In *Sociopolitical perspectives on language policy in the USA*, ed. Thom Huebner and Kathryn A. Davis, 297–319. Amsterdam: John Benjamins.

Roca, Ana and John B. Jensen, eds. 1996. *Spanish in contact: Issues in bilingualism*. Somerville, MA: Cascadilla Press.

Roca, Ana and John Lipski, eds. 1993. *Spanish in the United States: Linguistic contact and diversity*. Berlin: Mouton de Gruyter.

Sánchez, Rosaura. 1983. *Chicano discourse: Socio-historic perspectives*. Rowley, MA: Newbury House.

Silva-Corvalán, Carmen. 1994. *Language contact and change: Spanish in Los Angeles*. Oxford: Clarendon Press.

Silva-Corvalán, Carmen, ed. 1995. *Spanish in four continents: Studies in language contact and bilingualism*. Washington, DC: Georgetown University Press.

Varela, Beatriz. 1992. *El español cubano-americano*. New York: Senda Nueva de Ediciones.

Veltman, Calvin. 1988. *The future of the Spanish language in the United States*. New York and Washington, D.C.: Hispanic Policy Development Project.

Wherritt, Irene and Ofelia García, eds. 1989. U.S. Spanish: The language of the Latinos. *International Journal of the Sociology of Language* 79.

Zentella, Ana Celia. 1997. *Growing up bilingual: Puerto Rican children in New York*. Malden, MA: Blackwell.

Back to Zero or Ahead to 2001? Issues and Challenges in U.S. Spanish Research

John M. Lipski
The Pennsylvania State University

1. Introduction

I got the idea for this paper while running a little computer diagnostic program to determine compatibility with the year 2000. The program set the computers' clocks ahead to the final seconds of 1999 and I watched as the new millennium approached. At the (virtual) stroke of midnight, two of my three computers rolled over to the year 2000 and the program happily announced that they were 'Y2K compatible.' On the third computer a buzzer sounded and the date was suddenly 1900. My computer was, the program warned me, not Y2K compliant, and until I manually reset the clock back to reality my word processors would not acknowledge the hundreds of files – nearly all of my research over the past 15 years – which had been written in the 'future.' As flashes of the 'sciences' of generations past – astrology, alchemy, phrenology, phologisten, spiritism, the luminiferous ether, and spontaneous generation – flitted across my mind, I wondered if it would ever be possible to set back so much scholarship so easily. If I were Stephen King I would have written a story about an unremarkable individual suddenly awakening to a bizarre return to beginnings, and if I had been Gene Roddenberry I would have had Commander Data unexpectedly stumble into himself 100 years in the past, embodying one of the temporal paradoxes that so delight *Star Trek* fans. Instead, I wrote this paper.

Any possible claim I might have to a special perspective on the situation of Spanish in the United States results from my linguistic studies, that is, from sticking my nose and most importantly my ears into the immense whirlwind of voices and variations created by millions of people from all parts of the world who somehow manage to speak the same language. The following remarks attempt to trace the parallel evolution of scholarship on U.S. Spanish and the social and political realities of Hispanophone populations in the United States.

 Research on Spanish in the U.S., ed. Ana Roca, 1–41. Somerville, MA: Cascadilla Press.

Major research milestones are paired off with the events and attitudes that have shaped the usage of Spanish in this country.

The selection is personal and representative, rather than canonical and exhaustive; instead of simply enumerating the hundreds of relevant studies (which, after all, appear in the many valuable research bibliographies that have appeared over the years), I have chosen to dwell on certain vignettes in time and space that best exemplify the embedding of research on Spanish in the United States within the sociocultural milieu of the times. Given the exponential growth of research on U.S. Spanish, a treatment of the earliest years yields an almost complete list of the major players, while a summary of the last two decade's writings can at best hit the high spots of major anthologies, monographs, and events. There is no slight intended to those whose work is not explicitly mentioned; all antecedent scholarship has helped us arrive at the event we are celebrating today, but my cross-sectional slices inevitably force choices. In the spirit of the computer-driven demon that inspired this paper, I roughly follow a time line, with enough sidestepping and backtracking to ensure that no one will mistake the results for a computer-generated data scan.

2. U.S. Spanish: The early 20th century

Writings on the Spanish language in the United States appeared sporadically in the late 19th century in the form of newspaper columns and comments in popular magazines (e.g. Bourke 1896), but linguistic scholarship on U.S. Spanish as it is known in academe is a 20th century phenomenon. In the early decades of the 20th century, Spanish in the United States – then described only for the Southwest – was not treated as an immigrant language, a minority language, a bilingual dancing partner, or a language in transition. It was simply a variety of Spanish coincidentally found within the United States and spilling across its borders, like Italian in Switzerland, Albanian in Serbia, German in Hungary, or Haitian Creole in the Dominican Republic.

In 1906 E.C. Hills published an extensive article on "New Mexican Spanish" in the new periodical *PMLA*, a journal which then as now includes studies of both the English-speaking 'self' and the xenoglossic 'other.' Following this well-written but little-cited beginning, the most complete linguistic descriptions of a U.S. variety of Spanish come in the pioneering studies of Aurelio Espinosa (1909, 1911, 1911–12, 1914–15, 1925, 1946, 1975). Espinosa did most of his research before New Mexico became a state. As a territory, New Mexico was unknown to most Americans – and even today some people in other regions of the country believe that New Mexico is a foreign nation. New Mexico was also unabashedly Spanish-speaking.

In 1909 the Panama Canal was under construction, the U.S. had recently pulled out of Cuba and was still trying to determine what to do with its new colonies of Puerto Rico and the Philippines, and *National Geographic* published an article on settling the 'arid west,' which included forbidding scenes from

New Mexico and featured a first glimpse of the all-but-unknown Colorado desert. In the same year, Espinosa's first scholarship, derived from his doctoral dissertation completed the same year, was published in the inaugural issue of the *Bulletin of the University of New Mexico* (1909). The University itself was in its infancy, having been founded by the newly arrived Anglo-American settlers.

Two years later (1911), in the midst of the Mexican Revolution and the year before the U.S. invasion of Nicaragua, Espinosa published a popularizing description of New Mexico / Southern Colorado Spanish in Santa Fe. Significantly, these seminal studies were written in English and directed at a non-Spanish-speaking readership; the scholarship is nonetheless first-rate. At no point is Spanish referred to as anything but the natural and inevitable language of New Mexico. Astoundingly, in the year New Mexico became a state, University of New Mexico president Edward Gray (1912) published an article in the *University of New Mexico Bulletin* entitled "The Spanish language in New Mexico: A national resource," assuming a stance that moved beyond academic curiosity-seeking and liberal posturing. Few others shared his positive view of Spanish; an article in another New Mexico journal just a few years later (Morrill 1918) entitled "The Spanish language problem in New Mexico" exemplified the more common attitude. This was the year after Puerto Ricans were granted U.S. citizenship, after having lived in political limbo for nearly twenty years. It was three years after the 'new' Ku Klux Klan was formed, adding antagonism towards Jews, Catholics, and immigrants to their long-standing hatred of blacks. During the same years, I.W.W. 'Wobblie' miners – many of whom were foreign-born – were massacred by mobs in Colorado, Montana, and Washington. There was also considerable persecution of Germans and German culture during World War I. A long, bleak period of intolerance had arrived.

3. Linguistic scholarship in the 1920s

By the 1920s, President Warren Harding called for a "return to normalcy," but the definition of 'normal' varied widely. The United States had fully digested the horrors of the Great War and had moved into a period of isolationism which greatly impeded the teaching of 'foreign' languages – including the home languages of substantial portions of the U.S. population – in schools and universities. In 1920 the United States Congress defeated the last attempt to join the League of Nations, guaranteeing that the U.S. would not be part of any major world organization for the next quarter century. Despite this isolationism, the U.S. maintained occupying armies in Haiti, the Dominican Republic, and Nicaragua. Throughout the Southwest, Mexican-American newspaper columnists such as 'Jorge Ulica' (Julio Arce) and 'Kaskabel' (Benjamín Padilla) delighted their readers, and a (recently rediscovered) early Chicano novel was published: Daniel Venegas' *Las aventuras de Don Chipote o cuando los pericos maman* (1928).

In the first issue of *Language*, journal of the recently founded Linguistic Society of America (1925), the theoretical linguist Espinosa published an article on syllabic consonants in New Mexico Spanish, a tantalizing phenomenon which was not taken up again by linguists until Lipski (1993a), by that time operating at a level of theoretical abstraction unheard of in the Roaring 20s. Two years later Espinosa (1927–28) again published in *Language*, this time a linguistic description of New Mexico Spanish based on folk tales, reflecting the founding of the LSA with a strong admixture of anthropological orientation and descriptive linguistics. Espinosa also published specialized articles in Spanish in linguistics journals overseas (1909–15, 1913, 1934 and several others).

Espinosa's masterful works on the phonology (1930) and morphology (1946) of New Mexico Spanish were translated into Spanish and published in the Biblioteca de Dialectología Hispanoamericana, a prestigious collection of monographs edited by the linguists Amado Alonso (Spain) and Angel Rosenblat (Venezuela) and published by the University of Buenos Aires. Since all of the other titles of this series were studies of Spanish as the indisputably national language of independent countries, it is clear that Espinosa and others regarded New Mexico Spanish as a de facto 'national' language. Although New Mexico lacked the strictly hegemonic criteria of a passport, a flag, and military allegiance, New Mexicans formed a distinct demographic group like that of an independent nation.

The closest that Espinosa ever came to casting New Mexican Spanish as a language on the defensive came in 1917, in a mainstream historical anthology, when he wrote of "Speech mixture in New Mexico: The influence of the English language on New Mexican Spanish." In the same year that the American Association of Teachers of Spanish (now AATSP) held its first annual meeting, Espinosa openly acknowledged that "race antagonism has always been very pronounced . . ." Although in the first years of the American occupation newly arrived Americans married Spanish women, Espinosa wrote, "with the introduction of the railroads and the very rapid commercial progress of the last thirty years . . . there has come a check in the race fusion and the mutual contact and good feeling between the two peoples . . . in the new cities . . . where the English speaking people are numerically superior, the Spanish people are looked upon as an inferior race . . ." However, "outside of a few of these very recent American cities . . . the Spanish element is still the all important and predominant one . . . and in these places the English influence in language, customs and habits of life is very insignificant." Although his predictions missed the mark geographically, Espinosa was surely prescient when he postulated that "Some of the very isolated places like Taos and Santa Fé are yet thoroughly Spanish and will continue so, perhaps, for more than a century." Espinosa's comments came at a time when English-language schooling was just beginning to make significant inroads in the newly minted state, but his candid acknowledgment of racist repression is unique among early scholarship on U.S. Spanish.

Espinosa's role as a respected spokesman for an established and relatively prosperous Hispanophone population was also an exception. Most work on languages other than English in the United States was being done without the participation of ingroup members. Instead, research was written by outgroup scholars for the consumption of other academicians. Scholars of Spanish in the United States did not yet fully appreciate the fact that Spanish was now a permanent facet of the U.S. linguistic profile. Academicians shared the opinion of working-class Americans, who saw Spanish as a struggling urban immigrant language which could eventually be eliminated by ordering its speakers to 'get back on the boat.'

4. U.S. Spanish in the pre-World War II years

As statehood overtook New Mexico, other native or adopted New Mexicans continued to describe New Mexican Spanish, always in scholarly terms and directed at academic specialists. Kercheville (1934) offered a glossary of New Mexico Spanish terms, and McSpadden (1934) briefly described a rather unusual dialect spoken in an isolated New Mexican village. Juan Rael (1937), in a dissertation completed at Stanford University, described New Mexican Spanish based on a corpus of oral folktales, a brilliant work which unfortunately was never to slip beyond the pale of obscure university microfilm collections. Although a brief note by Rael (1934) in *Modern Language Notes* (curiously published in Spanish) took a neutral tone, Rael presented his work in the strait-laced *Hispanic Review* (1939, 1940) under the ominous title "Associative interference in New Mexican Spanish." The 'interference' is not from English; rather, it is a language-internal analogy: *cuerpo espín* < *puerco espín*, *nublina* < *neblina*, *descudriñar* < *escudriñar* and the like, and the article is strictly philological as befits the journal's editorial standards. Nearly all the items mentioned by Rael are found in rural dialects of Spanish throughout Spain and Latin America. Nonetheless the focus is exclusively on forms which were sure to arouse hilarity and derision among the normatively-trained perusers of this periodical. New Mexico Spanish was inadvertently portrayed to outsiders as an infelicitous patchwork: ". . . it is quite remarkable that so many of the blends and malapropisms . . . should have found such a wide acceptance in New Mexican Spanish, in view of the fact that blends and malapropisms are generally considered individual peculiarities which are not repeated by others" (Rael 1939).

The 1930s and early 1940s saw a number of articles, theses, and dissertations dealing with Southwest Spanish, centered on New Mexico; these almost inevitably dealt with perceived deficiencies of Spanish speakers in school achievement, in learning English, and when taking intelligence tests.[1] Many of these studies were written by educators seriously preoccupied by the educational difficulties of Spanish-speaking children, even though their work on bilingualism was often hopelessly entangled with ethnocentric views of mental disabilities, equating limited proficiency in English with mental retardation or personality disorders. Since the work was undertaken primarily by educators and psychologists there was little denigration of the characteristics of Spanish, but the entire discourse is permeated with the notion that knowledge of Spanish is a cognitive liability. A 1950s study (Marx 1953) referring to the 'problem' of bilingualism among Spanish-speaking Americans, and a 1960s thesis addressing the 'handicaps of bi-lingual Mexican children' (Marcoux 1961) demonstrate that such notions did not disappear easily. One departure from this tendency was a brief article on Tampa Spanish (Ramírez 1939) published in a newly founded Puerto Rican journal.

Arizona achieved statehood even later than New Mexico, and when Anita Post presented her work to the professional organization American Association of Teachers of Spanish in 1932 and published in the journal *Hispania* in 1933, Spanish was still the dominant language in most of the state. Post's article briefly describes phonetic traits widely found in other vernacular varieties of Spanish, and offers some oral folktales and songs; there is little in the article to distinguish Arizona Spanish from other rural dialects. Aware of the growing Anglicization of Arizona, Post remarks: "It is difficult to predict what the Spanish of the future will be. Many archaic forms are disappearing; new words are coming in from Mexico; many more are being formed from English words. The Spanish of the future may be purer or it may disappear." In fact, much of the archaic Spanish of the turn of the century has been supplanted by modern Mexican reintroductions while bilingualism with English characterizes all but the state's most recent Spanish-speaking immigrants.

5. U.S. Spanish research in the 1940s and 1950s

The time period roughly spanned by the California Pachuco riots and the beginning of the Bracero program, both in 1943, and the assassination of John Kennedy in 1963 and passage of the Civil Rights Act the following year is one of relative homogeneity for the study of Spanish in the United States. The end of World War II and the immediate postwar years brought little research on Spanish-speaking groups (cf. Woodbridge 1954), as the nation and the world grappled with the wrenching issues of the atomic bomb, the Holocaust, and the beginnings of the Cold War. Normal life returned at colleges and universities, many of which had virtually ground to a halt during the war, and the nation experienced the beginnings of a dramatic economic recovery.

Not all Americans reaped the benefits of peace and prosperity. Blacks, Chicanos, and Puerto Ricans who had served in the armed forces returned to a divided society which still denied them their basic rights (even the U.S. armed forces were not officially integrated until 1948). Previously recruited laborers from Mexico now became an undesirable surplus. The new immigration laws of the 1950s, collectively dubbed 'Operation Wetback' in government circles, further dehumanized an expendable migratory labor force. These facts were not reflected in academic journals, however.

A few exceptional studies stand out in this period; in the middle of World War II Keniston (1942) summarized research to date on U.S. Spanish, based on a paper he originally delivered in 1940, Porges (1949) studied Anglicisms in 'New York Spanish,' while Patterson (1946) provided information on the Spanish of San Antonio, Texas and Díaz (1942) described Anglicisms in California Spanish.

The 1950s brought the balmy complacency of the Eisenhower years. On the TV and in comic books Superman protected 'truth, justice, and the American way,' while Dick Tracy, Batman, and Elliott Ness effortlessly nabbed bad guys, an increasing number of whom were portrayed as dark, foreign, and disturbingly 'alien.' The McCarthy era cast immediate suspicion on any intellectuals dealing with non-American, hence 'un-American' topics, and free speech became a precious commodity. The Soviet Union launched the first Sputnik satellite in 1957, taking the United States by surprise and unleashing a frantic race for space and a technological and strategic competition that would impinge on academia in the form of the National Defense Education Act, which set up institutes and training programs for 'strategic' languages, including Spanish.

There were also rumblings of discontent among oppressed peoples in America. In 1955 Rosa Parks and Martin Luther King, Jr. struck the first major blow against the denial of civil rights to African-Americans. Chicano and Puerto Rican nationalist groups criticized the U.S. as a colonial power in its own right. In 1950 Pedro Albizu Campos railed against the recruitment of Puerto Ricans for military service in Korea; Puerto Ricans on the island had elected their first governor only two years before, while those on the mainland lived in ghettoes and were denied the most basic human dignity. Chicano activists were deported throughout the Southwest. However, the full implications of the impending struggle did not yet make an impression on middle-class Americans.

Several descriptive studies of U.S. varieties of Spanish were written during the 1950s and early 1960s; most were coolly objective. Bowen 1952, Hardman 1956, Ornstein 1951, 1972, Cherry 1966, Galván 1955, Phillips 1967, Sawyer 1958, 1964 and many other theses and dissertations, while not unsympathetic to Spanish, described particular U.S. Spanish communities with an air of insurmountable distance, as if they were dialect studies of far-flung speech communities in foreign lands. Scholars often focused on groups who purportedly descended from white, European Spaniards without New World admixture (e.g. MacCurdy 1950, 1959 for Louisiana; Ortiz 1947, 1949, Hayes 1949, and Canfield 1951 for Tampa, Friedman 1950 for Minorcans in St. Augustine).

Lozano 1961, a precocious article on codeswitching, was an early testimony to the fact that Spanish and English were in a symbiotic relationship throughout the Southwest. While Tsuzaki 1963, 1971 and Beck 1970 were not overly helpful in defining English influence on Spanish – limiting their observations to unremarkable loanwords not indicative of heavy cross-fertilization – they acknowledged the growing Hispanophone population in the urban midwest.[2] Kreidler (1958) continues the tradition of describing immigrant varieties of Spanish – in this case Puerto Rican Spanish in New Jersey – in terms of influence from English.

Perhaps the first commercially published textbook for native Spanish speakers in the U.S., Paulline Baker's *Español para los hispanos*, was published in 1953 and reprinted many times in the following four decades. Baker, teaching in rural New Mexico, offered the book as a supplement to traditional Spanish courses; speaking of U.S. Spanish speakers she notes in her introduction that "estamos presenciando una decadencia lamentable del español de los Estados Unidos," and "Cada día se hace sentir más la necesidad de corregir los errores del mal español que se deben evitar y desarrollarse el buen uso del español que se debe emplear." The book, in her words, "trata de los equívocos gramaticales o las faltas en el vocabulario de la gente de habla española de los Estados Unidos," and chapter headings include "barbarismos," "pachuquismos," and "faltas gramaticales." In the 1975 bibliography (Teschner, Bills, and Craddock 1975: 46), Richard Teschner compares this work to the *Appendix Probi,* in that it gives a wealth of authentic examples of vernacular speech all the while purporting to 'correct' such language. The book also contains sections on letter writing and parliamentary procedure in Spanish for setting up and conducting a Spanish club. Although Baker's book appears heavy-handed more than 45 years later, many of its observations and recommendations continue to figure prominently in Spanish courses for native speakers.

The study of social registers of Spanish made its first appearance in the 1950s, invariably choosing socially marked underclass speech for individual attention. It was during the 1950s that 'Pachuco' Spanish was first studied by scholars, almost all of whom were from outside the Mexican-American community. Barker (1950), like the German scholar Max Wagner (1953), described Pachuco in Tucson as "an American-Spanish argot." Barker extracts the term 'argot' from Webster's dictionary as "a secret language or conventional slang peculiar to a group of thieves, tramps or vagabonds; or, more broadly, a cant or class jargon." While he does not fully commit himself to the claim that Pachuco language has criminal connotations, Barker does cite informants' accounts that Pachuco originated among "grifos, or marijuana smokers and dope peddlers, in the El Paso underworld." "It seems probable," he writes, "that these individuals, in turn, obtained a substantial part of their vocabulary from the *Caló* or argot of the Mexican underworld." He cites sources which claim that the language first reached Los Angeles when a group of El Paso hoodlums received suspended prison sentences in return for self-banishment. Although he describes Pachucos as in effect youth gangs, Barker is judicious in describing the kangaroo court justice that befell many of the participants. He also acknowledges that many young Chicano war veterans became disillusioned by the shabby treatment they received from a society whose freedom they had risked their lives to protect. However, there remains an undercurrent of disapproval in his work: "the habitual use of the argot, then, may be taken to indicate that the speaker is not interested in raising his social status above that of the laboring group. Such usage may also indicate his rejection of some of the conventional values of Mexican and American culture." Barker concludes – not without some justification – that ". . . only when the goals of American society can be demonstrated as obtainable to him – perhaps then through such means as vocational education – will the pachuco as a linguistic and social type disappear . . ."

Paulline Baker's textbook for native Spanish speakers in the U.S. (Baker 1953: 49) uncompromisingly refers to Pachuco language as "the slang of the dead-end kids," and cautions that "A veces se expresa por medio del caló un muchacho de una familia buena y culta . . . ¡Pero nunca una señorita!" In addition to unequivocal Pachuquismos of the time, Baker also includes such tried and true Mexicanisms as *chamaco*, *feria* 'small change,' ¡*Hórale*! [sic] and even *chicano*. The chapter also contains an exercise entitled "Para ser tonto no es necesario estudiar."

Lurline Coltharp's monograph *The tongue of the Tirilones* (1965) was first presented as the author's doctoral dissertation in 1964, then published the following year by the University of Alabama Press. Coltharp was the first woman to publish research on *caló*, then regarded as an exclusively male-oriented language:

> It was and is a male language. The females who use it are the prostitutes of the area or the mates of the gang members. While law-abiding males use the language, no female of this level would admit that she even understood one word of the language. I have watched girls listening to boys who were speaking this *caló*. Their reactions assured me that they understood the language, but they were horrified by my suggestion that they help by taping. They were adamant that they neither spoke nor understood a single word (Coltharp 1965: 32).

Indeed, it was not until the work of the late Letticia Galindo (1992, 1995) that the role of women as speakers and researchers of *caló* was readdressed. Coltharp describes the El Paso Pachuco culture in strictly anthropological terms, stressing the poverty and alienation of the key neighborhoods covered by her research. In dealing with the topics of crime, drugs, sexuality, and gang activities, Coltharp largely refrains from value judgments, reiterating instead the rejection of El Paso's Chicano youth by the rest of American society. Although nearly all her informants were bilingual, "Spanish is rated as the school subject in which the children do most poorly. They are ashamed of the level of their Spanish" (p. 30). In contrast to Barker, Coltharp cites evidence that *caló* had non-criminal beginnings, and "is in reality an inoffensive type of jargon that started during the time of World War I." In addition to serving as a shield by means of which criminal elements can verbally disguise their activities, "this language also provides protection to the law-abiding element. These people knowingly learn and use the language as an identification with the group so that they will not suffer physical harm at the hands of the unlawful element" (p. 31). However, she does affirm that "this language was used originally as a cover for illegal activities, mainly fighting, smuggling and dope peddling" (p. 32).

At the same time that William Labov was first struggling with the difficulties faced by outgroup observers in obtaining linguistic material from inner-city black youth, Coltharp managed to secure cooperation – if not necessarily the most authentic language – from her informants: "The fact that I am a female had surprisingly few drawbacks in this endeavor . . . during the recording and listening sessions I maintained a detached attitude as though I did not understand the language. Because of this, they did not have to worry about the propriety of what they were saying. In fact, they could maintain a male superiority in front of the uncomprehending female." Eventually Coltharp gleaned enough information to enable her to participate in the conversations and carry out a vocabulary survey. While today's researchers might find Coltharp's advantageous use of stereotypes demeaning and insincere, the fact remains that the ensuing dictionary is both accurate and thorough – although by no means exhaustive – and *caló* is stripped of much of its threatening connotation.

Coltharp's assessment of *caló* as an inoffensive jargon clashed with the prevailing attitude towards Pachuco and contact-induced varieties of Southwest Spanish. Braddy (1953, 1956, 1965) wrote of "Pachucos and their argot" together with "smugglers argot" and "narcotic argot" in Texas. R. J. González (1967) believed that Pachuco was becoming a creole (taking this term to entail language degeneration), a view also shared by Webb (1976, 1980). Griffith (1947) referred to the "Pachuco patois," while May (1966) wrote of "tex-mex" and Ranson (1954) wrote of "viles pochismos." Pachuco and *caló*, often maligned as the sole purview of criminals and vicious nonconformists, has benefited from the increasingly sophisticated linguistic approaches described above, and although many segments of society (both Anglo and Latino) continue to regard Pachuco as synonymous with trouble, linguists appreciate its status as a coherent register with a wide range of non-malignant uses.

6. Linguistic currents in the 1960s

The '60s were the decade of massive social change, of school desegregation, voting rights activism, and civil disobedience. The Civil Rights Act of 1964 and the Voting Rights Act of 1965 ensured legal protection for minority groups, but the effective realization of these protected rights was much longer in coming. The Watts riot of 1965 and the 1967 riots which gutted the largest northern cities brought the painful message that racism was not confined to the South. The war in Vietnam and the violent government response to civil protest created deep fractures in the white middle class. America's neighbor, Cuba, became a major concern with the failed Bay of Pigs invasion, the Cuban Missile Crisis, and the hundreds of thousands of Cuban refugees who, it now appeared, were in for a long stay.

In 1966, Jane and Chester Christian described Spanish–English bilingualism in the Southwest from a socio-historical perspective which traced the gradual decline in the prestige and use of Spanish, from colonial times through American territorial status and statehood. Although some observations may strike contemporary readers as patronizing (e.g. equating Hispanic culture with "anarchism" and Anglo culture with "order"), the article offers a penetrating historical analysis of the dilemmas faced by a population torn between maintaining its ethnic heritage and achieving economic survival through assimilation.

In 1968, the Brown Berets, MECHA, La Raza, the Teatro Campesino, Corky González, César Chávez, and Reies López Tijerina were the order of the day. The United Farm Workers' grape boycott was in its second year. The politically radicalized Mexican-American community began to demand acceptance of the term *Chicano* by all sectors of society. In this same year Joshua Fishman, Robert Cooper, and Roxanna Ma delivered to the U.S. Department of Health, Education, and Welfare the final report of a project entitled "Bilingualism in the barrio: measurement and description of language dominance in bilinguals." A refined version of the report was published by Indiana University in 1971 and an expanded edition appeared in 1975. This study, based on the Puerto Rican community of Jersey City, New Jersey, exemplified the newly emerging intersection of sociology, linguistics, and quantitative analysis. It is not exaggerating to suggest that this study, together with the early work of William Labov, established the framework for much of the subsequent sociolinguistic research on Spanish-speaking communities in the United States. For the first time the full human scope of a bilingual community was coherently discussed by a multidisciplinary group of scholars, and language usage was integrated into a total community perspective; ghettoized Puerto Ricans were portrayed with the same care and in equally positive terms as more prestigious groups of French, Scandinavian, and German speakers had enjoyed.

7. The 1970s: Turning point for U.S. Spanish research

For the United States the 1970s were the most turbulent of times, and linguistic research rode the shifting and surging waves of political, social, and economic upheaval that were permanently transforming the country. Like Alice in Wonderland, Americans were perplexed by signs pointing in every direction, as the country seemed to move backward, forward, and in circles on political and social issues. This was a time for optimism and pessimism, for activism and ultra-conservatism, a time for every purpose under heaven. It was also the time in which the study of Spanish in the United States as a major scholarly pursuit came into existence.

Chicano literature entered the canon in the 1970s with great fanfare. Major works of the 1970s include Rodolfo Anaya's *Bless me Ultima*, Rolando Hinojosa's *Estampas del Valle*, Miguel Méndez' *Peregrinos de Aztlán*, Tomás Rivera's *Y no se lo tragó la tierra*, Alejandro Morales' *Caras viejas y vino nuevo*, Alurista's *Floricanto en Aztlán*, Sabine Ulibarrí's *Tierra Amarilla*, and many others. Poetry and narrative incorporating codeswitching appeared prominently as U.S. Latino writers emerged as a new literary voice. Intertwined language created a third code, in defiance of the colonialist literary canon which had held bilingual authors hostage to a single language or, at best, to the use of one language per work.

University departments began to include mention of U.S. Spanish language and literature. At Michigan State University in 1976 I taught a new course on an avant-garde topic, Spanish in the United States, scrambling for a bibliography but not short on students. A promising young writer from the newly founded Chicano Studies program at the University of Minnesota was passing through and visited my class; Rolando Hinojosa gave an inspirational talk and discussed bilingual speech and writing with an enthralled group of students. The following year a colleague in literature proposed a one-quarter course in Chicano literature, but since the senior faculty demurred due to a perceived lack of sufficient 'literature' it was agreed that half the course would be Chicano-oriented, while the crazy linguist who was talking about U.S. Spanish would teach Puerto Rican literature from the island and from the United States. U.S. Latino literature was casually tossed off to assistant professors trained in other areas (my adventurous colleague specialized in Peninsular literature). Tradition-bound Spanish departments reacted to the incorporation of linguistic and literary communities that were not to be found in the pages of Angel del Río's anthologies with indifference or mild amusement, benevolently tolerating impetuous young faculty who would soon come to their senses. The last throes of this academic backlash were still felt in the 1980s.

In 1974 the United States Supreme Court handed down the landmark Lau vs. Nichols decision, mandating schooling in languages other than English for students with little or no abilities in English. Bilingual education had come of age. One by one, individual states began to pass bilingual education legislation and more importantly to take concrete steps towards providing the services required by the law, whose groundwork had already been laid by Title VI of the Civil Rights Act of 1964. School systems throughout the nation scrambled to cobble together bilingual education programs, and colleges and universities were besieged with requests to provide guidance and training in a discipline which still did not exist. Many Hispanists and linguists, myself included, were pressed into service to design courses, certify teachers, and ensure compliance with the new mandates.

Yet another landmark of the 1970s is the publication of the first commercially successful textbooks designed to teach Spanish grammar and literacy to bilingual native speakers in the United States. As textbook publishers ventured into the 'Spanish for native speakers' market, the first steps sometimes resulted in smashed toes. For example, one of the early textbooks designed specifically for Spanish for native speaker courses (Barker 1966) states in the introduction that nonstandard speech is not to be despised, but it is recommended that "educated" language be used. However, throughout the book the author mentions *barbarismos* and *expresiones viciosas*, most of which are socially unaccepted Anglicisms, popular pronunciations, or morphological variants such as *asigún*, *truje*, and *maiz* (*maíz*). This book was written by an individual who learned Spanish as a second language, presumably in the strait-laced academic tradition. In a preface to a later edition, Christian (1971: vi) speaks approvingly of the author's stance:

> In an era which attempts to be so linguistically democratic that the jargon of adolescents is as nearly 'correct' as that of the most universally recognized writer, and in which the academician feels free, like the adolescent, to create a jargon that only he and a few of his colleagues can understand, this book goes against one of the strong currents of contemporary culture. The author assumes that standards are proper to a language, and should be imposed upon students. This is still, in spite of protestations to the contrary, a universal process. When authorities in general were more nearly sacrosanct, teachers had stronger convictions regarding the propriety of their beliefs and viewpoints, and were less hesitant about making them clear.

The "contemporary" culture referred to in this lament for the loss of canonical authority existed thirty years ago, a time in which few Spanish courses for native speakers existed, and even fewer teachers were so enamored of "adolescents' jargon." Today's bilingual educators, while not denying the importance of literacy in the educated standard and awareness of literary texts, see the home vs. school language dichotomy as symbiosis rather than antagonism.

Although a few educators had addressed the issue of teaching Spanish to bilingual students in the United States during the 1960s (e.g. Barker 1966, Whittier Union High School District 1966), the convergence of linguists and educators in developing materials for university-level teaching of Spanish to Spanish-speaking students occurred during the 1970s. In 1970 the American Association of Teachers of Spanish and Portuguese commissioned a report on teaching Spanish to native speakers in high school and college (AATSP 1970). Two years later the U.S. Office of Education (1972) issued a similar report. A number of school districts, especially in the Southwest, prepared reports and teaching materials directed at bilingual Spanish-speaking students (e.g. Corpus Christi Independent School District 1975). In 1976 Guadalupe Valdés and Rodolfo García-Moya edited an important collection of articles on teaching Spanish to Spanish speakers in a U.S. setting. In the following year the first major textbook for bilingual students in the United States, Valdés and Teschner's *Español escrito* (1977a), was published. Valdés and Teschner (1977b) also published a bibliography of materials on teaching Spanish to bilinguals in the same year. *Español escrito* was, as the title indicates, primarily devoted to teaching literacy and standard grammatical forms to students who were already fluent native speakers of some vernacular variety of Spanish. Although written by authors based in the Southwest, *Español escrito* does not incline towards Mexican/Chicano Spanish in particular. Rather, in the introduction the authors briefly mention Mexican, Cuban, and Puerto Rican regional expressions, while stressing three key components of the pedagogical approach. First, they stress differences in style, underscoring the need to apply formal styles in formal contexts while fully accepting the home vernacular in the appropriate domains. Second, irrespective of phonetic differences of style, register, and region, there is a single correct spelling for Spanish words, which the educated speaker must master. Finally, bilingual speakers are warned that use of non-internationalized Anglicisms with interlocutors from other countries may impede comprehension. And all of this without undermining the fundamental integrity of the home language, which as the authors point out, is not 'bad Spanish,' whatever else it may be.

Appearing at nearly the same time was Quintanilla and Silman's textbook (1978), giving basic Spanish grammar and orthography as well as frequent Anglicisms, but making no mention of the characteristics of Spanish varieties spoken in the United States. The authors suggest that the book be accompanied by a book of Mexican-American readings when used in bilingual programs. De la Portilla and Varela's (1979) text, entitled *Mejora tu español*, implicitly includes the substantial Cuban-American population, many of whom were already literate in Spanish and required less primary instruction and more fine-tuning to achieve parity with educated Spanish speakers in other countries.

As bilingual educators' desperate searches for published research yielded meager gleanings, scholarship on U.S. Spanish began a gradual upsurge. By the end of the decade a torrent of new studies appeared, spurred in part by bilingual education programs but also by the growing power and social consciousness of underclass groups, many of whom spoke Spanish. Latino scholars entered the discussion in ever-increasing numbers, representing not only elitist perspectives but also the reality of the barrios, the migrant farmworker communities, and the ever-permeable southern borderlands. U.S. Spanish gradually ceased to be described as a museum specimen and was instead portrayed as a living entity vital to the communities in which it was used and as an instrument of social change.

Canonical works on U.S. Spanish became widely available for the first time. Several journals which would become instrumental in spreading the appreciation and study of U.S. Spanish were founded in the 1970s: *Aztlán* in 1970, the *Revista Chicano-Riqueña* in 1973, the *Bilingual Review/Revista Bilingüe* in 1974. The latter two journals gave increased output to scholarship on Puerto Rican and Cuban Spanish in the United States and expanded the study of Mexican and Mexican-American varieties. The *Journal of the Linguistic Association of the Southwest* (LASSO), later to become the *Southwest Journal of Linguistics*, began publication in 1975. The Southwest Areal Languages and Linguistics Workshops (SWALLOW) were begun in 1971, and several influential sets of conference proceedings added to the bibliography on the linguistic behavior of Spanish–English bilinguals, beginning with Bills (1974). In 1970 Daniel Cárdenas published a brief document in the ERIC/Center for Applied Linguistics series, describing the most salient linguistic characteristics of some U.S. Spanish dialects. The Fishman et al. (1968, 1971, 1975) study of a bilingual Puerto Rican neighborhood first became widely disseminated through the Indiana University editions of 1971 and 1975. Also appearing in 1975 is Casiano Montañez' phonological study of New York Puerto Rican Spanish, a little-known monograph which gives sparse variational data.

The Academia Norteamericana de la Lengua Española was founded in 1973; its inaugural meeting was held the following year. At least half of the members were originally from outside the United States, and the list of academicians contained more literary scholars than linguists. That U.S.-born Spanish speakers or working-class immigrants were not the primary intended beneficiaries of the academy is suggested by the tone of the president's inaugural remarks:

> Los españoles e hispanoamericanos residentes en este país forman un verdadero pueblo dentro de la gran familia norteamericana . . . este conglomerado étnico naturalmente se identifica con todas las modalidades idiomáticas del español que se habla en sus países de origen y necesita más que ningún otro un idioma castellano claro, libre de localismos y provincialismos, que le sirva como instrumento de fácil comunicación con sus hermanos de idioma y destino. (McHale 1976: 91)

In 1976 the first issue of the Academy's *Boletín* appeared. The academy's own statement of purpose declares that the members will work for "la preservación de la unidad, universalidad, pureza, belleza y mayor difusión del idioma español en los Estados Unidos" (Academia Norteamericana de la Lengua Española 1976: 99). The editor's introduction (Chang-Rodríguez 1976: 5–6) notes that "los estatutos de nuestra Academia señalan una serie de tareas en defensa de la pureza de nuestro castellano," and concludes by saying "Antes estos múltiples retos lingüísticos, agravados por el actual prestigio del inglés, ofrecemos amor al castellano y nuestra propia interpretación de la ardua tarea de limpiarlo, fijarlo y darle esplendor." Despite these inauspicious words, the first issue contains a bibliography of studies on U.S. Spanish (Beardsley 1976) and an overview of the phonetics of U.S. Spanish varieties (Canfield 1976), as well as the more usual fare of literary study and lists of 'approved' words. Subsequent numbers would reflect this ambivalence, combining objective linguistic studies with literary accolades and official pronouncements.

In 1972 Rosaura Sánchez, then a graduate student, published in a journal directed at socially committed Chicano intellectuals "Nuestra circunstancia lingüística," an impassioned if innocent description of rural and urban varieties of Chicano Spanish. It is the *nuestra* of the title which presages what was to become one of the most compelling voices in Chicano social and linguistic scholarship, for Sánchez unabashedly juxtaposes her university training with her membership in a community whose language had been ignored or mistreated – by speakers of English and Spanish alike – for more than a century. Although having done Master's work in Latin American literature and in the process of writing a doctoral dissertation in the fashionable generative grammar paradigm, Sánchez took a strong stance in defense of the "circunstancia" of Chicano Spanish, using the intersection of her graduate training and activist credentials to add weight to her arguments. The fact that the article is written in Spanish is also of significance, since Sánchez observes (1972: 47):

> Un pueblo que participa en la economía de este país sin gozar de los bienes materiales que disfrutan los adinerados o los de la clase media necesita un esfuerzo colectivo para cambiar una situación que puede compartir con gran parte del mundo. Nuestra lengua, lo que podríamos denominar un dialecto popular del español, nos une a un gran número de personas por todo el sudoeste de EEUU y por toda la América Latina. No vamos a dejar perder este vínculo, convirtiéndonos en un pueblo monolingüe, agringado. Ahora que nuestro idioma se ve amenazado con la desaparición, es imprescindible llegar a un acuerdo en cuanto a fines lingüísticos.

Sánchez' article became required reading for students of U.S. Spanish and is still included in core bibliographies of Chicano studies.

Jerry Craddock (1973) published a comprehensive article on United States Spanish in the *Current Trends in Linguistics* series, bringing the topic to the attention of linguists throughout the world and legitimizing the study of U.S. Spanish as a major research domain. The volume is entitled *Linguistics in North America*, and Spanish is grouped together with English and French in the category "Major languages of North America." Reflecting the available bibliography of the time, Craddock makes brief mention of Puerto Rican, Sephardic, and Louisiana Spanish, even briefer mention of Cuban-American Spanish (citing only articles on traditional Tampa Spanish), and gives considerable attention to Spanish in the Southwest. Craddock (1973: 475–476) presciently speaks of "a good reason to expect a resurgence of interest in MA [Mexican-American] Spanish," while cautioning that "unless a much larger proportion of the basic research and development is taken over by the Mexican-Americans themselves, many current efforts to expand our knowledge of the varieties and vicissitudes of MA Spanish may be doomed to sterility." He was perhaps prematurely optimistic when he observed that "it may be possible to foresee the disappearance of the insane spectacle of our schools' systematic attempts to eradicate native speakers' Spanish while vainly striving to teach the language to countless unwilling and incompetent Anglo youths" (Craddock 1973: 476). All in all, Craddock gives a penetrating review of previous scholarship on Southwest Spanish.

In 1975 the Center for Applied Linguistics, a growing clearinghouse for scholarly work on the languages of the United States, published the anthology *El lenguaje de los Chicanos*, compiled by Eduardo Hernández-Chávez, aided by Andrew Cohen and Anthony Beltramo. The CAL had contacted Hernández-Chávez several years earlier in response to a growing awareness of the need for a sourcebook on Mexican-American language. The book contains twenty articles, ranging from the classic studies reviewed previously to more recent work, plus a thorough bibliography of works on U.S. Spanish and an extensive editors' introduction. For more than a decade this anthology served as the primary reader for courses on Mexican-American Spanish throughout the country, gradually supplanted by studies with a more modern orientation. The latter, however, have never been anthologized, thus making *El lenguaje de los Chicanos* the most comprehensive collection of research on a single variety of U.S. Spanish ever published. The editors end their introduction (1975: xvii) with a plea for the integration of academic research and social concerns:

> There is the strong feeling among Chicanos, not entirely unjustified, that much of the research in their communities has not been for the benefit of the communities themselves. It has benefited scholars who have used the results of studies in their publications or, less unkindly, it has been of general benefit to human knowledge. Even so, a flaw in much of the work is a profound lack of understanding on the part of researchers of the people and of their culture.

Although the editors acknowledge that matters were changing even as they were writing these words, their concerns are still a relevant mirror in which to examine ourselves as we continue the research enterprise a quarter century later.

In the same year, Richard Teschner, Garland Bills, and Jerry Craddock (1975) published a comprehensive and richly annotated bibliography on the language behavior of Spanish–English bilinguals in the United States, also published by the Center for Applied Linguistics. This bibliography includes work on Cuban, Puerto Rican, Mexican-American, and some isolated varieties of U.S. Spanish, and constitutes the most comprehensive bibliography published to date on the Spanish language in the United States (Solé had previously included U.S. dialects in his 1970 bibliography of Latin American Spanish dialectology). The compilers' introduction traces the evolution of scholarship on U.S. Spanish, which was only then appearing over the horizon in academic departments.

Also in 1975 Roberto Galván and Richard Teschner (1975) published their *Diccionario del español tejano*, the first commercially published dictionary of an explicitly U.S. variety of Spanish, not a dictionary of Mexicanisms published in Mexico, nor a glossary of forms found in a single Spanish-speaking community in the United States. In the second edition (1977), the authors included data from California, Arizona, New Mexico, Colorado and even Florida, thus making the dictionary into the *Diccionario del español chicano.* The year 1976 saw the publication of another important anthology, *Studies in Southwest Spanish*, edited by J. Donald Bowen and Jacob Ornstein (1976). The nine articles cover dialectology, grammatical systems, phonology, lexicon, and bilingual language switching, and many of the studies continue to figure in the core bibliography of U.S. Spanish. In the same year the volume *Bilingualism in the bicentennial and beyond* (Keller, Teschner, and Viera 1976) provided a diverse collection of articles spanning a larger range of issues and bilingual groups in the United States. Jorge Guitart (1976) published a scholarly treatise on Cuban Spanish phonology, in reality representing the first monograph on Cuban Spanish in the United States (Castellanos 1968 and Lamb 1968 are unpublished descriptions of the first wave of Cuban immigrant Spanish). Hammond (1976) also used Miami Cuban Spanish data to bolster a theoretical phonological model, while Domínguez (1974) offered a scheme for classifying dialect variants in New Mexican Spanish.

For linguists, sociologists, and bilingual educators, the 1970s marked the beginning of serious inquiry into the linguistic and social constraints on Spanish–English codeswitching, which had hitherto been regarded as a degenerate practice symptomatic of the undesirability of bilingualism and the confounding effects of language contact. The dual languages of bilingual communities were studied as a coherent system rather than as language deterioration punctuated by slips and errors. Scholars rapidly transformed the perception of language-switching from sociopathic behavior to mainstream research paradigm, vehicle of literary expression, and instrument of ethnic pride.[3] The next decade of codeswitching research was dominated by the Spanish–English findings from the United States, only gradually moving beyond the linguistic and social configurations of U.S. Latino bilingualism to discover the relative uniqueness of Chicano and U.S. Puerto Rican codeswitching, particularly as regards the density and flexibility of intrasentential shifts. Although derogatory comments about *Spanglish*, *pocho*, *Tex-Mex* and other content-free misnomers for fluid codeswitched language continue to appear in the media to this day, it is now possible for the more enlightened sectors of the general public to rebut ignorance and bigotry with solid research.

By the middle 1970s the generative grammar paradigm was in full swing, and linguists were surging beyond the study of English and standard varieties of western European languages to incorporate data from regional and social dialects as well as less commonly studied languages. Harris (1974) employed data from "Chicano Spanish" (taken from some of the classic descriptive accounts) to refine theoretical proposals in generative phonology, Reyes (1976) did the same for grammatical patterns, while Saltarelli (1975) included mention of analogical verb forms in Southwest Spanish in a comparative morphological analysis.

The 1970s ended with an event whose consequences we continue to celebrate. In 1979 the first conference *Spanish in the United States/El español en los Estados Unidos* was held at the University of Illinois–Chicago Circle. The presentations covered a range of topics and varieties of U.S. Spanish, and provided the most comprehensive forum to date for discussing U.S. Spanish as a national and not simply a regional concern. The venue itself was striking, for Chicago is the quintessential city of immigrants and a primary example of the growing presence of U.S. Spanish as a language of recent immigration in addition to an already present imperialist inheritance. The documentary film on Mexican immigration to the urban midwest, appropriately titled "Pilsen port of entry," confirmed the linguistic reality of Chicago, whose Latino population was then almost evenly divided between Mexican and Puerto Rican. For several years the congeners of this seminal conference were deliberately held in northern cities in Indiana, New York, Illinois, and Iowa, highlighting the fact that U.S. Spanish was not just the concern of the Southwest and New York City.

8. Setbacks and advances of the 1980s

In the 1980s the United States continued its surreal ride down the political and social roller coaster which was to bring out the best and the worst of human nature; academic scholarship was often beleaguered by the priorities of Cold War politics and anti-intellectualism. All of Latin America – then dominated by right-wing military dictatorships – was turned into a bloody chessboard, where superpower confrontations created living nightmares which included aiding government repression of peasant groups and the arming of paramilitary and counterrevolutionary militias. The United States invaded Grenada and Panama, launched a surrogate invasion of Nicaragua and taught us that former members of murderous police forces were really "freedom fighters." *Soldier of Fortune* magazine encouraged gun-toting renegades to try their luck in toppling popularly elected Third World governments, much as the American mercenary William Walker had done more than a century before as a prelude to his invasion of Central America. The nation denied refugee status to hundreds of thousands of Spanish-speaking Central Americans displaced by scorched earth campaigns and urban death squads. The Mariel boatlift brought more than 125,000 new Cuban refugees to the United States, shattering the previous solidarity of the Cuban-American community and placing ugly and grotesquely exaggerated images before the American public. In a macabre neo-McCarthyist world academic scholarship was once again regarded as potentially subversive. Many scholars working with Spanish-speaking groups did become involved in sanctuary movements and solidarity organizations.

This decade saw the rise of virulent anti-immigrant fervor throughout the nation, exemplified by the vituperative English Only movements. In nearly all states, counties, and municipalities where the English Only movement has been visible, Spanish has been the language targeted for exclusion. The motivations behind such movements are many, and while some proponents claim to have immigrants' well-being in mind, others appear to be responding only to personal resentment. Some advocates of English Only resent seeing Spanish translations of official documents and signs, expressing dismay over the use of public funds for the translations and suggesting that such translations retard immigrants' acquisition of usable proficiency in English. Others resent bilingual education programs in public schools, frequently equating bilingual education with the refusal to "wean" immigrants from excessive dependence on their native languages and the slow acquisition of English. In such areas as South Florida and parts of Texas and California, many non-Spanish speakers feel (at times with justification) that their chances for employment or advancement have been hindered by lack of abilities in Spanish; some may resent what they feel to be the usurping of their linguistic birthright by speakers of languages other than English. Finally, some stances in favor of English Only can only with difficulty be classified as anything other than petty meanness: this includes the 'my ancestors learned English, why don't you?' reaction, and the frank dislike of being in the presence of people who speak an unintelligible language.

Many proponents of English Only have a hazy vision of a world in which no public funds are spent on matters bilingual. They even hope to make it illegal for people who are racially or culturally different from them to communicate in a foreign language. This type of totalitarian vision is no more realistic than 'putting them back on the boat,' but there is little that stands in the way of attempts to make it real. Once a basis is created for outlawing use of languages other than English, there is no moral or legal impediment to the massive violation of the most basic human rights: the right to receive emergency and social services and schooling in one's native language, and more broadly, the First Amendment guarantees of freedom of expression. The ultimate situation could be far worse than the days when non-English speakers languished in jails and suffered police brutality because of the simple fact that they did not speak the dominant language.

Although the notion of declaring English as the 'official language' of states and the nation had been heard long before on talk shows and op-ed pages, the 1980s witnessed the commercialization of this xenophobic effort. In 1981 Senator S.I. Hayakawa of California proposed an amendment to the U.S. constitution which would declare English as the official language of the nation. In 1983, Hayakawa founded the lobbying organization U.S. English, which has spearheaded subsequent English-only campaigns across the country. Currently at least 21 states have passed measures declaring English to be the official and only state language. Efforts to declare English the official language at the national level have not been abandoned. House Resolution 123, originally proposed in 1996, was reintroduced in 1999 by Rep. Barr of Georgia.

The 21 states currently sporting English-only policies include all of the Southeast and most of the midwestern and western states. In most of these historically right-wing states, there are no large communities which speak languages other than English. Their English-only statutes are token gestures of anti-government/anti-liberal scorn. In other cases, however, Spanish is clearly the target language; the supporters of English-only laws in California, Arizona, Colorado, Florida, Illinois, and Indiana surely cannot have overlooked the growing Hispanophone populations of those states.

Early English-only proclamations were largely symbolic and unenforceable, carrying no more weight than the designation of the official state bird. As English-only activists gained in experience by observing the ineffectiveness of earlier initiatives, later laws made more serious attacks on the civil liberties of American citizens who speak in other languages. A 1988 Arizona law, eventually overturned by the Arizona Supreme Court (a decision which was sustained by the U.S. Supreme Court), contained the ominous wording that the state "shall act in English and no other language." English-only laws passed in California (1986) and Florida (1988) included language enabling the state assemblies to enforce the laws by appropriate legislation. Initially it was feared that such laws would curtail even the most essential uses of languages other than English, for example in emergency services, but recent visits to California and Florida have convinced me beyond a doubt that the voters who approved these laws were only exercising *el derecho del pataleo*. The wording nonetheless remains as a potential weapon of future legislatures and citizen groups determined to thwart the natural use of several languages in American society.

Xenophobic movements continue to grow in vehemence and to broaden their bases of support. A recent arrival is the organization English First, which opposes Puerto Rican statehood primarily because of the radically non-English linguistic foundations of that territory.

English-only legislation does not fit easily into a single category, but runs the full gamut from empty gestures to true attacks on civil liberties. Recent initiatives in Connecticut, Massachusetts, Maryland, Ohio, Wisconsin, Michigan, and Iowa may also result at least in part from resentment against Spanish-speaking groups. So far, Texas, New York, Pennsylvania, and New Jersey have resisted English-only legislation in the midst of significant Spanish-speaking populations, while New Mexico, Rhode Island, Oregon, and Washington have implemented symbolic 'English-plus' legislation. The battle of English vs. other languages is far from over, and today's social and political signs point in contradictory directions.

Despite the increasingly fractious political climate in the United States and its totalitarian allies, the 1980s produced some of the most incisive scholarship on U.S. Spanish. Fernando Peñalosa's monograph *Chicano sociolinguistics* (1980) offered the balanced perspective of a sociologist who was also an ingroup member, giving a full overview of the linguistic and sociocultural issues facing the Chicano community. The year 1981 saw the publication of two anthologies which became required reading for research and teaching on U.S. Spanish. Roberto Durán's *Latino language and communicative behavior* (1981) contains original scholarship on Chicano and Puerto Rican bilingualism, including codeswitching and grammatical contact. In the same year Guadalupe Valdés, Anthony Lozano, and Rafael García-Moya (1981) edited *Teaching Spanish to the Hispanic bilingual*, specifically addressing issues related to language teaching in bilingual communities. Maintenance of Spanish, rather than acquisition of English, was the focus of this collection, which includes theoretical studies in dialectology, recommendations for classroom implementation of Spanish for bilingual students courses, sample course designs, and evaluation procedures. Although Spanish had been taught to bilingual students for decades, the unique sociolinguistic constraints on U.S. Latino bilingual communities were never fully acknowledged until the publication of this volume. During this decade several more Spanish textbooks for bilingual students appeared: Mejías and Garza-Swan's (1981) *Nuestro español*, Burunat and Starčević's (1983) *El español y su estructura*, Marqués' (1986) *La lengua que heredamos* are exemplary of this trend. All three go beyond the implicit Southwest focus of the first textbooks for Spanish–English bilinguals, and all continue to stress literary, standard grammar, elimination of or at least conscious awareness of Anglicisms, and cultural awareness of the Spanish-speaking world within the United States and abroad. Except for the fact that they are written in Spanish and offer introductory comments aimed at bilingual students, these books are not easily distinguishable from intermediate-level textbooks aimed at second-language learners of Spanish. However, linguists offered explicit comparisons of U.S. Spanish varieties and dialects from other countries with an eye to legitimizing the pedagogical use of the former; Hidalgo (1987) is among the best examples, following on the earlier work of García (1975).

In 1982 Jon Amastae and Lucía Elías-Olivares edited *Spanish in the United States: Sociolinguistic aspects*, the first comprehensive sourcebook on a broad range of issues and dialects of U.S. Spanish, including Chicano, Puerto Rican, and Cuban varieties. Most of the articles are reprints of work done in the 1960s and 1970s, and the prestige of the Cambridge University Press imprint added further impact to a field of study which by this time had indisputably established itself as a major domain of scholarship and pedagogy. Particularly noteworthy are the reprints of several influential articles on codeswitching. In the same year Joshua Fishman and Gary Keller (1982) published the anthology *Bilingual education for Hispanic students in the United States*, also containing reprints of recently published articles or reports as well as studies appearing for the first time. There is considerable emphasis on child language acquisition and language attitudes, in addition to studies on language variation and educational techniques.

In 1983 Rubén Cobos published his *Dictionary of New Mexico and Southern Colorado Spanish*, the first modern dictionary of a non-immigrant variety of Spanish in the United States. In the same year Rosaura Sánchez published *Chicano discourse*, which combines a sociolinguistic analysis of Chicano Spanish with a scathing portrayal of Chicano society at the heart of a ruthless class struggle. Sánchez takes the stance that Chicano language and culture are under assault, and views with pessimism the possibilities for significant linguistic and cultural retention in view of the heavy pressure to assimilate to Anglo-American society. Cast in a neo-Marxist framework, Sánchez' monograph examines the root causes for Chicano language behavior, rather than confining herself to simply describing the end product. Her description of Chicano Spanish is considerably more mature than the "Nuestra circunstancia" article (Sánchez 1972), both in terms of descriptive detail and in encompassing the entirety of Mexican-American language usage. She distinguishes among "standard Spanish," "popular urban Spanish," and "popular rural Spanish" in describing Mexican-American speech, and treats all Chicano language usage from a discourse perspective. Language usage is set in terms of domains of usage, integration into distinct strata of United States society, linguistic and cultural attitudes, and rural/urban origin. Particularly useful is the careful delineation of rural vs. urban variants, based on field data. Sánchez convincingly demonstrates that not all Mexican-American Spanish is "archaic" or even "non-standard"; despite the relative socioeconomic disadvantage with respect to the Anglo-American population, the Mexican-American community contains an variety of styles and registers comparable to those used by monolingual native speakers of English.

Other influential anthologies, many stemming from the Español en los Estados Unidos conferences, were to appear in the 1980s: Bixler-Márquez, Green, and Ornstein (1989) and Green and Ornstein-Galicia (1986) on Mexican-American Spanish; Elías-Olivares (1983), another collection containing articles on several U.S. Spanish dialects; Elías-Olivares, Leone, Cisneros, and Gutiérrez (1985), with emphasis on language planning and public policy; Barkin, Brandt, and Ornstein-Galicia (1982) on bilingual language contacts; Aguirre (1985) on Chicano Spanish; Wherritt and García (1985) on U.S. Spanish; McKay and Wong (1988) with articles on Cuban, Mexican-American, and Puerto Rican communities in the United states, in addition to other bilingual groups; Ornstein-Galicia, Green, and Bixler-Márquez (1988) on several U.S. Spanish dialects; Blansitt and Teschner (1980) contains several articles on U.S. Spanish; Ferguson and Brice Heath (1981) also contains articles on U.S. Spanish.

During the 1980s most research on U.S. Spanish concentrated on Chicano and Puerto Rican varieties (cf. Alvarez 1989, Attinasi 1978, 1979, Flores, Attinasi, and Pedraza 1981, 1987, Milán 1982, Pousada and Poplack 1982, Reyes 1981, Torres 1989, Zentella 1981a, 1981b, 1981c, 1983, 1985, 1988 for samples of the latter), with comparatively little work done on Cuban-American Spanish (what little research was done was still largely based on Cuban-born expatriates). Noteworthy exceptions, including work on Cuban-American communities, include Fernández (1987), García and Otheguy (1988), Solé (1979, 1980, 1982), and Roca (1988). As hundreds of thousands of Central Americans poured into the United States, a few studies on Central American Spanish in the U.S. setting became available (Lipski 1986a, 1989 for Salvadoran Spanish); Peñalosa's (1984) survey of Central Americans in Los Angeles stands as the only monographic treatment (Varela 1998–99 updates the still scanty bibliography).

The most far-reaching linguistic survey of any U.S. variety was conceived in the late 1980s and carried out in the following decade. Garland Bills and Neddy Vigil received funding from the National Endowment for the Humanities to collect materials for an atlas of the traditional Spanish of northern New Mexico and southern Colorado, a region in which relatively little demographic turmoil has occurred over the past three centuries. During a three-year period, over 1000 hours of field recordings were made, covering all Spanish-speaking areas of New Mexico and Colorado, persons of all age ranges and backgrounds, and including free conversation, lexical and grammatical surveys, stories, and oral folklore. Numerous reports have already emerged from the survey (e.g. Bills and Vigil 1998, Vigil and Bills 1997, Vigil et al. 1996), and funding is now being sought to convert the recordings to digital format to facilitate use by other scholars. Similar projects have been contemplated in other southwestern states, with the California proposal coming the closest to realization, but to date the New Mexico/Colorado survey is the only comprehensive linguistic atlas of a language other than English carried out in the United States.

9. Interlude: Foreign-based studies of U.S. Spanish

Spanish in the United States has not typically been a topic of scholarly interest in the countries of origin of the principal U.S. Hispanophone populations. Puerto Rican linguists on the island have not traditionally included mainland U.S. Puerto Rican varieties in their studies, possibly discouraged by prevailing sentiments which stigmatize 'Nuyoricans' for their language and cultural behavior. In the Dominican Republic, whose expatriates now rival Puerto Ricans as the largest Spanish-speaking group in New York City, 'Dominican-York' speech has never been seriously broached as a research topic. Within Cuba, the entire Cuban-American population is regarded simply as expatriate counterrevolutionaries, ignoring the fact that the second generation of U.S.-born Cuban-Americans has already emerged, speaking a language which is no longer the unaltered Spanish of Cuba. The Central American nations which have contributed the largest numbers of expatriates to the United States – El Salvador, Nicaragua, and Guatemala – have been too burdened by political, social, and economic challenges to address the linguistic dimensions of Central American communities in the United States.

Within Spain, research on Spanish in the United States has centered on demographic concerns, the need to preserve the language, and the maintenance or establishment of cultural links between Spain and Spanish-speaking groups in the U.S. Peñuelas (1964, 1978) gives a sociohistorical perspective on Chicanos from a Spanish perspective, including mention of language, folklore, and literature. Montero de Pedro (1979) describes the remnants of Spanish language and culture in New Orleans. In 1980 there appeared the first panoramic book on Spanish in the United States from a scholar outside of the U.S.: Ernesto Barnach-Calbó's *La lengua española en Estados Unidos*. The focus is exclusively historical, legislative, and demographic; there are no linguistic details, and the author's stated intention is the defense of Spanish as a legitimate language in the United States.

In Mexico, where the term 'Chicano' has highly negative connotations, interest in 'Chicano Spanish' has, not surprisingly, been a late-blooming phenomenon. A noteworthy exception to this trend is the interest of Mexican dialectologists and sociolinguists, headed by Juan Lope Blanch (himself an expatriate Spaniard) in documenting the traditional Spanish spoken in the U.S. Southwest. The Universidad Nacional Autónoma de México (UNAM) held a conference in 1988 (already adumbrated in Lope Blanch 1987) in which plans were laid for systematic collection of samples of 'traditional' Spanish dialects in New Mexico, Colorado, California, Arizona, and Texas. The results of the symposium are summarized in Lope Blanch (1990b). Lope Blanch himself made several trips to the U.S. Southwest in the 1980s, collecting speech samples and writing brief analyses of several dialects (Lope Blanch 1990a, 1990c). Although explicitly referring only to 'traditional' Southwest Spanish, i.e. presumably leaving out the thousands of more recent Spanish-speaking arrivals and their descendants, the ambitious "Proyecto de estudio coordinado del español del Suroeste de los Estados Unidos" promises to place the study of Southwest Spanish on the same firm dialectological footing as the masterful *Atlas lingüístico de México* (Lope Blanch ed. 1990). A possible shortcoming of this project is the fact that it is modeled after dialect atlases of sedentary populations in which stable regional varieties and isoglosses can be easily traced. With the exception of northern New Mexico and southern Colorado, the 'traditional' (i.e. colonial) Spanish of the U.S. Southwest has been so completely overlaid by immigration from many regions of Mexico as to render the regionalist/isogloss approach untenable. As the data are collected researchers will face the challenge of developing dynamic models of U.S. Spanish which go beyond the classic European dialect atlas format, particularly in urban and suburban areas marked by a highly heterogeneous immigrant population.

10. U.S. Spanish research at the end of the century

The decade of the 1990s has been a time of immense international turmoil and internal strife. After the Persian Gulf War, the United States struggles not to reenter the endless morass of skirmishes and international isolation that accompanied earlier U.S. invasions of Western Hemisphere nations. The economy of Cuba has become increasingly tied to the U.S. dollar and small private businesses, but U.S.–Cuban relations remain marked by ambivalence and halting missteps. The Cuban-American community is irreconcilably split over liberalization of contacts with Cuba. By the end of the 1990s most of Latin America is under freely elected civilian governments, and in several countries former military dictators have been tried for atrocities committed during the previous decades. As the Americans with Disabilities Act opens new vistas for thousands of Americans, the dismantling of affirmative action programs, racially engineered congressional districts, and minority recruitment initiatives slams other doors. Amnesty of undocumented foreign workers has been followed by massive deportation of Mexican, Central American, and Caribbean 'illegals.' Research on U.S. Spanish in the last decade of the 20th century embodies the spirit of the times: satisfaction at obstacles overcome, tempered by frustration at the tenacious refusal of many sectors of American society to accept the language and culture of U.S. Latinos.

In the 1990s academia is no longer seen as subversive, but increasingly as redundant, bloated, self-serving and self-righteous. Ethnic studies continue to thrive at many universities, but potential beneficiaries of such programs often overlook or deliberately avoid such programs, while entering en masse into career tracks reputed to provide a rapid and substantial monetary payoff. 'Spanish for native/bilingual speakers' tracks are found at colleges and universities throughout the country, but in many departments their presence has become so routinized that the constant reevaluation and calibration essential to the success of booster programs does not take place at regular intervals. Spanish-

and English-speaking communities are divided over the meaning of bilingual education, and over whether such programs should be sustained or phased out.

This decade has been one of business as usual for the study of U.S. Spanish, although the publication of anthologies and monographs has slowed a bit. Several of the major publishers which had produced volumes on U.S. Spanish have shown reluctance to accept new collections, arguing that the topic is no longer innovative and therefore that matters are sufficiently settled. Among the anthologies which have overcome that reaction, Bergen (1990) and Roca and Lipski (1993) are derived from the Español en los Estados Unidos conferences; other anthologies stemming from conference presentations include Klee and Ramos-García (1991), a collection of articles on the sociolinguistics of the Spanish-speaking world containing articles on U.S. Spanish, as do Colombi and Alarcón (1997), devoted to teaching Spanish to native speakers. Silva-Corvalán (1995) and Roca and Jensen (1996), cover Spanish in bilingual contact environments, including the United States. Galindo and Gonzales (1999) is an anthology of Chicana language studies. Coulmas (1990) contains overview articles on U.S. Spanish.

In contrast to the relative scarcity of anthologies on U.S. Spanish, the 1990s have seen several important monographs on the sociolinguistic setting of U.S. Spanish varieties. Varela (1992) published the first comprehensive monograph on Cuban-American Spanish. Silva-Corvalán (1994) models the highly complex Los Angeles bilingual community; Zentella (1997) covers developmental bilingualism among Puerto Ricans in New York while Torres (1997) offers a discourse analysis of a suburban Puerto Rican community, the first monograph on suburban Spanish in the United States. Gutiérrez González (1993) provides a lexical survey of New York Puerto Rican Spanish. The vestigial dialects of Louisiana once more returned to the spotlight (Armistead 1992, Coles 1991a, 1991b, 1993; Lipski 1990 for the Isleños; Holloway 1997 for the Brulis), and the linguistic significance of semifluent bilinguals or isolated vestigial language speakers was also a recurring research topic (Harris 1994, Lipski 1985b, 1986b, 1987a, 1987b, 1987c, 1993b, 1996a, 1996b, Martínez 1993). Arnulfo Ramírez (1992) published *El español de los Estados Unidos: el lenguaje de los hispanos*. This book combines a brief overview of the linguistic characteristics of Chicano, Cuban, Puerto Rican, and Louisiana Isleño Spanish with more extensive chapters dealing with the sociolinguistics of language contact. Dominican Spanish, the burgeoning new kid on the block in the barrios of Nueva York, is beginning to accrete a research bibliography (e.g. García and Otheguy 1997), which has yet to grow in proportion to the Dominican-American population.

During the 1990s several of the principal textbooks of Spanish for bilingual students have come out with revised editions, while a number of important new books have been published, among the most noteworthy of which are DeLeon's (1993) *Español: material para el hispano*, Alonso-Lyrintzis' (1996) *Entre mundos*, Schmitt's (1997) *Nosotros y nuestro mundo*, and most recently Roca's (1999) *Nuevos mundos*.

11. Looking backward and forward at the gates of the new millennium

Although it includes a not inconsiderable number of maverick authors, the bibliography of U.S. Spanish studies closely follows the social and political undulations of the past century. As the nation moved backwards into intolerance and xenophobia again and again, scholarship on U.S. Spanish retreated with it. Every progressive societal thrust was also accompanied by a surge in the quantity and quality of research on Spanish in the United States. Although no one can question the sincere acts of good faith which have produced scholarship on U.S. Spanish over the past few decades, we must remain ever vigilant lest our work slip back over the brink into the chasm of esoterica. It is gratifying to encounter U.S. dialects of Spanish cited as data sources for linguistic analysis. The question we must ever pose, given the research trajectories described previously, is: are we traveling in an upward spiral, or caught in an endless whirlpool of stagnation? Is the current dearth of bombastically ideological approaches to Spanish in the United States a sign that U.S. Spanish has triumphed over its adversaries – internal and external – or just a temporary pause in an ongoing struggle? Universities have recently smiled on sociolinguistics and ethnic studies, but we cannot become complacent. Recently language and linguistics programs have been downsized, consolidated, or completely eliminated at several of the nation's most prestigious universities, bilingual education has been assaulted from all points on the political compass, and the ill-defined but vociferous public outcry against too much 'political correctness' has continued.

Our greatest fears are aroused by things that are different and unknown; as Spanish becomes neither, its place in American life will cease to be called into question. Demographics alone, however, will not suffice; our society, however reluctantly, still turns to scholars for answers to social dilemmas. Although change may be frustratingly slow, our legitimizing of Spanish as a national language through our research, teaching, and public presentations is a potent antidote to xenophobia and ignorance.

We, the authors and readers of this book, represent the bridge between the intellectually curious 'self' (our students and colleagues) and the anti-intellectual, incurious but politically and economically powerful 'other'; to the extent that we speak out with our voices and our words, we are variously reviled and respected, but seldom ignored. Let us continue to subvert what many construe as a dubious vulnerability into an asset, maintaining the healthy symbiosis of civil conscience and academic scholarship and never loosening our grasp on the lifeline that joins research and society.

Notes

1. Ajubita 1943, Baugh 1933, Blackman 1940, Callicut 1934, Coan 1927, Conway 1942, Fickinger 1930, Flores 1926, Hanson 1931, Haught 1931, Herriman 1932, Hoben and Hood 1937, Jackson 1938, Johnson 1938, Kelly 1935, Mahikian 1939, Manuel and Wright 1929, Montoya 1932, O'Brien 1937, Page 1931, Sánchez 1931, 1934a, 1934b, Vincent 1933, inter alia.

2. Only Decker 1952, describing Puerto Rican Spanish in Lorain, Ohio, and Maravilla 1955, dealing with Spanish in Indiana, antedate the Detroit study, while Humphrey (1943–1944) is a very early precursor of work on Midwestern Spanish.

3. Aguirre (1978), Anisman (1975), Barkin (1976, 1978a, 1978b), Dearholt and Valdés-Fallis (1978), DiPietro (1978), Gingras (1974), Gumperz and Hernández-Chávez (1975), Jacobson (1977a, 1977b, 1978a, 1978b), Lance (1975), Lipski (1977, 1978, 1979, 1982), McClure and Wentz (1975), McMemenamin (1973), Pfaff (1979), Poplack (1980), Redlinger (1976), Sánchez (1978), Timm (1975), and Valdés-Fallis (1975, 1976a, 1976b, 1978, 1979).

References

Academia Norteamericana de la Lengua Española. 1976. Noticias. *Boletín de la Academia Norteamericana de la Lengua Española* 1: 95–106.

Aguirre, Adalberto. 1978. *An experimental sociolinguistic analysis of Chicano bilingualism*. San Fransicso: R & E Associates.

Aguirre, Adalberto, ed. 1985. Language in the Chicano speech community. *International Journal of the Sociology of Language* 53.

Ajubita, María Luisa. 1943. Language in social relations with special references to the Mexican-American problem. M.A. thesis, Tulane University.

Alonso-Lyrintzis, Deana. 1996. *Entre mundos: An integrated approach for the native speaker*. Upper Saddle River, NJ: Prentice-Hall.

Alvarez, Celia. 1989. Code-switching in narrative performance: A Puerto Rican speech community in New York. In *English across cultures, cultures across English*, ed. Ofelia García and Ricardo Otheguy, 373–386. Berlin: Mouton de Gruyter.

Amastae, John and Lucía Elías-Olivares, eds. 1982. *Spanish in the United States: Sociolinguistic aspects*. Cambridge: Cambridge University Press.

American Association of Teachers of Spanish and Portuguese (AATSP). 1970. *Teaching Spanish in school and college to native speakers of Spanish*. Wichita, KS: AATSP.

Anisman, P. 1975. Some aspects of code-switching in New York Puerto Rican English. *Bilingual Review* 2: 56–85.

Armistead, Samuel. 1992. *The Spanish tradition in Louisiana: Isleño folklore*. Newark, DE: Juan de la Cuesta.

Attinasi, John. 1978. Language policy and the Puerto Rican community. *Bilingual Review/Revista Bilingüe* 5.1–2: 1–40.

Attinasi, John. 1979. Language attitudes in New York Puerto Rican community. In *Ethnoperspectives in bilingual education research*, ed. R. Padilla, 408–461. Ypsilanti, MI: Bilingual Review Press.

Baker, Paulline. 1953. *Español para los hispanos*. Dallas: B. Upshaw. Subsequent printings by National Textbook Company, Skokie, IL.

Barker, George. 1975. Pachuco: An American-Spanish argot and its social function in Tucson, Arizona. In *El lenguaje de los chicanos*, ed. Eduardo Hernández-Chávez, Andrew Cohen, and Anthony Beltramo, 183–201. Arlington, VA: Center for Applied Linguistics. Originally published in *University of Arizona Social Sciences Bulletin* 18 (1950): 1–38.

Barker, Marie. 1966. *Español para el bilingüe*. Skokie, IL: National Textbook Company.

Barkin, Florence. 1976. Language switching in Chicano Spanish: Linguistic norm awareness. *LEKTOS: Interdisciplinary working papers in language sciences, special issue*: 46–64.

Barkin, Florence. 1978a. Language switching in Chicano Spanish: A multifaceted phenomenon. In *SWALLOW VI*, ed. H. Key, G. McCullough, J. Sawyer, 1–10. Long Beach: California State University.

Barkin, Florence. 1978b. Loanshifts: An example of multilevel interference. In *SWALLOW VII*, ed. Anthony Lozano, 1–10. Boulder: University of Colorado.

Barnach-Calbó, Ernesto. 1980. *La lengua española en Estados Unidos*. Madrid: Oficina de Educación Iberoamericana.

Baugh, Lila. 1933. A study of pre-school vocabulary of Spanish-speaking children. M.A. thesis, University of Texas.

Beardsley, Theodore, Jr. 1976. Bibliografía preliminar de estudios sobre el español en los Estados Unidos. *Boletín de la Academia Norteamericana de la Lengua Española* 1: 49–73.

Beck, Mary. 1970. The English influence on the Spanish spoken in Bowling Green, Ohio. M.A. thesis, Bowling Green State University.

Bergen, John, ed. 1990. *Spanish in the United States: Sociolinguistic issues*. Washington, DC: Georgetown University Press.

Bills, Garland, ed. 1974. *Southwest areal linguistics*. San Diego: Institute for Cultural Pluralism, San Diego State University.

Bills, Garland and Jacob Ornstein. 1976. Linguistic diversity in Southwest Spanish. In *Studies in Southwest Spanish*, ed. J. Donald Bowen and Jacob Ornstein, 4–16. Rowley, MA: Newbury House.

Bills, Garland and Neddy Vigil. 1998. Ashes to ashes: The historical basis for dialect variation in New Mexican Spanish. Ms., published in *Romance Philology* 53.1.

Bixler-Márquez, Denis, George Green, and Jacob Ornstein, eds. 1989. *Mexican-American Spanish in its societal and cultural contexts*. Brownsville: University of Texas Pan American at Brownsville.

Blackman, Robert. 1940. The language handicap of Spanish-American children. M.A. thesis, University of Arizona.

Blansitt, E. and R. Teschner, eds. 1980. *Festschrift for Jacob Ornstein*. Rowley, MA: Newbury House.

Bourke, J. 1896. Notes on the language and folk usage of the Rio Grande Valley. *Journal of American Folklore* 9: 81–116.

Bowen, J. Donald. 1952. The Spanish of San Antonito, New Mexico. Ph.D. dissertation, University of New Mexico.

Bowen, J. Donald and Jacob Ornstein, eds. 1976. *Studies in Southwest Spanish*. Rowley, MA: Newbury House.

Braddy, Haldeen. 1953. Narcotic argot along the Mexican border. *American Speech* 30: 84–90.

Braddy, Haldeen. 1956. Smugglers argot in the Southwest. *American Speech* 21: 96–101.

Braddy, Haldeen. 1965. The Pachucos and their argot. *Southern Folklore Quarterly* 24: 255–271.

Burunat, Silvia and Elizabeth Starčević. 1983. *El español y su estructura: Lectura y escritura para bilingües*. Fort Worth: Harcourt, Brace, Jovanovich.

Callicut, Laurie. 1934. Word difficulties of Mexican and non-Mexican children. M.A. thesis, University of Texas.

Canfield, D. Lincoln. 1951. Tampa Spanish: Three characters in search of a pronunciation. *Modern Language Journal* 35: 42–44.

Canfield, D. Lincoln. 1976. Rasgos fonológicos del castellano en los Estados Unidos. *Boletín de la Academia Norteamericana de la Lengua Española* 1: 17–23.

Cárdenas, Daniel. 1970. *Dominant Spanish dialects spoken in the United States*. Washington, DC: ERIC Clearinghouse for Linguistics/Center for Applied Linguistics.

Casiano Montañez, Lucrecia. 1975. *La pronunciación de los puertorriqueños en Nueva York*. Bogotá: Ediciones Tercer Mundo.

Castellanos, Sister Mary C. 1968. English lexical and phonological influences in the Spanish of Cuban refugees in the Washington metropolitan area. M.A. thesis, Georgetown University.

Chang-Rodríguez, Eugenio. 1976. Palabras del director del *Boletín*. *Boletín de la Academia Norteamericana de la Lengua Española* 1: 5–6.

Cherry, Adrian. 1966. *Tampa Spanish slang with English translation*. Tampa: Lamplight Press.

Christian, Chester, Jr. 1971. Introduction to *Español para el bilingüe* by Marie Esman Barker. Skokie: National Textbook Company.

Christian, Jane and Chester Christian, Jr. 1966. Spanish language and culture in the Southwest. In *Language Loyalty in the United States*, ed. Joshua Fishman, 280–317. The Hague: Mouton.

Coan, Mary. 1927. The language difficulty in measuring the intelligence of Spanish-American students. M.A. thesis, University of New Mexico.

Cobos, Rubén. 1983. *A dictionary of New Mexico and southern Colorado Spanish*. Santa Fe: Museum of New Mexico Press.

Coles, Felice. 1991a. The *isleño* dialect of Spanish: Language maintenance strategies. In *Sociolinguistics of the Spanish-speaking world: Iberia, Latin America, United States*, ed. Carol Klee and Luis Ramos-García, 312–328. Tempe: Bilingual Press/Editorial Bilingüe.

Coles, Felice. 1991b. Social and linguistic correlates to language death: Research from the *Isleño* dialect of Spanish. Ph.D. dissertation, University of Texas, Austin.

Coles, Felice. 1993. Language maintenance institutions of the *isleño* dialect. In *Spanish in the United States: Linguistic contact and diversity*, ed. Ana Roca and John Lipski, 121–133. Berlin: Mouton de Gruyter.

Colombi, M. Cecilia and Francisco X. Alarcón, eds. 1997. *La enseñanza del español a hispanohablantes: Praxis y teoría*. Boston: Houghton Mifflin.

Coltharp, Lurline. 1965. *The tongue of the tirilones: A linguistic study of a criminal argot*. University, AL: University of Alabama Press.

Conway, T. F. 1942. The bilingual problem in the schools of New Mexico. *Alianza* 36 (Feb. 1942): 13, 17.

Corpus Christi Independent School District. 1975. *Speaking Spanish for native speaker: Teaching guide*. Corpus Christi, TX: CCISD.

Coulmas, Florian, ed. 1990. Spanish in the USA: New quandaries and prospects. *International Journal of the Sociology of Language* 84.

Craddock, Jerry. 1973. Spanish in North America. In *Linguistics in North America, Current trends in linguistics v. 10*, ed. Thomas Sebeok, 467–501. The Hague: Mouton.

De la Portilla, Marta and Beatriz Varela. 1979. *Mejora tu español: Lectura y redacción para bilingües*. New York: Regents Publishing Company.

Dearholt, D. and G. Valdés-Fallis. 1978. Toward a probablistic automata model of some aspects of code-switching. *Language in Society* 7: 411–419.

Decker, Bob. 1952. Phonology of the Puerto Rican Spanish of Lorain, Ohio: A study in the environmental displacement of a dialect. M.A. thesis, Ohio State University.

DeLeon, Fidel. 1993. *Español: Material para el hispano*. New York: McGraw Hill.

Díaz, Rosario. 1942. A vocabulary of California Spanish words of English origin used by first generation Spaniards of California. Ph.D. dissertation, Stanford University.

DiPietro, Robert. 1978. Code-switching as a verbal strategy among bilinguals. In *Aspects of bilingualism*, ed. Michel Paradis, 275–282. Columbia, SC: Hornbeam Press.

Domínguez, Doingo. 1974. A theoretical model for classifying dialectal variations of oral New Mexico Spanish. Ph.D. dissertation, University of New Mexico.

Durán, Roberto, ed. 1981. *Latino language and communicative behavior*. Norwood, NJ: Ablex Publishing.

Elías-Olivares, Lucía, ed. 1983. *Spanish in the U.S. setting: Beyond the Southwest*. Rosslyn, VA: National Clearinghouse for Bilingual Education.

Elías-Olivares, Lucía, Elizabeth Leone, René Cisneros, and John Gutiérrez, eds. 1985. *Spanish language use and public life in the USA*. The Hague: Mouton.

Espinosa, Aurelio. 1909. Studies in New Mexico Spanish, Part 1: Phonology. *Bulletin of the University of New Mexico* 1: 47–162. Translated and printed as "Estudios sobre el español de Nuevo Méjico" in *Biblioteca de Dialectología Hispanoamericana* 1 (1930): 19–313.

Espinosa, Aurelio. 1911. *The Spanish language in New Mexico and southern Colorado*. Santa Fe: New Mexican Publishing Company.

Espinosa, Aurelio. 1911–12. Studies in New Mexican Spanish, Part 2: Morphology. *Revue de Dialectologie Romane* 3: 241–256; 4: 251–286; 5: 142–172.

Espinosa, Aurelio. 1913. Nombres de bautismo nuevomejicanos. *Revue de Dialectologie Romane* 5: 356–376.

Espinosa, Aurelio. 1914–15. Studies in New Mexican Spanish, Part 3: The English elements. *Revue de Dialectologie Romane* 6: 241–317.

Espinosa, Aurelio. 1917. Speech mixture in New Mexico: The influence of the English language on New Mexican Spanish. In *The Pacific Ocean in history*, ed. H. Morse Stephens and Herbert Bolton, 408–428. New York: Macmillan. Also in *El lenguaje de los chicanos*, ed. Eduardo Hernández-Chávez, Andrew Cohen, and Anthony Beltramo, 99–114. Arlington, VA: Center for Applied Linguistics.

Espinosa, Aurelio. 1925. Syllabic consonants in New Mexican Spanish. *Language* 1: 109–118.

Espinosa, Aurelio. 1927–8. The language of the cuentos populares españoles. *Language* 3: 188–198, 4: 18–27, 4: 111–119.

Espinosa, Aurelio. 1934. El desarrollo fonético de las dos palabras 'todo' 'y' en la frase 'con todo y' + sustantivo en el español de Nuevo México. *Investigaciones Lingüísticas* 2: 195–199.

Espinosa, Aurelio. 1946. Estudios sobre el español de Nuevo Méjico, parte II: Morfología. *Biblioteca de Dialectología Hispanoamericana* 2: 1–102.

Fernández, M. 1987. Spanish language use among Cuban Americans of the first and second generation in West New York. M.S. thesis, City College of New York, School of Education.

Fickinger, Paul. 1930. A study of certain phases of the language problem of Spanish-American children. M.A. thesis, University of New Mexico.

Fishman, Joshua, Robert Cooper, and Roxana Ma, eds. 1975. *Bilingualism in the barrio, 2nd edition*. Bloomington: Indiana University.

Fishman, Joshua and Gary Keller, eds. 1982. *Bilingual education for Hispanic students in the United States*. New York: Columbia University, Teacher's College.

Flores, Juan, John Attinasi and Pedro Pedraza. 1981. La carreta made a U-turn: Puerto Rican language and culture in the United States. *Daedalus* 110: 193–217.

Flores, Juan, John Attinasi and Pedro Pedraza. 1987. Puerto Rican language and culture in New York City. In *Caribbean life in New York City: Sociocultural dimensions*, ed. Constance Sutton and Elsa Chaney, 221–234. New York: Center for Migration Studies of New York.

Flores, Zella. 1926. The relation of language difficulty to intelligence and school retardation in a group of Spanish-speaking children. M.A. thesis, University of Chicago.

Friedman, Lillian. 1950. Minorcan dialect words in St. Augustine, Florida. *American Dialect Society* 14: 81.

Galindo, Letticia. 1992. Dispelling the male-only myth: Chicanas and caló. *Bilingual Review/Revista Bilingüe* 17: 3–35.

Galindo, Letticia. 1995. Language attitudes towards Spanish and English varieties: A Chicano perspective. *Hispanic Journal of Behavioral Sciences* 17: 77–99.

Galindo, Letticia and María Dolores Gonzales, eds. 1999. *Speaking Chicana: Voice, power and identity*. Tucson: University of Arizona Press.

Galván, Roberto. 1955. El dialecto español de San Antonio, Texas. Ph.D. dissertation, Tulane University.

Galván, Roberto and Richard Teschner. 1977. *El diccionario del español chicano, 2nd edition*. Silver Spring, MD: Institute of Modern Languages.

García, Ernest. 1975. Chicano Spanish dialects and education. In *El lenguaje de los chicanos*, ed. Eduardo Hernández-Chávez, Andrew Cohen, and Anthony Beltramo, 70–76. Arlington, VA: Center for Applied Linguistics.

García, Ofelia and Ricardo Otheguy. 1988. The language situation of Cuban Americans. In *Language diversity: Problem or resource?*, ed. Sandra McKay and Sau-ling Cynthia Wong, 166–192. Cambridge and New York: Newbury House.

García, Ofelia and Ricardo Otheguy. 1997. No sólo de estándar vive el aula: Lo que nos enseñó la educación bilingüe sobre el español de Nueva York. In *La enseñanza del español a hispanohablantes: Praxis y teoría*, ed. M. Cecilia Colombi and Francisco X. Alarcón, 156–174. Boston: Houghton Mifflin.

Gingras, Rosario. 1974. Problems in the description of Spanish–English code-switching. In *Southwest areal linguistics*, ed. Garland Bills, 167–174. San Diego: Institute for Cultural Pluralism, San Diego State University.

González, R. J. 1967. Pachuco: The birth of a creole. *Arizona Quarterly* 23: 343–356.

Gray, Edward. 1912. The Spanish language in New Mexico: A national resource. *University of New Mexico Bulletin Sociological Series* 1.2: 37–52.

Green, George and Jacob Ornstein-Galicia, eds. 1986. *Mexican-American language: Usage, attitudes, maintenance, instruction, and policy.* Brownsville, Texas: Pan American University at Brownsville, Rio Grande Series in Language and Linguistics No. 1.

Griffith, Beatrice. 1947. The pachuco patois. *Common Ground* 7: 77–84.

Guitart, Jorge. 1976. *Markedness and a Cuban dialect of Spanish.* Washington, DC: Georgetown University Press.

Gumperz, John and Eduardo Hernández-Chávez. 1975. Cognitive aspects of bilingual communication. In *El lenguaje de los chicanos*, ed. Eduardo Hernández-Chávez, Andrew Cohen, and Anthony Beltramo, 154–163. Arlington, VA: Center for Applied Linguistics.

Gutiérrez González, Heliodoro. 1993. *El español en El Barrio de Nueva York: Estudio léxico.* New York: Academia Norteamericana de la Lengua Española.

Hammond, Robert. 1976. Some theoretical implications from rapid speech phenomena in Miami–Cuban Spanish. Ph.D. dissertation, University of Florida.

Hanson, Edith. 1931. A study of intelligence test results for Mexican children based on English and Mexican test forms. M.A. thesis, University of Southern California.

Hardman, Martha. 1956. The phonology of the Spanish of El Prado, New Mexico. M.A. thesis, University of New Mexico.

Harris, James. 1974. Morphologization of phonological rules: An example from Chicano Spanish. In *Linguistic symposium on Romance languages*, ed. Joe Campbell et al., 8–27. Washington, DC: Georgetown University Press.

Harris, Tracy. 1994. *Death of a language: The history of Judeo-Spanish.* Newark, DE: University of Delaware Press/London and Toronto: Associated University Press.

Haught, B. F. 1931. The language difficulty of Spanish-American children. *Journal of Applied Psychology* 15: 92–95.

Hayes, Francis. 1949. Anglo-Spanish speech in Tampa, Florida. *Hispania* 32: 48–52.

Hernández-Chávez, Eduardo, Andrew Cohen, and Anthony Beltramo, eds. 1975. *El lenguaje de los chicanos*. Arlington, VA: Center for Applied Linguistics.

Herriman, G. W. 1932. An investigation concerning the effect of language handicap on mental development and educational progress. M.A. thesis, University of Southern California.

Hidalgo, Margarita. 1987. Español mexicano y español chicano: Problemas y propuestas fundamentales. *Language Problems and Language Planning* 11: 166–193.

Hills, Elijah. C. 1906. New Mexican Spanish. *P.M.L.A.* 21: 706–753. Spanish translation "El español de Nuevo Méjico" in *Biblioteca de Dialectología Hispanoamericana* 4: 1–73.

Hoben, N. and J. Hood. 1937. Help the language handicapped. *Texas Outlook* 21 (June): 38–39.

Holloway, Charles. 1997. *Dialect death: The case of Brule Spanish.* Amsterdam and Philadelphia: John Benjamins.

Humphrey, Norman. 1943–44. The education and language of Detroit Mexicans. *Journal of Educational Psychology* 17: 534–542.

Jackson, Lucille. 1938. An analysis of the language difficulties of the Spanish-speaking children of the Bowie High School, El Paso, Texas. M.A. thesis, University of Texas.

Jacobson, Rodolfo. 1977a. How to trigger code-switching in a bilingual classroom. In *Southwest areal linguistics then and now*, ed. B. Hoffer and B. Dubois, 16–39. San Antonio: Trinity University.

Jacobson, Rodolfo. 1977b. The social implications of intra-sentential code-switching. In *New directions in Chicano scholarship*, ed. R. Romo and R. Paredes, 227–256. Special issue of *The New Scholar*.

Jacobson, Rodolfo. 1978a. Anticipatory embedding and imaginary content: Two newly identified codeswitching variables. In *SWALLOW VII*, ed. Anthony Lozano, 16–25. Boulder: University of Colorado.

Jacobson, Rodolfo. 1978b. Code-switching in South Texas: Sociolinguistic considerations and pedagogical applications. *Journal of the Linguistic Association of the Southwest* 3: 20–32.

Johnson, Loaz. 1938. A comparison of the vocabularies of Anglo-American and Spanish-American high school pupils. *Journal of Educational Psychology* 29: 135–144.

Keller, Gary, Richard Teschner, and S. Viera, eds. 1976. *Bilingualism in the bicentennial and beyond*. Jamaica, NY: Queen's University Press.

Kelly, Victor. 1935. The reading ability of Spanish and English speaking pupils. *Journal of Educational Research* 29: 209–211.

Keniston, Hayward. 1942. Notes on research in the Spanish spoken in the United States. *Bulletin of the American Council of Learned Societies* 34: 64–67.

Kercheville, F. M. 1934. A preliminary glossary of New Mexican Spanish. *University of New Mexico Bulletin* 5.3: 9–69.

Kreidler, Charles. 1958. A study of the influence of English on the Spanish of Puerto Ricans in Jersey City, New Jersey. Ph.D. dissertation, University of Michigan.

Lamb, Anthony. 1968. A phonological study of the Spanish of Havana, Cuba. Ph.D. dissertation, University of Kansas.

Lance, Donald. 1975. Spanish–English code switching. In *El lenguaje de los chicanos*, ed. Eduardo Hernández-Chávez, Andrew Cohen, and Anthony Beltramo, 138–153. Arlington, VA: Center for Applied Linguistics.

Lipski, John. 1977. Code-switching and the problem of bilingual competence. In *Fourth LACUS Forum*, ed. Michel Paradis, 263–277. Columbia, SC: Hornbeam Press.

Lipski, John. 1978. Code-switching and bilingual competence. In *Aspects of bilingualism*, ed. Michel Paradis, 250–264. Columbia, SC: Hornbeam Press.

Lipski, John. 1979. Bilingual competence and code-switching. *Langue et l'Homme* 42: 30–39.

Lipski, John. 1982. Spanish–English language switching in speech and literature: Theories and models. *Bilingual Review* 9: 191–212.

Lipski, John. 1985a. *Linguistic aspects of Spanish–English language switching*. Tempe: Arizona State University, Center for Latin American Studies.

Lipski, John. 1985b. Creole Spanish and vestigial Spanish: Evolutionary parallels. *Linguistics* 23: 963–984.

Lipski, John. 1986a. Central American Spanish in the United States: El Salvador. *Aztlán* 17: 91–124.

Lipski, John. 1986b. El español vestigial de los Estados Unidos: Características e implicaciones teóricas. *Estudios Filológicos* 21: 7–22.

Lipski, John. 1987a. El español del Río Sabinas: Vestigios del español mexicano en Luisiana y Texas. *Nueva Revista de Filología Hispánica* 35: 111–128.

Lipski, John. 1987b. Language contact phenomena in Louisiana *isleño* Spanish. *American Speech* 62: 320–331.

Lipski, John. 1987c. The construction *pa(ra) atrás* among Spanish–English bilinguals: Parallel structures and universal patterns. *Ibero Americana* 28/29: 87–96.

Lipski, John. 1989. Salvadorans in the United States: Patterns of sociolinguistic integration. *National Journal of Sociology* 3.1: 97–119.

Lipski, John. 1990. *The language of the isleños: Vestigial Spanish in Louisiana*. Baton Rouge: Louisiana State University Press.

Lipski, John. 1992. Language – varieties of Spanish spoken, English usage among Hispanics, Spanish in business, the media and other social environments, bilingualism and code-switching. In *The Hispanic-American almanac*, ed. Nicolás Kanellos, 209–227. Detroit: Gale Research Inc.

Lipski, John. 1993a. Syllabic consonants and New Mexico Spanish: The geometry of syllabification. *Southwest Journal of Linguistics* 12: 109–127 [published 1998].

Lipski, John. 1993b. Creoloid phenomena in the Spanish of transitional bilinguals. In *Spanish in the United States: Linguistic contact and diversity*, ed. Ana Roca and John Lipski, 155–182. Berlin: Mouton de Gruyter.

Lipski, John. 1996a. Patterns of pronominal evolution in Cuban-American bilinguals. In *Spanish in contact: Issues in bilingualism*, ed. Ana Roca and John B. Jensen, 159–186. Somerville, MA: Cascadilla Press.

Lipski, John. 1996b. Los dialectos vestigiales del español en los Estados Unidos: Estado de la cuestión. *Signo y Seña* 6: 459–489.

Lipski, John. Forthcoming. The linguistic situation of Central Americans. In *Language diversity: Problem or resource? (2nd ed.)*, ed. Sandra McKay and Sau-ling Cynthia Wong.

Lope Blanch, Juan. 1987. El estudio del español hablado en el suroeste de los Estados Unidos. *Anuario de Letras* 25: 201–208.

Lope Blanch, Juan. 1990a. El español hablado en el suroeste de los Estados Unidos. Mexico: Universidad Nacional Autónoma de México.

Lope Blanch, Juan. 1990b. El estudio coordinado del español del suroeste de los Estados Unidos (memoria de un coloquio). *Anuario de Letras* 28: 343–354.

Lope Blanch, Juan. 1990c. La estructura del discurso en el habla de Mora, Nuevo México. *Romance Philology* 65: 26–35.

Lope Blanch, Juan, ed. 1990. *Atlas lingüístico de México, vol. I*. Mexico City: Colegio de México/Fondo de Cultura Económica.

Lozano, Anthony. 1961. Intercambio de español e inglés en San Antonio, Texas. *Archivum* 11: 111–138.

MacCurdy, Raymond. 1950. *The Spanish dialect of St. Bernard Parish, Louisiana*. Albuquerque: University of New Mexico.

MacCurdy, Raymond. 1959. A Spanish word-list of the 'Brulis' dwellers of Louisiana. *Hispania* 42: 547–554.

Mahikian, Charles. 1939. Measuring the intelligence and reading capacity of Spanish-speaking children. *Elementary School Journal* 39: 760–768.

Manuel, Herschel and Carrie Wright. 1929. The language difficulty of Mexican children. *Pedagogical Seminary and Journal of Genetic Psychology* Sept. 1929: 458–468.

Maravilla, Frederick. 1955. Los anglicismos en el español de Indiana Harbor, Indiana. M.A. thesis, University of Chicago.

Marcoux, Fred. 1961. Handicaps of bi-lingual Mexican children. M.A. thesis, University of Southern California.

Marqués, Sarah. 1986. *La lengua que heredamos: Curso de español para bilingües*. New York: Wiley.

Martínez, Elizabeth. 1993. *Morpho-syntactic erosion between two generational groups of Spanish speakers in the U.S.* New York: Peter Lang.

Marx, Meyer. 1953. *The problem of bi-lingualism among Spanish speaking groups in the United States: A review of the literature*. Project Report, University of Southern California, August 1953.

May, Darlene. 1966. Notas sobre el tex-mex. *Boletín del Instituto Caro y Cuervo* 70: 17–19.

McClure, E. and J. Wentz. 1975. Functions of code-switching among Mexican-American children. In *Papers from the parasession on functionalism, Chicago Linguistic Society*, ed. R. Grossman, L. San, and T. Vance, 421–432. Chicago: Chicago Linguistics Society

McHale, Carlos. 1976. Discurso de D. Carlos McHale al instalarse la Academia Norteamericana de la Lengua Española. *Boletín de la Academia Norteamericana de la Lengua Española* 1: 89–94.

McKay, Sandra and Sau-ling Cynthia Wong, eds. 1988. *Language diversity: Problem or resource?* Cambridge and New York: Newbury House.

McMenamin. J. 1973. Rapid code-switching among Chicano bilinguals. *Orbis* 22: 474–487.

McSpadden, George. 1934. Some semantic and philolgical facts of the Spanish spoken in Chilili, New Mexico. *University of New Mexico Bulletin* 5.2: 72–102.

Mejías, Hugo and Gloria Garza-Swan. 1981. *Nuestro español: Curso para estudiantes bilingües*. New York: Macmillan.

Milán, William. 1982. Spanish in the inner city: Puerto Rican speakers in New York. In *Bilingual education for Hispanic students in the United States*, ed. Joshua Fishman and Gary Keller, 191–206. New York: Columbia University, Teacher's College.

Montero de Pedro, José. 1979. *Españoles en Nueva Orleans y Luisiana*. Madrid: Ediciones Cultura Hispánica del Centro Iberoamericano de Cooperación.

Montoya, Atanasio. 1932. Removing the language difficulty. *American Childhood* 17: 12–15.

Morrill, D. B. 1918. The Spanish language problem. *New Mexico Journal of Education* 14 (May): 6–7.

O'Brien, Mary. 1937. A comparison of the reading ability of Spanish-speaking with non-Spanish-speaking pupils in grade 6A of the Denver Public Schools. M.A. thesis, University of Denver.

Ornstein, Jacob. 1951. The archaic and the modern in the Spanish of New Mexico. *Hispania* 34: 137–142. Also in *El lenguaje de los chicanos*, ed. Eduardo Hernández-Chávez, Andrew Cohen, and Anthony Beltramo, 6–12. Arlington, VA: Center for Applied Linguistics.

Ornstein, Jacob. 1972. Toward a classification of Southwest Spanish non-standard variants. *Linguistics* 93: 70–87.

Ornstein-Galicia, Jacob, George Green, and Dennis Bixler-Márquez, eds. 1988. *Research issues and problems in United States Spanish: Latin American and southwestern varieties.* Brownsville: Pan American University at Brownsville.

Ortiz, Carmelita. 1947. English influences on the Spanish of Tampa. M.A. thesis, University of Florida.

Ortiz, Carmelita. 1949. English influence on the Spanish of Tampa. *Hispania* 32: 300–304.

Page, Dorothy. 1931. Performance of Spanish-American children on verbal and non-verbal intelligence tests. M.A. thesis, University of New Mexico.

Paradis, Michel, ed. 1978. *Aspects of bilingualism.* Columbia, SC: Hornbeam Press.

Patterson, Maurine. 1946. Some dialectal tendencies in popular Spanish in San Antonio. M.A. thesis, Texas Women's University.

Peñalosa, Fernando. 1980. *Chicano sociolinguistics.* Rowley: Newbury House.

Peñalosa, Fernando. 1984. *Central Americans in Los Angeles: Background, language, education.* Los Alamitos, CA: National Center for Bilingual Research.

Peñuelas, Marcelino. 1964. *Lo español en el suroeste de los Estados Unidos.* Madrid: Ediciones Cultura Hispánica.

Peñuelas, Marcelino. 1978. *Cultura hispánica en Estados Unidos: Los chicanos, 2nd ed.* Madrid: Ediciones Cultura Hispánica del Centro Iberoamericano de Cooperación.

Pfaff, Carol. 1979. Constraints on language mixing. *Language* 55: 291–318.

Phillips, Robert. 1967. Los Angeles Spanish: A description analysis. Ph.D. dissertation, University of Wisconsin.

Poplack, Shana. 1980. Sometimes I'll start a sentence in English y termino en español. *Linguistics* 18: 581–618.

Porges, Ana. 1949. The influence of English on the Spanish of New York. M.A. thesis, University of Florida.

Post, Anita. 1933. Some aspects of Arizona Spanish. *Hispania* 16: 35–42.

Pousada, Alicia and Shana Poplack. 1982. No case for convergence: The Puerto Rican Spanish verb system in a langauge-contact situation. In *Bilingual education for Hispanic students in the United States*, ed. Joshua Fishman and Gary Keller, 207–240. New York: Columbia University, Teacher's College.

Quintanilla, Guadalupe and James Silman. 1978. *Español: Lo esencial para el bilingüe.* Washington, DC: University Press of America.

Rael, Juan. 1937. A study of the phonology and morphology of New Mexico Spanish based on a collection of 400 folktales. Ph.D. dissertation, Stanford University.

Rael, Juan. 1939. Associative interference in New Mexican Spanish. In *El lenguaje de los chicanos*, ed. Eduardo Hernández-Chávez, Andrew Cohen, and Anthony Beltramo, 19–29. Arlington, VA: Center for Applied Linguistics. First published in *Hispanic Review* 7 (1939): 324–336.

Rael, Juan. 1940. Associative interference in Spanish. *Hispanic Review* 8: 346–349.

Ramírez, Arnulfo. 1992. *El español de los Estados Unidos: El lenguaje de los hispanos.* Madrid: MAPFRE.

Ramírez. Manuel. 1939. Some semantic and linguistic notes on the Spanish spoken in Tampa, Florida. *Revista Inter-Americana* 1: 25–33.

Ranson, Helen. 1954. Viles pochismos. *Hispania* 37: 285–287.

Redlinger, Wendy. 1976. A description of transference and code-switching in Mexican-American English and Spanish. In *Bilingualism in the bicentennial and beyond*, ed. Gary Keller, Richard Teschner, and S. Viera, 41–52. Jamaica, NY: Queen's University Press.

Reyes, Rogelio. 1976. Studies in Chicano Spanish. Ph.D. dissertation, Harvard University.

Reyes, Rogelio. 1981. Independent convergence in Chicano and New York City Puerto Rican bilingualism. In *Latino language and communicative behavior*, ed. Roberto Durán, 439–448. Norwood, NJ: Ablex Publishing.

Roca, Ana. 1986. Pedagogical and sociolinguistic perspectives on the teaching of Spanish to Hispanic bilingual college students in South Florida. D.A. dissertation, University of Miami.

Roca, Ana. 1999. *Nuevos mundos*. New York: Wiley.

Roca, Ana and John B. Jensen, eds. 1996. *Spanish in contact: Issues in bilingualism.* Somerville, MA: Cascadilla Press.

Roca, Ana and John Lipski, eds. 1993. *Spanish in the United States: Linguistic contact and diversity*. Berlin: Mouton de Gruyter.

Saltarelli, Mario. 1975. Leveling of paradigms in the Southwest. In *Colloquium on Spanish and Portuguese linguistics*, ed. William Milan et al., 123–131. Washington DC: Georgetown University Press.

Sánchez, George. 1931. A study of the scores of Spanish-speaking children on repeated tests. M.A. thesis, University of Texas.

Sánchez, George. 1934a. Bilingualism and mental measurement. *Journal of Applied Psychology* 18: 765–772.

Sánchez, George. 1934b. The implications of a basal vocabulary to the measurement of the abilities of bilingual children. *Journal of Social Psychology* 5: 395–402.

Sánchez, Rosaura. 1972. Nuestra circunstancia lingüística. *El Grito* 6: 45–74.

Sánchez, Rosaura. 1978. Denotations and connotations in Chicano code-switching. In *SWALLOW VII*, ed. Anthony Lozano, 187–198. Boulder: University of Colorado.

Sánchez, Rosaura. 1983. *Chicano discourse*. Rowley, MA: Newbury House.

Sawyer, Janet. 1958. A dialect study of San Antonio, Texas: A bilingual community. Ph.D. dissertation, University of Texas.

Sawyer, Janet. 1964. Spanish–English bilingualism in San Antonio, Texas. *Publications of the American Dialect Society* 41: 7–15. Also in *El lenguaje de los chicanos*, ed. Eduardo Hernández-Chávez, Andrew Cohen, and Anthony Beltramo, 77–98. Arlington, VA: Center for Applied Linguistics.

Schmitt, Conrad. 1997. *Nosotros y nuestro mundo*. New York: Glencoe/McGraw Hill.

Silva-Corvalán, Carmen. 1994. *Language contact and change: Spanish in Los Angeles.* Oxford: Clarendon Press.

Silva-Corvalán, Carmen, ed. 1995. *Spanish in four continents: Studies in language contact and bilingualism.* Washington, DC: Georgetown University Press.

Solé, Carlos. 1970. Bibliografía sobre el español en América, 1920–1967. Washington, DC: Georgetown University Press.

Solé, Carlos. 1979. Selección idiomática entre la nueva generación de cubano-americanos. *Bilingual Review/Revista Bilingüe* 6: 1–10.

Solé, Carlos. 1980. Language usage patterns among a young generation of Cuban-Americans. In *Festschrift for Jacob Ornstein*, ed. E. Blansitt and R. Teschner, 274–281. Rowley, MA: Newbury House.

Solé, Carlos. 1982. Language loyalty and language attitudes among Cuban-Americans. In *Bilingual education for Hispanic students in the United States*, ed. Joshua Fishman and Gary Keller, 254–268. New York: Columbia University, Teacher's College.

Teschner, Richard, Garland Bills, and Jerry Craddock. 1975. *Spanish and English of United States Hispanos: A critical, annotated, linguistic bibliography*. Arlington, VA: Center for Applied Linguistics.

Timm, Lenora. 1975. Spanish–English code-switching: El porque y how-not-to. *Romance Philology* 28: 473–482.

Torres, Lourdes. 1989. Code-mixing and borrowing in a New York Puerto Rican community: A cross-generational study. *World Englishes* 8: 419–432.

Torres, Lourdes. 1997. *Puerto Rican discourse: A sociolinguistic study of a New York suburb*. Mahwah, NJ: Lawrence Erlbaum.

Tsuzaki, Stanley. 1963. English influences in the phonology and morphology of the Spanish spoken in the Mexican colony in Detroit, Michigan. Ph.D. dissertation, University of Michigan.

Tsuzaki, Stanley. 1971. *English influence on Mexican Spanish in Detroit*. The Hague: Mouton.

U.S. Office of Education. 1972. *Teaching Spanish in school and college to native speakers of Spanish*. Washington, DC: Department of Health, Education and Welfare.

Valdés, Guadalupe and Rodolfo García-Moya, eds. 1976. *Teaching Spanish to the Spanish speaking: Theory and practice*. San Antonio: Trinity University.

Valdés, Guadalupe, Anthony Lozano, and Rafael García-Moya, eds. 1981. *Teaching Spanish to the Hispanic bilingual*. New York: Columbia University, Teacher's Press.

Valdés, Guadalupe and Richard Teschner. 1977a. *Español escrito: Curso para hispanoparlantes bilingües*. New York: Scribner's.

Valdés, Guadalupe and Richard Teschner. 1977b. *Spanish for the Spanish speaking: A descriptive bibliography of materials*. Austin: National Educational Laboratory.

Valdés-Fallis, Guadalupe. 1975. Code-switching in bilingual Chicano poetry. In *Southwest languages and linguistics in educational perspective*, ed. G. Cantoni Harvey and M. Heiser, 143–170. San Diego: Institute for Cultural Pluralism, San Diego State University.

Valdés-Fallis, Guadalupe. 1976a. Code-switching in bilingual Chicano poetry. *Hispania* 59: 877–885.

Valdés-Fallis, Guadalupe. 1976b. Social interaction and code-switching patterns: A case study in Spanish/English alternatives. In *Bilingualism in the bicentennial and beyond*, ed. Gary Keller, Richard Teschner, and S. Viera, 53–85. Jamaica, NY: Queen's University Press.

Valdés-Fallis, Guadalupe. 1978. Code-switching and language dominance: Some initial findings. *General Linguistics* 18: 90–104.

Valdés-Fallis, Guadalupe. 1979. Is code-switching interference, integration or neither? In *Festschrift for Jacob Ornstein*, ed. E. Blansitt and R. Teschner, 314–325. Rowley, MA: Newbury House.

Varela, Beatriz. 1992. *El español cubano-americano*. New York: Senda Nueva de Ediciones.

Varela, Beatriz. 1998–99. Discurso de incorporación: El español centroamericano de Luisiana. *Boletín de la Academia Norteamericana de la Lengua Española* 9–10: 1–40.

Vigil, Neddy and Garland Bills. 1997. A methodology for rapid geographical mapping of dialect features. In *Issues and methods in dialectology*, ed. Alan Thomas, 247–255. Bangor, Wales: University of Wales, Department of Linguistics.

Vigil, Neddy, Garland Bills, Ysaura Bernal-Enríquez, and Rodney Ulibarrí. 1996. El atlas lingüístico de Nuevo México y el sur de Colorado: Algunos resultados preliminares. In *Actas del X Congreso Internacional de la Asociación de Lingüística y Filología de la America Latina*, ed. Marina Arjona Iglesias et al., 651–663. Mexico: Universidad Nacional Autónoma de México.

Vincent, Henrietta. 1933. A study of performance of Spanish-speaking pupils on Spanish tests. M.A. thesis, New Mexico State Teachers College.

Wagner, Max. 1953. Ein mexicanisch-amerikanischer Argot: Das Pachuco. *Romanistisches Jahrbuch* 6: 237–266.

Webb, John. 1976. A lexical study of "calo" and non-standard Spanish in the Southwest. Ph.D. dissertation, University of California, Berkeley.

Webb, John. 1980. Pidgins (and creoles?) on the U.S.–Mexican Border. In *Festschrift for Jacob Ornstein*, ed. E. Blansitt and R. Teschner, 326–331. Rowley, MA: Newbury House.

Wherritt, Irene and Ofelia García, eds. 1989. U.S. Spanish: The language of the Latinos. *International Journal of the Sociology of Language* 79.

Whittier Union High School District. 1966. *Spanish for the bilingual student*. Whittier, CA: Whittier Union High School District.

Woodbridge, Hensley. 1954. Spanish in the American South and Southwest: A bibliographical survey for 1940–1953. *Orbis* 3: 236–244.

Zentella, Ana Celia. 1981a. Tá bien: You could answer me in cualquier idioma: Puerto Rican code-switching in bilingual classrooms. In *Latino language and communicative behavior*, ed. Roberto Durán, 109–131. Norwood, NJ: Ablex Publishing.

Zentella, Ana Celia. 1981b. Language variety among Puerto Ricans. In *Language in the U.S.A.*, ed. Charles Ferguson and Shirley Brice Heath, 218–238. Cambridge: Cambridge University Press.

Zentella, Ana Celia. 1981c. Hablamos los dos. We speak both: Growing up bilingual in El Barrio. Ph.D. dissertation, University of Pennsylvania.

Zentella, Ana Celia. 1983. Spanish and English in contact in the U.S.: The Puerto Rican experience. *Word* 33.1–2: 42–57.

Zentella, Ana Celia. 1985. The fate of Spanish in the United States: The Puerto Rican experience. In *The language of inequality*, ed. N. Wolfson and J. Manes, 41–59. The Hague: Mouton.

Zentella, Ana Celia. 1988. The language situation of Puerto Ricans. In *Language diversity: Problem or resource?*, ed. Sandra McKay and Sau-ling Cynthia Wong, 140–165. Cambridge and New York: Newbury House.

Zentella, Ana Celia. 1997. *Growing up bilingual: Puerto Rican children in New York*. Malden, MA: Blackwell.

Bilingualism from Another Perspective: The Case of Young Interpreters from Immigrant Communities

Guadalupe Valdés, Christina Chávez, Claudia Angelelli, Kerry Enright, Marisela González, Dania García, and Leisy Wyman

Stanford University

1. Introduction

Contrary to the claims made by supporters of U.S. English, immigrants to the U.S., including Latinos, are regularly acquiring English and shifting away from the use of their ethnic languages (de la Garza et al. 1992).[1] Solé (1990) demonstrated that many young Latinos have shifted entirely to English. Support for Solé's conclusions has been provided more recently by Portes and Hao (1998), who found that fewer than half of the Latino students they surveyed were fluent bilinguals.

The phenomenon of language shift raises important questions for people who are concerned about the future of Spanish in the United States, especially those individuals engaged in the teaching of Spanish to first-, second-, third-, and even fourth-generation Latinos. These questions are: (1) How can direct instruction in a heritage language be used to reverse the processes of language change and language shift? and (2) Are our current goals for heritage speakers of Spanish coherent with the personal and professional goals of these young people? All too often our goals for heritage language students are dictated by departmental traditions and curricula. Responding to pressures from colleagues, we often focus almost exclusively on preparing students for the next-level classes. At both the high school and college levels, we may know little about our students' lives or about their struggles to succeed academically. Even though we speak our students' heritage language, we may know little about the communities in which they live. We may have only a superficial awareness of

 Research on Spanish in the U.S., ed. Ana Roca, 42–81. Somerville, MA: Cascadilla Press.

the strengths that they display in both their languages when they use them in real-life settings.

This paper attempts to provide a more complete view of young immigrant students as bilinguals who use two languages in their homes and communities. We report on research carried out on young interpreters whose proficiencies in English and Spanish were not equal. We present evidence that these young interpreters, who are often considered by their teachers to be very low-level English speakers, are able to communicate effectively using flawed but very functional English when they interpret for their families. These youngsters displayed the ability to understand English at a sophisticated level. Similarly, many youngsters who were second- and third-generation immigrant students, and who had been schooled exclusively in English since their elementary school years, retained important strengths in Spanish. While Spanish language teachers might frown on the non-standard nature of their speech, these youngsters effectively interpreted for newly arrived immigrants of different ages and educational backgrounds.

We begin this paper with a description of the larger project of which this study is a part. We proceed to a discussion of bilingualism and an overview of the translation/interpretation field. We focus specifically on the difficulty of evaluating naive or young interpreters using criteria established for professional interpreters. We then describe the youngsters who took part in the study and the procedures followed in gathering the data. We present a detailed examination of the demands made by the interpretation task and describe and evaluate the youngsters' performance. We conclude that these youngsters have already developed unique linguistic abilities that must be nurtured through special classes designed for bilingual heritage-language students.

2. The study of linguistically and culturally talented youngsters

This study is one part of a larger project entitled "Identifying, Teaching, and Assessing the Talented through Linguistic and Cultural Lenses." This project was funded by the National Research Center on the Gifted and Talented. The purpose of the study was to broaden the definitions of intelligence that schools currently use to identify "giftedness" by focusing on abilities that are not generally identified or valued in formal education. It focused on bilingual youngsters who are selected from among their siblings to serve as interpreters for their families. The project included: (1) a study of young interpreters in communities, (2) the development and implementation of an instrument to identify tacit knowledge of interpretation and translation, (3) the implementation of a validation study involving a simulated interpretation task, and (4) the development of guidelines for an interpretation and translation curriculum at the high school level.

To date, the majority of schools around the country have been largely unsuccessful at identifying gifted bilingual students and at developing programs that might enhance the unique abilities of these youngsters. Current definitions of giftedness (U.S. Department of Education 1993) include a range of abilities, including general intellectual abilities, specific academic abilities, creative or productive thinking, leadership, visual abilities, and performing arts and psychomotor skills. This shift in official definitions, however, has not necessarily changed existing practices. Surveys conducted by Patton et al. (1990) and Gubbins et al. (1993), for example, reveal that there is a distinct discrepancy between educators' assumptions about identification practices in gifted education and actual practices. Gubbins et al. argue that the challenge is to create a broad range of procedures to identify gifted students in order to carry out this inclusive vision of giftedness.

According to Baldwin (1991), both African-Americans and Latinos continue to be under-represented in gifted and talented education programs and are over-represented in special education. In theory, teachers, educators, and state officials recognize that all communities have gifted and talented students, but their practices, including their over-reliance on IQ tests to identify gifted students, favor white students. According to leaders in the field of gifted education, one of the major challenges facing gifted education is the development of "identification procedures and programming practices that guarantee participation of more culturally and linguistically diverse students without falling prey to criticisms such as tokenism, watering down, and quota systems" (Renzulli 1997: 1). Equally important, according to Frasier 1992, Frasier et al. 1994, Gallagher 1996, and Kitano 1992 is the design and implementation of special programs for gifted minority students once they are identified.

Our research, then, hoped to provide data that would help school administrators and classroom teachers identify the special talents of children who are not normally viewed by schools as gifted. The particular focus of one segment of our project was the study of young interpreters, whom we conjectured would exhibit high performance in what Treffinger and Renzulli (1986) have termed "gifted behaviors."

3. Bilingualism and cognitive development

For many educators, including individuals who work closely with immigrant students, the categories *gifted and talented* and *bilingual* are mutually exclusive. Many educators have been influenced by the early research on bilingualism and intelligence from the beginning of the 20th century. The studies from this era were fueled by a desire to limit the flow of immigration. They argued that the reason that bilinguals did not perform as well as monolinguals on IQ tests was that bilingualism had a detrimental effect on cognitive development (see Darcy 1953, Diaz 1983, Hakuta 1986, Hakuta, Ferdman, and Diaz 1986).

Beginning in 1962 with the work of Peal and Lambert, later research on the impact of bilingualism on cognitive development (e.g. Balkan 1970, Cummins

1978, Genesee, Tucker, and Lambert 1975, Ianco-Worrall 1972) has sought to demonstrate the strengths, rather than the deficiencies, of bilinguals. This research has established that there are important areas where bilinguals perform better than monolinguals.

Some researchers have given special attention to metalinguistic skills. Metalinguistic skills involve the manipulation of language as a formal system, the use of language to talk about or reflect on language, and the ability to attend to units of language such as words and sentences. Researchers focusing on these abilities have been influenced by the work of Vygotsky (1962), who maintained that because bilingual children expressed the same thought in different languages, they would come to see their language as one system among many and develop an awareness of linguistic operations. Research conducted to date indicates that bilinguals are superior to monolinguals in the development of metalinguistic abilities, which include: the capacity to compare words on the basis of semantic features (Ianco-Worrell 1972); awareness of the conventional nature of words and language (Ben-Zeev 1977, Feldman and Shen 1971), and metalinguistic awareness (Cummins 1978, Hakuta and Diaz 1984). Metalinguistic awareness is defined by Malakoff and Hakuta (1991: 147) as "the awareness of the underlying linguistic nature of language use."

Some researchers have argued that for all of its promise, much of the current research on the cognitive advantages of bilingualism is methodologically flawed and leaves many important questions unanswered (e.g. Hakuta 1986, Reynolds 1991). Reynolds (1991: 148), in particular, has argued that the dependent variables used in the various studies conducted to date are "trivial, theoretically questionable, or psychometrically faulty."

For those concerned about minority immigrant children, the recent work on the cognitive advantages of bilingual experience presents other difficulties as well. Most of the more exciting findings concerning the positive consequences of bilingualism have been based on the study of middle-class children who are considered to be "balanced" in their bilingualism. Bilinguals are said to be balanced when they are proficient in both their first and second languages. Individuals who are more proficient in one language than in the other have often not attained the age-appropriate abilities that are typical of monolinguals in their other language. These second language learners are not included in major studies and are often termed "pseudo-bilinguals."

This emphasis on balanced bilinguals has serious implications. Studies which base their conclusions on notions of bilingual balance, including the well-known work of Cummins (1973, 1979, 1981),[2] have had a widespread influence on educators. Consequently, teachers overlook many of the manifestations of sophisticated bilingualism among their less "balanced" students. Because immigrant youngsters frequently fall further and further behind their mainstream same-age peers, teachers and administrators see them as a problem with very few solutions, rather than as students with special bilingual talents.

Interestingly, while educational communities focus on the low achievement of bilingual immigrant children, families call upon these same youngsters to play the role of interpreters and translators. Some research suggests that even very young bilingual interpreters develop the capacity to retain the meaning of the message as they translate from one language to the other (Harris 1977, Harris and Sherwood 1978, Shannon 1987, Vásquez, Pease-Alvarez, and Shannon 1994, Zentella 1997). Since both translation and interpretation are complex information processing activities that require the ability to uncover the underlying meaning of language, it is remarkable that young bilingual children can translate and interpret effectively.

Unfortunately, most language teachers know little about these abilities. Even when they are aware that bilingual youngsters interpret for their families, few teachers consider them to be uniquely talented or recognize their ability to carry out complex real-world tasks. Because language-teaching professionals often serve as ad-hoc interpreters or hire out as translators themselves, they frequently believe that all "good" interpreters must possess certain linguistic strengths. They sometimes find it hard to believe that students who are not native-like or highly educated in both languages can actually interpret successfully. They are not aware that these youngsters bring with them specialized proficiencies in two languages that can be nurtured by teachers like themselves.

4. Professional interpreters: The case of highly skilled bilingual individuals

4.1. Translators and interpreters

In this paper, we use the term "translation/interpretation" to refer to both written and oral transmission and "interpretation" to refer exclusively to oral transmission. There are three basic categories of interpreters. *Conference interpreters* help government officials and other formal bodies communicate with one another. *Court interpreters* help judges and attorneys communicate officially with individuals who do not speak the language of the court. Finally, *community* or *public service interpreters* help individuals carry out the various tasks of everyday life, such as enrolling children in school, obtaining information about insurance, applying for a position, or obtaining health care. Conference interpreters ordinarily work in the simultaneous mode. Court interpreters interpret for the defendant in the simultaneous mode and transmit witness testimony in the consecutive mode. Community interpreters work exclusively in the consecutive mode.

Conference interpreters are highly trained and well-paid professionals. They obtain professional certification through rigorous training programs. In comparison, most court interpreters are trained informally or receive training in short, specialized programs. They are generally certified through state or federal examinations, such as the Federal Court Interpreters Examination in Spanish/English. Both conference and court interpreters see themselves as members of the translating and interpreting profession and follow strict rules of procedure. Professional standards for translators emphasize three primary goals: accuracy of the message in its content and form, ethical behavior, and maintenance of professional stance.

Community interpreters, on the other hand, are usually untrained bilingual individuals who interpret as volunteers or as part of their job. Many of these individuals are members of the minority communities for whom they interpret. They are often called upon to serve as advocates for members of the minority community (Kaufert and Putsch 1997, Müller 1989, Wadensjö 1995, 1997). In some situations, community interpreters find that the absolute accuracy of the interpretation is less important than achieving mutual understanding and establishing good relations between the interlocutors.

4.2. *Characteristics of interpreters and potential interpreters*

There has been much debate about the differences between experienced professional interpreters and untrained "naive" (Harris 1978), "natural" (Harris 1977, 1978, Harris and Sherwood 1978) or "novice" (Dillinger 1994) interpreters. One position claims that interpretation ability is a natural consequence of bilingualism. Lörscher (1991), for example, suggests that every individual who has two or more languages also possesses what he terms a "rudimentary" ability to mediate between them. Other scholars insist that interpretation skills can only be acquired through training. Sherrill Bell (1995: 95) maintains that "the ability to use two or more languages, even at a high standard, is no guarantee of a person's capacity to work between them or to operate as an interpreter or translator for sustained periods of time or at reasonable speeds." Neubert (1984: 57) further argues that "any old fool can learn a language . . . but it takes an intelligent person to become a translator." Many others believe, as Weber (1984) does, that only exceptionally gifted people can become top-level professionals without direct instruction and supervision. Gile (1995) and Toury (1984) find a middle road between these positions. They argue that natural aptitude is a prerequisite for becoming a translator and interpreter, but they also accept that training and practice can help individuals develop skills more rapidly and fully realize their potential.

4.3. *Translation/interpretation as a process*

Roger T. Bell (1991: 44–45) best describes the complexity of the translation/interpretation process.[3] He sees translating/interpreting as a special case of human information processing which takes place in both short-term and long-term memory. This process requires devices for decoding text in one language and encoding it into another language via non-specific language representations. For Bell, the process operates at the linguistic level of the clause and integrates both bottom-up and top-down approaches. The style of operation is both cascaded and interactive, so that analysis or synthesis at one stage need not be completed before the next stage is initiated. Bell's model requires seven modules for each language: (1) a visual word-recognition system, (2) a syntactic processor, (3) a frequent lexis store and lexical search mechanism, (4) a frequent structure store and a parser, (5) semantic and pragmatic processors, (6) an idea organizer, and (7) a planner. At the same time that the translator moves through these six stages, he or she also carries out analysis, synthesis, and revision. Bell (1998) maintains that during analysis interpreters draw on background knowledge, specialist knowledge, domain knowledge, and knowledge of text conventions to comprehend the features of the source text. They process information at the syntactic, semantic, and pragmatic levels and conduct micro and macro analyses of text. During the synthesis stage, interpreters produce text and evaluate it against the sender's intended meaning. Finally, they undertake revision as needed.

Overall, Bell (1998) describes translation/interpretation as a problem-solving procedure. Translators and interpreters encounter problems of comprehension, interpretation, and expression and evolve strategies for coping with them. Many other scholars share this view. For example, Levy (1967: 1171) argues that "translating is a *decision process* – a series of consecutive situations – moves, as in a game – situations imposing on the translator the necessity of choosing among a certain (and very often exactly definable) number of alternatives." Gran (1998) gives examples of some of these decisions. Interpreters have to make an intelligent selection of what is being said in the original message. Once they identify the significant parts of the incoming speech, they must decide whether to transmit these parts entirely, abstract them, or compress them. Abstracting, according to Gran, requires a complete analysis of the incoming utterances based on a communicative or functional understanding of the text. Compressing requires the ability to quickly find the briefest and most efficient form to express what was understood. Interpretation/translation, then, involves the creative use of multiple strategies. Riccardi (1998: 172) argues that:

> From a limited set of cues or elements continuously unfolding, with no interruption or thinking longer than a few seconds, the interpreter has to come to a correct conclusion or be able to anticipate the message in such a way that he can organize his language output correctly. In doing so, s/he is not simply repeating something said by somebody else, but also engaging in a creative or productive process.

There is little agreement in the field about how this decision-making procedure works (Wilss 1996), but the problem-solving perspective still suggests that translation/interpretation is an extraordinarily complex information processing activity. It is especially complex for community or face-to-face interpreters who are engaged both in interpreting the text and in managing the interaction between the primary parties. As Wadensjö (1998: 150) points out, such interpreting involves simultaneous attentiveness to the pragmatic and the linguistic levels of the text.

5. The study of young interpreters

The work to be presented here focuses on the examination of the performance of young interpreters on a simulated interpretation task. It complements work carried out as part of the larger study (Valdés et al. 2000) which determined that Latino immigrant parents select only certain children in the family to serve as interpreters. We hypothesized that students who interpreted routinely for their families would have developed expertise in interpretation and translation and that they would be able to perform competently in a simulated interaction. The research task was to describe skilled performance in interpretation and to identify its systematic characteristics.

5.1. Methods

In order to examine the behaviors of experienced young interpreters in interpretation, we developed a script involving an interaction between a school principal and a mother. The scripted interaction was deliberately designed to resemble typical institutional interactions which, according to Drew and Heritage (1992), are generally asymmetrical. In this script, a mother whose daughter had been accused of stealing met with the principal to discuss the incident. The principal was sarcastic and condescending, and the mother was hostile. She argued that her daughter was being accused of stealing primarily because she was Mexican. We deliberately included a number of face threatening acts (FTAs)[4] in the script to test the students' ability to broker a tense and emotional exchange. The script also included an extensive narrative of the event that led to the accusation.

The simulated interpretation task consisted of a total of 18 turns of talk. The principal and the mother each held the floor for a total of 9 turns. The initial 4 turns involved routine greetings and were not analyzed. The remaining 14 turns were each extended turns, most of which involved several communicative actions.[5] Figure 1 lists the communicative actions in Turn 3.

Figure 1: Communicative actions in Turn 3

Turn 3: Principal		
Move	Scripted utterances	Communicative actions[6]
1	Hold on, hold on here.	• interrupts • reprimands (FTA)
2	Let's just get started the right way.	• expresses disapproval of interpreter's and mother's behavior (off record FTA)
3	Tell her	• requests action
4	I'm going to answer all her questions about her kid.	• establishes purpose of meeting • uses offensive term (FTA)
5	We talk like civilized people here.	• establishes ground rules • challenges competence of mother to behave appropriately (off record FTA)

In this particular turn, the principal makes five different interactional moves including four face-threatening acts, a direction to the interpreter, and a communicative act that establishes the purpose of the meeting.

A total of 25 youngsters from two different high schools participated in the interpretation task. At Camelot High School,[7] 13 entering ninth graders who were enrolled in a remedial summer school program volunteered to participate. All students from Camelot were Latino and spoke Spanish at home. At Willow High School, 12 seniors and juniors who were enrolled in Advanced Placement Spanish took part in the study. The group included 10 Latinos and 2 students originally from India. The Indian students were studying Spanish as a foreign language; both were immigrant students who had experience interpreting for their parents.

Two members of the research team read the parts of the principal and the mother. Students carried out the interpretation task in an empty classroom where they were both audio- and video-taped. Because members of the research team were reading scripts during the procedure, it was clear to the youngsters that the situation was fictitious. The "mother" and the "principal" deviated from the script as little as possible, even when a student was not entirely successful in transmitting the original.[8] Youngsters had the option of interpreting in an extended consecutive mode (listening to the entire turn and then interpreting) or in a paused consecutive mode (interpreting move by move).

The most obvious challenge for the young interpreters was that they were being asked to perform under very unusual circumstances. They were being audio- and video-taped in a school setting, and they were aware that their performance was being evaluated. Moreover, both readers were Latino and bilingual and could understand both the English and Spanish parts of the interaction. We conjecture that these unusual circumstances created additional stress for the young interpreters.

The interpretations produced by the youngsters were transcribed in their entirety. Notations about other characteristics of the youngsters' speech (e.g. lowered volume, segment spoken rapidly, segment spoken after giggling or chuckling) were also made.

5.2. Assessing quality of interpretation

There is at present no agreed-upon view about quality assessment in translation and interpretation. In her recent review of quality of translation, for example, House (1998) explains that approaches to the assessment of quality include three different procedures: anecdotal and subjective, response-oriented approaches, and text-based approaches. House criticizes the anecdotal and subjective approaches for using difficult to define concepts such as "faithfulness of the interpretation" or "natural flow of the translated text." She also criticizes response oriented approaches (e.g., Nida 1964, Nida and Taber 1969) because they focus on what has been termed "dynamic equivalence," that is, on ways in which the people who receive the translated/interpreted text respond to it. Response-oriented approaches are also dependent on vague and non-verifiable criteria such as "general efficiency of the communicative process" and "comprehension of intent." In contrast, text-based approaches, which include linguistically-based and functional/pragmatic approaches, have more verifiable criteria. Linguistically-based approaches involve the comparison of the source text and the target text in order to determine how accurately syntactic, semantic, stylistic, and pragmatic aspects of the original have been transferred. Functionally-based approaches such as Skopos theory (Reiss and Vermeer 1984) focus on the purpose of the translation and distinguish between equivalence and adequacy. Functional-pragmatic approaches (e.g. House 1981, 1997) stress both the linguistic and the situational particularities of target texts. This type of evaluation requires that the target text be functionally equivalent to the original on both ideational and interpersonal levels.

Equivalence is itself a term about which there is little agreement. Gentzler (1993: 4), for example, argues that "standards of translation analysis that rely on equivalence or non-equivalence" and other associated judgmental criteria "imply notions of substantialism that limit other possibilities of translation practice, marginalize unorthodox translation, and impinge upon real intercultural exchange." Newman (1994), on the other hand, describes translation equivalence as a common-sense notion: most individuals would expect an original and its translation to be equivalent. In spite of existing disagreements in the field, most interpreter trainers (e.g., Gile 1995) believe that there are quality criteria that are independent of context. These include ideational clarity, linguistic acceptability, and terminological accuracy. Fidelity, although not well defined, is considered essential as is professional behavior.

Questions of quality in interpretation have become more pronounced in the case of the evaluation of the performance of community interpreters. As the field of community interpreting has expanded, the broader field of interpretation/ translation has become increasingly concerned about the impact of "self-proclaimed" interpreters on the profession. Many individuals (e.g., Bell 1995, Roberts 1995) worry about the need to protect members of the public, especially linguistic and cultural minorities, from incompetent practitioners. As a result, a number of individuals (e.g. Bell 1995, Roberts 1995) have attempted to develop assessment instruments for certifying such face-to-face or liaison interpreters. Unfortunately, the evaluation of community interpreters has itself confronted the same questions that plague the larger field. Roberts (1995), for example, has favored a subjective equivalence approach involving the transmission of vital units. Wadensjö (1998: 275), on the other hand, argues that community interpreting is "dialogic" and involves an interaction between participants in a social event. She directly criticizes the equivalence preoccupation in translation studies. She points out that closeness of an interpreted renditions to the original is relative. Some could be linguistically close but functionally divergent, while others could be linguistically divergent but functionally close.

A number of individuals consider debates about the evaluation of community interpreting premature. They consider community interpreting a special kind of interaction that must be more completely understood before standards for evaluation can be imposed. Gentile (1997) argues that we know very little about what constitutes acceptable performance in *ad hoc* interpreting settings. He fears that in attempting to certify individuals who perform these services "the tendency will be to concentrate on the evaluation of language skills rather than transfer skills, in part because it is easier to justify one's assessment in terms of language than in terms of communication" (Gentile 1997: 116).

In examining the performance of young interpreters, we took the position that the youngsters who took part in our study are untrained community interpreters who serve as mediators, brokers, advocates, and guides for their loved ones. Their performance, therefore, cannot be evaluated using the norms that might be applied either to conference or to court interpreters even if the field were to agree on what these norms might be. In evaluating their performance, we were mindful of the debates in the broader field of translation/interpretation surrounding assessment of quality of interpretation and elected to use several approaches while viewing equivalence as a commonsense notion. We followed Gran's advice and focused our attention on transfer or communication skills as opposed to language proficiency. We were also guided by Wadensjö (1998: 286–267), who argues that an evaluation of community interpreters should not only examine talk as text but also should include other criteria such as ability to attend simultaneously to various key details in the discourse as well as flexibility in positioning themselves in the interactional exchange.

We expected that the young interpreters would be involved in a process of problem solving that required their being simultaneously attentive to a number of different challenges. We also expected that they would use a variety of strategies[9] for coping with the challenges encountered in order to transmit the original communicative actions. We did not expect that these transmissions would be verbatim or word-for-word renditions of the originals. Rather, we conjectured that as Gran (1998) suggested, young interpreters would make an intelligent selection of what was being said and identify significant parts of the incoming speech in order to decide what to abstract, reduce, expand, and omit. We thus examined both the information transmitted by the young interpreters as well as the strategies they used (1) to convey essential information, (2) to communicate the tone and stance of the original, (3) to keep up with the information flow, and (4) to cope with momentary lexical difficulties. We also briefly examined the ways in which youngsters coped with other linguistic limitations.

We present our analysis of these various aspects separately here, but it is important to emphasize that in transmitting the communicative actions, youngsters were simultaneously engaged in making decisions about the significant elements of the original utterances, the potential impact of conveying the full force of insulting remarks, the challenges posed by the speed and flow of the interaction, and the linguistic difficulties encountered.

6. The transmission of communicative actions

6.1. Scoring the transmission of essential communicative actions

We used a largely text-based approach to score the 25 youngsters' transmission of communicative actions (CAs) in the script. Following Roberts (1995), we identified the "essential" communicative actions in the original script.[10] For example, for Turn 3 in Figure 2, the essential communicative action for the turn was determined to be: "Explains purpose of meeting." In this turn, we considered CAs 1, 2, and 5 non-essential because they only conveyed tone and stance. CA 3 and all other similar instructions to the interpreter were considered non-essential as well.

Figure 2. Essential communicative action in turn 3

Turn 3	Original utterances	Essential CA
Action 1	Hold on, hold on here.	
2	Let's just get started the right way.	
3	Tell her	
4	I'm going to answer all her questions about her kid.	**explains purpose of meeting**
5	We talk like civilized people here.	

Students' renditions of each of the 13 essential communicative actions were scored using the following scale: completely conveyed (2 points), conveyed but not completely (1 point), and not conveyed (0 points). The maximum number of points obtainable was 26. All the students who participated in the study successfully conveyed the essential communicative actions. When the raw scores were converted into a percentage of the total essential information score possible, students received a mean score of .86 (86%) with a standard deviation of .08 and a range of .27. These scores suggest that young interpreters were able to carry out the task of transmitting the essential elements of the communication at a level that would be considered acceptable for adult community interpreters. The scores obtained by the young interpreters are especially noteworthy because Roberts' (1995) examination for the certification of community interpreters in Canada used a 70% cut-off score for accreditation of community interpreters and a 65% minimum cut-off score for entry into formal training programs.[11]

6.2. Strategies used to transmit communicative actions

In order to obtain a more complete picture of the strategies used by young interpreters to transmit the original utterances, we conducted a more detailed text-based analysis of their renditions. Rather than looking only at essential communicative actions, we examined students' renditions of each of the 45 total original CAs contained in the script. Each of the renditions was coded following the system proposed by Wadensjö (1998), which included:

- close renditions (include propositional content found in original)
- expanded renditions (include more information than original)
- reduced renditions (include less information than original)
- substituted renditions (combine a reduced and expanded rendition)
- summarized renditions (correspond to two or more prior originals)
- non-renditions (do not correspond to original)
- zero-renditions (not translated)

We expected that students would make errors in transmitting original utterances. These errors are termed here *non-renditions*, and include translated utterances that could not be understood, utterances that were begun and abandoned, utterances that depended on a single lexical item that was mistranslated, and utterances that directly contradicted or seriously distorted the content of the original. Table 1 lists the various types of renditions produced by the young interpreters.

Table 1. Mean number of types of renditions produced by young interpreters

Types of renditions	Mean	SD	Range
Close	18.6	5.55	22
Expanded	4.40	2.45	10
Reduced	5.56	2.43	11
Substituted	0.60	0.82	3
Summarized	1.96	0.81	6
Non-renditions	3.72	2.20	9
Zero renditions	10.12	4.06	16

Students primarily produced either close renditions or zero renditions. They also produced a much smaller number of reduced and expanded renditions. They produced very few summarized, substituted, or non-renditions.

The students who scored highest in the transmission of essential communicative actions did not produce the greatest number of close renditions. For example, even Ernesto and Ulises, who received scores of 26 and 25 in the transmission of essential CAs, produced only 13 and 17 close renditions respectively out of the total 45 CAs.

Students used multiple strategies in a single turn. In Figure 3, Hilda conveys the essential communicative actions by producing a combination of expanded, substituted, close, and reduced renditions.

Figure 3. Expanded, reduced, and zero renditions

	Original utterances Turn 9: All CAs in turn	Interpreter's rendition (Hilda)
1	Tell her	Zero rendition
2	that it's clear that she does not agree with Mrs. Murphy.	Expanded rendition DICE QUE CLARAMENTE USTED NO VA: A ACEPTAR QUE (PAUSE) ROCIO SE LA QUERIA ROBAR--O:, UM (PAUSE) QUE LA SEÑORA MURPHY TIENE LA RAZON 'She says that you clearly are not going to accept that Rocío wanted to steal or, um that Mrs. Murphy is right.'
3	Mrs. Murphy can't prove that Rohw – (corrects herself) Rocío was going to steal her wallet.	Reduced rendition Y QUE TAMPOCO TIENE NINGUNA PRUEBA. 'And she also doesn't have any proof.'

4	But she knows students. She can tell the difference between thieves and honest kids.	Reduced rendition PERO DICE QUE LA SEÑORA MURPHY CONOCE A LOS ESTUDIANTES. (takes quick breath) 'But she says that Mrs. Murphy knows students.'
5	and she could see Rocío's face..... Mrs. Murphy thinks that she just got caught in the middle of stealing.	Zero rendition

* Throughout these figures, the following notations are used: interpreted segments are in upper case, ? indicates rising intonation (not necessarily a question), a period indicates a fall in tone (not necessarily at the end of a sentences), a comma indicates continuing intonation (not necessarily between clauses or sentences), a colon indicates an extension of sound or syllable, (PAUSE) indicates untimed intervals longer than 1 second, .. indicates a very short pause, ... indicates a slightly longer pause, [X] indicates inaudible, brackets [] indicate transcriptionist's doubt, and parentheses () are used for descriptions of delivery or other phenomena.

The students produced zero renditions strategically primarily to avoid rendering a particularly offensive FTA or to avoid a linguistic difficulty. They did not, however, always transmit the original utterances successfully. Occasionally, for example, a lexical limitation caused them to communicate something quite different from what was originally intended. For example, in the segment presented in Figure 4, Homero begins to translate the original Spanish verb *discutir*, with an English term beginning with "*di-*" intending, perhaps, to say *discuss*. Conscious immediately that the term is an inappropriate translation, he then asks for repetition/clarification twice before producing a mistranslation using the very term that he rejected initially. Homero's difficulty in translating the original is based on the fact that the Spanish word *discutir* can be translated as either 'to argue' or 'to discuss.' Since for most speakers of Mexican Spanish, such as Homero, *discutir* connotes being involved in a heated, rather than a neutral, discussion, he realizes the English term 'discuss' is an inappropriate translation of the original. He nevertheless is unsuccessful at accessing a more appropriate equivalent.

Figure 4. Non-rendition (mistranslation of original lexical item)

	Original utterances Turn 10: CA 1	Interpreter's rendition (Homero)
1	Muy bien, yo no le discuto que eso piense la mis Murphy. 'Fine, I'm not arguing that that's what she thinks.'	SHE DI – SHE DOESN'T – SHE SAYS THAT (PAUSE) COMO?
	(original repeated)	(PAUSE) AH, [X] (sounds like: 'see that') THAT'S HARD. ¿COMO? COMO?
	(original repeated)	SHE'S NOT <u>DISCUSSING</u> THAT THE TEACHER WOULD – [X] IS LYING (PAUSE) BUT FOR HER TO JUST TELL HER. JUST THINKING NOT, JUST TELL HER.

In other cases, students produced non-renditions that directly contradicted the original utterance.

Figure 5. Non-rendition (contradiction of original)

	Original utterance Turn 4: CA 5	Interpreter's rendition (Ulises)
5	que son mentiras que Rocío quería robarle la cartera a esa vieja 'that it's a lie that Rocío wanted to steal that old bag's wallet'	SHE THAT THAT'S A LIE. THAT ROCIO WOULDN'T STEAL THE LADY'S WALLET. PURSE.

We conjecture that students produced utterances that were the direct opposite of what was said in the original because their attention was on other aspects of the interpretation task. Many of these renditions are inadvertent errors that would have been noted in a real interaction. The principal parties would notice an obvious error such as "she stole your wallet" instead of "she stole the teacher's wallet" and question it immediately. Because our role play required that the "principal" and the "mother" not attempt to clarify inadvertent errors or momentary misunderstandings, there was no opportunity for students to make corrections.

It is interesting to note that in comparison with the professional court interpreters investigated by Berk-Seligson (1990), the young interpreters did not monitor the understanding of their interlocutors; that is, they did not inform either the principal or the mother of suspected misunderstandings. This does not mean, however, that youngsters do not have the skills to carry out such monitoring. Rather, we believe that because they were aware that the two role-playing researchers spoke both languages, the youngsters did not feel a need to carry out such monitoring. We conjecture that when interpreting for their parents, students are indeed able to ascertain whether one or the other of the interlocutors misunderstood the intent or the content of the message.

As Wadensjö (1998) has suggested, the various kinds of "divergent" renditions (expanded, reduced, substituted, summarized, and zero renditions) served functional purposes. For example, reduced renditions were used to eliminate redundancy, to concentrate on the perceived main force of the communicative act, and to mitigate direct FTAs. Expanded renditions were used to explain an idea more fully and to make certain that the exact sense of the original was conveyed. In a few cases, expanded renditions were used to convey the interpreter's strong sense of what needed to be said at a certain point in the interaction. Such expansions directly reflected the momentary alignment of the interpreter with one or the other of the two speakers.[12] Zero renditions were used strategically to focus on the essential elements of a turn, to convey or avoid conveying the original tone and stance, to manage the flow of information, and to avoid momentary linguistic difficulties.

7. Conveying tone and stance

Our script was deliberately designed to portray a tense interaction between two individuals whose power relationship was unequal. Students needed to be especially conscious of the original tone and stance of each utterance. The mother's lines included an aggressive and direct attack on the credibility of the teacher who made the original accusation, the racism of the institution, and the attitude of the principal toward her personally. The principal's lines featured off-record face-threatening actions (FTAs) that suggested contempt for the mother, her daughter, and possibly a certain category of students.

The young interpreters had to decide how essential the tone and stance were to a speaker's message. They then chose whether to transmit the FTAs at all. If they did not omit the FTAs, they had to choose the best linguistic form to convey the precise level of aggression that they wanted to transmit. These decisions required the students to monitor potential conflicts between the speakers and anticipate the effect of offensive remarks. Table 2 presents the mean number of each type of strategy used by the young interpreters to render the 17 face-threatening acts (FTAs).

Table 2. Strategies used to convey tone and stance

Strategy	Mean	SD	Range
Conveyed	3.88	1.83	7
Conveyed with reluctance	0.84	0.94	3
Omitted	6.32	2.67	9
Aggravated	0.28	0.54	2
Mitigated	3.28	1.94	7
Other	3.40	1.93	8

The young interpreters directly conveyed a mean number of only 3.88 FTAs. They omitted a mean number of 6.32 FTAs, communicated a mean number of 3.28 FTAs in mitigated form, and transformed a mean number of 3.40 FTAs in other ways. It is evident that young interpreters preferred to omit, mitigate, or otherwise transform original offensive remarks rather than convey them directly.

All youngsters provided clear evidence that they were aware of the possible impact of the face-threatening remarks made by the mother on the principal. Decisions about how to convey these offensive remarks were frequently marked by pauses, hesitations, giggles, and complete breaking of role. Given the unpredictability of how the dialogue would develop,[13] the youngsters had to decide whether to convey, mitigate, or omit offensive remarks made by the mother on a turn-by turn basis. When the mother directly insulted the principal, some youngsters directly interpreted some of the offensive remarks, but omitted and mitigated others.

In Figure 6, the student uses a combination of strategies that include omitting, mitigating and conveying offensive remarks. She omits *vieja* entirely, and renders *mugres* as ‘stuff,’ rather than, for example, ‘shit.’ However, she conveys the slightly veiled accusation of racism completely.

In Figure 7, the student omits a particularly offensive FTA by producing a zero rendition and reducing other originals to a bare minimum. In this particular case, the young interpreter conveys what is pragmatically correct, given his assumption that the mother should try to be polite to the principal. Omitting the FTAs is a deliberate strategic choice.[14]

Figure 6. Conveying mitigating and omitting offensive remarks

	Original utterances Turn 8: All CAs in turn	Interpreter's rendition (Micaela)
1	Primero que todo, dile que mi hija se llama Rocío, no Róhwceeo. 'First of all, tell her that my daughter's name is Rocío, not Róhwceeo.'	FIRST OF ALL... HER DAUGHTER'S NAME IS RÓCIO.
2	A la vieja claramente se le había caído la bolsa de su escritorio. 'The old bag's purse had clearly fallen from her desk.'	WELL, OBVIOUSLY THE PURSE JUST FELL FROM THE DESK.
3	Mi hija por buena gente le estaba ayudando a recoger sus mugres. 'My daughter, because she's a nice person, was just helping her pick up her junk.'	HER DAUGHTER WAS JUST BEING NICE IN TRYING TO PICK UP THE STUFF.
4	No se iba a meter nada a la bolsa. 'She wasn't going to put anything in her pocket.'	SHE WASN'T GONNA PUT ANYTHING IN HER BAG.
5	La están acusando porque creen que todos los mexicanos somos unos ladrones. 'They're/you're accusing her because they/you think that we Mexicans are all thieves.'	THEY'RE JUST ACCUSING HER BECAUSE THEY THINK ALL MEXICANS ARE THIEVES.
6	¿Cómo sabe que se la iba a robar? ¿Qué come que adivina? 'How does she know that she was going to steal it? Does she eat something that makes her psychic?'	HOW DO YOU KNOW THAT SHE WAS GONNA TAKE? HOW DO THEY FIGURE THAT?

Figure 7. Use of zero and reduced renditions

	Original utterances Turn 14: All CAs in turn	Interpreter's rendition (Adolfo)
1	A usted también que le vaya bien, doña se-cree-mucho 'You have a good day too, Mrs. really-stuck-up'	Zero rendition
2	y gracias por creernos a todos una bola de ladrones. 'and thanks for thinking that we are all a bunch of thieves.'	Reduced rendition THANKS FOR SERVING HER – FOR ATTENDING HER.

In a few cases, students elect to convey and aggravate an offensive remark. In these instances, the students clearly aligned themselves with the position of the mother. In Figure 9, Sonia adds her own interpretation of the mother's implied meaning and aggravates the original communicative action by directly accusing the principal of racism.

Figure 8. Aggravating offensive remarks

	Original utterance Turn 8 : CA 5	Interpreter's rendition (Sonia)
5	La están acusando porque creen que todos los mexicanos somos unos ladrones. 'They're/you're accusing her because they/you think that we Mexicans are all thieves.'	AND SHE WANTS TO KNOW HOW CAN YOU ACCUSE HER. SHE SAYS THAT, UM, YOU GUYS ONLY ACCUSE MEXICANS. YOU GUYS ARE LIKE RACIST AGAINST MEXICANS.

In other cases, students giggled or chuckled as they anticipated the effect of the mother's FTA. In Turn 14, for example, only two youngsters transmitted the original. The other youngsters either omitted large segments of the turn or deliberately distorted the original meaning. Given the brevity of the turn and its function in the leave-taking move, some youngsters struggled with how to proceed. In several cases, the young interpreters stalled for time and asked for repetition in order to decide exactly how to proceed. In Figure 9, Vicente begins to interpret, breaks role to comment on the aggressiveness of the remark, and then uses a youth slang alternative ('hard') to interpret the original 'really-stuck-up.'

Figure 9. Breaking role and conveying offensive remarks

	Original utterance Turn 14: CAs 1 & 2	Interpreter's rendition (Vicente)
1	A usted también que le vaya bien, doña se-cree-mucho 'You have a good day too, Mrs. really-stuck-up'	SHE SA- – SHE SAID, UM (PAUSE) QUE FUERTE. DIGO? SHE SAID, LIKE, YOU THINK YOU ARE HARD?
2	y gracias por creernos a todos una bola de ladrones. 'and thanks for thinking that we are all a bunch of thieves.'	AND SHE SAID THANK YOU FOR, LIKE, LIKE, THINKING THAT – THAT WE ARE, LIKE, STEALERS. ROBBERS.

Given the fact that the youngsters were participating in a simulated interpretation task, breaking role was a tactical choice. Students broke role in order to express their belief that certain remarks were unacceptably aggressive.

When the principal made offensive remarks, a number of students directly interpreted what was said (e.g. "we talk like civilized people here," "we don't need any drama here"). It is possible the students did not understand the connotations of the remarks or the attitude of the principal toward the mother. As a result, they simply rendered the content directly. It is also possible that the students did not find the principal's remarks particularly offensive. Because of their experience in interpreting in situations where powerful majority members were routinely rude to Latinos, they may have seen the principal's behavior as normal. One might also argue, however, that the youngsters had aligned themselves with the mother. By conveying all the offensive remarks, they deliberately provided her with information that might help her perceive the principal's attitude toward her.[15] We choose not to conjecture about the plausibility of one or the other of our interpretations. What we do suggest is that students' experiences in real-life interactions with majority group members will determine their reading of the particular tone and stance used by such individuals when they are engaged in communication with members of their community.

Finally, in a number of cases the offensive remarks were transformed in other subtle ways. Students expanded the original, began and abandoned renditions, changed the meaning of the original utterance, or miscommunicated entirely. Several of these meaning changes and miscommunications neutralized the original offensive remark. For example, instead of referring to the teacher's possessions as 'junk' or 'stuff,' several youngsters chose to use the terms 'wallet' or 'purse.' They thus changed the meaning of the original in a way that mitigated its hostility.

The students were fully aware of the potential impact of the original face-threatening acts. We view their decisions to convey, omit, mitigate, or aggravate these actions as conscious solutions to the problem of brokering the communication between two individuals. We emphasize once again that scoring procedures that expect close renditions for all original utterances mask the strategic sophistication involved in selecting the parts of incoming speech that must be retained and omitting those parts that may or should be left out.

8. Keeping up with communication demands

Students in the study also used multiple strategies in order to keep up with the pace of the interaction. These included: (1) asking for repetition, (2) producing zero renditions for elements of the original, (3) reordering segments in the original, (4) reducing the original, and (5) stalling by complaining about some other difficulty. The most common strategy used by all students was a combination of reduced and zero renditions. By omitting segments, young interpreters were able to catch up with the pace of the interaction. The second most common strategy used by the young interpreters to keep up with the communication demands was asking for repetition.

In Figure 10, for example, the student interprets in the extended consecutive mode; that is, the mother holds the floor for several seconds, and in theory, the interpreter would then interpret her entire series of CAs. She first stalls for time by complaining about the pace of the interaction and then produces a reordered, substituted rendition of the original communicative actions.

Figure 10. Stalling for time

	Original utterance Turn 4: All CAs in turn	Interpreter's rendition (Lola)
1	Bueno, a mí lo que me dijo Rocío fue que la maestra la acusó de robarse su cartera y que la quieren correr de la escuela. 'Well, what Rocío told me was that the teacher accused her of stealing her wallet and that they want to expel her from school.'	[interpreter listens]
2	Yo vengo aquí a decirles que mi hija será· muchas cosas, pero ratera, no es. 'I'm here to tell you that my daughter may be a lot of things, but she is not a thief.'	[interpreter listens]
3	Tú dile 'You tell her'	
4	que son mentiras que Rocío quería robarle la cartera a esa vieja. 'that it's a lie that Rocío wanted to steal that old bag's wallet.'	[interpreter listens]
5	Si Rocío ya la conoce a la maestra. Y sabe que es una maldita. 'Rocío already knows the teacher. And she knows that she is wicked.'	[interpreter listens]
6	Hay maestros que no quieren a los muchachos. 'There are teachers that are not fond of kids.'	(LAUGH) VA MUY RECIO. 'you're going too fast.' UM, SHE'S SAYING THAT HER DAUGHTER IS NOT A STEALER AND THAT EVERYONE IS SAYING THAT SHE STOLE A PURSE FROM SOMEBODY. AND THAT SHE'S NOT A STEALER. AND WHY WOULD YOU WANT TO KICK HER OUT FROM SCHOOL?

The youngsters in the study kept up with the pace of the interaction by transmitting essential elements and producing zero renditions for utterances they momentarily viewed as non-essential. They also asked for repetition or clarification. Requests for repetition and clarification compensated for what may have been lapses of memory, lack of understanding, lack of sufficient attention, or uncertainty about how best to proceed. In sum, the young interpreters used the same strategies that professional interpreters use to keep up with the pace of an interaction (Berk-Seligson 1990).

9. Compensating for linguistic limitations

Youngsters needed to choose the best linguistic forms and structures for conveying particular meanings. In order to do so, they needed to be able to search rapidly for appropriate equivalents, respond to linguistic and lexical challenges, try out and discard possible forms and structures, and monitor their performance for both form and content.

For young interpreters, proficiency in both English and Spanish is a central issue. Compared to conference and court interpreters, who have highly developed abilities in both of their languages, the youngsters who participated in this study were "unbalanced" in their Spanish and English proficiencies. They had different strengths in each of the two languages – as members of a linguistic minority group, their exposure to the two languages was not equivalent.

The two students who were not raised in homes where Spanish was spoken were strikingly different from the other 23 students. They experienced many difficulties in understanding original Spanish utterances and asked for repetition and clarification numerous times, as illustrated in Figure 11.

Figure 11. Asking for repetition and clarification

	Original utterance: Turn 6	Interpreter's rendition (Gozo)
4	que me explique bien qué pasó y...por qué la misus Murphy le vio cara de ratera 'to explain to me what happened and why Mrs. Murphy thought she looked like a thief.'	(PAUSE) REPITE [X]. 'Repeat' (inaud.)
	(original repeated)	SHE WANTS – SHE WANTS TO [X] SHE WANTS A GOOD EXPLANATION FOR THIS. AND WANTS TO KNOW THAT (PAUSE). SORRY BUT – LO SIENTO, REPITELA [X] 'I'm sorry, repeat it.'
	(original repeated)	UM, I THINK THAT SHE'S SAYING THAT – WHY DID THE TEACHER EXC – ACCUSE HER OF STEALING THE – AH, THE PURSE. WHATEVER.

Some of the other 23 students might superficially be described as English-dominant or Spanish-dominant given external criteria (e.g., age of arrival in this country, years of English language education, language spoken at home, standardized test scores). However, our evaluation of students' strengths and weaknesses in the simulated interpretation task led us to question commonly held views concerning constructs such as limited-English-proficient, English-dominant, Spanish-dominant, and the like that are commonly used in schools. For example, students are classified as limited-English-proficient using assessment instruments that may not accurately evaluate students' differing abilities in receptive and productive abilities. The assumption is often made that students who produce flawed English are incapable of understanding oral presentations in this language.

Swain, Dumas, and Naiman (1974) have argued that correct translation requires the subject to make use of separate comprehension and production systems for both the source language and the target language. In second language acquisition, the comprehension grammar and the production grammar can develop at different paces. As Swain and her colleagues predicted, we found that students' comprehension grammars clearly outpaced their production grammars in their weaker language. They had surprising abilities to communicate their understanding of what was said in the weaker language and were able to transmit even subtle meanings conveyed by the tone and stance of the original. Camelot High School, however, did not consider a number of these students proficient enough to profit from instruction conducted totally in English.

In a number of cases, the demands of our task caused flawed production in students' stronger language as well as in their weaker language. As students attended to the challenge of transmitting the force of particular communicative actions, they failed to monitor their speech and produced a number of performance errors in what – from the evidence of other segments – was clearly a competent language.

In this section, we discuss the accuracy of students' production and focus on the ways in which students compensated for either general or momentary linguistic limitations. We discuss first the students' responses to lexical challenges and then the students' use of flawed language.

9.1. Responding to lexical challenges

We built 30 lexical challenges into the script for the simulated interaction. Students also had difficulty finding equivalents for several words that we had assumed would be familiar terms. Lexical challenges included idiomatic expressions (e.g. *give her the benefit of the doubt*), American school terms that do not have exact Spanish equivalents (*language arts*), and terms (*mugres*, *cara de ratera*) that were deliberately chosen for their subtle offensive nuances which are difficult to transmit with the same connotation. Figure 12 lists a number of the lexical items which most students found difficult.

Figure 12. Principal lexical challenges in English and Spanish

English	Spanish
civilized people	cara de ratera 'a sneaky look on her face'
get to the bottom of this	maldita 'wicked woman'
language arts	mugres 'junk, stuff'
purse, wallet, and pocket	¿Qué come que adivina? 'Does she eat something that makes her psychic?'
does not agree	yo no le discuto que eso piense la Miss Murphy 'I don't argue that Miss Murphy may think that'
can't prove	pero que sepa es otra cosa 'but, that she knows it for a fact is a different story'
benefit of the doubt	tiene que ajustar 'you handle the teacher'
she knows students	yo me encargo de mi hija 'I'll take care of my daughter'
came back into the room	doña se-cree-mucho 'Mrs. really-stuck-up'
got caught	bola de ladrones 'bunch of thieves'

Students had to respond to these lexical challenges while carrying out a number of other tasks. Several of these lexical difficulties, moreover, involved more than simply finding an equivalent in the other language. To accurately convey the events that led to the accusation of the daughter, for example, students had to select terminology to distinguish clearly between 'purse,' 'wallet,' and 'pocket' in Spanish. If students selected, for example, the term *cartera* for purse, they were then forced to select *billetera* for 'wallet.' However, they could then use the term *bolsa* for pocket. On the other hand, if they selected the term *bolsa* for purse, they then could use *cartera* for wallet, but they needed to use another term for pocket other than *bolsa*. Similarly, when students encountered the English phrase 'she knows students,' they were forced to choose between *saber* and *conocer* in Spanish. Several students transmitted the phrase as *ella conoce a los estudiantes* without difficulty. Other students produced an unacceptable Spanish equivalent, *ella sabe los estudiantes*. In Figure 13, the student struggles to repair the error.

Figure 13. Responding to lexical challenges

	Original utterance Turn 9: CA 8	Interpreter's rendition (Adolfo)
8	But she knows students..... she can tell the difference between thieves and honest kids.	PERO ELLA, – she – PERO ELLA SABE ESTUDIANTES. PUES, LES CONOCE. Y PUEDE DECIR LA DIFERENCIA DE LOS ESTUDO- LOS ESTUDIANTES (PAUSE) MALOS Y LOS ESTUDIANTES BUENOS. 'But she, – she knows (wrong verb used) students since she knows (correct verb used) them and can tell the difference between stu- bad students and good students.'

Table 3. Strategies used to cope with lexical challenges

Strategy	Mean	StdDev	Range
Conveyed lexical item accurately	10.96	2.96	13
Used substitution strategy	10.96	2.64	11
Executed obvious search successfully or unsuccessfully	0.68	1.14	5
Omitted difficult lexical item	2.68	1.31	5
Broke role	0.68	0.85	2
Produced a zero rendition	4.04	2.65	10

Table 3 shows that out of 30 lexical challenges, students were able to find a close equivalent in the other language for a mean number of 10.96 items. When they could not access a needed term, a few students executed obvious searches that involved pauses, hesitations, and rephrasings, or they simply broke role and admitted not knowing a particular word. In some cases (mean=4.04), students produced zero renditions. It is not possible, however, to determine whether certain elements were deliberately eliminated in order to get around lexical problems. In other cases (mean=2.68), the students rendered the original utterance but omitted the item in question. For the most part, however, when students could not recall or did not know a particular term, they tended to use a substitution strategy that included: (1) producing a related term (+/– expansion), (2) producing a circumlocution, (3) producing a literal translation, (4) using fuzzy language, (5) using a false cognate, borrowing or switch, (6) using an invented form, and (7) using an inaccurate or unrelated term (+/– expansion). The mean number of substitutions produced was 10.96, the exact equivalent of the mean number of items conveyed. Not all substitutions, however, successfully conveyed the original. Figure 14 contains examples of a number of the strategies used.

Figure 14. Strategies used to cope with lexical challenges

Original utterance	Interpreter's rendition
Successful search and use of circumlocution (Adolfo)	
that it's clear that she does not agree with Mrs. Murphy	EXCUSE ME? (SIGH) O QUE USTED NO, PUES, (PAUSE) NO (PAUSE) QUE NO (PAUSE) QUE NO AL- AGRU- [X] AGREED, UM (PAUSE). QUE USTED NO (PAUSE) TIENE LA MISMA OPINION QUE LA MAESTRA. 'Excuse me? (SIGH) or that you aren't, well, (PAUSE) don't (PAUSE) that you don't (PAUSE) that you don't agru (unclear) agreed, um (PAUSE) that you don't (PAUSE) have the same opinion as the teacher.'

Unsuccessful search and abandonment of attempt to render (Horacio)	
Si Rocío ya la conoce a la maestra. Y sabe que es una maldita. 'Rocío already knows the teacher. And she knows that she is wicked.'	SHE THINKS THERE'S – (PAUSE) THAT, UM, HER DAUGHTER KNOWS THAT THE TEACHER IS, LIKE (Rendition of CA abandoned. Interpreter continues with next CA.)
Use of substitution: literal translation plus fuzzy language (Ulises)	
We're going to give her the benefit of the doubt on this one.....	DICE QUE SE CALME (PAUSE) QUE LE VAN A DAR EL BENEFICIO DE – (PAUSE) DE ESTA. 'She said to calm down (PAUSE) that they are going to give her the benefit of (PAUSE) of this.'
Use of substitution: inaccurate term plus expansion (Micaela)	
that it's clear that she does not agree with Mrs. Murphy.	ES CLARO QUE NO- QUE NO, UM, NO ESTAS EN COMPROMISO CON LA PROFESORA QUE NO L-LA CREAS. 'It's clear that you don't – that you don't, you aren't in engagement with the teacher – that you don't believe her.'
Use of substitution strategy: invented term (Homero)	
La están acusando porque creen que todos los mexicanos somos unos ladrones. 'They're/you're accusing her because they/you think that we Mexicans are all thieves.'	YOU'RE TRYING TO ACCUSE HER 'CAUSE YOU THINK ALL MEXICANS ARE (PAUSE) STEALERS.

In the majority of cases, when students chose to interpret a segment that contained a lexical challenge, they were able to provide an accurate equivalent for the item encountered. In a number of cases, however, students produced inaccurate terms or unrelated forms. In spite of such momentary failures, students did not stop interpreting. They went on to the next communicative action. Most youngsters took lexical problems in stride. Some youngsters, however, appeared disturbed by their failure to access an appropriate term. They continued to focus on the difficulty as they transmitted the segments that followed. In several cases, this monitoring backward resulted in the production of disfluencies not typical of their language in other parts of the interpretation. When questioned about their response to the interpretation task, most young interpreters said that these lexical limitations were their principal difficulty.

When students coped with lexical difficulties, they once again displayed the ability to simultaneously attend to the many different demands made by the process of interpreting. They used many of the same strategies that second language learners use to cope with difficulties in an imperfectly known second language (Bialystok 1990, Faerch and Kasper 1983, 1984, Kasper and

Kellerman 1997, Tarone 1981, Yule and Tarone 1997). However, in our simulated interpretation task, students encountered specific production or combined reception-production problems in both their L1 and their L2. Because the task required them to transmit the original communicative actions produced by two other individuals, it made much greater demands on them than ordinary interactions in which they only attempt to communicate their own meanings. Their use of strategies, then, involved unique communication challenges.[16]

9.2. Communicating using flawed language

The young interpreters used what we have termed "flawed" language. They produced a number of pauses, hesitations, and rephrasings, as well as disfluencies that are not a part of monolingual varieties of either English or Spanish. These included single violations of acquired grammatical rules in Spanish as well as other errors reflecting partial acquisition of certain English language features or transfer of elements from one language to the other. Additionally, several students produced a number of segments using a non-standard variety of English, perhaps reflecting their interaction with African-American speakers in their schools and their community. Tables 4 and 5 show the mean number of disfluencies of different types produced in English and in Spanish by the entire group of young interpreters.

Table 4. Disfluencies produced in English by all students (n=25)

Type of disfluency	Mean	SD	Range
Errors in idiomaticity	1.80	1.29	4
Syntactic transfer	0.52	0.82	3
Errors in verb tense/form	0.48	1.05	4
Errors in verb agreement	0.40	0.58	2
Errors in preposition selection	0.32	0.63	2
Non-standard usage	1.08	2.40	11
Other	0.04	0.20	1

Table 5. Disfluencies produced in Spanish by all students (n=25)

Type of disfluency	Mean	SD	Range
Errors in idiomaticity	0.56	0.82	3
Syntactic transfer	0.40	0.76	3
Errors in verb tense	0.16	0.62	3
Errors in verb agreement	0.08	0.28	1
Errors in verb form	0.28	0.46	1
Errors in verb mood	0.20	0.41	1
Errors in object pronoun gender	0.64	0.91	3
Errors in noun gender/number	0.16	0.47	2
Errors in noun–adjective agreement	0.28	0.68	3
Preposition omission	0.44	0.58	2
Preposition selection	0.08	0.28	1
Other	0.40	0.70	3

The students at Willow High School, who were enrolled in an advanced placement Spanish class, were quite fluent in English. None were enrolled in English as a Second Language courses. Students at Camelot High School, however, were entering ninth graders who were considered at risk by the school. The majority of these students were identified by the school as English language learners. Tables 6 and 7 show a comparison of the number of disfluencies produced by the two groups of students in English and Spanish. The two groups produced disfluencies at somewhat different rates. The Willow students, who were enrolled in an AP Spanish class, produced a mean number of 3.33 English disfluencies, while the Camelot students, who were largely ESL students, produced a mean number of 5.84 English disfluencies. Both groups, however, primarily produced disfluencies in Spanish that appeared to be momentary slips of the tongue; the Camelot students produced a mean number of 2.52 Spanish disfluencies, while the Willow students produced a mean of 3.53 Spanish disfluencies. Perhaps the Camelot students produced fewer Spanish disfluencies because they were first-generation immigrants.

Table 6. English disfluencies produced by Willow and Camelot students

Willow students (n=12)		Camelot students (n=13)	
Mean	3.33	Mean	5.84
StdDev	2.06	StdDev	4.23
Range	6	Range	16

Table 7. Spanish disfluencies produced by Willow and Camelot students

Willow students (n=12)		Camelot students (n=13)	
Mean	4.17	Mean	3.23
StdDev	3.69	StdDev	2.52
Range	13	Range	8

A number of students produced at least one disfluency in English in the production of conventionalized or genuinely idiomatic language. Errors in idiomaticity include ungrammatical substitutions and deletions, semantic substitutions and deletions, and errors in word order, as well as errors not directly attributable to surface language errors. Examples of these are presented in Figure 15. Students also produced constructions that reflected direct transfer from Spanish. Examples of this type of disfluency are included in Figure 16.

Figure 15. Errors in idiomaticity

Student	Disfluency
Marta:	SHE SAID THE HER CHILD MAY DO A LOT OF STUFF BUT ROBBING A PURSE
Antonio:	[PAUSE] THAT SHE WAS JUST TRYING TO PUT THE [PAUSE] WALLET BACK TO HER

Figure 16. Syntactic transfer

Student	Disfluency
Ernesto:	THE – [PAUSE] THE PURSE FALL DOWN THE- [PAUSE] THE DESK OF THE TEACHER. HER DAUGHTER [PAUSE] FOR A GOOD PERSON THAT HER – [X] THAT SHE IS [PAUSE], SHE WAS HELPING HER –
Lola:	THAT SHE WASN'T GOING TO PUT INSIDE U:M [PAUSE] HER POCKET [PAUSE] THE-THE WALLET

A number of students produced disfluencies that involved verb tense or verb form such as the following:

Figure 17. Verb disfluencies

Student	Disfluency
Yesenia:	UM, SHE SAID THA:T ROCIO, HER DAUGHTER [PAUSE] TOLD HER THAT – [PAUSE] THAT THE TEACHER ACCUSED HER OF STEALING THE PURSE [PAUSE] BUT THAT SHE DIDN'T DID IT – [PAUSE] SHE DIDN'T EXACTLY STO:LE THE PURSE.

Examples of disfluencies in verb agreement and preposition selection were also common.

Figure 18. Verb agreement and preposition selection disfluencies

Student	Disfluency
Rosa: (verb agreement)	SHE SAI:D HER DAUGHTER'S NOT GONNA GIVE HER ANY PROBLEMS. [PAUSE] THE PROBLEMS [X] [PAUSE] THE PROBLEMS [PAUSE] STARTS WITH MISS MURPHY.
Lola: (preposition selection)	AND WHY – [PAUSE] WHY WOULD YOU WANT TO KICK HER OUT FROM SCHOOL

Finally, 9 students produced constructions that contained features typical of non-standard varieties of English. Even though we have counted these constructions as disfluencies here, our position is that the students have simply acquired a variety of English that is influenced by African-American Vernacular English, perhaps through their contact with African-American classmates.

Figure 19. Non-standard English

Student	Disfluency
Ulises:	SHE SAID THAT [PAUSE] SHE ALREADY KNOW HER DAUGHTER, THAT [PAUSE] THAT PROBABLY THAT TEACHER DON'T LIKE HER
Vicente:	SHE SAID THAT SHE WASN'T GONNA GET NOTHIN' IN – [PAUSE] SHE WASN'T GONNA PUT NOTHIN' IN HER PURSE

This group of youngsters, many of whom were considered to be at-risk English language learners by their schools, produced few English disfluencies. Moreover, most of the utterances they produced did not contain disfluencies. It is also not clear whether the disfluencies they did produce under these stressful circumstances actually reflect the kind of English that these students would produce under other circumstances. A few students, for example, were able to immediately correct the mistakes they made.

It is evident from our analysis that many youngsters were able to communicate effectively in English, while occasionally using language that was non-native-like in character. They coped with linguistic difficulties by searching for, rephrasing, correcting, and abandoning constructions. Ultimately, however, they simply came as close as they could to the original and went on. In spite of momentary failures, students persisted in their efforts to interpret the communicative actions as successfully as they could.

The disfluencies produced in Spanish by most students in both groups appear to be primarily uncorrected performance errors. Only a few students produced disfluencies that suggest a partial acquisition of Spanish language rules or a serious breakdown of linguistic control (Figure 20). Two students produced examples of non-native-like syntactic transfer (Figure 21).

Figure 20. Spanish disfluencies

Type	Disfluency
Verb form	Y QUE PUEDE DECIR LA VERDAD DE – [PAUSE] DE NIÑOS QUE SON HONESTOS She could see Rocío's face ELLA PUDE VER LA CARA DE ROCIO (Enrique)
Verb tense	SU – [PAUSE] SU BOLSO ESTABA EN – EN EL SUELO and the contents were spilled out [PAUSE] Y TODO LO QUE TIENE ADENTRO ESTABA A FUERA, [PAUSE] TODO (Ada)
Syntactic transfer	ELLA CONOCE A LOS ESTUDIANTES, QUE PUEDE: UM DECIR LA DIFERENCIA [PAUSE] DE NIÑOS HUMILDES Y NIÑOS RATEROS (Rosa)
Noun & pronoun gender	ESTABA LA CARTERA DE ELLA TIRADA EN EL SUELO: Mmmm Y CON: UNOS [PAUSE] COSAS [PAUSE] TIRADAS, [PAUSE] FUERA DE LA CARTERA [PAUSE] Y QUE::, ROCIO [PAUSE] TRAIA LA – UNA CARTERA QUE ESTABA ADENTRO DE ESE BOLSO [pitch rises on last syllable] Mmhmm Y QUE PARECE – LO IBA A PONER A DENTRO (Yesenia)
Idiomaticity	[PAUSE] DICE QUE: AHORITA LE VAN A DAR EL BENEFICIO DE ESO, PERO PARA LA SI – SI – SI PASA ESO SEGU:NDA VEZ, [PAUSE] QUE NO VAN A:: NO VAN A TENER [PAUSE] DUDAS YA

Figure 21. Non-native-like disfluencies

Type	Disfluency
Syntactic transfer	A parent came to the door [PAUSE] Y UN – UN [PAUSE] PADRES RE- [PAUSE] PADRE'S REUNION EN LA CLASE (Antonio)
	her purse was on the floor [PAUSE] SU: – AH [PAUSE] SU PUR – [PAUSE] SU BOLSA DE [X] [quickens pace] COSAS LO ESTABAN ALLI EN EL SUELO (Antonio)

Except for the two students from India, most students generally produced native-like Spanish. We conjecture that disfluencies were the result of momentary inattention and failure to monitor language production, rather than a reflection of actual linguistic limitations. When they produced these disfluencies, students were often engaged in transmitting complicated details on which the entire accusation hinged. Their attention was not on forms, and they made momentary slips that would have been corrected immediately in other circumstances.

From the data we have analyzed, a few students appear to be clearly English-dominant. However, we cannot simply label the other students as Spanish-dominant. Several students displayed an impressive range of communicative abilities in both languages. Many of these youngsters used flawed language in at least a few segments; they did not appear to be able to monitor their own performance while attending to the other demands of the task. Other students were simply English language learners at a relatively early point in the acquisition process. Given its limitations, their performance in this language can in many ways be seen as exceptional.

10. Understanding the bilingualism of young interpreters

It is not clear whether or how direct instruction in a heritage language can be used to reverse or retard the processes of language change and language shift. Neither is it clear that our current goals for the direct instruction for heritage speakers of Spanish are coherent with the personal and professional goals of these young people *as functioning bilinguals*. What we do know is that in high schools around the country, many immigrant students of Latino background do not graduate.

The young interpreters who took part in our study were ordinary high school students. They were unusual only in that they had used their two languages to broker communication between English and Spanish speakers in their families and communities. All were experienced family interpreters, and all were confident in their ability to carry out our simulated task. The students from Willow High School had achieved some level of academic success. Their enrollment in AP Spanish suggests that they were either college-bound or that teachers had encouraged them to continue their study of Spanish. Someone had cared enough about them to give them the guidance that they needed. The students at Camelot High School were not as lucky. As entering ninth graders, they had been enrolled in a special support program for students bused in to the school from outside the district. They were viewed by the teachers as at risk for academic failure. The students, not surprisingly, were angry, rebellious, and fully determined to leave school as soon as possible. Many thought more ESL classes would be a waste of their time.

It is clear that as valuable as it is for at-risk bilingual students to focus on the development of their Spanish, much more needs to be done to help them survive academically. Many of these students respond to discouraging experiences at school by simply not attending. They are convinced that they are learning little in their classes, and they long to start working and earning money. Unfortunately, many new immigrant youngsters and their families have not yet understood how necessary a high school diploma will be for them in the future.

We believe that developing the bilingual abilities of immigrant youngsters, even the most disillusioned and angry ones, can encourage them to excel at school. While there are many ways that the unique abilities of these youngsters could be fostered in elementary school, we suggest that at the high school level schools should create special classes in interpretation and translation. In these classes, bilingual youngsters can be encouraged to consider careers in which their special language skills will be an advantage. As students begin to form career goals, they are more likely to form academic goals as well.

As a part of our larger project, we have produced guidelines for instructors as they develop curricula for classes in translation and interpretation for students of heritage backgrounds.[17] A curriculum designed to nurture the special linguistic abilities of young interpreters offers them an opportunity to see themselves as uniquely talented individuals. At a time in their lives in which many immigrant youngsters are confused and troubled, the knowledge that their school recognizes them as outstanding and the support of a class designed to develop their existing abilities may very well make the difference between continued engagement and dropping out of school. A curriculum focusing on interpretation and translation, moreover, can give youngsters genuine preparation to become part of a group of respected professionals. As part of a school-to-work program, classes in interpretation and translation can foster connections between students and community organizations and agencies.

If Spanish language teaching professionals pay attention to bilingual children and to their special gifts, it could make an important difference in how these youngsters are perceived by schools and in the ways that they perceive themselves. The development of young Latinos' existing abilities in interpretation and translation is one of the ways that language teaching professionals can make a difference in the lives of young people who have much to offer to their communities and to this country.

Notes

1. The Latino National Political Survey (LNPS) was designed to collect basic data describing Latino political values, attitudes and behavior. Supported by the Ford, Spencer, Rockefeller, and Tinker Foundations, the survey was conducted between 1989 and 1990 in 40 Standard Metropolitan Statistical Areas and involved a sample representative of 91 percent of the Mexican, Puerto Rican, and Cuban populations of the U.S.

2. Cummins (1973, 1979, 1981) proposed two hypotheses: the developmental interdependence hypothesis and the minimal threshold of linguistic competence hypothesis. According to the first hypothesis, second language development is dependent upon development of a first language. According to the second hypothesis, in order for children to benefit from the cognitive advantages of bilingualism they must reach an upper threshold of first language development. In order to avoid cognitive deficits, they must cross a lower threshold of first language development.

3. For an overview of other models of the interpretation process, the reader is directed to Lörscher (1991).

4. Face-threatening acts (FTAs) are defined by Brown and Levinson (1978) as acts that threaten face (the public image that every member of society wants to claim for him or herself). FTAs include orders, contradictions, challenges, threats, warnings, expressions of disapproval, criticism, strong negative emotion, accusations, reprimands, and insults.

5. We are using the term "communicative actions" following Geis (1995). He argues that communicative actions are social as well as linguistic acts through which speakers seek to achieve particular communicative goals.

6. In annotating the script for communicative actions, we follow the strategies employed by Valdés (1986).

7. In order to protect the privacy of children involved in the study, the schools have been given fictitious names.

8. The decision to follow the script offered both advantages and disadvantages. On the one hand, following the script allowed us to compare and contrast the performance of young interpreters on the exact same challenges. On the other hand, following the script prevented us from investigating ways in which young interpreters might have solved problems of misunderstanding and confusion.

9. According to Piotrowska (1998), the concept of strategy has not been unequivocally defined in the field of translation studies. Lörshcher (1991: 78) defines a translation strategy as "a potentially conscious procedure for the solution of a problem which an individual is faced with when translating a text segment from one language into another."

10. Five members of the research team independently marked each communicative turn and identified the essential message for that turn. The differences encountered were resolved, and a final scoring sheet was designed in which the essential communicative action for each turn was identified.

11. It is important to point out that Roberts et al.'s (1995) assessment procedure consists of the evaluation of the reproduction of original information at three levels (vital points, important points, and less important points) as well as the evaluation of language proficiency including general vocabulary, grammar, level of language and pronunciation. Omissions and partial omissions are not seen as strategic choices.

12. We are using the term "alignment" here to refer to an interpreter's feeling of sympathy for one of the two individuals for whom she is interpreting. Berk-Seligson (1990) points out that interpreters may consciously or unconsciously establish an ethnic bonding with one of the interlocutors.

13. As Hatim and Mason (1997: 51) point out, liaison or community interpreters involved in face-to-face communication receive a first installment of a longer text which they must treat as a self-contained. They must cope with an "unpredictability at the outset as to how the dialogue will develop and what the long-term significance of current lexical choice or local cohesion will be."

14. Had we been evaluating students' performance as Roberts (1995) does, by giving points to each CA contained in the text, students would have received no points for zero renditions. The strategic use of omissions would not have been taken into account.

15. Current work being carried out by Marisela González for her honors thesis at Stanford University is focused on this possibility.

16. For a very complete overview of the concept of strategy in communication and in translation, the reader is referred to Chesterman 1995/1996.

17. The guidelines are entitled "Developing the talents and abilities of linguistically gifted bilingual students: Guidelines for developing curriculum at the high school level." They are available as part of the final report submitted to the National Research Center on the Gifted and Talented.

References

Baldwin, A.Y. 1991. Ethnic and cultural issues. In *Handbook of gifted education*, ed. Nicholas Colangelo and Gary A. Davis, 416–427. Boston: Allyn & Bacon.

Balkan, Lewis. 1970. *Les effets du bilinguism Français–Anglais sur les aptitudes intellectuelles*. Bruxelles: Aimav.

Bell, Roger T. 1991. *Translation and translating: Theory and practice*. London: Longman.

Bell, Roger T. 1998. Psycholinguistic/cognitive approaches. In *Routledge encyclopedia of translation studies*, ed. Mona Baker, 185–190. London: Routledge.

Bell, Sherrill J. 1995. The challenges of setting and monitoring the standards of community interpreting: An Australian perspective. In *The critical link: Interpreters in the community*, ed. S.E. Carr, R. Roberts, A. Dufour, and D. Steyn, 93–108. Amsterdam: John Benjamins.

Ben-Zeev, Sandra. 1977. The Influence of bilingualism on cognitive strategy and cognitive development. *Child Development* 48: 1009–1018.

Berk-Seligson, Susan. 1990. *The bilingual courtroom*. Chicago: University of Chicago Press.

Bialystok, Ellen. 1990. *Communication strategies: A psychological analysis of second-language use*. London: Blackwell.

Brown, Penelope and Stephen Levinson. 1978. Universals in language usage: Politeness phenomena. In *Questions and politeness: Strategies in social interaction*, ed. E.N. Goody, 56–289. London: Cambridge.

Chesterman, Andrew. 1995/1996. Communication and learning strategies for translators. *AILA Review* 12: 79–86.

Cummins, Jim. 1973. A theoretical perspective on the relationship between bilingualism and thought. *Working Papers on Bilingualism* 1: 1–9.

Cummins, Jim. 1978. Bilingualism and the development of metalinguistic awareness. *Journal of Cross-Cultural Psychology* 9: 139–149.

Cummins, Jim. 1979. Linguistic interdependence and the educational development of bilingual children. *Review of Educational Research* 49: 222–251.

Cummins, Jim. 1981. The role of primary language development in promoting educational success for language minority students. In *Schooling and language minority students: A theoretical framework*, ed. California State Department of

Education, Office of Bilingual Bicultural Education, 3–49. Los Angeles: California State University Evaluation Dissemination and Assessment Center.

Darcy, N.T. 1953. A review of the literature on the effects of bilingualism upon the measurement of intelligence. *Journal of Genetic Psychology* 82: 21–57.

de la Garza, Rodolfo O., Louis DeSipio, F. Chris Garcia, John Garcia, and Angleo Falcon. 1992. *Latino voices: Mexican, Puerto Rican, and Cuban perspectives on American politics*. Boulder, CO: Westview Press.

Diaz, Rafael M. 1983. The impact of bilingualism on cognitive development, *Review of Research in Education* 10: 23–54.

Draper, Jamie B. and June H. Hicks. 1996. Foreign language enrollments in public secondary schools, fall 1994. *Foreign Language Annals* 29.3: 303–306.

Drew, Paul and John Heritage, eds. 1992. *Talk at work*. London: Cambridge.

Faerch, Claus and Gabriele Kasper, eds. 1983. *Strategies in interlanguage communication*. London: Longman.

Faerch, Claus and Gabriele Kasper. 1984. Two ways of defining communication strategies. *Language Learning* 34: 45–63.

Feldman, Carol and Michael Shen. 1971. Some language-related cognitive advantages of bilingual five-year-olds. *Journal of Genetic Psychology* 118: 235–244.

Frasier, Mary M. 1992. Response to Kitano: The sharing of giftedness between culturally diverse and non-diverse gifted students. *Journal of Education for the Gifted* 15: 20–30.

Frasier, Mary M. and A. Henry Passow. 1994. *Toward a new paradigm for identifying talented potential*. Storrs, CT: National Research Center on the Gifted and Talented.

Gallagher, James J. 1996. Issues in the education of gifted students. In *Handbook of gifted education*, ed. Nicholas Colangelo and Gary A. Davis, 10–23. Boston: Allyn and Bacon.

Geis, Michael L. 1995. *Speech acts and conversational interaction*. London: Cambridge.

Genesee, Fred, G. Richard Tucker, and Wallace E. Lambert. 1975. Communication skills of bilingual children. *Child Development* 46: 1010–1014.

Gentile, Adolfo. 1997. Community interpreting or not? Practices, standards and accreditation. In *The critical link: Interpreters in the community*, ed. Silvana E. Carr, Roda Roberts, Aideen Dufour, and Dini Steyn, 109–130. Amsterdam: John Benjamins.

Gentzler, Edwin. 1993. *Contemporary translation theories*. London: Routledge.

Gile, Daniel. 1995. *Basic concepts and models for interpreter and translator training*. Amsterdam: John Benjamins.

Gran, Laura. 1998. In-training development of interpreting strategies and creativity. In *Translators' strategies and creativity*, ed. Ann Beylard-Ozeroff, Jana Králová, and Barbara Moser-Mercer, 145–162. Amsterdam: John Benjamins.

Gubbins, E. Jean., Del Siegle, Joseph S. Renzulli, and S. Brown. 1993. Assumptions underlying the identification of gifted and talented students. *The National Center on the Gifted and Talented Newsletter* Fall 1993: 3–5.

Hakuta, Kenji. 1986. *Mirror of language: The debate on bilingualism*. New York: Basic Books.

Hakuta, Kenji and Rafael Diaz. 1984. The relationship between bilingualism and cognitive ability: A critical discussion and some new longitudinal data. In *Children's Language, Vol. 5*, ed. Keith E. Nelson, 319–344. Hillsdale, N.J.: Erlbaum.

Hakuta, Kenji, Bernard M. Ferdman, and Rafael M. Diaz. 1986. *Bilingualism and cognitive development: Three perspectives and methodological implications.* Los Angeles: UCLA Center for Language Education and Research.

Harris, Brian. 1977. The importance of natural translation. *Working Papers In Bilingualism* 12: 96–114.

Harris, Brian. 1978. The difference between natural and professional translation. *Canadian Modern Language Review* 34: 417–227.

Harris, Brian and Bianca Sherwood. 1978. Translating as an innate skill. In *Language interpretation and communication*, ed. David Gerver and H. Wallace Sinaiko, 155–170. New York: Plenum Press.

Hatim, Basil and Ian Mason. 1997. *The translator as communicator*. London: Routledge.

House, Juliane. 1981. *A model for translation quality assessment.* Tubingen: Gunter Narr.

House, Juliane. 1997. *Translation quality assessment: A model revisited.* Tubingen: Gunter Narr.

House, Juliane. 1998. Quality of translation. In *Routledge encyclopedia of translation studies*, ed. Mona Baker, 197–200. London: Routledge.

Ianco-Worrall, Anita. D. 1972. Bilingualism and Cognitive Development. *Child Development* 43: 1390–1400.

Kasper, Gabriele and Eric Kellerman, eds. 1997. *Communication stategies: Psycholinguistic and sociolinguistic perspectives*. London: Longman.

Kaufert, Joseph M. and Robert W. Putsch. Communication through interpreters in healthcare: Ethical dilemmas arising from differences in class, culture, language, and power. *The Journal of Clinical Ethics* 8.1: 71–87.

Kitano, Marjie. 1992. A multicultural educational perspective on serving the culturally diverse gifted. *Journal for the Education of the Gifted* 15: 4–19.

Levy, Jiri. 1967. Translation as decision process. In *To honor Roman Jakobson, Vol. 2,* 1171–1182. The Hague: Mouton.

Lörscher, Wolfgang. 1991. *Translation performance, translation process and translation strategies*. Tubingen: Gunter Narr.

Malakoff, Marguerita and Kenji Hakuta. 1991. Translation skill and metalinguistic awareness in bilnguals. In *Language processing in bilingual children*, ed. Ellen Bialystok, 141–166. London: Cambridge.

Neubert, Albrecht. 1984. Translation studies and applied linguistics. *AILA Review* 1: 46–64.

Newman, Aryeh. 1994. Translation equivalence: Nature. In *The encyclopedia of language and linguistics*, ed. R.E. Asher and Y.M.Y. Simpson, 4694–4700. Oxford: Pergammon Press.

Nida, Eugene A. 1964. *Toward a science of translating*. Leiden: E.J. Brill.

Nida, Eugene A. and Charles R. Taber. 1969. *The theory and practice of translation.* Leiden: E.J. Brill.

Patton, James M., Douglas Prillamon, and Joyce Van Tassel-Baska. 1990. The nature and extent of programs for the disadvantaged gifted in the United States and territories. *Gifted Child Quarterly* 34.3: 94–96.

Peal, Elizabeth and Wallace Lambert. 1962. The relation of bilingualism to intelligence. *Psychological Monographs* 76.546: 1–23.

Pease-Alvarez, Lucinda. 1993. *Moving in and out of bilingualism: Investigating native language maintenance and shift in Mexican-descent children. Research Report #6.*

Santa Cruz, CA: National Center for Research on Cultural Diversity and Second Language Learning, University of California, Santa Cruz.

Piotrowska, Maria. 1998. Towards a model of strategies and techniques for teaching translation. In *Translators' strategies and creativity*, ed. Ann Beylard-Ozeroff, Jana Králová, and Barbara Moser-Mercer, 207–211. Amsterdam: John Benjamins.

Portes, Alejandro and Lingxia Hao. 1998. E pluribus unum: Bilingualism and loss of language in the second generation. *Sociology of Education* 71: 269–294.

Reiss, Katarina and Hans. J. Vermeer. 1984/1991. *Grundlegung einer allgemeinen Translationstheorie, 2nd edition*. Tubingen: Niemeyer.

Renzulli, Joseph S. 1986. The three-ring conception of giftedness: A developmental model for creative productivity. In *Conceptions of giftedness*, ed. R.J. Sternberg and J.E. Davidson, 53–92. Cambridge: Cambridge University Press.

Renzulli, Joseph S. 1997. Major issues and challenges facing the field. Paper presented at the Jacob K. Javits Program Meeting, Washington, DC.

Reynolds, Allan G. 1991. The cognitive consequences of bilingualism. In *Bilingualism, multiculturalism, and second language learning: The McGill conference in honour of Wallace E. Lambert*, ed. A. G. Reynolds, 145–182. Hillsdale, NJ: Erlbaum.

Riccardi, Alessandra. 1998. Interpreting strategies and creativity. In *Translators' strategies and creativity*, ed. Ann Beylard-Ozeroff, Jana Králová, and Barbara Moser-Mercer, 171–179. Amsterdam: John Benjamins.

Roberts, Roda P. 1995. An assessment tool for community interpreting. In *Proceedings of the 36th annual conference of the American Translators Association*, ed. Peter W. Krawutschke, 135–145. Medford, NJ: Information Today.

Roberts, Roda P. 1997. Community interpreting today and tomorrow. In *The critical link: Interpreters in the community*, ed. Silvana E. Carr, Roda Roberts, Aideen Dufour, and Dini Steyn, 7–26. Amsterdam: John Benjamins Publishing Company.

Shannon, Shiela M. 1987. *English in el barrio: A sociolinguistic study of second language contact*. Ph.D. dissertation, Stanford University.

Solé, Yolanda R. 1990. Bilingualism: Stable or transitional? The case of Spanish in the United States. *International Journal of the Sociology of Language* 84: 35–80.

Sternberg, Robert. J. 1985. *Beyond IQ: A triarchic theory of human intelligence*. New York: Cambridge University Press.

Sternberg, Robert J. and Janet E. Davidson. 1986. *Conceptions of giftedness*. Cambridge: Cambridge University Press.

Swain, Merrill, Guy Dumas, and N. Naiman. 1974. Alternatives to spontaneous speech: Elicited translation and imitation as indicators of second language competence. *Working Papers on Bilingualism* 3: 68–79.

Tannenbaum, Abraham J. 1986. Giftedness: a psychosocial approach. In *Conceptions of giftedness*, ed. R.J. Sternberg and J.E. Davidson, 21–52. Cambridge: Cambridge University Press.

Tarone, Elaine. 1981. Some thoughts on the notion of 'communication strategy.' *TESOL Quarterly* 15: 245–295.

Terman, Lewis. M. 1925. *Genetic studies of genius: Vol. 1. Mental and physical traits of a thousand gifted children*. Stanford, CA: Stanford University Press.

Toury, Gideon. 1984. The notion of 'native translator' and translation teaching. In *Translation theory and its implementation in the teaching of translating and interpreting*, ed. Wilss Wolfram and Gisela Thome, 186–195. Tubingen: Gunter Narr.

Treffinger, Donald and Joseph Renzulli. 1986. Giftedness as potential for creative productivity: Transcending IQ scores. *Roeper Review* 8.3: 150–154.

US Department of Education. 1993. *National excellence: A case for developing America's talent*. Washington, DC: Office of Educational Research and Improvement.

Valdés, Guadalupe. 1986. Analyzing the demands that courtroom interaction makes upon speakers of ordinary English: Towards the development of a coherent descriptive framework. *Discourse Processes* 9.3: 269–303.

Valdés, Guadalupe, Christina Chávez, and Claudia Angelleli. 2000. *The selection of young interpreters* (Report to the National Research Center on the Gifted and Talented). Stanford, CA: Stanford University.

Vásquez, Olga A., Lucinda Pease-Alvarez, and Sheila. M. Shannon. 1994. *Pushing boundaries: Language and culture in a Mexicano community*. London: Cambridge.

Vygotsky, Lev S. 1962. *Thought and language*. Cambridge, MA: MIT Press.

Wadensjö, Cecilia. 1998. *Interpreting as interaction*. London: Longman.

Wadensjö, Cecilia. 1997. Recycled information as a questioning strategy: Pitfalls in interpreter-mediated talk. In *The critical link: Interpreters in the community*, ed. Silvana E. Carr, Roda Roberts, Aideen Dufour, and Dini Steyn, 35–52. Amsterdam: John Benjamins.

Wadensjö, Cecilia. 1995. Dialogue interpreting and the distribution of responsibility. *Journal of Linguistics* 14: 111–129.

Weber, Wilhelm. 1984. *Training translators and conference interpreters*. New York: Harcourt Brace.

Wilss, Wolfram. 1996. *Knowledge and skills in translator behavior*. Amsterdam: John Benjamins.

Yule, George and Elaine Tarone. 1997. Investigating communication strategies in L2 reference: Pros and cons. In *Communication stategies: Psycholinguistic and sociolinguistic perspectives*, ed. Gabriele Kasper and Eric Kellerman, 17–30. London: Longman.

Zentella, Ana Celia. 1997. *Growing up bilingual*. Oxford: Blackwell.

The Spanish Speaker + Interpreter Services = Equal Access to the Judicial System: Is the Equation Accurate?

Virginia Benmaman
College of Charleston

1. Introduction

Court interpreters for litigants with minimal English skills have become an increasingly familiar sight in recent years. This increased presence has paralleled the dramatic increase in minority linguistic populations throughout the United States, especially within the Hispanic community. Demographic predictions estimate that the United States will have a population of 40 million Hispanics by 2005. This population will swell to 96 million by the middle of the 21st century. Hispanics will account for 16.3% of the U.S. population by 2020, and 24.5% by 2050. (Hispanic Business 1999, Census Bureau 1997).

Although the Constitution of the United States does not guarantee the right to an interpreter, the rights of all individuals facing our system of justice are based on the Fifth, Sixth, and Fourteenth Amendments. These amendments guarantee due process, fundamental fairness and equal protection under the law. The Fifth Amendment imparts the right to be publicly charged with a crime in an indictment returned by the grand jury, and to be held to answer to those charges according to established legal procedures before being deprived of life, liberty, or property. This amendment also guarantees the right of a criminal defendant to refuse to be a witness against himself or herself, and safeguards the accused against being tried twice for the same crime. The Sixth Amendment states that a defendant has the right to be "meaningfully present" at his or her own trial. This presence implies not only the defendant's physical presence, but also his or her 'mental presence,' i.e. direct knowledge about court proceedings. A clear understanding of those proceedings is crucial for the defendant to be able to assist in his or her own defense through active participation, receive effective assistance from counsel and provide counsel with informed and intelligent input, and confront government's witnesses and cross-examine them on the testimony presented. The Fourteenth Amendment extends the application of these rights to resident citizens of any and all states. Case law frequently invokes these amendments and attorneys regularly cite them in their appellate briefs.

Non-English-speaking litigants must rely on the renditions of all colloquies and witness testimony as interpreted into the foreign language, and the English version of testimony as interpreted from the foreign language. The accuracy and completeness of the interpreted renditions is rarely monitored. Even more significant, the record preserves only the English version of what is said in the courtroom. If a problem arises, a litigant has the right to raise a timely and substantiated objection on the record. If an interpretation-related problem arises and is not addressed immediately, subsequent redress is usually futile. As a rule, guilty decisions are reversed and cases are remanded for retrial only when an abuse of discretion has been confirmed by court records. I will argue that evidence needed to prove an abuse of discretion in interpreted proceedings is difficult to obtain. As a result, violation of a litigant's right of due process becomes a significant issue.

Courts of Appeals are reluctant to reverse trial court decisions regarding matters related to the appointment of an interpreter or interpreter performance. Historically, broad discretion has been granted the lower courts in these matters. In only a few instances have the two major standards of review, abuse of discretion and demonstration of plain error, warranted a judgment of reversible error. A U.S. Court of Appeals ruling in 1989 clearly illustrates this position.

> Appointment of an interpreter is a matter within the trial judge's discretion. In matters of handling translation issues, the trial judge must be given wide discretion in assessing the complexity of the proceedings and testimony, and the defendant's knowledge of English, as well as a variety of other factors. . . . In such instances the trial judge must balance the defendant's 6th Amendment rights against the public's interest in the economical administration of criminal law, and that such balancing is reversible only on a showing of abuse. Valladares v United States (CA 11 GA, 1989)

2. Precedent in modern case law

The landmark case United States ex rel. Negrón v New York (1970) set the stage for modern case law. An indigent Puerto Rican defendant who did not speak English was tried and convicted of murder. His court-appointed attorney spoke no Spanish. No communication existed between counsel and defendant. None of the trial proceedings were made comprehensible to the defendant except for brief instances in which the court interpreter translated the proceedings into Spanish in summary fashion for Negrón. The interpreter had been hired by the prosecution. Negrón's own testimony and that of two Spanish-speaking witnesses was translated into English for the benefit of the court. Twelve of the fourteen state witnesses testified against him in English. None of this testimony was comprehensible to Negrón. Circuit Judge Irving Kaufman commented that the trial must have sounded like "a babble of voices" surrounding the defendant. The Court of Appeals held that Negrón's trial lacked the fundamental fairness required by the due process clause of the Fourteenth Amendment and the Sixth Amendment's guarantees extended to the states. The Spanish-speaking defendant in a state homicide prosecution was entitled to the services of a translator. The state's failure to provide a translator rendered the trial constitutionally infirm (1970: 388).

3. Federal and state legislation

The Federal Court Interpreter's Act of 1978 (amended 1988) mandates the presence of certified interpreters when a litigant has limited English language skills. This mandate is supported by the recently formed consortium organized by the National Center for State Courts, which currently involves 22 states. This legislation is significant because it establishes minimal qualifications for practicing interpreters. It reflects society's gradual acknowledgment that interpreting is a skill which goes well beyond the ability to speak two languages. It also implies that education and training will eventually become prerequisites for entering this emerging profession.

In spite of these positive steps, decisions about who qualifies for interpreter services, who is appointed to serve as interpreter, and who assesses interpreters' performance are frequently arbitrary. Judicial practice varies from state to state. More significantly, the decisions rendered in appellate court rulings have been inconsistent.

A review of several hundred appellate decisions has revealed that Courts of Appeals consistently grant broad discretion to the trial court in the selection of interpreters and in all other matters pertaining to interpreter performance. The predominant pattern has been for appellate judges to uphold the rulings of lower courts, and to reject defense claims that the right to due process was violated by inadequate interpretation.

4. Issues on appeal

To date, very few appeals have been based solely on an interpreter-related matter. Rather, concerns about interpretation have been raised as one of a variety of contested procedural issues, in the hope that the court would include interpretation issues in a serious review of all the problems with the case. In the following sections I outline the predominant issues that have been raised on appeal. Unless otherwise specified, the word 'court' refers to the appellate court.

4.1. Appointment of interpreter

Failure to appoint an interpreter was the overwhelming reason for appeal in the 1970s and early 1980s. The ruling issued in State of Kansas v Van Pham (1984) was typical of the wording of other rulings during this period: "... determining and propriety of appointing person as interpreter lies within discretion of trial court, and such determination will be reversed on appeal only in most extreme cases." While this is no longer as prevalent, courts in at least 35 states still rely on judicial or administrative discretion in the appointment of interpreters. A court must determine how much English a litigant is able to speak and understand. All too often, this determination of the litigant's ability is based on the personal perceptions of monolingual judges or English-speaking and even bilingual defense attorneys, rather than fact. Although a judge may hold an evidentiary hearing to determine the litigant's English language skills, the questions asked often include a number of yes or no questions, instead of questions which will elicit sufficient language on which to make a valid assessment of English language ability. I often hear court personnel comment that the assistance of an interpreter is an unnecessary expense for the court, since simple statements when spoken slowly are generally understood by a litigant who claims to speak "a little English." However, counsel and the judge rarely reduce their rate of speech during legal discourse, much less simplify the language of legal oratory.

A related issue is payment for interpreter services. It has been argued that if counsel is privately retained, the defendant should also be responsible for payment of interpreter services, when needed. So ruled the Court of Appeals in State v Guzman (NJ, 1998). However, in Texas, the statute does not distinguish between indigent and non-indigent defendants in this way (Villareal v State, Tex, 1993). According to Texas Code of Criminal Procedure (Art. 3830 (a) Sup 1993), the court must provide an interpreter for the accused whenever the litigant lacks proficiency in the English language.

4.2. The appointed interpreter

Once the court has determined that an interpreter is needed, it must determine who will serve in that capacity. Once again, courts across the country do not conform to uniform standards for interpreters' qualifications. It is generally held that an interpreter assigned to assist a defendant must be competent enough to render an accurate and complete oral translation of all communication. Some jurisdictions employ staff interpreters, who serve as needed. Standards for these employees vary. However, in jurisdictions with no staff interpreters, the situation becomes much less clear. The selection of the interpreter rests wholly within the discretion of the trial judge. Court administrators feel pressure to avoid a delay in the trial while they locate a qualified interpreter or to avoid the added expense of paying an interpreter.

Faced with the usual backlog of cases, the court often quickly appoints someone who is readily available and who claims to speak the language of the litigant. Interpreters are expected to be unbiased towards the parties and disinterested in the outcome of the case. Nevertheless, appeals records show that appointments of interpreters have included a bailiff (People v Montoya, Tex, 1991), an arresting police officer (Gonzalez v State, Del, 1977), a co-defendant (State v Tamez, La, 1987), a family member (State v Van Pham, Kan, 1984; Balderrama v State, Fla, 1983), and defense counsel. This last category merits discussion.

On occasion, bilingual attorneys believe their language skills are sufficient to render the presence of an interpreter unnecessary. The court often welcomes this decision because it saves time, tax and budget resources. However, ethical questions linger. What if the accused enters a plea on advice of his attorney and then attempts to set it aside? Or if the accused makes an incriminating statement unwittingly, can counsel assert attorney–client privilege? Also, the quality of both legal representation and interpretation goes down when a single person attempts to play both roles. While counsel is speaking for his client or examining a witness, who is interpreting the proceedings for the defendant? While counsel is interpreting, who is representing the client's interest? Finally, bilingual abilities, however well-developed, do not guarantee interpreting skills. It is questionable whether the defendant's right to due process can be preserved when both the attorney–client relationship and the quality of interpretation are compromised.

Appellate courts have had differing opinions on this issue. For instance, in Briones v Texas (1980) and State v Zambrano (Ohio, 1989) the courts held that the attorney's bilingual competence was adequate to protect the defendant's Fourteenth Amendment rights. In State v Zambrano, the ruling stated that, as an officer of the court, the attorney takes an oath which obligates him to represent his client faithfully, thereby eliminating any concerns about deception or fraud. This oath bound the attorney to render a true translation of the questions and answers which were directed to his client. However, in Giraldo-Rincon v Dugger (MD Fla, 1989) and in State v Kounelis (NJ, 1992), the Courts of Appeals reversed the trial court rulings. In the Florida case, the court ruled that the trial judge violated the petitioner's constitutional rights by denying a request for the appointment of an interpreter. The defendant could not comprehend the testimony in English of eleven witnesses, although occasionally counsel would relate what was transpiring during the trial. The court ruled that counsel did not give the defendant a "word for word" translation of testimony and the proceedings, and therefore did not serve as an interpreter. In this case also, the trial judge had denied the appointment of an interpreter stating that, since the attorneys had been privately retained, the petitioner could secure his own interpreter. In the New Jersey case, the trial judge was apprised of the need for an interpreter just before commencement of the trial. The co-defendant's lawyer informed the judge that both he and the defendant's attorney spoke Greek. The conviction was reversed when the court found nothing in the transcript to indicate that anyone had translated any part of the trial to the defendant. According to the court ruling, failure to appoint an interpreter violated the defendant's rights to confrontation and assistance of counsel.

It is reassuring to learn of more recent cases which have been reversed because of due process violations involving the attorney acting as an interpreter. However, I am currently consulting with an attorney in another state on just such an issue. The petitioner, who speaks no English, is seeking to have his conviction overturned. He claims that his attorney, serving as interpreter, advised him to plead guilty with the assurance that he would receive a short sentence in exchange for his plea. The sentence was much more severe than he had been led to believe. The petitioner asserts that the plea was not rendered knowingly and voluntarily, because it was based on the interpretation and advice of an attorney who was not competent in Spanish. The current attorney handling this case has documentation which confirms the limited bilingual abilities of the defendant's previous counsel. This example illustrates that many courts today still do not consider this practice a due process violation.

4.3. Role(s) of interpreter

Interpreters perform several functions in court. As proceedings interpreter, they translate all the verbal exchanges of the various court players into the foreign language in the simultaneous mode for the defendant. As witness interpreters, they translate for any witness who cannot communicate easily in English. Witness testimony is normally interpreted in the consecutive mode from the witness stand, and the English questions and the interpreted answers form part of the official permanent record of the proceeding. In most federal courts and some state courts, interpreters work in teams during trials and long evidentiary hearings. This allows for one interpreter to provide simultaneous interpretation of the proceedings for the defendant and facilitate communication between counsel and client as needed, while a second interpreter provides consecutive interpretation at the witness stand. However, such a practice is considered a luxury in the majority of state courts. Generally one interpreter serves as both proceedings and witness interpreter, and may also be the sole interpreter for a multi-defendant case.

Once again, appellate courts have not had a consistent response to claims of due process violations resulting from "shared" or "borrowed" interpreter services. Several convictions were overturned on these grounds in the 1980s. In People v Resendes (CA, 1985), the appellant contended that providing only one interpreter for himself and his co-defendant violated his constitutional rights to an interpreter throughout the proceedings and to effective assistance of counsel. The court ruled that in joint criminal prosecutions of two defendants who did not speak English, requiring the defendants to share one interpreter inhibited effective communication with counsel and therefore constituted reversible error.

The court relied on the Supreme Court decision in People v Aguilar (Cal, 1984). In that case, the Supreme Court held that the defendant, who was appealing a murder conviction, was deprived of his constitutional right to a proceedings interpreter when the trial court borrowed the interpreter to translate testimony of two state witnesses. Yet, in People v Rodriguez (NY, 1990) the court held that a Spanish-speaking defendant was not entitled to appointment of a second interpreter when the court used the defendant's interpreter to translate testimony of Spanish-speaking witnesses. The court reasoned the second interpreter was unnecessary because the defendant was able to comprehend testimony of the witness and the interpreter was permitted to return to the defense table whenever the defendant needed to confer with counsel through the interpreter. The court also affirmed the conviction in People v Chavez (Cal, 1991). The appellant alleged that the trial court made an error in requiring the non-English-speaking defendant, who was charged with grand theft, to share the interpreter with a co-defendant. The court held that sharing an interpreter was harmless beyond a reasonable doubt as there was no evidence of prejudice suffered by the defendant. Similarly in U.S. v Yee Soon Shin and Yong Woo Jung (Cal, 9th Cir, 1991), an appeal of a money laundering conviction, the court ruled that two defendants sharing one interpreter did not violate the defendant's rights under the Fifth and Sixth Amendments, nor did the Federal Court Interpreter Act require separate interpreters for each defendant in multi-defendant cases.

4.4. Appointment of uncertified interpreters

Generally, a presiding judge's appointment of an uncertified interpreter does not constitute a reversible error unless a timely objection is raised, a substantial objection is made to the selection or performance of an interpreter, or it was demonstrated that a certified interpreter was available. In State v New Chue Her (Minn, 1990) the state did not examine the qualifications of two Hmong-speaking interpreters. Despite subsequent claims that the interpreters mistranslated a number of statements made by the victim and state witnesses, no objection was raised at trial. All parties subsequently agreed that errors were made, but disagreed about the extent of the impact the errors made on the interpreted testimony. The court affirmed the conviction, ruling that there was no tangible prejudice or harm to the defense. The defense counsel in State v Puente-Gomez (Idaho, 1992) did not raise objections during the proceedings to the performance of an "otherwise qualified interpreter" appointed by the trial judge during the proceedings. A post-conviction objection was overruled. The court stated that the determination of an interpreter's qualification is a matter of the trial court's discretion, and an objection with supporting evidence is required to preserve an error on the record.

4.5. Substantive challenges to the accuracy of interpretation

A brief description of several cases will further highlight the divergence in appellate rulings in cases of substantial challenges to fitness of the interpreter. In U.S. v Anguloa (Ariz, 1979), the appeal was based on poor translations and prejudicial comments made by the interpreters in open court. The services of three different interpreters were used; each was replaced because of reported mistranslations and objections raised by both prosecutor and defense counsel. On several occasions, the judge admonished the interpreter and asked the jury to disregard the interpreter's comments. The defendant was convicted. On appeal the court concluded that no prejudicial error was made since the records did not show any inaccuracies in translation, nor was there any prejudice evident by the interpreters' actions.

Nearly fifteen years later in State v Mora (RI, 1993), the Appeals Court sustained the denial of a mistrial motion which alleged that there were numerous deficiencies in a court-appointed interpreter's translation of the defendant's testimony. The defense claimed the interpreter was not able to keep up with defendant's testimony, a failure which significantly altered the course of the questions and answers and made the defendant appear distraught and evasive before the jury. Since the interpreter could not remember whole answers, the defendant's narratives has to be split into parts. Despite the fact that the defense objected and noted discrepancies between the defendant's testimony and the interpreter's translation for the record, the court found that the trial judge used proper discretion in allowing the same interpreter to continue. The court justified its affirmation of the conviction by asserting that the trial judge had controlled the length of the defendant's answers so that the interpreter could be more effective. This court ruling echoed a Minnesota court ruling issued six years earlier:

> Translation is an art that will inevitably lead to some disagreement. When interpreter's translation is generally accurate and adequate and conveys the essence of what was said, the fact that another interpreter disagrees with the translation in a few particulars does not warrant relief in the accused's favor. . . . There is no such thing as a perfect translation, and in every case there will be room for dispute among expert translators over some aspects of the interpretation. (State v Mitjins, MN, 1987)

A different appellate view was expressed in State of Illinois v Starling (Ill, 1974). On appeal of a conviction of simple robbery, the court focused on the central question of whether the testimony of the sole prosecution witness was "understandable, comprehensible and intelligible." Both prosecutor and defense counsel complained repeatedly of the ineffectiveness of the interpreter, and the trial judge frequently admonished the interpreter for engaging in unrecorded discussions with the witness. The court held that the defendant was denied his right to confront the state's sole witness. The trial judge abused his discretion in not replacing the interpreter. The judgment was reversed and the case was remanded for a new trial. The appellate ruling also stated, "The only cure upon discovery of an incompetent interpreter is to appoint another interpreter, one who will translate truly, competently, and effectively, each question and answer with due regard for his or her oath to do so."

5. Standard of review

I now turn to a closer examination of the standards that are applied by appellate courts when an appeal asserts that a violation of due process has occurred.

5.1. Abuse of discretion

Appellate courts have held that failure to appoint an interpreter, failure to provide complete translations of specific testimony, or failure to interpret accurately does not warrant relief from conviction in and of itself. A court can only be charged with an abuse of discretion under the following conditions: (1) The accused must make a timely and specific objection. The objection must be raised during the proceedings and must appear in the record to be preserved for appeal. (2) Proof must be presented to the trial court that there is a problem with an interpreter-related issue that is prejudicial to the defendant's case.

Relief is *not* warranted if:

1. The alleged error is not prejudicial,
2. The evidence involving an error is irrelevant or inconsequential. Sketchy arguments of the importance of untranslated remarks or mistranslated remarks cannot be the basis for a finding that the trial judge abused his discretion in handling the matter, or that the errors were substantial as to the outcome of the case,
3. The error was corrected once it was brought to the attention of the trial judge,
4. Cross-examination was made concerning the matter,
5. Untranslated evidence was presented in the defendant's own language and therefore did not require translation, or
6. The evidence against the accused was so overwhelming that errors in interpretation were of little consequence.

On these premises, an appellate review of errors usually results in a decision that the errors were "harmless" and an affirmation of the conviction.

A question that immediately comes to mind is: Who can determine whether an interpretation is accurate? Three possibilities exist: (1) The judge is bilingual and can monitor interpreter performance; (2) The defendant knows enough English to know that an interpretation is inaccurate; (3) The defense attorney is sufficiently bilingual to object to any inaccuracies. If no objections are made by counsel *in a timely manner* and *preserved on the record*, there can be no grounds for appeal unless the admission of the translation was plain error which affected substantial rights of the objecting party. Absent any of these possibilities, errors can remain undetected.

In her discussion of several high-profile cases in Minnesota (State v Lee, 1992 and State v Her, 1992), Hovland (1993: 490–492) describes additional barriers to objecting in a timely manner. Attorneys who make too many objections run the risk of appearing obstructionist and trying to conceal information. The objections may also draw more attention to the evidence than it would normally receive. New Chue Her, who spoke English, did not object to the errors in interpretation at his trial because he did not want the jury to think negatively of him. King Buachee Lee, himself an interpreter, did complain to his attorney, but the judge reprimanded him for attempting to shake the jury's faith in the interpretation.

Various rules of evidence, criminal procedure and civil procedure state that if errors do not affect substantial rights of a party, the court should disregard them. However the definition of what constitutes a "substantial right" or a "prejudicial error" is unclear. The Supreme Court has held that substantial rights are affected if the error "substantially swayed the jury's verdict" or "materially affected the deliberations of the jury" (Hovland: 492). Although the 'harmless doctrine' serves as a useful barrier to frivolous appeals, it presents a potentially severe obstacle to the serious review of interpretation errors.

5.2. Plain error doctrine

If an error was not objected to at trial, the error cannot be raised on appeal. However, the court may review the issue under the plain error doctrine. In this situation, the court will rule in favor of the appellant *only* if the error was severely egregious, if it affected substantial rights, if it represented a miscarriage of justice, or if it resulted in an unfair trial. This standard is stricter than the standard applied to objections made in a timely fashion during trial. Reversals based on 'plain error' seldom occur. To illustrate, in Spruance v State (Del, 1994), the court affirmed a conviction of armed robbery and unlawful sexual intercourse and rejected the claim that the victim's testimony was not translated verbatim in English. The court stated that "Some difficulty is insufficient to rebut the presumption of adequate interpretation and the accused's substantial rights are not violated absent a showing that the translation is subject to serious doubt." This view reflected an earlier opinion issued in People v Rivera (NY, 1993): "Unspecified inadequacies of translations cannot be basis for a reversal of a conviction. When no record is made of serious translation error there is no basis for reversing conviction even though some discrepancies in translation are found and there is no showing of serious error."

Hovland (1993) argues convincingly that defendants raising objections based on interpretation errors must satisfy a higher standard for appellate review than objections for other types of errors. For many courts the error must be reflected in the trial transcript. However, the trial transcript only records statements made in English; it is impossible to check an interpreter's translation against the witness' original statement. The only way the transcript can indicate an interpretation error is if the trial judge addresses the interpreter on matters of the interpretation or the complaining party raises repeated objections which were recorded in a timely manner. It is impossible to determine the extent of error or to determine the extent to which the contested issue has influenced the jury. In U.S. v Anguloa (AZ, 1979), the court wrote:

> We acknowledge that there is an inherent difficulty in attempting to evaluate the accuracy of interpretation on appellate review. The reporter's transcript can only contain the questions in English and the answers after they have been translated into English, and nobody knows how accurate the interpretation may have been except the interpreter and he is the wrong person to look to for an impartial assessment of his performance.

If an oral recording of the proceeding were made of both languages spoken, and a transcript were provided in both languages when necessary, then it would be easy to assess the quality of interpretation. However, courts are unlikely to adopt such a tedious and costly procedure. In light of this reality, Hovland suggests, "Because it is unrealistic to assume that defendants or attorneys can make timely objections to interpretation errors, appellate courts should waive the mandate of timely objections for interpretation errors or in the alternative, apply a less stringent standards of review than that applied under the 'plain error' doctrine" (Hovland: 493–494). Such an exception to the plain error rule would allow for greater scrutiny of errors, and permit the presentation of evidence that did not appear in the transcript of the proceeding to support claims of interpretation.

Errors in interpretation are likely to occur even under optimal trial conditions. When errors do occur, the courts must give recourse to correct interpretations that could change the outcome of a case. Unless there are major institutional changes in the way interpreted proceedings are handled, errors will persist *and* go undetected. Surely there must be a better way to ensure that non-English speakers receive justice than to assume that all translation errors are harmless.

6. Conclusion

Considering these constraints, do non-English-speaking defendants or defendants whose trials include testimony from non-English-speaking witnesses have the same access to the appellate process as English-speaking defendants? I think not. The two stringent standards of review, abuse of discretion and plain error, virtually eliminate the possibility that defendants will be able to substantiate errors in interpretation. If no accommodation in the appeals procedure can be made for appellants raising interpreter-related issues, then the onus falls on the trial courts to ensure that interpreted proceedings are held under optimal conditions. In conclusion, I offer several suggestions: (1) The quality of interpretation must be vastly improved. Education and training programs must be developed to adequately prepare individuals to serve as court interpreters. (2) Courts must set minimum standards of performance and require certification as a prerequisite for employment. (3) Tape recordings should be made of all interpreted proceedings, and provided upon request by either party. (4) A defendant must have access to an interpreter who will provide a simultaneous foreign language version of all spoken discourse during the proceedings. A second interpreter should be provided for witness testimony. (5) Team interpreting for trials is essential. A team of interpreters can monitor the accuracy of the interpretation, assist each other as needed, and provide relief for one another so that mental fatigue will not undermine the interpreter's performance. The trial courts must be put on notice that accurate interpretation is essential to a fair trial. Only when these recommendations are adopted by courts throughout the country can all individuals, not only English speakers, have equal access to our system of justice.

References

Davis, Lynn W. and William E. Hewitt. 1994. Lessons in administrating justice: What judges need to know about the requirements, role, and professional responsibilities of the court interpreter. *Harvard Latino Law Review* 1.1: 121–176.

Davis, Lynn W. and Michael Gardner. 1996. Justicia para todos: Ensuring equal access to the courts for linguistic minorities. *Utah Bar Journal* 9.2: 21–25.

Grabau, Charles and Joseph Gibbons Llewellyn. 1996. Protecting the rights of linguistic minorities: Challenges to court interpretation. *New England Law Review* 30.2: 231–274.

Hammond, Ruth. 1993. Lost in translation. *The Washington Post* Oct. 2: C3.

Hispanic Business. 1999. *Who are we?* April. 21.4: 38–42.

Hovland, Debra. 1993. Errors in interpretation: Why plain error is not plain. *Law and Inequality- A Journal of Theory and Practice.* 11: 473–495.

Piatt, Bill. 1990. Attorney as interpreter: A return to babble. *New Mexico Law Review* 20: 1–16.

Piatt, Bill. 1990. *¿English only? Law and language policy in the United States.* Albuquerque, NM: University of New Mexico Press.

Schulman, Charles. 1993. No hablo inglés: Court interpretation as a major obstacle to fairness for non-English-speaking defendants. *Vanderbilt Law Review* 46: 175–196.
U.S. Census Bureau. 1997. Presentation at Workshop for Federal Court Interpreters sponsored by the Federal Judicial Center. Albuquerque, New Mexico.
U.S. Code Public Law 95–539. 1978. Title 8, Sec. 1827 and 1828.
U.S. Code Public Law 100–702. 1988. Title 7, Sec. 701–12.

Cases Cited

Balderrama v State (1983, Fla App) D2 433 So 2d 1311
Briones v Texas (1980, Tex Crim) 595 SW2d 546
Giraldo-Rincon v Dugger (1989, MD Fla) 707 F Supp 504
Gonzalez v State (1977, Del Supp) 372 A2d 191
People v Aguilar (1984, 35 Cal) 3d 785
People v Chavez (1991, 4th Dist) 231 Cal App 3d 1471
People v Montoya (1991, Tex App) Corpus Christi 811 SW 2d 671
People v Resendes (1985, 5th Dist) 164 Cal App 3d 812
People v Rodriguez (1990, 1st Dept) 165 App Div 2d 705
Spruance v State (1994, Del Supp) LEXIS 106
State v Her (1992, Minn Appeal) LEXIS 25
State v Guzman (1998) 313 NJ Super 712, 712 A2d 1233
State of Illinois v Starling (1974, 1st Dist) 21 Ill App 3d 217
State of Kansas v Van Pham, (1984) 234 Kan 649
State v Kounelis (1992) 258 NJ Super 420
State v Lee (1992, Minn) 494 NW 2d 475
State v Mitjins (1987, Minn) 408 NW2d 824
State v Mora (1993, RI) 618 A2d 1275
State v New Chue Her (1994, Minn App) 510 NW2d 218
State v Puente-Gomez (1992, App) 121 Idaho 702
State v Tamez (1987, La App 1st Cir) 506 So 2d 531
State v Van Pham (1984) 234 Kan 649
State v Zambrano (1989, Ohio App, Sandusky Co) 1989 Ohio App LEXIS 3951
U.S. v Anguloa (1979) Ariz 598 F.2d 1182
U.S. v Yee Soon Shin (1992, CA9 Cal) 953 F2d 559
United States ex rel. Negrón v New York (1970, 2nd Dept) 434 App Div 2d 386
Valladares v United States (1989, CA11 Ga) 871 F2d 1564
Virrareal v State (1993, Tex, App Corpus Christi) 853 SW2d 170

Sociolinguistic Categorization of Spanish–English False Cognates for Court Interpreting Strategies

Erik Camayd-Freixas
Florida International University

False cognates are a familiar problem for all translators and interpreters. Translators know that they must first recognize a potential false cognate if they are to take the precaution to look up the correct equivalent. Otherwise a false sense of security will keep them from questioning the problematic term at all. In court interpreting, however, the problem is particularly acute because interpreters must make split-second decisions and errors can have serious consequences. Given the linguistic acculturation of many Hispanics in the United States, the use of Spanish words with English meanings rather than their original Spanish meanings has become increasingly common. By virtue of being bilingual, interpreters are probably the most linguistically acculturated individuals in the courtroom. They must constantly struggle against lexical and syntactic contamination. The interpreter's awareness of false cognates and correct usage is only half the solution, though. An interpreter must also be able to decide whether a witness is using a Spanish word 'correctly' or inadvertently using it with an 'incorrect' (or English) meaning. Interpreters must know when *violación* means 'rape' and when it simply means *infracción*; when *crimen* means 'murder' and when it simply means *delito*. Because interpreters must be primarily guided by popular speech (or *parole*) and not by rules (or *langue*), giving the 'correct' translation of a false cognate can be a serious interpreting mistake.

Incomplete but useful lists of false cognates can be found in books, journals, and even the Internet, and frequently circulate among interpreters. These lists can help interpreters recognize potential false cognates and their correct usage. However, because these lists are not broken down into categories, they tell us nothing about which meaning a particular speaker intends. Common sense dictates that you make out the meaning from context, but often – and this is particularly true of a word's first occurrence – the semantic context may not be

 Research on Spanish in the U.S., ed. Ana Roca, 95–109. Somerville, MA: Cascadilla Press.

enough to settle the issue. Interpreters often overlook the fact that the sociolinguistics of the courtroom and the level of linguistic acculturation of the speakers are also subtle aspects of a word's context. Moreover, false cognates are not all the same, but can be grouped in sociolinguistic categories which help us determine the appropriateness or probability of a particular meaning.

The sociolinguistic categorization of false cognates has useful implications not only for the practice of court interpreting, but also for interpreter training, pedagogy, and testing. The interpreter should assess the level of acculturation of witnesses and be aware of her own acculturation in order to utilize these categories strategically. She should also create a personalized list of words which are relevant to her individual situation.

This paper proposes such a categorization of Spanish–English false cognates and suggests interpreter strategies for dealing with each type. Some false cognates are field-specific or, in this case, courtroom-specific (e.g., conviction = *condena* vs. *convicción* = belief or certainty; process = *procedimiento* vs. *proceso* = trial). By virtue of the global influence of English, some are not dependent on acculturation, but are widely used even in Hispanic countries (e.g., *renta* for *alquiler*, *asumir* for *suponer*, *aplicación* for *solicitud*). The probability of English meaning in these cases is quite high. Other false cognates are the product of linguistic acculturation; of these, some are relevant to the acculturated witness (e.g., *carpeta* for *alfombra*, *embarazada* for *avergonzada*). Others are simply common mistakes of the acculturated interpreter (e.g., *realizar* for *percatarse*, *asalto* for *acometimiento*, *registrar* for *inscribir*, *injuria* for *lesión*). Yet others are typically generated by both interpreters and highly acculturated witnesses (e.g., *utilidades* for *servicios públicos*, *compromiso* for *acuerdo*, *pretender* for *fingir*). Finally, there are those false cognates which no competent interpreter should ever fall prey to, and which indicate bilingual deficit.

I have divided false cognates into six sociolinguistic categories which are relevant to court interpreting:

1. Courtroom-specific false cognates.
2. Widely used false cognates.
3. False cognates likely to be used by the acculturated witness.
4. False cognates likely to be used by the acculturated interpreter.
5. False cognates likely to be used by both acculturated witnesses and interpreters.
6. False cognates that indicate bilingual deficit.

Before I comment on each of these categories' utility for interpreting strategies, a word about my methodology is in order.

The present compilation is not exhaustive, but it is part of the ongoing collection effort that every interpreter must undertake. The classification of many of these items is open to debate. Many are so ubiquitous that they belong in two or more categories. I have sought to avoid annoying repetitions in the attached list, and thus, I have placed each word in the closest fitting category, repeating only the most treacherous ones.

I have not undertaken a word frequency study to establish the frequency with which each cognate appears in the speech of different categories of speakers: witnesses, interpreters, and other interlocutors. Since only two or three false cognates appear in the interpretation of most court sessions, such a study would be prohibitively expensive and would quickly become obsolete. This essay is grounded instead in my observation of live courtroom speech and classroom interactions with a range of translators. I also gathered words from translation documents, where I could not directly correlate a word occurrence with a particular type of speaker. In many cases, my classification was based on whether the false cognate originated from a common Spanish word or a common English word. Witnesses are more likely to use false cognates based on common Spanish words, while interpreters and other English speakers are more likely to use false cognates based on common English words.

1. Courtroom-specific false cognates

Courtroom-specific false cognates are based on those words that belong to the specialized vocabulary of the courts or that are otherwise common in legal proceedings. Some of them, in fact, are only false cognates in the legal setting (such as: accuse = *inculpar* vs. *acusar* = to charge or indict). In the question "Has anyone accused you of not paying your bills on time?" the context suggests that "accused" be translated as *culpado,* not *acusado,* which would connote 'charged' or 'indicted.' In some cases, the semantic scope of the cognates is quite different in each language, even though one of the acceptations may be the same. Such is the case with *defraudar* and "defraud"; *honesto* and "honest"; *tráfico* and "traffic." Since the particular meaning the court context requires is usually quite different, a non-cognate alternative should be used to avoid confusion; otherwise, gross misinterpretation might result. Consider the question "Which occurrence is that?", and the translation "*¿Qué ocurrencia es ésa?*", instead of "*¿A qué ocasión se refiere?*"

Courtroom-specific false cognates will most likely be put into play by the attorneys or the judge. It is then the interpreter's responsibility to use the correct and unequivocal Spanish equivalents, both when interpreting simultaneously for the defendant and when translating attorneys' questions during interrogatories. However, such "court cognates" – as we may call them for short – may occasionally be used by defendants or witnesses who speak little or no English, particularly if they have been in custody for some time and have picked up a degree in "Spanish for jurisprudence" from their fellow inmates. They now come to testify in court and, in the middle of otherwise exemplary Spanish, they talk the talk, interjecting with unshakable authority: "*Me cargaron con una ofensa*" instead of "*Me acusaron de un delito.*" The more the interpreter knows about her client, the better off she will be. However, the interpreter should never condescend by using court cognates from the start in an attempt to be better understood by the witness. Quite the opposite might happen: you may translate "*¿Alguna vez ha sido convicto de un crimen?*", and you may get "*No, a mí nada más me cogieron robando carros.*" On the whole, the court cognates classification is one of the least problematic of the six.

Table 1. Courtroom-specific false cognates

English	Spanish
Accuse = inculpar	Acusar = to charge, to indict
Allegation = insinuación, alegación (alleged = presunto)	Alegato = legal argument, pleading
Argument = alegato; disputa, trifulca	Argumento = plot of a movie or story; reasoning, argument
Assault = acometimiento, intento de agresión	Asalto = hold up, robbery, mugging
Attest = dar fe, certificar, atestar	Atestar = to cram, stuff, crowd; to attest
Battery = agresión, golpiza, abuso físico (assault & battery = acometimiento & agresión)	Batería = set of drums, electric battery
Charge = imputar (un delito), acusar, instruir (al jurado)	Cargar = to carry, to load (but: cargos = charges)
Conference = reunión, consulta; congreso	Conferencia = a talk, a lecture, a speech
Confront = enfrentar(se), encarar	Confrontar = to compare, to collate
Consistent = coherente, consecuente; compatible (con), conforme (con)	Consistente = solid, having consistency
Consists of = consta de	Consiste en = it is a matter of, it lies in
Conspiracy = confabulación, conjura	Conspiración = political conspiracy
Constraint = restricción, impedimento	Constricción = shrinkage, contraction
Contempt = contumacia, desacato	Contento = happy, content, satisfied
Contend = sostener, afirmar, arguir	Contender = to fight, combat, dispute, litigate
Contention = argumento	Contienda = battle, bout
Convene = reunirse; entrar en sesión; acordar, convenir	Convenir = to be appropriate, advantageous or advisable; to agree
Conviction = condena; convencimiento	Convicción = belief, certainty, certitude
Court = tribunal, juzgado; sala	Corte = king's and queen's court
Crime = delito	Crimen = murder, violent crime
Criminal = delincuente; (adj.) penal	Criminal = murderer; criminal
Deception = engaño	Decepción = disappointment
Decline = rehusar, rechazar, no aceptar; decaer	Declinar = to lean, fall, decline, degenerate
Defraud = estafar, defraudar	Defraudar = to disappoint, to defraud

Depose = tomar(le) declaración; deponer (deposition = declaración jurada)	Deponer = remove from office; depose (option: destituir)
Deputy = (adj.) auxiliar; suplente, sustituto	Diputado = representative, delegate
Discovery = recabar (pruebas)	Descubrir = to find out, discover
Disorder = desarreglo, desorden, caos; trastorno, padecimiento (med.)	Desorden = disturbance, riot; mess
Evidence = prueba; indicios	Evidencia = obviousness, manifest certainty
Execute = desempeñar; llevar a cabo; firmar	Ejecutar = to put to death; to execute
Expire = caducar, vencerse	Expirar = to die
Fault = culpa; defecto; falla	Falta = lack, missing; mistake
Felony = delito mayor o grave	Felonía = disloyalty, unfaithfulness
Forge = falsificar	Forjar(se) = to carve or forge (a destiny or a future)
Guardian = tutor	Guardián = a guard
Habit = vicio (drugs); hábito	Hábito = custom, tendency, habit
Honest = sincero, franco; honesto	Honesto = just, straight, law-abiding; pure, chaste; honest
Injury = lesión	Injuria = insult
Intend = proponerse	Intentar = to try, to attempt
Intent = intención	Intento (de) = attempt(ed - adj.)
Motorist = conductor, chofer	Motorista = motorcyclist
Occurrence = vez, caso, situación, aparición	Ocurrencia = (extravagant) idea; occurrence
Offense = delito	Ofensa = insult
Outrage = indignación, ultraje	Ultraje = rape; outrage
Process = procedimiento; proceso	Proceso = trial; process
Proprietary = de propiedad, registrado	Propietario = proprietor, owner
Provision = disposición, estipulación; medida (but: disposition = attitude)	Provisión = supply, stock, provision
Register = inscribir(se); radicar, hacer constar	Registrar = to search
Sanity = cordura	Sanidad = public health
Scenario = circunstancia, panorama, contexto	Escenario = stage
Sympathy = compasión	Simpatía = congeniality
Trace = rastro; (v.) rastrear; trazar (sketch)	Traza(r) = sketch, blueprint; to design, to draw
Traffic = tránsito	Tráfico = trafficking (drugs)
Transpire = suceder, ocurrir, acontecer	Transpirar = to sweat, exhale, transpire
Trespass = entrar sin derecho, transgredir, translimitar; violar, infringir	Traspasar = to go through, pierce (option: atravesar)
Violation = infracción (tránsito); violación de la ley (o de derechos)	Violación = rape; violation (of law or rights)

2. Widely used false cognates

The classification of widely used false cognates, like the previous classification, leaves little room for debate. In this case, equivocal usage is so widespread that it appears to be almost "accepted," but not quite. Words like *renta*, *aplicación*, and *asumir* are so common that the interpreter might look first to the false meaning. Special care should be exercised with *discutir* because of its crucially divergent meaning (to fight vs. to discuss). In any case, the interpreter should learn to recognize these words and interpret them in context, but never generate them in her own translation. Fortunately, widely used false cognates are few in number, and the errors they tend to promote are generally benign.

Table 2. Widely used false cognates

English	Spanish
Actual = real, efectivo	Actual = current, present
Apply for = solicitar, postular	Aplicar = to apply something (e.g., glue)
Apply oneself = dedicarse	Aplicarse = to be more studious
Application = solicitud, planilla, formulario	Aplicación = studiousness, discipline
Assume = suponer	Asumir = to take on (e.g., responsibility)
Discuss = comentar, ventilar, conversar, explicar	Discutir = to argue, quarrel
Stranger = desconocido; forastero	Extraño = strange (extranjero = foreigner)
Notary Public = testigo notarial	Notario Público = notary attorney
Panel = mesa redonda; debate	Panel = wood panel
Postpone = aplazar, postergar, atrasar	Posponer = to put behind in order, rank, value, or estimation
Relevant = pertinente, relacionado	Relevante = noteworthy, remarkable, outstanding, important, of note
Rent = alquiler; to rent = alquilar	Renta = income, revenue
Role = papel (play a r. = desempeñar un p.)	Rol = list, roll
Seminar = cursillo	Seminario = seminary
Shock = susto, sacudida; postración nerviosa; corrientazo; (v.) sacudir; ofender; escandalizar, horrorizar	Choque = crash; clash
Sophisticated = avanzado	Sofisticada(o) = wordly, artificial, unnatural, false, lacking in simplicity
Tentative = provisional; inseguro	Tentativa = attempt, trial; (adj.) experimental
Topic = asunto, cuestión, tema	Tópico = common place, cliché
Versus = contra, frente a	Versus = towards

3. False cognates likely to be used by the acculturated witness

By far the most debatable classifications are those for acculturated witness, interpreter, or both. With regard to the acculturated witness, two rationales guided my classification. First, I included here those words that are very commonly used in Spanish, and that the witness will probably use with 'correct' Spanish meaning, but that the interpreter may erroneously render as an English false cognate. I refer to such words as *asistir*, *cuestión*, *eventual*, *ilusión*, *molestar*, and others which, though less common, are still likely to be used correctly by the witness. I have also included those typical non-standard forms of the acculturated witness: *carpeta*, *furnitura*, *la troca* 'the truck,' *la rufa* 'the roof,' etc. Still others, like *ganga*, *grosería*, and *producto* (for 'produce'), are equally likely to be used correctly or incorrectly by the witness. The likelihood that a speaker intends the English meaning depends on his or her level of acculturation. For this reason, it is of capital importance that the interpreter at least get a feeling for the level of linguistic acculturation of the witness, so that she can adjust to each individual speaker.

When studying this category of false cognates, it would be helpful for the interpreter to *visualize* a witness speaking these words on the witness stand, and herself interpreting consecutively in a real-life interrogatory. This visualization will help establish a contextual link between the word and the situation where it is likely to appear in court. The interpreter's response to these false cognates will become second nature.

The study of witness cognates will certainly help, but it will not eliminate every interpreting difficulty, nor is it a substitute for the interpreter's own resourcefulness. Two brief anecdotes may illustrate the point. The first one relates to a cognate somewhat 'correctly' used by a witness. In a recent immigration case, a deportable alien claimed to have been given a "*permiso eventual*" to cross the border. In a split second I considered various options as the interpreter. From my knowledge of false cognates, I was sure it could not be an "eventual permit"; that is, a written promise of a *future* permit or a permit that would become effective in the future. I did not think he meant a "special," "incidental," or "ad hoc" permit, meanings that did not match the speaker's uneducated register. I thought he meant a permit to go back and forth to work across the border. So I looked for an equivalent that would be at least as awkward as the original, hoping to prompt a follow-up question that would clarify the matter. I said "a *sporadic* permit" and waited for the follow-up question. Instead, the prosecutor used my rendition to ridicule the witness in front of the jury: "*Sporadic permit? What in the world is a sporadic permit?*" She even called an immigration officer to the stand later to testify that there was no such thing. As the interrogatory proceeded and I was able to make out more of the context, I realized that he was trying to say "provisional" or "temporary" permit. I adapted accordingly, but it was too late to erase the previous impression. I left with the feeling that I had contributed "sporadically" in destroying this witness' credibility.

The second anecdote relates to a non-standard form generated by a witness. An indigent old man, who was being questioned about his occupation, replied: "*Bueno, yo vivo del golfeo.*" Since the man is not from Spain, I ruled out "pimping" as a translation, but my solution prompted the following exchange: "Do you mean to say, sir, that you are a professional golfer?" "*No, chico, del golfeo, del golfeo que me da el gobierno*" (welfare). Acculturated witnesses often have trouble communicating. They may speak some broken English, but their Spanish is not much better. They simply have trouble communicating accurately in either language, let alone in a mixture of both. When all else fails, the interpreter can always look to the judge for help: "Your Honor, the interpreter needs to inquire." "You may." "*Señor, ¿usted quiere decir que sufrió una 'ruptura' o un 'rapto'?*"

Table 3. False cognates likely to be used by the acculturated witness

Spanish	**English**
Abandonado = neglectful, irresponsible, forgetful; abandoned, derelict	Abandoned = olvidado, abandonado; renunciado
Asistir = to attend; to help, aid, assist	Assist = ayudar, auxiliar, asistir
Bachiller = high school graduate; baccalaureate	Bachelor = soltero; licenciado (bachelor's degree = licenciatura)
Carpeta = binder, file	Carpet = alfombra
Colegio = school (usually private)	College = universidad
Constipado = congested, with a cold	Constipated = estreñido
Convocación = calling, summon, notice	Convocation = asamblea
Cuestión = the matter, issue, or question	Question = pregunta
Disgusto = disagreement, falling out; displeasure; grudge, hurt, anger	Disgust = repugnancia, asco, aversión; hastío
Doctor = (frequently) attorney, lawyer	Doctor = médico
Editar = to publish	Edit = corregir, enmendar
Editor = publisher	Editor = jefe de redacción
Eventual = incidental, subject to contingencies or chance; occasional, sporadic; temporary	Eventual(ly) = consiguiente (que ocurrirá de seguro); finalmente, con el tiempo
Fino = refined, sophisticated; fine, pure; thin	Fine = delicado; bueno; excelente; sutil
Franco, de = off duty; zona franca = duty free zone	Frank = sincero, honesto
Ganga = bargain	Gang = pandilla
Grado = rank; degree; grade	Grade = nota, calificación; grado
Grosería = rudeness, rude comment	Grocery store = bodega, almacén, supermercado

Ilusión = hope, expectation, dream; illusion (forjarse ilusiones = to delude oneself)	Illusion = falsedad, espejismo, engaño, alucinación
Licenciado = attorney	Licensed = titulado, certificado, con licencia
Molestar = to bother, annoy	Molest = ultrajar (sobre todo a un menor)
Presumir = to put on airs or be conceited	Presume = suponer
Producto = product	Produce = cosechas, vegetales
Redactar = to write, to compose	Redact = corregir, preparar para imprenta
Troca = [he/she] exchanges, barters	Truck = camión

4. False cognates likely to be used by the acculturated interpreter

This category of false cognates demands most careful attention, because these are the ones that interpreters are most likely to generate themselves. Included here are some English words which are frequently used in court. They are likely to be put into play, with correct usage, by officers of the court, and then rendered erroneously as Spanish false cognates by the acculturated interpreter. To study them, interpreters should visualize themselves in court, in the process of interpreting simultaneously for the defendant. As with previous categories, the interpreter should practice using each word in a natural-sounding sentence or brief dialogue, and then supplying a correct written translation underneath. This exercise reinforces the learning process by placing each cognate in a meaningful context.

For witness cognates, the troublesome word appears first in the Spanish source message, and the danger arises in the process of translating it into English. For interpreter cognates, the false cognate appears in English and must be translated into an appropriate Spanish term. However, there is a second distinction between these categories. Interpreters are assumed to be more highly educated, and therefore more linguistically competent than your average witness. As a result of this sociolinguistic difference, interpreter cognates tend to belong to a higher register; they are fancier words, if you will. Conversely, witness cognates tend to belong to a lower register. This is immediately apparent when you compare both lists.

Table 4. False cognates likely to be used by the acculturated interpreter

English	Spanish
Adhere (to) = observar, acatar, atenerse	Adherir(se) = to glue, stick to
Advise = aconsejar, asesorar, amonestar	Avisar = notify
Advice = consejo	Aviso = notice, warning
Agency = organismo, dependencia, departamento; agencia	Agencia = agency; dealer (e.g. car)
Aggregate = total, la suma de	Agregado = added; attaché (diplomatic)

Aggressive = dinámico, activo, emprendedor	Agresivo = belligerent, offensive; combative
Allocate(d) = asignar, distribuir	Alocar (-ado) = to make crazy; crazed, wild
Appreciate = comprender, reconocer; agradecer; valorar; apreciar	Apreciar = to esteem; to observe; to appreciate or increase in value
Assessment = evaluación; recargo	Asesoría = counseling
Attend = asistir, acudir	Atender = to pay attention; to tend to (e.g., a patient or a client)
Attitude = (mala) disposición; actitud	Actitud = demeanor, state of mind, attitude
Candid = franco	Cándido = ingenuous, simple, guileless
Capable = capaz, apto	Capable = castratable
Collar = cuello	Collar = necklace
Complacent = descuidado, despreocupado, incauto, laxo	Complaciente = accommodating
Compromise = arreglo, término medio; comprometer	Compromiso = obligation, engagement
Concurrence = de modo simultáneo; de acuerdo	Concurrencia = public, those in attendance, the participants; agreement
Condescending = arrogante, que rebaja o ningunea	Condescendiente = indulgent, lenient
Convenient = oportuno, favorable, aconsejable	Conveniente = appropriate
Crude = descarnado, lascivo; grosero, burdo, rudimentario	Crudo = raw; cruel, ruthless
Desire = anhelo	Deseo = wish
Domestic = nacional, interno; doméstico	Doméstico = household (adj.); (a) maid
Dramatic = drástico; espectacular, llamativo	Dramático = theatrical, exaggerated
Expedient = necesario, oportuno, conveniente	Expediente = file, record
Expedite = acelerar (un trámite)	Expedir = to issue
Extensive = considerable	Extensivo = including, inclusive
Extravagant = derrochador	Extravagante = eccentric, odd, flashy
Font = tipo (de letra)	Fuente = source; fountain
Genial = simpático, afable	Genial = brilliant, of genius
Gentle = suave, blando; lento; amable, paciente	Gentil = kind, courteous, gracious
Gracious = cortés	Gracioso = funny
Ignore = no hacer caso, hacer caso omiso	Ignorar = not know
Ineffective = ineficaz	Inefectivo = not actual, unreal, null
Inpatient = paciente hospitalizado (outpatient = paciente ambulatorio)	Impaciente = impatient
Literature = bibliografía, escritos; folletos	Literatura = creative writings, literary works
Major = principal, importante, significativo	Mayor = larger, greater, bigger

Minimize = aminorar, reducir al mínimo, evitar	Minimizar = to take away importance, minimize
Misery = tristeza, sufrimiento, congoja	Miseria = poverty
Occurrence = vez, caso, situación, instancia	Ocurrencia = (extravagant) idea, occurrence
Offense = delito	Ofensa = insult
Pretend = fingir	Pretender = to attempt, try, aspire to, seek
Process = procedimiento; proceso, trámite	Proceso = trial; process
Range = alcance, campo, dominio; mirilla	Rango = rank
Realize = darse cuenta, percatarse, advertir, comprender	Realizar = to carry out; accomplish
Register = inscribir(se); anotar, asentar	Registrar = to search
Render = emitir (un veredicto); volver, convertir, hacer, dejar; (r. into) traducir, verter; prestar (servicio, ayuda, auxilio)	Rendir(se) = surrender; pay (homage) (rendir planilla = file a return)
Resume = reanudar, continuar	Resumir = summarize
Revise = corregir, enmendar, poner al día	Revisar = to review, look over (option: estudiar = to review)
Routine = sistema, práctica establecida; rutina; (adj.) usual, habitual; rutinario	Rutina, rutinario = routine, senseless repetition
Subject = asunto, tema; sujeto, individuo; súbdito	Sujeto = guy, individual, subject; liable; secure
Sympathy = compasión	Simpatía = congeniality

5. False cognates likely to be used by both acculturated witnesses and interpreters

These 'shared cognates' are those which in fact belong to both lists; I do not segregate them merely to avoid repetition. Each category requires a different training approach and a different decision-making strategy. Shared cognates require the combined strategies of both the witness' and the interpreter's categories. This middle-of-the-road category includes words that tend to belong to a *middle* register that is not distinctive of either the witness or the interpreter. It also includes words that are equally common in English and in Spanish, and therefore are equally likely to arise from either direction.

Table 5. False cognates likely to be used by both acculturated witnesses and interpreters

English	Spanish
Addition = ampliación (de casa); suma; adición	Adición = extension; addition
Affection = cariño, afecto	Afección = disease, affliction
Afflicted = que padece (enfermedad)	Afligido = anguished
Agony (-izing) = sufrimiento	Agonía (-zar) = to be dying
Balance = equilibrio	Balance = remainder, residue, balance
Confront = enfrentarse, encarar	Confrontar = to compare, to collate
Courage = valor, valentía	Coraje = often: "anger"
Definitely = por seguro	Definitivamente = for good
Disagreeable = descortés, rudo, impropio	Desagradable = unpleasant
Disgrace = bochorno, deshonra, ignominia	Desgracia = misfortune; tragedy
Disgraced = deshonrado	Desgraciado = wretch, unfortunate person
Education = instrucción, escolaridad	Educación = upbringing, manners
Extension = plazo, aplazamiento	Extensión = length, breadth
Facility = edificio, plantel	Facilidad = ease
Facilities = medios; edificio y equipos	Facilidades (de pago) = layaway, credit, payment terms
Fastidious = melindroso, quisquilloso	Fastidioso = annoying; boring
Fatality = muerte accidental; desgracia; baja	Fatalidad = fateful happening; destiny; bad luck
Figure = cifra; figura; calcular, imaginar (It figures = tenía que ser, me lo figuraba)	Figura = figure, shape, silhouette; build, looks, physique Figurar = to figure, fancy, imagine, come to mind; to appear
Inconvenient = molesto, poco práctico, incómodo; inoportuno	Inconveniente = (n.) objection; delay, disadvantage; (option: percance, imprevisto)
Infirm = inválido, débil, enfermizo, achacoso	Enfermo = ill, sick
Infirmity = debilidad, achaque, impedimento físico	Enfermedad = illness, sickness, malady
Inhabitable = habitable	Inhabitable = uninhabitable
Instructed = mandado, ordenado	Instruido = educated, knowledgeable
Intoxicated = borracho, ebrio	Intoxicado = having food poisoning; poisoned
Involve(d) = incluir, comprender, inmiscuir, implicar, involucrar; complicado	Envolver = to wrap
Policy = regla, norma, política	Póliza = insurance policy
Qualifications = credenciales, títulos	Calificaciones = grades
Remove = sacar, eliminar, quitar; expulsar	Remover = to stir (a liquid)

Sensible = sensato, razonable, prudente	Sensible = sensitive, perceptible
Serious = grave; serio (for people only)	Serio = serious, stern
Suburbs = barrio residencial	Suburbios = outskirts; commuter towns; slums (in some countries)
Susceptible = propenso, vulnerable	Susceptible = sensitive, easily hurt or insulted
Utilities = servicios públicos	Utilidades = profits
Utility = utensilio; de utilería	Utilidad = usefulness
Vicious = despiadado	Vicioso = full of vices; gambler

6. False cognates that indicate bilingual deficit

I should point out that I am not concerned here with the bilingual deficit of the witness, who does not need to be bilingual, but with the limitations of the interpreter. For the most part, these are words that should pose little or no problem to anyone with bilingual proficiency. However, I have deliberately excluded words like *pan* (bread) and "pan," the cookware, because they are too elementary for our purpose.

In contrast to the previous categories, this list has little to do with training and performance strategy. Rather, it is *diagnostic* in nature. Teachers can incorporate this material into diagnostic tests and students should use it to assess their own bilingual proficiency. Trouble with, or even surprise at, a few of these words may already be a sign that the student needs to take remedial courses in his or her weak language. Obviously, this is only one symptom which indicates general bilingual deficit. Memorizing this list will do nothing to remedy the student's underlying deficit in bilingual skills.

Table 6. False cognates that indicate bilingual deficit

English	Spanish
Ancient = antiguo	Anciano = elderly
Allocate = asignar, distribuir	Alocar = to make crazy
Appoint = nombrar, designar	Apuntar = to point to; to write down
Arm = brazo	Arma = weapon (arms - only in the plural)
Attempt = intento	Atento = attentive
Casualty = accidente, desastre, siniestro; víctima; baja; caso fortuito	Casualidad = chance; coincidence
Character = reputación; carácter, índole; sujeto, personaje; signo, letra	Carácter = temper, nature, personality; character
Commodity = mercancía cotizada	Comodidad = comfort
Contest = disputar, debatir	Contestar = to answer, to reply
Date = fecha; cita; dátil	Dato = fact, piece of information
Distress = angustia, malestar, zozobra	Destreza = skill
Deprived = privado de, despojado	Depravado = depraved, perverse

Destitute = indigente, necesitado, menesteroso, desvalido, desposeído	Destituir (-ido) = to dismiss from office; to deprive or make destitute
Diversion = distracción; desviación	Diversión = amusement
Embarrassed = avergonzado	Embarazada = pregnant
Exit = salida	Exito = success
Gang = pandilla	Ganga = bargain
Injury = lesión	Injuria = insult
Invert = invertir (el orden)	Invertir = invest; invert
Invest = invertir (dinero)	Investir = to confer upon, to invest with
Jubilation = regocijo, júbilo	Jubilación = retirement
Large = grande	Largo = long
Lechery = lujuria, lascivia	Lechería = dairy (farm, shop)
Lecture = conferencia	Lectura = reading
Library = biblioteca	Librería = bookstore
Local = (adj.) de la región, local	Local = n. site, premises; adj. local
Luxury = lujo	Lujuria = lust, lechery
Molest = ultrajar (sobre todo a un menor)	Molestar = to bother, annoy
Notice = aviso, advertencia	Noticia = news
Parents = padres	Parientes = relatives, kin
Patron = cliente; patrocinador	Patrón = boss, foreman, benefactor Patrono = employer
Pendency = estar pendiente algo	Pendencia = fight, argument
Resort = recurso, recurrir; combinado turístico	Resorte = spring; elasticity
Rest = descanso(-ar); resto	Restar = to subtract; to remain
Revolve = girar (en torno a)	Revolver = to stir up, to mix up
Sanity = cordura	Sanidad = public health
Scholar = erudito, estudioso, especialista	Escolar = n. school kid; adj. school related
Solar = relativo al sol	Solar = lot, plot of land; sometimes 'tenement'
Sort = ordenar, repartir	Sortear = to raffle
Staff = plantilla, personal	Estafa = swindle
Stir = remover, batir; instigar	Estirar = stretch
Succeed = tener éxito, triunfar, lograr; heredar, suceder (seguir, venir después)	Suceder = to happen; to succeed (as in: to follow, come after)
Success = éxito	Suceso = event
Support = apoyar, sostener; mantener (con $); confirmar, corroborar, reforzar	Soportar = endure, bear, put up with, withstand

7. Conclusion

The categorization of false cognates can be useful for the practice of court interpreting as well as for interpreter training, pedagogy, and testing. Practicing court interpreters should study these lists and highlight all items that may tend, even remotely, to cause them trouble. They should continue expanding these lists by categorizing new items they may encounter. Most importantly, they should review their lists periodically in order to maintain alertness and standard usage. Spanish in the United States is heavily Anglicized. Interpreters are constantly exposed to false cognates, to the point that equivocal usage will in time begin to sound correct. Their struggle against lexical and syntactic interference must be ongoing. In addition to periodic review, interpreting students should work actively with these lists as part of their training. This means using the terms in conversational context and in translation exercises, both written and oral, and applying the visualization techniques described earlier as appropriate to each category. Training should proceed progressively from passive to active engagement, from recognition to recall, and from mere reception to actual production, until items are internalized and become second nature. Interpreter testing should include items from every category. This categorization enhances the diagnostic and pedagogical value of testing by revealing those categories where a particular student or candidate needs improvement. The last category in particular should be carefully incorporated into screening and certification exams for professional interpreters. Whether free-lance or staff, interpreters with bilingual deficit clearly have no place in the judiciary. Having said this, let me conclude with a word of caution about the use of cognates in interpreter testing. One does not speak by cognates alone. No test other than a classroom quiz should ever be composed entirely, or even primarily of cognates, least of all a screening or certification exam. The validity and reliability of such a test would be virtually nil. I don't know of any study that correlates cognates with general bilingual proficiency, but I suspect the correlation will be too weak to have any statistical significance. What is wise, in my opinion, is to *incorporate* cognates into a broad-based test of bilingual proficiency.

Perspectiva histórica del paradigma verbal en el español de California

Rebeca Acevedo
Loyola Marymount University

En los albores de un nuevo siglo, es indiscutible la pujante vitalidad que ha adquirido nuestra comunidad en los Estados Unidos. La última década ha sido testigo de un considerable aumento en la población hispana, la cual representa el 54.5% de la población que habla una lengua diferente del inglés (Valdés 1997). Las estadísticas del año 1996 indican que la población hispana en Estados Unidos ha llegado a los 28 millones de habitantes, lo que significa el 10.5% de la población total. Antes de lo previsto y debido a un acelerado crecimiento, nos hemos establecido como la primera minoría del país. Hemos logrado, a fuerza de nacimientos, una legitimidad indiscutible. Continúa, no obstante, el esfuerzo por lograr el reconocimiento cultural y social que nuestra comunidad merece; un instrumento indispensable para lograr este objetivo será la valorización de nuestra lengua.

Mi participación, a través de este artículo, se enfoca hacia la descripción histórica del paradigma verbal en una importante variedad lingüística del suroeste de los Estados Unidos: el español californiano.[1] En mi opinión, el enfatizar la riqueza histórica que caracteriza a nuestra lengua ya en territorio norteamericano y definir, a través de esa historia, el origen de los rasgos peculiares que la caracterizan, constituye una óptima estrategia para facilitar el camino hacia la legitimación del español de los Estados Unidos. Además, por medio de este conocimiento histórico, se puede lograr una mejor explicación de los fenómenos lingüísticos del habla actual. Por otro lado, desde un punto de vista teórico, las circunstancias sociohistóricas que rodean el desarrollo de la lengua española en California, con diversas etapas de colonización y una constante nivelación lingüística debido a las olas continuas de inmigración hispana, constituyen un excelente laboratorio donde comprobar muchas de las hipótesis planteadas en nuestro campo.

 Research on Spanish in the U.S., ed. Ana Roca, 110–120. Somerville, MA: Cascadilla Press.

La investigación lingüística diacrónica sobre la variedad específica que nos ocupa ha sido limitada y se centra principalmente en las áreas de lexicología (Blanco 1971). Afortunadamente, otras variedades, tanto del suroeste de los Estados Unidos, como del mismo México, han recibido mayor atención desde un punto de vista histórico y constituyen fuentes de información invaluable (Espinosa 1946, Lozano 1976, Orstein 1951, 1972, Lope Blanch 1985, Parodi 1995). Prevalecen, sin lugar a dudas, estudios sincrónicos que tratan en particular del sistema verbal en la variedad californiana (Phillips 1967, Silva-Corvalán 1994, Gutiérrez 1995, Villa 1997). A través de toda esta literatura se ha podido comprobar un fenómeno constante en lo que se refiere al paradigma verbal, su notable simplificación.[2] El presente análisis ofrece evidencias concretas de cómo en el español californiano ya se había activado, desde sus orígenes, el proceso de simplificación del sistema verbal.

Quiero aclarar que los resultados obtenidos en este trabajo representan solo una primera etapa de mi investigación sobre el análisis del paradigma verbal en el área de California durante los siglos XVIII y XIX. Deberán ser considerados solo como resultados preliminares, debido a que el corpus se basa exclusivamente en material impreso escrito en español por oficiales, frailes, militares y civiles que vivieron en el área geográfica de la Alta California durante el período estudiado.[3]

La presencia del español en territorio californiano inició en el siglo XVI, a partir del año 1542 en que se descubre el puerto de San Diego; no obstante, debemos esperar hasta el último tercio del siglo XVIII para hablar de la verdadera colonización española del territorio. Ya que fue solo hasta esa época en que se estableció Presidio y Misión en San Diego y Monterrey; además de una ruta terrestre que comunicaba desde Sonora a Monterrey. Por esa razón, parto para este estudio del período misional, establecido a partir de 1770 y analizo manuscritos escritos hasta el año de 1880. Considero un período de 110 años en mi análisis porque fue el período en que se mantuvo en territorio californiano el idioma español como lengua oficial; aún durante los últimos 34 años en que ya se había llevado a cabo la ocupación americana.

Mi análisis comprende las formas personales del verbo en los modos indicativo y subjuntivo. Los manuscritos del siglo XVIII nos ofrecen un paradigma verbal muy completo; reflejo claro del que describe la gramática prescriptiva, por lo menos en lo que a morfología verbal se refiere. Registré quince formas verbales diferentes, a saber: cinco conjugaciones simples de indicativo y cuatro formas compuestas; además de los tres tiempos verbales del subjuntivo con sus correspondientes morfologías compuestas.

La única forma del paradigma verbal que no se empleó en mi data fue el pretérito anterior. Esto no sorprende ya que la forma "hube cantado" nunca prosperó realmente y se mantuvo limitada al registro escrito (Penny 1991: 144). Se ha sugerido aún la ausencia de esta forma verbal en todo el territorio americano. Es decir, que este morfema no llegó nunca a formar parte de nuestra "koiné" ya que su decadencia se registra antes del siglo XVI (Lope Blanch 1985, Moreno de Alba 1978). Fuera de esta conjugación, todas las otras formas verbales aparecen, aunque sea en forma esporádica.

Registré una sola aparición del "futuro perfecto de subjuntivo"; producida por el gobernador de la Alta California ya a fines del siglo XVIII: "Exceptuando los casados . . . que *hubieren ofrecido* domiciliarse en él" (D. 6: 1799).

En la misma posición, con un solo testimonio, se encuentra el "futuro perfecto de indicativo." Mc parece pertinente añadir que este caso registrado se refiere al uso hipotético o de conjetura presente y no al empleo temporal: "No sé si *habrán dado* a V.M. algo de carne fresca; si así *haya sucedido* . . . " (D. 4, 1777). Por lo anterior, podríamos presuponer que la vigencia de esta forma con valor temporal se habría ya perdido durante este último tercio del siglo XVIII en que se ubica los orígenes del español en California. Además, ésta parece ser la tendencia en la simplificación de las formas del futuro y condicional, como veremos más adelante, en la que se pierden primero los valores temporales, mientran sobreviven sus usos modales. Por otra parte, podemos ver en el mismo ejemplo anterior, como la conjugación del verbo en la segunda oración condicional se olvida de los futuros y lo sustituye por la forma compuesta del presente de subjuntivo, evidencia clara del desuso de los futuros perfectos.

Por lo que respecta al "condicional perfecto," se registró una mayor vitalidad; principalmente en las cláusulas condicionales hipotéticas. No obstante, presuponemos una pérdida también temprana, desde el último tercio del siglo XVIII, al identificar sustituciones por medio de la forma simple correspondiente:

(1) No *sería* de estrañar que huviesemos hallado al (sic) puerto
de Monterrey (D. 1, 1770)
(Por: "no habría sido de estrañar")
y si no *puse* el reservo de las miciones no *comerían* los pocos (D. 8, 1836)
(Por: "no habrían comido")

Como se puede observar, corresponde exclusivamente a los tiempos compuestos iniciar el proceso de reducción del paradigma verbal en la variedad dialectal que nos ocupa. Tendencia general en el idioma, a pesar de que se trataba de un paradigma de reciente formación en el sistema verbal romance.

La forma del "futuro de subjuntivo" también mostró poca vitalidad y pronto se ve relegada a frases hechas como:

(2) Y si la fortuna me fuere en favor, pienso (D. 6, 1773)
Cada uno lo que *tuviere* y Pedidle lo que *quisieres* (D. 9, 1875)

No obstante, todavía se registraron diversos ejemplos durante el siglo XVIII que denotan cierta vitalidad. Por lo que no me sorprendió tanto su falta de vitalidad en la variante lingüística que nos ocupa, como su presencia. Sobre todo si consideramos que esta forma verbal, junto con la conjugación compuesta correspondiente "declined from the eighteenth century onwards" (Penny 1991: 144):

(3) Se les suplica [. . .] que si a pocos días [. . .] *abordaren* a
esta plaia (D. 1, 1770)
Yo escribiré cuando *pudiere* (D. 2, 1772)

La identificación de esta forma en nuestro corpus confirma que su pérdida en la variedad californiana no se dio, previa al siglo XIX.[4]

Por su parte, el "pluscuamperfecto de subjuntivo" registra algunos casos aislados en los documentos pertenecientes al siglo XVIII. Identificamos los dos morfemas -RA y -SE, en una aparente alternancia libre: "si [. . .] *huviesemos* intentado [. . .] huvieramos tenido" (D. 1, 1770).

No obstante, como la mayoría de las formas que constituyen el paradigma compuesto, no se registran en nuestros datos durante el siglo XIX. Al caer en desuso y sustituirse por las formas simples, la hipótesis irreal ya no es viable por medio de morfología verbal y se deja solo al apoyo contextual o a la transparencia del sentido: "y si no *puse* el reservo de las miciones (sic) no *comerían* los pocos" (D. 7, 1836).

Identificamos así, durante estos primeros años de presencia del idioma español en territorio de la Alta California, una evidente simplificación del paradigma verbal; orientada principalmente, a la reducción del sistema en sus formas compuestas. De las formas compuestas restantes que se mantuvieron durante el siglo XIX, es el "presente perfecto de subjuntivo" el de menor vitalidad: Que *hayan cometido* (D. 9, 1867)

El "pluscuamperfecto" y el "presente perfecto" del modo indicativo continúan activos en la mayoría de los documentos del siglo XIX que incluye nuestro corpus:

(4) Vi lo que nunca *había visto* (D. 9, 1875)
He procurado disuadir a los que saven (sic) (D.8, 1836)

Sin embargo, al haberse perdido casi por completo el paradigma de las formas compuestas (con el auxiliar "haber"), se provoca un desequilibrio morfológico y también estas formas restantes empiezan a caer en desuso, siendo frecuentemente sustituidas por las formas simples correspondientes: ". . . es forzoso se hagan de adobe, por lo que no emprende la fundación del Presidido del Canal hasta el inmediato año luego que *terminen* las aguas" (D. 7, 1781) (por "hayan terminado").

Por lo que respecta a las formas simples de indicativo, especial atención merecen otras dos morfologías verbales de creación romance. Me refiero a los tiempos "futuro" y "condicional" que, como podemos observar en el ejemplo anterior, ya era común su sustitución por el tiempo presente ("emprende" en lugar de "emprenderá"). Este proceso de sustitución de las formas sintéticas del futuro y condicional, en particular por su contraparte analítica, ha atraído la atención de varios estudiosos. Se ha comprobado cómo esta sustitución se presenta de manera más acelerada en la variedad estadounidense en donde el español pervive en una situación de contacto (Villa 1997, Gutiérrez 1995); en contraste con una variedad como la mexicana, que aunque parece abocarse en la misma dirección, el proceso de sustitución ha sido más lento (Moreno de Alba 1978). A pesar de estas diferencias dialectales de aceleración del fenómeno, no debemos olvidar que el origen de la forma perifrástica "ir a + inf." con sentido de futuro se ha identificado aún antes de transplantarse la lengua a América, alrededor de los siglos XIII o XIV en las lenguas romances (Fleischman 1982). Considerando la aceleración del proceso en la variedad dialectal estadounidense, atendimos en nuestra investigación a esta morfología y se pudo comprobar que el germen de este fenómeno ya estaba sembrado desde los orígenes mismos de esta variedad lingüística según testimonio del registro escrito que comprende nuestro corpus. No quedó duda, sin embargo, que las formas sintéticas, tanto del futuro como del condicional, predominan sobre las perifrásticas a través de todo nuestro corpus. Ofrezco a continuación algunos de los ejemplos perifrásticos:

(5) Cogieron 5 fanegas que *van a sembrar* (D. 3, 1773)
Tengo asignados ministros para la [misión] que se *iba a fundar* (D. 2, 1772)
Ahora nos causa gran gusto/ lo que nos *van a decir* (D. 9, 1867)

Los estudios sincrónicos sobre estos morfemas futuros sugieren una tendencia a restringir las funciones modales para el morfema sintético y dejar a la construcción perifrástica su función temporal. Por la evidencia que ofrece nuestro corpus se confirma que, en los limitados casos en que se usan las formas perifrásticas, su función es temporal. Se puede también identificar, ya que estas formas perifrásticas subsisten con las sintéticas, que la diferencia temporal implicaría mayor cercanía al tiempo verbal de referencia: "Y al fin que *se va a exponer*, (en la presente carta) conduce mucho la primera compañía [. . .] la Real Hacienda no se *libertará* jamás del gasto" (D. 7, 1795).

Vemos como la acción de "exponer" es inmediata posterior, en contraste con la acción de "liberar." La vigencia del morfema sintético de los tiempos futuro y condicional durante el período que corresponde a nuestra investigación es patente. Es también ilustrativo el hecho de que el único manuscrito de nuestro corpus que representa de manera más cercana el lenguaje oral – una pastorela – sea a su vez el que incluya un mayor número de sustituciones perifrásticas; por lo menos por lo que respecta al tiempo futuro, ya que las formas perifrásticas del condicional fueron mucho más escasas en nuestro corpus. Lo anterior nos permite presuponer que el avance de la forma analítica era mayor en los registros orales. Por otro lado, también se percibe que la sustitución analítica del condicional se desarrolla a partir de la construcción de futuro. Esto se deduce debido al hecho de que la sustitución del condicional por la forma sintética del imperfecto aparece también en nuestros documentos, como lo ejemplifica la siguiente oración: "Si esta villa se lograse, *merecía* con razón el título de Branciforte" (D. 5, 1795).

Por lo que corresponde a los tiempos del pasado y con base en el análisis de documentos de nuestro corpus, se pudo comprobar que, al igual que la variedad mexicana (Acevedo 1997: 79–114), se identifica una preferencia por el morfema -RA para el "imperfecto de subjuntivo"; principalmente, en los ejemplos que corresponden al siglo XIX.: "Es preciso que el gobernador se *ingiera* en los autos" (D. 8, 1836).

No obstante lo anterior; los ejemplos del siglo XVIII todavía presentan una alternancia entre los dos morfemas -SE y -RA, como se pudo ver también en las formas compuestas analizadas más arriba:

(6) fue necessario abrir una poza [. . .] que *recibiera* su corto caudal y aguardar a que se *llenara* para dar agua a las bestias (D. 1, 1770)
dieronnos otros guias que nos *condujesen* (D.1, 1770)
di orden que *mandase* echar a cada uno [. . .] y que *siguieran* (D. 4, 1774)

Esta alternancia no parece estar motivada por ningún criterio de selección específico. Refleja, sin embargo, una identificación directa con la variedad mexicana.[5]

De la misma forma, las funciones temporales del "pretérito perfecto" o "antepresente" parecen haberse delimitado en la época de nuestro análisis en la misma dirección que lo hizo la variedad mexicana (Lope Blanch 1983: 131–143, Acevedo 1997: 115–149).[6] En el español californiano del siglo XVIII, como en la variedad mexicana, se muestra una clara ventaja de la forma compuesta para expresar el pasado abierto o de modo imperfectivo:

(7) Ninguna *ha estado* ni está tan socorrida (D. 2, 1749)
El padre *ha venido* cuatro ocasiones (D. 2, 1749)
a más de los muchos aprietos antiguos en que me *vi*, *he experimentado* a la presente tener [. . .] sin ración de maíz (D. 4, 1776)

Este valor aumenta, de manera evidente, durante el siglo XIX:

(8) *he procurado* desuadir a los que saven (D. #8, 1836)
Ya la tentación pasó (D. #9, 1867)
Siempre la mujer *ha sido* más piadosa que mujer (D. #9, 1875)

Por lo que respecta al uso de los tiempos "presente," "pretérito" e "imperfecto" de indicativo, no se identificó simplificación alguna en sus usos temporales; por el contrario, son éstas precisamente las formas verbales que han ampliado su campo de acción para suplir las funciones perdidas por la reducción del paradigma verbal.

Quiero, antes de concluir, relacionar los resultados del presente trabajo, con los de otras dos investigaciones que tratan sobre el paradigma verbal de variantes lingüísticas directamente relacionadas con la que ahora nos ocupa y que sirvieron como punto de partida para mi investigación. Me refiero al libro de Silva-Corvalán (1994) titulado *Language contact and change: Spanish in Los Angeles*;[7] y el de Moreno de Alba (1978) sobre los *Valores de las formas verbales en el español de México*. Estos estudios sincrónicos ofrecen evidencias concretas del proceso de simplificación y reducción que caracteriza al sistema verbal de las variantes californiana y mexicana respectivamente. Silva-Corvalán (1994: 22) divide el corpus de su análisis en tres grupos generacionales en situación bilingüe para identificar las tendencias de simplificación y reducción del paradigma verbal. Los resultados obtenidos demuestran claramente "acceleration of change in language in contact." Al describir Silva-Corvalán (1994: 3) el fundamento teórico de su investigación, juzga pertinente aclarar que el concepto de simplificación que ella maneja debe considerarse "as a process" y no como "an end-state."

Este "proceso" de simplificación y reducción del paradigma verbal se observa, de una manera muy evidente, con la descripción que ofrece por su parte Moreno de Alba y que representa la comunidad monolingüe "culta" del Distrito Federal en la segunda mitad del siglo XX.[8] Ambos estudios nos brindan, desde una perspectiva sincrónica, una clara gama horizontal de los grados de simplificación identificados en el paradigma verbal del español, como podremos ver en las siguientes columnas.

Tabla 1. Simplificación del paradigma verbal

Tiempos verbales	California S. XVIII y XIX	México S. XX	California S. XX. 1a. generación	California S. XX. 2a. generación	California S. XX. 3a. generación
Presente	•	•	•	•	•
Pretérito	•	•	•	•	•
Imperfec.	•	•	•	S	S
Pres. Subj.	•	•	•	S	ø
Pres. Perf.	•	•	•	S	ø
Pret. Subj.	•	•	•	S	ø
Cond. M.	•	•	•	•	ø
Cond. T.	•	S	ø	ø	ø
Futuro	•	S	S	ø	ø
Pluscuam.	•	S	S	ø	ø
P. Pf. Sub.	S	S	ø	ø	ø
Plusc. Sub.	S	S	ø	ø	ø
Cond. Perf.	S	ø	ø	ø	ø
Fut. S.	S	ø	ø	ø	ø
Fut. Perf.	ø	ø	ø	ø	ø
Fut. Perf. S.	ø	ø	ø	ø	ø
Pret. Perf.	ø	ø	ø	ø	ø

• = vigencia, S = simplificación, ø = pérdida

Los resultados de mi análisis diacrónico (presentados en la primera columna de la izquierda) complementan de manera perfecta este testimonio de la simplificación y reducción del paradigma verbal a través del tiempo. Queda confirmada, con ello, la hipótesis con la que concluye Silva-Corvalán (1994: 208) en el trabajo mencionado anteriormente, la cual implica que "in language-contact situations a number of changes affecting the secondary language have an *internal motivation* in that they are *in progress in the 'model' monolingual variety* before intensive contact with another language occurs." Identificamos durante el primer siglo de presencia activa del español en la Alta California que este proceso de reducción ya estaba en marcha.

Así pues, se pudo confirmar también con este trabajo la continuidad del constante proceso simplificador del paradigma verbal en la lengua española. Observamos cómo esta reducción se da de manera sistemática y por influencia interna; es decir, pertenece al sistema mismo del idioma español. Corrobora lo anterior la repetición de procesos identificados en nuestro corpus y que pertenecen a la historia de nuestra lengua. Así como sucedió entre el latín y las lenguas romances, en el español californiano (y en la mayoría de las variantes hispanas) en contraste con el llamado español estándar, observamos una misma secuencia jerárquica, en la cual primero se pierden las formas perfectas o compuestas, seguidas inmediatamente por los tiempos futuros. Con ello se evidencia la inestabilidad de estos morfemas. Observamos también los mecanismos del sistema que ante "el desgaste de todos estos tiempos determina que las formas verbales restantes amplíen su campo de acción para cubrir las lagunas originadas por el desuso de aquéllos" (Lope Blanch 1983: 154–155). Otra tendencia común que pudimos identificar fue la sustitución de las formas sintácticas por construcciones analíticas, como ha sido el caso del futuro y condicional con la construcción "ir a + inf." Por último, pudimos comprobar con evidencia morfosintáctica que, desde sus orígenes, el español californiano presenta una conexión directa con la variedad lingüística mexicana; como sucede con el resto de las variantes del suroeste de los Estados Unidos.[9]

Los resultados del presente trabajo nos permitirán entender mejor los mecanismos del idioma y reconocer los procesos históricos que han influido en la variedad lingüística que nos ocupa. Confío en que con este tipo de estudios diacrónicos logremos un conocimiento más profundo del español hablado en el suroeste de los Estados Unidos. Con ello podremos enfrentarnos de manera confiada a las tareas urgentes de nuestra comunidad, como son: la enseñanza del idioma o la educación bilingüe y la legitimación de nuestra lengua en la sociedad norteamericana.

Notas

* La base de la presente investigación fue posible gracias al apoyo recibido del "Summer Research Grant 1997" de LMU.

1. La población hispana en el estado de California constituye más del 20% de la población total (Clare Mar-Molinero 1997) y cuenta con la presencia continua en el territorio por más de dos siglos.

2. Esta tendencia ha sido interpretada, desde el punto de vista diacrónico, por el proceso de la "koineización" o nivelación en donde, al reunirse diferentes dialectos en una área de colonización se logra la convergencia de las variantes de uso anteriores en una modalidad lingüística común (Fontanella 1993, Granda 1994); y, desde el punto de vista sincrónico, bajo una perspectiva de lenguas en contacto o bilingüismo (Silva-Corvalán 1994).

3. Comprende este análisis los siguientes manuscritos: Doc. #1 El diario de Miguel Constansó, escrito en los años 1769–1770; Doc. #2, Cartas escritas por Fray Junípero Serra, en el año de 1772; Doc. #3, Cartas escritas por Fray Francisco Palou, en 1773; Doc. #4, Diario de Fernando de Rivera y Moncada, escrito entre 1774–1777; Doc. #5, Carta escrita por José María Beltrán, en 1795; Doc. #6, Carta escrita por Diego de Borica, en 1799; Doc. #7, Carta del Gobernador Felipe de Neve, en 1781; Doc. #8, Carta escrita por Mariano Chico, en 1836; Doc. #9, Dos versiones de la Pastorela escrita por Florencio Ibáñez, una de 1867 y la otra de 1875. Con excepción de los documentos 1 y 4, todos los otros manuscritos se tomaron del libro de Blanco (1971).

4. No debemos olvidar, aunque se ha reportado la pérdida de estas formas futuras del subjuntivo en nuestra lengua (Penny 1991), que Granda (1978: 98) identifica "la supervivencia de las formas del futuro hipotético (formas en -re)" hasta el presente en una amplia zona del español atlántico.

5. Para la segunda mitad del siglo XVIII, cuando el español se establece en territorio californiano, el español del altiplano mexicano se caracterizaba por tener una alternancia de 72% del morfema -RA; frente a un 28% del morfema -SE para el imperfecto de subjuntivo (Acevedo 1997: 108).

6. El paradigma verbal implantado en México a principios del siglo XVI presentaba una clara competencia entre dos formas verbales del pasado: el pretérito y el antepresente. Durante la época colonial se mantuvo en aumento constante la preferencia por el uso del antepresente con valor de tiempo presente y aspecto imperfectivo; no obstante, todavía se presentaba un tercio del uso antepresente con valor perfectivo. La solución ofrecida por la variedad mexicana consistió en diferenciar el aspecto de los dos tiempos verbales. A pesar de que esta distinción aspectual está perfilada en forma relativamente clara desde el primer siglo de la colonia, fue sólo hasta el siglo XIX en que el antepresente limita su uso perfectivo y se emplea principalmente para expresar acciones repetidas o habituales en el pasado; acciones negativas o acción anterior que se prolonga hasta el presente o tienen un marcador de tiempo presente (Acevedo 1997: 115–149).

7. En particular hago alusión a los capítulos 2 y 3 que tratan sobre la reducción del paradigma verbal.

8. Esta investigación pertenece al "Proyecto de estudio del habla culta de las principales ciudades de Hispanoamérica" presentado por Juan M. Lope Blanch (Moreno de Alba 1978: 7).

9. Esta evidencia se opone a lo que mantiene Blanco (1971: 259) cuando dice que "Hasta 1830 aproximadamente, se conservó firmemente no solo la estructura, sino el léxico, la morfología, la sintaxis, y tenemos razones fundadas para suponer que la fonética también, que forman la base de la lengua castellana. Pocas influencias mexicanas de léxico y modos de expresión encontramos, debido a dos razones que ya tenemos explicado: el ser un baluarte de los españoles-americanos y de los españoles-europeos y el enorme aislamiento."

Referencias

Acevedo, Rebeca. 1997. El español del altiplano central mexicano durante la época colonial: Reducción del paradigma verbal. Tesis de doctorado, University of Michigan.

Blanco, Antonio S. 1971. *La lengua española en la historia de California.* Madrid: Ediciones Cultura Hispánica.

Espinoza, Aurelio M. 1946. *Estudios sobre el español de Nuevo Méjico, Parte II: Morfología.* Buenos Aires: Facultad de Filosofía y Letras de la Universidad de Buenos Aires.

Fleischman, Suzanne. 1982. *The future in thought and language: Diachronic evidence from Romance.* Cambridge: Cambridge University Press.

Fontanella de Weinberg, María Beatriz. 1993. *El español de América.* Madrid: MAPFRE.

Granda, Germán de, ed. 1978. *Estudios lingüísticos hispánicos, afrohispánicos y criollos.* Madrid: Editorial Gredos.

Granda, Germán de. 1994. *Español de América, español de Africa y hablas criollas hispánicas: Cambios, contactos y contextos.* Madrid: Gredos.

Gutiérrez, Manuel J. 1995. On the future of the future tense in the Spanish of the Southwest. En *Spanish in four continents: Studies in language contact and bilingualism*, ed. Carmen Silva-Corvalán, 214–226. Washington, DC: Georgetown University Press.

Lope Blanch, Juan M., ed. 1983. *Estudios sobre el español de México.* México: UNAM.

Lope Blanch, Juan M. 1985. *El habla de Diego de Ordaz: Contribución a la historia del español americano.* México: UNAM.

Lozano, Anthony G. 1976. The Spanish language of the San Luis Valley. En *The Hispanic contribution to the state of Colorado*, ed. J. de Onís, 191–207. Boulder: Westview Press.

Mar-Molinero, Clare. 1997. *The Spanish-speaking world.* New York: Routledge.

Moreno de Alba, José 1978. *Valores de las formas verbales en el español de México.* México: UNAM.

Orstein, Jacob. 1951. The archaic and the modern in the Spanish of New Mexico. *Hispania* 34: 137–141.

Orstein, Jacob. 1972. Toward a classification of Southwest Spanish nonstandard variants. *Linguistics* 93: 70–78.

Parodi, Claudia. 1995. *Orígenes del español americano, vol. 1.* México: Universidad Nacional Autónoma de México.

Penny, Ralph. 1991. *A history of the Spanish language.* Cambridge: Cambridge University Press.

Phillips, R.N. Jr. 1967. Los Angeles Spanish: A descriptive analysis. Tesis de doctorado, University of Wisconsin.

Silva-Corvalán, Carmen. 1994. *Language contact and change: Spanish in Los Angeles.* Oxford: Clarendon.

Valdés, Guadalupe. 1997. The teaching of Spanish to bilingual Spanish-speaking students: Outstanding issues and unanswered questions. En *La enseñanza del español a hispanohablantes*, ed. M. Cecilia Colombi y Francisco X. Alarcón, 8–44. Boston: Houghton Mifflin.

Villa, Daniel. 1997. *El desarrollo de futuridad en el español.* México: Grupo editorial EóN.

Factores socio-históricos en la pérdida del español del suroeste de los Estados Unidos y sus implicaciones para la revitalización

Ysaura Bernal-Enríquez
University of New Mexico

1. Introducción

La pérdida del español chicano tanto en la Nueva México[1] como en el resto del suroeste estadounidense es un problema de grandes proporciones. Hace tiempo Ortiz (1975), Floyd (1982), y Hudson-Edwards y Bills (1982) encontraron que el aumento del dominio y uso del inglés afectaba negativamente el uso y la habilidad del español en el hogar. Existen varios estudios más recientes que demuestran claramente la pérdida de habilidad en el idioma a causa del gran desplazamiento del español a favor del inglés, especialmente entre los jóvenes (véanse por ejemplo Hernández Chávez 1993a, Bernal-Enríquez 1994, 1998a, 1998b, Hudson, Hernández Chávez, y Bills 1995).

Es muy importante entender la relación entre el uso y la habilidad en una lengua, sea en la materna o en una segunda lengua, ya que la adquisición de habilidad requiere el uso regular y suficiente de un idioma, lo que Krashen (1981) y Harris (1992) llaman *sufficiency of input*. Por otra parte, el desuso, o la falta de suficiente uso, resulta en la pérdida lingüística, es decir en la adquisición dilatada o parcial de habilidad. A causa del uso insuficiente o de un cambio en el uso, los jóvenes adquieren una habilidad parcial en el idioma o no la adquieren del todo.

Dadas estas relaciones, para que se transmita un idioma de una generación a otra, es esencial mantener el uso a un nivel lo suficientemente alto para llegar a la adquisición completa porque la adquisición parcial no asegura la transmisión a la siguiente generación (Bernal-Enríquez y Hernández-Chávez 1998). Además donde una de las lenguas es más fuerte, es decir de mayor uso y valor en la sociedad, la tendencia es usar menos la lengua más débil, y esto a su vez finalmente lleva a la pérdida (Seliger y Vago 1991).

Desde la renombrada declaración de la UNESCO (1953), el idioma materno se reconoce como el instrumento idóneo para el desarrollo cognoscitivo del ser humano. De igual importancia, la lengua materna, aprendida en el seno de la familia, sirve como medio esencial para la integración a la comunidad, y el mantenimiento de esta lengua significa la transmisión a la siguiente generación no sólo del idioma mismo, sino también de la tradición moral, los valores, la cultura, y la identidad que forman parte integral de esa lengua ancestral (Hernández Chávez 1978, 1993b, Jalava 1988, Fishman 1996).

Al perderse la lengua, y con ello estas tradiciones morales, una de las consecuencias más serias para los chicanitos es la enajenación, no sólo de la comunidad sino, lo que es más destructivo, de sí mismos (Jalava 1988). Este enajenamiento hasta pudiera ser vinculado a la incidencia tan alta del disfuncionalismo social, como lo son la deserción de las escuelas, el embarazo en la adolescencia, el alcoholismo, la drogadicción, la participación en las pandillas, y el crimen que se encuentra en la comunidad chicana (Hernández Chávez 1993a).

Existe una creencia general entre muchos grupos étnicos que si uno ya no habla la lengua, deja de ser miembro del grupo (Adley-Santamaria 1999). Aunque sea posible ser parte del grupo sin hablar la lengua étnica, el ser miembro por medio de ella lleva consigo diferencias cualitativas (McCarty, Watahomigie, y Yamamoto 1999). Así es que cuando se pierde la habilidad en la lengua, se pierde con ello la posibilidad de aprovechar todo lo que la lengua simboliza, no sólo para el individuo, sino también para los miembros de la comunidad y para todas sus generaciones futuras.

En este estudio presentaré un análisis de los factores que afectan la pérdida de la lengua materna de los chicanos. El objeto principal es saber cuáles son los patrones de uso que influyen en el mantenimiento o pérdida del español chicano con el fin de entender cómo contrarrestar la pérdida. En última instancia, mi propósito es idear, junto con la comunidad afectada, estrategias y programas que puedan revitalizar la lengua.

Los datos para el análisis vienen de 209 consultantes entrevistados para la *Encuesta sobre el Español de Nuevo México y el sur de Colorado (NMCOSS)* (Vigil, Bills, Bernal-Enríquez, y Ulibarrí 1996, Vigil y Bills 1997). Las entrevistas se hicieron con el propósito de crear un atlas lingüístico que documentara la variedad de la lengua española hablada en esta región e incluyen tanto un cuestionario dialectológico como información demográfica y sociolingüística. Además contienen narrativas orales en las cuales se encuentran datos autobiográficos, experiencias, actitudes, y muchos otros aspectos de la vida de los encuestados. Se transcribieron todas las secciones de las narrativas que tuvieran que ver con el lenguaje, la discriminación, la etnicidad, y todo lo que informara sobre el estado actual de la habilidad de los consultantes en español y en inglés.

Los análisis presentados enfocan en la relación de ciertas variables socio y psicolingüísticas y sociales con la habilidad en español de los encuestados, la cual fue evaluada globalmente por cada uno de los entrevistadores. Las variables sociales de interés son la edad actual de los entrevistados y sus años de educación. De importancia sociolingüística son el uso lingüístico actual con amistades, con los niños, y entre esposos; y el idioma o idiomas usados en el hogar durante la niñez. Las variables psicolingüísticas son la edad de aprender inglés y la habilidad actual en inglés.

2. La pérdida de habilidad en español

Los hallazgos de este estudio confirman los resultados citados arriba que documentan el desplazamiento del español entre los hispanohablantes en el suroeste de los Estados Unidos. A través de las generaciones en la Nueva México, se ve una clara disminución de habilidad en español, la cual pronostica la desaparición del idioma en generaciones venideras.

2.1. La habilidad en español en relación con la edad y con la generación

En la tabulación de cruce de *Habilidad en español* con *Edad* en el Cuadro 1, vemos la pérdida a través de las generaciones. En este análisis los "jóvenes" son de la edad de 20 a 40, los de "edad mediana" de 41 a 59, los de "edad madura" de 60 a 72, y los "ancianos" de 73 a 96 años.

En el cuadro, el porcentaje según el nivel de habilidad indica que el 100% de los de "pobre" o "poco o nada" de habilidad en español son los jóvenes. (Véase los números en negrita.) Es decir, aunque muchos jóvenes tienen habilidad regular o más, sólo este grupo sufre de habilidad pobre o menos.

Examinando estas cifras por edad, vemos que el porcentaje de aquellos hablantes que tienen habilidad de hablar el español "muy bien," o sea excelente, sube dramáticamente por edad. Entre los jóvenes, únicamente el 26% tiene habilidad excelente, mientras que el 50% de los de edad mediana y el 62% de los de edad madura tienen esta habilidad. Al otro extremo, el 87% de los ancianos tiene habilidad excelente.

Este aumento de habilidad en español por mayor edad no significa que los mayores hablan mejor español sólo porque son mayores, ni tampoco que los jóvenes adquirirán mucho más español a través de los años. Lo que sí representa es la adquisición diferencial del español a través de las generaciones: las generaciones más jóvenes – todos adultos – tienden a no adquirir habilidad completa en español, lo cual tiene serias implicaciones para la posibilidad de trasmitir el español a sus hijos. Tomando en cuenta que estos encuestados no fueron escogidos al azar sino que todos tenían que saber algo de español para poder participar en la Encuesta NMCOSS, la realidad de la pérdida entre la población general de la región se ve aún más seria de lo que indican estas cifras.

Cuadro 1. La relación entre la habilidad en español y la edad/generación

	Habilidad en Español					
Edad	Muy Bien	Bien	Regular	Pobre	Poco o Nada	Núm Tot Pct
Joven	12	15	13	5	1	46
Pct Col	10.6	30.6	44.8	***100.0***	***100.0***	23.4
Pct Fila	***26.1***	32.6	28.3	10.9	2.2	
Pct Total	6.1	7.6	6.6	2.5	0.5	
Edad Mediana	26	19	7			52
Pct Col	23.0	38.8	24.1			26.4
Pct Fila	***50.0***	36.5	13.5			
Pct Total	13.2	9.6	3.6			
Adulto Maduro	28	10	7			45
Pct Col	24.8	20.4	24.1			22.8
Pct Fila	***62.2***	22.2	15.6			
Pct Total	14.2	5.1	3.6			
Anciano	47	5	2			54
Pct Col	41.6	10.2	6.9			27.4
Pct Fila	***87.0***	9.3	3.7			
Pct Total	23.9	2.5	1.0			
Número Columna	113	49	29	5	1	
Tot Pct Col	57.4	24.9	14.7	2.5	0.5	
Número Total de Observaciones						197

Valor Pearson Chi-square 56.14; p<.00000

2.2. Evidencia de la pérdida de habilidad en el uso actual

El uso actual normalmente se considera como indicador del desplazamiento o del mantenimiento (véase por ejemplo Fishman 1968, Hayden 1966, Laosa 1975, Faltis 1976). Por otra parte, el presente estudio enfoca en la relación de la habilidad lingüística con el uso actual, encontrando alguna evidencia adicional de la pérdida a través de las generaciones además de dar un entendimiento más detallado de los procesos sociolingüísticos.

En general, las tabulaciones de cruce de habilidad en español con el uso actual demuestran que los adultos que tienen mucha habilidad en español tienden a usarlo más entre sí. Así es que el *Uso entre amistades* se correlaciona fuertemente con *Habilidad en español* (Cuadro 2).

Cuadro 2. Uso con amistades en relación con la habilidad

	Habilidad en Español					
Uso con Amistades	Muy Bien	Bien	Regular	Pobre	Poco o Nada	Núm
Todo en Inglés	5	5	8		4	22
Más Inglés	3	7	10		1	21
Ambos Iguales	42	21	4		1	68
Más Español	15	5				20
Todo en Español	14	2	1			17
Número Total de Observaciones						148

Valor Pearson Chi-square 64.90; p<.00000

También muestran la misma tendencia el *Uso entre esposos* (valor Chi-square 20.56, p <.19) y el *Uso actual con los niños* (valor Chi-square 24.37, p<.08). (Los datos no se presentan aquí, ya que sus valores estadísticos no alcanzaron significancia.) En todos estos casos, el uso del idioma, o sea su manutención, depende directamente de la habilidad adquirida, especialmente en estos contextos de intimidad. En vista de la disminución de habilidad por edad visto en el Cuadro 1, estos datos tienden a confirmar la pérdida lingüística intergeneracional.

3. Los efectos de la transmisión temprana

Las fuentes de la pérdida se encuentran en las experiencias lingüísticas tempranas, especialmente la edad de adquisición del inglés y la lengua o lenguas usadas en el hogar durante la niñez. La habilidad actual en español (y su uso actual, como ya vimos) se relaciona directamente con estas experiencias.

3.1. La habilidad en español en relación con la lengua del hogar durante la niñez

En el Cuadro 3, *Habilidad en español* con *Lengua del hogar durante la niñez*, vemos que mientras más español se usó como idioma del hogar en la niñez, mejor es la habilidad actual en español. Así vemos que en la columna titulada "muy bien," el 88.5% de los que tienen ahora excelente español se criaron en hogares donde sólo el español se usaba, mientras que el porcentaje baja al 9.7% del total en los hogares con ambos idiomas, y al 1.8% del total cuando se criaron con solamente inglés en la casa durante su niñez (números en negrita).

Cuadro 3. Habilidad en español por idioma del hogar en la niñez

Idioma del Hogar	Habilidad en Español Muy Bien	Bien	Regular	Pobre	Poco o Nada	Núm Tot Pct
Sólo Español	100	38	14	2	1	155
Pct Col	**88.5**	77.6	50.0	40.0	100.0	79.1
Pct Fila	***64.5***	24.5	9.0	1.3	0.6	
Pct Total	51.0	19.4	7.1	1.0	0.5	
Ambos	11	10	11	2		34
Pct Col	**9.7**	20.4	39.3	40.0		17.3
Pct Fila	***32.4***	29.4	32.4	5.9		
Pct Total	5.6	5.1	5.6	1.0		
Sólo Inglés	2	1	3	1		7
Pct Col	**1.8**	2.0	10.7	20.0		3.6
Pct Fila	***28.6***	14.3	42.9	14.3		
Pct Total	1.0	0.5	1.5	0.5		
Número Columna	113	49	28	5	1	
Tot Pct Col	**57.7**	25.0	14.3	2.6	0.5	
Número Total de Observaciones						196

Valor Pearson Chi-square 27.91; p<.00049

Además, se puede notar que entre los que tuvieron exclusivamente el español como lengua del hogar en la niñez, casi dos tercios (64.5%) tienen muy buena habilidad en español, mientras que entre los que pasaron los primeros cinco o seis años de su vida con dos idiomas, menos de un tercio de éstos (32.4%) tienen excelente español. Y entre los de una niñez con puro inglés en casa, poco más de una cuarta parte (28.6%) de ellos habla español muy bien. La mayoría de este grupo (57.2%) lo habla menos de "bien." (Los del grupo de únicamente inglés en su hogar tienen que haber tenido algún contacto con el español para poder adquirir lo que sí saben, pero ha de haber sido o fuera de su propio hogar o en visitas u otro contacto esporádico en el hogar con personas hispanohablantes.)

3.2. La Habilidad en español en relación con la edad de aprendizaje del inglés

El Cuadro 4, *Habilidad en español* en relación con la *Edad de aprender inglés*, demuestra que mientras más temprano se aprende el inglés, menor es la habilidad en español como adulto.

Primero observemos las últimas dos columnas de *Habilidad en español.* El 100% (en negrita) de los de español "pobre" o "poco o nada" son los que adquirieron inglés antes de entrar a la escuela. Ahora observemos los porcentajes por *Edades.* El 90.9% de los que no aprendieron inglés hasta después de ser adolescentes hablan muy buen español. En contraste, el 65.5% de los que esperaron hasta por lo menos los cinco o seis años lo habla muy bien, y sólo el 34.5% de los que adquirieron inglés antes de los cinco años tiene excelente español.

Cuadro 4. Habilidad en español por edad de aprendizaje del inglés

	Habilidad en Español					
Edad de aprender inglés	Muy Bien	Bien	Regular	Pobre	Poco o Nada	Núm Tot Pct
Pre-escolar	20	20	14	3	1	58
Pct Col	18.5	41.7	50.0	***100.0***	***100.0***	30.9
Pct Fila	***34.5***	34.5	24.1	5.2	1.7	
Pct Total	10.6	10.6	7.4	1.6	.5	
Primaria	78	27	14			119
Pct Col	72.2	56.3	50.0			63.3
Pct Fila	***65.5***	22.7	11.8			
Pct Total	41.5	14.4	7.4			
Pos-pubertad	10	1				11
Pct Col	9.3	2.1				5.9
Pct Fila	***90.9***	9.1				
Pct Total	5.3	.5				
Número Columna	108	48	28	3	1	
Tot Pct Col	57.4	25.5	14.9	1.6	.5	
Número Total de Observaciones						188

Valor Pearson Chi-square 26.90; p<.0007

4. El efecto de la educación en la transmisión del español

Volvamos la atención al efecto de la educación sobre la habilidad en español dentro de la comunidad neomexicana. En el Cuadro 5, *Habilidad en español* por *Años de educación*, se ve una relación inversa entre estas dos variables: menos años de educación implican mejor español; más años implican más inglés y menos español.

Tiene excelente español el 92.9% de los que no llegaron más allá del cuarto grado y el 88.9% de los que estudiaron solamente hasta el grado ocho. El porcentaje baja al 43.9% en el grupo que fue a la *high school*, y al 46.2% en los que fueron a la universidad – básicamente la mitad de los que tuvieron sólo educación primaria o ninguna escuela (números en negrita). Estas cifras tienden a confirmar los hallazgos de Hudson et al. (1995) sobre datos censales, mostrando que, en los estados del Suroeste, cuanto más años de educación, menos se usaba el español.

Cuadro 5. Habilidad en español por años de educación

	Habilidad en Español					
Años de Educación	Muy Bien	Bien	Regular	Pobre	Poco o Nada	Núm Tot Pct
0–4 años	13		1			14
Pct Col	12.7		3.6			7.6
Pct Fila	***92.9***		7.1			
Pct Total	7.0		0.5			
5–8 años	24	3				27
Pct Col	23.5	6.1				14.6
Pct Fila	***88.9***	11.1				
Pct Total	13.0	1.6				
9–12 años	29	20	13	3	1	66
Pct Col	28.4	40.8	46.4	60.0	100.0	35.7
Pct Fila	***43.9***	30.3	19.7	4.5	1.5	
Pct Total	15.7	10.8	7.0	1.6	0.5	
Más de 12 años	36	26	14	2		78
Pct Col	35.3	53.1	50.0	40.0		42.2
Pct Fila	***46.2***	33.3	17.9	2.6		
Pct Total	19.5	14.1	7.6	1.1		
Número Columna	102	49	28	5	1	
Total Pct Col	55.1	26.5	15.1	2.7	0.5	
Número total de observaciones						185

Valor Pearson Chi-square 29.43; p<.00339

5. Discusión y conclusiones

En este estudio se han presentado datos que confirman los hallazgos de un creciente número de investigadores con respecto a la pérdida del español en la Nueva México. En general, la adquisición del español entre los jóvenes es incompleta, hecho reflejado en su habilidad actual en español y, como consecuencia, en el uso del idioma. Estos hablantes tienden a usar el español solamente en ciertas ocasiones y en contextos restringidos, limitando severamente la transmisión de la lengua a la generación subsecuente.

Hemos visto también que el uso histórico – es decir el idioma del hogar en la niñez, la edad de aprender inglés, y los años de educación en inglés, especialmente durante la niñez – afecta directamente la habilidad en español de la persona como adulto, según la suficiencia del *exposure* y del *input*, o sea el CONTACTO, con esta lengua. Estos resultados nos llevan a concluir lo siguiente: (1) la habilidad completa en español y el mantenimiento del idioma en la comunidad requieren el uso predominante del español durante la niñez y la adolescencia; y (2) la introducción demasiado temprana del inglés perjudica la habilidad en español.

Estas conclusiones están basadas tanto en los resultados de este estudio como en los requisitos psicolingüísticos y sociolingüísticos para la adquisición del idioma materno. El desarrollo normal de la lengua – que conduce a la habilidad y el uso completos – se determina no sólo por el conocimiento innato del ser humano (Chomsky 1964, 1972, 1983, 1986) y el desarrollo cognoscitivo del niño (Piaget 1974, Vygotsky 1962), sino también por la *experiencia lingüística*. Esta experiencia lingüística requiere el uso frecuente, suficiente, y significativo del idioma con el aprendiz desde la infancia hasta la adolescencia (véanse por ejemplo Krashen 1981, Bruner 1983, Heath 1983, Moskowitz 1985, Karmiloff-Smith 1986, Wells 1987, Garton y Pratt 1989, Garton 1992, Harris 1992). Esto explica la habilidad parcial en español de las personas que aprendieron el inglés muy temprano y por lo tanto usaron ambos idiomas en la niñez.

Este uso de dos idiomas en el hogar a temprana edad, lo cual promueve un bilingüismo simultáneo, tiene un efecto erosivo para la adquisición completa del español, un idioma minoritario y socialmente subordinado, aun en la Nueva México. En este caso, el bilingüismo, en vez de decir "*twice as much*," como proclama el lema de la educación bilingüe, ¡se reduce a decir "*half as much*"! Precisa aclarar que no es la presencia del inglés en el hogar en sí la que causa la pérdida lingüística, sino la erosión de contacto con el español durante el período crítico de su aprendizaje. El uso de un idioma en dado contexto excluye la posibilidad de usar el otro en ese mismo contexto. Bajo estas condiciones, "*the forceful presence of English*" (Haugen 1950, citado en Ornstein 1975: 10) y las presiones sociolingüísticas en la comunidad (Dulay, Burt, y Hernández Chávez 1978) interrumpen el desarrollo completo del español.

Un estudio reciente (Winsler, Díaz, Espinosa, y Rodríguez 1999) apoya la posibilidad del desarrollo de un bilingüismo equilibrado en la educación preescolar. Sin embargo, los mismos investigadores conceden que el contacto continuo con el inglés en los años de escuela primaria y secundaria, sea en dos idiomas o sólo en inglés, puede causar un cambio en el uso que lleva a la pérdida del español.

En efecto, la presencia preescolar del inglés en el hogar, la cual promueve el aprendizaje del inglés antes de la edad de seis años, equivale a las condiciones de "demasiado inglés, demasiado temprano" que llevan al niño al más serio empobrecimiento de habilidad en la lengua materna (Wong-Fillmore 1991a, 1991b, Liu, Bates, y Li 1992). Estas son en sí las condiciones citadas por Hernández Chávez (1999) que resultan en un bilingüismo malogrado el cual "contiene el germen de su propia destrucción." Es decir, el bilingüismo demasiado temprano impide el desarrollo pleno de la lengua materna.

Hudson et al. (1995), en su estudio sobre el desplazamiento del español en el suroeste de los EE.UU. usando datos del censo, encontraron que el menor uso del español se correlacionaba con más años de educación. Estos resultados motivaron a los investigadores a concluir que el aprovechamiento escolar y socioeconómico de los grupos hispanohablantes en el Suroeste se logra a costa de la lengua materna. Esta conclusión asombrosa es apoyada por los hallazgos presentados en este estudio que muestran que las personas que tienen más años de educación tienden a tener menos habilidad en español.

¿Por qué sucede esto? En primer lugar, no es la educación en sí la que causa la falta de habilidad en español, sino el hecho de que la escolaridad es conducida predominantemente en inglés. Salvo tres personas, todos los entrevistados recibieron su educación completamente o principalmente en inglés ya que la educación en el estado de Nuevo México ha sido en inglés desde el principio de siglo con la excepción de algunas zonas rurales (Espinosa 1911, González 1967, Meyer 1977, Milk 1980, Hernández Chávez 1995, 1998). A consecuencia de esto, si la persona recibe mucha educación, experimenta más contacto con el inglés y por lo tanto lo usa más; por otro lado, si *no* se recibe mucha educación, el uso del inglés es indeterminado, pero tiende a ser menos.

En efecto, la educación en Nuevo México ha sido el instrumento principal de la pérdida del español no sólo por ser en inglés sino por la represión del español por medio de castigos físicos o psicológicos, una forma potente de violencia institucionalizada, lo que llamo *school-sponsored child abuse.* (MacGregor-Mendoza 1999, expone algunas formas de esos castigos contra los niños en Nuevo México. Véase también Skutnabb-Kangas 1981, Skutnabb-Kangas y Cummins 1988.) Esta represión contra los niños de lenguas minoritarias, impuesta por políticas oficiales del sistema educativo (Hernández Chávez 1996, Sims 1999) después llevó a muchos de estos individuos, como adultos, a la decisión de no usar el español del todo con sus hijos para que no sufrieran los mismos castigos en la escuela.

Como se ha notado anteriormente, el uso histórico, o sea la experiencia lingüística, es esencial para el desarrollo de la habilidad lingüística. Por otro lado, el uso actual es, en gran parte, una función de la habilidad adquirida históricamente. Así es que existe un ciclo de uso-habilidad-uso que, según las condiciones socio y psicolingüísticas, es o autoperpetuante o autodestructiva.

6. Implicaciones para la revitalización

La revitalización de una lengua que está en peligro de desaparecer implica un esfuerzo masivo que requiere la reintroducción de la lengua en todos los sectores de la sociedad: en el hogar, las escuelas, el gobierno y los servicios sociales en que se deben de ensanchar los derechos lingüísticos, los medios de comunicación, las instituciones económicas, la cultura popular, etc (Hernández Chávez 1993b, 1995, 1999, Holm 1999a). En este estudio, hemos visto que dos de estas instituciones son indispensables para el desarrollo completo de la lengua: el hogar y la escuela.

6.1. El papel del hogar

En el hogar, y por extension en la comunidad, los padres y otros adultos que quieran revitalizar el español de sus hijos tendrán que crear un ambiente donde predomine el español, donde oigan los hijos el español constantemente – de personas monolingües si es posible – y donde se protejan su valores sociales y culturales. Los padres deberán usar el español todo el tiempo posible, aun cuando haya visitas. Este uso se podrá facilitar utilizando materiales y recursos en español como los libros, la música, y los medios de comunicación, tanto como por la participación en las actividades culturales, sociales, y religiosas de la comunidad hispanohablante.

Para algunos será muy difícil usar el español constantemente, pero con el tiempo se les hará más cómodo y fácil. Aunque el nivel de habilidad en español de los padres sea parcial, un poco de español es preferible a nada porque el ejemplo de los padres que lo usan es vital para valorizar el idioma. No cabe duda que necesitarán aprovechar todas las oportunidades para aprenderlo mejor por medio de la lectura, el estudio, y la utilización de la radio, la televisión, y las grabaciones, así como por el roce con personas hispanoparlantes. De esta manera, los modelos adultos podrán regenerar su propio español a la vez que se esfuerzan por ampliar los contextos en que ellos mismos usan el español oral y escrito.

El español necesita ser no sólo la lengua de la niñez sino una parte integral de la comunicación cotidiana durante toda la vida. Como ya hemos observado en este estudio, mientras más español se habla en el hogar (y mientras más tarde se aprende el inglés) mejor es la habilidad en español del individuo como adulto. El uso engendra la habilidad, la cual da cabida a más uso.

Los padres no deben de temer que sus hijos falten de aprender completamente la lengua dominante. Dentro de una sociedad donde prepondera el inglés en casi todos los contextos, este idioma se desarrollará automáticamente, el español no. El predominio del inglés en la escuela, los medios de comunicación, el comercio, y los demás sectores de la sociedad asegura que, muy pronto, los niños recibirán más que suficiente contacto con la lengua dominante para su desarrollo completo. En efecto, los datos de este estudio (no presentados aquí) demuestran que ambas lenguas se pueden aprender con excelente habilidad, ya que el 30.5 porciento de los consultantes calificaron como completamente bilingües. Además, otros estudios también han mostrado que el desarrollo completo del idioma materno no sólo *no impide* el aprendizaje de la segunda lengua sino que lo aumenta (véanse por ejemplo Cummins 1991, Krashen 1981).

6.2. El papel de las escuelas

La preocupación de las escuelas por la introducción temprana y la adquisición completa del inglés, antes de que la niña haya desarrollado adecuadamente su primer idioma, es una de las causas fundamentales de la pérdida lingüística. Esto es cierto especialmente donde la lengua materna no se valoriza. Aun dentro de los programas bilingües en los cuales la meta principal y final es el *mainstreaming* (esencialmente la asimilación a la lengua y cultura anglosajona), el español es visto muy rápidamente por los alumnos como una lengua sin importancia.

Este enfoque continuo en el inglés erosiona más y más la lengua nativa. Como hemos visto, el número de años de escolaridad está negativamente correlacionado con la habilidad en español. Esto de ninguna manera significa que debemos de privar al niño de una educación para mantener o revitalizar su idioma materno. Al contrario, significa que la niña debe de recibir una educación completa y que la escuela tiene que asegurar el contacto adecuado con la lengua materna. Para cumplir con este propósito, es indispensable que el español sea la lengua de instrucción; que los estudiantes, los maestros, y el personal de la escuela usen la lengua para todas las interacciones – tanto con los estudiantes como con los padres; y que estas condiciones persistan por lo menos hasta que los estudiantes entren a la *high school.*

Es más, el desarrollo completo del idioma requiere que se continúen enseñando las destrezas académicas y cognoscitivas en español a través de todos los grados. No es suficiente que el estudiante aprenda bien la lengua familiar; para el mantenimiento y la transmisión natural del idioma, los hablantes tendrán que aprenderlo bien en todos los registros y en todas las modalidades. Además, existe un cuerpo amplio de estudios e investigaciones que indican que la enseñanza de las destrezas académicas y cognoscitivas por medio de la lengua materna ayuda a desarrollar la segunda lengua y refuerza estas mismas destrezas (Lambert 1977, Swain y Cummins 1979, y Cummins 1981).

Existen algunos proyectos activos que podrían servir como modelos para esta clase de cambios. Como lo están haciendo en partes del Hawai'i (Video: 'Aha Pūnana Leo 1997), en Maori, en el Pueblo de Cóchiti, Nuevo México, en selectos programas en la reserva Navajó, y en varios otros lugares del mundo (Holm 1999b), con el apoyo de sus padres y sus abuelos, estos cambios requieren el activismo informado de los jóvenes, que son los que tendrán que esforzarse y unirse para que no se les vaya del todo la lengua y la cultura de sus antepasados.

Notas

* Este estudio ha recibido apoyo de dos becas para la tesis doctoral ortorgadas por el Centro de Estudios Regionales (*CRS*) de la Universidad de Nuevo México y por la Asociación Americana de Mujeres Universitarias (*AAUW*).

1. La región de la Nueva España en lo que hoy es el norte de Nuevo México y el sur de Colorado fue inicialmente designada en los mapas de la época como *la Nueva México.* El nombre se cambió más tarde al masculino *Nuevo México*, se supone a causa de la [o] en México. Utilizo el nombre original en este estudio por razones históricas y porque la región bajo estudio forma un área lingüística y culturalmente unida. El uso de *la Nueva México* nos permite también referirnos a la región entera con un solo término. Véase la discusión de Kloss (1977) sobre la división política de *la Nueva México* en 1861 por el gobierno de los Estados Unidos y la subsecuente incorporación de la parte norteña al nuevamente creado estado de Colorado (1876), en efecto dividiendo a la población hispanohablante y, por consiguiente, su voto.

Referencias

Adley-Santamaria, Bernadette. 1999. Interrupting White Mountain Apache language shift: An insider's view. En *Reversing language shift in indigenous America: Collaborations and views from the field*, ed. Teresa L. McCarty, Lucille J. Watahomigie, y Akira Y. Yamamoto, 16–19. (*Practicing Anthropology* 20.2).

'Aha Pūnana Leo. 1997. E Ola Ka'Ōlelo Hawai'i. *The story of the revitalization of Hawaiian language through Hawaiian medium schools: Success in the face of challenges*. Video. Hilo, Hawai'i: 'Aha Pūnana Leo.

Bernal-Enríquez, Ysaura. 1994. La relación entre el uso y la proficiencia en el español de un barrio de Albuquerque. En *University of New Mexico Working Papers in Linguistics* 2, ed. Patricia M. Escarraz, Laurent D. Thomin, Sally A. Weller, y Bushra Zawaydeh, 117–121. Albuquerque: University of New Mexico Department of Linguistics.

Bernal-Enríquez, Ysaura. 1998a. Factores psicolingüísticos, sociolingüísticos y socio-demográficos en la pérdida del español chicano en la Nueva México: Sus implicaciones para la revitalización. Simposio Internacional sobre Lenguas Indígenas e Interculturalidad, Casa Escuela DIF, Creel, Chihuahua, México, Mayo 21–23.

Bernal-Enríquez, Ysaura. 1998b. La pérdida del español en la Nueva México. VII Annual Conference of the Ibero-American Society and the XVI Annual Conference of El Español en Estados Unidos. Albuquerque, NM, Febrero 13–14.

Bernal-Enríquez, Ysaura y Eduardo Hernández Chávez. 1998. La enseñanza del español a los chicanos: ¿Revitalización o erradicación de la variedad chicana? manuscrito inédito.

Bruner, Jerome Seymour. 1983. *Child's talk*. Cambridge: Cambridge University Press.

Chomsky, Noam. 1964. Review of B.F. Skinner's "Verbal Behavior." En *The structure of language*, ed. Jerry A. Fodor y Jerrold J. Katz, 547–578. Englewood Cliffs, NJ: Prentice-Hall.

Chomsky, Noam. 1972. *Language and mind*. New York: Harcourt Brace Jovanovich.

Chomsky, Noam. 1983. An interview (por John Gliedman). *Omni* 6: 112–118.

Chomsky, Noam. 1986. *Knowledge of language: Its nature, origin, and use*. New York: Praeger.

Cummins, James. 1981. The role of primary language development in promoting educational success for language minority students. *Schooling and language minority students: A theoretical framework*, ed. California State Department of Education, 3–49. Los Angeles: California State University Evaluation, Dissemination, and Assessment Center.

Cummins, James. 1991. Interdependence of first and second-language proficiency in bilingual children. En *Language processing in bilingual children*, ed. Ellen Bialystok, 70–89. Cambridge: Cambridge University Press.

Dulay, Heidi C., Marina K. Burt, y Eduardo Hernández Chávez. 1978. The process of becoming bilingual. En *Diagnostic procedures in hearing, language, and speech*, ed. Sadanand Singh and Joan Lynch, 251–303. Baltimore: University Park Press.

Espinosa, Aurelio Macedonio. 1911. *The Spanish language in New Mexico and southern Colorado*. Santa Fe, NM: New Mexico Printing Co.

Faltis, Christian Jan. 1976. *A study of Spanish and English usage among bilingual Mexican Americans living in the Las Calles Barrio of San José, California*. M.A. thesis, California State University San José.

Fishman, Joshua. 1968. Societal bilingualism: Stable and transitional. *Sociology of language* VI: 91–106. Rowley, MA: Newbury House.

Fishman, Joshua. 1996. Maintaining languages: What works and what doesn't. En *Stabilizing indigenous languages*, ed. Gina Cantoni, 186–198. Flagstaff, AZ: Northern Arizona University.

Floyd, Mary Beth. 1982. Spanish language maintenance in Colorado. En *Bilingualism and language contact: Spanish, English, and Native American Languages*, ed. Florence Barkin, Elizabeth A. Brandt, y Jacob Ornstein-Galicia, 290–303. New York: Teachers College Press.

Garton, Alison F. 1992. *Social interaction and the development of language and cognition.* Hillsdale, NJ: Lawrence Erlbaum.

Garton, Alison F. y Chris Pratt. 1989. *Learning to be literate: The development of spoken and written language*. Oxford: Blackwell.

González, Nancie. 1967. *The Spanish Americans of New Mexico: A distinctive heritage.* Los Angeles: Division of Research, Graduate School of Business Administration, University of California.

Harris, Margaret. 1992. *Language experience and early language development: From input to uptake.* Hillsdale, NJ: Lawrence Erlbaum Associates.

Haugen, Einar. 1950. Review of Leo Pap's Portuguese-English speech. *Language* 25: 438–439.

Hayden, Robert G. 1966. Some community dynamics of language maintenance. En *Language loyalty in the United States*, ed. Joshua A. Fishman, 190–205. The Hague: Mouton.

Heath, Shirley Brice. 1983. *Ways with words: Language, life and work in communities and classroom*. Cambridge: Cambridge University Press.

Hernández Chávez, Eduardo. 1978. Language maintenance, bilingual education, and philosophies of bilingualism in the United States. En *International dimensions of bilingual education: Georgetown University roundtable on languages and linguistics*, ed. James E. Alatis, 527–550. Washington, DC: Georgetown University Press.

Hernández Chávez, Eduardo. 1993a. La pérdida del español entre los chicanos: Sus raíces sociopolíticas y las consecuencias para la identidad cultural. Ponencia plenaria en el III Congreso Anual de La Sociedad Iberoamericana sobre la Lengua Española y la Identidad Social, Albuquerque, Febrero 13–15.

Hernández Chávez, Eduardo. 1993b. Native language loss and its implications for revitalization of Spanish in Chicano communities. En *Language and culture in learning*, ed. Barbara J. Merino, Henry T. Trueba, y Fabián A. Samaniego, 58–74. London: Falmer Press.

Hernández Chávez, Eduardo. 1995. La reivindicación del español en el Suroeste. Ponencia plenaria en el First Annual Conference on Spanish for Native Speakers: New Directions for the 21st Century, Universidad Estatal de Nuevo México, Las Cruces, NM, Mayo 17–19.

Hernández Chávez, Eduardo. 1996. The role of language policy in the loss of Spanish in New Mexico. Ponencia en la Quinta Junta Anual de la Rocky Mountain Modern Language Association, Albuquerque, NM, Octubre 24–26.

Hernández Chávez, Eduardo. 1998. Los derechos lingüísticos en Nuevo México: El llamado bilingüismo oficial estatal. Ponencia en el XVI Congreso de El Español en

Estados Unidos y el VII Congreso Anual sobre Sociedad y Cultura Iberoamericana, Albuquerque, NM, Febrero 12–14.

Hernández Chávez, Eduardo. 1999. Imperativo para la sobreviviencia cultural: La revitalización del español chicano de Nuevo México. Ponencia en el XVII Congreso del Español en Estados Unidos, Miami, FL, March 11–13.

Holm, Wayne. 1999a. The goodness of bilingual education for Native American students. Ponencia plenaria en el VI Annual Stabilizing Indigenous Languages Conference: One voice, many voices . . . Recreating indigenous language communities. American Indian Language Development Institute, University of Arizona, Tucson, June 3–5.

Holm, Wayne. 1999b. Personal e-mail letter to Ysaura Bernal-Enríquez, June 18, 1999.

Hudson, Alan, Eduardo Hernández Chávez, y Garland D. Bills. 1995. The many faces of language maintenance: Spanish language claiming in five southwestern states. En *Spanish in four continents*, ed. Carmen Silva-Corvalán, 165–183. Washington, DC: Georgetown University Press.

Hudson-Edwards, Alan y Garland D. Bills. 1982. Intergenerational language shift in an Albuquerque barrio. En *Spanish in the U.S.: Sociolinguistic aspects*, ed. Jon Amastae y Lucía Elías-Olivares, 135–153. Cambridge: Cambridge University Press.

Jalava, Antti. 1988. Mother tongue and identity. En *Minority education: From shame to struggle*, ed. Tove Skutnabb-Kangas y James Cummins, 161–185. Clevedon, England: Multilingual Matters.

Karmiloff-Smith, Annette. 1986. Some fundamental aspects of language development after five. En *Language acquisition*, 2a. edición, ed. Paul Fletcher y Michael Garman, 455–474. Cambridge: Cambridge University Press.

Kloss, Heinz. 1977. *The American bilingual tradition*. Rowley, MA: Newbury House.

Krashen, Stephen. 1981. Bilingual education and second language theory. En *Schooling and language minority students: A theoretical framework*, ed. California State Department of Education, 51–79. Los Angeles: California State University Evaluation, Dissemination, and Assessment Center.

Lambert, Wallace. 1977. Culture and language as factors in learning and education. En *Current themes in linguistics: Bilingualism, experimental linguistics and language typologies*, ed. Fred Eckman, 15–21. Washington, DC: Hemisphere Publishing Co.

Laosa, Luis. 1975. Bilingualism in three United States Hispanic groups: Contextual use of language by children and adults in their families. *Journal of Educational Psychology* 67.5: 617–627.

Liu, Hua, Elizabeth Bates, y Ping Li. 1992. Sentence interpretation in bilingual speakers of English and Chinese. *Applied Psycholinguistics* 13: 451–484.

MacGregor-Mendoza, Patricia. 1999. Aquí no se habla español: Stories of linguistic repression in Southwest schools. Ponencia, XVII Congreso del Español en Estados Unidos, Miami, FL, March 11–13.

McCarty, Teresa L., Lucille J. Watahomigie, y Akira Y. Yamamoto. 1999. Introduction: Reversing language shift in indigenous America – collaborations and views from the field. *Practicing Anthropology* 20.2: 2–4.

Meyer, Doris L. 1977. The language issue in New Mexico, 1880–1900: Mexican American resistance against cultural erosion. *Bilingual Review/Revista Bilingüe* 4.1–2: 99–106.

Milk, Robert Dale. 1980. The issue of language education in Territorial New Mexico. *Bilingual Review* 7.3: 212–221.

Moskowitz, Breyne Arlene. 1985. The acquisition of language. En *Language*, 4th edition, ed. Virginia P. Clark, Paul A. Eschholz, y Alfred F. Rosa, 45–73. New York: St. Martin's Press.

Ornstein, Jacob. 1975. The archaic and the modern in Spanish of New Mexico. En *El lenguaje de los Chicanos: Regional and social characteristics of language used by Mexican Americans*, ed. Eduardo Hernández Chávez, Andrew D. Cohen, y Anthony F. Beltramo, 6–12. Arlington, VA: Center for Applied Linguistics.

Ortiz, Leroy I. 1975. A sociolinguistic study of language maintenance in the northern New Mexico community of Arroyo Seco. Ph.D. dissertation, University of New Mexico.

Piaget, Jean. 1974. *The language and thought of the child*. New York: New American Library.

Seliger, Herbert W. y Robert M. Vago. 1991. The study of first language attrition: An overview. En *First language attrition*, ed. Herbert W. Seliger y Robert Michael Vago, 3–15. Cambridge: Cambridge University Press.

Sims, Chris. 1999. Issues in language maintenance in the Native American communities of New Mexico. Colloquio patrocinado por la facultad de lingüística y el colegio de educación, Universidad de Nuevo México, Albuquerque, NM.

Skutnabb-Kangas, Tove. 1981. *Bilingualism or not: The education of minorities*. Clevedon, England: Multilingual Matters.

Skutnabb-Kangas, Tove y James Cummins, eds. 1988. *Minority education: From shame to struggle*. Clevedon, England: Multilingual Matters.

Swain, Merrill Kathleen y James Cummins. 1979. Bilingualism, cognitive functioning and education. *Language Teaching and Linguistics: Abstracts* 12: 4–18.

UNESCO. 1953. The use of vernacular languages in education. Paris: UNESCO.

Vigil, Neddy A. y Garland D Bills. 1997. A methodology for rapid dialect mapping of geographic features. En *Issues and methods in dialectology*, ed. Alan Thomas, 247–255. (Selected proceedings from the Ninth International Conference on Methods in Dialectology at the University of Wales). Bangor: University of Wales Press.

Vigil, Neddy A., Garland D. Bills, Ysaura Bernal-Enríquez, y Rodney A. Ulibarrí. 1996. El atlas lingüístico de Nuevo México y el sur de Colorado: Algunos resultados preliminares. En *Actas del X congreso internacional de la Asociación de Lingüística y Filología de la América Latina*, ed. Marina Arjona Iglesias, Juan López Chávez, Araceli Enríquez Ovando, Gilda C. López Lara, y Miguel Angel Novella Gómez, 651–663. México: Universidad Autónoma de México.

Vygotsky, Lev Semenovich. 1962. *Thought and language*. Cambridge: MIT Press.

Wells, C. Gordon. 1987. *The meaning makers*. London: Hodder and Stoughton.

Winsler, Adam, Rafael M. Díaz, Linda Espinosa, y James L. Rodríguez. 1999. When learning a second language does not mean losing the first: Bilingual language development in low-income, Spanish-speaking children attending bilingual preschool. *Child Development* 70.2: 349–362.

Wong-Fillmore, Lily. 1991a. Loss of a native language ability due to premature exposure to English. Ponencia plenaria en la junta de la Society for Research in Child Development. Seattle, WA.

Wong-Fillmore, Lily. 1991b. When learning a second language means losing the first. *Early Childhood Research Quarterly* 6: 323–346.

The Continuity of Change: Nahuatlisms in New Mexican Spanish

Garland D. Bills and Neddy A. Vigil
University of New Mexico

1. Introduction

This paper explores the occurrence in New Mexican Spanish of Nahuatlisms, that is, borrowings from Nahuatl, the language of the Aztecs of central Mexico and their descendants. New Mexican Spanish has many words that derive from the Nahuatl language, as does Southwest Spanish in general. Smead and Clegg (1990), for example, report finding 268 Nahuatlisms, and Emiliano (1976) lists some 130 basic (non-derived) Nahuatlisms 'commonly used by Chicanos.' Many of these Nahuatlisms were brought in by the first Spanish-speaking colonizers as much as 400 years ago. But others are the result of the four centuries of sustained, though hardly intimate, contact with the evolving Spanish of Mexico.

The data reported here derive from the New Mexico–Colorado Spanish Survey, the objectives of which are to document as comprehensively as possible the range of Spanish spoken in this region at the end of the 20th century. This project began in 1991 with funding from the National Endowment for the Humanities. Tape-recorded interviews were carried out with a diverse group of consultants distributed around the state of New Mexico and 16 counties of southern Colorado. The geographical scope of the project is shown in Map 1.

Several criteria went into the selection of consultants. First, all of our consultants were born and raised in the survey region. No immigrants were included because we assumed that the nature of a variety is determined primarily by those who acquire it in situ. Second, consultants had to have been exposed to Spanish as children and to have developed sufficient skill in the language to complete an interview that lasted a minimum of two hours. Third, consultants were selected to provide broad geographical distribution and balanced representation of both genders and three adult age groups within each sub-region.

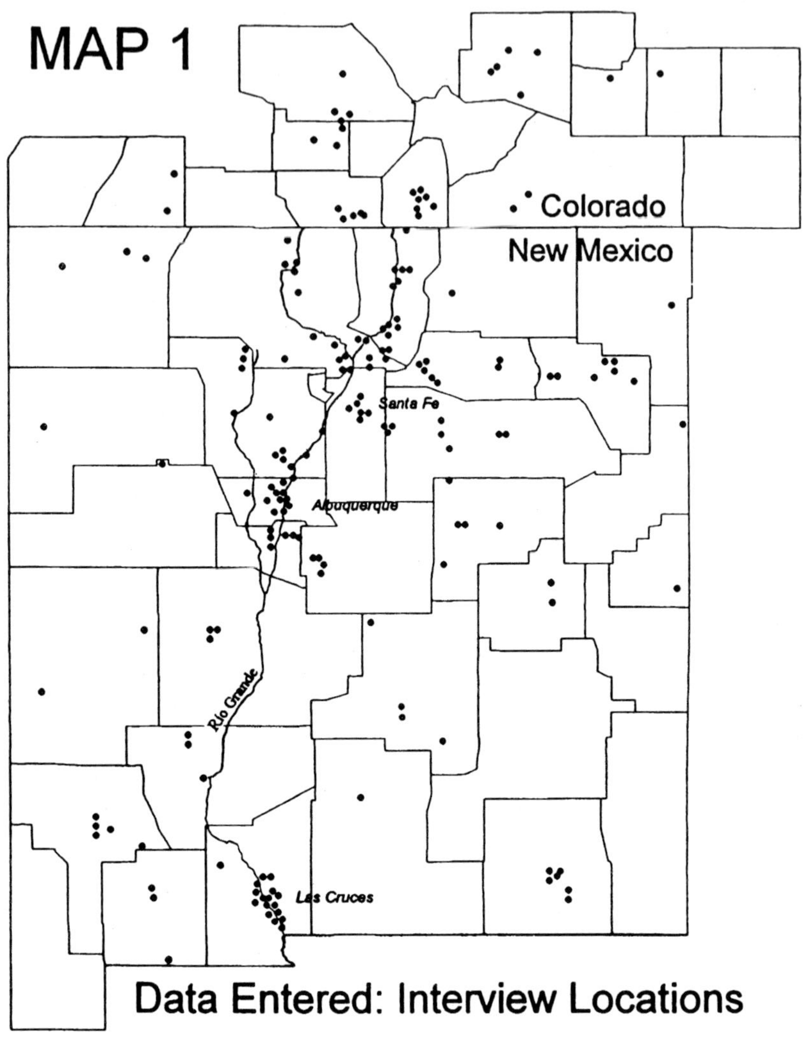

Interviews were conducted with a total of 350 individuals, and data collection was completed in 1995. Analysis of the approximately 1,200 hours of tape-recorded data is ongoing. While very little of the conversational discourse material has been examined as yet, the specifically elicited data – totaling more than 800 items per interview – have been entered into the computer for 181 consultants, just over half of the total. The geographical spread of these 181 individuals is represented by the black dots on Map 1.

Three highlights of the history of the region provide a broad understanding of the linguistic situation. First, the Spanish language was brought up from

Mexico into New Mexico 400 years ago, when the first permanent Spanish-speaking settlement was established in northern New Mexico in 1598. This was a remote colony. It was separated from central Mexico by a thousand miles of rugged desert terrain, and periodic conflicts with Indian groups along the route made communication still more difficult. Nevertheless, for 250 years almost all contact with the outside world was through Mexico. During the 17th century, that contact was pretty much limited to the trade and resupply caravans that usually arrived once a year. As settlement along the corridor to New Mexico expanded under the Spanish crown in the 18th century and under Mexican rule in the first half of the 19th century, the isolation of the region diminished, but the increasing contact was not strong enough to restrain the independent development of the New Mexico dialect.

The second historical highlight is the 1848 transfer of this region to the United States under the terms of the Treaty of Guadalupe Hidalgo following the Mexican–American War. Previously, distance had formed a barrier to communication with the rest of the Spanish-speaking world. Now a political boundary reinforced the New Mexicans' isolation from the main currents of their mother tongue.

The third historical circumstance is modern immigration, which has heightened contact with Mexico. In the late 19th century, the construction of railroads brought large numbers of Mexican immigrants into the U.S. Southwest. Additional masses of immigrants fled Mexico as a consequence of the Mexican Revolution of 1910. The U.S. had a great need for agricultural workers at the time. Finally, the economic expansion of the United States during the four decades following World War II has attracted massive numbers of immigrants.

Numerous scholars of the traditional New Mexico dialect have emphasized that the reduced contact with the mainstream of Spanish yielded a unique variety of Spanish (e.g. Hills 1906, Espinosa 1909, Rael 1937, Bowen 1952). At the same time, scholars have recognized that New Mexican Spanish remained closely related to Mexican Spanish. Like Southwest Spanish more generally, New Mexican Spanish is a variety of Mexican Spanish, that is, a sub-dialect of the Mexican macrodialect (Lozano 1977, Smead and Clegg 1990: 23). These varieties are united by commonalities in all aspects of linguistic structure: phonology, morphology, syntax, and lexicon. The extensive incorporation of loanwords from Nahuatl is perhaps the most apparent of these commonalities.

When the Spanish conquerors arrived in Mexico in 1527, the new foods, flora, fauna, and cultural artifacts they encountered required a new lexicon, partly created out of Spanish resources and partly borrowed from other languages. Nahuatl was the politically and economically dominant Native American language of the region at that time. Moreover, it was accepted as a lingua franca by the Spaniards, especially by the priests, who used it for the proselytization of Native Americans (Moreno de Alba 1988: 45). Need, influence, and opportunity conspired to make the Nahuatl language one of three major Native American contributors to the lexicon of New World Spanish.

All of the early settlers in New Mexico came up from Mexico, bringing a variety of Spanish which had developed across three-quarters of a century in Mexico. Many Nahuatl loanwords were already firmly established. Mexican Spanish has remained in contact with Nahuatl. As in the last century, whenever New Mexican Spanish has been in close contact with Mexican Spanish, new Nahuatlisms have entered the lexicon of New Mexican Spanish. Thus, even though there has been no direct contact between Nahuatl and the Spanish of New Mexico for four centuries, Nahuatlisms have continued to enter New Mexican Spanish.

We have organized the following discussion of Nahuatlisms in New Mexico by the probable time that each group of terms entered the region. We infer the probable time of entrance of each term primarily from its current spatial distribution in the area surveyed, though we also draw support from textual and other evidence in some cases. First, we present terms that were brought up from New Spain by early settlers and that thereby form part of the 'traditional Spanish' (Lope Blanch 1987) characteristic of northern New Mexico. Second, we discuss Nahuatlisms that were introduced over the past 100–150 years, including those that have only recently arrived. We conclude the treatment of later Nahuatlisms with some brief comments on the recent influences that are having a negative impact on the use of some Nahuatl borrowings.

2. Early Nahuatlisms

The early appearance of Nahuatlisms into New Mexico is associated with Spanish colonization in the 16th and 17th centuries. There were two key episodes in this early settlement. The first was the entrance of the original colonists led by Juan de Oñate in 1598. Eighty years later, in 1680, the entire colony was expelled from the territory by the Pueblo Revolt, a general uprising of the local Native Americans. In 1693, a second wave of settlers from Mexico joined with some of the original colonists to repopulate New Mexico with Spanish speakers. We can assume that the new settlers introduced some new Nahuatlisms from 17th century Mexican Spanish, but also employed many of the same Nahuatlisms as the first colonists.

Some Nahuatlisms are still in widespread use in both New Mexico and in Mexico with more or less the same general meaning they had for the early borrowers. An example of this type of maintenance, and possibly even expansion, can be seen in Map 2, which shows the distribution of one word for 'kite,' *papalote*, from Nahuatl *papalotl* 'butterfly.' (In order to focus on the distribution pattern of the Nahuatlism, these maps display only the Nahuatl-derived variants of the lexical variable, even though each variable has at least one other variant. Each data point is created from the geographical location represented by the consultant and is based on his or her first response to the stimulus, which was typically a picture illustrating the variable.)

The fact that *papalote* is used throughout the region indicates that it was brought into the area in the early period. It is also the first form offered by 101 of the 181 consultants. The other variant commonly used in New Mexico is a much later borrowing from English, *kite* [kajt], sometimes more phonologically integrated as *caite*.

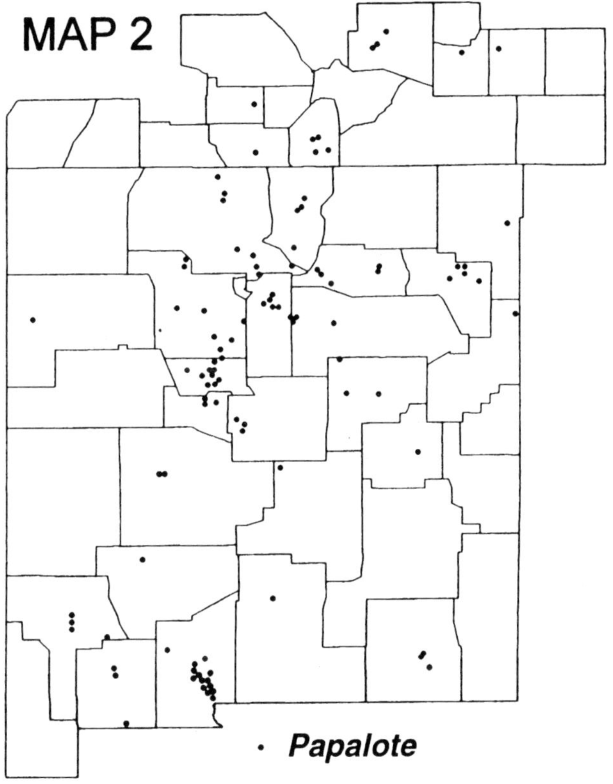

The distribution of *jacal* (from Nahuatl *xacalli*) for 'hut' in Map 3 shows a broad distribution pattern similar to that of *papalote* in Map 2, but with somewhat less density. The other two most widely used variants for the 'hut' variable are two borrowings from English, *chaque* (from *shack*) and *chante* (from *shanty*). Both *jacal* and *papalote* can be found in Mejías' list of Nahuatlisms that are documented in Mexico for both the 16th and 17th centuries and that continue to be borrowings of absolute general knowledge in Mexico in the 20th century (Mejías 1980: 153).

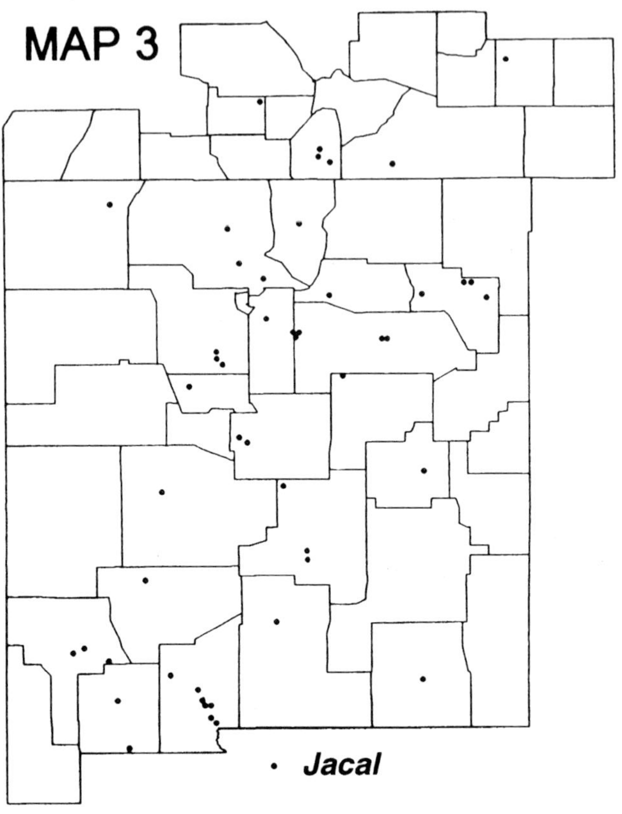

Many other Mexican Spanish words derived from Nahuatl remain in general use in New Mexico and were probably brought in during the colonial period. A sampling of some of the most common includes: *cuates* 'twins,' *cacahuates* 'peanuts,' *chocolate*, *jumate* 'dipper,' *tamal*, *tecolote* 'owl,' *zacate* 'grass,' *zoquete* 'mud,' *chapulín* 'grasshopper, locust,' *capulín* 'chokecherry,' *coyote*, *atole* 'blue corn gruel,' *posole* 'hominy stew with pork and chile,' *talache* 'pickaxe,' *chile*, *chichi* 'nipple,' and *mitote* 'gossip.'

A second category of early Nahuatl borrowings includes forms that were once in widespread use but are now disappearing. Such forms have a special distribution pattern: they are generally found only in the northern part of the survey region in rural areas where the early colonists settled. As is characteristic of relic forms, they are also used only by a small percentage of the consultants, typically the elderly. Map 4 shows two such forms elicited as labels for 'string': *mecate* (from Nahuatl *mecatl*) and *íchite* (from Nahuatl *ixtli*). In early New Mexico both forms probably referred to a cord made of vegetable fiber. As the artifact has developed into more refined manufactured string, the label has shifted to a more standard Spanish word, *cordón*.

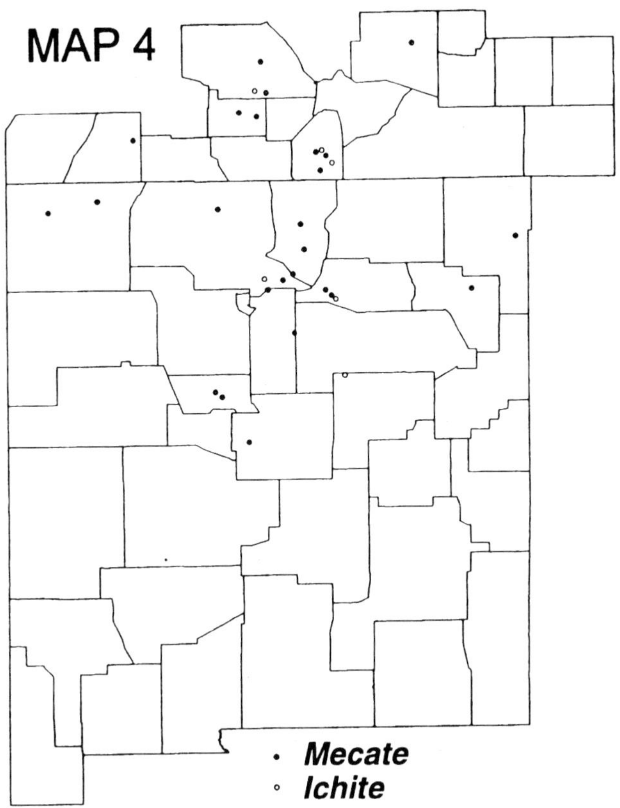

Another example of a form that is disappearing is *milpa* 'cornfield.' *Milpa* was apparently once in widespread use in New Mexico. There is, for example, a reference to "las milpas de Santa Fe" at the time of the Pueblo uprising (Twitchell 1914: 9). This Nahuatlism is rapidly being replaced by the English borrowing *fil* 'field.'

The third type of early Nahuatlisms are those that continue to be widely used but show a substantial change in form or meaning in comparison with the variant typical of Mexico. Such independent developments are one of the two major diachronic processes that contribute to the divergence of the Spanish dialect of New Mexico from that of Mexico (the other is borrowing from English). An example of this type of Nahuatlism is seen in Map 5, which shows the distribution patterns for two variants of the variable 'buzzard.' In Mexico the most general pronunciation for the Nahuatl borrowing is *zopilote* (from Nahuatl *zopilotl*). This form is also preferred by a number of New Mexican Spanish speakers (marked by black dots in Map 5). The most common variant in New Mexico, however, is *chupilote* (marked by open circles), illustrating an innovation in form independent from Mexico.

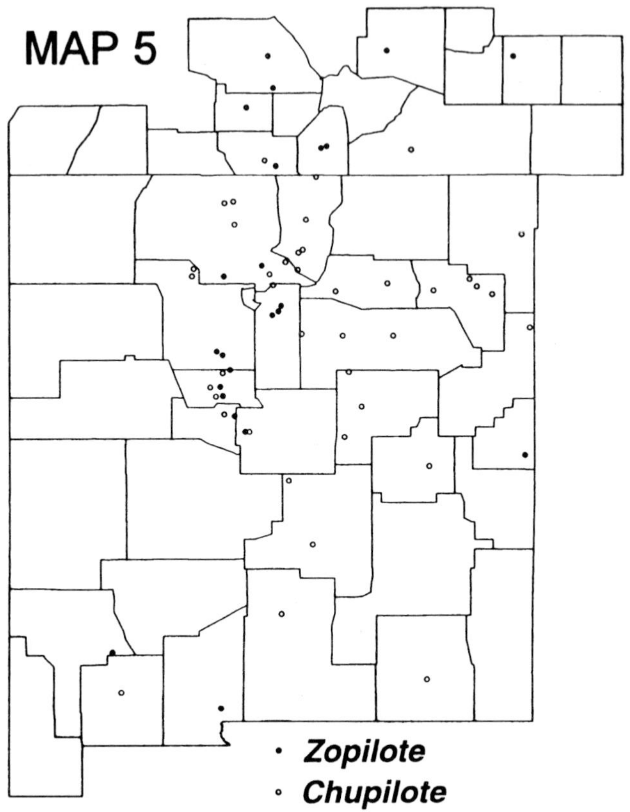

The term for 'water salamander' has undergone a more significant change. In Mexican Spanish, the form is *ajolote*, which derives from the Nahuatl *axolotl*. This is quite likely the form that was brought into New Mexico in the early period. However, the overwhelmingly common form in New Mexico today is *guajolote* (sometimes realized as *guajalote*). *Ajolote* was offered by only three consultants in southeastern Colorado. Semantic matters make this case more interesting. The forms *guajolote* and *guajalote* also have the meaning 'turkey,' deriving from Nahuatl *uexolotl* 'turkey.' The synonymy of *guajolote* may well be contributing to the rapid expansion of the English borrowing *torque* for 'turkey.'

An early Nahuatlism that shows a substantial change in meaning is *cajete*, a form whose geographical distribution is presented in Map 6. Like the Nahuatl source, *caxitl*, the word *cajete* in modern Mexican Spanish refers to an 'earthen bowl.' In New Mexico, the word has been extended to mean a 'metal tub' (marked by dots on Map 6) and the original meaning of an earthen bowl is generally lost. Map 6 also shows that the meaning of *cajete* has been further extended to 'bathtub' (marked by open circles) by some, generally younger, speakers.

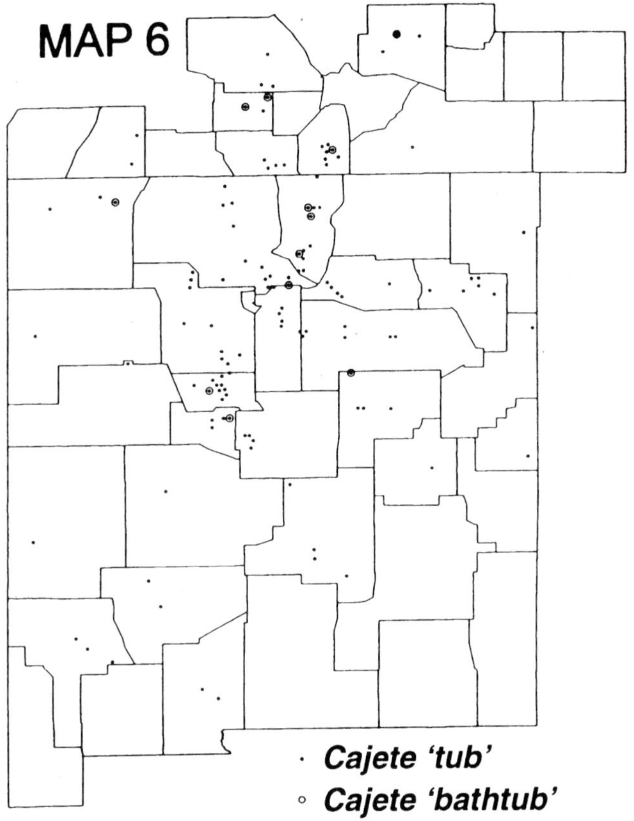

This kind of semantic extension has also occurred with the word *comal* (from Nahuatl *comalli*), which for the Aztecs was a flat earthen plate used for cooking corn tortillas. In Mexico that meaning is retained. In New Mexico, *comal* is now typically used to refer to a metal griddle (see Cobos 1983: 33). Moreover, some older respondents have even extended the meaning of this word to include 'frying pan.'

Another early Nahuatl borrowing that has changed meaning is the term *mitote*, derived from Nahuatl *mitotl*. For the Aztecs, a *mitotl* was a type of dance with drinking (Santamaría 1959: 728). Cobos reports that in colonial New Mexico *mitote* referred to "a dance with drinking and a great deal of noise." He supports this claim with a translation from the *Colección de documentos inéditos* of the Espejo expedition into New Mexico: "And day and night, during the three days that we stayed there, they always made *mitotes* and balls, and dances" (Cobos 1983: 112). The early meaning of a loud party has been retained in Mexico, while in New Mexico *mitote* appears to now be restricted to the meaning 'gossip.'

An example of change in both form and meaning can be demonstrated with Map 7, which shows the distribution of two Nahuatlisms for 'trunk': *petaca* (black dots) and *petaquilla* (open circles).

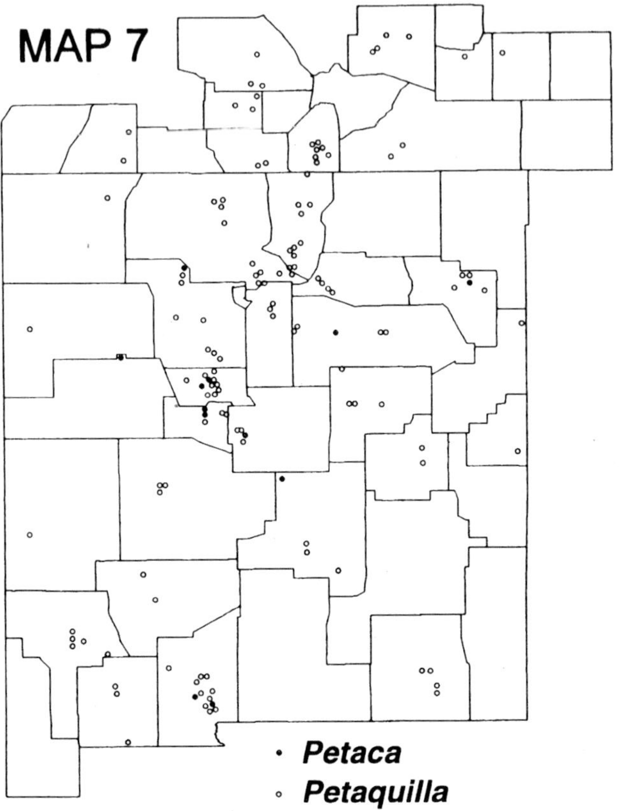

Petaquilla appears to be a diminutive form of the earlier *petaca* (derived from Nahuatl *petlacalli*). *Petaca* continues to refer to a kind of trunk in Mexico. The diminutive form, *petaquilla*, is documented in the 16th and 17th centuries, but is not generally known in the 20th century (Mejías 1980: 53). It meant 'a woven basket for carrying fruits and such' in Mexico (Santamaría 1959: 838), though it can now also mean 'a small trunk or suitcase.' Lope Blanch (1979) found that *petaca* is widely known in Mexico City nowadays, but *petaquilla* does not even fall into his 'almost unknown' category. Conversely, in New Mexico the form *petaquilla* has almost totally replaced *petaca.*

3. Later Nahuatlisms

The 1848 Treaty of Guadalupe Hidalgo transferred a large part of Mexico to the United States at the end of the Mexican-American War. Suddenly there was a political border separating Mexico from New Mexico. The immediate border area remained porous to the coming and going of people who spoke the same language and had once been under the same flag. The presence of an already established population and the lack of economic opportunities, however, discouraged movement further north into New Mexico. In fact, the population was so dense in northern New Mexico that settlers from that area left to colonize the San Luis Valley in southern Colorado in the middle of the 19th century.

Several events over the last 150 years have contributed to the deeper penetration of modern Mexican influence into most parts of New Mexico and southern Colorado. During the late 19th century, Mexican immigrants came to the U.S. to work on the railroads, in the mines, and in the expanding agricultural industry (Martinez 1957: 7–11). From 1910 to 1917 the political, social, and economic instability created by the Mexican Revolution encouraged Mexicans to emigrate to the American Southwest. The loss of young American men in the First World War also created a need for braceros, laborers admitted legally for a short period.

Yet, "of the four border states, New Mexico in 1920 had the smallest Mexican population. . . . The absence of agricultural or industrial diversification has always kept the number of Mexican immigrants comparatively low in New Mexico" (Martinez 1957: 67–68). Many of the braceros were migratory because of the seasonal nature of the crops and returned to Mexico for the winter. Those who moved to Colorado were less likely to be transitory, since they could work in the mines during the cold season. The Great Depression era and implosion of cotton during the 1930s reduced Mexican immigration to New Mexico even further. Immigration increased strongly again during World War II. In the decades after the war, the powerful United States economy has continued to lure Mexican workers north.

The Nahuatlisms that entered later into New Mexico reflect this history of immigration. Quite naturally, the geographical distribution of later borrowings tends to conform to those areas that have received the bulk of the immigration from Mexico over the last 100 years: the southern third of the state closest to the border; agricultural areas of the eastern plains, the San Luis Valley of south-central Colorado, and along the Arkansas River of southeastern Colorado; the mining and industry areas of northwestern New Mexico; and the major cities. On the other hand, these words tend not to occur in the rural areas of north-central New Mexico where the traditional Spanish is strongest, though there is evidence that the new terms are displacing some traditional forms.

An example of a later Nahuatlism is the adjective used for a spoiled child. Map 8 shows that *chiple* (from Nahuatl *tzipitl*) is most strongly represented in the southern part of New Mexico, with scattered occurrences elsewhere, particularly in and around Albuquerque and Santa Fe. This borrowing is conspicuously absent in the rural north, where the most common term for the same concept is *echado a perder*.

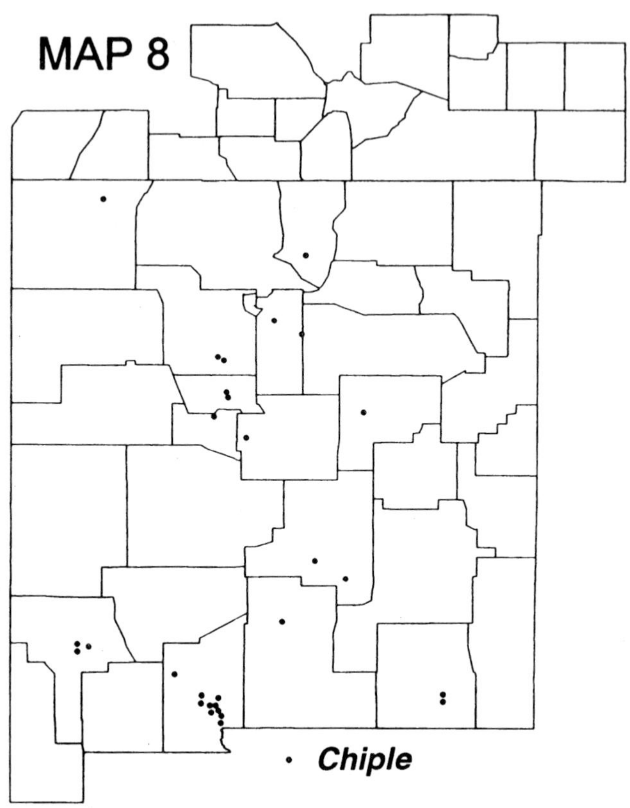

Another example of a term that entered later into New Mexico is *ejote* (from Nahuatl *exotl*) for 'green bean,' illustrated in Map 9. This Nahuatlism has a distribution pattern very similar to that for *chiple* in Map 8, though here we also see a couple of occurrences along the Arkansas River in Colorado. The traditional term for a green bean in New Mexican Spanish is *frijol* or *frijol verde*.

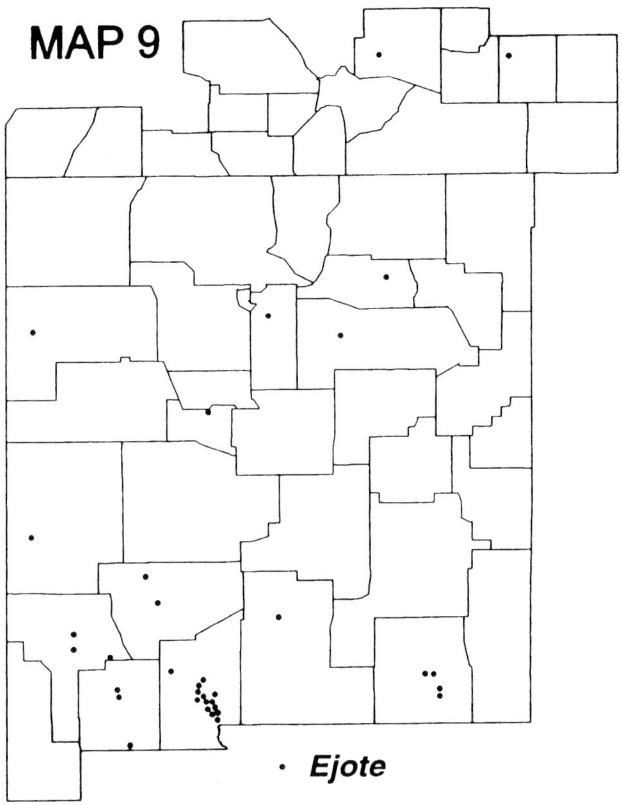

Nahuatlisms of very recent entry are found mostly in the far southern part of the state along the border. Map 10 demonstrates the pattern very clearly. The geographical distribution of *esquite* (from Nahuatl *izquitl*) for 'popcorn' is much more limited than those of *chiple* and *ejote* in Maps 8 and 9. *Esquite* is restricted, except for two respondents, to the far south. It is the weakest of the competing forms in the survey region; much more prominent are the traditional *rositas* or *rositas de maíz*, the general Mexican *palomitas*, and the English borrowing *popcorn*.

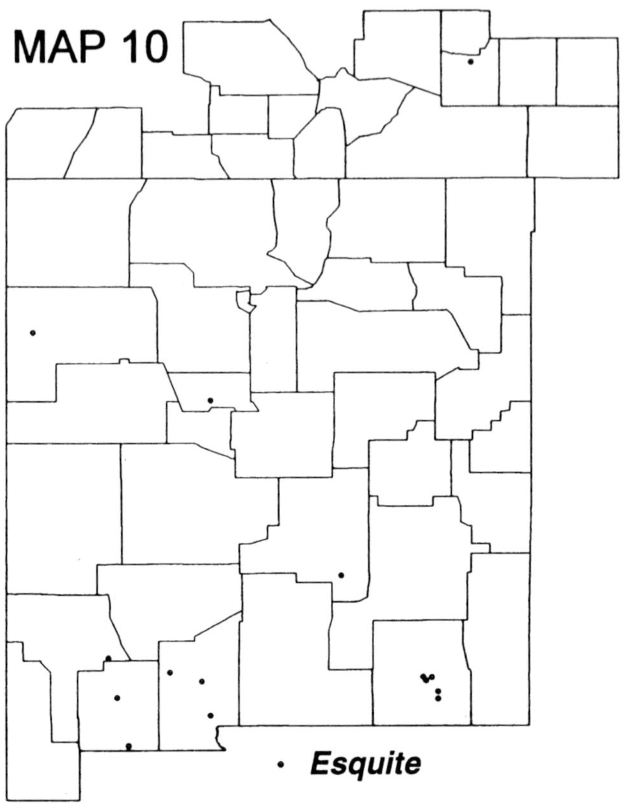

Another very recent entry is *piocha* (from Nahuatl *piochtli*) for 'chin' (see Map 11). This term only occurs in the extreme south, indicating that it crossed the border only recently. The general variant for 'chin' in the survey region is *barbilla*.

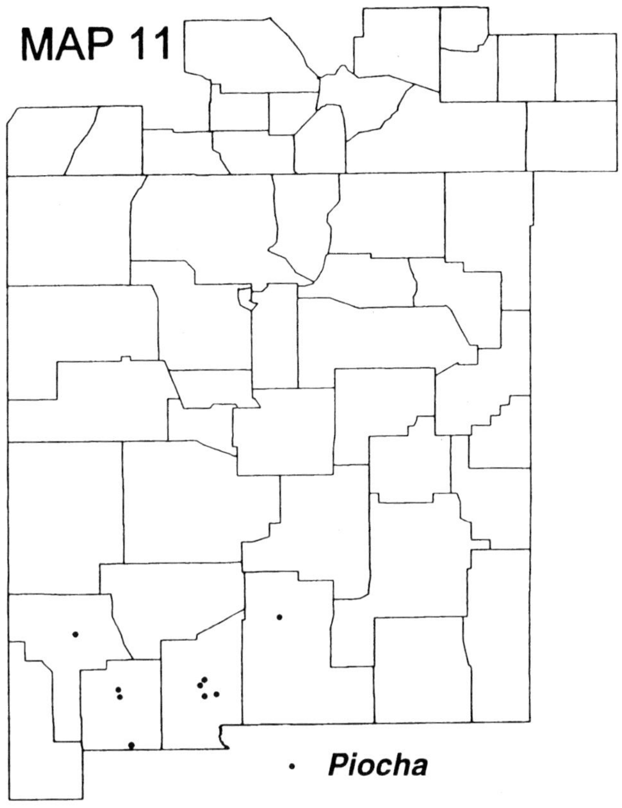

Another Nahuatlism with restricted distribution in the southern part of New Mexico is *moyote* (Nahuatl *moyotl*) for 'mosquito.' A prominent form in the northern part of the state and southern Colorado is *jején*, a borrowing from the Taíno language of the Caribbean that must have been brought by the earliest settlers. Yet a third form, *mosquito*, appears to have the greatest strength, no doubt because of its identity with the English form.

While later immigration from Mexico has brought in a variety of new Nahuatlisms, it has also introduced other lexical items. Sometimes these other forms wind up in competition with the Nahuatlisms that entered earlier. One example of this external pressure on the maintenance of traditional Nahuatlisms is the third variant for 'buzzard.' The standard form *aura* has the distribution pattern of a very recent entry from Mexico. It will now be competing with the early Nahuatlism *zopilote* and its derivative *chupilote* (see Map 5).

In addition, some English borrowings are expanding at the expense of Nahuatl borrowings. *Kite* and *caite*, for example, are making inroads on the *papalote* form of Map 1. While nearly 90 percent of the consultants over age 72 offered *papalote*, only 45 percent of those under 40 did so. Similarly, the Anglicism *torque* seems to be rapidly replacing the traditional Nahuatlisms *guajolote*, *cócano*, and *güíjalo* as the preferred label for 'turkey.' A form that has all but disappeared is *tequesquite* 'baking soda' (from Nahuatl *tetl* 'stone' and *quizquitl* 'efflorescent'; Cobos 1983: 162). The word was certainly used in the region; one now-abandoned Hispanic village in northeastern New Mexico which had a post office in 1879–90 was named Tequesquite (Williams 1986: 139). When asked to identify the contents of a box of baking soda, however, not one of these 181 consultants responded with *tequesquite*. The two most common forms used in New Mexico today are *salaruta* and *soda de martillo*.

4. Conclusion

The examination of the geographical distribution of a small set of lexical items, these Nahuatlisms, provides a fascinating glimpse into the linguistic interchange that has marked, and continues to mark, the development of the Spanish language in New Mexico. Much remains to be done, of course. There are four ways that we hope to enhance the scope of our findings in the future. First, completion of the computerized database of specifically elicited data for all 350 consultants will provide crisper pictures of geographical distributions, though it is unlikely to significantly affect the results discussed here. Second, examination of the conversational and narrative portions of the interviews will provide useful supplementary documentation of Nahuatlisms. Third, analysis of the relationship of Nahuatlisms to sociological variables such as age, gender, education, and formal study of Spanish will enable us to perceive more clearly the directions of present trends in lexical choice. Finally, and of utmost importance, publication of the lexical volumes of the Atlas Lingüístico de México (Lope Blanch et al. 1990–) will permit us to relate our findings to the situation in Mexico and determine more accurately the historical relationship between the two varieties of Spanish, including perhaps the influence of immigration from specific areas of Mexico.

References

Bowen, Jean Donald. 1952. *The Spanish of San Antoñito, New Mexico.* Albuquerque, NM: University of New Mexico dissertation.

Cobos, Rubén. 1983. *A dictionary of New Mexico and southern Colorado Spanish.* Santa Fe: Museum of New Mexico Press.

Emiliano, Ramón. 1976. Nahuatlan elements in Chicano speech. *Grito del Sol* 1.4: 89–108.

Espinosa, Aurelio M. 1909. Studies in New Mexican Spanish, part I: Phonology. *University of New Mexico Bulletin/Language Series* 1.2: 47–162.

Hills, Elijah Clarence. 1906. New Mexican Spanish. *PMLA* 21: 706–753.

Lope Blanch, Juan M. 1979. *Léxico indígena en el español de México. 2a ed. aumentada.* México: Colegio de México.

Lope Blanch, Juan M. 1987. El estudio del español hablado en el suroeste de los Estados Unidos. *Anuario de Letras* 25: 201–208.

Lope Blanch, Juan M. et al. 1990–. *Atlas lingüístico de México*. México: El Colegio de México/Fondo de Cultura Económica.
Lozano, Anthony G. 1977. El español chicano y la dialectología. *Aztlán* 7: 13–18.
Martínez, John Ramon. 1957. *Mexican emigration to the United States, 1910–1930*. Berkeley, CA: University of California dissertation.
Mejías, Hugo A. 1980. *Préstamos de lenguas indígenas en el español americano del siglo XVII*. México: Universidad Nacional Autónoma de México, Instituto de Investigaciones Filológicas.
Moreno de Alba, José G. 1988. *El español en América*. México: Fondo de Cultural Económica.
Rael, Juan B. 1937. *A study of the phonology and morphology of New Mexican Spanish based on a collection of 410 folk-tales*. Stanford, CA: Stanford University dissertation.
Santamaría, Francisco J. 1959. *Diccionario de mejicanismos*. México: Editorial Porrúa.
Smead, Robert N. and J. Halvor Clegg. 1990. Aztequismos en el español chicano. In *Spanish in the United States: Sociolinguistic issues*, ed. John J. Bergen, 23–30. Washington, DC: Georgetown University Press.
Twitchell, Ralph Emerson. 1914. *The Spanish archives of New Mexico. Vol. 2*. Cedar Rapids, IA: Torch Press.
Williams, Jerry L. 1986. *New Mexico in maps. 2nd ed.* Albuquerque: University of New Mexico Press.

Morphological Adaptation of Anglicisms into the Spanish of the Southwest

J. Halvor Clegg
Brigham Young University

1. Introduction

Borrowing in the Spanish of the Southwest is a phenomenon recorded as early as Hills (1906) and Espinosa (1909). The studies done by Espinosa (1909–1913) are still considered to be the most complete of any U.S. variety (Teschner, Bills, and Craddock 1975). Espinosa not only noted the presence of Anglicisms in the Spanish of the Southwest, but made limited generalizations as to the processes that take place in their adaptation. He noted that the process allows for multiple influences, but his morphological analysis deals with deviations from Standard Spanish and does not treat morphological adaptation of Anglicisms. These early observations are typical of work done to the present which repeat the same theme of deviation from Standard Spanish, including phenomena which are essentially lexical in nature, such as noun gender. The only partially morphological analyses in relatively recent times come from Anthony Beltramo (1972) and J. Donald Bowen (1975). Bowen's work is largely phonological in nature, but some morphological data can be extracted from it. Beltramo actually deals with morphological adaptation as a given phenomenon; his work is done on a more general plane but gives some direction into types of adaptation.

Nevertheless, the morphological adaptation of Anglicisms merits additional study and is important to linguistics in general because it provides an insight into how language works. In order to study this phenomenon more completely and systematically, corpora were created using Galván and Teschner's *The Dictionary of Chicano Spanish/Diccionario del español chicano* (DEC) and the *Diccionario de la Real Academia Española* (DRAE). The DRAE corpus was included to provide a comparison to the corpus from the DEC. In each case the Anglicisms were extracted and detailed analyses were done on the borrowed forms.

2. Word creation

Three processes are typical of word creation in the Spanish and English languages: word compounding, morphological synthesis, and loanwords. Word compounding may be accomplished through the use of multiple words or phrases, e.g. *black tie event*, *high school*, *hombre rana*, *ballena macho*. Word compounding is very common in English but is not as common in Spanish. An evolution of word compounding is word combining, in which the multiple words become one word, e.g. *mailman*, *grandmother*, *sinvergüenza*, *sabelotodo*. Word combining occurs in both languages but again is more common in English.

Morphological synthesis is the normal pattern in all languages and has more manifestations in some languages than in others. Spanish is more highly inflected than English and consequently has greater possibilities of synthesis. The normal pattern of synthesis in both languages is to begin with a root or base form. This form is semantic in nature and carries the weight of meaning for the entire word. In fact, the root often appears alone as a free word or morpheme: *skate*, *song*, *toro*, *silla*, etc. Other forms may be added to the root. These may be other root morphemes, as in *television*, *astrodome*, *pelirrojo*, and *cabizbajo*, or the root form may be combined with derived forms which are semantic forms that never occur separately (called bound morphemes), as in *skater*, *unacceptable*, *torero*, and *sillón*. A second bound form that may be added to all the other morphemes is an inflected form. Inflected morphemes are grammatical in nature as opposed to semantic and are called inflected because they apply to all the members of a given grammatical category. Examples of inflected morphemes are the plurals on nouns (*house/houses*, *casa/casas*) and verb conjugations (*run/runs*, *correr/corre*). Inflected morphemes are much more common than derived morphemes in usage.

Loanwords are words that come from other languages. The general pattern for the use of loanwords is for a foreign concept to enter into the host language. The host speaker then must choose what form to use to represent the concept. This may be accomplished by using a suitable synonym (*gaseosa/soda*), by using a host form with a new meaning (*baloncesto/basquetbol*) called a calque, or by simply borrowing the foreign word form and meaning (*sputnik*, *spaghetti*). Borrowings show at least two interesting motivations. Either the word is new or the speaker chooses this form to emphasize English usage. The speaker may be trying to use the prestige language (English) to show his/her superiority. A second purpose is commercial; products with an English name are considered more desirable. Consequently, throughout the Hispanic world there are products and establishments with English names or English-like names such as *Lupe's Beauty Parlor*, *Firestone* (pronounced in Spanish), or *Sears* (pronounced in Spanish as well), the prestige department store chain in Mexico.

If a loanword endures in the language it invariably becomes adapted to the linguistic structures of the host language. The two most important adaptations are phonological and morphological. The basic rule in both cases is for the host language to follow the nearest neighbor principle and adapt the borrowing to its own nearest approximation in the foreign structure either phonologically (Clegg and Smead 1991) or morphologically. For example, the word *volleyball* adapted to Spanish has the form *voleibol*. The phonological processes follow the written form in the {o} > [o], reduce the {ll} > [l], follow the written form in the {ey} > [ei]. The form [ból] can be either a phonological adaptation of {*ball*} or a morphologically adapted form to [ból] < {*bola*}. There is even an accent shift to better reflect Spanish phonotactics.

3. Possible forms of adaptations

Which are the possible forms that could be adapted into the Spanish of the Southwest? An analysis of the Juilland and Chang-Rodríguez (1964) *Frequency dictionary of Spanish words* shows the following proportions for a total of the 5024 most commonly used words:

(1) Inflected forms in Juilland and Chang-Rodríguez 1964

Nouns	2549	50.7%
Adjectives (including articles)	1205	24.0%
Verbs	957	19.1%
Pronouns	52	1.0%

(2) Non-inflected forms in Juilland and Chang-Rodríguez 1964

Prepositions	15	0.3%
Conjunctions	19	0.4%
Adverbs	185	3.7%
Interjections	7	0.1%
Cardinal numbers	35	0.7%

These statistics indicate that borrowings should fall among the more common word forms: the nouns, adjectives, and verbs. The percentages represent a part of the total (5024) and are included to provide a comparison with the forms that actually do get borrowed in the Spanish of the Southwest.

An analysis of Galván and Teschner's (1977) *El diccionario del español chicano / The dictionary of Chicano Spanish* shows a total of 888 Anglicisms. As would be expected, 98% of these fall among the nouns, adjectives, and verbs.

(3) Anglicisms in the DEC

Nouns	632	71%
Adjectives	28	3%
Verbs	213	24%
Interjections	14	2%

An analysis of the *Diccionario de la Real Academia Española* shows a total of 350 Anglicisms. Again, 99% of these fall among the nouns, adjectives, and verbs.

(4) Anglicisms in the DRAE

Nouns	308	88%
Adjectives	14	4%
Verbs	26	7%
Interjections	2	1%

An examination of the statistics shows that the borrowing is generally the same for both sources. Nouns are the form most borrowed. They are also the most numerous form in the Spanish language in general (50.7% according to Juilland and Chang-Rodríguez). The majority of words accepted by the DRAE have entered into the language through educated sources, in particular the written page, and have been highly filtered through the institutional resistance of the Real Academia Española. The borrowings in the Southwest have largely entered through oral sources and gone into a community with no effective filter since the Hispanics in the Southwest have little or no education in Spanish. As a result, a borrowing from English is a more logical alternative for them than a learned Spanish form since they tend to be more educated in English than in Spanish. In addition to education, Hispanics in the Southwest live in an English-dominant society. This also contributes to borrowing because it allows a more semantically precise loanword to be used for a concept in place of a linguistically imposed approximation.

4. Types of adaptation

How are these words adapted? There are five types of adaptation: visual, oral, calques, partially adapted forms, and non-adapted forms. These same types of adaptation function not only in the Spanish of the Southwest but in the Spanish language in general.

Visual adaptations occur when the word is seen in written form rather than pronounced. Some examples taken from the DRAE and the DEC are *boxear*, *iceberg*, and *pijama* from the DRAE, and *zíper*, *escúrer* (scooter), and *mopear* from the DEC. Visual adaptations are more frequent in Spanish in general than in the Spanish of the Southwest. This is because the medium through which the Anglicism is exposed to other Spanish speakers is more likely to be written.

Oral adaptations occur when the word is heard rather than seen in written form. Some examples are *beibisira* (babysitter), *chahua* (shower), and *morosaico* (motorcycle) from the DEC, and *crup* (croup), *interviú*, and *drenar* (to drain) from the DRAE. Oral adaptations are much more common in the

Spanish of the Southwest since the medium of exposure is largely the spoken language.

Calques are words that have Spanish form with an English meaning. Some examples are *baloncesto*, *interfaz*, and *tranvía* (< tramway) from the DRAE, and *ignorar* (not pay attention to), *electar*, and *mayor* (city mayor) from the DEC.

Partially adapted forms are words that are adapted only in part and thus retain vestiges of English form. Examples are *beicon*, *hamburguesa*, and *voleibol* from the DRAE, and *jámborger*, *jey fíver*, and *tícher* from the DEC.

Non-adapted forms are words that are incorporated phonologically but not morphologically. Some examples are *gángster*, *récord*, and *clip(e)* from the DRAE, and *blóaut*, *cartún*, and *fultaim* from the DEC.

5. The process of adaptation as seen in the Spanish of the Southwest

The first step in adaptation is to begin with a loanword. The loanword may then undergo any of the types of adaptation shown previously. To be adapted, the loanword functions as a root, which in turn undergoes normal morphological synthesis for Spanish. In the example (5) the loanwords *wine*, *milk*, and *spell* function as root forms which then undergo morphological synthesis adding both derived and inflected forms.

(5) Word formation

en + guayn (< wine) + ar(se) = enguaynarse
a + milc (< milk) + ado (analogy with *aguado)* = amilcado
e + spel (< spell) + et (analogy with *deletrear)* + ear = espeletear

As part of the process, the root form is adapted phonologically and phonotactically following the nearest neighbor principle. The purpose of phonotactic adaptation is to eliminate foreign consonant clusters as well as foreign consonant endings.

(6) Phonological adaptation of the root

clutch [klʌ́ʧ] > [klóʧ]; *plug* [plʌ́g] > [plóg]; *bat* [bǽt] > [bát];
cookie [kʊ́ki] > [kúki]; *natch (<naturally)* [nǽʧ] > [náʧ];

dodge [dáʤ] > [dóʧ]; *antifreeze* [ǽntɪfriḭz] > [antifrís]; *rim* [rɪm] > [r̄ín];
cheating [ʧiíʔən]/[ʧiíɾɪŋ] > [ʧírin]; *starter* [stáɾɚ] > [estár];
pickle [pɪkəɫ] > [píkl]

(7) Phonotactic adaptation of the root

a. Vowel endings /a/, /e/, /o/ *(/i/ < English /j/)
[klóʧ] + [e] = cloche (DRAE); [plóg] + [a] = ploga;
[bát] + [e] = bate (DRAE); [náʧ] + [o] = nacho; [kúki] = cuqui;
[dóʧ] + [e] = doche

b. Consonant endings /s/, /n/, /l/, /r/, /x/, /d/
[antifrís] = antifrís; [r̄ín] = rin; [ʧírin] = chirin; [stárɚ] > [estár] + [a];
[píkl] + [e] = picle; raid, detur, pul, fain, beis

The other part of the process involves normal morphological synthesis for Spanish. In the example (8), the loanwords that function as root forms undergo morphological synthesis adding either derived or inflected forms. The morphological adaptation generally follows the same pattern as the phonological one: the nearest neighbor principle.

(8) Morphological adaptation: inflected endings

Noun forms (-(*e*)*s*)
mompe*s* (mumps), moni*s* (money plural), chapa*s* (choppers)
Verb forms (*-ar*, *-ear*/*iar*)(*-ado*/*a*,*-ido*/*a*)
chus*ar*, chus*ear*, chus*iar*
feil*ar*, feil*ear*, feil*iar*
soc*ado* (soaked), trimiada, entosequ*ido* (intoxicated)
Adjective forms (*-o*/*-a*)(*-s*)(**ado*/*a*)
fone (funny), escante (scant), jaitón (high-toned)
tabaque*ado* (tobacco-smelling), naque*ado* (knocked-out),
soc*ado* (soaked)

The inflected forms are standard forms for the nouns. This is to be expected because of the similarity in noun inflection between the two languages. There are some interesting cases of loanwords that end in {-y} in English. These often are pronounced as an [i] in the Spanish of the Southwest, for example *poni*, *moni*, etc.

In the case of the verbs, the most frequent inflected form in our corpus is the /-ear/ ending with 85, followed by /-iar/ with 68, /-ar/ with 59, /-er/ with two and /-er/ with one. These latter two forms occur in calques (*asumir* and *atender*) along with two other calques ending in /-izar/ (*realizar* and *enfatizar*). These numbers change significantly when the two forms /-ear/ and /-iar/ are counted as allomorphs, giving a total of 153 for the variant forms of that morpheme. If the /-e/i-/ vowel is considered as part of the root, the result is basically an all /-ar/ inflection. There is considerable flexibility in which form is chosen. In the examples given, all three endings appear as possibilities. Multiple options are not uncommon.

The majority of the adjective forms are past participles used as adjectives. Some of these show delightful ingenuity in their formation. *Amilcado* was created by analogy with the Spanish *aguado* meaning "watered down," only the case here is "milked down." *Tiniado* has no equivalent in English and was created to describe a person high on paint thinner. *Tabaqueado* is the same type of word which means "smelling of tobacco." Other creations are *craqueado*, *entosequido*, *trimiado*, and *estraquiado* for *cracked*, *intoxicated*, *trimmed*, and *struck*.

(9) Derived forms

-ito/a: forc*ito* (Fordcito) babito (Bobby), chequead*ita*
-azo/a: hit*azo*, fon*azo*, por*azo* (big pore < party)
-ero/era: guain*ero*, troqu*ero*, lonch*era*
-udo/a: tof*udo* (real tough)

6. Conclusions

The creation of corpora of borrowings allows us to analyze the morphological adaptation of Anglicisms into the Spanish of the Southwest. This adaptation follows the general pattern of word creation, including morphological synthesis and the use of loanwords. Word compounding is also used, though less frequently. Those forms which most readily lend themselves to borrowing are the inflected forms, specifically nouns, verbs, and adjectives, which comprise 94% of the words of the Spanish language. 98% of the Anglicisms in the DEC and 99% of those found in the DRAE are nouns, verbs, and adjectives.

There are five general types of adaptation: (1) visual, which is the case in Spanish in general, (2) oral, which is generally the case in the Spanish of the Southwest, (3) calques from English, (4) partial adaptations which have mixed phonotactics, and (5) non-adapted forms appearing as Spanish phonological pronunciations of English words. The process of adaptation involves the use of a loanword which functions as a root form and is adapted phonologically and phonotactically. The root form also goes through normal morphological synthesis in which either derived or inflected forms are added. Throughout this process the nearest neighbor principle is followed.

The normal processes of language are evident in the morphological adaptation of Anglicisms into Spanish. Both the speakers and the institutions that preserve the Spanish language are also active in the innovation and enrichment that takes place.

References

Beltramo, Anthony F. 1972. Lexical and morphological aspects of linguistic acculturation by Mexican-Americans in San Jose, California. Ph.D. dissertation, Stanford University.

Bowen, J. Donald. 1975. Adaptation of English borrowing. In *El lenguaje de los chicanos*, ed. Anthony F. Beltramo et al., 115–121. Arlington, VA: Center for Applied Linguistics.

Clegg, J. Halvor and Robert N. Smead. 1991. Phonological adaptation of English lexicon in the Spanish of the Southwest. Paper read at the XIIth Annual Conference on Spanish in the United States and 1st International Conference on Spanish in Contact with Other Languages, November 7–9, University of Southern California, Los Angeles, CA.

Espinosa, Aurelio Macedonio. 1909. Studies in New Mexican Spanish. Part I: Phonology. *University of New Mexico Bulletin, Language Series* 1.2.53: 141–150. Albuquerque: University of New Mexico Press.

Espinosa, Aurelio Macedonio. 1911–13. Studies in New Mexican Spanish. Part II: Morphology. *Revue de Dialectologie Romane* 3: 251–286 (1911); 4: 241–256 (1912); 5: 142–172 (1913).

Espinosa, Aurelio Macedonio. 1914–15. Studies in New Mexican Spanish. Part III: The English elements. *Revue de Dialectologie Romane* 6: 241–317.

Galván, Robert A. and Richard V. Teschner. 1977. *El diccionario del español chicano / The dictionary of Chicano Spanish*. Silver Spring, MD: Institute of Modern Languages.

Hills, Elijah Clarence. 1906. New Mexican Spanish. *PMLA* 21: 739–753.

Juilland, Alphonse and E. Chang-Rodríguez. 1964. *Frequency dictionary of Spanish words*. The Hague: Mouton.

Real Academia Española. 1995. *Diccionario de la lengua española, vigésima primera edición, edición en CD-ROM*. Madrid: Espasa-Calpe.

Reyes, Rogelio. 1981. Independent convergence in Chicano and New York City Puerto Rican bilingualism. In *Latino language and communicative behavior*, ed. Richard P. Duran, 39–48. Norwood, NJ.

Teschner, Richard V., Garland D. Bills, and Jerry R. Craddock. 1975. *Spanish and English of United States Hispanos: A critical, annotated, linguistic bibliography*. Arlington, VA: Center for Applied Linguistics.

Phrasal Calques in Chicano Spanish: Linguistic or Cultural Innovation?

Robert N. Smead
Brigham Young University

1. Introduction

Recent forays into lexical borrowing from English among bilingual Hispanics have proven quite fruitful. In addition to Smead and Clegg (1996) on calquewords and Smead (1998) on loanwords, other researchers have recently considered another important albeit controversial category, the phrasal calque. For example, Lipski (1985) provides a detailed analysis of *pa(ra) (a)trás* 'back' in Spanish–English contact varieties the world over, while Otheguy (1991, 1995a, 1995b), using examples from Cuban-American Spanish, has reexamined phrasal calquing from a theoretical perspective. Other researchers who have recently considered calquing at both the word and phrase level include Silva-Corvalán (1994, 1995) in her study of Spanish in East Los Angeles, and Montes-Giraldo (1985) for Colombian Spanish. Example (1) illustrates and defines the phrasal calque in conjunction with the loan(word) and calqueword.

(1) **A typology of Anglicisms**

Loan: *high school* or *jaiscul* [háiskul]
Both the form (signifier) and the meaning (signified) derive from English.

Calqueword: *colegio* 'college or university'
Composed of a simple Spanish form with an English meaning overlaid.

Phrasal calque: *escuela alta*
A multiword or compound unit which employs native elements but is patterned after English. These can be classified as collocations (fixed or semi-fixed expressions).[1]

Running Lope Blanch's (1990) data through *Word Cruncher* (1989) provides contextualized, real-life examples of these Anglicisms. (The coding material at the end of each citation identifies the consultant as male or female, provides his or her age and place of residence at the time the interview was conducted, indicates the extent of formal education or the social class of the consultant and includes the page and paragraph number from the published version).

(2) Lo que les pidía es que acaben su escuela, porque mi esposo acabó la escuela, pos – ¿cómo se dice? – la **high school**. Y graduó del **colegio** de aquí.

'What I asked them to do was to finish their schooling, because my husband finished his schooling – well, how do you say it? – (up through) high school. And he graduated from college here.'

(F, 37, San Marcos, Texas, grade school, 108: 3)

(3) Ahora lo echaron afuera de la **high school**, de la **escuela alta**, porque fallaba mucho.

'Now they threw him out of high school because he was failing a lot.'

(F, 55, Tucson, Arizona, some high school, 237: 1)

With respect to the phrasal calque *escuela alta*, three representative features should be noted. First, while this phrasal calque does include common translation equivalents for both *high* and *school* the replica does not calque the model's syntax, but instead follows the unmarked word order for Spanish (that is, **alta escuela* does not obtain). Second, what is linguistically innovative about this lexical item is the semantic stretching of *alta*; here it does not refer to something physically higher or taller (its primary usage), rather it refers to an education advanced beyond the primary or elementary level. In other words, *alta* acquires the meaning usually associated with terms like *superior*, *secundaria* or *preparatoria* in monolingual varieties of Spanish. The only other important linguistic consequence of this process is the creation of a new collocation (as a prefabricated element it is entered in the mental lexicon or "phrasicon"). Third, the expression itself will only be semantically transparent to Spanish speakers who are familiar with American English and the mainstream culture of the United States.

This chapter will reexamine and evaluate the category of phrasal calques as it is manifest in Chicano Spanish. The 155 putative phrasal calques that comprise our corpus have been extracted from a computerized version of Galván and Teschner (1977) with additions from Galván (1995) and Aguilar Melantzón (1985). While I will not attempt any sort of descriptive statistical analysis (given the relatively small corpus at my disposal), I will illustrate four major subcategories and discuss their importance. Also, Otheguy's (1991) contention that some phrasal calques are merely mislabeled semantic extensions and that the remainder are instances of "cultural or conceptual modeling" will be carefully considered in light of the analyses performed on our corpus.

2. Preliminary analyses: DRAE

In the case of related languages it is often difficult if not impossible to definitively determine whether or not borrowing has occurred. Often coincident forms descend from a common ancestor. In fact, while not infallible, the one consistent proof that is offered is the date for which a form is first attested: if an earlier date exists for one language, a case can be made that it is the source language for the borrowing in question. However, it may be that the form in question was borrowed from a third language. It is also possible that one of the two languages served as the intermediary in its transmission to the other. Only a careful and diligent effort will reveal, so far as possible, the actual word history.

This situation is even more complicated in the case of parallel expressions, since even less documentation exists for these collocations. In some instances, it is clear that an expression derives culturally or linguistically from English/U.S. mainstream culture. There can be little doubt that *día de dar gracias* or *día de acción de gracias* 'Thanksgiving Day' is culturally modeled on the observance of such a holiday in the U.S. However, the source for other collocations like *entrar(le) por un oído y salir(le) por el otro* 'to go in one ear and out the other' is much less clear. Is it a borrowing? If so, is it an Anglicism or is it a Hispanicism or did both Spanish and English borrow it from a third source?

In order to ascertain which of the putative calques in our corpus also exist in Standard Spanish (and thus may not be calques at all), the electronic version of the *Diccionario de la Real Academia Española* (DRAE) was consulted. The results of that investigation can be summarized as follows: a few collocations had exactly the same form and same meaning (e.g., *cuatro ojos* 'four eyes,' *dar lumbre* 'give a light,' *hacer dinero* 'to make money') while ten other expressions were variants of those which appear in the DRAE. These items are included in Table 1.

Table 1. Forms which vary from the DRAE

DRAE	Corpus	English gloss
pena capital	castigo capital	capital punishment
coger calor	coger frío	to catch cold/get cold or hot
dar gas	darle al gas	to give it some gas, accelerate
estación de servicio	estación de gasolina	service station; gas station
perrito caliente	perro caliente	hot dog; wiener
piedras	piedras en la vejiga	(gall)stones
tener flojos los tornillos	tener un tornillo suelto	to have a screw loose (fig.)
echar flores	tirar flores	to throw flowers (fig.)
dormir como un leño	dormir como un tronco	to sleep like a log

Other collocations were referenced with other authoritative works. On the one hand, Lorenzo (1996) considers *espalda mojada* 'wetback' an Anglicism and cites corroborative Mexican sources. On the other, Santamaría (1992) considers *mamá/papá grande* 'grandmother or grandfather' to be Mexican child language and Elías-Olivares (1980) states specifically that these expressions do not derive from English. With regards to some putative phrasal calques in the corpus, it is less than certain that English is the source language or that the source of the innovation or variation is linguistic in nature.

3. Lexico-semantic innovation

3.1. Incorporation of calquewords and loans

Otheguy (1991) has claimed that many so-called phrasal calques are merely mislabeled semantic extensions or, in other words, the collocation incorporates one or more calquewords. Such phrasal calques are certainly in evidence in our corpus. Examples include (calquewords in bold): ***yarda*** *de madera* 'lumberyard,' ***correr*** *para una* ***oficina*** 'to run for office,' *dar* ***quebrada*** 'to give someone a break,' and ***hacer tiempo*** 'to make or do time.' Other phrasal calques incorporate a naturalized/nativized loanword (in bold): *andar* ***juqui*** 'to play hookey,' *ir al* ***baibai*** 'to go out, to go bye-bye,' ***bil*** *de la luz* 'light bill,' *llevar a los* ***clíners*** 'to take to the cleaners (fig.),' and *tener* ***fon*** 'to have fun.' To summarize, this subcategory of phrasal calques includes hybrid elements: its English origins are manifest in form and/or meaning. Furthermore, the fact that one or more contact neologisms form an integral part of a prefabricated slab of Spanish language could have at least one significant linguistic consequence. Specifically, the Anglicism in question may come to be utilized outside the confines of the set expression or phrase, possibly affecting or displacing Spanish equivalents in the speech of the bilingual (cf. Silva-Corvalán 1994: 172–178).

3.2. N + N

English possesses a syntactic pattern wherein two nouns are agglutinated to form a compound. As Whitley (1986: 153, 167) notes, this is a highly productive pattern which results in the creation of compounds like *lake bottom* and *metal furniture screw manufacturer*. Butt and Benjamin (1995: 2.1.7 and 4.2.3) analyze the Spanish counterpart to this pattern as either N + N (only the first element is pluralized: e.g., *años luz/*años luces* 'light years') or as N + Adj (the adjective is invariable in terms of gender agreement but sometimes is pluralized: *cabeza monstruo* 'monstrous head,' *chaquetas sport* 'sports jacket,' and *palabras tabú(es)* 'taboo words'). Although Penny (1991: 252) also includes this pattern in his review of compounding for Spanish, it appears to be limited in productivity. Some of the examples he cites are long-standing compounds (e.g., *telaraña* 'spider web, lit. cloth spider,' *aguanieve* 'sleet, lit. water snow,' and *zarzamora* 'blackberry (bush), lit. bramble berry') and it is unlikely that language contact has played a role in their creation. Other such compounds (e.g., *lengua madre* 'mother tongue' and *punto clave* 'key point'), while parallel to English, are probably best analyzed as internal innovations in the Spanish system or as mutually inherited forms. Recently, however, a veritable plethora of such parallel compounds have surfaced in the Spanish language: *avión espía* 'spy plane,' *coche bomba* 'car bomb,' *escuela modelo* 'model school,' and *pluma fuente* 'fountain pen,' for example. Notably, the DRAE also includes a few such compounds: *ciudad dormitorio* 'bedroom city,' *coche cama* 'Pullman or sleeper car,' and *hombre rana* 'frogman,' among others. There can be little doubt that these compounds are modeled at least culturally on American English usage. Furthermore, *coche bomba* calques the syntax in the source language; most other parallel Spanish compounds invert the English word order.

These recent innovations in Spanish are representative of what Vázquez-Ayora (1977) has termed "anglicismos de frecuencia." That is, while the pattern of N + N is attested to in Spanish without language contact being posited as its source, it is a syntactic pattern which, on the whole, has been less frequently utilized. There can be little disagreement that Spanish prefers N + prep (usually *de*) + N as a solution in these cases, as collocations such as *máquina de lavar* 'washing machine' and *corbata de seda* 'silk tie' illustrate. Thus, a rise in frequency or a change in preference which parallels English usage may be attributable to language contact.

Our corpus contains only two such forms: *baile-cena* 'dinner-dance' and *caja idiota* 'idiot box, television.' Neither is particularly remarkable, aside from the fact that they are unique to our corpus. It is possible to analyze the second compound as N + Adj (*idiota* does not agree in gender but could be pluralized; it functions as both a noun and an adjective). Other potential compounds do not obtain: **bolas carne/*carne bolas* are not attested (although *bolas de carne* 'meatballs' is); neither are **casa cortes/*cortes casa* (the form, in this instance, is *casa de cortes* 'courthouse'). None of the compounds cited in our sources appear in Lope Blanch (1990). It is possible that wire service translations and the media have played the major role in the creation and dissemination of a large number of these *anglicismos de frecuencia.* Indeed, Whitley (1986: 167) indicates that this pattern is becoming more frequent in Spanish "at least in journalistic or technical writing."

3.3. English Adj + N; Spanish Adj + N or N + Adj

It is well-known that English and Spanish differ with regard to adjective placement. However, rather than characterize the difference strictly in terms of the position that a predetermined type of adjective usually occupies, it is useful to note that English can only prepose adjectives while Spanish may both prepose and postpose. Thus, English expressions like *brick red* (a particular shade of red) or *red brick* (a brick which is red) differ due to the lexical or syntactic category of the word in question (*red* is nominal in post-position and adjectival in pre-position). In Spanish, where an adjective can occupy both positions, syntax has semantic consequences, but is not responsible for categorial change. For example, *buena parte* can mean 'a good amount' while *parte buena* may be glossed in English as 'good part.' In either case *buena* retains its function as an adjective.

If English syntax were to influence Spanish in this instance, we would first expect to find an increase in the number of preposed adjectives, particularly those which according to meaning and monolingual usage would usually be postposed. This is precisely what Silva-Corvalán (1994: 182–183) found in her study of Spanish in East Los Angeles. She provides the following examples noting that this phenomenon is most frequent among the least proficient Spanish speakers in her sample.

(4) **Preposing of adjectives among bilinguals speaking Spanish**

a. Ella hablaba como yo más o menos, machucado español. . . .
'She spoke more or less like me, chopped up Spanish. . . .'

b. es el número uno gastador de petróleo
'it is the number one user of oil'

c. la más importante persona
'the most important person'

d. compré una 'king-size' cama
'I bought a 'king-size' bed'

In our corpus, only collocations which incorporate what Hernanz and Brucart (1987: 171) term an *adjetivo valorativo* (one that expresses a subjective judgment) utilize pre-position. These include (adjectives in bold): *hacer* ***buenos/malos*** *grados* 'to make good/bad grades,' *tener* ***buena*** *cabeza* 'to have a good head, to be intelligent,' *tener* ***buen/mal*** *tiempo* 'to have a good/bad time,' *el* ***mejor*** *lado* 'the best (most photogenic) side,' and ***mejor*** *mitad* 'better half (husband or wife).' Lope Blanch (1990) provides one instance in which a fragment of one of these collocations occurs:

(5) La Rita fue la del **buen tiempo**. . . . era la (d)el novio.
'Rita was the good-time girl . . . she was the one that had a boyfriend.'
(F, 45, Mora, New Mexico, middle class, 179: 1)

Since Spanish allows for and even prefers pre-position in the case of the *adjetivo valorativo*, it is unlikely that English has played a significant role in determining adjective placement in the examples extracted from the corpus. Furthermore, all other instances utilize post-position (adjectives in bold): *trabajo* ***cochino*** 'dirty work,' *delincuente* ***juvenil*** 'juvenile delinquent,' and *pelo* ***derecho*** 'straight (not wavy) hair' are illustrative.

3.4. Prepositional usage and creation

English and Spanish also frequently differ with regard to which preposition (if any) may accompany a verb in complement position. For example, monolingual varieties of Spanish employ *depender de* (contrasting with 'depend on/upon') and *consistir en* (as opposed to 'consist of'). A rather simple variation attested to in our corpus occurs when, on the basis of the English model, the bilingual recasts the *régimen verbal* of these two as *depender en* and *consistir de*. In practice, the calquing of English prepositional usage in such cases has little effect on Spanish syntax – verb valency remains unchanged, and the substitution of prepositions is not unlike what occurs in non-contact varieties of Spanish with verbs like *entrar* 'to enter, go in' (which may collocate with either *a* or *en*) or *preocuparse* 'to worry' (which, in turn, may collocate with either *de* or *por*). Lope Blanch (1990) provides two contextualized examples of *depender en* by a bilingual Chicano:

(6) Sí está frío. **Depende en** cuál mes uno esté allá.
'Yes, it feels cold. It depends on which month one is there.'
(M, 34, San José, California, some college, 278: 29)

(7) **Depende en** lo que – lo que ande buscando uno
'It depends on what – what one is looking for'
(same consultant, 281: 15)

Another type of bilingual innovation, termed relexification by Silva-Corvalán (1994: 184), occurs when figurative expressions like *(named) after* or *to look forward to* are rendered as *después de* (a temporal preposition) and *mirar adelante para* (not a collocation in monolingual Spanish, but would likely be interpreted in a spatial sense). Both of these are found in our corpus; they constitute somewhat more radical innovations and would not be semantically transparent to the monolingual Spanish speaker.

As mentioned in the introduction, one prepositional phrase, *pa(ra a)trás,* merits (and has received) special attention. It is worth noting that this collocation which is thought to calque the English 'back' (in two-word verbs like *call back, give back, talk back, go back, take back, put back*, etc.) has limited, sporadic usage in monolingual Spanish (particularly in popular varieties). For example, Alvar (1960: 537) in a transcript of a conversation titled "Córdoba, escena de siega [Cordoba, harvest scene]," records the following line: *"Ámono* ***pa'tráh****, no ay na mah que hasé*"; ignoring the phonetic detail, this is *Vámonos para atrás, no hay nada más que hacer* 'Let's go back, there's nothing more to do.' As Elías-Olivares (1980) points out, it is quite possible that this collocation has its origins in pleonasms like *salir pa'fuera* 'to go out,' *subir pa'rriba* 'to go up,' and *bajar pa'bajo* 'to go down,' where both the verb and the prepositional phrase indicate in which direction the subject is moving. Our own corpus includes at least two such redundant expressions: *devolver(se) pa'tras* 'to take back, return' and *volver pa'tras* 'to return, go back.' Lope Blanch (1990) provides the following contextualized example where the usage is clearly pleonastic:

(8) Él piensa irse al servicio, pa dispués cuando **regrese pa'trás**, tiene la oportunidá de ir al colegio.
'He plans to go into the service, so later when he comes (lit., returns) back, he has the opportunity to go to college.'
(M, 39, San Marcos, Texas, grade school, 118: 1).

However, not all uses of *pa'tras* may be considered pleonastic. In other collocations, it contributes independently to the meaning of the verb phrase. In these cases, it may refer to a literal, physical return (spatial) or it may acquire the meaning of 'again.' The following examples from Lope Blanch (1990) also illustrate these two meanings (all but one of these verb phrases are also found in our corpus):

(9) Fuimoh a vihitar la Virgen de San Juan. Allá estuvimoh un día y **loh vinimoh pa'tráh.**
'We went to visit the Virgin of Saint John. We were there for a day and then came back.'
(M, 39, San Marcos, Texas, grade school, 120: 10)

(10) ¡Vamos de aquí! ¡**Vamos pa'trás**, pa la casa!
'Let's get out of here! Let's go back to the house.'
(F, 45, Mora, New Mexico, middle class, 179: 3)

(11) Posiblemente **se fue pa'trás**, pa Méjico.
'Possibly, he went back to Mexico.'
(M, 45, Mora, New Mexico, middle class, 185: 4)

(12) Y yo jui y la **compré pa'trás**.
'And I went and I bought it back.'
(M, 51, San Marcos, Texas, grade school, 162: 1)

(13) Pues se los **dan pa'trás**, y si no, under adoption los niños, ¿no?
'Well, they'll give them back, and if not, the children (will be) under adoption, right?'
(F, 55, Tucson, Arizona, some high school, 232: 11).

Talmy (1985) points out that English tends to express movement and path by means of a verb and particle (or preposition): *fall off, go down, move up*, etc. Non-contact varieties of Spanish, on the other hand, tend to conflate both path and movement in the verb itself: *caer(se), bajar, subir*, etc. In adapting and extending *pa'tras*, bilingual varieties of Spanish demonstrate convergence with English in this use of a typically English syntactic pattern.

4. Conclusion

We have examined four categories of putative phrasal calques. We noted that many of these collocations are hybrid in nature and contain either loans or calquewords as constituent elements. Nonetheless, this first category of putative phrasal calques does not demonstrate syntactic influence from English. As for the second category, the agglutination of two nouns to form a compound, we maintained that the rise in frequency of this pattern in some varieties of Spanish may be due to contact with English, but discovered that only two of our forms could be analyzed as N + N. We then observed that it is unlikely that English had influenced adjective placement for the collocations contained in the corpus, since no item in this third category deviated from monolingual usage. However, we stated that it is possible that English has influenced our fourth category, bilingual prepositional usage, by recasting certain instances of *régimen verbal*, relexifying, and extending the monolingual usage of *pa'tras*. To conclude, in two of the four categories we found no evidence that syntactic input from English had played a significant role in the creation of those collocations.

In the title of this chapter, we asked, "Are phrasal calques instances of cultural or linguistic innovation?" The answer is not clear-cut. Some so-called phrasal calques show no evidence of syntactic transference and are simply instances of cultural innovation. Others, like those included in categories two and four, do demonstrate minor linguistic innovations in that an underutilized pattern may become more frequent or be extended to new contexts. In the final analysis, one must decide whether the frequency of occurrence of a particular structure or form has any direct relationship with linguistic competence. If we dismiss frequency as merely an artifact of linguistic performance, we are unlikely to see any relationship to linguistic competence. However, if we recognize that quantitative differences can and frequently do lead to qualitative differences, we may be more likely to assume that frequency has an important relationship with linguistic competence. Nonetheless, the question is not easily answered – ultimately, it may depend not such much on the linguistic facts themselves but on our interpretation of the facts.

Notes

1. The fields of phraseology and translation/interpretation have studied collocations (as well as other phraseological units). On phraseology, see Cowie (1998) and Corpas Pastor (1996). Larson (1998: 155–167) deals with the difficulties of translating language-specific collocations.

References

Aguilar Melantzón, Ricardo. 1985. *Glosario del caló de Ciudad Juárez: Primera aproximación*. Las Cruces, NM: Joint Border Research Institute, NMSU.

Alvar, Manuel. 1960. *Textos hispánicos dialectales: Antología histórica. Tomo II*. Madrid: CSIC.

Butt, John and Carmen Benjamin. 1995. *A new reference grammar of Modern Spanish, 2nd edition*. Lincolnwood: NTC.

Corpas Pastor, Gloria. 1996. *Manual de fraseología española*. Madrid: Gredos.

Cowie, Anthony Paul, ed. 1998. *Phraseology: Theory, analysis, and applications*. Oxford: Clarendon.

Elías-Olivares, Lucía. 1980. The analysis of mixed Spanish: A critique of existing studies. In *Speaking, singing, and teaching: A multidisciplinary approach to language variation. Proceedings of the eighth annual Southwestern Areal Language and Linguistics Workshop*, ed. Florence Barkin and Elizabeth Brandt, 332–336. Tempe, AZ: ASU.

Galván, Roberto A. and Richard Teschner. 1977. *El diccionario del español chicano / The dictionary of Chicano Spanish*. Silver Spring, MD: Institute of Modern Languages.

Galván, Roberto A. 1995. *El diccionario del español chicano / The dictionary of Chicano Spanish*, 2nd edition. Lincolnwood: NTC.

Hernanz, María Llüisa and José María Brucart. 1987. *La sintaxis: Principios teóricos. La oración simple*. Barcelona: Crítica.

Larson, Mildred L. 1998. *Meaning-based translation: A guide to cross-language equivalence*. New York: University Press of America.

Lipski, John. 1985. The construction *pa(ra) atrás* among Spanish–English bilinguals: Parallel structures and universal patterns. *Revista Interamericana* 15: 91–102.

Lope Blanch, Juan M. 1990. *El español hablado en el suroeste de los Estados Unidos: Materiales para su estudio*. Mexico, D.F.: UNAM.

Lorenzo, Emilio. 1996. *Anglicismos hispánicos*. Madrid: Gredos.

Montes Giraldo, José Joaquín. 1985. Calcos recientes del ingés en español. *Thesaurus* 15: 17–49.

Otheguy, Ricardo. 1991. A reconsideration of the notion of loan translation in the analysis of U.S. Spanish. *CUNY Forum* 16: 101–121.

Otheguy, Ricardo. 1995a. A reconsideration of the notion of loan translation in the analysis of U.S. Spanish. In *Spanish in the U.S.: Linguistic contact and diversity*, ed. Ana Roca and John Lipski, 21–45. New York: Mouton de Gruyter.

Otheguy, Ricardo. 1995b. When contact speakers talk, linguistic theory listens. In *Meaning as explanation: Advances in linguistic sign theory*, ed. Ellen Contini-Morava and Barbara Sussman Goldberg, 213–242. New York: Mouton de Gruyter.

Penny, Ralph. 1991. *A history of the Spanish language*. New York: Cambridge.

Real Academia Española. 1995. *Diccionario de la lengua española, vigésima primera edición, edición en CD-ROM*. Madrid: Espasa-Calpe.

Santamaría, Francisco J. 1992. *Diccionario de mejicanismos, quinta edición*. Mexico D.F.: Porrúa.

Silva-Corvalán, Carmen. 1994. *Language contact and change: Spanish in Los Angeles*. Oxford: Clarendon.

Silva-Corvalán, Carmen. 1995. Lexico-syntactic modeling across the bilingual continuum. *Linguistic change under contact conditions*, ed. Jacek Fisiak, 253–270. New York: Mouton de Gruyter.

Smead, Robert N. and J. Halvor Clegg. 1996. English calques in Chicano Spanish. In *Spanish in contact: Issues in bilingualism*, ed. Ana Roca and John B. Jensen, 123–130. Somerville, MA: Cascadilla Press.

Smead, Robert N. 1998. English loanwords in Chicano Spanish: Characterization and rationale. *Bilingual Review/Revista Bilingüe* 23.2: 113–123.

Talmy, Leonard. 1985. Lexicalization patterns: Semantic structure in lexical forms. In *Language typology and syntactic description, vol. III: Grammatical categories and the lexicon*, ed. Timothy Shopen, 57–149. New York: Cambridge University.

Vázquez-Ayora, Gerardo. 1977. *Introducción a la traductología: Curso básico de traducción*. Washington, DC: Georgetown University.

Whitley, M. Stanley. 1986. *Spanish/English contrasts: A course in Spanish linguistics*. Washington, DC: Georgetown University.

WordCruncher 4.30. March 1989. Provo, UT: Electronic Text Corporation.

El español cubanoamericano

Beatriz Varela
University of New Orleans

Desde que en 1992 publiqué mi libro *El español cubano-americano*, este dialecto ha seguido evolucionando de la misma forma que se predijo en la introducción al libro. La mayoría de las veces – salvo quizás en los cubanismos *guagua, máquina, trusa*, que resultan incomprensibles para otros hispanos, y que son fáciles de sustituir por *ómnibus, automóvil, carro, coche, traje de baño* – se conservan otras voces propias de Cuba como *buchipluma, cachumbambé, quilo, tareco*, así como préstamos del inglés como *bíper, membresía, pulóver, taipear* y *teipear*. En la fonología continúan predominando los rasgos fonéticos de la Isla como la aspiración o la pérdida de la *-s* final de sílaba o de palabra y la apócope de sonidos. También sobresalen en el sistema vocálico dos sonidos ingleses: la schwa o vocal central relajada /ə/ y una vocal anterior baja /æ/ que no existían ni existen en el español cubano. La morfología se destaca por un tuteo evidente en todos los hablantes, la casi eliminación del futuro sintético de indicativo y por influencia del inglés el escaso uso del modo subjuntivo. La sintaxis se caracteriza por la anteposición del pronombre *tú* al verbo en las oraciones interrogativas, construcción que es común a todo el español del Caribe. Se nota asimismo la falta de concordancia entre las partes variables, rasgo tan típico del inglés: "mi primer corbata. . . ."

Conviene subrayar el interés de las escuelas, las universidades y la población estadounidense así como la cubanoamericana, en el estudio de la lengua española. Ésta se enseña en todos los niveles desde la primaria hasta el doctorado. Además se publican periódicos y revistas, y se transmiten programas de radio y televisión. No cabe duda que el español cubanoamericano es una variante importante del español de los Estados Unidos, y éste a su vez lo es del español de América. En esta presentación me concentraré en los préstamos y calcos del inglés que se han divulgado en los últimos años.

Lo más difícil de determinar es el nivel en que se usa cada préstamo o cada calco. La mayoría pertenece a un nivel bajo de hablantes con poca cultura que no hablan bien ni el inglés ni el español. Otros ejemplos se observan en hablantes de educación media que utilizan anglicismos puros o hispanizados

 Research on Spanish in the U.S., ed. Ana Roca, 173–176. Somerville, MA: Cascadilla Press.

porque quieren formar parte de la corriente de moda para así lograr objetivos comerciales, sociales o políticos. En un tercer plano se hallan individuos de alto nivel cultural o académico, cuyas construcciones anglicadas resultan más difíciles de captar.

Al nivel bajo corresponden expresiones incomprensibles para el hispano que no resida en los Estados Unidos, pero que desgraciadamente han alcanzado una gran difusión entre hablantes de pocos conocimientos. Registro ejemplos documentados en Varela (1992): *correr para mayor* 'postularse para alcalde,' *darle una vacuneadita a la carpeta* 'limpiar la alfombra con la aspiradora,' las muchas construcciones verbales con el adverbio *para atrás* calcadas de otras tantas locuciones anglo-americanas con *back*: *caminar para atrás* 'regresar,' *llamar para atrás* 'devolver la llamada' *morder para atrás* 'devolver la mordida' y otras que no cito. Los estudiantes de los primeros cursos universitarios emplean con frecuencia los verbos *cuitear* 'abandonar,' *dropear* 'dejar' y *flonquear* 'no aprobar' y el sustantivo *grados* por 'notas.'

En el nivel medio predominan los cantantes de música popular como Gloria Estefan ("Mi cuerpo, mi salsa") y Willy Chirino ("Mister, Don't Touch the Banana" 'Señor, no toque el banano') que emplean la alternancia de código en sus canciones. También usan el cambio constante del inglés y el español, – a veces con errores garrafales en las dos lenguas o en una de las dos – los compositores de "rap," de "rock," de "pop balada." Realmente cuesta trabajo entenderlos.

Para analizar los préstamos y calcos del tercer nivel los hemos separado en tres categorías: (1) los de autores que dominan el inglés y el español y que escriben lo mismo en una lengua que en la otra, (2) los de escritores que por haber nacido en los Estados Unidos o haber venido de Cuba cuando eran niños, se criaron en este país, se educaron en escuelas americanas y utilizan el *Spanglish, espanglés* o como diría Olimpia Rosado, la *angliparla*. En la tercera categoría están los anglicismos que ha aceptado la Real Academia Española (RAE) en su diccionario de 1992 y los que está preparando para documentar en la próxima vigésima segunda edición del diccionario que verá la luz en el año 2000 o en el 2001. Entre los escritores de la primera división se encuentran Roberto G. Fernández (1981, 1988), Cristina García (1992), y Gustavo Pérez Firmat (1994, 1996), todos pertenecientes a una segunda generación de autores cubano-americanos, cuyos temas, escritos lo mismo en inglés que en español, giran siempre alrededor de la historia y la cultura cubana. A veces inyectan el sentido del humor al traducir literalmente al inglés o al español expresiones idiomáticas de un idioma o del otro, canciones, nombres de cantantes y comidas de Cuba. Así, Roberto G. Fernández (1981: 40) traduce *take it easy* como *cógelo suave* y en Fernández (1988: 48) calca el nombre del cantante cubano Barbarito Diez: *Little Barbaro X* y el del Trío Matamoros: *the Moorkiller Trío*, famosos por la canción "Son de la loma" cuya traducción *They Are from the Hills* no significa nada para el que no esté familiarizado con la letra y la música de la popular canción cubana. Al describir la inauguración de una elegante "boutique" en Miami, Fernández (1981: 47) indica que se repartieron "little crabs," traducción del cubanismo *cangrejitos* ('pasta de hojaldre rellena con jamón y otras carnes, cuya forma imitaba la muelita de un cangrejo'). Los menús de conocidos restaurantes de Miami sirven especialidades de la cocina cubana como ropa vieja, moros y cristianos y tocino del cielo, cuyas traducciones al inglés – *old clothes*, *Moors and Christians* and *bacon of the sky* – las comprende todo residente de la Florida.

Para analizar el "espanglés" nos basamos en la obra de los editores de la revista *Generation ñ* (Abril 1996–Septiembre 1998), cuyo nombre, muy original por cierto, abarca a los jóvenes que aunque formados en la cultura estadounidense retienen con orgullo la grafía *ñ* que los identifica con la cultura hispánica de sus padres y abuelos. Pues bien, en *Generation ñ*, Bill Cruz publica una sección titulada *Cubanamericanisms*, que incluye una lista de palabras y expresiones propias del habla cubana, las cuales son traducidas al inglés y clasificadas como: (1) *transliteration* 'préstamo hispanizado,' (2) *descriptive* 'préstamo puro' y (3) *traditional* 'calco o préstamo,' según Cruz, *más viejo que andar a pie*. El éxito de esta columna de cubano-americanismos se evidencia en la página *Hooked on Cubonics* que publicó Lydia Martin en el *Miami Herald* (27 de enero de 1997) con la ayuda de Bill Teck, editor de *Generation ñ*, Bill Cruz, el citado autor de los *Cubanamericanisms*, y otros colaboradores del *Miami Herald*. Asimismo, Cruz et al. acaban de publicar *The Official Spanglish Dictionary* (1998) que contiene más de 300 palabras y frases, las quales como no son ni español ni inglés, pertenecen al dialecto mencionado. Cito la traducción de varios cubanismos de mucho uso: "He sang the peanut vendor" *cantó el manicero* que significa 'murió'; "he sandpapers himself" *se da lija* con la acepción de 'he takes very good care of himself.' Vale la pena citar algunos términos de la informática, aunque no los incluya *The Official Spanglish Dictionary*. Para el correo electrónico se prefiere el anglicismo *e-mail* /i-méil/ y el verbo */i-meileár/*, que en algunos países hispanoamericanos se ha hispanizado en *emilio*. *Daunlodear* 'download' por descargar archivos, y desde luego *internet* por red electrónica internacional.

Dado el enorme caudal de voces inglesas que han influido en el léxico español en las últimas décadas, la Real Academia Española, con mucho tino, ha registrado unos cuantos anglicismos en su última edición, la de 1992, y propone otros para su vigésima segunda edición. Estoy de acuerdo con esta política, pero debo hacer tres objeciones. Si existe un sinónimo en español para la voz inglesa, su aceptación en el *Diccionario de la lengua española* (DRAE) no es necesaria. Por ejemplo, en español tenemos *payaso*, hermosísima palabra, que no ha de ser reemplazada por el horrible anglicismo *clon*, que documenta el DRAE de 1992, y que como procedente del inglés *clown* debe escribirse *claun*, hispanización fonológica más exacta, y que además evita la confusión con el homógrafo *clon* qe significa 'estirpe celular' o "copia genética.' Otro anglicismo innecesario que registrará la próxima edición del DRAE es *braun*, del inglés *brown*. Son numerosas las voces que existen en la lengua española para este color: *café, carmelita, castaño, marrón, pardo*. Vale reconocer, no obstante, que esta vez la hispanización se ha realizado respetando el sonido de la palabra inglesa y que al mismo tiempo su extensión geográfica es mayor que la del citado *clon* pues abarca no solo a España sino también a Puerto Rico. Quizás Ricardo Alfaro (1964: 19) hubiera clasificado estos dos anglicismos como superfluos, viciosos e injustificados.

Mi segunda objeción es quizás la más difícil de cumplir, ya que no siempre se puede acomodar el anglicismo a la fonología y a la morfosintaxis de la lengua española. Si en la próxima edición del DRAE se incluye el préstamo *airbag* 'bolsa de aire' – que no hace falta – ¿cuál será la ortografía correcta? ¿Se escribirá igual que en inglés para facilitar su reconocimiento por el mundo extranjero? Si esto ocurre, tendremos un puro extranjerismo, que el que no sepa inglés pronunciará mal. ¿Deberá deletrearse *erbag* para que se articule adecuadamente? ¿Será conveniente escribir *airbag* y a continuación la transcripción fonética o la fonológica? Les dejo con estas interrogaciones problemáticas.

Mi última observación se refiere a la acentuación de los compuestos. Si la RAE acepta *cóc*tel y coc*tel*, *fútbol* y fut*bol*, ¿por qué no basquet*bol* y *bás*quetbol, *béis*bol y beis*bol*, volei*bol* y *vó*leibol. En esta última es importante eliminar el diptongo *-ei-* pues en Hispanoamérica se dice *vólibol*, con acentuaión proparoxítona, así como *básquetbol* esdrújula y *beisbol* aguda. Aunque el habla cubana no emplea los citados anglicismos *brown, clown, airbag* sí usa mucho las voces hispanizadas – con un acento distinto – *básquetbol, beisbol* y *vólibol*.

Notas

* Deseo agradecerle a la Dra. Ana Roca su gentil invitación a que yo participara en esta mesa sobre el bilingüismo cubano-americano y además felicitarla calurosamente por la magistral organización de este décimo-séptimo Congreso del Español en los Estados Unidos.

Referencias

Alfaro, Ricardo J. 1964. *Diccionario de anglicismos*. Madrid: Editorial Gredos.

Cruz, Bill, Bill Teck, and the Editors of *Generation ñ* magazine. 1998. *The official Spanglish dictionary*. New York: Simon and Schuster.

Fernández, Roberto G. 1981. *La vida es un "special."* Miami: Ediciones Universal.

Fernández, Roberto G. 1988. *Raining backwards*. Houston: Arte Público Press.

García, Cristina. 1992. *Dreaming in Cuban*. New York: Ballantine Books.

Pérez Firmat, Gustavo. 1994. *Life in the hyphen: The Cuban-American way*. Austin: University of Texas Press.

Pérez Firmat, Gustavo. 1996. *Next year in Cuba: A Cubano's coming-of-age in America*. New York: Doubleday.

Real Academia Española. 1992. *Diccionario de la lengua española*. Madrid: Espasa Calpe.

Varela, Beatriz. 1992. *El español cubano-americano*. Prólogo de Samuel G. Armistead. New York: Senda Nueva de Ediciones.

Adapted Borrowings in Spanish: A Morphopragmatic Hypothesis

Mónica Cantero

Berry College

1. Introduction

In the Spanish classes that I have taught in the United States, I have always found that, at one moment or another, someone will say "no problemo" for no seemingly apparent reason. I have also observed the occurrence of such morphological output using Spanish inflectional or derivational elements occurs frequently in public discourse in the U.S. What are the consequences of the intentional use of such strategies? These observations have led me to ponder the structural and intentional mechanisms that operate in the creation of new lexical items in a given language, which in this case is focused on Spanish word formation rules.

I will explore data in this paper that characterize the morphological linguistic productivity of a concrete region: Hispanic communities of the Southwest, where bilingual speakers create lexical items by means of what I propose to call morphological stem-switching mechanisms (for further discussion and data see Cantero 1996). This is a type of codeswitching within a word, which I believe is the most complex type of codeswitching and requires a high degree of proficiency in both languages.

2. Nominal adaptations

This section will look at various strategies used to adapt English nouns into Spanish. In Spanish, gender and number paradigms are obligatory and distinctive; all nouns have an assigned inflectional class. Stems coming from other linguistic systems that Spanish speakers then incorporate must be assigned to an inflectional class in order to be activated as "native" lexemes within the language in which they are employed. We are investigating English lexemes that

 Research on Spanish in the U.S., ed. Ana Roca, 177–183. Somerville, MA: Cascadilla Press.

Spanish speakers incorporate into the language, particularly lexemes lacking nominal gender features (Aronoff 1994 explores this process in Hebrew).

I argue that when this type of "foreign" lexeme is adopted in another system that distinguishes gender category – whether syntactically or through a rule – an automatic process must exist to assign this distinct features to this lexeme which allow it to be introduced as a unit within the system as a whole, where it is then used in derivative morphological processes. Let us consider the introduction of the following lexemes in Tables 1–3:

Table 1. Phonological adaptations of nouns

bil **bale**

De una vez pegó un bil de zacate con la llanta grande de la roca . . . (Sagel 1983: 26)

The huge tire of the truck immediately collided with a bale of hay . . . (Sagel 1983: 27)

-¡cuidado con estos biles, americano! (Sagel 1983: 33)

elque **elk**

Parado atrás de un pino, le esperó el elque en silencio profundo y profesional (Sagel 1983: 56)

He was waiting for the elk, standing behind a pine in absolute and professional silence (Sagel 1983: 57)

fon **fun**

Yo también tenía mi fon más antes cuando era jovencita, pero ya no (Sagel 1983: 20)

I used to have my fun too when I was younger, but not anymore (Sagel 1983: 21)

jaiskul **high school**

. . . animalito oficial del jaiskul del Sagrado Corazón (Sagel 1983: 53)

. . . todavía tenía la cara redonda y vacía de un chamaquito de jaiskul (Sagel 1983: 80)

. . . he still possessed the round, vacant face of a high school kid (Sagel 1983: 81)

jalo **hello**

. . . en lugar de decir amén, dijo, en un tono bien político, jalo (Sagel 1983: 31)

. . . when Darryl arrived in front of the priest he didn't say Amen. He said hello, in a polite introduction to the Holy Eucharist. (Sagel 1983: 30)

juisque **whiskey**

. . . dijo su tío, levantando una botella fresca de juisque (Sagel 1983: 41)

. . . la Alicia tomó otro trago de juisqui (Sagel 1983: 123)

pantes **panties**

con su levita de seda roja y el cabello lleno de toritos, se bajó los pantes a mearse (Sagel 1983: 35)

troca **truck**

Darryl Galván le miró a su tío borracho gritándole que manejara la troca para la izquierda y a su abuelo enseñándole que iría para la derecha (Sagel 1983: 27)

Darryl Galván looked at his drunken uncle yelling at him to turn the truck to the left and at his grandfather signalling to the right (Sagel 1983: 26)

yaque **jack**
Su abuelo tuvo que pasar toda la tarde renegando con el yaque y la rondanilla . . . (Sagel 1983: 29)
yeli **jelly**
. . . llenándose con tortilla y yeli de cerezo que su tía le sacó del trastero (Sagel 1983: 39)

Table 2. Spanish forms of English truncations

bro **brother**
Con un barullo se salieron –después de que el pollo dio la mano a todos, diciendo: "bueno, bro." (Sagel 1983: 91)
caf **cafeteria**
Cuando yo veo a las parejas besando ahí atrás del "caf," pues, me pongo muy triste (Sagel 1983: 53)

Table 3. Derivational stem-switching: combining forms using a foreign base

jungl*ista* **jungle**
El sonido dub-a-delic de "Evolve" desemboca en un océano polirrítmico y junglista (*RDL* 1996: 128:52)
speéd*ica* **speed**
Como guindas, speedicas "rock cover songs . . ." (*RDL* 1996: 128:44)
troqu*ita* **truck**
Y muchas veces se paseaban en la troquita Ford con el barandal quebrado y el tapón amarrado con alambre (Sagel 75)
soundtrak*grafía* **soundtrack**
lo mejor, la sound-trackgrafía de Danny Elfman (*RDL* 1996: 128:23)
soul*eros* **soul**
. . . sin asumir el rol de acompañantes souleros. . . (*RDL* 1996: 128:47)
pop*ero* **pop**
. . . para desmarcarse de ese aire muzak popero que les caracteriza. . . (*Boogie* 1988: 2:29)

In the examples presented above, the adaptation of a foreign unit into the Spanish system involves the immediate acquisition of the morphological features characterizing the nominal categories of the Spanish language. I wish to reinforce the idea that this is a required morphological process: every lexeme that is incorporated into the Spanish language is given either syntactically or through the assignation of rules the necessary features in order for it to conform to an inflectional class within the language. This process is necessary for the borrowing to work as a derivational base within the language.

In Spanish, lexeme rule formation output provides the gender and inflectional categories of the base. This is especially important to point out in the case of borrowings that do not belong to but that do get assigned to a morphological category through the above-mentioned mechanism. The acquisition of inflectional features must occur in conjunction with a process of incorporating the new linguistic unit in order for it to work within the "other" system.

We can see in Tables 1–3 three ways in which these English forms are adapted into Spanish. Table 1 shows examples of simple phonological adaptations of English nouns to make the forms sound more Spanish. Table 2 shows truncations of English words. Table 3 shows derivational stem-switching, where an English stem is combined with a Spanish suffix to create a Spanish form.

3. Verbal adaptations

Spanish verbal formation uses a specific set of verbal suffixes. Morphemes available for creating verb forms are limited, in contrast to adjectival or nominal suffixation which uses an open inventory of suffixes.

Spanish spoken in the Southwestern states incorporates English verbs into the Spanish language through the addition of suffix [*–ear*] to the English base. The [*–ear*] suffix is one of the most productive verbal formatives in contemporary Peninsular Spanish, as well as in Spanish spoken in the U.S. In Tables 4–7, the base used is an English verb to which the suffix [*–ear*] has been added in order for the adapted form to be conjugated as a verb within the Spanish verbal paradigm.

Table 4. Adaptations of English verbs in Peninsular Spanish

resetear

. . . y la estabilidad sólo podrá ser restaurada por intervención manual o *reseteando* el regulador. (*Universidad Politécnica de Barcelona Ingenieros industriales: Regulación automática*)

rapear

. . . como el que imprime rapeando Avenda Khadija Ali. . . (*Rock de Luxe (RDL)* 1996: 126:43)

. . . sobre la que los invitados rapean con toda normalidad. (*RDL* 1996: 127:52)

surfear

. . . con la que solía *surfear* por encima del público. (*Popular* 1996: 1.267:29)

rockear

Allí se puede escuchar *rockear* en catalán a ELS 4 GATS. . . (*RDL* 1996: 127:58)

samplear

. . . y cuando más se acerca a Portishead es *sampleando* a Carmel. (*RDL* 1996: 126:6)

Table 5. Literary examples of adaptations of English verbs in Southwest Spanish

parquear
Y *parqueó* el van ahí en el lado del camino mientras que la Alicia . . . (Sagel 1983: 125)
snapear
Y el Librado, cuando al fin *snapeó* a lo que había hecho, trató a la Alicia un poco mejor (Sagel 1983: 129)
spotear
. . . que los chamacos grandes lo *spotearon* como a un chico diferente (Sagel 1983: 30)
taipiar
. . . y lo usaba liberalmente como agente de su "justicia," particularmente en la clase de *taipiar* (Sagel 1983: 135)

Table 6. Colloquial speech production examples of adaptations of English verbs in Southwest Spanish

batear	to bat
bloquear	to block (sometimes spelled: *bloqiar, bloquiar*)
chutear	to shoot
danciar	to dance
donquiar	to dunk (sometimes spelled: *donqiar*)
dompear	to dump
dropear	to drop
lonchear	to eat lunch
pickiar	to pick
taipiar	to type (sometimes also spelled: *typiar*)
wekiar	to wake up (pronounced:*wekear*)

Table 7. MCI Tecnoguia. Techno-NoNo's. Top ten most common incorrectly used "Spanglish" verbs.

"Incorrect" form	Meaning	Correct form
beepear	to beep	localizar electrónicamente
printiar	to print	imprimir
escapiar	to escape	abandonar
faxiar	to fax	mandar/enviar por fax
postiar	to post	registrar
surfiar	to surf	navegar por la red
taipiar	to type	escribir a máquina
clickear	to click	pinchar/hacer clic
e-mailiar	to e-mail	enviar por correo electrónico
atachear	to attach	adjuntar

In Spanish, verbs must be assigned to an inflectional class in order to indicate particular verb forms. The inflectional class names a set of instructions for constructing inflected (conjugated) verb forms. The three paradigms for Spanish verbs are *-ar*, *-er*, and *-ir*; verbs can only be inflected within one of these three paradigms.

The English bases in Tables 4–7 don't demonstrate a correlation to the Spanish verbal system, so the suffix [*–ear*] is applied. The [*-ear*] suffix does not modify the syntactic category of the Spanish output nor does it add any semantic connotation to the base, though the suffix [*–ear*] does add negative semantic connotations when added to Spanish verbal forms (*llorar* → *lloriquear*). I believe that the suffix [*-ear*] is used to create a verbal stem-switching category.

4. Morphopragmatics and adaptations of borrowed forms

Dressler and Barbaressi (1987) proposed using morphopragmatics as a theoretical framework, arguing that distinct universal pragmatic principles could be applied fruitfully to morphological inquiry. They also posited the existence of a relationship between morphological rules and their interpreters, such as those used to interpret the results of word formation rules (WFR), whether real or as conceptualized by a speaker.

This framework provides a useful approach to understanding the adaptations of borrowed forms as discussed in this paper. In the incorporation of foreign elements, the native language is maintained but altered. The first elements to be adopted are lexical items. The native language is changing – we are approaching a macroprocess of language change; therefore, the notion of 'linguistic choice' is expanding beyond the intentional meaning it tends to carry for microcommunicative events (see Verschuren 1987 for a discussion of microprocesses and macroprocesses of adaptation). The degrees of adaptation in the microprocesses of day-to-day communication involve notions such as implicitness, indirectness, and metaphoric use (Meeuwis 1991). For instance, the use of *pantes* 'pantyhose' instead of the Spanish *medias* reflects a strategy of avoidance of intimacy, because the speaker may be embarrassed to use that term in his native language, while in the loanword, that directness is nonexistent. When a speaker uses *troquita*, the loanword with the suffixed *–ita*, that denotes "smallness," he is not meaning a "small truck," but rather a noun that in that specific context could connote endearment, intimacy, sarcasm, etc.

Other words like *troca*, frequently used without any apparently specific strategy in the discourse, denote another degree of adaptation in the process of linguistic integration of the borrowing: the foreign origin is no longer transparent for the speakers of the language in question. One could argue that this word is situated in the macrolevel of language change.

References

Aronoff, Mark. 1994. *Morphology by itself: Stems and inflectional classes*. Cambridge: MIT Press.

Boogie. 1988. Barcelona.

Cantero, Mónica. 1996. Formación de palabras en español: Morfopragmática. Ph.D. dissertation, Universitat de Barcelona. Barcelona: Serveis de publicació de la Universitat de Barcelona.

Dressler, Wolfgang U. and Lavinia M. Barbaressi. 1987. Elements of morphopragmatics. Paper presented at the International Pragmatics Conference, Antwerp, Belgium. Reproduced by L.A.U.D. Linguistic University of Duisberg.

Meeuwis, Michael. 1991. A pragmatic perspective on contact-induced language change: Dynamics in interlinguistics. *Pragmatics* 1.4: 481–516.

Popular. 1996. Barcelona.

Rock de Luxe (RDL). 1996. Barcelona.

Sagel, Jim. 1983. *Tunomás Honey*. Tempe, AZ: Bilingual Press/Editorial Bilingüe.

Verschuren, Jef. 1987. Pragmatics as a theory of linguistic adaptation. First working document drafted for the International Pragmatics Association in preparation of a Handbook of Pragmatics. *IPRA Working Document* 1.

Once upon a time en un lugar muy lejano . . . Spanish–English Codeswitching across Fairy Tale Narratives

Almeida Jacqueline Toribio
The Pennsylvania State University

This chapter explores the syntactic regularities that underlie language alternation in Spanish–English bilingual speech, and the methodologies that prove most informative in this exploration. The study introduces three tests of codeswitching competence and performance, examining the form that language alternation takes and its potential differential status in the reading, recounting, and writing of codeswitched narratives. The findings reveal speakers' strong sensitivity to syntactic well-formedness in all three tasks.

1. Preliminary overview

1.1. Codeswitching as rule-governed bilingual behavior

Codeswitching (CS) refers to the ability on the part of bilinguals to alternate between their linguistic codes in the same conversational event. With respect to its linguistic form, CS may be intersentential or intrasentential, as exemplified in the Spanish–English sentences in (1a-b) respectively.

(1) a. *Érase una vez una linda princesita blanca como la nieve*. Her stepmother, the queen, had a magic mirror on the wall.

b. *Por la noche, los siete enanitos* found her on the ground, seemingly dead.

The status of intrasentential CS in particular had been much in dispute. Some linguists viewed it as indicative of imperfect language acquisition, extreme crosslinguistic interference, or just poor sociolinguistic manners. Labov (1971) is frequently cited as referring to CS as the "irregular mixture" of two

 Research on Spanish in the U.S., ed. Ana Roca, 184–203. Somerville, MA: Cascadilla Press.

linguistic systems, and numerous others had despaired of finding any constraints on what Lance (1975) called a "willy-nilly" combination. However, subsequent studies have revealed that CS is rule-governed and systematic (cf. Gingràs 1974, Timm 1975, Pfaff 1979), demonstrating grammatical regularities which reflect the operation of underlying syntactic restrictions (cf. Poplack 1980, McClure 1981, Zentella 1981, Woolford 1983, 1984, Lipski 1985, Belazi, Rubin, and Toribio 1994, MacSwan 1997). For example, Spanish–English bilingual speakers will agree that the sentences in (2) represent possible codeswitches, whereas those in (3) do not, although they may be unable to articulate exactly what accounts for this differential judgment.

(2) a. *Al cumplir ella los veinte años, el rey invitó* many neighboring princes to a party.
b. Since she was unmarried, he wanted her to choose *un buen esposo.*
c. Princess Grace was sweet *y cariñosa con todos.*
d. *Juro por Dios que te casaré con el primer hombre* that enters this room!
e. At that exact moment, a beggar arrived *en el palacio.*

(3) a. * Very envious and evil, the *reina mandó a un criado que matara a la princesa.*
b. * *El criado la llevó al bosque* and out of compassion abandoned *la allí.*
c. * *La reina le ofreció a Blancanieves una manzana que había* laced with poison.
d. * *En la cabina vivían siete enanitos que* returned to find Snow White asleep.
e. * *Los enanitos intentaron pero no* succeeded in awakening Snow White from her sleep.

Moreover, speakers render these judgments in the absence of overt instruction – bilinguals are not taught how to codeswitch. And yet, just as monolingual native speakers of Spanish and English have an intuitive sense of linguistic well-formedness in their language, Spanish–English bilinguals are able to rely on unconscious linguistic principles in distinguishing between permissible and unacceptable codeswitches.

1.2. Accessing and assessing CS competence

Works addressing the grammar of CS in bilingual speech have made use of a wide variety of methodologies, most commonly interviews and naturalistic recordings. Unfortunately, these approaches are of limited value to a study of linguistic competence. Interviews and self-reports about bilingual speech are unreliable. Bilinguals often find it difficult to remember which language was used in any particular speech exchange. Furthermore, the problem of self-reporting is exacerbated in situations of social stigma. A speaker may refrain from switching when being observed or recorded owing to a variety of subjective factors (cf. Gumperz 1971). Recordings of naturalistic utterances face a more acute criticism: the linguistic performance of a speaker, in the form of natural data, may not be indicative of that speaker's underlying linguistic competence. In fact, given performance data alone, we might erroneously conclude that there are no exceptionless constraints on the form that language takes (cf. Poplack 1980).

The problem adduced here is endemic in almost all of the CS research reported to date. Especially noteworthy in this respect is the work of Mahootian and Santorini (1996), who admit only recordings of spontaneous speech on the grounds that linguistic theory must account for natural occurrences of the data for which it has been constructed. This focus on natural CS data is incompatible with current syntactic modes of inquiry, since the absence of violations of principles in spontaneous utterances cannot be unequivocally ascribed to a constraint that exists on the speaker's grammar. In assessing a speaker's competence, linguistic studies normally test his or her ability to judge a given sentence as a grammatical or ungrammatical string of the language, the correct response indicating the application of the principle which sanctions the structure of the target sentence. As aptly noted by McClure (1981: 72), "without native speakers' judgments about the grammaticality of an utterance, it is often difficult to determine whether the utterance clearly reflects the speaker's competence and so should be included in the corpus for which rules must account or whether it has been affected by performance factors, such as lapses of attention, and hence should be excluded from consideration." Thus, recordings of spontaneous speech must be complemented by elicitation of speakers' beliefs about ungrammatical sentences.

However, we must concede that grammaticality judgments, too, are susceptible to confounding factors, as a speaker or researcher may accept or reject a codeswitched sentence or response for non-linguistic reasons. Therefore, caution must be taken in soliciting and interpreting CS judgments. Consider in this respect MacSwan's (1997) dismissal of items such as that in (3d) which indicate the ill-formedness of switches between a complementizer and its IP complement. His dismissal of such items as "erroneous data" is founded on the informally elicited judgments of two bilinguals, who report that a short pause before the codeswitch improves the ill-formed sentences considerably. This fact bears directly on the issue at hand – it may represent the speakers' attempt to comply with the injunction against switching at this site – yet it is overlooked by the researcher, who concludes that "there is no ban on switches at this juncture" (MacSwan 1997: 241). Thus the ease with which counterexamples to any proposed constraint on CS are found may be attributable not only to differences in the methods of data collection, but also to the subsequent selection of the data for which linguistic constraints are formulated.[1]

2. The present study

The study outlined in this section seeks to redress the aforementioned failures in the research literature. The objective is to access and assess the syntactic co-occurrence constraints attested in Spanish–English bilinguals' CS behavior, while circumventing the methodological difficulties that have flawed previous efforts.

2.1. Methodologies: Test instruments and participants

Three instruments for testing CS competence and performance were designed and deployed: a reading task, a recounting task, and a writing task. For the reading task, participants are instructed to read aloud two fairy tales – "Snow White and the Seven Dwarfs," which includes grammatically unacceptable CS, and "The Beggar Prince," prepared in well-formed codeswitched sentences – and respond to questions that reference readability, comprehension, enjoyability, and grammatical form. The reading recital and responses to the questions that followed are recorded and subsequently transcribed. For the recounting task, participants are instructed to recount the ending of "Snow White" or "The Beggar Prince" in CS; the narratives are recorded and subsequently transcribed. For the writing task, participants are instructed to retell, in writing, the tale of "Little Red Riding Hood / La Caperucita Roja," as depicted in a sequence of color drawings.

The reading task required the bilingual participants to draw on their languages automatically, without forethought, while eliciting judgments about acceptable and unacceptable codeswitched texts. The recounting task was intended to engage the participants in CS, thereby offering a measure of CS performance. The writing task was devised to elicit texts that would be illustrative of the creativity of bilingual code alternation and revealing of the notions of grammatical well-formedness that modulate bilingual speakers' CS expression.[2] All ten participants selected for analysis – Yanira, Federico, Guadalupe, Carlos, Carmen, Belinda, Emma, Sara, Noemí, and Lorenzo[3] – are native Spanish speakers of Mexican heritage who had lived in Santa Barbara County for a minimum of fifteen years.[4]

2.2. Results: Reading

In the first of the CS narrative tasks, participants were instructed to read two fairy tales aloud and then respond to the questions that followed. The two narrative texts were of similar length and incorporated a comparable number of switches, though they differed significantly in the type of CS presented: "Snow White and the Seven Dwarfs" included switching at boundaries known to violate CS norms: e.g., between auxiliary and main verb, between object pronoun and main or auxiliary verb, and between noun and modifying adjective. "The Beggar Prince" included switches at those boundaries that are thought to serve as common switch sites in bilingual speech: e.g., between subject and predicate, between verb and object, and between noun and subordinate clause. Brief excerpts of each fairy tale appear in (4).

(4) Narrative reading text excerpts

a. "Snow White and the Seven Dwarfs / *Blancanieves y los siete enanitos*"

El criado la llevó al bosque y out of compassion abandoned *la allí.* A squirrel took pity on the princess and led her to a *pequeña cabina en el monte. En la cabina, vivían siete enanitos que* returned to find Snow White asleep in their beds. Back at the palace, the stepmother again asked the *espejo: "Y ahora, ¿quién es la más bella?" El espejo otra vez le* answered, without hesitation, "Snow White!" The queen was very angry and set out to find the *casita de los enanitos. Disfrazada de vieja, la reina le ofreció a Blancanieves una manzana que había* laced with poison. When Snow White bit into the apple, she *calló desvanecida al suelo. Por la noche, los enanitos la* found, seemingly dead. . . .

b. "The Beggar Prince / *El príncipe pordiosero*"

El rey Arnulfo tenía una hija muy hermosa que se llamaba Graciela. Al cumplir ella los veinte años, el rey invitó many neighboring princes to a party. Since she was unmarried, he wanted her to choose *un esposo.* Princess Grace was sweet *y cariñosa con todos. Tenía solamente un defecto*: she was indecisive. Surrounded by twelve suitors, she could not decide and the king *se enojó. Gritó, "¡Juro por Dios que te casaré con el primer hombre* that enters this room!" At that exact moment, a beggar, who had evaded *a los porteros, entró en la sala. . . .*

Based on their performance, we can conclude that all ten participants read the well-formed codeswitched "Beggar Prince" text with little effort, but had consistent problems with the ill-formed codeswitched "Snow White," demonstrating various types of disfluency, including pauses, false starts, breakdowns, even laughter. Some participants unknowingly corrected ill-formed switches in their reading, e.g., by changing 'she *calló*' to '*se calló*,' '*el* mirror' to 'the mirror,' or 'a *pequeña cabina*' to 'a *pequeña* cabin'; other attempts at self-corrections included the rendering of 'found *la*' to '*la* found her.' And some participants stammered in producing phrases such as 'the – the – the *espejo*,' as if verifying that a switch was intended at a particular inopportune juncture. Their actions, however unconscious, were substantiated by their introspections on the two texts. As shown in (5), "The Beggar Prince" was reported to be easy to read and understand. Several participants believed their reading fluency owed to their facility with English and Spanish; others reported that their success was due to the fact that the text reflected their own CS practice. In contrast, "Snow White" was deemed confusing, despite participants' acquaintance with the familiar story. Some found the text unnatural and harsh, and several offered up ways of editing the text to make it "sound right."

(5) Narrative reading task questions: Was the segment of the fairy tale easily read? Was it easily understood?

a. Comments about "The Beggar Prince"

Sí, siento que el fragmento del cuento fue fácil de leer y fácil de entender; porque puedo leer en los dos idiomas, me imagino que al mismo nivel; no me causó ninguna angustia leer este cuento. (Federico)

I think this one flowed a little bit better; it was easier to go from back to forth in English and Spanish; [. . .] it was pretty well understood; there was [sic] no harsh grammatical errors that made it hard to transition. (Lorenzo)

b. Comments about "Snow White"

Too much switching made it confusing. (Yanira)

It was harder to read – and, because it was so hard to read, it was harder to understand. (Carmen)

It was hard to shift from English to Spanish or vice versa. (Belinda)

Este fragmento del cuento de "Blancanieves" fue un poco más difícil de leer, no fue difícil de entender, pero se me hizo un poco más difícil la lectura – en el aspecto de que no llevaba un ritmo, o sea que el ritmo de la lectura fue un poco interrumpida por el hecho que unas palabaras las usaron en el cuento en una manera que yo no las uso generalmente en ocasiones que he mezclado el lenguaje. (Federico)

Había algunas oraciones que – didn't make sense. (Sara)

The segment of the fairy tale was somewhat easily read, although what it is that some of the sentences could've changed from Spanish to English in a better way; there are certain places that really weren't really right to break from English to Spanish or from Spanish to English. The story was easily understood because I understand English and Spanish, but I just think, like, for example the last sentence, "When Snow White bit into the apple, she cayó desvanecida al suelo," that I wouldn't say it, it doesn't sound right. I would probably say, "When Snow White bit into the apple, ella se cayó al suelo." Or "she fell desvanecida al suelo." (Lorenzo)

The participants were then asked to compare the two texts, again on measures of readability, comprehension, and enjoyability. Consistent with their reading and evaluations of the individual fragments, most expressed a preference for "The Beggar Prince," as articulated in (6a). However, there were exceptions: one participant, Lorenzo, stated that he just didn't like the stories (6b), and two other participants indicated a preference for "Snow White," though, as shown in (6c), they favored the text for the familiar plot and vocabulary, rather than for its grammatical form.

(6) Narrative reading task questions: In comparing the two texts, which one was more easily read? understood? enjoyable?

a. Comments indicating preference for "The Beggar Prince"

"The Beggar Prince" flowed better. You didn't get stuck on the switches . . . it didn't mix the languages so often. (Yanira)

The first one. Why? Because it was easier to read and I actually understood the story. (Carmen)

b. Comments indicating no preference

I'd have to say that they're both the same; me dio igual los dos. I don't know I guess I really don't like stories. (Lorenzo)

c. Comments indicating preference for "Snow White"

Se me afigura que el fragmento de "Caperucita Roja" ["El Príncipe Pordiosero"] fue un poco más fácil y de entenderse también. . . . Me gustó más el de "Blancanieves," pero eso es porque me gusta más ese cuento no necesariamente la manera en que está escrito, pero si tuviera yo que leerle el cuento a otra persona me gustaría leerle mejor el de "Caperucita Roja" ["El Príncipe Pordiosero"].[5] (Federico)

I think the "Snow White" was more easy to read, because there was [sic] some words in "The Beggar Prince" that I didn't really know before . . . . . . so, I enjoyed the one about Snow White and the seven dwarfs more. (Emma)

Finally, participants were asked to comment specifically on the CS forms represented in the two texts. All ten participants recognized the differential CS patterns, which they perceived to be more abrupt, more frequent, and less patterned in "Snow White" than in "The Beggar Prince." Sample comments are transcribed in (7):

(7) Narrative reading task question: Was there a difference in the mixing across the two texts?

There is mixing in "The Beggar Prince," but it makes sense. "Snow White" changes without a pattern. (Yanira)

Como mencioné anteriormente la diferencia en el tipo de mezcla es un poco más inadecuada de mi punto de vista el de "Blancanieves." Se me hizo un poco más difícil la manera en que se fragmentaron las frases del español al inglés. (Federico)

I don't know really what the difference is, but, the other one ["The Beggar Prince"] was half in Spanish and half in English, and so was this one ["Snow White"], but the other one was just easier to read, I don't know exactly if it's the way part of the sentence or which words you use Spanish and which you don't. (Carmen)

The changes in "Snow White" were harder to understand. (Belinda)

There is more mixing in the first one, "Snow White and the Seven Dwarfs." (Emma)

"The Beggar Princess" . . . didn't have such breaks in between sentences, it didn't go where they wouldn't connect. Blancanieves . . . if it began in English and went into Spanish, it was a point where it shouldn't, or it just didn't sound right. (Lorenzo)

"Snow White" [. . .] that's not how I mix languages. (Sara)

Thus, the reading task proved useful in accessing judgments on distinct CS forms. Specifically, all of the participants demonstrated a more positive disposition towards the language forms in "The Beggar Prince" with respect to readability, comprehension, enjoyability, and patterns of language alternation. More generally, then, our participants' responses revealed a marked sensitivity to CS well-formedness.

2.3. Results: Recounting

Two elicitation tasks were developed to investigate the CS performance of the bilingual participants. Though it is unusual to divorce CS production from its social context, such 'isolated' tasks are a necessary step in controlling for the variables that would otherwise confound the inferences drawn from the study. For instance, an extensive background questionnaire indicated that some participants seldom engaged in CS in their natural speech productions, for lack of opportunity or inclination, and thus CS had to be elicited (Toribio 2000). In the recounting component, participants were instructed to select one of the fairy tale fragments previously presented and recount the ending in codeswitched speech. The productions were recorded, and subsequently transcribed and analyzed for linguistic content. Nine of the ten story-telling narratives produced in this condition were well-elaborated in codeswitched speech; two representative excerpts appear in (8).

(8) *Por la noche los enanitos* – they found uhhh *Blancanieves* seemingly dead. *Se pusieron muy tristes y a llorar* – and then one of them had an idea to bury her. *Arriba en la montaña donde estuviera rodeada por todos sus heridos queridos* . . . all the little birds, the little possums, all the little animals of the forest because she loved them so much – *entonces se la llevaron este* – in a procession they marched up there. *Y como, como eran . . . muy imaginativos ellos, muy – este* – they, they built a casket of ahhh clear crystal casket. *Y allí es donde la metieron y la velaron por un día, dos días y todos los animalitos del bosque* were there with them – all sad because she was a very beautiful *doncella – ya ya que habían pasado unos dos – tres días – pasó por allí* a very handsome prince. (Sara)

Después que encontraron los enanitos a a Blancanieves, umm, they were crying and were sad about about what had happened to her because they thought that she was dead. Ummmm. *Y en eso vino, llegó un umm príncipe y vio a Blancanieves* and he ahh, ahh he approached her and he gave her a kiss. *Cuando la, después de que la besó, Blancanieves despertó y los enanitos estaban* very happy, *porque ella se ummm ella se* she came back to life . . . *Cuando la reina se dio cuenta de esto, ehh*, she got very angry. (Noemí)

Even a cursory overview of the oral narratives reveals a broad use of both languages. The vast majority of language switches occurred at sentence boundaries, many preceded by pauses signaling principal discourse breaks required in recalling and reformulating the story. The narratives additionally included other stylistic features commonly marked by language alternations in bilingual speech; as shown in (9), some of these stylistic strategies are especially germane to storytelling.

(9) Stylistic language alternations[6]

a. CS for reported speech
pero dijo ella, "I'll give it some time," (Lorenzo)

b. CS for repetition or emphasis
un príncipe, Prince Charming – *estaba pasando por el bosque . . .* (Yanira)
un gran palacio, a great palace, *y allí entonces la princesa* (Belinda)

c. CS for qualification or elaboration
por todos sus queridos – all the little birds, the little possums, all the little animals of the forest (Sara)
qué tipo de animales habían, what type of trees, flowers (Lorenzo)
she wanted to experiment, *quería ver qué había allá fuera* (Lorenzo)
No había cuartos, there was no living room, there was no, not even a bathroom. (Lorenzo)

d. CS for fixed or formulaic phrases
Y así vivieron, they lived happily ever after. (Belinda)

Also attested were lexical insertions and tag-switches. Lexical insertions, exemplified in (10a), represent the introduction of individual items into a recipient language; such insertions may be occasioned by lexical unavailability or temporary lapses in memory, and often trigger a language switch for ensuing material. Tag-switches, such as *okay*, *so*, *pues*, and *verdad*, function as sentence fillers or reveal a speaker's disposition towards an utterance; tags typically occur at phrase or clause boundaries. Lexical insertions and tags are manifested in both monolingual and bilingual modes of interaction. In contrast, CS is illustrative of a bilingual speech mode that requires a high degree of bilingual competence.

(10) Other features common in bilingual speech

a. Lexical insertions
because she was a very beautiful *doncella* (Sara)
ella estaba acostumbrada a todas las, umm, luxuries of her palace (Belinda)

b. Tag-switches
se quedó unos, you know, *ella dijo, me voy a quedar aquí un mes . . .* (Lorenzo)

As noted, intersentential switches predominated in the oral narratives. However, there were also attested numerous examples of intrasentential CS, especially at major phrase boundaries. The excerpts shown in (11) illustrate switching between clauses, between coordinated clausal conjuncts,[7] between coordinated phrasal conjuncts, between subject and predicate, between verb and complements, between noun and relative clauses, and between clause and sentential modifiers.

(11) CS produced in narrative story-telling task

a. CS between sentential clauses, with pause
They don't know what to do and they pick her up, *y la llevan a la casa* . . . (Yanira)
They prepared for a funeral, *y pusieron muchas flores* (Guadalupe)
He saw that she was very beautiful, *y la besó*. (Emma)
Se pusieron muy tristes y a llorar . . . and then one of them had an idea to bury her. (Sara)

b. CS between coordinated clausal conjuncts
Se asomó a la casa de los enanitos and he saw that . . . (Yanira)
Llegó un príncipe y vió a Blancanieves and he approached her and gave her a kiss. (Noemí)
y la sacó del ataúd and without knowing why . . . he kissed her on the lips. (Sara)

c. CS between coordinated phrasal conjuncts
Her mother *le habló* and sent her to make, to take . . . (Carlos)
He wanted to see her up close *y se le acercó*. (Sara)
accepted the decision that the husband had made *y se fueron al bosque* . . . (Lorenzo)

d. CS between subject and predicate
Ellos se enamoraron y el príncipe wanted to get married. (Emma)
*Y todos los animalitos del bosqu*e were there with them. (Sara)
y su belleza took him by surprise. (Sara)
*Y Blancanieves y el príncipe y los siete enanito*s were very happy. (Noemí)

e. CS between verb and complements
Al fin, ella decidió to go back her palace. (Carmen)
Blancanieves despertó y los enanitos estaban very happy. (Noemí)
She wanted to see *la belleza que tenía* . . . (Lorenzo)

f. CS between noun and relative clause
se fueron al bosque where they would both live in the little house. (Lorenzo)
the beauty *que el bosque le daba*. (Lorenzo)

g. CS for sentential modifiers
Al mismo tiempo, the wolf continued on the original path[8] (Carlos)
Al llegar a la casita, she noted . . . (Lorenzo)

While the grammatically-sanctioned switches illustrated in (11) proceed smoothly, others, representing potential ill-formed switches, occasioned disfluencies. For example, as shown in (12), switching after a coordinating conjunction, subordinating complementizer, and determiner is preceded by pauses or prevented by an immediate reiteration:

(12) Circumventing ill-formed switches

a. Disfluency in CS
not frowns but – *un poco tristes* (Yanira)
they continued working and – *en eso iban pasando un príncipe* . . . (Yanira)
dijo que – all of a sudden . . . (Belinda)

b. Repair in CS
el – the queen was not happy that she was still alive[9] (Guadalupe)
Ella se she came back to life (Noemí)
y umm he and he fought with her and he killed her. (Noemí)
con las, with the leaves of the tree. (Lorenzo)
Y, the house was just a one-room house. (Lorenzo)

In addition, there were no incidences of CS at the boundary between auxiliary and main verb, between negative marker and verb, or between demonstrative and noun, among other syntactic junctures where grammatical norms do not favor CS. In fact, not one of the participants who elected to tell the ending to the "Snow White" fairy tale replicated the ill-formed switching modeled in the exemplar; this finding is significant, as it suggests that the switching in the fairy tale is indeed incompatible with fluent bilingual production.

The remaining participant, Federico, experienced difficulty in meeting the demands of the task, and gave verbal expression to his frustration. As shown in the transcript (13), he recounted the ending of "The Beggar Prince" fully in Spanish, and was apologetic in his resignation. He made a second attempt to comply with the instructions, this time relating the segment fully in English, with a single insertion of an adverbial modifier.

(13) [. . .] *Nunca más quiso todas las riquezas que quería antes porque antes era una, una niña fresa, no trataba bien a sus compañeros, y ahora era mas buena de corazón . . . como ven Se me hizo un poco difícil mezclar el inglés con el español. No es que no lo puedo hacer pero casi siempre pienso o estoy pensando en español. No estoy pensando en inglés y – y – y a veces es más es más fácil terminarlo de una manera pero, y* – I guess I could do it both ways. I don't know. It's hard for me though, yeah, you know if I start talking in one language I keep talking in one language so it's kind of hard. I can't concentrate on doing that. Umm – so I'm not gonna try to do it – umm – she lived happily ever after, *humildemente*, umm, without all the riches that the – see, I can't, I don't know, for some reason I hold myself back sometimes. (Federico)

However, Federico's behavior does not impugn the validity of the storytelling task; rather, it makes evident that not all bilinguals possess the communicative competence to engage in CS. As often noted in the research literature (cf. Valdés 1976, Aguirre 1977), competence in two languages is a necessary but not sufficient prerequisite in determining successful CS performance: membership in a community in which CS is practiced may also be required.[10] This mitigating factor is controlled for in the narrative writing task.

2.4. *Results: Writing*

In the final narrative task, participants were asked to review a sequence of color illustrations depicting the "Little Red Riding Hood" fairy tale and recount the story in mixed speech, but this time in written form. To be sure, this task was not intended to yield speech samples that would be equivalent to the oral narratives produced in the preceding task. Lipski (1985) has pointed to the "obvious limitations" inherent in the use of written samples of bilingual CS as representative of speaker norms. However, the task at hand did not elicit literary artifacts, but written-out renditions of a familiar fairy tale narrative, and, as such, the texts were expected to more closely approximate unmarked verbal behavior than prose or poetry. Thus, while the task was designed to examine speakers' creative manipulation of two languages, its greater purpose was to elicit speakers' notions of CS well-formedness while abstracting away from the demands of performance and practice.

All participants successfully completed the task, producing well-elaborated narratives that were permeated by intrasentential CS. Lorenzo's writing sample is reproduced, without editorial correction, in (14).

(14) Once upon a time, *en un lugar lejano*, there was a little girl *que se llamaba Caperucita Roja*. She liked walking through the forest, *escuchando los pajaritos, oliendo las flores, y apreciando la belleza natural*. One day, *su mamá la mando a la casa de su abuelita*. She told L.R.R.H. *que su abuelita ocupaba* some medicine for some sickness. *Caperucita* went to her grandmother's house, *a llevarle medicina*. On the way to the house, *se topo con un lobo feo*. The wolf gave her flowers and asked where she was heading. *Ella le contesto que iba a la casa de su abuelita*. The wolf then left her and headed to the grandmother's house, *corriendo lo mas pronto posible par ganarle a Caperucita*. When he arrived, *se metio y persiguido a la abuelita. Caperucita luego llegó* and began to knock. The wolf changed into the grandmother's clothes *y se metio de bajo de las cobijas*. L.R.R.H. went inside and noticed *que su abuelita* looked different. She began to ask questions about the wolf's nose, eyes, ears, and mouth. *Cuando Caperucita* asked the last question, *el lobo brincó y la empeso a corretiar*. At the same time, a little squirrel had warned a hunter in the forest about this big bad wolf. *El hombre corrio en seguida, a la casa de la abuelita*. There he found

> the wolf, *persiguiendo a Caperucita.* L.R.R.H. ran outside, *y el lobo la siguio. Entonces el hombre levanto su rifle* and fired it at the wolf, *matandolo. Caperucita entonces empeso a llorar.* The man asked her *porque estaba llorando, y ella le dijo que porque el lobo se había comido a su abuelita.* At that same time, the grandmother came out of the dog's house. *Ella se había escondido el la casa del perro durante todo ese tiempo. Asi que feliz termina este cuento de* Little Red Riding Hood. [sic]

As in the oral production task, the participants demonstrated a broad use of both languages in achieving a diversity of stylistic effects: e.g., in signaling a change in roles (15a), marking direct or indirect speech (15b), shifting for declarative or interrogative (15c), attracting attention (15d), heightening an interjection or exclamation (15e), and inserting fixed or formulaic phrases (15f).

(15) Stylistic CS

a. CS for change in roles
"Oh grandma what a big nose you have" "*Para olerte mejor mijita*" (Sara)

b. CS for reported speech
El wolf *le pregunto* – where are you going *Caperucita*? And she told him "*A la casa de mi abuelita* (Noemí)

c. CS for declarative or interrogative
El lobo le preguntó where did she live (Emma)

d. CS for attracting attention
Mira so that you get to her house sooner *vete por este camino* (Belinda)

e. CS for interjections or exclamation
"Oh *que bien*, where does she live?" [sic] (Sara)

f. CS for fixed or formulaic phrases
Once upon a time *había una niña llamada Caperucita Roja* (Carmen)
Y la historia termina con un happy ending. (Emma)

Just as with the oral narratives, the written narratives incorporated lexical insertion of nouns, such as *wolf*, *ardillita*, *hunter*, *mom*, *abuelta, grandma*, and *mi'ja* [sic]. The example in (16) demonstrates two such insertions:

(16) Lexical insertion

> On the way to *abuela*'s house she runs into the *lobo* and he asks her where she is going. After she tells him they both go on their way. (Federico)

Unlike the oral narrative production task, this third task produced no tag switches, which is expected given their typical discourse functions. More notably, unlike the previous task, the written narrative task gave rise to various types of transfers. Examples such as '*la* house of the grandmother,' modeled on '*la casa de la abuela*,' and '*hablar con* strangers' modeled on 'talk to strangers,' demonstrate the influence of the structure of one language on the other.

A longer view of the Spanish and English segments of discourse produced in these written narratives reveals that the participants generally possess an advanced degree of bilingual competence; this ability was used in producing texts that included intersentential and intrasentential CS. Interestingly, the intersentential CS attested in the written narratives is significantly reduced when compared with that produced in the oral narratives; intrasentential CS predominated in this task, as evidenced in the examples in (17). Again, the written texts are faithfully reproduced without editing.

(17) CS in written narratives

a. CS between coordinated clausal conjuncts
Le dispara and the wolf dies. (Yanira)
Ella anda perdida so she asks him for directions (Carmen)
She thanked him for this advice *y se despidieron.* (Belinda)
knew of a short cut *y Caperucita se fue por ahi.* [sic] (Emma)

b. CS between coordinated phrasal conjuncts
En eso llega la niña saludándola but points to her big teeth (Yanira)
She suspects something *y le hace muchas preguntas.* (Federico)
Llego a la casa de la habuela and scared her off. [sic] (Carlos)
Caperucita lo encontro sospechoso and pointed out that . . . [sic] (Emma)
El hombre lobo se le acerco a Caperucita and said where are you going mija. [sic] (Sara)
Caperucita luego llegó and began to knock. (Lorenzo)
el hombre levantó su rifle and fired it at the wolf (Lorenzo)

c. CS between subject and predicate
The story *empieza en que su mamá le hace un encargo* . . . (Federico)
When the wolf *she iba a comer a Caperucita* the hunter came [sic] (Emma)
cada quien went on their own way (Sara)
Cuando Caperucita asked the last question . . . (Lorenzo)

d. CS between verb and subordinate clause
Caperucita told him *que iba a visitar a su* grandmother. (Emma)
El lobo le preguntó where did she live (Emma)
after telling him *donde vive la* grandma *cada quien* went on their own way. (Sara)
The man asked her *porque estaba llorando.* [sic] (Lorenzo)

e. CS between verb and complements
La madre de Caperucita le da a jar of honey. (Yanira)
In the title frame we see *Caperucita Roja en el bosque* (Federico)
que ella lleva some food to her gradmother [sic] (Guadalupe)
siempre traía a red cloth over her head. (Carmen)
para que le llevara food to her grandmother. (Sara)
que su abuelita ocupaba some medicine for some sickness. (Lorenzo)
Caperucita went to her grandmother's house *a llevarle medicina.* (Lorenzo)

f. CS between preposition and objects
El lobo platica con Little Red Riding Hood for a while. (Yanira)
goes to *la casa de la abuelita* (Federico)
and sent her to take honey to *su abuela.* (Carlos)
recuerda no hables con strangers along the way (Sara)

g. CS between noun and relative clause
there was a little girl *que se llamaba Caperucita Roja.* (Lorenzo)

h. CS for phrasal modifiers
directions *para llegar a la casa de su abuela.* (Carmen)
Esta es la historia of the "Little Red Riding Hood." (Emma)

i. CS for sentential modifiers
As Little Red Riding Hood is walking along the forest *se encuentra con un lobo.* (Yanira)
y llego when the wolf was chasing Little red riding Hood. [sic] (Guadalupe)
to take this path *por que era mas corto.* [sic] (Carlos)
Her mom had given her some soup *para que le llevara a su abuela . . .* (Carmen)
se mete en la cama to pretend that he is the grandmother (Carmen)
en el camino she met this *lobo feroz* that asked where she was going. (Belinda)
so that you get to her house sooner *vete por este camino* (Belinda)
to her grandmother's house *porque su abuelita estaba enferma.* (Emma)
Once upon a time, *en un lugar lejano*, there was a little girl . . . (Lorenzo)

Finally, in the creative alternating use of Spanish and English, there were ill-formed switches produced – remarkably, only two, shown in (18):

(18) Ill-formed CS

a. CS of a clitic pronoun/complex verb
Una ardilla que lo escucho le fue a tell a hunter and he went to look for the wolf. [sic] (Emma)

b. CS before a coordinating conjunction
El hombre lobo beat *Caperucita* to *abuelita*'s house and *la asusto*. [sic] (Sara)

Thus, the written mode did not constrain but encouraged switching at a variety of syntactic junctures. However, though the number and variety of switch sites increased, the written narratives were similar to the oral narratives in revealing a preference for switching at major syntactic boundaries.

3. Summary and conclusion

The findings for the reading, recounting, and writing components are robust across subjects and tasks. The reading task, a grammatical acceptability task of sorts, accessed speaker's sensitivity to CS patterns. By their reading performance and by their introspection on the differential CS in the two model texts, the participants demonstrated knowledge of the grammatical coherence that underlies language alternations. While the language alternations in "The Beggar Prince" were thought to be systematic and more correct, the CS in "Snow White" was rejected as affected and forced. Several participants unconsciously self-corrected the ill-formed switches in their readings, and others offered explicit editing recommendations for improving the ill-formed text. And our participant, Federico, who was unable to produce a CS narrative was nevertheless successful in identifying and articulating the differences between the texts. These findings are telling of our participants' ability to draw on unconscious linguistic principles in distinguishing between permissible and unacceptable switches.

The task of CS competence was complemented by two performance tasks in which participants were required to recount fairy tales in oral and written code-switched speech. The productions in both tasks reflected a strict compliance to CS norms. The oral narratives incorporated intersentential CS and intrasentential CS at major phrasal boundaries (in addition to the lexical insertions and formulaic expressions that are commonly evidenced in bilingual productions). Moreover, alternations that would violate phrasal coherence were circumvented or repaired, such that there were no true violations of CS norms attested in oral speech. Such overall well-formedness is unexpected in informal speech, where speakers are less apt to "watch their ps and qs" (Zentella 1997: 135). However, while the oral production task should not have evoked a formal, careful speech style, the condition itself – a lone speaker directing speech into a microphone in an individual carrel – does not foster the environment in which speakers allow themselves the privilege of 'relaxing' their grammars.[11] This condition also precludes the casual interchange in which intrasentential CS is favored, accounting for the multitude of alternations at sentence boundaries.

Our participants were able to more effectively draw on their bilingual resources in the written production task; the quantity and types of intrasentential CS was significantly increased in the writing task, as compared with the oral production task. In fact, the CS produced in this condition, especially as compared with the reduced CS modeled in "The Beggar Prince," attests to our participants' creative manipulation of Spanish and English. The abundance of intrasentential CS was likely fostered by the specifics of the task itself: the visual aids and lack of time constraints for formulating the story were certain to reduce anxiety. However, the task engendered reflection and self-correction, and as a consequence, CS well-formedness was maintained.[12] These differential and at once convergent findings speak to the benefit of multiple measures in the study of CS.

Notes

1. For a discussion of factors that enter into an accurate characterization of CS, see Toribio and Rubin 1996 and Toribio 2000.

2. As these tasks represent the elicitation of CS, the linguistic forms produced will not necessarily duplicate the forms observed in spontaneous speech. Nevertheless, the language samples yielded by these tasks provide important insights into speakers' sensitivity to CS norms.

3. The fictional names correspond to participants 121776YS, 040173FR, 091868GG, 041373CV, 051076CB, 122273BV, 010478ER, 070375SR, 020477NP, 091675LR, randomly selected from a larger study of 50 Spanish–English bilinguals from Southern California.

4. The study on which this work is based was carried out in 1997–98 at the University of California, Santa Barbara, in the context of a research group convened and directed by the author. The group was motivated by an interest in the historical and continued presence of Spanish and Spanish–English bilingualism in the city of Santa Barbara. The aim was to identify those factors, including linguistic, social, and psychological, which influence the form of the local language. The author gratefully acknowledges the support of the National Endowment for the Humanities (grant FA 34144–96) and various intramural funding agencies, among these, the Interdisciplinary Humanities Center, UC Mexus, the Academic Senate, and the Center for Chicano Studies, and expresses sincere appreciation to seven student researchers for their commitment and abilities in completing the project: Renée Basile, Mimi Beller, Cecilia Montes-Alcalá, Silvia Pérez-López, Christina Piranio, Guillermo Vásquez, and Patxi Zabaleta.

5. Federico later corrected his 'error' in misidentifying the fairy tale, saying, "Quiero hacer una corrección a lo que dije anteriormente. Me equivoqué con el título del cuento

que había leído. Se llama 'El Príncipe Pordiosero,' no 'Caperucita Roja;' estaba confundido."

6. The reader is referred to Gumperz 1971 and Valdés-Fallis 1976 for discussion of the discursive functions achieved by CS.

7. The possibility of null subjects in Spanish makes it difficult to distinguish between coordination of full clauses and coordination of predicates. The analysis here errs on the side of conservatism: coordination of clauses must include two distinct subjects, indicated by overt content or morphology.

8. Carlos recounted both "The Beggar Prince" and "Little Red Riding Hood" fairy tales.

9. This example does not represent a correction for misassignment of gender; the remainder of the oral text confirms that *reina* is marked with the default masculine gender in the speaker's lexicon. Her uncertainty regarding grammatical gender is verified in the written CS task and in a separate Spanish-language narrative task, not reproduced here (cf. Toribio 1999).

10. As corroborated in his sociolinguistic profile, Federico participates in largely monolingual-speaking Spanish- and English-language communities.

11. Zentella (1981: 56–57) reports that "codeswitchers sometimes jump from one language to another at points that break up constituents that are usually kept together, e.g., between determiner and subject noun as in 'the *demonio*' (devil)."

12. Though not its principal aim, the present work can be interpreted as presenting strong experimental evidence of the extent to which the grammatical coherence and co-occurrence restrictions attested in Spanish–English codeswitching adhere to the Functional Head Constraint (Belazi et al. 1994).

References

Aguirre, Adalberto, Jr. 1977. Acceptability judgment of grammatical and ungrammatical forms of intrasentential code alternation. Ph.D. dissertation, Stanford University.

Belazi, Hedi, Edward Rubin, and Almeida Jacqueline Toribio. 1994. Code switching and X-bar theory: The Functional Head Constraint. *Linguistic Inquiry* 25: 221–237.

Gingràs, Rosario. 1974. Problems in the description of Spanish/English intrasentential code-switching. In *Southwest areal linguistics*, ed. Garland D. Bills, 167–174. San Diego, CA: University of California Institute for Cultural Pluralism.

Gumperz, John. 1971. *Language in social groups.* Stanford, CA: Stanford University Press.

Labov, William. 1971. The notion of system in creole languages. In *Pidginization and creolization of languages*, ed. Dell Hymes, 447–472. Cambridge: Cambridge University Press.

Lance, Donald. 1975. Spanish/English code-switching. In *El lenguaje de los Chicanos,* ed. Eduardo Hernández-Chávez, Andrew Cohen, and Anthony Beltramo, 138–153. Arlington, VA: Center for Applied Linguistics.

Lipski, John. 1985. *Linguistic aspects of Spanish–English language switching.* Tempe, AZ: Arizona State University, Center for Latin American Studies.

MacSwan, Jeffrey. 1997. A minimalist approach to intrasentential code switching: Spanish-Nahuatl bilingualism in Central Mexico. Ph.D. dissertation, University of California, Los Angeles.

Mahootian, Shahrzad and Beatrice Santorini. 1996. Codeswitching and the complement/adjunct distinction. *Linguistic Inquiry* 27: 464–479.

McClure, Erica. 1981. Formal and functional aspects of the code-switched discourse of bilingual children. In *Latino language and communicative behavior,* ed. Richard Duran, 69–94. Norwood, NJ: Ablex Publishing.

Pfaff, Carol W. 1979. Constraints on language mixing: Intrasentential code-switching and borrowing in Spanish/English. *Language* 55: 291–318.

Poplack, Shana. 1980. Sometimes I'll start a sentence in Spanish y termino en español: Toward a typology of code-switching. In *Spanish in the United States: Sociolinguistic aspects,* ed. Jon Amastae and Lucía Elías-Olivares, 230–263. Cambridge: Cambridge University Press.

Timm, Leonore A. 1975. Spanish–English code-switching: El porque and how-not-to. *Romance Philology* 28: 473–482.

Toribio, Almeida Jacqueline. 1999. Code-switching and minority language attrition. Forthcoming in *Proceedings of the 1999 Conference on the L1 and L2 Acquisition of Spanish and Portuguese*, ed. Ronald Leow and Cristina Sanz. Washington, DC: Georgetown University Press.

Toribio, Almeida Jacqueline. 2000. Spanglish?! Bite your tongue! Spanish–English code-switching among US Latinos. In *Reflexiones 1999*, ed. Richard Flores, 115–147. Austin, TX: Center for Mexican American Studies.

Toribio, Almeida Jacqueline and Edward J. Rubin. 1996. Code-switching in generative grammar. In *Spanish in contact,* ed. Ana Roca and John B. Jensen, 203–226. Somerville, MA: Cascadilla Press.

Valdés-Fallis, Guadalupe. 1976. Social interaction and code-switching patterns. In *Bilingualism in the bicentennial and beyond*, ed. Gary Keller, Richard Teschner, and Silvia Viera, 52–85. Jamaica, NY: Bilingual Press.

Woolford, Ellen. 1983. Bilingual code-switching and syntactic theory. *Linguistic Inquiry* 14: 520–536.

Woolford, Ellen. 1984. On the application of wh-movement and inversion in code-switching sentences. *Revue Quebecoise de Linguistique* 14: 77–86.

Zentella, Ana Celia. 1981. Hablamos los dos: We speak both: Growing up bilingual in el barrio. Ph.D. dissertation, University of Pennsylvania.

Zentella, Ana Celia. 1997. *Growing up bilingual.* Malden, MA: Blackwell Publishers.

Codeswitching and Language Use in the Classroom

Florencia Riegelhaupt
Northern Arizona University

Research in codeswitching in the United States started to unfold when the nation began to address the academic inequalities that make it difficult for Spanish/English bilinguals and speakers of Black English to succeed. In 1954, the groundbreaking Supreme Court decision in Brown vs. Board of Education declared that "separate but equal" education was unconstitutional and required schools to integrate. Title VI of the 1964 Civil Rights Act declared a ban on discrimination on the basis of "race, color, or national origin," and the Bilingual Act of 1968 provided assistance to schools that served linguistic minorities. In 1974, the landmark U.S. Supreme Court decision in Lau vs. Nichols defined the legal responsibilities of schools serving limited-English-proficient students in any federally assisted program. The court declared that children have a civil right to be taught in their home language while they acquire English. Equal access and equal educational opportunity did not mean merely providing students with the same materials, teachers, and facilities. Rather, it required that students be given an educational experience that was socially, linguistically, and academically meaningful. In 1974, the Equal Educational Opportunities Act provided legislative backing to the Lau vs. Nichols Supreme Court decision. It required public school districts to implement programs to meet the needs of bilingual students. In 1975, the Lau Remedies were developed. They provided specific procedures for assessing language proficiency and outlined appropriate instructional treatment and professional standards for teachers of language minority students. Many teachers sought out retraining, especially in Spanish and the native languages of other minority students.

The language of the classroom became an important concern of educators and linguists in the mid 1960s, and by the early 1970s numerous studies were being published. One of the first sources to discuss classroom language using sociolinguistic theory and ethnographic methodology was *Functions of*

 Research on Spanish in the U.S., ed. Ana Roca, 204–217. Somerville, MA: Cascadilla Press.

Language in the Classroom by Cazden, Vera, and Hymes (1972). Their edited volume was an outgrowth of a 1965 meeting of anthropologists, linguists, psychologists, and sociologists. The group, called together by Edmund Gordon, and including participants Joshua Fishman, Joan Gussow, Vivian Horner, Alfred Hayes, Courtney Cazden, Dell Hymes, and John Vera "believed that school problems could be better explained by differences in language use between home and school, and the need for future research became a nagging theme throughout our discussions" (Cazden et al. 1972). The participants worked to establish a research agenda for the study of the relationship between children's language use and school success.

When educators began to study the languages, dialects, and registers of their students, they discovered that bilingual students utilize their second language English, their first language, and the alternation of the two, or codeswitching, when interacting with other bilinguals. This phenomenon of codeswitching sparked many new questions. Should codeswitching be permitted in the classroom? What types of codeswitching should be used? Does codeswitching indicate a weakness in the language being acquired? Or is it another resource to be developed and used to the student's advantage?

This article provides an overview of the primary issues surrounding the use of codeswitching in the bilingual classroom. First, I discuss the importance of placing language use in its social context and the value of the ethnographic method for classroom research. I then describe how codeswitching can promote cognitive development, increase comprehension, and mark changes in context. Finally, I explore two central questions facing educators today: what role should codeswitching play in classrooms, and how do we teach bilingual students about the appropriate use of their two languages?

1. Ethnography in the classroom

In the 1960s, the new and blossoming field of theoretical linguistics concentrated on language universals and the capacity of humans to acquire language. Theoretical linguists sought to uncover linguistic competence, rather than performance. At the same time, a field that bridged the gap between what humans are capable of doing with and through language and what they actually do in real social settings was about to be born. This field, called sociolinguistics or the sociology of language, recognized the importance of placing language within the contexts of its use. A central question was appropriateness: where, with whom, and when do people use each variety of the language in question?

In *Functions of Language in the Classroom*, Hymes (1972: xi) notes that few linguists had considered the problems related to language use in classroom settings. Some linguists, he writes, "have come to deny any claim to authority in classroom matters, saying that the present state of linguistic theory is so confused that linguists can tell teachers nothing useful at all." Hymes recognizes the fact that new research would be necessary if "we are to say something valid and helpful." According to Hymes (1972: xii):

> The primary difficulty for linguistics is that such improvements do not depend on language alone, but on language in social context. What is crucial is not so much a better understanding of how language is structured, but a better understanding of how language is used, not so much what language is, as what language is for. Linguists have generally taken questions of use and purpose for granted. They have not related the structure of language to the structure of speaking. Yet if one thing is abundantly clear, it is that the problems in many American classrooms have to do precisely with that relationship.

The task of sociolinguistic research in educational settings, then, is to make "explicit and objectively systematic what speakers of the language, or members of the community, in a sense already know" (Hymes 1972: xv).

In order to study codeswitching in classroom interactions, we need to document conversational and pedagogical language use in context. We must also learn the particular rules that govern interaction and appropriate language use in the classroom setting. To be effective, the study of functions of language in the classroom must focus on all the different forms of communication that take place in educational settings. These must include small and large group instruction, teacher interaction with individuals in private and public contexts, peer tutoring sessions, and other child/child interactions. Codeswitching may occur in none, some, or all of these contexts.

Ethnography can be a powerful method of gaining insight into classroom interactions. Traditionally, ethnography was only used by anthropologists to study cultures other than their own. However, the ethnographic study of classroom interaction gained popularity in the early 1970s.

Carrasco (1984: 19) notes that "the central aim of ethnography is to understand another way of life from the native point of view." Ethnography can be used as a collaborative tool that allows the practitioner and researcher to examine the classroom together, from both emic and etic perspectives, as outsider and insider. When the teachers are engaged in teaching, they rarely notice their own or their students' language behavior. The ethnographer's observations allow the teacher to see his or her own behavior as an outsider and to become aware of the quality of interaction during daily activities. This opportunity for self-reflection helps to develop an "expanded awareness" (Carrasco 1981) of individual student competencies and can have an immediate effect on teacher (and student) behavior. In particular, it can make teachers aware that codeswitching is an effective communicative and pedagogical strategy.

It is also important to view classroom language in its wider social context. Gumperz and Hernández-Chávez (1972) and Blom and Gumperz (1972) show that codeswitching patterns among adults in bidialectal/bilingual contexts outside the classroom also hold true for the bilingual classroom. The more we know about how language is used in the surrounding communities, the more we will be able to understand the functions of codeswitching in the classroom.

Each linguistic community is different and continues to change. While research in one community at a particular moment in time might shed light on the linguistic reality of another, specific recommendations about language use and codeswitching in the classroom must be predicated upon research in that community and the schools within it. Contextual information about the overall linguistic reality of a community must include:

1. the social, cultural, political, linguistic, and economic characteristics of the individuals and communities involved,
2. the attitudes of the minority linguistic community toward codeswitching, its own language(s), bilingualism, and the language of the mainstream, or perhaps the official language of a nation,
3. the language and overall attitudes of the majority community toward the various groups and their languages,
4. the educational opportunities within and outside the communities in question,
5. the opportunities available to access linguistic resources within and outside the communities, and
6. the overall relationships between the communities and their members.

2. Codeswitching and cognitive development

Early studies on codeswitching were undertaken to investigate whether bilingualism itself causes bilinguals to lag behind the majority in school achievement. The low achievement of some bilinguals may be attributed to differences between home and school culture, low socioeconomic class and low self-esteem. It may also be caused by the differential treatment of minorities in schools. It is not true, however, that bilingualism impedes students' ability to learn.

If codeswitching were detrimental to the child's linguistic, cognitive, or academic development, it would be necessary to discourage its use, at least in academic settings. However, there is no research whatsoever that indicates any negative effects of codeswitching on linguistic or academic achievement or cognitive development. In fact, bilingual teachers and students who codeswitch often demonstrate a particular sensitivity to the nuances of language. They are also acutely aware of the grammar of codeswitching. A codeswitch cannot just take place anywhere in a sentence. It needs to occur at appropriate places. Nouns, for example, can be switched relatively easily according to context, but other types of switches require specific conditions (Barkin and Rivas 1978, Poplack 1978, 1980, Lipski 1978, 1982). Only certain codeswitches are considered acceptable to native speakers who codeswitch (Aguirre 1976).

Sociolinguistic research has developed a basic explanation of codeswitching in bilingual communities: (1) speakers who codeswitch between languages are indeed bilingual, perhaps with varying degrees of proficiency in the two languages, (2) these bilinguals interact with each other, and (3) when they do interact with one another, their communicative needs may be met by either of the two languages alone, but are often more appropriately and comfortably met when the two languages are used alternately.[1] Codeswitching represents a third or additional code available to bilinguals in certain social circumstances.

Genishi (1976) hypothesizes that children may begin to learn situational as well as conversational switching at a very early age. In an environment where codeswitching is used as part of the family's verbal repertoire, it is also acquired by their children (Huerta-Macías 1981). It differs significantly from the kind of language mixing found in early simultaneous and sequential bilingual acquisition. When children learn codeswitching from their parents, their codeswitching is seldom ungrammatical and is used in adult-like ways. For example, these children use codeswitching as a strategy to mark changes in context.

Hudelson (1983) shows that classroom codeswitching behavior can be used as an assessment tool for the Spanish and English development of bilingual students. She illustrates how Beto, a bilingual eight-year-old, switches codes depending upon the language ability of particular individuals. He can speak either language without inserting elements from the other. When he does choose to codeswitch, he codeswitches according to the norms of interaction appropriate for his home and learning communities. Hudelson's study demonstrates "that children in bilingual classrooms possess sociolinguistic skills not evidenced by test scores" (Hudelson 1983: 48). Ethnographic monitoring and taped language interactions can help train teachers to tune in to what their students are doing and saying (Carrasco, Vera, and Cazden 1981). In this way, teachers may acquire more realistic pictures of their pupils' abilities and provide more opportunities for children to demonstrate and increase their bilingual skills.

3. The functions of codeswitching

3.1. Codeswitching to increase comprehension

Bilinguals use the language that the people they speak to know best. They are aware that in order to communicate with monolingual English speakers, they must speak in English and only in English. Similarly, Spanish is the language of interaction with monolingual Spanish speakers. When bilinguals of the same languages interact with each other, codeswitching is often the appropriate and preferred code.

Children are extremely sensitive to language use around them. Genishi (1976) found that children at a kindergarten and affiliated day care center where maintenance of Chicano/Mexican culture is emphasized generally followed the situational rule "Speak the language your listener knows best." This finding holds true in other classroom settings (Cazden 1988, Carrasco 1984, Olmedo-Williams 1980). For example, Feldman and Wertsch (1972) notes that five-year-old bilingual Spanish/English kindergarten children know not to speak Spanish with strangers, although they codeswitch among themselves to emphasize points, to quote directly from another's speech, and to single out an addressee. Mallory (1971) documents that during role-play children choose Spanish or English depending on the person and the situation to be simulated, and they can even explain reasons for their choices. Shultz (1975) notes that children are highly sensitive to the addressee's language ability, and use the language they determine to be the stronger language.

Codeswitching also occurs when one speaker uses one language consistently, while the second persists in using another language. For example, grandparents may use their first, stronger, or only productive language when interacting with their grandchildren, while the latter answer in English. Both speakers have well-developed receptive skills for both languages. They understand what they hear, but must switch languages to answer because they can only speak one language productively. Such is the case with Veronica, as reported in Carrasco 1981. The teacher explains a tutoring task to Veronica in English, which the bilingual child later conveys to her tutee in Spanish. The task, however, involves an English phonics lesson. The teacher never witnesses this switch in languages, nor does she notice Veronica's expertise in teaching the lesson presented to her in English. The teacher, due to her involvement with the research, is surprised to find out that Veronica knows more English than she thought.

Carrasco (1984) notes that lessons occurring predominantly in Spanish may include some codeswitching into English. Often students are beginning to acquire English, but are not yet able or required to use it productively. When the teacher introduces English, even during a Spanish reading lesson, he or she helps the students improve their English comprehension and transfer their Spanish reading skills to reading in English.

3.2. Codeswitching to mark a change in context

Codeswitching is an important discourse strategy in both monolingual and bilingual communities and classrooms. It often marks a change in context, formality, or mood. In monolingual situations, it involves a change in register, dialect or modality rather than a change in language. Monolingual speakers also utilize switches in body posture, movements, and eye gaze to make a transition from one context to another. Bilinguals use all of these strategies, but also have the option of changing languages.

In a classroom, the setting and participants remain constant. However, linguistic behavior changes as the contexts shift from formal to informal and back again. Teachers proficient in their students' home languages often switch languages to mark context changes, such as the transition from one academic subject to another, or from one topic to another within discussion of a particular academic subject. A codeswitch may indicate that a new person has entered the room. It may also may mark a change of attitude. Codeswitches can be used to make a reprimand or praise stand out from the rest of the lesson. Children also use codeswitching to make an utterance stand out. As Genishi (1976: 6) observes, "By changing languages, the child conveys the message, "I really want your attention."

4. Pedagogical approaches

Educators are only beginning to explore codeswitching as a pedagogical strategy to increase language and content acquisition and promote cognitive development. As they create programs for bilingual students, schools must decide how they want each language to be used in the classroom. Milk (1990: 32) describes the importance of the language distribution issue:

> Clearly, issues related to language distribution must be at the heart of any substantive discussion of bilingual methodology, for there is no more fundamental decision to be made by a bilingual teacher than which language(s) to use when (i.e. with which subjects), and in what manner (i.e. concurrently or following a strict separation of codes).

Unfortunately, none of the current language distribution models has been studied in depth. Educators do choose particular language distribution models, and often strongly believe that a particular model is effective. However, there is little data on which to base these convictions.

First, some teachers present content in one language, and then directly translate the material into the other language. Some educators believe that direct translation of everything said in one language into the other is an ineffective codeswitching strategy, since it cuts the amount of material a teacher can cover in a lesson period in half. Instead of learning how to express a concept in both languages, students "space out" the information delivered in their weaker language. As Jacobson writes (1990a: 7):

> It has been argued that the translation into the child's vernacular of everything that is being taught may prevent him/her from ever developing the kind of English language proficiency that must be one of the objectives of a sound bilingual program.

On the other hand, teachers who directly translate all the material may feel more confident that their students understand the content of the lesson.

Second, many bilingual programs use a language separation approach or LSA. Some programs maintain a one language per subject model. In these situations, students learn history in one language, and science in the other. Other programs provide a one language per teacher model. When students are with teacher A they hear and use English, and when they are with teacher B they hear and use only Spanish. In this model, the English-speaking teacher is frequently monolingual. However, since the school is in the United States, it is more than likely that the Spanish-speaking teacher can speak English. Especially if the Spanish-speaking teacher is from the bilingual community served by the school, he or she may use codeswitching despite the program's goal of language separation. Jacobson (1990a: 4) has pointed out that the idea that teachers should avoid codeswitching "was felt to be so self-evident that no research was ever conducted to support this argument."

Jacobson (1977a, 1990a, 1990b, 1997) has devised a model of teaching involving concurrent use of two languages, "where a highly structured approach to codeswitching is introduced." He proposes that there be "no intra-sentential codeswitching, the alternation is not random but purposeful, the use of both languages is fully balanced and the structure of the lesson does not encourage the child to tune out whilst his/her weaker language is spoken." (Jacobson 1990: 7). He believes that the New Concurrent Approach, or NCA, increases academic learning time, thereby increasing the acquisition of content. Moreover, by providing equal status for the two languages and a climate conducive to the use of the home language, the NCA encourages a closer relationship between school and community and further acquisition of both languages (Milk 1980). The NCA model requires highly trained and linguistically proficient bilingual teachers.

This kind of codeswitching resembles Cazden's scaffolds (1988: 101–110). Scaffolds are "a series of questions designed to provide minimum help at first and then increasingly specific help as needed" (1988: 106). In the NCA, the teacher creates a scaffold by using both languages alternately to convey increasingly specific and complex information, while connecting the new information to the information already presented.

When Jacobson compared the effectiveness of the language separation and the concurrent models, he found that "no significant difference emerged between groups regardless of whether the languages were separated or used concurrently" (1990b: 15). He recommends that effective bilingual teaching practices are better uncovered when researchers shift their focus from "Which language should I use?" to "How can learning best be achieved?" (Jacobson 1990b: 33). Ultimately, the acquisition of the skills necessary to function in an academic environment is the goal. If codeswitching enhances learning and helps children acquire the skills they need to succeed, then it should be considered an essential part of bilingual teachers' verbal repertoire. It should also be covered in training programs for bilingual teachers.

I would take Jacobson's argument one step further. According to the NCA, language alternation should only occur intersententially. When Milk analyzed the use of Spanish and English in two NCA classrooms, he found that only 2.2% of the teachers' 3450 alternations were intrasentential. However, research suggests that educators' fear that intrasentential switches will result in ungrammatical language is unfounded. Functionally bilingual individuals are able to codeswitch without violating the grammatical principles of either language. Therefore, if intrasentential switches will help bilingual children learn, then they too should be welcomed in the bilingual classroom.

5. Codeswitching, power, and appropriate language use

School is one of the principal environments where children acquire new registers. One of the objectives of schooling is to help expand children's repertoires, so that they will be able to communicate appropriately in a variety of settings. Children need to know where, when, how, and to whom to use which languages as well as which registers of those languages. They also need to learn the appropriate "time and place" to use codeswitching in and out of class. Students tend to follow their teachers' codeswitching patterns (Valdés-Fallis 1978, Phillips 1975). Whether they intend to or not, bilingual teachers model appropriate language use for their students.

Timm (1993) points out that while codeswitching represents a valuable communication strategy among bilinguals, it is often considered problematic when used by teachers and students in bilingual classrooms. Timm notes that when the teacher accepts codeswitching in the classroom it "will probably be conducive to a more relaxed classroom atmosphere, which, in turn, can enhance learning" (1993: 107). However, she argues that codeswitching as "an intimate and spontaneous form of communication among people who feel comfortable with one another" (1993: 108) may not be possible in the classroom between teacher and student, since the relationship between teachers and students is implicitly one of social distance. Because codeswitching is a somewhat informal register, bilingual teachers may avoid codeswitching in situations that require formality.

Timm also argues that teachers can better help their students if they are aware of parental and community attitudes toward codeswitching. She suggests that teachers and parents should communicate with each other about what research says about codeswitching. They should also have the opportunity to share their own attitudes about the role of codeswitching both in the home and in the school. Timm notes that even when codeswitching is frequently used at home, parents may consider it inappropriate at school.

Sapiens (1982) finds that English is used twice as often as Spanish for delivery of key concepts and for classroom management (see also Phillips 1975 and Valdés-Fallis 1978). This approach to language use in the classroom appears to foster further development of English and a language shift from Spanish to English for academic purposes. When English is the principal language used for establishing control over the class and for conveying key concepts, students also learn that English is the language of power. Researchers have also found that bilingual teachers tend to codeswitch more often during Spanish instruction than during English instruction, a pattern that tells students that English is preferred. If bilingualism is to be nurtured and encouraged, a more equitable language distribution model must be employed.

At the same time, bilingual students are aware of the power of knowing another language in a monolingual environment. Carrasco (1984) describes an incident where during a lesson taught by a monolingual English-speaking teacher, students switch to Spanish to interact socially about an off-task topic. The students cleverly use the rhythmic English reading lesson sentences to transition over to a similar-sounding rhythmic Spanish utterance. The students use codeswitching to undermine the teacher's authority by mocking her and the lesson. Since the teacher does not speak Spanish, she does not understand the content of their off-task conversation. Nevertheless, it serves as an annoyance and distraction, especially since 20% of the students' utterances in this lesson are in Spanish, unlike the 4–5% in previous lessons. Here, codeswitching is used to exclude the teacher and to sabotage the lesson.

6. Conclusion

Language use in multilingual classrooms must be pedagogically and linguistically sound, culturally relevant, and socially responsive. It must involve well-trained teachers who understand the sociocultural reality of their students and know how to appropriately interact within the greater community while using linguistic strategies which support bilingualism and cognitive development. Language use in the classroom must not only mirror the community's language use but also must provide an effective model and learning environment for bilingual students. When researchers are knowledgeable about all aspects of the surrounding communities and how they interact, they can help teachers respond to the linguistic and cultural realities of their students. Such knowledge can help make the classroom a place where we promote equality and try to avert the prejudices often found outside the school.

Notes

1. Barkin 1976, 1978, 1980, 1981, Blom and Gumperz 1972, Cazden, John, and Hymes 1972, Elías-Olivares and Valdés-Fallis 1979, Genishi 1976, Gumperz and Herasimchuk 1975, Gumperz and Hernández-Chávez 1972, Huerta 1977, 1978a, 1978b, Huerta-Macías 1981, McClure and Wentz 1975, McClure 1977, 1978, 1981, Poplack 1978, 1980, 1998, Riegelhaupt-Barkin 1976, Scotton 1983, 1988a, 1988b, Scotton and Ury 1977, Silva-Corvalán 1983, Timm 1975, 1978, Valdés-Fallis 1975, 1976, 1978, and Zentella 1981.

References

Aguirre, Adelberto. 1976. Acceptability judgments of code-switching phrases by Chicanos: Some preliminary findings. Arlington, VA: Center for Applied Linguistics. (ERIC Document Reproduction Service no. ED129122.)

Barkin, Florence. 1976. Language switching in Chicano Spanish: Linguistic norms of awareness. In *Sociolinguistics and teaching of modern languages (LEKTOS/special issue),* ed. R. St. Clair and G. Valdés-Fallis, 46–65. University of Louisville, Louisville, Kentucky.

Barkin, Florence. 1978. Language switching in Chicano Spanish: A multifaceted phenomenon. *Proceedings of the Southwest Areal Language and Linguistics Workshop (SWALLOW VI)*, ed. H. Key, G. McCullough, and J. Sawyer, 1–10. Long Beach: California State University.

Barkin, Florence. 1980. Codeswitching. In *Speaking, singing and teaching: A multidisciplinary approach to language variation*, ed. Florence Barkin and Elizabeth Brandt, 371–374. Arizona State University Anthropological Research Papers No. 20. Tempe: Arizona State University.

Barkin, Florence. 1981. Language switching in Chicano Spanish: Norms of awareness. In *Social and educational issues in bilingualism and biculturalism.* ed. R. St. Clair, 102–122. Washington, DC: University Press of America.

Barkin, Florence and Alberto Rivas. 1978. The underlying structure of bilingual sentences. Paper presented at the Third Annual Conference for Bilingualism and Bilingual Education, Amherst, MA, November.

Blom, Jan Petter and John Gumperz. 1972. Social meaning in linguistic structures: Codeswitching in Norway. In *Directions in sociolinguistics: The ethnography of communication*, ed. J. Gumperz and D. Hymes, 407–443. New York: Holt, Rinehart and Winston.

Carrasco, Roberto L., Arthur Vera, and Courtney Cazden. 1981. Aspects of bilingual students: Communicative competence in the classroom. In *Latino language and communicative behavior. Discourse processes: Advances in research and theory*, ed. Richard Duran. Norwood, NJ: Ablex Publishing.

Carrasco, Roberto L. 1981. Expanded awareness of student performance: A case study in applied ethnographic monitoring in a bilingual classroom. In *Culture and the bilingual classroom: Studies in classroom ethnography*, ed. H.T. Trueba, G.P. Guthrie, and K.H. Au, 153–177. Rowley, MA: Newbury House.

Carrasco, Roberto L. 1984. *Collective engagement in the segundo hogar: A microethnography of engagement in a bilingual first grade classroom.* Ph.D. dissertation, Harvard University.

Cazden, Courtney. 1988. *Classroom Discourse*. Portsmouth, NH: Heinemann.

Cazden, Courtney, Vera John, and Dell Hymes, eds. 1972. *Functions of language in the classroom*. New York: Teachers College Press.

Elías-Olivares, Lucía and Guadalupe Valdés-Fallis. 1979. Languge diversity in Chicano speech communities: Implications for language teaching. Working Papers in Sociolinguistics, Southwest Educational Development Laboratory.

Feldman, Carol and Jim Wertsch. 1972. Analysis of syntactic and semantic elements found in the classroom speech of teachers. (ERIC Document Reproduction Service no. ED142077.)

Genishi, Celia. 1976. *Rules for code-switching in young Spanish–English speakers: An exploratory study of language socialization*. Ph.D. dissertation, University of California, Berkeley.

Gumperz, John and Eleanor Herasimchuk. 1975. The conversational analysis of social meaning: A study of classroom interaction. In *Sociocultural dimensions of language use*, ed. M. Sanches and B. Blount, 81–116. New York: Academic Press.

Gumperz, John and Eduardo Hernández-Chávez. 1972. Bilingualism, bidialectalism and classroom interaction. In *Functions of language in the classroom*, ed. Courtney Cazden, Vera John, and Dell Hymes. New York: Teachers College Press.

Hudelson, Sarah. 1983. Janice: Becoming a writer of English. Paper presented at the Annual Meeting of the Teachers of English to speakers of other Languages, 17th, Toronto, Ontario, March 16–19, 1983.

Huerta, Ana. 1977. The acquisition of bilingualism: A code-switching approach. *Working Paper in Sociolinguistics*, No. 39. Austin: Southwest Educational Development Laboratory.

Huerta, Ana. 1978a. Code-switching among Spanish–English bilinguals: A sociolinguistic perspective. Paper presented at the National Conference on Latino Discourse Behavior, Princeton, NJ, April 17–19.

Huerta, Ana. 1978b. *Code-switching among Spanish–English bilinguals: A sociolinguistic perspective*. Ph.D. dissertation, University of Texas, Austin.

Huerta-Macías, Ana. 1981. Code-switching: All in the family. In *Latino language and communicative behavior, vol. 6*, ed. R.P. Durán, 153–168. Norwood, NJ: Ablex Publishing.

Hymes, Dell. 1972. Introduction. In *Functions of language in the classroom*, ed. Courtney Cazden, Vera John, and Dell Hymes, xi–lvii. New York: Teachers College Press.

Jacobson, Rodolfo. 1977. How to trigger code-swtiching in a bilingual classroom. In *Southwest areal linguistics then and now*, ed. B. Hoffer and B. Dubois, 16–39. San Antonio: Trinity University Press.

Jacobson, Rodolfo. 1990a. Code-switching as a worldwide phenomenon. In *Code-switching as a worldwide phenomenon, vol. 11*, ed. Rodolfo Jacobson, 1–14. New York: Peter Lang.

Jacobson, Rodolfo. 1990b. Socioeconomic status as a factor in the selection of encoding strategies in mixed discourse. In *Codeswitching as a worldwide phenomenon*, ed. Rodolfo Jacobson. New York: Peter Lang.

Jacobson, Rodolfo, ed. 1997. *Code-switching worldwide*. Trends in Linguistics, Studies and Monographs 106. Berlin: Mouton de Gruyter.

Lipski, John. 1978. Code-switching and the problem of bilingual competence. In *Aspects of bilingualism,* ed. M. Paradis, 250–264. Columbia, SC: Hornbeam Press.

Lipski, John. 1982. Spanish–English language switching in speech and literature: Theories and models. *Bilingual Review/Revista Bilingüe* 9: 191–212.

Mallory, Gloria Elaine Griffin. 1971. Sociolinguistic considerations for bilingual education in an Albuquerque community undergoing language shift. Ph.D. dissertation, University of New Mexico.

McClure, Erica and John Wentz. 1975. Functions of code-switching among Mexican-American children. In *Papers from the Parasession on Functionalism*, ed. R. Grossman, L. San, and T. Vance, 421–432. Chicago: Chicago Linguistic Society.

McClure, Erica. 1977. Aspects of code-switching in the discourse of bilingual Mexican-American children. In *Linguistics and anthropology*, ed. M. Saville-Troike, 93–115. Washington, DC: Georgetown University Press.

McClure, Erica. 1978. Aspects of code-swtiching in the discourse of bilingual Mexican American children. Paper presented at the National Conference on Latino Discourse Behavior, ETS, Princeton, NJ.

McClure, Erica. 1981. Formal and functional aspects of the code-swtiched discourse of bilingual children. In *Latino Language and Communicative Behavior*, ed. R. Durán. Norwood, NJ: Ablex Publishing.

Merritt, Marilyn, Ailie Cleghorn, Jared Abagi, and Grace Bunyi. 1992. Socialising multilingualism: Determinants of code-swtiching in Kenyan primary classrooms. In *Code-switching*, ed. C. Eastman, 103–122. Clevedon: Multilingual Matters.

Milk, Robert D. 1980. The issue of language education in Territorial New Mexico. *Bilingual Review* 7.3: 212–221.

Milk, Robert D. 1990. TESOL. Can foreigners do "foreigner talk"?: A study of the linguistic input provided by non-native teachers of EFL. *Texas Papers in Foreign Language Education* 1.4: 274–188.

Olmedo-Williams, Irma. 1980. Function of code-switching in a Spanish/English bilingual classroom. *Reports-ResearchTechnical* 4.11: 1–24.

Phillips, Jean McCabe. 1975. Code-switching in bilingual classrooms. Master's thesis, California State University, Northridge. (ERIC Document Reproduction Service no. ED111222.)

Poplack. Shana. 1978. Syntactic structure and social function of code-switching. Working Paper 2: Centro de Estudios Puertorriquenos. The City University of New York.

Poplack, Shana. 1980. Sometimes I'll start a sentence in Spanish y termino en español: Toward a typology of code-switching. *Linguistics* 18: 581- 618.

Poplack, Shana. 1998. Contrasting patterns of code-switching in two communities. In *The sociolinguistics reader, volume 1: Multilingualism and variation*, ed. Peter Trudgill and Jenny Cheshire, 44–65. London: Arnold.

Riegelhaupt-Barkin, Florence. 1976. The influence of English on the Spanish of bilingual Mexican American migrant workers in Florida. Ph.D. dissertation, SUNY Buffalo.

Sapiens, Alexander. 1982. Instructional language strategies in bilingual Chicano peer tutoring and their effect on cognitive and affective learning outcomes. Ph.D. dissertation, Stanford University.

Scotton, Carol M. 1983. The negotiation of identities in conversation: A theory of markedness and code choice. *International Journal of the Sociology of Language* 44: 115–136.

Scotton, Carol M. 1988a. Differentiating borrowing and code-switching. In *Proceedings of the sixteenth annual Conference on New Ways of Analyzing Variation*, ed. K. Ferrara, B. Brown, K. Walters, and J. Baugh, 318–325. Austin: University of Texas Department of Linguistics.

Scotton, Carol M. 1988b. Code-switching as indexical of socialnegotiations. In *Code-switching: Anthropological and sociolinguistic perspectives*, ed. M. Heller, 151–186. Berlin: Mouton de Gruyter.

Scotton, Carol and W. Ury. 1977. Bilingual strategies: The social functions of code-switching. *Linguistics* 193: 5–20.

Shultz, J. 1975. Language use in bilingual classrooms. Unpublished ms., Harvard Graduate School of Education.

Silva-Corvalán, C. 1983. Code-shifting patterns in Chicano Spanish. In *Spanish in the U.S. setting: Beyond the Southwest*, ed., L. Elías-Olivares, 69–88. National Clearinghouse for Bilingual Education..

Timm, Lenora. 1975. Spanish–English code-switching: El porque y how-not-to. *Romance Philology* 28: 473–482.

Timm, Lenora. 1978. Code-switching in *War and Peace*. In *Aspects of Bilingualism*, ed. M. Paradis, 302–315. Columbia, SC: Hornbeam Press.

Timm, Lenora. 1993. Bilingual code-switching: An overview of research. In *Language and culture in learning: Teaching Spanish to native speakers of Spanish*, ed. Henry T. Trueba and Fabian A. Samaniego. Washington, DC and London: The Falmer Press.

Valdés-Fallis, Guadalupe. 1975. Code-switching in bilingual chicano poetry. In *Southwest languages and linguistics in educational perspective*, ed. G. Harvey and M. Heiser, 143–170. San Diego, CA: Institute for Cultural Pluralism.

Valdés-Fallis, Guadalupe. 1976. Social interaction and code-switching patterns: A case study of Spanish/English alternation. In *Bilingualism in the bicentennial and beyond*, ed. G. Keller, R. Teschner, and S. Viera, 53–85. New York: Bilingual Press/Editorial Bilingue.

Valdés-Fallis, Guadalupe. 1978. Code switching and the classroom teacher. *Language in Education, Theory and Practice*, #4. Arlington: Center for Applied Linguistics.

Zentella, Ana Celia. 1981. "Tá bien, you could answer me en cualquier idioma": Puerto Rican code-switching in bilingual classrooms. In *Latino language and communicative behavior, vol. 6*, ed. R. Durán, 109–132. Norwood. NJ: Ablex Publishing.

Attitudes Towards Oral and Written Codeswitching in Spanish–English Bilingual Youths

Cecilia Montes-Alcalá
University of California, Santa Barbara

The present study is part of a larger-scale project which investigates various aspects of the linguistic behavior of Spanish speakers in California. My particular work focuses on codeswitching, the alternating use of two languages in the discourse of bilingual individuals. More specifically, I considered how attitudes towards codeswitching affect the type of codeswitches produced in both oral and written narratives. We would expect those subjects who have positive attitudes towards codeswitching to codeswitch more and in a more complex mode than those who have negative attitudes. The findings are quite surprising, indicating a shift in attitudes towards codeswitching among the new generations of college-educated Spanish–English bilingual individuals.

1. Introduction

1.1. Codeswitching as a social stigma

Codeswitching is a natural linguistic phenomenon commonly attested in bilingual communities in which two (or more) languages are in contact. It consists of the alternating use of two languages within the discourse, at the word, clause, or sentence level. Unfortunately, this phenomenon has been socially stigmatized by monolinguals and bilinguals alike, and has been given derogatory labels such as "Tex-Mex" or "Spanglish." Codeswitching is often attributed to illiteracy, lack of formal education, or lack of proficiency in one or both languages. Nevertheless, numerous studies of codeswitching over the last three decades have revealed specific regularities at both a grammatical level (syntactic restrictions) and a pragmatic level (socio-psychological functions). Codeswitching has proven to be a far from random or arbitrary phenomenon. My initial hypothesis is that bilingual individuals can engage in codeswitching in writing tasks as much as they do when they speak. However, given that

 Research on Spanish in the U.S., ed. Ana Roca, 218–227. Somerville, MA: Cascadilla Press.

codeswitching has typically been socially unacceptable in speech, I would expect to find a greater degree of disapproval towards codeswitching in writing. In this study, I ask: Is there a correlation between these language attitudes and the complexity of a speaker's actual codeswitching? How do the young, college-educated generations of Spanish–English bilinguals perceive this phenomenon?

1.2. Types of codeswitching

The literature on codeswitching has made a distinction between two main types of codeswitching: switches between sentences (intersentential codeswitching) and switches within sentences (intrasentential codeswitching). Weinreich (1953), one of the founders of language contact research, stated that "the ideal bilingual switches from one language to the other according to appropriate changes in the speech situation (interlocutors, topic, etc.), but not in an unchanged situation, and certainly not within a single sentence." Ironically, just three decades afterwards, researchers like Poplack (1980), Lipski (1982), and Myers-Scotton (1988) show that intrasentential switching is idiosyncratic of the "true" or "balanced" bilinguals.[1] Nowadays, many researchers accept that intrasentential codeswitching is more complex and elaborated than intersentential switching. Switching within a sentence requires the bilingual individual to be proficient enough in both languages to create a smooth blend without violating the grammatical rules of either language.

Leaving aside the question of what a "true" bilingual is, we agree that the type of codeswitching produced may vary according to an individual's degree of bilingualism, his or her age of second language acquisition, and other factors. Therefore, we divided the codeswitches found in our corpus into intersentential and intrasentential categories.[2] Our corpus included the following examples of each type:

(1) Intersentential (oral) codeswitching
She wanted to experiment. Quería ver qué había allá afuera del palacio.
(LR 9/16/75)

(2) Intrasentential (written) codeswitching
El lobo went to the old lady's house and la echó.
(DT/12/8/75)

We hypothesized that subjects with a positive attitude towards codeswitching would produce the more complex intrasentential type more often than those who hold negative attitudes against codeswitching.

2. Methodology

2.1. Data collection

One of the main problems in obtaining reliable data for this type of sociolinguistic study is the high sensitivity of linguistic behavior to contextual features. It is exceedingly difficult to gain access to naturalistic bilingual behavior, especially when dealing with a socially stigmatized linguistic phenomenon. To minimize the possibility that our subjects would be intimidated by a physically present interlocutor, the data collected for this study was primarily self-recorded by the subjects in a language laboratory. Data was collected during one-hour sessions on three non-consecutive days at the University of California in Santa Barbara. Additionally, subjects were required to fill out a background questionnaire at home with specific questions about their language attitudes.

For the oral narrative part, the subjects were asked to finish a fairy tale of their choice in "mixed speech." The choices were "The Beggar Prince" or "Snow White and the Seven Dwarfs." The subjects were given the beginning of each tale in Spanish–English codeswitching. Each subject used earphones and a microphone to record his or her speech on a tape-recorder in a separate booth.

For the written part, the subjects were given two excerpts of fairy tales written in codeswitched mode. Then the subjects were asked to write a different fairy tale ("Little Red Riding Hood"), also "mixing the two languages."

Because we required the subjects to codeswitch in their narratives, both types of switches were elicited in a relatively artificial situation. We expected that those individuals who engage in codeswitching on a daily basis would have no problems performing this task, while those who do not regularly mix languages would still be able to produce some codeswitches.

2.2. The subjects

The criteria for the general selection process required our subjects to be at least 18 years old, be native speakers of Spanish or bilingual in Spanish and English, have lived in California for 15 years or longer, and be relatively communicative. Out of a total of 50 subjects, I randomly selected 10 individuals for this particular study.

Table 1 shows the profiles of my subjects. This group consisted of six males and four females, whose ages ranged from 19 to 27 years old. Seven of them were born in California. Of these, one was a second-generation Hispanic-American and the six others were first generation Hispanic-Americans. Three of the group were immigrants; two were born in El Salvador and one was born in Mexico. Spanish was the first language of all the subjects. Each subject learned English at an early age, ranging from 3 to 10 years old. Eight of them rated their own ability as high in both Spanish and English, and the other two rated themselves medium-high in Spanish, but high in English. However, English was the dominant language for all the subjects.[3]

Seven of the subjects were college students or students with a part-time job, and the other three held clerical positions. The highest level of schooling completed was high school for nine of the subjects, and the remaining one had already completed a college education.

In spite of our painstaking efforts to reach out in the Spanish-speaking community to get a wide variety of subjects, our group was relatively homogeneous. The study was conducted at a university, which would explain why the bulk of our informants were college students or college employees. The data obtained in this study should not be extrapolated to the general Hispanic community in Santa Barbara, let alone in California.

Table 1. Subject profiles

Code and gender	Age	Place of birth	Generation	Occupation	Schooling completed
DBG8/15/76 (m)	22	Calif.	2nd	Student	HS
LR9/16/75 (m)	23	Mexico	Immigrant	Student/ T. A.	HS
BV12/22/73 (f)	25	El Salv.	Immigrant	Adm. Assistant	HS
DQ5/4/79 (m)	19	El Salv.	Immigrant	Student	HS
CG3/22/77 (m)	21	Calif.	1st	Student	HS
LT8/26/71 (f)	27	Calif.	1st	Assistant	College
PD3/31/77 (f)	21	Calif.	1st	Recreat. leader	HS
SR7/3/75 (f)	23	Calif.	1st	Student	HS
DT12/8/75 (m)	23	Calif.	1st	Office clerk	HS
CS3/24/76 (m)	22	Calif.	1st	Student Work	HS

3. Results

The data was analyzed both quantitatively and qualitatively. I looked at the background questionnaire for general information about language attitudes, sociopragmatic reasons and appropriate settings for both oral and written codeswitching. I then analyzed the actual production of the subjects after carefully transcribing each and every of the tapes and manuscripts. The approximate time of the segments actually transcribed was two and a half hours. After all the transcribing was done, a quantitative analysis was carried out for all the answers in the self-reports, and also for the real production samples.

3.1. Oral codeswitching

As part of the general background questionnaire, subjects were asked to express their opinions about codeswitching. Using a scale from 1 to 7, in which 1 represented total agreement, and 7 represented total disagreement, they had to respond to a number of statements regarding attitudes towards this linguistic mode. An answer of 1–2 would constitute "agree," whereas 6–7 would constitute "disagree," and 3–5 would be regarded as neutral opinion.

Table 2 shows our overall interpretation of the subjects' general attitudes toward both oral and written codeswitching. These percentages are based on the responses to the following statements on the questionnaire:

(3) It sounds pretty when speakers mix Spanish and English in the same conversation. (#1)

(4) It bothers me when speakers talk in Spanish and English at the same time. (#2)

(5) It looks pretty when somebody mixes Spanish and English in writing. (#12)

Table 2. General attitudes toward codeswitching

	Oral codeswitching	Written codeswitching
Positive	60%	40%
Negative	10%	20%
Neutral	30%	40%

Surprisingly, we find that a majority of our subjects hold positive attitudes towards oral codeswitching. The written mode is less accepted, but we find a low percentage of negative opinions for both modes. Since this phenomenon has traditionally been stigmatized by monolinguals and bilinguals alike, the findings here are unexpected. I would suggest that codeswitching is highly regarded in the communities where our subjects live, or at least among people in the same age group. It is worth remembering that we are dealing primarily with university students.

The next statements on the questionnaire dealt with the relationship between codeswitching and the loss or maintenance of Spanish:

(6) In my opinion, the mixing of Spanish with English leads to the loss of Spanish. (#3)

(7) In my opinion, the mixing of English with Spanish helps to maintain Spanish. (#4)

Table 3. Codeswitching leads to the maintenance or the loss of Spanish

Language maintenance	30%
Language loss	30%
Neutral	40%

While no significant results emerge, we do not find a strongly negative view. Traditionally, bilingualism in general, and codeswitching in particular, have been seen as a "disease" threatening or undermining the purity of either of the languages (Keller 1976: 131). The fact that we find more subjects who remain neutral on the subject than subjects who see codeswitching as a cause of language loss might indicate a shift of attitude within the young college-educated generations of bilinguals.

Our subjects' responses to the statement: "The mixture of English and Spanish reflects who I am" (#6) are shown in Table 4:

Table 4. Codeswitching reflects identity

Yes	60%
No	30%
Neutral	10%

Most of our subjects feel that codeswitching reflects their identity. This result correlates with the fact that a significant portion of our subjects hold codeswitching in high regard. We suspect that those subjects who believe that codeswitching reflects their identity are more likely to codeswitch in their everyday speech. However, we cannot verify this theory here because it is extremely difficult to really know who does and who does not codeswitch based solely on their self-assessments.[4]

Table 5 shows our subjects' responses to the statement: "When I mix languages, I am more respected by my community." (#8)

Table 5. Codeswitching earns respect

Yes	10%
No	80%
Neutral	10%

The communities in which our subjects live do not necessarily reward codeswitching with respect. While our informants' attitudes were predominantly positive, this shift towards the acceptance of codeswitching may be limited to the younger, college-educated generation. At the same time, our informants do not believe that the general public has an overtly negative response to codeswitching. 80% of our informants did not agree with the statement (#7): "When I mix languages, others regard me as less intelligent."

We used the next two statements to gauge whether our informants felt more segregated or integrated in society when they mixed their languages:

(8) When I mix languages, I feel more integrated with my community. (#9)

(9) When I mix languages, I am segregated from society. (#10)

We found that 40% feel more integrated in society, but an equal number feel neither segregated nor integrated when they codeswitch. It is significant that a very small percentage (20%) actually feel segregated from society when they engage in codeswitching. In general, our subjects do not seem to associate codeswitching with any negative social consequences.

3.2. Written codeswitching

In the next section of the questionnaire, we asked about our subjects' attitudes towards written codeswitching. The first statement (#13) was: "When I read bilingual texts, I can relate better to the author." A significant majority (70%) agreed that they could relate better to the author in bilingual texts, as opposed to monolingual texts. Even subjects who did not perform well on our codeswitching tasks declared a preference for bilingual texts. This result indicates a general positive attitude towards codeswitching in writing, despite the fact that only 40% agreed that written codeswitching "looks pretty" (#12). It is becoming fashionable for bilingual/bicultural authors to express themselves more naturally in both languages. Publishers no longer see codeswitched texts as deviant, and the amount of bilingual literature published has noticeably increased over the last two decades.[5]

90% of our subjects did not agree with the following statement (#14): "People mix languages when they write because they do not know either language well." One of the long-lasting criticisms of codeswitching has been that it indicates a lack of proficiency in one or both languages. During the past two decades, researchers have proven that in order to codeswitch the bilingual individual must have an excellent command of both languages. Only someone who is proficient in both languages can produce a "good mix" that will not violate the grammatical rules of either language. Our informants' overwhelming rejection of this traditional criticism reveals a similar shift in the attitudes of young, educated bilinguals.

However, bilingual texts do not necessarily reflect the speech of bilingual communities any better than monolingual texts. Keller (1976: 146) claims that "the bilingual language of literary texts is not the same as the language of a given bilingual community. To presume that bilingual literature directly corresponds to usage in a given community entails a total misapprehension about the relationship between literary language and communal language." Keller (1979: 283) also states that literary codeswitching is necessarily different from codeswitching in natural discourse. Codeswitching is used mainly for stylistic purposes in texts, and it constitutes foregrounding in itself. Our subjects were evenly divided (50% agreeing and 50% disagreeing) on the question (#15):

"Bilingual texts reflect my speech community better than monolingual texts." We conclude that, as Keller predicts, our informants perceive a difference between bilingual texts and the bilingual speech of their communities.

3.3. Types of switches

A total of 331 switches were counted in the whole corpus of data. 153 switches were made in the oral portion (46%), while 178 (54%) were made in the written portion. This result confirms my initial hypothesis that bilingual speakers can engage in codeswitching when they write as much as they do when they speak.

Table 6 shows the percentages of intersentential and intrasentential switches made in the oral and written tasks. We find that intrasentential switches are more frequent in writing than in oral production. Because intrasentential switches constitute a more complex and elaborated mode of production, individuals who do not regularly codeswitch would be unlikely to attempt this type of switching in speech. However, since writing is a more self-conscious process, even individuals who do not have a lot of experience with codeswitching were able to produce intrasentential switches.

Table 6. Types of switches

	Oral	Written
Intersentential	53%	30%
Intrasentential	47%	70%

Table 7 compares the types of switches made by those subjects who had a positive attitude toward codeswitching to the types made by those who had a negative attitude. Our hypothesis was that those individuals who do not like to codeswitch would produce intersentential switches rather than intrasentential ones in a forced codeswitching task.

Table 7. Types of switches across attitudes towards codeswitching

	Oral		Written	
	Intersent.	Intrasent.	Intersent.	Intrasent.
Positive attitudes	48%	52%	28%	72%
Negative attitudes	27%	73%	32%	68%

However, our findings contradict this hypothesis. The subjects with negative attitudes towards codeswitching had a significantly higher percentage of intrasentential switches in the oral production than the subjects with positive attitudes had. At the written level, the individuals who like codeswitching have a slightly higher percentage of intrasentential switches than those who do not like it, but the two groups are much closer than we expected. In both the oral and the written tasks, far more intrasentential switches than intersentential switches were produced. We conclude that even those individuals who do not approve of codeswitching have the bilingual competence required to produce the most complex and elaborated type of switch on a forced codeswitching task.

4. Conclusions

We find that bilingual individuals are equally capable of codeswitching in speech and in writing. We also find that our subjects have a generally positive attitude towards codeswitching. In direct opposition to the traditional views, our subjects do not ascribe a negative value to codeswitching, do not think it will lead to language loss, and do not consider it to be a sign of a lack of language proficiency. They believe that oral codeswitching reflects their identity, and that written codeswitching allows them to relate better to the author of a text. We believe that the young generations of college-educated bilinguals have developed a more positive attitude towards codeswitching.

Surprisingly, attitudes towards codeswitching are not a determining factor in the types of codeswitching that bilingual individuals produce. The complex and elaborated intrasentential type was produced more often than the intersentential type in both the written and the oral modes, even among those subjects who held negative attitudes toward codeswitching. Therefore, it is not the case that subjects with negative attitudes towards codeswitching will necessarily produce the less elaborated intersentential type when they are forced to alternate languages.

The homogeneity of our subjects may prevent us from extrapolating our results to wider populations. More research needs to be done in this field to corroborate the findings presented here. However, this study gives us hope that this particular way of speaking and writing will no longer carry a social stigma among the future generations of Spanish–English bilinguals.

Notes

* The general project was carried out between October 1997 and April 1998 at the University of California, Santa Barbara by a research group in which the present author took part. The research group was convened and directed by Almeida Jacqueline Toribio and the work was supported by various funding agencies with grants to Dr. Toribio, among these, the Interdisciplinary Humanities Center, UC Mexus, the Academic Senate, and the Center for Chicano Research. The general purpose of the study was to examine different morphosyntactic aspects of the Spanish spoken in California, as well as issues on language attitudes, language and ethnicity, and code-switching in the context of a bilingual community such as the City of Santa Barbara. The author gratefully acknowledges the support of Dr. Toribio for directing and funding the project, as well as the other six student researchers for their commitment in completing the study: Patxi

Zabaleta, Guillermo Vásquez, Silvia Pérez López, Renée Basile, Mimi Beller, and Christina Piranio.

1. See also Jacobson (1977) for the social implications of this type of switching.

2. While isolated lexical items can be considered a separate category, I included those in the intrasentential group for practical purposes of our present discussion.

3. Language dominance was primarily based on frequency of use of one language over another, according to the subjects' self-reports. I am grateful to Patxi Zabaleta for his collaboration in determining this variable.

4. Since the comparative purposes of this study required a forced elicitation of codeswitching, we cannot predict what our subjects' speech patterns would be in a natural setting. We did find, however, that the performance of some individuals who claim that they never codeswitch suggests that they actually have practiced codeswitching. Even though our informants express a positive attitude towards codeswitching, the social stigma may still influence their reports of their own linguistic behavior.

5. Alurista, one of the most important bilingual Chicano poets, reports in an interview with Bruce-Novoa (1980) that he was the first modern Chicano writer who dared send bilingual work to an editor. The reactions of the editors ranged from a "Why can't you write either in Spanish or in English?" to "It is the decadence of our Spanish language."

References

Bruce-Novoa, Juan. 1980. *Chicano authors: Inquiry by interview.* Austin, TX: University of Texas Press, 276.

Jacobson, Rodolfo. 1977. The social implications of intra-sentential code-switching. *New Directions in Chicano Scholarship* 6 (special issue of *The New Scholar*): 227–256.

Keller, Gary. 1979. The literary stratagems available to the bilingual Chicano writer. In *The identification and analysis of Chicano literature*, ed. Francisco Jiménez, 262–316. Ypsilanti, MI: Bilingual Press.

Keller, Gary. 1976. Towards a stylistic analysis of bilingual texts: From Ernest Hemingway to contemporary Boricua and Chicano literature. In *The analysis of Hispanic texts: Current trends in methodology*, ed. Mary Ann Beck et al., 130–149. New York: Bilingual Press.

Lipski, John M. 1982. Spanish–English language switching in speech and literature: Theories and models. *The Bilingual Review* 3: 191–212.

Myers-Scotton, Carol. 1988. Code-switching as indexical of social negotiations. In *Codeswitching: Anthropological and sociolinguistic perspectives*, ed. Monica Heller, 151–186. Berlin: Mouton de Gruyter.

Poplack, Shana. 1980. Sometimes I'll start a sentence in Spanish y termino en Español: Toward a typology of code-switching. In *Spanish in the United States: Sociolinguistics aspects*, ed. Jon Amastae, and Lucia Elías-Olivares, 230–263. Cambridge, UK: Cambridge University Press.

Weinreich, Uriel. 1968. *Languages in contact.* The Hague: Mouton.

The Use of the Past Tense in the Narratives of Bilingual Children: The Acquisition of Aspectual Distinctions

Liliana Paredes and Vicky Nova-Dancausse
University of North Carolina, Greensboro

Research on Spanish as a second language (L2) has been concerned mostly with the use of Spanish in naturalistic settings. Studies of bilingualism and languages in contact have examined the occurrences of innovative Spanish structures in relation to sociolinguistic as well as linguistic factors (Escobar 1994, Landa 1993, Silva-Corvalán 1994, Paredes 1996, among others). Few of these studies focus on the development of discourse in Spanish as L2. In this paper we explore children's acquisition of L2 Spanish in the non-naturalistic context of an immersion program.[1] In particular, we examine the structure of temporal relations in narratives.

There are two important domains in which one could examine children's acquisition of discourse strategies: first, how children encode given and new information and second, how children encode spatial and temporal relations (Hickmann 1995). The givenness or newness of the information is related to the perception of mutual (shared) knowledge among speakers involved in the interaction. Temporal and spatial relations are related to the perception of the flow of the events involved in the text.

The expression of temporal relations in the discourse is an explicit illustration of the interaction between pragmatic and semantic elements operating at the discourse level. Thus, looking at this area of children's performance in Spanish will shed light on how children manage the construction of a cohesive text through the interaction of functional elements with morphosemantic elements (verb inflection).

1. Tense and aspect

Tense and aspect are categories used in the description of verbs. Tense refers to the way the grammar encodes the time when the event expressed by the verb took place. Grammatical aspect describes how the grammar marks the type of temporal activity denoted by the verb. Aspectual distinctions will refer to whether a situation is viewed as temporally bounded (perfective) or unbounded (imperfective).

In the structure of a narrative, aspectual distinctions interact with tense selection. This interaction defines the manner in which the narrative has been structured. Hopper (1979) proposed that in a narrative, perfective "is the aspect used for narrating sequences of discrete events in which the situation is reported for its own sake, independent of its relevance to other situations." Perfective aspect describes the event or situation as having temporal boundaries, as being a single, unified, discrete situation. The function of perfective aspect may be better understood in terms of its contrast partner, imperfective aspect, which presents a situation without regard to temporal boundaries. An imperfective situation may be viewed as in progress at a particular time, either in the past or present. Imperfective forms are typically used in discourse for setting up background situations, in contrast with perfective forms which are used for narrating sequences of events (Hopper 1979, 1982). Imperfective aspect may be applicable to past, present, or future time, but is more commonly restricted to the past; for example, in Spanish and French the imperfective covers both ongoing and habitual situations, but only in the past.

In Spanish, tense and aspect information along with person and number are expressed through inflectional morphemes. Aspectual distinctions such as perfective/imperfective, progressive, and perfect have been grammaticized in the Spanish verb forms. This semantic complexity imposes a further difficulty in the acquisition of aspectual distinctions for the past tenses (perfective and imperfective).

The interaction of grammatical aspect with lexical aspect of the verbs or 'aktionsart' is also relevant in the structure of the narrative. Certain verbs tend to carry either perfective or imperfective aspect depending on their inherent semantic nature. For instance, states will tend to carry imperfective grammatical aspect as presented in (1), while punctual verbs will tend to carry the perfective aspect as in (2):

(1) El niño *pensaba* que el sapo *estaba* en la jarra.
'The child thought (Ipfv) that the frog was (Ipfv) in the jar.'

(2) El venado *se alto (detuvo)* muy rápidamente.
'The deer stopped (Pfv) very quickly.'

Thus, the degree to which a bilingual speaker is able to coordinate grammatical aspect with aktionsart is a good indicator of his or her level of development.[2]

2. The study

One aspect of discourse organization focuses on the linguistic devices used to provide connections to the events told in the story. The use of such linguistic devices will determine the cohesion of a text. The choice of tense and aspectual distinctions, for example, shows how events are related in the narrative. Choice of tense and aspect provides the temporal links to the story which are evidence of how grounding functions operate in the text.

Grounding universals, as originally proposed by Hopper (1979), state that backgrounded events refer to evaluations, observations, and commentaries that can provide new information within the story, but do not move the story line along, whereas foregrounded events move the narrative line forward. This pattern is observed in Sebastian and Slobin's (1994) study of the acquisition of Spanish by monolingual children. They examine narratives based on the story 'Frog, where are you' and determine different stages of tense and aspect use. According to their study of monolingual children's narratives, until age 5 children oscillate in the selection of a dominant tense. This early tense-shifting can not always be attributed to narrative purposes. By age 9 children seem to have acquired a better sense of tense and aspect choice for the purpose of narration. At this age, children are also more able to use other narrative mechanisms such as connectors and discourse markers. The preference for the present tense in 9-year-olds places them together with the general tendency by adults.

It is clear from Sebastian and Slobin's research that the grammatical forms marking tense and aspect are acquired early by Spanish-speaking children (age 3–4).[3] However, the grounding functions of tense and aspect choice start to operate at age 5, "with perfective serving to encode plot-advancing events and imperfective used for various kinds of background" (Sebastian and Slobin 1994: 253).

The focus of this paper is narrative organization and structure in bilingual children. We are interested in determining whether the use of tense and aspect is motivated by the situations narrated in the stories or by other factors, such as the semantics of the verbs or the level of proficiency reached by the child. We are also interested in examining the hierarchy of the elements structuring the bilingual narratives. We examine the use of connective words in the narratives, expecting that complex forms will occur in the narratives of children whose Spanish is more advanced at the sentential level. To a large extent, this is a pilot study that explores the issue of what bilingual narratives can tell us about L2 learning and L2 production by examining the temporal organization of the events.

The data was elicited by showing the children the pictures of the story *¿Sapo dónde estás?* 'Frog, where are you?' and then asking them to narrate a story based on the pictures. The children were always able to look back at the pictures. Each narrative was tape-recorded, transcribed, and coded for statistical analysis.

The analysis of the children's narratives aims to understand whether tense choice goes along with grounding universals as defined by Hopper (1979). The data examined and discussed in this paper come from the narratives of six children whose only connection with Spanish is through schooling. The children were all English speakers in a Spanish immersion program. Some of the results obtained by Sebastian and Slobin (1994) will be used as a reference to analyze both grammatical choices of tense and aspect with narrative purposes and the developmental stages of our targeted bilingual children.

3. Analysis

In our analysis, we examine tense choice and the use of linguistic devices to structure the narratives. The narratives show two main tendencies. First, tense selection is clearly oriented towards the use of the present, preterit, and imperfect tenses. Second, the sequences of events in the narratives are structured through the use of some connective words. Table 1 displays the frequencies of tense forms selected.

Table 1. Tense selected in the six children's narratives

Tense	Number / Total	Percentage
Present	106/244	43%
Preterit	81/244	33%
Imperfect	29/244	12%
Present progressive	17/244	7%
Past progressive	11/244	5%

The most frequently used tense is the present, followed by the preterit and then much less frequently the imperfect. The use of progressive forms is infrequent. Since the unmarked tense for telling a sequence of events is the past, the predominant use of the present tense in monolingual narratives (Slobin and Berman 1994, Silva-Corvalán 1983) entails an advanced developmental stage. At this stage, speakers adopt a more marked narrative use of the present (the historic tense). The frog story makes the use of the present tense appropriate because the events can be viewed as ongoing and the speaker can choose to make the story more vivid by narrating it in the present.

The dominant use of the present tense in a bilingual narrative, however, does not necessarily represent an advanced developmental stage in L2. The ability to narrate a story in L2 should not be restricted to the correct and appropriate use of the grammar and vocabulary (which could indicate a high oral proficiency in other situational contexts). Narrating a story requires the presence of other elements providing cohesion and coherence. These are elements that, together with tense selection, will structure the text. The more complex the structure, the greater the ability to narrate a story. A spatial organization of the text, characterized by the use of adverbs such as *aquí* 'here' or *en este dibujo* 'in this picture,' would represent an initial stage in terms of story-telling, whereas a temporal organization of the text, characterized by the intentional choice of tense and aspect and the use of connectors and discourse markers, would represent an advanced stage. Examples (3–7) illustrate different stages found among these children. A first stage would be represented by a narration using mostly the present tense[4]; this stage is represented by examples 3 and 4.

(3) pero después el venado **empieza** a correr y después detrás el perro y y el vena y **hay** un . . . y el venado para y el niño y el perro **caen caen** en el agua después y cuan y el perro **está** arriba del niño cuando el **mira** arriba del agua el perro **está** en su cabeza y *aquí* y ellos después el niño **está diciendo** al perro que como silencio. . . .

'But then the deer starts (Ipfv) running and then the dog is behind and and the deer and there is a . . . and the deer stops (Ipfv) and the boy and the dog fall, fall (Ipfv) into the water then, and, when and the dog is (Ipfv) on top of the boy when he looks (Ipfv) up the water an the dog is (Ipfv) on his head and *here* they then the boy is telling (Ipfv) the dog like silence. . . .'

(4) El niño **tiene** una rana y también **tiene** un perro y cuando **va** a la cama la rana se **sale** de la jarra y cuando le levantan **ven** la rana no **está** y entonces **van** a mirar para el sapo y de primero **miran** en el cuarto del niño y después **miran** afuera . . . y pero **cae** (el perro) . . . y **miran** están están **tratando** de encontrar a la rana o el sapo por gritarle y el niño **está mirando** en el hueco pero otro animal **vive** ahí, y después y el perro **está mirando** a las ovejas abejas y cuando el niño el niño **mira** dentro de un árbol . . . el niño **mira** en el árbol y **hay** una lechuza adentro entonces y ahora las abejas **están** muy enojados con el perro . . .

'The boy has (Ipfv) a frog and (he) also has (Ipfv) a dog and when (he) goes (Ipfv) to bed, the frog leaves (Ipfv) the jar, and when (they) get up (Ipfv), (they) see that the frog is not there (Ipfv) and then (they) go (Ipfv) to look for the frog and, first (they) look (Ipfv) in the boy's room and then (they) look (Ipfv) outside . . . and the dog falls (Ipfv) . . . and (they) look (Ipfv) they are, are trying to find the frog (Ipfv) by yelling and the boy is looking (Ipfv) in the hole but another animal lives (Ipfv) there, and then and the dog is looking (Ipfv) the sheep, the bees and when the boy, the boy looks (Ipfv) inside the tree . . . the boy looks inside the tree and there is (Ipfv) an owl inside then, and, now the bees are (Ipfv) very angry with the dog . . .'

Notice the difference between these narratives. Example (3) represents more a description of events; in particular the use of an spatial adverb such as 'aquí' *'here'* places the text into one close to a picture description. On the other hand, (4) the story flows smoothly and the presence of adverbs such as 'primero' *'first'* connected with 'y después' *'and then'* indicates a certain level of narrative organization that goes beyond picture description.

A second stage can be represented by the use of past tenses. Examples 5 and 6 illustrate uses of the past tenses.

(5) **Había** un día que un niño **tenía** una, un sapo en una jarra y cuando él **se fue** a dormir el sapo **se escapó**. En la mañana el niño **se levantó** y el sapo no **estaba** en la jarra. El primero **miraba** todo por su cuarto y no **podía** encontrar. El perro **tenía** la jarra en su cabeza y cuando **miró** afuera de la ventana [el perro] **se caí** y [la jarra] **se rompió**.

'There was (Ipfv) a time that a boy had (Pfv) a frog in a jar and when he went (Pfv) to bed, the frog escaped (Pfv). In the morning, the boy woke up (Pfv) and the frog was not (Ipfv) in the jar. He first looked (Ipfv) around his room and could not (Ipfv) find it. The dog had (Ipfv) the jar on his head and when he looked (Pfv) out the window, he falled (Pfv) and [the jar] broke (Pfv).'

(6) cuando el niño **estaba mirando** para él, el perro **se pusí** su cabeza en el jarro después **se cayó** de la ventana y el jarro **se rompió** y después el niño no **estaba** muy feliz.

'When the boy was looking (Ipfv.Prog) for it, the dog put (Pfv) his head in the jar and then, he falled (Pfv) out of the window and the jar got broken (Pfv) and then the boy was (Ipfv) not very happy.'

(5) and (6) are excerpts of the narratives that exhibit an appropriate structure in terms of tense and aspect selection: events that move the story forward are expressed through the use of the perfective, whereas background situations and evaluations are expressed through the imperfective. The presence of form errors (underlined in the text), do not interfere with the choice of perfective or imperfective aspect.[5]

In our sample, the contrast between preterit and imperfect is motivated by grounding functions: 69% of the use of the imperfect tense is related to background events and 14% to evaluation and commentaries. The use of the preterit for foreground events is almost categorical. The use of the imperfect for foreground events is relatively low (17%), which parallels the scarce use of the preterit to refer to background events (5%). Table 2 displays these results.

Table 2. Percentages of Choice of Tense[6] and Grounding Functions (n=216 clauses)

	Imperfect	Preterit	Present
Background	**20/29 = 69%**	4/81 = 5%	13/106 = 12%
Foreground	5/29 = 17%	**73/81 = 90%**	86/106 = 81%
Evaluation & commentaries	4/29 = 14%	4/81 = 5%	7/106 = 7%

Compare these examples with one by a monolingual nine-year-old child (from Sebastian and Slobin 1994: 245):

(7) Esto es un niño y un perro -no?- que encuentran una rana y la meten en un bote. Entonces el niño se va a dormir y la rana se escapa. Al día siguiente el niño y el perro disgustados miran el bote. El niño se levanta, se viste, y ve el vaso de cristal que estaba la rana.

'This is (Ipfv) a boy and a dog - right? that find (Ipfv) a frog and they put (Ipfv) her in a jar. Then the boy goes (Ipfv) to sleep and the frog escapes (Ipfv). The next day the boy and the dog, (both) upset, look (Ipfv) at the jar. The boy gets up (Ipfv), gets dressed (Ipfv) and sees (Ipfv) the glass jar that the frog was (in).'

There is definitely a gap between monolingual and bilingual narratives. By age nine monolingual children have reached a developmental stage that enables them to organize a narrative following a temporal perspective. By the same age, but with only 5 years of exposure to Spanish, an L2 learner is able to construct a text based on pictures, but his or her performance corresponds more closely to that of a 5-year-old monolingual.

Another relevant piece of information given by Table 1 is that these children have acquired at least 5 tense forms: present, present progressive, imperfect, preterit and past progressive. None of the children, however, used any of the Spanish perfect forms, which could have fit in these narratives. The monolingual children in Sebastian and Slobin's study had a wider range of verb forms in their repertoire. Another difference between monolingual and bilingual production is the number of clauses in a narrative text. Monolingual English-speaking children had an average of 200 clauses per narrative prompted by 'Frog, where are you?' (Berman and Slobin 1994). The average number of clauses in the data used for this study is 40 clauses per child.

The use of connectors provides evidence of the development of narrative strategies. Simple connectors such as *y* 'and' or *entonces* 'then' would represent early stages, whereas the use of adverbial phrases such as *había una vez* 'once upon a time' would represent advanced stages. Table 3 displays the presence of connectors in the narratives. All the children used *y* 'and,' *entonces* 'then,' *después* 'then.' Adverbial phrases with a narrative function were *primero* 'first,' *a la mañana siguiente* 'the next morning,' *en la noche* 'at night.' Only three out of six children used these adverbial phrases with narrative functions. Under 'other' we consider phrases or words that refer to the beginning or to the end of the story.

Table 3. Connective words used in the six children's narratives

	y, (y) entonces, (y) después	Adverbial phrases	Other (había una vez, fin de la historia)
Niño A	+	+	+
Niño B	+	–	–
Niño C	+	+	+
Niño D	+	+	+
Niño E	+	–	–
Niño F	+	–	–

Connective words such as *entonces, después* 'then,' and *y* 'and' function primarily as linking words in text. These connectors do not have a complex discourse function, but rather reflect a simple discourse strategy. These forms connect clauses without having a narrative purpose. Example (8) illustrates this:

(8) . . . y el perro pone su cara en el frasco y él y ellos están mirando afuera de la ventana y el perro cae y el frasco rompe y entonces el niño está enojado.

'. . . and the dog puts (Ipfv) his face in the jar and he and they are looking (Ipfv) outside the window and the dog falls (Ipfv) and the jar breaks (Ipfv), and then the boy is upset.'

4. Conclusion

The data we have examined indicate that the contrast between perfective and imperfective in the past tense is well motivated in these bilingual children. The use of the present tense, however, does not follow the patterns observed in monolingual 9-year-olds. It is possible that the dominant use of the present tense in some of the narratives corresponds to a lack of acquisition of not only the forms for the past tenses, but also the absence of a distinction of tense and aspect for narrative purposes.[7]

Many of the children in this study used connectors to keep the story moving. The use of connectors indicates a first level of narrative cohesion in L2.[8] The story is organized from a spatial perspective following a picture description strategy. The use of tense and aspect with narrative purposes definitely represents a more advanced stage of discourse organization in L2. The use of a variety of tense forms and tense functions would indicate an advanced level of proficiency in L2. The bilingual child not only knows the verb forms and endings, but their narrative functions.

Finally, it is interesting that the trends for narrative structure found in these six narratives correspond to the trends found for monolingual children age 3 to 5. An explanation for this gap could correspond to the five year difference of exposure to Spanish. A direction for future research would be to study how language development in L1 (in this case English) affects linguistic behavior in L2, particularly when referring to narrative structure.

Notes

1. The bilingual children targeted in this analysis are fifth-grade students attending an immersion program in Greensboro, NC. This program started in 1990 at David D. Jones Elementary School with one kindergarten class. Over the following nine years the program grew very rapidly. The elementary immersion students follow the regular school curriculum, but are taught entirely in Spanish. The students also maintain progress in the development of English skills. The immersion students develop native-like proficiency in Spanish in listening, reading, and writing and at the same time they develop efficient and appropriate communication skills for a variety of purposes.

2. A factor of language development in L1 may have an effect on the development in L2. This paper, however, does not look at bilingual children's performance in L1.

3. Variation in tense choices relate to regional varieties of Spanish.

4. Not the historic present tense, which corresponds to a more advanced stage.

5. We examined the effect of the semantics of the verbs on the selection of aspect. For young narrators (3 years old), Sebastian and Slobin (1994) observed a correlation between aktionsart and aspect of the verb. In fact, they suggested that aspect choice was motivated by the semantics of the verb in 3-year-old and 4-year-old children. We analyzed the relationship between aspect and the dynamics, telicity and punctuality of verbs in our data. The only category that correlated positively with aspect is punctuality. This is one of the areas that must be explored more carefully to compare bilingual with monolingual behavior.

6. Progressive forms were not included in this study because they were infrequent. We found only 7% of present progressive (17/244) and 5 % (11/244) of past progressive.

7. The results of a correlation between tense and number of errors in the narratives show that 40% of the present tense is used by children who have more than 13 errors in their text. Discarding these narratives from our study would probably result in a clear picture of the role of the present tense among the most proficient bilingual children.

8. Bilingual speakers presumably will be able to create a more complex narrative in their native language.

References

Berman, Ruth and D. Slobin. 1994. Relating events in narrative: A crosslinguistic developmental study. Hillsdale, NJ: Lawrence Erlbaum Associates.

Escobar, A.M. 1990. *Los bilingües y el castellano en el Perú*. Lima: IEP.

Hickmann, Maya. 1995. Discourse organization and the development of reference to person, space, and time. In *Handbook of child language*, ed. Paul Fletcher and Brian MacWhinney, 194–218. Oxford: Blackwell.

Hopper, Paul. 1979. Aspect and foregrounding in discourse. In *Syntax and semantics, Vol 12, Discourse and Syntax*, ed. T. Givón, 213–241. New York: Academic Press.

Hopper, Paul. 1982. Aspect between discourse and grammar: An introductory essay for the volume. In *Tense-Aspect*, ed. Paul Hopper, 3–17. Amsterdam: John Benjamins.

Landa, Alazne. 1993. Conditions of null objects in Basque Spanish and their relation to leísmo and clitic doubling. Dissertation prospectus. University of Southern California, ms.

Paredes, Liliana. 1996. The Spanish continuum in Peruvian bilingual speakers: A study of verbal clitics. Ph.D. dissertation, University of Southern California.

Sebastián, Eugenia and Dan Slobin. 1994. Development of linguistic forms in Spanish. In *Relating events in narrative: A crosslinguistic developmental study*, ed. Ruth Berman and Dan Slobin, 239–284. Hillsdale, NJ: Lawrence Erlbaum Associates.

Silva-Corvalán, Carmen. 1983. Tense and aspect in oral Spanish narrative: Context and meaning. *Language* 59: 60–80.

Silva-Corvalán, Carmen. 1994. *Language contact and change: Spanish in Los Angeles*. Oxford: Clarendon Press.

Discourse Connectedness in Caribbean Spanish

Bárbara I. Ávila-Shah
State University of New York at Buffalo

1. Introduction

Several studies have established that coreferentiality is a significant discourse-pragmatic factor in determining whether subjects are expressed in Spanish (Ávila-Jiménez 1995, 1996, Cameron 1992, Morales 1986, Silva-Corvalán 1982, 1994). These studies have found that subjects which are coreferential with the subject in the previous utterance have a lower probability of being expressed. Conversely, a change in referent increases the likelihood that a subject pronoun will be expressed. Nevertheless, this application of the concept of 'same' versus 'switch' reference cannot explain the many instances which do not fit the general patterns of coreferentiality. These exceptions signal that we must consider other discourse factors in order to account for the complexities of referential meaning in discourse and its correlation with subject expression in Spanish.

In this study, I investigate clausal relationships in the discourse as a key factor in determining subject expression. I adopted a modified version of the hierarchy of discourse which Paredes-Silva (1993) devised to investigate pronominal expression in written personal letters in Brazilian Portuguese. This analysis captured subtle changes in the connection between clauses which previous analyses had failed to reveal.

More recently, researchers have begun to study the effect of language background on coreferentiality and subject expression in contact phenomena (Ávila-Shah 1998, Bayley and Pease-Álvarez 1996, Silva-Corvalán 1994). Of these studies, only Silva-Corvalán (1994) has found significant effects. In her study, Mexican-American speakers who were born and raised in Los Angeles with parents also born in Los Angeles showed some loss of coreferentiality restrictions on subject expression.

 Research on Spanish in the U.S., ed. Ana Roca, 238–251. Somerville, MA: Cascadilla Press.

This study tests two hypotheses: (1) coreferentiality by itself does not adequately account for subject expression in Spanish, and (2) English–Spanish language contact has affected subject expression in Spanish. Therefore, as we move from Spanish monolingualism into English-dominant bilingualism, discourse-pragmatic functions are weakened and rates of subject expression gradually increase.

2. Methodology

The data for this study was obtained through the analysis of approximately 11 hours of transcribed speech of 32 Spanish informants. The informants included:

6 adult heritage speakers of Puerto Rican Spanish
14 adult bilingual speakers from Puerto Rico
12 adult monolingual Spanish speakers from Cuba

The 6 adult heritage speakers of Puerto Rican Spanish (hereafter HS), 3 men and 3 women, ranged in age between 19 and 23 years. These speakers were of Puerto Rican descent and were born and raised in the state of New York. None had received formal instruction in Spanish. Their speech showed evidence of lexical, phonological, and grammatical interference from English.

All of the 14 adult bilingual speakers from Puerto Rico were born or had lived in the San Juan metropolitan area since age 5. They had studied English formally for a minimum of 13 years and had been in the United States either for vacation or for work or study. Six of these informants (3 women and 3 men between 19 and 23 years of age, hereafter YPR) were university students in the state of New York at the time of the interviews. The remaining eight Puerto Rican Spanish interviews were taken from *La Norma Culta de San Juan* (Vaquero and Morales 1990). The speakers included 5 women aged 24 to 57 years and 3 men aged 30 to 43 years. For the sake of comparison, I selected the interviews with speakers who were closer in age to the Spanish monolingual speakers from Cuba. The 8 Norma Culta informants (hereafter APR) were interviewed between 1968 and 1971 as part of the "Proyecto de Estudio Coordinado de la Norma Lingüística de las Principales Ciudades de Iberoamérica y de la Península Ibérica." All APR informants had completed a college education, most with a Master's or Ph.D. degree. The interviews were semi-directed and were mostly related to their job experience.

Finally, the 12 adult Cuban Spanish speakers (hereafter CS) had recently arrived in the United States. They included 8 women and 4 men between 26 and 55 years of age. The length of their stay in Miami ranged from 2 days to 2 years. Most of the speakers had been born in Havana or had lived there since age 5, and they had little if any exposure to English prior to their arrival in Miami. Many of those who had been living in Miami for more than 6 months were enrolled in English as a Second Language courses. All the Cuban speakers had completed studies leading to a career; while in Cuba some had been teachers, business owners, and hospital technicians. These interviews were recorded as part of the Norma Culta project for Havana. Most of the interviews were semi-directed and were focused on describing the type of life they led in Cuba prior to the revolution as well as the adaptation process to their new life in the United States.

3. Data

All the possible occurrences of a tensed verb with a subject pronoun, whether overt or null, in a declarative statement were considered for this study (2984 in total). However, there were some exclusions. I omitted discourse markers that occur with an obligatory subject pronoun, such as *tú sabes* 'you know,' *tú ves* 'you see,' and *tú entiendes* 'you understand' (1). I also omitted discourse markers like Ø *viste* 'you see' and Ø *digo* 'I say' that occur obligatorily without a subject pronoun (2).

(1) . . . y en las carreras él gana dinero, tú sabes, la última carrera . . .
. . . and in the races he wins money, you know, the last race . . .

(2) . . . a él le gusta el dulce, Ø digo, yo creo . . .
. . . he likes sweets, I mean, I think so . . .

Impersonal constructions with *hacer*, *ser*, existential *haber*, and *se* were excluded since these constructions are subjectless (3–5).

(3) yo lo llamé . . . hace como dos o tres semanas y le dije . . .
I called him . . . two or three weeks ago and I told him . . .

(4) . . . es diferente así porque . . .
. . . it is different that way, because . . .

(5) había un letrero que decía 'se venden alcapurrias'
there was a sign that read 'alcapurrias for sale'

Relative clauses in which the head is the subject of the verb in the subordinate clause (6) were not included in this study because they rarely occur with a resumptive pronoun.

(6) Los dominicanos que Ø han estado aquí, que Ø son tercera o segunda generación . . .

The Dominicans who have been here, who are third o second generation . . .

Infinitives and participles can sometimes occur with an overt subject, but none of these forms are inflected for person, number, or tense (7–8). Therefore, they were not included in the study.

(7) Yo estar ahí y ver . . .
I to be there and see . . .

(8) ella comiendo y yo estudiando
she eating and I studying

4. Discourse connectedness

In this section, I present the levels of Paredes-Silva's (1993) hierarchy of coreferentiality and discourse cohesion. I also discuss the ways I modified this hierarchy in order to apply it to the spoken discourse of the Caribbean Spanish speakers.

Level 1: A subject pronoun in this level is optimally connected to the previous clause because both subjects share the same referent as well as the same verb tense, aspect, and mood. In most instances, these subjects occur between closely related events (9).

(9) Porque el año que yo vine, yo llegué en enero – y – en enero del '83 y vine con papi y mami.

'Because the year that I came, I arrived in January – and – in January of 1983 and I came with mom and dad.'

Level 2: Subject pronouns in this level have a nearly optimum connection to the previous clause since the same subject referent is maintained. However, there is a change in the tense, aspect, or mood of the verb (10). These alternations signal changes in temporal reference in narratives or events. They also mark changes from event to action, from narration to direct speech, from mental reaction to specific actions, or from facts to opinions (Flashner 1987, Givón 1987, Paredes-Silva 1993).

(10) . . . vine con papi y mami. Recuerdo que ellos iban a buscarme una almohada . . .

'. . . I came with mom and dad. I remember that they were going to look for a pillow for me . . . '

Level 3: The connection among the subject pronouns is slightly weakened. There is a change in referent from the subject in the previous utterance, but there is no rival candidate for subject that might render the reference ambiguous (11). The intervening clause can be an impersonal sentence, a sentence with an inanimate or indefinite subject.

(11) pues $Ø_i$ se dió por vencida porque $nadie_j$ quiso hablar, aunque $Ø_k$ nos llevaron a la oficina . . .

'So she gave up because no one spoke up, although they took us to the office . . .'

Level 4: A change in subject weakens the connection between clauses. The referent last occurred in the previous utterance, but it performed some other syntactic function, such as a direct or indirect object, possessive, or object of a preposition (12).

(12) . . . cuando ella $\underline{me}_i$ lo dijo, yo_i sentí el corazón "fum" . . .
' . . . when she told me (it), I felt my heart "fum" . . . '

Level 5: In this level the connection is severely weakened. The token subject has a different referent than the subject of the previous clause. Furthermore, there is another possible candidate for subject between the target subject pronoun and its last occurrence. In contrast with Paredes-Silva, I only counted intervening subjects that were similar in person and number to the target subject as possible candidates. Since Spanish verbs are inflected, the hearer could easily rule out a subject that had a different person and number than the verb in question. However, if the previous subject had the same person and number and the subject pronoun that had switched referent was omitted (as subject b in 13 is), then the reference could become ambiguous. I must emphasize, though, that in the over 3,000 tokens I have examined, I have not found a single case in which the context would not disambiguate the reference.

(13) una vez, $\underline{\text{un amigo de nosotros}}_a$ cogió y tenía una cucaracha de la casa, muerta y $Ø_a$ la puso en la silla y cuando $Ø_b$ se sentó, que $Ø_b$ se iba a parar, $Ø_b$ tenía la – la – la desto, la ropa atrás manchá y desto . . .

('José' is talking about the pranks that his classmates used to play on a particular sixth-grade teacher)

'one time, a friend of ours took and had a roach from his house, dead and he placed it in the chair and when she sat down, that she was going to stand up, she had the – the – thing, her clothes stained . . . '

Level 6: The connection between subjects is disrupted. I divided Paredes-Silva's Level 6 into two levels in order to capture two different types of discourse disruption. In Level 6, the same referent is maintained but some change in topic is introduced. In oral interviews, the interviewer introduces most new topics into the discourse. Nevertheless, the interviewees often make tangential comments about a particular individual. In example 14, the informant was explaining how he thought the music at a Latin party that was taking place the next day would be organized.

(14) No, well si $Ø_i$ van a hacer lo que hicieron el año pasado, Ø van a tener el grupo que hace como salsa y merengue y después $Ø_i$ van a tener un DJ también para poner la música. . . . So, la última vez, $Ø_{j/i?}$ me trataron de enseñar, you know, cómo bailar merengue y salsa y I hope I haven't forgotten.

'No, well if they are going to do what they did last year, they are going to have a group that does like salsa and merengue and afterwards they are going to have a DJ also to play music. . . . So, the last time, they tried to teach me, you know, how to dance merengue and salsa and I hope I haven't forgotten.'

Level 7: At this level the discourse topic and the subject referent are changed (15).

(15) . . . y lo informan en una reunión de . . . asamblea anual de todos los miembros de la congregación. Pasando al último tópico que Ø señalé, al principio, o sea, la . . . situación de la iglesia en el . . . medio ambiente cultural . . . (XIIM APR)

' . . . and they report it in a meeting of . . . the annual assembly of all the members of the congregation. Moving to the last topic I indicated, at the beginning [of the recording], that is, the . . . situation of the church in the . . . cultural setting . . . '

Paredes-Silva does not account for the difficulty that plural subjects present to coreferentiality. These subjects are considered contained inferables, which are entities whose reference can be determined either from the same NP or pronominal or from the direct object, indirect object or the object of a preposition in the previous discourse (see Prince 1981). In this study, I considered first-person plural forms same in reference if the preceding clause contained the referents to the *nosotros* form. In example 16, the reference of the null *nosotros* (c) is contained in the subject (a) and object (b) of the preposition in the previous clause.

(16) Yo_a fui con mi $novia_b$ a casa de su hermano. $Cogimos_c$ la Greyhound.
'I went with my girlfriend to her brother's house. We took the Greyhound.'

Likewise, if the subject of a clause was first-person plural and the subject of the next reference was a single member of the plural set, then I considered the latter subject same in reference (17).

(17) Entonces este muchacho$_a$ lo que hace es comparando la proteína . . . Pero $Ø_{a+b}$ estamos encontrándonos toda una serie de dificultades. $Ø_{a+b}$ Tenemos como 3 ó 4 experimentos parados esperando que llegue cierto equipo. Y tal vez, hasta cierto punto, la culpa es mía porque yo$_b$ tal vez he debido de pensar, en experimentos más sencillos . . . (IIIM APR)

'Then this young man what he does is comparing the protein . . . But we are facing a series of difficulties. We have like 3 or 4 experiments stopped waiting for some equipment to arrive. And perhaps, to a certain degree, it is my fault because I should have thought of more simple experiments . . . '

I tested the validity of this treatment of *nosotros* by comparing an analysis in which *nosotros/yo* references were considered same in reference to an analysis in which they were classed as switches in reference. I found no statistically significant differences between the two analyses. Furthermore, the Varbrul weights obtained for the two analyses did not vary. These speakers do not appear to consider a set-to-member or member-to-set change as a switch in reference.

I put inferables whose reference could be determined from the direct object, indirect object, or the object of a preposition in Level 4. Finally, deictic pronouns are used differently in an interview context than in the written narratives of Paredes-Silva's study. If an informant answered a question using *tú* or *usted* with *yo,* or answered a question using *ustedes* with *nosotros*, the subjects were considered same in reference.

5. Results

The results presented in Table 1 reveal that Level 1 connectedness, where the referent is maintained as well as the verb tense, mood, and aspect, favors null pronouns. At a first glance it appears that the YPR and HS groups had lower rates of null pronoun expression than the other two groups, but a Chi-square test showed that the differences are not statistically significant.

Table 1. Subject expression by discourse connectedness levels among informant groups

	CS		APR		YPR		HS	
	Expression	%	Expression	%	Expression	%	Expression	%
Level 1	84/323	26%	56/220	25%	61/194	31%	80/245	33%
Level 2	60/176	34%	62/161	39%	61/153	40%	36/118	31%
Level 3	181/351	52%	167/314	53%	94/185	51%	88/165	53%
Level 4	41/79	52%	26/61	43%	33/63	52%	45/81	56%
Level 5	11/18	61%	4/6	67%	6/9	67%	6/10	60%
Level 6	3/4	75%	0/1	–	5/9	56%	0/4	–
Level 7	10/14	71%	1/1	100%	7/7	100%	4/4	100%

When changes in temporal reference occur (Level 2), informants are less likely to leave subject pronouns unexpressed. Moving down the continuity hierarchy, all groups of informants show a significant increase in the expression of pronouns from Level 2 to Level 3, where there is an intervening clause that ruptures referential continuity. The intervening clause does not present a viable competing subject between the clause being analyzed and the one preceding it, and this fact could explain the almost equal favoring of expression or non-expression of subject pronouns by all groups which range between 51% and 53% of expression. In other words, there is an increase in expression between Level 2 and Level 3, however, speakers are not clearly favoring overt pronominal expression in Level 3 partly because there has not been a 'true' switch in reference.

In Level 4 discontinuity, reference is bound to less-topical syntactic positions in the previous utterance, such as direct or indirect object, possessive, or object of a preposition (see Givón 1987). CS, YPR and HS groups slightly favored the expression of the subject pronoun, but APR informants did not. Level 5 disruption, where the token subject has a different referent than the subject of the previous clause and another possible candidate for subject appears between the target subject pronoun and its last occurrence, caused a significant increase in the expression of overt subjects among all groups. Even though the contextual information was sufficient to avoid any ambiguity between each token switched subject and the intervening subject in the previous clause, informants still marked this possible conflict by increasing the rates of pronominal expression from Level 4 to Level 5.

In Level 6, there were wide differences in the selection of subject expression among the different groups of speakers. CS speakers favored expression at a higher rate than YPR speakers while APR and HS speakers did not express the subject at all, even when there was a switch in topic but the subject referent was the same. For Level 7, there was some discrepancy as well in the results for all groups. APR, YPR, and HS speakers expressed all subjects when both switched in reference and topic. CS speakers however, showed a 71% rate of expression in these cases. The differences in rates of expression between Levels 6 and 7 seemed to point to a stronger effect of a switch in reference than a switch in topic over subject expression. Nevertheless, except for one case in the HS group, all the unexpressed pronouns in Level 6 are first-person singular references. Furthermore, the 4 cases of unexpressed pronouns in Level 7 for CS speakers are also first-person singular references. Thus, what seems to be causing these differences is an effect of the interview context. Since the new referent is the speaker himself or herself, the informant seems to have the option of whether or not to signal this change.

I suspected that the significant difference in subject expression demonstrated by APR informants for Level 4 was related to an unattested hierarchy of subject expression based on the syntactic position that the coreferential argument occupied in the previous utterance. Therefore, I looked at the syntactic positions in which the referent of each Level 4 subject had last occurred in the previous clause. Table 2 shows the rates of expression for each group of informants for each of six syntactic positions.

Table 2. Subject pronoun expression by syntactic function of the coreferential argument in the previous clause

	CS		APR		YPR		HS	
	Expression	%	Expression	%	Expression	%	Expression	%
Direct object	2/13	15%	2/7	29%	4/11	36%	8/16	50%
Indirect object	20/40	50%	12/28	43%	18/35	51%	16/33	48%
Oblique argument	3/7	43%	4/11	36%	6/10	60%	8/13	62%
Possessive	10/12	83%	8/14	57%	4/6	67%	8/14	57%
Nominal attribute	1/1	100%	0	–	0	–	4/4	100%
Other (vocative)	5/6	83%	0/1	0%	1/1	100%	1/1	100%

Few trends were observed in the data. Cases of nominal attributes or other positions were too scarce for any conclusions to be made. Subject pronouns whose referent last occurred as a direct object were mostly not expressed, and those whose referent last occurred as a possessive adjective or pronoun were mostly expressed.

All the groups except for APR informants showed rates of expression close to 50% for indirect objects. Those subjects whose referent last occurred as an oblique argument were expressed more by YPR and HS informants than by CS and APR informants. The indirect and oblique object positions account for more than half of the cases present in the corpus. At this point, APR informants' preference for unexpressed subjects at Level 4 seems to result from this group's higher rates of null subjects for these two positions.

6. Discussion

My first hypothesis was that coreferentiality by itself does not adequately account for subject expression in Spanish. If coreferentiality were the only factor that determined subject expression, I would expect to find that none of the token subjects that were same in reference were expressed, while all of the token subjects that were switched in reference were expressed. In Table 3, we see that coreferentiality is an important factor in determining whether subject pronouns will be expressed; subjects that are switched in reference are expressed more often than those that maintain the reference. However, approximately a third of subjects that are same in reference are expressed, while nearly half of subjects that are switched in reference are left unexpressed. Clearly coreferentiality alone cannot account for subject expression in Spanish.

Table 3. Subject expression by switch or maintenance of coreferentiality

	CS	APR	YPR	HS
Same in reference	144/499 29%	118/381 31%	122/347 35%	116/363 32%
Switch in reference	246/466 53%	198/383 52%	145/273 53%	143/264 54%

The discourse connectedness hierarchy creates a more detailed account of the interaction between expression of subject pronouns in Spanish and the coreferentiality of subjects; verb tense, aspect, and mood; the cognitive accessibility of subjects; and topic. This study demonstrates that subject pronoun expression is sensitive to several factors other than changes in the reference of the subject of the clause. The expression of subject pronouns reacts to changes in temporal reference (Level 2). I also find that an intervening clause which poses no 'rival candidate' for reference can still affect the expression of a subject pronoun. The argument position of the referent in the previous utterance can affect pronoun expression as well.

In general, my application of the connectedness hierarchy to spoken speech yielded similar gradient results to those obtained by Paredes-Silva (1993) for written Brazilian Portuguese and Bayley and Pease Álvarez (1997) for written Mexican-American Spanish (see Table 4). I found higher percentages for subject pronoun expression than these studies found, but this difference is mostly attributable to the fact that I studied spoken rather than written discourse. Both of these studies found the same pattern that I found: subject pronoun expression increases as subject coreferentiality becomes weaker in the discourse. Thus, we are observing a constraint that operates across dialects and related languages.

Table 4. Subject pronoun expression per degrees of discourse connectedness for written Brazilian Portuguese (Paredes Silva 1993) and written Mexican-American Spanish (Bayley and Pease Álvarez 1997)

	Brazilian Portuguese (first-person subjects only)		Mexican-American Spanish	
Level 1	3/212	(1%)	44/378	(12%)
Level 2	59/395	(15%)	41/212	(19%)
Level 3	35/178	(20%)	48/217	(22%)
Level 4	23/78	(30%)	84/237	(35%)
Level 5	148/410	(36%)	N/A	
Level 6	111/377	(30%)	162/505	(32%)

My second hypothesis was that English–Spanish language contact has affected subject expression in Spanish. If language contact were a motivating force behind the increased expression of subject pronouns in Caribbean Spanish, I would expect higher probabilities of expression for APR, YPR, and HS speakers (in that order) than for CS speakers. That is, if Spanish varieties in a close contact situation with English showed evidence of grammatical convergence, then CS speakers would show significantly lower rates due to their minimal if non-existent contact with English. Probability weights (Goldvarb 2.0) for subject expression by discourse connectedness appear in Table 5.

The weights in Table 5 do not provide support for the second hypothesis. Overall, the informants in this study showed a gradual decrease in subject expression as discourse connectedness weakened with mostly similar weight values. Thus, discourse-pragmatic functions had similar effects on the expression of subject pronouns for all groups.

Table 5. Probability weights for subject pronoun expression by levels of discourse connectedness

	CS	APR	YPR	HS
Level 1	.68	.70	.63	.60
Level 2	.59	.57	.56	.63
Level 3	.35	.32	.36	.31
Level 4–DO	.76	.77	.56	.50
Level 4–IO	.44	.54	.44	.47
Level 4–OBL	.35	.57	.27	.29
Level 5	.24	.43	.21	.27
Level 6	.17	–	.39	–
Level 7	.24	.34	–	.43

Overall, the informants in this study showed a gradual decrease in subject expression as discourse connectedness became weaker. Thus, discourse-pragmatic functions had similar effects on the expression of subject pronouns for all groups. HS informants seem to have blurred the distinctions between Levels 1 and 2. However, this phenomenon is caused by imperfect acquisition of tense, aspect, and mood in Spanish rather than the influence of discourse-pragmatic conventions from English. The HS informants in this study had never studied Spanish in school; all their Spanish was acquired at home through interactions with adult family members. It was evident from the interviews that their knowledge of Spanish tense, aspect, mood, and modality was limited. Thus, we would expect these speakers to lack many of the signs that mark temporal changes in discourse, not just as a transfer from English, but as a result of the manner in which they acquired Spanish.

Results for Level 4 do not support the generalization that if a speaker assumes that the hearer shares the reference for the subject of an utterance, he or she will not mark that information with an overt subject pronoun unless there is an implicit contrast (Haverkate 1976, Lipski 1996). Rather we found that token subjects which are coreferential with a syntactic position other than subject in the previous utterance (Level 4) are expressed slightly more often than token subjects which retained the same subject reference (Levels 1 and 2). As Table 2 showed, our speakers do not reveal any pattern in selection of expression based on the syntactic function of the coreferential argument in the preceding clause (cf. topicality hierarchy, Givón 1983). Moreover, informants in this study showed such a wide range of differences in expression within this level that a comparison with Silva-Corvalán's results (1994) for East Los Angeles Spanish (see Table 6 below) could not reveal any cross-dialect patterns of subject expression.

Table 6. Silva-Corvalán (1994) subject expression (NPs and pronouns) by syntactic function of the coreferential argument in the preceding clause

Sentential subject	30/42	63%
Switch in reference with all arguments	624/1080	57%
Coreference with oblique argument	18/36	50%
Coreference with direct object	28/86	33%
Coreference with indirect object	14/48	29%
Coreference with subject	176/873	20%

To conclude, this study provides evidence that the documented increase in subject pronoun expression in Caribbean Spanish is a language-internal change. All groups showed similarities in the overall rates of expression when analyzed using a discourse connectedness hierarchy as well as instability in expression at Levels 3 and 4. Speakers showed uncertainty in whether or not to mark the slight weakening of referential connection between contiguous clauses in which the coreferentiality moved away from the subject position in these levels. The rates become 'stable' once we move into Level 5, in which there is a clear switch in reference. Finally, there is also evidence of the extension of this change among the younger bilingual groups (YPR and HS) into Levels 1 and 2. Both groups showed a reduction of the gap between Levels 1 and 2 which can be attributed to the contact situation of English and Spanish. Language contact between these two languages has caused interference and convergence in the syntactic systems of bilingual speakers (cf. Morales 1986, Silva-Corvalán 1994). This contact situation seems to have triggered simplification of some tense, mood, and aspect distinctions between the languages which are critical in distinguishing between Levels 1 and 2 in Spanish. Further studies with similar bilingual groups will permit a better understanding of the extent of this phenomenon.

References

Ávila-Jiménez, Bárbara. 1995. Markedness reversal of discourse functions in Puerto Rican Spanish. Paper presented at the 25th Meeting of New Ways of Analyzing Variation (NWAVE), University of Nevada, Las Vegas.

Ávila-Jiménez, Bárbara. 1996. Subject pronoun expression in Puerto Rican Spanish: A sociolinguistic, morphological, and discourse analysis. Ph.D. dissertation, Cornell University.

Ávila-Shah, Bárbara. 1998. Subject pronoun expression in Cuban and Puerto Rican Spanish. Paper presented at the 27th Conference of the Linguistic Association of the Southwest, Arizona State University.

Bayley, Robert and Lucinda Pease-Álvarez. 1997. Null pronouns variation in Mexican-descent children's narrative discourse. *Language Variation and Change* 9: 349–371.

Cameron, Richard. 1992. *Pronominal and null subject variation in Spanish: Constraints, dialects and compensation*. Philadelphia: Institute for Research in Computer Sciences, IRCS Report 92–22.

Flashner, Vanessa. 1987. The grammatical marking of theme in oral Polish narrative. In *Coherence and grounding in discourse*, ed. R.S. Tomlin, 131–156. Philadelphia: John Benjamins.

Givón, Talmy. 1983. *Topic continuity in discourse: A quantitative cross-language study*. Amsterdam: John Benjamins.

Givón, Talmy. 1987. Beyond foreground and background. In *Coherence and grounding in discourse*, ed. R.S. Tomlin, 175–188. Philadelphia: John Benjamins.

Haverkate, W.H. 1976. Estructura y función del sujeto en el español moderno. *In Actes du XIII Congrès International de Linguistique et Philologie Romanes*, ed. M. Boudreault and F. Möhren, 1191–1197. Québec: Les Presses de l'Université Laval.

Lipski, John. 1996. Patterns of pronominal evolution in Cuban-American bilinguals. In *Spanish in contact: Issues in bilingualism*, ed. Ana Roca and John B. Jensen, 159–186. Somerville, MA: Cascadilla Press.

Morales, Amparo. 1986. La expresión de sujeto pronominal en el español de Puerto Rico. In *Gramáticas en contacto: Análisis sintácticos sobre el español de Puerto Rico*, ed. Amparo Morales, 89–100. San Juan: Editorial Playor.

Morales, Amparo and María Vaquero. 1990. *El habla culta de San Juan: Materiales para su estudio*. Río Piedras: Editorial de la Universidad de Puerto Rico.

Paredes-Silva, Vera Lúcia. 1993. Subject omission and functional compensation: Evidence from Brazilian Portuguese. *Language Variation and Change* 5: 35–49.

Prince, Ellen. 1981. Toward a taxonomy of given-new information. In *Radial pragmatics*, ed. P. Cole, 223–255. New York: Academic Press.

Silva-Corvalán, Carmen. 1982. Subject expression and placement in Mexican-American Spanish. In *Spanish in the United States: Sociolinguistic aspects*, ed. J. Amastae and L. Elías-Olivares, 93–120. New York: Cambridge University Press.

Silva-Corvalán, Carmen. 1994. *Language contact and change: Spanish in Los Angeles*. New York: Oxford University Press.

Nosotros somos dominicanos: Language and Self-Definition among Dominicans

Almeida Jacqueline Toribio
The Pennsylvania State University

This chapter examines the language situation of the immigrant and U.S.-born Dominican populations of New York, which, despite increasing numerical and socio-political prominence, have gone largely ignored. These Dominican communities exhibit a high degree of language loyalty, which is remarkable in the context of the dominant English language and in the proximity of other dialects of Spanish, from which the Dominican vernacular differs markedly. Many of these differences are stigmatized, and yet the dialect persists with minimal disturbance. The question arises as to why speakers don't abandon these low-prestige forms in favor of the more conservative General Latin American Spanish norm (through leveling) or in favor of the dominant language, English (through language displacement or loss). The answer lies in the unifying and separatist functions of the Dominican vernacular.

The first section of this chapter presents an overview of the linguistic features of the dialect at issue; though syntax is not the focus of the work, this section points to data that should prove of inherent interest to syntacticians. Section 2, the kernel of the work, considers Dominican Spanish in its socio-historical context, both in the Dominican Republic and in the United States. The data on linguistic forms, usage, and attitudes reveal that while Dominicans have viable alternatives for escaping linguistic prejudice, they remain fiercely loyal to their native dialect which binds them to their Hispanic past and isolates them from their African and African-American neighbors.

1. Dominican Spanish and its properly linguistic import

The diversity of the dialects of Latin American Spanish has stimulated significant popular interest and scholarly attention (cf. Lipski 1994). What invariably emerges from the literature is the uniqueness of the dialects of

Spanish spoken in the Caribbean, with the Dominican Republic at the forefront of linguistic innovation. Henríquez Ureña (1940) and Jiménez Sabater (1975) present the most complete analyses of the dialect, detailing the lexical, phonological, morphological, and syntactic characteristics that identify this dialect of Spanish and distinguish it from the Spanish spoken in other Latin American nations and from the established norm. As expected, variations in the lexicon abound. The introduction of Taíno/Arawak indigenisms such as *ají*, *cabuya*, and *guanábana* and Africanisms such as *ñame*, *cachimbo*, and *féferes* reflects historical contact, and continued innovations in the lexicon attest to the vitality of the language, and to Dominicans' tendency to language play in particular:[1]

(1) a. Hay un conjunto de frases propias del país, y hay cosas que se ponen de moda. . . . De un tiempo acá se ha usado mucho, cuando una persona es muy diestra en algo, decir esa persona es un *caballo* o un *toro*. En cualquier nivel social tú oyes, «Fulano, ve donde[2] ese médico, que es un caballo».

b. Yo recuerdo que en una compañía allá en Estados Unidos, un dominicano le dijo a un centroamericano, «Mira, pásame esa vaina para darle un coñazo a esta desgracia ahí». Él no entendió. Si me lo dice a mí, yo le doy cualquier cosa, porque eso es una vaina, eso es una desgracia, eso es una pendejada.

There are also regional variations in pronunciation, particularly of syllable-final consonants. Especially noteworthy are the processes that affect syllable-final liquids, the most prevalent being lambdacism, glide formation, and rhotacism. For example, the items *faltar, faltas,* and *faltaban* may be rendered with distinct pronunciations in the capital city of Santo Domingo, in the agricultural countryside of the Cibao Valley, and in the southern region:[3]

(2) a. Norm: [faltár], [fáltas], [faltáβãn]
b. Santo Domingo: [faltál], [fálta], [faltáβãŋ]/[faltáβã]
c. Cibao Valley: [fajtáj], [fájta], [fajtáβãŋ]/[fajtáβã]
d. Southern coast: [fartár], [fárta], [fartáβãŋ]/[fartáβã]

The dialect has also experienced a decrease in morphological distinctions which may be due to reduction of other alveolar consonants. A common feature is the weakening of syllable-final /s/, which may be subsequently elided altogether, as illustrated in (2).[4] While Henríquez Ureña's (1940: 139) early survey of the language revealed that "en la dicción culta se procura evitar la modificación," some fifty years later Lipski (1994) estimates the consonantal reduction to be so common as to be nearly categorical, even among educated speakers.

Also attested across regional and social dialects are the velarization and elision of syllable-final /n/, though, as indicated, the nasalization remains on the preceding vowel.[5] These consonantal changes have given rise to incipient phonological restructuring, and have had significant consequences in the verbal system, eliminating distinctions across numerous verbal paradigms: {-s} marks the second-person singular, and {-n} marks the third-person plural.[6] In the traditional linguistic literature, such distinctions encoded by richness of inflectional endings have been linked to the availability of null subjects.[7] Thus, we would predict that the loss of morphological distinctions would occasion the rise of overt pronominal subjects.[8] This is not the case in Dominican Spanish. In marked contrast to General Latin American Spanish, in which subject pronouns are typically expressed only for emphatic purposes, Dominican Spanish allows for subjects to be freely employed without added pragmatic meaning, as in (3). (Note that the morphophonological reductions at issue are not reproduced in the transcripts.)

(3) Overt subject pronouns with specific and non-specific human reference

a. Yo no lo vi, él estaba en Massachusetts, acababa de llegar, pero muy probable para el domingo pasado, que fue Día de las Madres allá, él estaba en Nueva York. . . . El estaba donde Eugenia, y yo creo que él se va a quedar allá hasta que . . .

b. Simplemente tus padres te dicen, «Bueno m'hijo, todo lo que tú me pidas yo te lo doy, pero tu carrera tú tienes que hacerla tú».

c. Déjeme yo contarle . . . yo le dije que no se le puede echar plato a la casa sin tú hablar con los otros hermanos tuyos, . . . porque después cuando yo me muera, tú te vas a hacer dueño de la casa tú solo.

d. Ellos me dijeron que yo tenía anemía. . . . Si ellos me dicen que yo estoy en peligro cuando ellos me entren la aguja por el ombligo, yo me voy a ver en una situación de estrés.

This marked use of subject pronouns has proliferated throughout the pronominal system, so that even verb forms that remain phonologically distinct with respect to person and number are nonetheless accompanied by the subject pronoun. These subject pronouns may be overtly expressed without emphatic force. Therefore, we might invoke paradigmatic pressure or parametric shift in accounting for the preponderance of subject pronouns in evidence, a proposal that finds support in the use of pronouns even with inanimate subjects, (4a), and the overuse of the impersonal neutral pronouns *tú* and *uno* (4b). And perhaps the most intriguing and most telling characteristic of the dialect is the introduction of the non-referential pronoun *ello*, which is completely devoid of content and force; the overt expression of the expletive, exemplified in (4c), is striking, as it has no equivalent expression in other varieties of Spanish.

(4) a. Overt subject pronoun with non-human reference

[Re: river] Él tiene poca agua.
[Re: buses] Ellas se saben devolver en Villa; ellas pasan de largo.
[Re: cistern] A la cisterna mía ya no le falta agua. Ella tiene agua.

b. Impersonal neutral pronouns *tú* and *uno*

Uno habla regularcito aquí.
A uno le dan una película y se desmaya.
A mí me gusta allá, pero entonces, como uno tiene su negocio aquí . . . uno no va a coger para allá para trabajarle a otro.
Uno se da cuenta que uno es adulto ya. . . . Tú haces lo que tú te propones hacer.

c. Overt expletive pronoun

Ello llegan guaguas hasta allá.
Ello había mucha gente en *lay-a-way* [stand-by].
Ellos querían renovar el centro para el turismo y ello hay mucha gente que lo opone.
Porque ello no hay luz, aquí no hay luz, no – Ya agua hay, y va a haber más agua todavía . . . sí, ello viene un poquitico ya en la llave ya.

Jiménez Sabater (1975: 164–165) provides an explicit statement of the interrelation of all of the aforementioned properties:

> En el habla dominicana actual parece sentirse cada vez más la necesidad de diferenciar la segunda de la tercera persona del singular utilizando los respectivos pronombres antepuestos al verbo. Estos se mencionan, cuando menos, una vez en cada oración o período. . . . En la zona del Cibao estas expresiones más o menos redundantes coinciden curiosamente con la utilización del pronombre fósil *ello* como sujeto antepuesto a verbos 'impersonales.'[9]

Another prominent feature of Dominican Spanish is the pattern of word order attested in declaratives, interrogatives, and infinitival constructions. The word order of declaratives in General Latin American Spanish is relatively free, demonstrating a sensitivity to pragmatic considerations such as theme-rheme requirements and syntactic considerations such as verb class. In contrast, word order in Dominican Spanish is relatively fixed – subject-verb-object –

irrespective of subject type or verb class, a fact frequently noted in the literature. Further corroboration for the fixing of the preverbal position for subjects is the fact that the pattern is maintained even in questions, where the General Latin American Spanish norm requires that the verb appear in second position, preposed to the subject. As shown in (5a), in Dominican Spanish the preverbal position is available to pronouns and full NPs alike. This lack of inversion in questions is noted in Henríquez Ureña (1940) and by Jiménez Sabater (1975: 169), the latter stating that the preverbal positioning of subject pronouns in questions "es prácticamente general en el español de la República Dominicana." The dialect also employs an additional strategy as a means of circumventing the inverted order, the pseudo-cleft illustrated in (5b). This could explain the focus strategy, in (5c), whose null operator is very pronounced in the Dominican vernacular (cf. Toribio 1992, 1993b).

(5) a. Interrogatives

¿Qué yo les voy a mandar a esos muchachos?
Papí, ¿qué ese letrero dice?
¿Qué número tú anotaste? . . . ahorita tú vas a ver si sale.
¿Cuánto un médico gana?
¿Y con quién Fredi está allá?

b. Pseudo-cleft

¿En qué es que tú te vas a graduar?
¿Dónde fue que tú estudiaste?
¿Qué es lo que ese muchacho me trae?
¿Cuánto fue que él me dijo que costaba?
¿Cuándo es que ustedes se van?

c. Focus strategy

Yo quiero es comida.
Ese niño está es enfermo.
Tú trajiste fue una sola maleta nada más.
Mamá tiene que ir es al mercado.

More interestingly, Dominican Spanish permits overt preverbal subjects in non-finite (infinitival and gerundive) clauses, as in (6). The attested subject-infinitive order stands in marked contraposition to that observed in General Latin American Spanish, in which the subject follows the infinitival verb (cf. Toribio 1993a).

(6) Infinitival clause

A la carne se le mezcla limón para usted lavarla.
Mira muchachito, ven acá, para nosotros verte.
Tienes que ir a cambiarle un dinero a estas mujeres antes de ellas irse para allá.
Ella vive enferma, sin los médicos encontrarle nada.
En tú estando con ella, nada te pasa.

While Henríquez Ureña (1940) reports the preverbal positioning of subjects in infinitival clauses as possible for the expression of pronouns, it is described by Jiménez Sabater (1975: 169) as having displaced the canonical postverbal positioning only three decades later:

> propagado ya a aquellos casos en que el infinitivo viene acompañado de un sustantivo y no de un simple pronombre como sujeto. Podríamos pensar que se está extendiendo un esquema 'sujeto-verbo' en el cual un orden riguroso de las palabras (sujeto precediendo al verbo) sería rasgo relevante.

To recapitulate, the linguistic patterns manifest in Dominican Spanish reveal that it has expanded to encompass phonological rules and grammatical constructions that are not uniformly reproduced in the dialects of other Latin American nations today.[10] Viewed from a properly linguistic perspective, these latter observations, which are systematically corroborated (cf. Toribio 1993b, 1996, 1999a, 1999b), suggest that Dominican Spanish is undergoing a shift from one grammar to another, "un hecho perfectamente explicable dentro de las posibilidades que ofrece el mismo sistema español" (Jiménez Sabater 1975: 169).[11] (Consult Toribio 1999a, 1999b for a syntactic-theoretical account of intralingual variation.)

2. Dominican Spanish in its social context

Aside from its import to theoretical linguistics, there are additional aspects of dialectal variation that merit scrutiny. For instance, are speakers aware of the linguistic novelty? If so, do they have a favorable judgment of the innovations? Would they abandon the vernacular for a more conservative variety? Are there any social correlates? Questions such as these were explored in interviews with Dominicans in the Dominican Republic and in New York in fall of 1998. The guiding inspiration and motivation for examining these and other affective and social factors that enter into language loyalty is found in Johnson's (1998) thesis on Dominican cultural and racial identity. While that work did not highlight the nature of the linguistic issues of interest here, the connection between language and cultural identity, on the one hand, and between language and race, on the other, was an essential underlying theme.

2.1. Language attitudes and language loyalty

As we saw in Section 1, the Spanish dialect of the Dominican Republic distinguishes itself in significant linguistic respects from the prescribed norm for the Spanish language. This assessment is substantiated in subjective evaluations culled from interviews with Dominicans of diverse backgrounds. The excerpts in (7) attest to Dominicans' sensitivity to variation and the remarkably low esteem in which the dialect is held:

(7) a. Los dominicanos tenemos el problema que hablamos con faltas ortográficas. . . . Aquí se habla con falta ortográfica, no sólo se escribe, sino que se habla también. (DR#2; upper class male; age 35)

b. Aquí es . . . como decimos allá en los Estados Unidos, es un *broke English*. . . . No sé por qué los niños no hablan un español mejor que el que hablan, que es tan pobre. (DR#9; middle class male returnee; age 62)

The Dominican vernacular remains stigmatized and aesthetically undervalued, especially among the Dominican middle and upper classes, for lacking certain features of an idealized standard – the Northern Peninsular Castilian variety:

(8) a. Me gusta como hablan los españoles. . . . Para como hablan los españoles y como hablamos nosotros aquí, hay mucha diferencia – Me gusta la forma de ellos hablar, su acento y todo, eso me gusta – ellos tienen más modalidad que uno hablando. (DR#37; middle class male; age 30)

b. El [español] de España es como más fino. La lengua española vino de España, ¿no fue? (DR#29; middle class male; age 54)

c. En España, que es la madre de la lengua española, hablan muy bien el español. (DR#24; middle class male returnee; age 55)

d. El argentino habla muy europeizado, para decirlo así. Tú aquí le dices a alguien, «Vos estáis» y te miran medio raro. (DR#2; upper class male; age 35)

Conversely, specific regional dialects are discounted or disparaged for incorporating other, less agreeable characteristics, namely, those of the Haitian Creole of the neighboring nation:

(9) a. La región que habla mal, que hablan medio cruzado, es en Vaca Gorda, porque ahí son todos prietos.[12] Es como la lengua que se les cruza, son gente medio haitianados. (DR#25; working class male; age 70+)

b. Por aquí en El Rodeo había una descendencia haitiana; en esa área del Rodeo no se hablaba bien el español. Ellos usaban a veces unas palabras dialécticas, que a veces uno mismo ni las entendía, esa misma clase de gente, haitianos, que se mestizaron ahí. Yo recuerdo que a veces ellos hablaban delante de uno y uno no entendía las palabras. (DR#24; middle class male returnee; age 55)

c. Los prietos ronchuses de por allá hablan como jmmpf, ¿no es verdad? Como cosa de bruto. (DR#3; middle class female; age 50+)

In this predilection for the northern Peninsular variety and emphatic disavowing of the inevitable influence of the Haitian Creole, Dominicans affirm their *hispanidad*, an historical obsession that is part and parcel of the Dominican national endowment (cf. Baud 1996).[13] This favoring of the Peninsular variety – *la lengua original y pura* – persists in the U.S., where the Dominican dialect is but one of many. As shown in (10), in the linguistic *potaje* that is New York, Dominican Spanish is characterized as *campesino*, while other dialects are merely "different."

(10) a. I think España [speaks Spanish best]; they have an <s> and a good accent. Everybody else speaks Spanish different. (NY#44; working class male; age 15)

b. Dominicans don't speak Spanish well. I'm not saying that I speak perfect Spanish or perfect English. . . . All you see is Dominicans that are from *el campo*. Everybody knows right away that they're Dominicans; you get embarrassed because of those people. (NY#42; working class female; age 30)

c. Si te pasaras un día en mi trabajo, te dieres cuenta que la forma de yo hablar es una mezcla de todos los diferentes tipos de razas de países. El problema es que donde yo trabajo es una faramacia y estoy ahí más porque puedo hablar español. Entonces hay muchas personas de diferentes países y cuando llega una persona por decir, de Puerto Rico, pues yo tengo que saber cómo es que ellos hablan y a qué es que ellos se refieren cuando hablan de algo específico. Entonces cuando viene otra persona de, vamos a decir, del Salvador, que hablan también español, yo tengo también que tratar de entenderlos a ellos. Entonces es un trabajo muy interesante. Y la gente me dice, «Pero tú no hablas como los dominicanos.» (NY#45; working class female; age 24)[14]

It is readily apparent from the foregoing excerpts that Dominicans are most conscious of their 'radical' pronunciation, especially in view of other highly conservative Latin American varieties, but their lexical regionalisms and syntactic innovations evade self-censure.[15] Thus, as noted by García et al.

(1988: 505), while Dominicans may regularly substitute *casimente* for *casi* and *auyama* for *calabaza*, the more educated Dominicans "have a more conservative pronunciation, that is, one that follows more closely the orthography of the language." Moreover, the aforementioned dialectal features (e.g., the overt expletive and reduplicative negation in *Ello no hay mangos no* and the assertive copula represented in *Las mujeres levaban canastas era*) are rarely abandoned, for they simply reflect *el habla dominicana.* In other words, radical pronunciation will identify one as poor and uneducated, whereas particular lexical regionalisms and grammatical constructions merely distinguish one as Dominican (Toribio 2000).[16]

These innovations may appear unsystematic, even deficient, to the untrained ear, but the Dominican dialect is neither. Indeed, as elaborated in Toribio 1993a, 1993b, the variety is both systematic in itself and is also related systematically to the standard. Still, this difference between local vernacular and conservative norm significantly impacts Dominicans in the U.S., where educational policy dictates that only the standard variety of the minority language is taught. Children and adolescents who are exposed to Dominican Spanish at home acquire a variety that is different from the standard modeled by educators. Indeed, the increased presence of Dominicans in the schools has raised difficult questions about the most appropriate means of accommodating the dialect while effectively promoting the school norm. The observation in (11) is offered by an informant who served as an instructor in a trade school in a large Dominican community in the U.S.:

(11) Yo conozco muchachos, que han nacido allá en Estados Unidos, que nunca conocían la República Dominicana y hablaban con una <i> más fuerte que cualquier gente de un campo de aquí. Ese caso lo vi yo en un muchacho que nació en Lawrence, Massachusetts. Y tú lo oías hablando y tú creías que estaba hablando con un muchacho de cualquier campo de Salcedo, porque los papás eso era lo que hablaban. Y ellos estudiando español en la escuela y estudiando inglés, y hablaban común y corriente como cualquier cibaeño, cibaeños de los que hablan malo. (DR#28; middle class male returnee; 51)

One solution has been to enroll students in introductory or 'remedial' Spanish classes where they can be taught how to speak 'properly.' In these classrooms, they are ridiculed by peers who openly demonstrate negative attitudes towards their dialect. They also receive little sympathy from educators who fail to appreciate the ways in which dialects differ or the practical difficulties and familial and community alienation that adopting a normative standard may impose:[17]

(12) Hay gente que dirían, «La hija de Nano vino privando en fisna,[18] pronunciando la 's' hasta donde no va», pero no: si tú aprendiste a hablarlo bien, tú aprendiste. (DR#28; middle class male returnee; age 51)

It is not surprising that many youngsters seek to distance themselves from their stigmatized language variety, even among in-group peers, reserving the language for the intimacy and safety of the community and home. In this situation, language displacement towards English may become an important option for escaping linguistic prejudice.

2.2. Language vitality: Spanish as an economically viable language in Dominican enclaves

The observed deprecation of the Dominican dialect by speakers themselves is at odds with the attested vitality of Dominican Spanish in the U.S. diaspora. Dominicans are extremely language-retentive, maintaining and advancing the Dominican Spanish dialect even in the context of other more conservative Latin American dialects. As the most monolingual of the Hispanic groups in New York (U.S. Bureau of the Census 1990), Dominicans demonstrate extensive Spanish language usage in the private home domain with family members, as well as with in-group members such as with friends, classmates, and co-workers, and in the extended out-group domains of the community (cf. García et al. 1988).

The continued use of the Dominican vernacular is a strong indicator that the immigrant community considers its language to be an important feature of its identity, a positive assertion of *dominicanidad.* (However, this sustained use is not necessarily a rejection of the negative evaluations that speakers themselves may harbor.) There are strong affective and instrumental factors that favor maintenance. The dialect provides a link with their past and with their fellow speakers abroad, and therefore it helps to promote the group's feeling of unity and national identity. In other words, the sustained language maintenance among Dominicans in the diaspora owes in large part to the nature and extent of their ties with their homeland; they are intensely loyal to their home country – they are Dominicans first, Latinos second – and for many, return to the homeland is not a myth, but a mandate.

Substantial numbers of Dominicans were driven to migrate, temporarily, they supposed, during the state of political turbulence and economic instability precipitated by the assassination of the ruling dictator, Trujillo, in 1961 (cf. Wiarda and Kryzanek 1992). Many entered as transient immigrants, and stayed to find employment, married citizens or resident aliens (the normal route to legalizing immigrant status), requested additional immigrant visas for family members, and stayed on (Johnson 1998):

(13) a. Nos fuimos [a los Estados Unidos] buscando un futuro mejor. Mis hijos nacieron allá. (DR#31; middle class female returnee; age 48)

b. Yo me fui para allá porque mis hijos me pidieron. (DR#40, working class female; age 80+)

Today, about one million Dominicans reside in the U.S., concentrated predominantly along the eastern seaboard with an estimated 69% in New York.[19] Dominicans have continued to immigrate in large numbers, at an average of over 22,000 per year between 1990 and 1994 (cf. Lobo and Salvo 1997). These *dominicanos ausentes* are received into communities that are culturally and linguistically familiar, thereby easing the settlement process (cf. Torres-Saillant and Hernández 1998).[20] Dominican presence is especially strongly felt in the social and economic life of Washington Heights in upper Manhattan (variously known as 'Quisqueya Heights,' '*el pequeño Cibao*,' and '*el platanal*'), where in the local *bodega*, *dominicanos* can find food stuffs such as *casabe* and *longaniza*, gamble on the illegal numbers game, and catch up on island politics, all in their native, regional island vernacular. As described by Suro (1998: 198–199), Washington Heights "was not built as a place where newcomers could start the process of becoming Americans. Instead, the purpose was to allow its inhabitants to become transnationals or simply to remain Dominicans."

In fact, most Dominicans, especially those of the older generations, are never fully integrated into the fabric of U.S. society; instead, they maintain *un pie aquí y el otro allá*, guarding the hope of returning to the Dominican Republic. And even the younger generations return to the island for regular visits for Holy Week and Christmas, summer vacations, and family weddings and funerals. As a result, they share this Dominican/American identity, "the state of mind that permits them to remain actively linked to life in the native land while also becoming acclimated to the values and norms of the receiving society" (Torres-Saillant and Hernández 1998: 156).

2.3. Contrasting cultural constructions of race: Language in its separatist function

Despite their notable advances, Dominicans in the U.S. have encountered a great deal of ill-fortune, and the 'American dream' of social advancement and the 'Dominican dream' of rapid return have remained elusive (cf. Guarnizo 1997, Wucker 1999). The great majority continue to toil long hours in blue-collar jobs in factories and service industries, earning just enough to send remittances to relatives left in the Dominican Republic. Their underemployment is variously attributed to a restructuring of New York City's manufacturing sector, high rates of (female) single-parent households, and low levels of English language acquisition (cf. Grassmuck and Pessar 1996). Further augmenting these disadvantages is the barrier of racial discrimination,[21] which proves especially disconcerting for Dominican immigrants, who, as noted by Pessar (1997: 144), "come from a society where to be partly white (which includes most Dominicans) is to be non-black."

Indeed, throughout its history, the Dominican Republic has held an unofficial policy against *negritude*, and an official policy of affirmation of the island's Spanish roots (cf. Baud 1997). The result has been the propagation of the sentiment that African heritage is negative and shameful and an enforcement of white supremacy, positions that Dominicans publicly disavow but privately uphold. In part this denigration of African heritage dates to the war of independence against Haiti, and to the subsequent Haitian occupation of Santo Domingo in the early nineteenth century.[22] More recently, the Trujillo dictatorship, which lasted three decades, further enhanced these racial attitudes in profound ways. Promoting his ideology of *hispanidad*, which defined Dominicans as the most pure Spanish people in the Americas, Trujillo began a national political effort to save the Dominican nation from 'Haitianization' that lives on today:[23]

(14) Nosotros perdimos unas elecciones porque al candidato lo acusaron de haitiano. Lo humillaron, le hicieron de todo. Cuando lo necesitaron para ir al Club de París a intervenir por República Dominicana con un atraso de una deuda era blanco y buen mozo, pero cuando quiso ser presidente ya es prieto y feo y haitiano. Y aquí hay negros, negros, más prietos que el haitiano . . . a mí me da pena y vergüenza como pensamos nosotros. (DR#28; middle class male returnee; age 51)

Many Dominicans continue to endorse the *limpieza de sangre*, opposing Haitian immigration and Dominican-Haitian intermarriage on the grounds that they threaten the national culture:

(15) a. Usted no quisiera que una hija suya se casaría con un haitiano, porque vemos la poquedad de ellos, y su color también. . . . Uno no quisiera que se unan para entonces uno tener esa raza. . . . ¿Racista? No. Es que ¿cómo es que una mujer tan buena moza, de una estatura buena se case con un haitiano? (DR#3; middle class female; age 50+)

b. Los haitianos . . . son demasiado brutos, los pobres. Yo no me casaría con una haitiana, no. Consuma lo nuestro que es mejor que lo extranjero. Para una haitiana, mejor una americana . . . es más blanca. ¿Usted sabe lo que es uno casarse con una haitiana? No conviene, no. (DR#29; middle class male; age 54)

Such anti-Haitian sentiment is frequently given voice by persons in power – politicians, scholars, and other social critics (cf. Wucker 1999). Haitians are blamed for all manner of social ills, from low wages and high unemployment, to malaria and syphilis, to overall moral deformity and societal stagnation:

(16) Aquí en el país hay alrededor de un millón de haitianos que viven aquí. Ya los obreros de la construcción en la República Dominicana son haitianos en un ochenta por ciento. . . . los picadores de caña de los ingenios azucarero en un noventa por ciento son haitianos también. Lo que son los trabajos más duros que se hacen actualmente: la caña y la construcción. Pero ¿qué pasa? Eso al mismo tiempo es una mano de obra barata, es una demanda agregada en la economía, pero también representa el atraso de la sociedad dominicana. Mientras aparezca un hombre que trabaje por pocos pesos una jornada de trabajo, una persona nunca va a tener un tractor en el campo, porque esa mano de obra está barata y está ahí. Igual sucede en la construcción: tú siempre vas a ver, durante mucho tiempo hasta que esto no cambie, un hombre con un pico y una pala. (DR#2; upper-class male; age 35)

The national propaganda proved so effective that many Dominicans believed, and continue to believe, that the Haitians were the only blacks on Hispaniola. To cite the historian Moya Pons (1981: 25), "Dominicans perceived themselves as a very special breed of Spaniards, living in the tropics with dark skins."

Today, light-skinned Dominicans, and even dark-skinned members of the upper class, call themselves 'white.' As one upper-class dark-skinned Dominican explained, "blanco es de la mente":

(17) Cuando aquí se dice que una persona es blanca es no solamente por la tez de la piel, se mira en el grado de astucia, de inteligencia, en la forma de sus pensamientos. Se dice fulano es blanco, piensa como blanco, o sea, que es una persona que no es bruto, que tiene una habilidad de ver las cosas un poquito más allá de la nariz. (DR#2; upper class male; age 35)

The vast majority call themselves *mestizo* or *mulato*, though even within these categories, numerous subtle shadings are recognized (e.g. *trigueño, grifo, indio claro, indio oscuro, jabao, canela, moreno*).[24] This classificatory strategy conflicts with the contrasting conceptions of race in the U.S., where to be partly black is to be non-white, and color ensures social marginalization:

(18) a. We don't consider ourselves black and we don't consider ourselves white. White people don't consider us white, we're like peach. And the black people consider them brown, so Dominicans are between black, brown, and peach. (NY#41; working class male; age 11)

b. Para los blancos caemos al negro. . . . El blanco no distingue entre claros y el negro, sino todo lo conceptúa en el mismo marco. (NY#46; working class male; age 60+)

As a consequence, even the better-educated, lighter-complexioned elite may struggle for day-to-day existence alongside African-Americans in the U.S. As aptly observed by Grasmuck and Pessar (1996: 290), the dilemma arises "when Dominicans with African features or dark skin, regardless of their social sense of self, find themselves identified by many in the United States as Black and are discriminated against on that basis (rather than language, for example), and are often not prepared to interpret discrimination on these grounds."[25] Just as in the preceding centuries of interaction with their Haitian neighbors, then, Dominicans have sought to firmly distinguish themselves from their African roots and African neighbors. In contemporary U.S. society, this emphasis on *hispanidad* has resulted in a strengthening of the Spanish language among immigrant and U.S.-born Dominicans:

(19) a. Sure, you're Hispanic, but you're considered black – when you talk, they can tell. (NY#42; working class female; age 30)

b. En el habla ya se sabe. Hay negros cubanos y hay de otros países. (NY#46; working class male; age 60+)

For while there exist a number of other markers of identity, such as social group, geography, religion, cultural traditions, and race, for many New York Dominicans language is the most salient. As articulated by one young informant:

(20) La cultura dominicana incluye mucho el idioma. Yo diría que ser dominicano y hablar [español] es importante, por no decir original. El dominicano que no hable [dominicano] puede sentirse igual de orgulloso, pero le falta algo. (NY#45; working class female; age 24)

3. Conclusion

To conclude, language loyalty in the Dominican diaspora is a strong indicator that the Dominican dialect is an important feature of Dominican ethnic identity. For although it may not be a full-fledged linguistic variety to which overt prestige is ascribed, the Dominican dialect enjoys a considerable measure of covert prestige as a symbol of national or group identity: it serves a unifying and separatist function, binding Dominicans to their Hispanic past and isolating them from their African and African-American neighbors.

Notes

1. This work draws on several primary sources. Preliminary speech samples were collected in the Dominican Republic in 1992 by the author, and additional data was gathered in New York in 1997 by Kimann Johnson. In 1998, the author again traveled to the Dominican Republic and New York to complete more extensive interviews for a larger study of Dominican Spanish; data was collected from 46 speakers in diverse geographical regions. The language samples presented in Section 1 are drawn principally from the 1992 data set, and those in Section 2 from the more recent interviews conducted in 1998. This research was generously funded by the Faculty Research Assistance Program and the Academic Senate of the University of California, Santa Barbara.

2. The *donde* is a locative, functionally equivalent to Italian *da* and French *chez*.

3. Of these forms, the lateral liquid of the *capitaleño* carries the greatest cultural and political capital, as expected, and the northwestern *cibaeño* pronunciation the least. As one informant acknowledges, "El capitaleño se mofa del cibaeño hasta en las comedias por la <i>. Cae gracioso. . . . En la televisión te ponen un cibaeño y le ponen la <i>, y te hace reír. [Y la <l> no?] No . . . la <l> no. . . . Quizás sean los cheques de la capital."

4. The two-step process is as follows: the segment loses its supralaryngeal features and only the aspiration remains, and then the consonant slot is lost altogether.

5. More precisely, the /n/ is velarized in syllable rhymes (cf. Harris 1983). The segment fails to undergo the customary assimilation of place features; it is rendered as the velar nasal, save in the context of labial consonants, to which it assimilates.

6. In most tenses and moods, the loss of syllable-final /s/ has resulted in the convergence of second and third persons; in the imperfect and conditional, first, second, and third persons are rendered homophonous.

7. Many researchers have tried to relate the null subject property to rich verbal inflection, pointing out that languages such as (General Latin American) Spanish have an agreement system which is quite complex, whereas languages such as English have one which is very poor. Chomsky (1981) suggests that in null subject languages, Agr(eement) in Infl makes it possible to recover the information made unavailable by the fact that the subject is phonetically missing. Elaborating, Rizzi (1982) proposes that the characteristic property of null subject languages is that their verbal inflection is specified with a feature [+pronoun], i.e., it has clitic-like pronominal properties. In this mode of inquiry, Lipski (1977) proposes that the Spanish subject pronoun cliticizes onto the verb, recovering the person and number features that may be lost by the weakening of verbal agreement. Such an account, fails, however, since these subject pronouns do not demonstrate the behavior common to clitics. For example, as noted by Suñer and Lizardi (1995), these pronouns can be separated from the verb by negation. In addition, unlike clitics which are, by definition, unstressed, pronouns such as *nosotros* and *usted(es)* must be stressed.

8. By some accounts, it is the paucity of inflectional distinctions which has caused the retention of subject pronouns as a means of identifying the subject of the verb (cf. Hochberg 1986). However, the diversity of inflectional systems that license null subjects makes clear the difficulty of arriving at an adequate notion of inflectional richness (cf. Toribio 1993b, 1999b).

9. It merits pointing out that null subject pronouns are indeed available to the speakers sampled; within one speaker's speech there are segments that are replete with overt referential subject pronouns, whereas others contain very few, and the overt *ello* appears in only a subset of the contexts where it is theoretically possible. Such intra-dialectal variability is central to the syntactic-theoretical analysis proffered in Toribio 1993b, 1999a.

10. One might conjecture that these innovations reflect the lasting contribution of the African languages that were carried to the Caribbean region. However, Lipski (1994: 133) presents extensive data which "suggests that no major innovation in pronunciation, morphology or syntax in Latin American Spanish is due exclusively to the former presence of speakers of African languages or of any form of Afro-Hispanic language, creole or otherwise." And speaking specifically to the continued contact with the Haitian creole of the adjoining nation, Lipski (1994: 237) states, "the impact of Haitian Creole on Dominican Spanish is largely confined to the rural border region, and to life on the sugar plantations."

11. Although not presenting an analysis for this change, Jiménez Sábater (1975: 168) cautions against attributing the influence to linguistic contact with English:

> Es de dudarse que estemos ante un fenómeno de interferencia del inglés o de ninguna otra lengua extranjera. Un rasgo morfosintáctico tan característico difícilmente habría podido calar de modo tan profundo en una masa analfabeta como la de nuestro país, donde predomina, antes bien, el arcaísmo castellano – o la evolución de tendencias lingüísticas netamente hispanas – y en la que apenas se cuentan escasos préstamos léxicos de otros idiomas, por oposición a lo que sucede con otras zonas antillanas como Puerto Rico en donde también es corriente este orden de palabras.

12. *Prieto* is a descriptor, typically used as a term of endearment, but also used derogatorily, for a person with dark skin.

13. We would be remiss not to invoke historical memory at this juncture: in 1937 the national military was mobilized to the western frontier, where soldiers were ordered to kill as many Haitians as they could find; these 'offending' Haitians were identified by their inability to offer a native Dominican pronunciation of the word *perejil* – the assumption being that the uvular trill of Creole speech would reveal the speaker's Haitian identity. Such maneuvers remain in place (cf. Toribio 2000).

14. This participant's pronunciation and syntactic constructions were the most demonstrative of dialectal leveling.

15. Several of the New York informants indicated that when they spoke Spanish, they were regarded as poor and uneducated, but when they spoke English, their pronunciation betrayed them only as Hispanic; the clear implication is that Dominicans, among all Hispanics, are most disadvantaged. This finding is consonant with those of García et al. (1988).

16. However, Dominicans' self-conscious evaluation of their pronunciation over other linguistic properties does not correspond to the assessments of other Hispanic groups towards the Dominican vernacular. Many of the phonological features (e.g., the /s/-reduction and /n/-velarization) may resonate with speakers from other Latin American nations, who signal the lack of inversion in questions and the overuse of subject pronouns as uniquely Dominican; in fact, this propensity for overt preverbal subject pronouns has earned Dominicans the appellation of "Joe's" (*yo's*), as argued by one informant.

17. These linguistic differences, or more accurately peer and teacher attitudes towards these distinguishing linguistic characteristics, probably play an important part in the educational underperformance of many Dominican students. See Torres-Saillant and Hernández 1998 and Grasmuck and Pessar 1996 for interpretations of the 1990 U.S. Census data on academic achievement.

18. *Privar en fina*, or 'to put on airs' with an epenthetic [s].

19. The 1990 Census reports 511,297 Dominicans in the U.S., a figure that does not account for undocumented residents (cf. Torres-Saillant and Hernández 1998, Grasmuck and Pessar 1996).

20. The characteristics of these Dominican communities coincide with those of the specific Dominican residents within its boundaries. To quote one informant (DR#33, middle class male returnee, age 62), "Aquí hay sitios que uno va a Nueva York y sabe de dónde son esa gente, de una parte de Santiago, de Jánico, de San José de las Matas. Desde que uno habla con unas de esas personas uno sabe que son de por ahí."

21. In the 1990 census, 50% of Dominicans in New York City identified themselves as mulatto or other and 25% self-identified as black. Grasmuck and Pessar (1996) note that skin color is a significant predictor of poverty, with black and mulatto Dominicans suffering higher poverty levels than white Dominicans.

22. As stated by Torres-Saillant and Hernández (1998: 4–5), "The fact that Dominican independence, the formal emergence of Dominicans as a people, occurred as a separation from the black republic of Haiti, and that racial self-differentiation has subsequently been used in nationalist discourse, has added levels of complexity to the racial identity of Dominicans, inducing in the population a reticence to affirm their own blackness openly despite the overwhelming presence of people of African descent in the country."

23. Though Dominicans disclaim charges of racism, the correlation between privilege and race is evident, and recent incidents of racial violence between Dominicans and immigrant Haitians have forced many to reevaluate the issue of race. However, discussions of race remain a somewhat taboo topic among Dominicans (cf. Cambeira 1997, Sorensen 1997).

24. These are buttressed by reference to related desirable or undesirable physical characteristics, e.g., hair textures and size of the nose, lips, hips, and buttocks.

25. This struggle to define themselves in terms of difference from Haitians at home has led to conflicts in relations with African-Americans abroad. This theme is further developed in Toribio 2000.

References

Baud, Michiel. 1997. 'Constitutionally white': The forging of a national identity in the Dominican Republic. In *Ethnicity in the Caribbean: Essays in honor of Harry Hoetink*, ed. Gert Oostindie. Macmillan Caribbean.

Cambeira, Alan. 1997. *Quisqueya la bella: The Dominican Republic in historical and cultural perspective.* Armonk, NY: M.E. Sharpe.

Chomsky, Noam. 1981. *Lectures on government and binding.* Dordrecht: Foris.

Ferguson, James. 1992. *The Dominican Republic: Beyond the lighthouse.* Latin America Bureau.

García, Ofelia, Isabel Evangelista, Mabel Martínez, Carmen Disla, and Bonifacio Paulino. 1988. Spanish language use and attitudes: A study of two New York City communities. *Language and Society* 17: 475–511.

Grasmuck, Sherri and Patricia Pessar. 1996. Dominicans in the United States: First-and Second-Generation Settlement, 1960–1990. In *Origins and destinies: Immigration, race, and ethnicity in America*, ed. Silvia Pedraza and Rubén G. Rumbaut, 280–292. Belmont, CA: Wadsworth.

Guarnizo, Luis Eduardo. 1997. "Going home": Class, gender and household transformation among Dominican return migrants. In *Caribbean circuits: New directions in the study of Caribbean migration*, ed. Patricia Pessar, 13–60. New York: Center for Migration Studies.

Harris, James. 1983. *Spanish phonology.* Cambridge: MIT Press.

Henríquez Ureña, Pedro. 1940. *El español en Santa Domingo.* Buenos Aires: Biblioteca de Dialectología Hispanomericana V.

Hochberg, Judith. 1986. Functional compensation for /s/ deletion in Puerto Rican Spanish. *Language* 62: 609–621.

Jiménez Sabater, Max. 1975. *Más datos sobre el español de la República Dominicana.* Santo Domingo: Ediciones Intec.

Johnson, Kimann. 1998. Dominican cultural and racial identity. Senior honors thesis, Program in Latin American and Iberian Studies, University of California, Santa Barbara.

Lipski, John. 1994. *Latin American Spanish.* New York: Longman.

Lipski, John. 1977. Preposed subjects in questions: Some considerations. *Hispania* 60: 61–67.

Lobo, Arun Peter and Joseph Salvo. 1997. Immigration to New York City in the 1990s: The saga continues. *Migration World Magazine* 25: 14–17.

Moya Pons, Frank. 1981. Dominican national identity and return migration. *Occasional Papers* #1. Center for Latin American Studies, University of Florida, Gainesville.

Pessar, Patricia. 1996. Dominicans: Forging an ethnic community in New York. In *Beyond black and white: New faces and voices in US schools*, ed. Maxine Seller and Lois Weis, 131–149. Albany: State University of New York.

Pessar, Patricia. 1997. Introduction: New approaches to Caribbean emigration and return. In *Caribbean circuits: New directions in the study of Caribbean migration*, ed. Patricia Pessar, 1–11. New York: Center for Migration Studies.

Rizzi, Luigi. 1982. *Issues in Italian syntax.* Dordrecht: Foris.

Sigurðsson, Halldór Armánn. 1993. Argument-drop in Old Icelandic. *Lingua* 89: 247–280.

Sorensen, Ninna Nyberg. 1997. There are no Indians in the Dominican Republic. In *Siting culture: The shifting anthropological object*, ed. Karen Fog Olwig and Kirsten Hastrup, 292–310. New York: Routledge.

Suñer, Margarita and Carmen Lizardi. 1995. Dialectal variation in an argumental/non-argumental asymmetry in Spanish. In *Contemporary research in Romance linguistics*, ed. John Amastae, Grant Goodall, Mario Montalbetti, and Marianne Phinney, 187–203. Amsterdam: John Benjamins.

Suro, Roberto. 1998. *Strangers among us: How Latino immigration is transforming America*. New York: Knopf.

Toribio, Almeida Jacqueline. 1992. Proper government in Spanish subject relativization. *Probus* 3: 291–304.

Toribio, Almeida Jacqueline. 1993a. Lexical subjects in finite and non-finite clauses. *Cornell Working Papers in Linguistics* 11: 149–178.

Toribio, Almeida Jacqueline. 1993b. Parametric Variation in the Licensing of Nominals. Ph.D. dissertation, Cornell University, Ithaca, NY.

Toribio, Almeida Jacqueline. 1996. Dialectal variation in the licensing of null referential and expletive pronouns. In *Aspects of Romance linguistics*, ed. Claudia Parodi, Carlos Quicoli, and Mario Saltarelli, 409–432. Washington, DC: Georgetown University Press.

Toribio, Almeida Jacqueline. 1999a. Setting parametric limits on dialectal variation. *Lingua* 110: 315–341.

Toribio, Almeida Jacqueline. 1999b. Minimalist ideas on parametric variation. Forthcoming, *NELS 30*.

Toribio, Almeida Jacqueline. 2000. Linguistic ideologies: The role of language in the (re)construction of Dominican national identity. Unpublished ms., Pennsylvania State University.

Torres-Saillant, Silvio and Ramona Hernández. 1998. *The Dominican Americans*. Westport, CT: Greenwood Press.

U.S. Department of Commerce, Bureau of the Census. 1991. *Persons of Hispanic origin in the United States: 1990*. Washington, DC: U.S. Government Printing Office.

Wiarda, Howard and Michael Kryzanek. 1992. *The Dominican Republic: A Caribbean crucible (2nd. ed.)*. Boulder, CO: Westview Press.

Wucker, Michele. 1999. *Why the cocks fight: Dominicans, Haitians, and the struggle for Hispaniola*. New York: Hill and Wang.

Spanish-Speaking Miami in Sociolinguistic Perspective: Bilingualism, Recontact, and Language Maintenance among the Cuban-Origin Population

Andrew Lynch
University of Miami

"Sometimes the American dream is written in Spanglish."
—Gustavo Pérez Firmat, 1994

1. Introduction

In the 1950s, Miami was an overgrown tourist center controlled by Anglos and Jews. Over the next 40 years, the metropolitan area experienced a dramatic social transformation. In the 1960s and 1970s, the city became the bastion of Cuban exile, followed by wide-scale Hispanic immigration in the 1980s. By 1999, Miami had established itself as the capital of Latin American trade and commerce, entertainment, television, pop culture, and U.S. Hispanic power (*Américas* 1992, Booth 1993, Olson and Olson 1995, MacSwan 1996). The expansion of English–Spanish bilingualism has characterized the sociocultural and economic growth of Miami since the 1950s.

At the new millennium, Miami meets all the criteria for being a bilingual metropolitan area, taking into consideration the number of speakers of English and Spanish there, the levels of bilingualism manifested, and the visibility, institutional and commercial support, and economic viability of both languages. Based on present social trends and population projections, this bilingual reality is unlikely to change very much in the coming decades. Resnick (1988: 89) identified three primary ways that Spanish is used in Miami: (1) as an immigrant language, (2) as the ethnic mother tongue of a large and socially predominant population of Cubans and their American-born children, and (3) as a language of the Miami marketplace, workplace, and government.

 Research on Spanish in the U.S., ed. Ana Roca, 271–283. Somerville, MA: Cascadilla Press.

Although Resnick did not assert that successive generations of Cuban-Americans in Miami would shift to the exclusive use of English, he did suggest that 'assimilation' in the Miami context was highly plausible. He stated:

> [T]he assimilatory force of American society continues to operate, and Cubans are too close to mainstream America in their values, ideologies, aspirations and physical characteristics for them not to join it. . . . We must wait to see whether an EMT (ethnic mother tongue) now in its third generation can survive the cultural assimilation of its speakers in America . . . (Resnick 1988: 100–101)

I suggest that in our research on the bilingual reality of Miami in the year 2000, use of the term 'assimilation' has become highly questionable.[1] In the sociological literature on other immigrant groups, 'assimilation' traditionally has referred to the adoption of an American mainstream culture in which non-immigrant social, economic, and political macrostructures are essential. This non-immigrant 'mainstream' does not exist in Miami (Portes and Stepick 1993: 8). Immigrant 'assimilation' by appeal to notions of economic and political power, upward socioeconomic mobility, and adaptation to American sociocultural mores is rendered amorphic in the Miami context, and so we are left essentially with the question of linguistic adaptation. My response is that Miami's mainstream has become English–Spanish bilingual.

Miami is the only major metropolitan area in the world where Spanish and English compete for social, economic, and political prevalence. A complete shift to English at the expense of bilingualism appears not to be a requirement for achieving the American dream in South Florida; as Gustavo Pérez-Firmat (1994) writes, "Sometimes the American dream is written in Spanglish." The purpose of this chapter is to put Miami's bilingual situation in sociolinguistic perspective forty years after the "Cubanization" of Miami (Boswell 1994) began.

2. Spanish–English bilingualism in the Miami context

I see two principal reasons that bilingualism has become the norm among second- and third-generation Cuban-origin Spanish speakers. First, the Spanish–English bilingualism of the social, economic, and political structures of Miami supports the continued use of Spanish by Miami-born bilinguals. In my observations, the current younger generation in Miami does not associate Spanish principally with economic disadvantage or with the older generation. For them, Spanish is not tied to nostalgia for life back on the island of Cuba, since the overwhelming majority of them have never been to Cuba. To many Miami-born bilinguals, Spanish is not just the language of their proud Cuban grandparents, but also a language of immense everyday social value. Spanish gives them access to a dynamic urban culture that depends on the economic power of the Spanish-speaking world and the linguistic and social power of the continuous influx of Spanish-speaking immigrants, visitors, and tourists.

Second, at the individual and family levels, Miami bilingualism is also characterized by recontact with the monolingual Spanish-speaking world (cf. Cisneros and Leone 1983). Recontact with the heritage language through Spanish-dominant social networks encourages young Miami-born bilinguals to maintain their Spanish skills.

2.1. Miami: Bilingual city?

Weinreich's (1953: 1) original definition of 'bilingualism' states that it is "the practice of alternately using two languages." The term 'bilingual' may refer to an individual, to an isolated or integrated speech community, to a society, or to a nation as a whole. I propose that Miami should be considered a bilingual city. As I describe below, Spanish and English in Miami are in close competition on a number of levels: number of speakers, visibility, institutional and commercial support, and economic viability.[2]

Boswell (1994) has described the demographic transformation of Miami as a "Cubanization" phase from 1960 through the middle 1970s, followed in the 1980s and 1990s by a "Hispanicization" phase. Nicaraguans, Colombians, Puerto Ricans, Dominicans, Mexicans, Hondurans, Peruvians, Salvadorans, and other nationalities arrived by the thousands. The 1990 census registered more than 953,000 Hispanics in a county whose total population numbered well under 2,000,000, making it 49.2% Hispanic (Boswell 1994). Several of the county's major municipalities had a majority Hispanic population, including: Miami (city proper), Miami Beach, Sweetwater, West Miami, Virginia Gardens, Medley, Islandia, Hialeah, and Hialeah Gardens. In two other municipalities, Coral Gables and Miami Springs, Hispanics represented nearly half of the population (Boswell 1994). In the year 2000, Miami–Dade's social makeup is as Hispanic as its national and international image.

The only other group which experienced steady growth from 1960 to 1990 were non-Hispanic Blacks (Boswell 1994). However, by 1990, non-Hispanic Blacks still only represented 21% of Miami–Dade's total population, and were residentially segregated from both Anglos and non-Black Hispanics (Boswell 1993).

Based on immigration trends and migration patterns, it appears that the Hispanic population has increased in Miami–Dade through the 1990s, while the non-Hispanic White population has continued to diminish. Demographic projections predict an even greater Hispanic presence in Miami–Dade in the future as immigration from the Spanish-speaking world will most likely remain steady (Boswell 1994).

As a group, Hispanics in Miami have a great deal of economic power. Indeed, Boswell (1995: 34) found that with the exception of Nicaraguans,

Mexicans, and Hondurans, the majority of Miami Hispanics have incomes which place them within the middle class.[3]

Miami has more Spanish-language television channels, radio stations, and newspapers than the cities of Los Angeles and New York combined (Fradd 1996: 9). On both the FM and AM radio dials in Miami, Spanish and English are equally heard. A wide variety of musical genres are broadcast in both languages, including traditional, classical, contemporary, and pop (*AdRatecard* 1999). In television, WLTV *Canal 23*, an affiliate of the Spanish-language Univisión network, claimed the top spot for both news and primetime programming in 1998's Nielsen ratings (*Business Wire* 1998, Pérez 1998). Cable access includes two major 24-hour Spanish-language news networks – CNN en español and CBS Telenoticias – that are very popular in Miami–Dade. The international Spanish-language television network conglomerates Univisión and Telemundo, whose programming is seen by millions throughout the U.S. and Latin America, both have their headquarters in Miami. The HBO Latin America Group, which operates and distributes the leading cable and satellite programming services in Latin America and the Caribbean, is also based in Miami (*Business Wire* 1999).

Newspapers, magazines, and books are highly visible in both languages. In addition to their usual English-language stock, the Miami–Dade stores of major nationwide bookstore chains boast large sections of Spanish-language books on a wide variety of topics and from nearly all literary genres. Miami's principal newspapers are the English-language *Miami Herald* (estimated readership of 851,000 daily and 1.2 million on Sundays) and *El Nuevo Herald* (estimated readership of 210,000 daily and 316,000 on Sundays), its Spanish-language offspring. *El Nuevo Herald* gained an independent newsroom in 1988 and separated from *The Miami Herald* in 1998. Another newspaper with a wide circulation in the metropolitan area is the Spanish-language *Diario de las Américas* (estimated readership of 133,440 daily and 140,200 on Sundays). All three newspapers are widely distributed throughout the metropolitan area in newsstands and in stores. Similarly, magazines in both languages are sold and distributed in newsstands and stores. Even most supermarkets and drugstore chains display both the English- and Spanish-language editions of such nationally popular magazines as *Time*, *Newsweek*, *People*, *Good Housekeeping*, and *Cosmopolitan* at the front registers. Dozens of Spanish-language magazines are based in Miami (Booth 1993).

In many nationwide chain stores in Miami–Dade, the aisle signs and store information appear in both languages. Similarly, store announcements may be heard in both languages. Numerous nationwide chain restaurants in Miami–Dade provide menus in both languages, as do a great number of local restaurants. The area's major hospitals post information in both languages and have bilingual receptionists. Miami International Airport reflects the same dynamic English–Spanish bilingualism, with directories, signs, announcements and counter service in both languages. The Greater Miami–Dade telephone directory is bilingual. All over the metropolitan area, billboard advertisements are seen in both English and Spanish. Street signs are generally posted in English in accordance with Florida's statewide traffic sign system, but are also sometimes found in Spanish, particularly if they announce construction-related road closings or traffic delays. Street names are highly visible in both languages, and since the 1960s some streets and avenues have taken on official Spanish-language names, e.g. Calle Ocho (Southwest 8th Street) in the city of Miami proper.

The arts in Miami flourish in both Spanish and English. Cinema, live theater, music concerts, formal lectures, and literary readings abound in both languages. In the music industry, however, the dominance of the Spanish language is undeniable. Miami is considered the pop music capital of Latin America (MacSwan 1996). The offices and recording studios of Sony Discos, the label of such internationally known top-selling artists as Gloria Estefan, Shakira, Alejandro Fernández, and Ricky Martin, are located in Miami Beach, along with WEA Latina and PolyGram Latino. Spanish-language MTV Latino, which is currently gaining wide popularity among younger cable television viewers throughout Latin America and the U.S., is also broadcast from studios located in Miami Beach. The great majority of the metropolitan area's large music stores distribute and sell remarkably high volumes of recordings of Spanish-language music.

In the educational realm, Spanish language instruction receives ample support. The 1997–98 enrollment for Spanish-S (Spanish for Native Speakers) classes in Miami–Dade's Public School System was 97,086 students. Another 62,896 students studied Spanish as a second language. In that year, 48,749 students were enrolled in ESOL programs, implying that they were Spanish-dominant (Miami–Dade Public Schools 1998). Figures for the 1998–99 academic year are quite similar (Fragas 1999). Amidst heated political debate in California over the efficacy and validity of bilingual programs, an article appeared in the May 25, 1998 issue of the *Los Angeles Times* (Anderson 1998) contrasting Los Angeles to Miami, calling the latter a "boomtown of bilingual education." A recently formed community task force on bilingual education in Miami–Dade has made proposals to employ dozens of Spanish–English bilingual teachers at all grade levels and to open 10 new two-way immersion programs in addition to the 30 two-way programs which are already in operation. The total cost of the initiative is estimated at $2.3 million.

The *Los Angeles Times* article noted that since South Florida's trade with Latin America amounts to billions of dollars a year, business leaders in Miami argue that they quite simply cannot afford to do without bilingual education. The business community is behind the recent push to bolster bilingual education in Miami–Dade schools. The article quoted James F. Partridge, chief of the Miami-based Latin American and Caribbean Operations Center for Visa International, as saying: "I don't give a hoot about the political aspects of it. . . . To me, that's a lot of garbage. I'm interested in the financial well-being of this community. We need bilingual people to survive" (Anderson 1998). Partridge's view reflects the economic importance and viability of Spanish in Miami area businesses.

Of a total of 245 businesses surveyed by Fradd (1996), 95.7% agreed that a Spanish–English bilingual workforce is essential to the economic future of Miami–Dade. Fradd pointed out that Miami controls 43% of all U.S. trade with the Caribbean, 28% of all U.S. trade with South America, and almost half of all trade with Central America. She also reported that nearly 129,000 Greater Miami businesses depend on markets located in countries to the south, and some 130 international corporations, including Texaco, General Motors, Sony, Nabisco, Komatsu, Airbus, and AT&T, have established their Latin American headquarters in Miami–Dade (Fradd 1996: 4). In response, many English speakers in Miami now learn Spanish for employment and professional purposes, according to a September 10, 1998 *Miami Herald* article (Santiago 1998).

2.2. Recontact and the social value of Spanish in Miami

In the fall of 1998, María was a 23-year-old college student completing a degree in physical therapy at the University of Miami. She was born in Miami and had always lived there. Her father was 6 years old when his parents immigrated to New York from Cuba, and at age 13 he moved to Miami. María's mother was also born in Cuba; she came to Miami as a child and was raised and educated there. María reported that she first learned Spanish from her mother, but quickly shifted to English after she began primary school at age 5. After that time, she primarily spoke English with her parents and Spanish with her Cuban grandmother. She did not attend a bilingual program, nor did she study Spanish during her school years; instead, she opted for classes in Italian to complete her high school foreign language requirement. She reported using English with her siblings.

Curiously though, María's written and spoken Spanish reflected remarkably high levels of proficiency. She reported that her Spanish skills began to develop fully only after she graduated high school and became friends with a number of recently-arrived immigrants of Argentine and Mexican origin. At the same time, she began to attend church with her grandmother, where services and fellowship were conducted exclusively in Spanish. She also held a number of jobs requiring bilingual skill, and she reported that she was able to quickly develop the particular registers of Spanish language proficiency necessary for each job. At the time of the interview, she was employed at a successful Miami-based import–export business where she reported using mostly Spanish for work-related purposes. In her final year of study at the University of Miami, she took a Spanish for Native Speakers course in which she developed formal and academic-register skills in written and spoken Spanish.

I believe that María's experience is a very fitting example of recontact with Spanish. She primarily used English through her school-age and adolescent years, yet when she became an adult living, studying, and working in the bilingual context of Miami, her Spanish skills were reborn through recontact with her parents' heritage language. Her case was similar to that of many second- and third-generation speakers whom I interviewed. In general, I observed that in cases where individual and family-level influences lead to language attrition, social-level influences can intervene and promote language use and language maintenance.

Lambert and Taylor (1996) also documented this pattern of recontact in Miami. Their findings show how strong a social force Spanish can be for young Cuban-Americans in Miami. The investigators compared the fluency and use of Spanish and English among first-generation Cuban-born mothers and their second-generation Miami-born offspring. Their sample of 108 families was divided into two groups according to socioeconomic class – one group of families they considered working-class and another group they considered middle-class.[4] Interestingly, Lambert and Taylor found that for the working-class families, the mothers' Spanish fluency was not statistically correlated with the Spanish fluency of any of their children, suggesting that outside-family influences are the primary cause of their children's high level of Spanish ability. Their data also revealed that the more fluent in Spanish the first-born child becomes, the more fluent the second- and third-born children of the family become. In contrast, there was a statistically significant correlation between the middle-class mothers' Spanish fluency and the fluency of the first- and second-born children, but no correspondence between the mother's fluency and the fluency of the third-born child. However, as with the working-class families, there were significant correspondences between the Spanish fluency of first-born children and second- and third-born children.

Lambert and Taylor (1996: 496) concluded that the working-class mothers appeared to promote subtractive bilingualism – a shift to English use for their children, probably for economic concerns in the broader U.S. context. But the researchers suggested that in Miami:

> the (working-class) mothers' values and wishes have to compete with those circulating in a vibrant Hispanic ethnic community that in certain instances can be strong enough to attenuate the assimilation process. The findings in fact suggest that social forces operating in Miami's Hispanic community may temper or even override parental orientations by sustaining and nurturing Spanish language skills, particularly for the first-born child, who in turn can have determining influences on the development of Spanish skills of younger siblings, quite independent of the mothers' inclinations.

As I found in my own research, the social-level forces that promote the use of Spanish in Miami sometimes override the cross-generational and individual-level forces that promote the simplification and loss of Spanish in most other U.S. contexts.

3. Spanish language maintenance among the Cuban-origin population

In one of the first sociolinguistic studies carried out in Miami in 1975, Solé (1979) determined that at the societal level Spanish was consistently renewed through the political and economic power of Spanish-speaking Cubans, the constant immigration of Spanish speakers into the city, and the use of Spanish in commerce and business. In this way, Solé highlighted the instrumental value of Spanish in Miami. He pointed out that, based on the societal importance of Spanish, it would be easy to assume that individual speakers would maintain their Spanish as they adopted English. However, Solé found that at the individual level, actual language use by the majority of second-generation bilinguals demonstrated a preference for English. He concluded that bilingualism in Miami was not stable. In a related article on language loyalty and attitudes, Solé (1982: 267) stated that "if language loyalty and language maintenance succeed in Dade County, they will probably respond more to instrumental needs than to deliberate maintenance efforts or ideological elaborations."

Indeed, the instrumental value of Spanish in Miami has grown immensely in the 25 years since Solé's study. More recently, García and Otheguy (1988) discussed five factors that Fishman (1977) thought were highly influential in any language maintenance situation. They are: (1) demographic, (2) sociocultural, (3) economic, (4) philosophical/ideological, and (5) political. García and Otheguy (1988: 186) argued that only the demographic factor was favorable to the maintenance of Spanish in Miami, whereas the sociocultural, economic, ideological, and political factors were creating pressures toward language shift.

Roca (1991) argued against the position of García and Otheguy (1988) by providing detailed evidence that several other of Fishman's (1977) theoretical factors do contribute to the maintenance of Spanish in Miami. Roca (1991: 248) wrote that sociocultural and economic factors "are difficult to divorce from demographic considerations, since the large and increasing numbers of Spanish speakers alone make Miami function today in a radically different manner from the way it did before the extensive Cuban migrations of the sixties and early seventies. . . ." She explained furthermore that "the growing number of . . . Hispanics who continue to arrive from the Caribbean, Central and South America, has had an overwhelming impact on the social, economic, and linguistic fronts." Roca concluded that the Miami bilingual context is vastly different from other U.S. urban situations. She suggested that the present evidence points to the sustained use and widespread visibility of Spanish in Miami well into the future.

In Miami–Dade, the linguistic value of this continuous influx of Spanish monolingual immigrants is quite significant. First, it points to the continued use of Spanish at the societal level. Second, in a city where new immigration is at such a high rate and where Hispanics are the demographic majority, there is a high probability that already established immigrants and their offspring will have intimate social contact with recently arrived Spanish monolinguals. A substantial number of U.S.-born bilinguals will experience generational recontact with the language as they interact with recently-arrived Spanish monolingual family members and form friendships, romances, marriages, and work partnerships with other recently-arrived immigrants.

Miami's sociocultural, economic and geographic intimacy with many countries of the Spanish-speaking world make its relationship to the Spanish language inevitable in the globalization of the coming decades. Miami will keep growing as an economic center for Latin American trade and finance, so Spanish will continue to have an instrumental value for Miami businesses and a bilingual workforce will be essential (Fradd 1996). The rise of Miami in the 1990s as the capital of world-wide Spanish-language mass communication and popular entertainment (MacSwan 1996) will additionally secure the vitality of the language there.

Miami will continue to attract young, contemporary middle and upper class Latin Americans and to host thousands of Spanish-speaking visitors, tourists, and vacation-home dwellers on a yearly basis. These visitors promote the use of Spanish in everyday social and service encounters throughout the metropolitan area. Their presence in trendy South Miami Beach and Coconut Grove enhances the positive image of the Spanish-speaking world among second-, third-, and fourth-generation speakers who have never traveled outside the U.S. (Gutiérrez 1998). In Miami, Spanish is not viewed as a language of the elderly or the poor, but as a world language of all generations of speakers of diverse educational and socioeconomic class backgrounds.

4. Conclusion

One of the first-generation Cuban speakers whom I interviewed commented that Miami is "closer to Havana than to Savannah" in every sense. But can it and will it remain this way? And how will the "American dream" be ultimately redefined in Miami in the new millennium? Will it be written in "Spanglish"? I propose that if anywhere in the U.S. context, it is in Miami that we find the greatest potential for sustained Spanish language use in the coming decades.

Although we cannot be certain what sociolinguistic reality future generations of Spanish–English bilinguals will create in Miami beyond the year 2000, we can rely on what we have observed during the 40 years of Spanish–English contact there. Since the beginning of their mass arrival in the 1960s,

Cuban Spanish speakers and their bilingual children have seen the importance of their language steadily increase. This expansion has occurred not only through wide-scale Hispanic immigration, but also through the use of Spanish in business, finance, trade, tourism, employment, education, mass communication, arts and entertainment, religion, and everyday social interaction in Miami's public domains.

At the same time, English language use has remained vital in Miami. The expansion of Spanish in the Miami context has not excluded English. Despite the unfounded beliefs held by some Americans outside of Miami, there is no empirical sociolinguistic evidence to suggest that English either is being socially lost, or is not being fully acquired by successive generations of Hispanic immigrants there. Every empirical source points to the contrary. All of the second- and third-generation bilinguals whom I interviewed in 1998, and all those with whom I have spoken informally within the past year, have insisted on the importance and, in most cases, preferred use of English in their educational, professional, and everyday lives. This affirmation of English, however, does not deny their proficiency in Spanish or the social and economic value which they place on being bilingual.

In conclusion, I suggest that the social and economic value of both Spanish and English will remain high and that processes of contact and recontact with the Spanish-speaking world will continue to support the acquisition, use, and maintenance of Spanish among subsequent generations of Miami bilinguals. Portes and Stepick (1993: xiv) described Miami in the following way:

> The city is several things at once: at the southern end of the land and astride two cultural worlds; about to complete its first century of existence; and, above all, on the edge of a future marked by uncertainty, but also by the promise of pathbreaking innovations in urban life. The multilingual, multicultural experiment that is Miami holds important lessons for what the American city will be about in a changed world.

Miami can teach us extremely important lessons about the sociolinguistic future of American cities far past the year 2000. My hope is that this article will stimulate further thinking, discussion, and empirical sociolinguistic research on bilingual Miami beyond the first and second generations and beyond the Cuban-origin population.

Notes

* I wish to humbly acknowledge the many years of guidance and unconditional support provided to me by my dissertation adviser, Carol Klee of the University of Minnesota, whose courses on Spanish in the United States, bilingualism, and Spanish language contact sparked my interest in those areas and inspired me to dedicate my

research to the situation of Spanish speakers in this country. Likewise, I am gratefully indebted to Ana Roca for so generously offering to me her valuable personal and professional insights as a Miami Cuban bilingual, as well as her constant support and encouragement throughout the completion of my dissertation research on the situation of bilingual Miami. I also extend to her my thanks for an invitation to read an earlier version of this paper as part of a panel session on bilingualism and Cuban-Americans at the Seventeenth Conference on Spanish in the United States. Many sincere thanks to the Department of Foreign Languages and Literatures of the University of Miami for providing me with a visiting semester lectureship during Fall 1998, and to Elena Grau-Lleveria, Lillian Manzor, and Celita Lamar for their kindness and help to me while I was there.

1. My observations are based on interviews carried out in Miami during the fall of 1998 with 45 first-, second-, and third-generation Cuban-origin speakers, as part of a project to empirically measure Spanish language proficiency and use. For the present purposes, I defined a first-generation speaker as one born in Cuba who arrived in Miami in post-adolescence, sometime after the age of 18. Second-generation speakers were defined as those who were born in Miami to first-generation parents, or who came to Miami from Cuba before the age of 10 (pre-adolescence). Third-generation speakers were those Miami-born bilinguals who had at least one parent who was a member of the second generation.

2. The theoretical criteria developed in Lynch 1999 to characterize Miami as a bilingual metropolitan area are: number of speakers of each language (monolinguals and bilinguals), levels of bilingualism (individual, familial, and societal), visibility of both languages (in aural mass communication, written mass communication, and public information), institutional and commercial support (through mass media, the arts, education, religion, government, and politics), economic viability (in employment, trade and commerce, and socioeconomic class), and geographic space (residential distributions).

3. Boswell (1993) and Boswell and Cruz-Báez (1997) offer highly insightful empirical considerations of residential segregation patterns in Miami–Dade based on the factors of race, ethnic and national background, and socioeconomic class.

4. Lambert and Taylor's (1996) study points to the impact of the variable of socioeconomic class in Spanish language acquisition, use, and maintenance processes in the Miami context. This variable was not taken into account in the methodology of the sociolinguistic analysis which I carried out in Lynch 1999. Based on the occupations and educational attainments of the interviewees (or their parents) included in my research, it is safe to estimate that the great majority came from middle-class socioeconomic backgrounds. I would also suggest that heritage language maintenance is more prevalent in Miami among middle- and upper-class Cuban-origin speakers than among those who come from lower-income backgrounds or, perhaps, other ethnic backgrounds. These key variables, along with those of race and gender, must be carefully investigated in future research on bilingual generations in Miami.

References

AdRatecard. 1999. Listing of radio stations, #11 market-Miami/Ft. Lauderdale, FL. Available from www.adratecard.com; Internet.

Américas: An Anthology. 1992. Video no. 10: "The Americans." New York: The Annenberg/CPB Collection.

Anderson, Nick. 1998. A Boomtown of bilingual education. *Los Angeles Times*, 25 May.

Booth, Cathy. 1993. Miami: The capital of Latin America. *Time Magazine*, 2 December.

Boswell, Thomas D. 1993. Racial and ethnic segregation patterns in Metropolitan Miami, Florida, 1980–1990. *Southeastern Geographer* 33: 82–109.

Boswell, Thomas D. 1994. The Cubanization and Hispanicization of Metropolitan Miami. Miami: The Cuban American National Council, Inc.

Boswell, Thomas D. 1995. Hispanic national groups in Metropolitan Miami. Miami: The Cuban American National Council, Inc.

Boswell, Thomas D. and Angel David Cruz-Báez. 1997. Residential segregation by socioeconomic class in Metropolitan Miami: 1990. *Urban Geography* 18: 474–496.

Business Wire. 2 December 1998. Univisión sweeps result in the largest November year-to-year ratings growth in its history. Available from www.elibrary.com; Internet.

Business Wire. 3 May 1999. Galaxy Latin America, LLC and HBO Latin America Group sign exclusive agreement for DIRECTV in Argentina. Available from news.excite.com; Internet.

Cisneros, René and Elizabeth Leone. 1983. Mexican-American language communities in the Twin Cities: An example of contact and recontact. In *Spanish in the U.S. setting: Beyond the Southwest*, ed. Lucía Elías-Olivares, 181–210. Rosslyn, VA: National Clearinghouse for Bilingual Education.

Fishman, Joshua A. 1977. The spread of English as a new perspective for the study of language maintenance and language shift. In *The spread of English: The sociology of English as an additional language*, ed. Joshua A Fishman, Robert L. Cooper, and Andrew W. Conrad, 109–133. Rowley, MA: Newbury House.

Fradd, Sandra H. 1996. The economic impact of Spanish-language proficiency in Metropolitan Miami. Miami: Greater Miami Chamber of Commerce and The Cuban American National Council, Inc.

Fragas, Oscar. Telephone conversation with author, Miami–Dade Public Schools Division of Bilingual Education, Miami, FL, 28 April 1999.

García, Ofelia and Ricardo Otheguy. 1988. The language situation of Cuban-Americans. In *Language diversity: Problem or resource?*, ed. Sandra Lee McKay and Sau-ling Wong, 166–192. New York: Newbury House.

Gutiérrez, Barbara. Interview with author, office of Executive Director of *El Nuevo Herald*, Miami, FL, 23 November 1998.

Lambert, Wallace E. and Donald M. Taylor. 1996. Language in the lives of ethnic minorities: Cuban American families in Miami. *Applied Linguistics* 17: 477–500.

Lynch, Andrew. 1999. The subjunctive in Miami Cuban Spanish: Bilingualism, contact, and language variability. Ph.D. dissertation, University of Minnesota, Minneapolis.

MacSwan, Angus. 1996. For Latin American stars, all roads lead to Miami. *Reuters*, 23 October.

Miami–Dade County Public Schools. 1998. 1997–98 District and School Profiles. Miami, FL: Miami–Dade Public Schools Office of Educational Planning.

Olson, James and Judith Olson. 1995. *Cuban American: From trauma to triumph*. New York: Twayne Publishers.

Pérez, Evan. 1998. In Miami, Spanish-language TV conquers 'ER.' *Denver Rocky Mountain News*, 26 April.

Pérez Firmat, Gustavo. 1994. *Life on the hyphen: The Cuban-American way*. Austin: University of Texas Press.

Portes, Alejandro and Alex Stepick. 1993. *City on the edge: The transformation of Miami*. Berkeley: University of California Press.

Resnick, Melvyn. 1988. Beyond the ethnic community: Spanish language roles and maintenance in Miami. *International Journal of the Sociology of Language* 69: 89–104.

Roca, Ana. 1991. Language maintenance and language shift in the Cuban American community of Miami: The 1990s and beyond. In *Language planning: Focusschrift in honor of Joshua A. Fishman*, ed. David F. Marshall, 245–257. Amsterdam: John Benjamins.

Santiago, Fabiola. 1998. A second language opens new doors in diverse region. *The Miami Herald*, 10 September.

Solé, Carlos. 1979. Selección idiomática entre la nueva generación de cubano-americanos. *The Bilingual Review/La Revista Bilingüe* 6: 1–10.

Solé, Carlos. 1982. Language loyalty and language attitudes among Cuban-Americans. In *Bilingual education for Hispanic students in the United States*, ed. Joshua A. Fishman and Gary D. Keller, 254–268. New York: Teachers College Press.

Weinreich, Uriel. 1953. *Languages in contact: Findings and problems*. New York: *Publications of the Linguistic Circle of New York*.

Linguistic Notions of Spanish among Youths from Different Hispanic Groups

Arnulfo G. Ramírez
Louisiana State University

1. Introduction

Sociolinguists have adopted the term language attitudes (Fishman 1972) to refer to evaluative reactions or feelings toward language use. This can include attitudes toward a language or dialect (Colombian vs. Argentinian Spanish), toward a feature of language ("doh" vs. "dos," "semos" vs. "somos"), toward language use (Spanish/English code-mixing at home vs. school), and toward language as a group marker (Spanish speakers as "lazy," "poor," and "uneducated" persons). Fasold (1984) argues for a broader definition of the concept to encompass such areas as attitudes toward language maintenance and planning efforts as well other types of language behaviors.

Studies of language attitudes of Hispanic youths have examined beliefs and opinions about the uses of Spanish (Mejías and Anderson 1988), varieties of Southwest Spanish (Ramírez 1983), and codeswitching (Fernández 1990). Some studies have explored the language attitudes of the major Hispanic groups in the United States: Cuban (Solé 1982), Mexican-American (Peñalosa 1980, Sánchez 1983), and Puerto Rican (Attinasi 1979, Zentella 1997).

The purpose of this study is to compare the language attitudes of bilingual youths from the three major Hispanic groups (Cuban, Mexican-American, and Puerto Rican) with respect to (1) the value of the Spanish language, (2) the concept of Spanish language proficiency, (3) notions about the local variety of Spanish, and (4) the place where "good" Spanish is spoken. The findings of this study might provide useful insights for designing Spanish language programs for bilingual students and, at the same time, offer valuable information about the linguistic notions of young Hispanics who make up the Latino Generation X, the emerging "generación ñ" (Larmer 1999).

2. Hispanic groups and their characteristics

The students in the study were all enrolled in a high school Spanish class at the time the language survey questionnaire was administered. All the participants in the Cuban group were from Miami, Florida. Those in the Puerto Rican group were from two locations in New York, the Bronx in New York City and Amsterdam, a mid-size town in the upstate region. The Mexican-American group involved youths from three major urban centers of the Southwest (San Antonio, Texas, Albuquerque, New Mexico, and Los Angeles, California). As noted in Table 1, the students had a mean age range of 15.6 to 16.7 years, studied Spanish as a subject from 2.1 to 4.7 years, attended bilingual programs from 1.7 to 4.2 years, and resided in the particular school location between 11.2 to 15.7 years.

Table 1. Characteristics of Hispanic groups

		Sex			Mean number of years		
	Sample size	M	F	Age	Attendance in school	Studying Spanish	Bilingual schooling
Cuban							
Miami	55	17	38	16.5	12.5	4.7	2.7
Puerto Rican							
Bronx	54	23	31	16.7	11.2	3.6	4.2
Amsterdam	60	33	27	15.7	15.7	2.1	1.7
Mexican-American							
San Antonio	50	22	28	15.6	15.0	2.1	2.2
Albuquerque	53	18	35	16.5	11.3	2.3	3.7
Los Angeles	55	26	29	16.5	14.7	2.6	2.3

3. Procedures

The students completed a language survey questionnaire which elicited personal background information, language proficiency ratings, language use patterns, language attitudes, opinions about local Spanish, concepts of Spanish language competence, and the notion of the place where the "best" Spanish is spoken. The results describing language use patterns and Spanish in the media have been reported elsewhere (Ramírez 1991, 1992).

Students' attitudes toward the value of Spanish were measured via a Likert format, using a 5-point rating scale from a "very good reason" (1) to "very bad reason" (5). The students expressed their opinions on five items involving both instrumental (finding a job, meeting educational goals, and meeting career goals) and integrative (making more Hispanic friends and interacting with different Hispanic persons) functions of language.

Concepts of Spanish language competence were determined on the basis of content analysis of students' responses on an open-ended question asking, "What does it mean to know Spanish?" A response-based category system was constructed to include all the language areas cited by the students. The areas comprise (1) levels of language (pronunciation, vocabulary, grammar, orthography), (2) language modalities (listening, speaking, reading, writing), (3) language proficiency issues (fluency, accuracy, topics, translation) (4) sociolinguistic concerns (standard language, registers, use in different contexts, communication with others), and (5) language, culture, and schooling matters. Some students referred to several language areas in their responses. For this part of the study, 20 students (10 male, 10 female) were randomly selected from the total sample of each location.

The evaluative reaction toward the local variety of Spanish was assessed through the use of semantic differential scales. Ten pairs of bipolar adjectives ("bad" ↔ "good"; "incorrect" ↔ "correct"; "useful" ↔ "useless") were included, based on the list of traits by Isaac and Michael (1982). Each trait was rated on a 6-point scale, using a "1" to "6" range for all items whether ordered in a negative or positive direction.

Finally, the students' responses to the question of "the place or country where the best Spanish is spoken" were classified according to geographic region with the respective Spanish-speaking countries or places. For this part of the study, twenty students (10 males, 10 females) were randomly selected from the total sample of each location.

4. Results and discussion

The value of Spanish for instrumental and integrative purposes (Gardner and Lambert 1972, Ely 1986) varies across the Hispanic groups, as can be found in Table 2. On the importance of Spanish for finding a job, Los Angeles (M=1.39) assigns the highest value, followed by Miami (M=1.55), San Antonio (M=1.58), and Albuquerque (M=1.83), with the Bronx (M=2.00) and Amsterdam (M=2.20) regarding it as less useful. On the value of the language for meeting educational goals, Miami (M=1.87) rates it the highest, followed by the three Southwestern cities, Albuquerque (M=1.92), Los Angeles (M=1.98), and San Antonio (M=2.10), with the lower assessment by the two New York locations, the Bronx (M=2.18) and Amsterdam (M=2.39). For meeting career goals, Spanish is rated the highest by Miami (M=1.87), followed by Los Angeles (M=1.89) and Albuquerque (M=2.02), then the Bronx (M=2.27), San Antonio (M=2.35), and Amsterdam (M=2.41).[1]

Table 2. Value of Spanish language

Language value/ Hispanic group	Mean	Level of importance: Very good reason (1) %	Good reason (2) %	Neither good/ bad reason (3) %	Bad reason (4) %	Very bad reason (5) %
Find a good job						
Miami	1.55	60.0	32.7	3.6	—	3.6
Bronx	2.00	34.7	36.7	24.5	2.0	2.0
Amsterdam	2.20	35.0	28.3	26.7	1.7	8.3
San Antonio	1.58	58.0	30.0	8.0	4.0	—
Albuquerque	1.83	38.5	40.4	21.2	—	—
Los Angeles	1.39	74.1	18.5	3.7	1.9	1.9
Make more Hispanic friends						
Miami	1.82	30.9	56.4	12.7	—	—
Bronx	1.71	46.9	38.8	10.2	4.1	—
Amsterdam	2.08	40.0	26.7	25.0	1.7	6.7
San Antonio	2.34	16.1	48.0	26.0	6.0	4.0
Albuquerque	1.58	61.5	19.2	19.2	—	—
Los Angeles	1.38	67.3	27.3	5.5	—	—
Interact with different persons						
Miami	1.46	58.2	38.2	3.6	—	—
Bronx	1.76	40.8	49.0	4.1	6.1	—
Amsterdam	1.83	45.8	30.8	20.3	1.7	1.7
San Antonio	1.52	54.0	40.0	6.0	—	—
Albuquerque	1.44	63.5	30.8	3.8	1.9	—
Los Angeles	1.29	74.5	21.8	3.6	—	—
Meet educational goals						
Miami	1.87	42.6	33.3	20.4	1.9	1.9
Bronx	2.18	28.6	32.7	34.7	—	4.1
Amsterdam	2.39	32.2	16.9	39.0	3.4	8.5
San Antonio	2.10	28.0	46.0	18.0	4.0	4.0
Albuquerque	1.92	33.3	43.1	21.6	2.0	—
Los Angeles	1.98	31.5	42.6	22.2	3.7	—
Meet career goals						
Miami	1.87	38.2	40.0	20.0	1.8	—
Bronx	2.27	27.1	29.2	37.5	2.1	4.1
Amsterdam	2.41	28.8	20.3	37.3	8.5	5.1
San Antonio	2.35	26.5	30.6	28.6	10.2	4.1
Albuquerque	2.02	30.9	36.5	32.7	—	—
Los Angeles	1.89	41.8	30.9	23.6	3.6	—

The benefit of Spanish for making more friends within the Hispanic community is rated most positively by Los Angeles (M=1.38) and Albuquerque (M=1.58), followed by the Bronx (M=1.71) and Miami (M=1.82), with Amsterdam (M=2.08) and San Antonio (M=2.34) assigning it less worth. The merit of the language for meeting and interacting with persons from different backgrounds is judged most favorably by Los Angeles (M=1.29) and Albuquerque (M=1.44), followed by Miami (M=1.46) and San Antonio (M=1.52), with the Bronx (M=1.76) and Amsterdam (M=1.83) viewing it as less advantageous. The Cuban (Miami) group views Spanish more favorably for instrumental purposes than for integrative reasons. The Mexican-American group (San Antonio, Albuquerque, Los Angeles) tends to assign favorable ratings to Spanish for both instrumental and ethnic purposes. The Puerto Rican group (Bronx and Amsterdam), on the other hand, appears to view Spanish as less important for meeting either instrumental or integrative language uses.

The students' notions about what it means to know Spanish include a broad range of linguistic competencies, sociolinguistic considerations, sociocultural issues about language in society, and the willingness to devote time and study to improve Spanish proficiency (see Table 3). Spanish language ability in terms of the four language-skill areas is mentioned most frequently (35.2%), with the productive abilities (speaking: 42.6%, writing: 23.4%) cited more often than the receptive skills (listening: 20.6%, reading: 13.4%).

Sociolinguistic issues about Spanish language variation are second in importance. Being able to communicate with people who speak differently (45.3%) is of major interest, followed by knowing the standard language variety (17.9%), understanding different dialects (14.7%), and knowing different registers (9.4%) and social varieties (8.4%) of Spanish. The third area of concern involves language proficiency matters, centered primarily on "accuracy" (58.7%) and "fluency" (30.7%) issues but also including questions about familiarity with a "range of topics" (6.7%) and translation skills (4.0%). Specific language areas that are cited involve the use of more standard grammatical elements (38.3%), a more extensive vocabulary (28.3%), and greater attention to pronunciation (21.7%). Sociocultural aspects of language use and the need for further study and practice of Spanish are fifth in the list of proficiency notions.

Table 3. Conception of Spanish language competence

Language concern	M	B	A	SA	ABQ	LA	Total	%
Aspect of language								
Pronunciation	4	1	2	1	2	3	13	21.7
Vocabulary	5	1	1	3	5	2	17	28.3
Grammar	7	2	2	5	2	5	23	38.3
Usage	—	1	—	—	2	—	3	5.0
Orthography	2	1	1	—	—	—	4	6.7
Total	18	6	6	9	11	10	60	
%	30	10	10	15	18.3	16.7		(15.0)
Language modality								
Listening	5	1	5	7	7	4	29	20.6
Speaking	6	9	11	11	12	11	60	42.6
Reading	—	2	—	3	6	8	19	13.4
Writing	7	3	5	5	5	8	33	23.4
Total	18	15	21	26	30	31	141	
%	12.8	10.6	14.9	18.4	21.3	22.0		(35.2)
Language proficiency								
Fluency	5	1	2	8	—	7	23	30.7
Accuracy	3	11	9	12	—	9	44	58.7
Topics/content	3	—	1	1	—	—	5	6.7
Translation skills	1	—	—	—	1	1	3	4.0
Total	12	12	12	21	1	17	75	
%	16	16	16	28	1.3	22.7		(18.7)
Sociolinguistic concern								
Standard language	3	5	3	1	1	4	17	17.9
Castilian Spanish	—	1	—	1	2	—	4	4.2
Registers of Spanish	2	1	—	—	2	4	9	9.4
Use in social contexts	1	1	2	2	2	—	8	8.4
Communicate w/others	7	8	5	8	7	8	43	45.3
Understand different dialects	1	2	3	3	4	1	14	14.7
Total	14	18	13	15	18	17	95	
%	14.7	18.9	13.7	15.8	18.9	17.9		(23.7)
Language, culture, and schooling								
Sociocultural issues	4	1	1	2	4	—	12	40
Lang. study & practice	5	2	1	3	2	5	18	60
Total	9	3	2	5	6	5	30	
%	30	10	6.7	16.7	20	16.7		(7.5)
Total	71	54	54	76	66	80	401	

* Cuban: Miami=M; Puerto Rican: Bronx=B, Amsterdam=A;
Mexican-American: San Antonio=SA, Albuquerque=ABQ, Los Angeles=LA

The students' multidimensional notion of language competence is in line with the current conceptions of proficiency (Byrnes and Canale 1987, Harley 1990, Brown 1996). Sociolinguistic concerns about language variation and the use of Spanish in society reflect a keen awareness about the linguistic dynamics Spanish in the United States. Furthermore, these students, all enrolled in Spanish classes, recognize the need to study and use the language in order to continue developing their proficiency.

The Hispanic groups place emphasis on different aspects of language competence. In the area of aspects of language, the Cuban group (30%) expresses a greater concern for the mastery of specific linguistic elements than either the Mexican-American (San Antonio 15%, Albuquerque 18.3%, Los Angeles 16.7%) or Puerto Rican group (Bronx 10%, Amsterdam 10%). In terms of language modalities, the Mexican-American group (San Antonio 18.4%, Albuquerque 21.3%, Los Angeles 22.0%) places a greater emphasis than either the Puerto Rican (Bronx 10.6%, Amsterdam 14.9) or Cuban group (12.8%). Language abilities seen in relation to fluency, accuracy, topic control, and translation skills are noted at similar levels by the Cuban (16%) and Puerto Rican group (Bronx 16%, Amsterdam 16%) but seen as much more relevant by Mexican-Americans from San Antonio (28%) and Los Angeles (22.7%). Sociolinguistic concerns appear to be of equal importance to all groups, ranging from Amsterdam (13.7%) to Albuquerque and the Bronx (both 18.9%). Language, culture, and schooling issues are a greater concern for Miami (30%), followed by the Mexican-American group (Albuquerque 20%, San Antonio and Los Angeles both 16.7%) and the Puerto Rican locations (Bronx 10%, Amsterdam 6.7%). The concept of what it means to know Spanish varies across the Hispanic groups and perhaps reflects local community standards as well as socioeconomic realities (Zentella 1990).

The overall evaluation of local Spanish is generally positive across the groups as can be seen in Table 4. Local Spanish is judged to be basically "good" (M=4.73), "interesting" (M=4.56), and a "rich" (M=2.71) language variety. It is seen as somewhat "simple" (M=4.53), "familiar" (M=2.25), and spoken at a relatively "fast" (M=2.85) pace. As a language system, it is rated as more "useful" (M=1.83) than "correct" (M=4.40) or "clear" (M=4.71), and it can be classified somewhere between "modern" and "traditional" (M=3.21).[2]

Table 4. Evaluation of local Spanish according to semantic traits

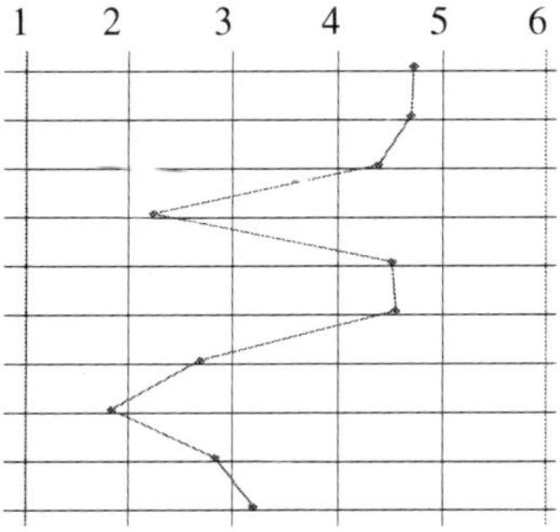

	1 2 3 4 5 6		Mean	S.D.
Bad		Good	4.73	1.36
Confusing		Clear	4.71	1.35
Incorrect		Correct	4.40	1.36
Familiar		Strange	2.25	1.51
Complicated		Simple	4.53	1.37
Boring		Interesting	4.56	1.32
Rich		Poor	2.71	1.38
Useful		Useless	1.83	1.21
Fast		Slow	2.85	1.57
Modern		Traditional	3.21	1.64

The Bronx and Los Angeles groups assign higher ratings to five of the ten attributes: "good" (Los Angeles M=5.10, Bronx M=5.04), "clear" (Bronx M=5.02, Los Angeles M=4.85), "correct" (Bronx M=4.74, Los Angeles M=4.62), "familiar" (Bronx M=2.04, Los Angeles M=1.84), and "simple" (Bronx M=4.91, Los Angeles M=4.57). Albuquerque (M=4.90) rates its local Spanish as most "interesting," followed by Los Angeles (M=4.81) and the Bronx (M=4.67). Los Angeles (M=2.23) rates its variety as "rich," followed by Albuquerque (M=2.55) and San Antonio (M=2.73). Similarly, the three Mexican-American locations rate its Spanish as most "useful" (Los Angeles M=1.37, San Antonio M=1.80, Albuquerque M=1.83).

Miami rates its Spanish less favorably on five of the attributes: "good" (M=4.42), "clear" (M=4.35), "correct" (M=3.89), "simple" (M=4.33), and "interesting" (M=4.15). San Antonio follows Miami with three relatively low ratings: "good" (M=4.40), "clear" (M=4.46), and "correct" (M=4.16). Compared to the other groups, Amsterdam tends to assign its Spanish more neutral ratings on seven of the attributes: "good" (M=4.48), "clear" (M=4.73), "correct" (M=4.47), "familiar" (M=2.22), "rich" (M=2.76), "useful" (M=1.85), and "fast" (M=2.86). It rates the local Spanish more negatively for its "simplicity" (M=4.38) and level of "interestingness" (M=4.39). Amsterdam (M=2.98) and Miami (M=2.74) view their Spanish as more "modern" compared to Albuquerque (M=3.42) and the Bronx (M=3.54) who regard it as somewhat "traditional." San Antonio (M=3.28) and Los Angeles (M=3.28) share similar views about their Spanish as being neither particularly "modern" nor "traditional."

The more favorable ratings of Spanish are found in the large metropolitan areas of New York (Bronx) and Los Angeles. These higher ratings might be due to a number factors such as favorable perceptions of ethnolinguistic vitality and strong intragroup relations (Giles and Byrne 1982), interethnic group relations (Giles 1977, Beebe and Giles 1984), Spanish/English language use patterns (Zentella 1997), and demographic strength along with institutional support

(Conklin and Lourie 1983). The Miami students, on the other hand, are less impressed with their local Spanish. With more years of formal Spanish study then the other groups, they appear to have greater concern about such matters as language norms and linguistic accuracy, which, in turn, seem to be associated with a higher level of negative stereotyping of local Spanish varieties in the United States.

Students' designation of the place where the prestige variety of Spanish is spoken is presented in Table 5. Spain (45%) is the country cited most frequently, followed by Mexico (27.5%) and Puerto Rico (14.2%). Differences among the Hispanic groups suggest a type of language loyalty to one's own ethnolinguistic group. The Miami group mentions Cuba and Miami as the places to find "good" Spanish. The Puerto Rican group (Bronx and Amsterdam) refers to Puerto Rico and New York City, while the Mexican-American locations (San Antonio, Albuquerque, Los Angeles) specify Mexico and New Mexico. Countries such as Costa Rica and Columbia are mentioned by the Miami group, indicating an awareness about other Spanish varieties perhaps due to the city's extensive commercial relations with Latin American nations. Only a few students (3.3%) from three of the locations responded with a "don't know" answer.

Table 5. Places where prestige variety of Spanish is spoken

Location	M	B	A	SA	ABQ	LA	Total	%
Caribbean								
Cuba	3	—	—	—	—	—	3	2.5
Puerto Rico	—	8	9	—	—	—	17	14.2
Central America	—	—	1	—	—	—	1	0.8
Costa Rica	1	—	—	—	—	—	1	0.8
North America								
Mexico	—	1	—	10	13	9	33	27.5
United States								
Miami	1	—	—	—	—	—	1	0.8
New Mexico	—	—	—	1	1	—	2	1.6
New York City	—	—	1	—	—	—	1	0.8
Other	—	—	—	1	—	1	2	1.6
South America: Columbia	1	—	—	—	—	—	1	0.8
Spain	14	10	8	8	4	10	54	45.0
Don't know	—	1	1	—	2	—	4	3.3

* Cuban: Miami=M; Puerto Rican: Bronx=B, Amsterdam=A;
Mexican-American: San Antonio=SA, Albuquerque=ABQ, Los Angeles=LA

From a diglossic perspective of "high dialect" and "low dialect" status (Ferguson 1972), Peninsular Spanish seems to be assigned the prestige status by all the Hispanic groups. Latin American varieties of Spanish, including those found in the United States, are viewed as having a lower status within the Hispanic constellation of dialects. These results are supported by the study of language attitudes conducted in Argentina by Solé (1991).

5. Conclusion

The attitudes and notions of Spanish among bilingual youths vary according to ethnolinguistic background. The three Hispanic groups have different perceptions about the usefulness of Spanish for instrumental and integrative purposes. Hispanic students have a multidimensional perspective of what it means to know Spanish, which encompasses the components of language, proficiency issues, and sociolinguistic concerns about Spanish variation. Differences exist between the groups with respect to the importance they assign to the various language components. The ratings of local Spanish are generally positive, suggesting that Hispanic youths are not ashamed of their dialect. The more favorable evaluations are among the students from the larger urban settings, the Bronx and Los Angeles. The Miami group tends to be more critical of its local Spanish, while the students from Amsterdam respond with generally neutral ratings. The designation of the place where the prestige variety of Spanish is spoken reflects in part a language loyalty orientation toward the ethnolinguistic group, and at the same time situates Peninsular Spanish as the high-status dialect among the Latin American varieties.

Finally, group differences might reflect particular local and regional socioeconomic realities (Zentella 1990), interethnic relations between the dominant and subordinate groups (Torres 1990), ethnolinguistic vitality (Giles and Byrne 1982), community expectations, demographic strength, and institutional support (Conklin and Lourie 1983). As Gardner (1985) points out, the social and cultural milieu in which learners grow up determines their beliefs about language and culture.

Notes

* This study was made possible with the financial support of the U.S./Spanish Joint Commission for Cultural and Educational Cooperation, Madrid, Spain. I am most grateful to Rolando Santiago, who assisted me with the development of the sociolinguistic questionnaire, data processing, and statistical analysis with the support of Carlos Colley-Capo and Angeles Pagán-Cáceres. I would also like to express my appreciation to those persons who dedicated much time and energy in making arrangements for the administration of the questionnaires at the various locations: Imelda Carey (Los Angeles), Erlinda González-Berry (Albuquerque), Caridad Iglesias (Miami), Robert Milk (San Antonio), Armando Pacheco (Bronx), and Cándida Santos (Amsterdam).

1. The correlation coefficients for the three instrumental-oriented language attitude items is from .49 to .78, significant at the .001 level. The correlation coefficient for the two integrative items is .42, also significant at the .001 level.

2. The inter-item correlations for the ten semantic traits reveal two types of associations, a positive set among five items ("good," "clear," "correct," "simple," and "interesting") and a negative set among five other items ("familiar," "rich," "useful," "fast," and "modern").

References

Attinasi, John. 1979. Language attitudes in a New York Puerto Rican community. In *Ethnoperspectives in bilingual education research, Vol. 1: Bilingual education and public policy in the United States*, ed. R. Padilla, 408–461. Ypsilanti, MI: Eastern Michigan University.

Beebe, Leslie and Howard Giles. 1984. Speech accommodation theories: A discussion in terms of second language acquisition. *International Journal of the Sociology of Language*, 46: 5–32.

Brown, Gillian, Kristen Malmkjaer, and John Williams, eds. 1996. *Performance and competence in second language acquisition*. Cambridge: Cambridge University Press.

Byrnes, Heide and Michael Canales, eds. 1987. *Defining and developing proficiency*. Lincolnwood, IL: National Textbook Company.

Conkin, Nancy F. and Margaret A. Lourie. 1983. *A host of tongues: Language communities in the United States*. New York: The Free Press.

Ely, Christopher M. 1986. Language learning motivation: A descriptive and causal analysis. *The Modern Language Journal* 70: 28–35.

Fasold, Ralph. 1984. *The sociolinguistics of society*. Oxford: Basil Blackwell.

Ferguson, Charles A. 1972. Diglossia. In *Language and social context*, ed. P.P. Giglioli, 232–251. Harmondsworth, England: Penguin Books.

Fernández, Rosa. 1990. Actitudes hacia los cambios de códigos en Nuevo México: Reacciones de un sujeto a ejemplos de su habla. In *Spanish in the United States: Sociolinguistic issues*, ed. J.J. Bergen, 49–58. Washington, DC: Georgetown University Press.

Fishman, Joshua. 1972. *Sociolinguistics: A brief introduction*. Rowley, MA: Newbury House.

Gardner, Robert C. 1985. *Social psychology and second language learning: The role of attitude and motivation*. London: Edward Arnold.

Gardner, Robert C. and Wallace E. Lambert. 1972. *Attitudes and motivation in second language learning*. Rowley, MA: Newbury House.

Giles, Howard. 1977. *Language, ethnicity and intergroup relations*. London: Academic Press.

Giles, Howard and J.L. Byrne. 1982. An intergroup approach to second language acquisition. *Journal of Multicultural and Multilingual Development* 3: 17–40.

Harley, Birgit, Patrick Allen, Jim Cummins, and Merrill Swain, eds. 1990. *The development of second language proficiency*. Cambridge: Cambridge University Press.

Isaac, Stephen and William B. Michael. 1982. *Handbook in research and evaluation, 2nd edition*. San Diego, CA: EDITS Publishers.

Larmer, Brook. 1999. Latino America. *Newsweek* July 12: 48–58.

Mejías, Hugo A. and Pamela L. Anderson. Attitudes toward use of Spanish on the South Texas border. *Hispania* 71: 401–407.

Peñalosa, Fernando. 1980. *Chicano sociolinguistics*. Rowley, MA: Newbury House.

Ramírez, Arnulfo G. 1983. Bilingüismo y actitudes hacia variedades del español entre estudiantes de Texas y California. *Lingüística Española Actual* 5: 249–268.

Ramírez, Arnulfo G. 1991. Sociolingüística del español-inglés en contacto entre adolesentes hispanos en Estados Unidos. *Hispania* 74: 1057–1067.

Ramírez, Arnulfo G. 1992. *El español de los Estados Unidos: El lenguaje de los hispanos*. Madrid: Editorial MAPFRE.

Sánchez, Rosaura. 1983. *Chicano discourse: Socio-historic perspectives*. Rowley, MA: Newbury House.

Solé, Carlos A. 1982. Language loyalty and language attitudes among Cuban Americans. In *Bilingual education for Hispanic students in the United States*, ed. J. A. Fishman and G. D. Keller, 254–268. New York: Teachers College Press.

Solé, Carlos A. 1991. El problema de la lengua en Buenos Aires: Independencia o autonomía lingüística. In *Sociolinguistics of the Spanish-speaking world: Iberia, Latin America, United States*, ed. C. A. Klee and L. A. Ramos-García, 92–112. Tempe, AZ: Bilingual Press/Editorial Bilingüe.

Torres, Lourdes. 1990. Spanish in the United States: The struggle for legitimacy. In *Spanish in the United States: Sociolinguistic issues*, ed. J. J. Bergen, 142–151. Washington, DC: Georgetown University Press.

Zentella, Ana Celia. 1990. El impacto de la realidad socio-económica en las comunidades hispanoparlantes de los Estados Unidos: Reto a la teoría y metodología lingüística. In *Spanish in the United States: Sociolinguistic issues*, ed. J. J. Bergen, 152–166. Washington, DC: Georgetown University Press.

Zentella, Ana Celia. 1997. *Growing up bilingual*. Oxford: Blackwell Publishers.

En vías del desarrollo del lenguaje académico en español en hablantes nativos de español en los Estados Unidos

M. Cecilia Colombi

University of California, Davis

El mantenimiento del español como lengua minoritaria depende del desarrollo de los registros y usos que van más allá del hogar y la comunidad, en otras palabras, si realmente queremos mantener el español como una lengua viva dentro de los Estados Unidos es importante desarrollar aspectos del discurso académico que le permitirán a sus hablantes desenvolverse en un ambiente público. En las últimas décadas ha emergido un gran número de estudios que describen el español que se usa en distintos contextos en los Estados Unidos (Elías-Olivares 1995, García 1995, García y Cuevas 1995, Gutiérrez 1990, 1995, Lipski, 1996, Ocampo 1990, Ramírez 1994, Silva-Corvalán 1994, Valdés 1988,Valdés y Geoffrion-Vinci 1998, Zentella 1997).

La alfabetización a nivel académico es un fenómeno complejo y multifacético que incluye conceptos básicos de puntuación, ortografía e imprenta. También hay aspectos textuales como poder comprender el formato (por ejemplo reconocer en un periódico qué partes corresponden a los anuncios clasificados, los titulares, editoriales, etc.) y dentro de cada texto podemos reconocer el género al que pertenece y sus constituyentes (por ejemplo en una narración: la situación, la complicación y el desenlace; o en un ensayo académico: una introducción, el desarrollo y la conclusión). La alfabetización también implica el activar un conocimiento del mundo de los lectores, y se puede argüir, el reconocimiento del fondo ideólogico de la autora del texto. Estos elementos son comunes a todas las lenguas. En la situación de una lengua minoritaria como el español en los Estados Unidos muchos de esos aspectos pueden haber sido adquiridos en la casa aunque generalmente se desarrollan en la escuela en el contexto de una lengua dominante. Entre los hablantes bilingües muchos de esos aspectos pueden ser transferidos de una lengua a otra, un proceso que si bien no está libre de problemas, es probablemente más fácil que la adquisición inicial, especialmente con lenguas como el inglés y el español que tienen bastante en común en sus concepciones acerca de los sistemas de escritura. En un estudio de estudiantes latinos bilingües en español e inglés (Schleppegrell and Colombi 1997) se vió que la estructura organizativa al nivel del discurso reflejaba el tipo de combinaciones que los estudiantes elegían al nivel de la cláusula, al mismo tiempo que los recursos de los estudiantes variaban entre sí se observó que utilizaban las mismas estrategias al escribir en español y en inglés. Sin embargo la alfabetización en las dos lenguas difiere de la alfabetización en una lengua en un número de áreas, especialmente aquellas prácticas de escritura que se basan en un aspecto cultural y en registros discursivos que emplean diferentes recursos gramaticales y léxicos en las dos lenguas.

Cummins en una serie de publicaciones ha descripto la proficiencia de la lengua minoritaria de los chicos en dos áreas: el lenguaje conversacional de todos los días: *basic interpersonal communicative skills* (BICS) y la proficiencia en el lenguaje académico cognitivo: *cognitive academic language proficiency* (CALP) (Cummins 1981, 1990, 1996). El último lo relaciona con la educación formal y la alfabetización enfatizando que esta última se adquiere principalmente en los contextos educativos. Si bien su modelo parte de un enfoque educativo y social, no particularmente lingüístico, Cummins hace una diferencia entre el lenguaje de todos los días que está inmerso en el contexto (*context embedded*) y el lenguaje académico que se da en un contexto reducido (*context reduced*).

Desde el punto de vista lingüístico y especialmente en inglés, Halliday (1978, 1985/89, 1993a, 1993b, 1994, 1998), Martin (1983, 1989, 1992, 1993, 1996) y Eggins (1994) entre otros han estudiado las características lingüísticas del registro académico. Halliday ha resuelto la dificultad de los diferentes textos que van del lenguaje diario más contextualizado y menos planeado a aquel que requiere más planeamiento y tiene un contexto más reducido, describiéndolos dentro de un continuo:

(1) 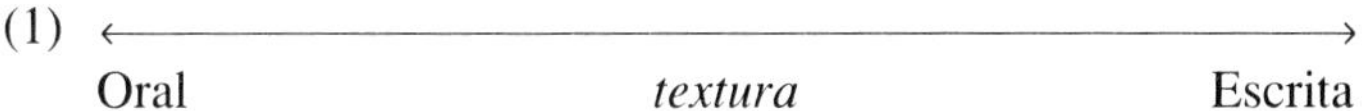

Se refiere a un "modo continuo" que tiene que ver con la forma de presentación del mensaje (escrito-oral) (Modo) pero también con los interactuantes (Tenor) y el tema/propósito (Campo) y van desde los contextos más contextualizados y menos planeados a los más descontextualizados y más planeados. Esta clasificación obviamente va más allá del medio oral o escrito e incorpora el próposito del mensaje, las características interpersonales de los interactuantes (mayor o menor solidaridad) y la situación en la cual se desarrolla el acto de habla. Sin duda el lenguaje académico en general se encuentra en el extremo derecho del continuo; es decir ya sea en una forma oral o escrita, la distancia entre los interactuantes es grande y no refleja una situación solidaria sino de poder, el propósito de los trabajos académicos generalmente es demostrar que se manejan los registros académicos y en la mayoría de los casos también está relacionado a una evaluación (por ejemplo un ensayo en un curso de lengua o una presentación oral en un seminario).

El análisis que presentaré en este capítulo forma parte de una investigación longitudinal del desarrollo del lenguaje académico escrito de 30 estudiantes hispanohablantes a nivel universitario durante un año escolar en el cual se recogieron todos los trabajos escritos en los cursos de español para hispanohablantes en una universidad pública de California.[1] El propósito de este estudio es describir el desarrollo léxico-gramatical a nivel de la combinación de las cláusulas y los procesos de nominalización que caracterizan el registro acádemico. Para ello he seleccionado los ensayos de Rosa (un nombre ficticio), una estudiante que representa el desarrollo de la mayoría del grupo. Rosa es méxico-americana, hija de padres mexicanos y primera generación que accede a una educación universitaria; no ha recibido instrucción formal en español pero lo habla fluidamente y por lo tanto ha podido ingresar a estos cursos de hispanohablantes de nivel avanzado cuyo propósito es desarrollar el lenguaje formal académico a nivel oral y escrito. En estos cursos se utiliza una pedagogía freiriana y se enfatiza la escritura como proceso, es decir se parte de la experiencia personal de los estudiantes y luego se expande el análisis a textos más académicos literarios y científicos. También se espera que los estudiantes interactúen individual y grupalmente con los textos reescribiéndolos dos y tres veces.

1. Hipótesis

Partiendo de una perspectiva de la lingüística sistémica funcional (LSF) que es una teoría semiótica del lenguaje en la cual se considera la relación entre el lenguaje y el contexto como constituyente e interdependiente, se espera ver una progresión desde los primeros ensayos que reflejen un lenguaje más oral y dependientes del contexto a los últimos que representen un lenguaje escrito (y académico) más descontextualizado. Esa progresión se puede ver en un aumento de la densidad léxica (mayor número de palabras de contenido en relación al número de palabras del texto) (Eggins 1994: 60) y una disminución en el "intricamiento" gramatical (Halliday 1994: 350) o sea el número cláusulas de encadenamiento (hipotácticas y paratácticas) en el texto en proporción con el número de oraciones en el texto. La combinación de cláusulas de encadenamiento son típicas del lenguaje oral (cláusulas relacionas por medio de los conectores *y*, *pero*, *porque*, etc.); el lenguaje oral elabora complejos de cláusulas constituidas de paratácticas e hipotácticas a diferencia del lenguaje escrito cuya densidad léxica es mayor e incorpora mayor información en cada oración por medio de nominalizaciones y cláusulas enganchadas.

El estudio se ha realizado a dos niveles: un micronivel tomando en cuenta las estrategias que usan los escritores al combinar las cláusulas y la interacción de esas estrategias con la organización discursiva de las asignaciones a un macronivel. Rosa es una escritora efectiva que maneja los conceptos del ensayo en el macronivel o nivel del género, es decir, sus ensayos están compuestos de los constituyentes funcionales de la introducción (que incluye la tesis), el desarrollo y la conclusión. La enseñanza de los constituyentes funcionales del género del ensayo forma parte de estos cursos y los participantes comienzan a aplicar estos conceptos desde el comienzo en sus propios ensayos. Sin embargo el tipo de combinación de cláusulas y léxico que caracteriza el lenguaje académico es algo que no se ha estudiado explícitamente en estos cursos avanzados para hispanohablantes. Basándose en un análisis funcional de la relación entre la gramática y el discurso, este estudio puede proveer un marco de referencia útil para incorporar una gramática funcional en clases de escritura, marcando cómo las diferentes elecciones gramaticales ayudan a los estudiantes a construir los tipos de textos que se requieren de ellos en los contextos académicos.

2. Estudio

El análisis de la combinación de las cláusulas sigue un enfoque sistémico funcional (Halliday 1994: 242), en el que se distinguen tres formas de combinar las cláusulas: paratácticas, hipotácticas y enganchadas, siguiendo las líneas de las últimas investigaciones que arguyen que la subordinación como categoría pone en el mismo grupo cláusulas que son constituyentes de otras cláusulas (enganchadas) junto a cláusulas que se encuentran en una relación de asociación, más que de enganche o incrustación, con otras cláusulas (hipotácticas).

(2) Rosa #2
//Aparte de esto la mayoría de la gente pobre era analfabeta //
1
y sufría problemas económicos a causa de la oligarquía// {Paratáctica}
2

(3) Rosa #2
//Sin embargo en los últimos años la esperanza de un futuro mejor ha
α
aumentado, /ya que un acuerdo de paz fue firmado en 1992 por el presidente
β
Alfredo Cristiani.// {Hipotáctica}

(4) Rosa #2
//Es cierto [que hasta hoy en día mucha gente todavía es víctima de la violencia y de la guerra [que continúa en el Salvador]. {Enganche}

El punto es diferenciar estructuras sintácticas que representan un encadenamiento de cláusulas (hipotácticas y paractácticas) y contrastar esas combinaciones con estructuras que representan una condensación de la información e integración de las cláusulas (enganchadas). Al hacer esta diferencia entre cláusulas paratácticas e hipotácticas por un lado, separándolas de las cláusulas incrustadas o enganchadas, se puede ir más allá de la categoría de subordinación y hacer una distinción más fina o específica entre las cláusulas que contribuyen al discurso de una forma independiente (hipotácticas y paratácticas) y aquellas otras que forman parte de otras cláusulas (incrustadas o enganchadas).[2]

Los resultados del análisis de la combinación de la cláusulas en los tres ensayos de principios, mediados y fines del año escolar de Rosa se presentan en la tabla 1.

Tabla 1. El desarrollo gramatical de los ensayos académicos de Rosa

Ensayos (Rosa)	#1. Primer trimestre (688 words)		#2. Segundo trimestre (555 words)		#3. Tercer trimestre (762 words)	
Tipo de cláusula	Núm.	%	Núm.	%	Núm.	%
Cláusulas principales en oraciones simples	14		7		6	
en oraciones complejas	14		17		28	
Total de cláusulas simples	**28**	**43.75%**	**24**	**51.%**	**34**	**46.57%**
Cláusulas hipotácticas	12		11		12	
Cláusulas paratácticas	9		6		6	
Total de cláusulas hipotácticas y paratácticas	**21**	**32.81%**	**17**	**36.1%**	**18**	**24.65%**
Cláusulas enganchadas	**15**	**23.47%**	**6**	**12.7%**	**21**	**28.76%**
TOTAL DE CLAUSULAS	64	100%	47	100%	73	100%

Se observa que el desarrollo gramátical de Rosa al nivel de la combinación de las cláusulas va progresivamente de un mayor número de paratácticas e hipotácticas en el primer ensayo, típicas del discurso oral (32.81%) a un mayor número de oraciones principales y enganchadas en el último ensayo del año escolar (46.57% y 28.76% respectivamente) más típicas del lenguaje académico. Es interesante notar que en el segundo ensayo analizado que corresponde a la mitad del año escolar, Rosa utiliza un alto número de oraciones principales (51%) junto a un alto número de paratácticas e hipotácticas (36.1%) pero el número de enganchadas ha disminuido. Sin embargo estos resultados junto con la densidad léxica del texto responden a la progresión en el continuo oral-escrito de textos puesto que no tan sólo la densidad léxica ha aumentado sino que el intricamiento gramatical ha disminuido lo que implica que a pesar de haber aumentado el número de cláusulas de enganche también ha aumentado en proporción la condensación de la información (nominalizaciones) (tabla 2). Es interesante notar que no ha habido un énfasis explícito en la combinación de las cláusulas a nivel de la instrucción que los estudiantes recibieron, y sin embargo el desarrollo que esta estudiante y que la mayoría de los estudiantes ha seguido refleja ese continuo desde lo oral a lo escrito.

Tabla 2. Densidad léxica e intricamiento gramatical de los ensayos

Ensayos	Densidad léxica	Intricamiento gramatical
#1	(297/688) 4.31%	(49/28) 1.75
#2	(255/555) 4.59%	(41/24) 1.70
#3	(387/762) 5.07%	(52/34) 1.52

El desarrollo del lenguaje académico sigue el continuo de un mayor intricamiento gramatical, caracterizado por un alto número de cláusulas parátacticas e hipotácticas en el extremo oral a un mayor índice de densidad léxica, caracterizado por un mayor número de cláusulas principales que contienen información condensada y compactada (Halliday 1994) por medio de nominalizaciones y cláusulas de enganche. Es interesante notar que este análisis nos muestra un desarrollo paulatino y lento del lenguaje académico, los resultados ejemplificados representan muestras de un año académico (9 meses de instrucción) y las diferencias entre los porcentajes no es significativa aunque van en la línea del continúo y de acuerdo a las hipótesis presentadas. Es decir, a mayor intricamiento gramatical corresponde menor densidad léxica (ensayo #1) y a mayor densidad léxica corresponde un menor intricamiento gramatical (ensayo #2 y 3).

Junto con la combinación de las cláusulas es necesario observar las estrategias que Rosa ha utilizado para compactar la información, especialmente el recurso de nominalización que le permite presentar mayor información con menos palabras.

Halliday (1994, 1997) denomina al proceso de nominalización "metáfora gramatical"; esencialmente él aduce que hay una relación primaria entre los significados y las formas que usamos para nombrarlos en las sociedades occidentales. Esa relación primaria se refleja en el orden en que aprendemos a hablar como niños y también esa relación tiende a desarrollarse primero en los textos. Las más importantes de esas correlaciones son:

- los nombres codifican a los participantes (personas, lugares, cosas, etc.)
- los verbos codifican procesos (acciones, pensamientos, sentimientos, etc.)
- los adjetivos codifican cualidades (tamaño, color, forma, etc.)
- las conjunciones codifican relaciones lógicas (causa, tiempo, contraste, etc.)

El lenguaje académico, por otra parte, presenta la información en una forma más condensada con correlaciones que no siguen las relaciones descriptas, observemos algunos ejemplos de los dos últimos ensayos de Rosa:

(5) Rosa #3
Al comienzo de la novela existe una división entre la familia Rubio, la cual demuestra la evolución del engaño que en ciertas formas se compara a la realidad de México.

En este enunciado los procesos "comenzar, dividir y engañar" se presentan como participantes "*comienzo, división, engaño*" al igual que la cualidad "real" es presentada como otro participante "*realidad.*" Halliday llama a estas correlaciones "metáforas" porque deben ser entendidas a dos niveles- literalmente en términos de la categoría de palabras que representan (en este caso, nombres) y figurativamente de acuerdo al significado que están presentando. Es decir, debemos comprender el proceso de dividir como participante que realiza el proceso de demostrar " la evolución del engaño (que se compara a la realidad de México)." Tanto cuando interpretamos como cuando escribimos frases con nominalizaciones, debemos reconocer esos dos niveles. La función primordial de la nominalización es la posibilidad de poder presentar más información léxica.

(6) Rosa #2
A través de la dominación del imperialismo y la oligarquía, el pueblo salvadoreño ha sido víctima de la opresión, el atropello y de guerras civiles.

En este ejemplo nuevamente vemos a los procesos (dominar, oprimir, atropellar) y a los atributos (imperial) funcionando como participantes. Estas ideas se pueden descompactar de la siguiente forma:

(7) El imperialismo y la oligarquía han dominado al pueblo salvadoreño.
El imperialismo y la oligarquía y las guerras civiles han oprimido y atropellado al pueblo salvadoreño.

Por medio de estas nominalizaciones, Rosa puede presentar estas ideas juntas en una oración con un alto contenido léxico. Las nominalizaciones, como la escritura, se aprenden en un contexto académico formal y el desarrollo es más efectivo si presentamos estas estrategias de una forma explícita en nuestras clases de escritura. En la mayoría de los cursos de escritura nos concentramos en aspectos de puntuación, ortografía y gramática que dan una mejor apariencia a los textos pero que no son suficientes si realmente queremos desarrollar un lenguaje académico.

(8) Rosa #3
A causa de éstos, el padre César Rubio engaña a su familia y a su patria haciéndoles creer que él es un revolucionario que murió muchos años atrás.

En este caso, Rosa utiliza una frase preposicional para unir los enunciados como una relación lógica de causalidad.

(9) Rosa #2
Debido a esto y la oligarquía que se estableció, el país enfrentó problemas entre la dominación de clases.

En este ejemplo un verbo realiza la conexión entre las ideas mencionadas y la que quiere presentar en vez de una conjunción. Si bien varios de estos ejemplos presentan nominalizaciones en una etapa de desarrollo hacia un lenguaje académico efectivo, es importante notar que comienzan a aparecer después de los primeros meses de instrucción cuando Rosa ha tenido mucho más contacto con textos literarios y académicos en español, a diferencia de sus primeros ensayos que reflejan un lenguaje mucho más oral. La escritura académica y científica en nuestras culturas generalmente presentan un gran número de metáforas gramaticales que produce una alta densidad léxica, o sea una mayor condensación de la información y un intricamiento gramatical menor.

3. Conclusión

Los hablantes nativos de español en los Estados Unidos a menudo utilizan estrategias del lenguaje oral cuando escriben (Colombi 1997) y es una ventaja que poseen, al mismo tiempo viendo estas diferencias entre los patrones de combinación de cláusulas como una elección entre un estilo más dialógico y oral, y otro más analítico y escrito, les puede ayudar a reconocer los recursos que el discurso académico demanda. El lenguaje académico requiere de los escritores que puedan ir más allá de los estilos que les son familiares y adopten una variedad de enfoques de acuerdo al tipo de asignación que deban realizar. Si los escritores se limitan a estilos y registros orales, no tendrán la flexibilidad para responder a la amplia gama de demandas académicas y más tarde de demandas que el mundo externo exija de ellos. Este trabajo describe cómo las características de la combinación de cláusulas y estrategias de nominalización contribuyen al desarrollo de un registro académico. En la escritura de los tres ensayos de Rosa recogidos durante el curso de un año académico se puede ver que existe una progresión de un mayor intricamiento al nivel gramatical en su primer ensayo hacia una mayor densidad léxica en los ensayos de mediados y finales del año. Este análisis de la escritura nos ofrece una forma de aproximarnos al texto que puede servirnos en el momento de presentar el lenguaje académico en nuestras clases de escritura.[3]

Apéndice

Primer ensayo

California y "el otro"

Hace muchos años atras, los Estados Unidos tuvo conflictos con razas que no eran o pertenecian a la cultura anglosajon. Nomas porque no querian aceptar la diversidad entre culturas. Lo cual pudo haber causado las barreras y divisiones entre muchas razas. Actualmente, todavia existe este problema, Simplemente en los países al este de los Estados Unidos, (como Virginia, Carolina de Sur), se niegan aceptar que el mundo se esta haciendo diverso cada vez más. ¿Por qué? Simplemente porque no conviven con diferentes razas y no quieren ver la realidad que ocupan y necesitan de las demás identidades, como los hispanos. En cambio, el estado de California, tiene tanta diversidad multicultural que, se puede decir que, California esta preparado para enfrentarse con "el otro" atravéz de diversos lenguajes, contribuciones y la diversidad racial.

California ha sido, uno de los pocos estados con mayor diversidad racial en los Estados Unidos. Desde mucho tiempo atras fue, y sigue siendo, la frontera para muchos individuos, especialmente para los hispanos. Una frontera que abre nuevos horizontes llenos de oportunidades. Y atravéz de esa frontera, California ha logrado ser un país multicultural. Ya que en muchas cuidades de este estado se puede encontrar diversos grupos étnicos. La ciudad de Los Angeles, por ejemplo, es una de las cuantas ciudades que uno puede observar la cantidad de razas que viven ahí. Entre esta grande ciudad uno se encuentra con gente hindú, salvadoreña, mexicana, guatemalteca, oriental, afroamericana, etc. Por la enorme cantidad de diversidad multicultural, Los Angeles convive y comparte diariamente con "el otro."

Apesar de que hay una gran multitud de diferentes razas étnicas en Los Angeles al igual que diversas lenguas, todos parecen entenderce bastante bien. ¿Cómo? Se puede preguntar uno. Simplemente que en donde quiera que uno se presente siempre hay alguien que sepa hablar o interpretar unos de los varios lenguajes que mas se habla. Especialmente el español, ya que la mayoria de los que habitan en esta ciudad son hispanos.

Otro aspecto de California que muestra el encuentro con "el otro" son las contribuciones que han dado diversos grupos. Por ejemplo, muchas razas han traído, en representación y costumbres de su país, elementos como la música, comida, arte y literatura. Casi en cada rincón de las calles de Los Angeles uno puede ver restaurantes mexicanos, salvadoreños u orientales. Cada uno de estos grupos han traido e incorporado una parte de su país natal. Al igual, la música típica de ciertos países ha llegado hasta California. Ritmos como la salsa, cumbia, banda, corridos, norteñas han logrado cruzar la frontera de los Estados Unidos. Junto con la música y comida también llego el arte y literatura. En ciertos barrios de la ciudad de Los Angeles uno puede observar y admirar murales creativos que han sido pintados como retratos o memorias de la cultura hispanohablante.

Aparte de la música y comida muchos individuos han traido con ellos las ganas de sobresalir y además trabajar. Principalmente porque California ocupa a los hispanos y otras minorias para beneficiarse. Sobre todo porque la economia los necesita para poder superar los Estados Unidos, ya que hay muchos trabajos que los anglosajones no quieren hacer. Come digo Carlos Fuentes, "el trabajador inmigrante mantiene bajos los precios y alto el consumo, y aunque desplaza a algunos obreros, no puede competir con los desplazamientos laborales provocados por la tecnología y la competencia extranjera."

Bastantes individuos creen que las minorias, como los hispanos, estan en los Estados Unidos nomás quitandole a los angloamericanos oportunidades. Pero la realidad es que California ocupa a toda esta gente. En los países del este, no quieren aceptar esta realidad. Pero claro esta que "el mundo hispanico no vino a los Estados Unidos, sino que los Estados Unidos vinieron al mundo hispanico," como lo explica Carlos Fuentes en El espejo enterrado. Y así de esta manera California tiene a Los Angeles como una prueba mundial, para todos los que se niegan aceptar el mundo multicultural, de que California esta verdaderamente preparado para enfrentarse con "el otro." ¿Si en Los Angeles todos pueden convivir con diferentes razas y culturas, por que otros estados no?

Segundo ensayo

La lucha continua

El Salvador, apesar de ser el país más pequeño y poblado de Centroamérica ha sido el que ha tenido bastantes conflictos entre el pueblo. Estos problemas se iniciaron cuando se estableció el colonialismo. Desde entonces la lucha contra éste y la liberación ha continuado. En los artículos "El Salvador: medio siglo de lucha" de Andres Fábregas, "Monseñor Romero un enviado de Dios para salvar a su pueblo" de Ignacio Ellacuría y la película Romero muestran acontecimientos sobre el inicio de esta lucha hasta hoy en día. A través de la dominación del imperialismo y la oligarquía, el pueblo salvadoreño ha sido víctima de la opresión, el atropello, y de guerras civiles.

Desde hace más de cien años El Salvador empezó con una situación colonial, la cual fue superando a lo largo del tiempo. Debido a ésto y la oligarquía que se estableció, el país enfrentó problemas entre la dominación de clases. Esto lo podemos ver en al artículo "El Salvador: medio siglo de lucha," el cual muestra estadísticas sobre el control del país desde los años setenta. Por ejemplo, ese año seis familias llegaron a controlar las propiedades del país. Asi de esta manera uno puede comprender porque casi la mitad de los campesinos no tienen propiedades. Aparte de esto la mayoría de la gente pobre era analfabeta y sufría problemas económicos a causa de la oligarquía. Debido a que esta junto con el imperialismo manipulaban el ingreso, la población no recibía un ingreso justo. Actualmente estos problemas todavia existen, ya que el pueblo sigue siendo reprimido.

Además del artículo de Andres Fábregas, la película Romero también nos muestra como el país de El Salvador ha enfrentado cuestiones políticas y sociales entre el pueblo. Basada en la vida del arzobispo Oscar Arnulfo Romero, la película se enfoca en eventos violentos que tomaron lugar en el país. Estos eventos muestran como la población de clase baja es diariamente asesinada, reprimida y humillada por la clase alta o la Guardia Nacional. Hasta que el padre Grande es asesinado, el arzobispo empezó a ver la realidad y fue entonces cuando se unió con la gente pobre del pueblo. Para esta gente la voz del arzobispo Romero era un gran paso hacia su lucha y esperanza de ser libres. "El pueblo sin voz hizo que su voz, la del obispo y la de la iglesia, retumbase no sólo en el país, sino internacionalmente" (Ignacio Ellacuría, pg. 38). Esto le costó la vida a Oscar Romero, pero al menos logró que el pueblo tuviera el valor para poder salir adelante.

Casos como el del arzobispo Oscar Arnulfo Romero eran comunes entre la población humilde de El Salvador. A causa del poder y la oligarquía la población salvadoreña ha sufrido bastante durante varios años. Pero apesar de esto siempre han logrado salir adelante de una manera u otra. Es cierto que hasta hoy en día mucha gente todavia es víctima de la violencia y de la guerra que continua en El Salvador. Sin embargo en los últimos años la esperanza de un futuro mejor ha aumentado, ya que un acuerdo de paz fue firmado en 1992 por el presidente Alfredo Cristiani. Tal vez en un rinconcito de El Salvador exista alguien que crea en la justicia y traiga finalmente la paz a este país que tanto ha sufrido!

Tercer ensayo

La verdad nos grita

El Gesticulador de Rodolfo Usigli es una novela dramática que trata el tema de la mentira entre una familia. Antes de publicarse en 1963, esta novela fue llevada al teatro en numerosas ocasiones. Inclusivemente, ha sido traducida en varios idiomas como el inglés, alemán y el francés. Tal y como lo indica su título, esta novela oculta los secretos de sus personajes. *El Gesticulador* refleja el engaño y la decepción que ocurre entre el sistema político de México representado a través de la familia Rubio.

Al comienzo de la novela existe una división entre la familia Rubio, la cual demuestra la evolución del engaño que en ciertas formas se compara a la realidad de México. Es así como se desenvuelve la ambición hacia el poder y el dinero. A causa de éstos, el padre César Rubio egaña a su familia y a su patria haciéndolos creer que él es un revolucionario que murio muchos años atrás. Tomando la personalidad de otro individuo, César logra obtener lo que siempre ha deseado: dinero y poder. Según él, su destino ha cambiado para ser un bien y seguir el ejemplo del general César Rubio. "Ahora conozco mi destino: sé que debo completar el destino de César Rubio" (Usigli 83). Tal parece que aquí César se está contradiciendo ante sus palabras, pues está llevando una vida, de un hombre, que no le pertenece. Como quien dice, César se está aprovechando de la situación no sólo para engañarse el mismo sino también a sus hijos y a su patria.

En comparación con México, igualmente el engaño y la decepción sucede entre la política. No cabe duda que cuando llegan las elecciones del gobierno, cada candidato lleva puesta su "máscara" para ganarse a la gente. Durante las elecciones la mayoría de los candidatos se convierten en gesticuladores, pues sólo así podrán obtener lo que desean. Ya una vez logrando su proposito, se quitan su máscara y se olvidan de las promesas que han hecho a su patria. En ciertos casos ni siquiera toman en cuenta el voto de la gente, pues no es extraño que ocurran fraudes con las votaciones.

No tarda mucho en descubrirse una mentira cuando rápidamente empiezan a surgir problemas por dondequiera. En el caso de César, podemos observar que a causa de su "reaparición" el candidato gobernal Navarro está dispuesto a todo con tal de que César le deje el camino libre para que gane las elecciones. "Quiero decirte que no seas tonto, que te retires de esto. Te puedes arrepentir muy tarde" (Usigli 81). Pero al igual que César, Navarro ha llegado a ser un general porque también ha cometido fraudes en el sistema del gobierno. Igualmente en México muchas figuras políticas están en una posición gobernal porque han hecho tranzas para llegar ahi. La ambición hacia el poder es tan enorme que hasta han llegado al extremo de eliminar a cualquier persona que lleve la ventaja de ganar. Un ejemplo de ésto sucedió hace unos años atrás cuando el candidato presidencial del PRI Luis Donaldo Colosio fue asesinado. Aunque no esté probado, se sospecha que los mismos colegas del partido son responsables por la muerte de Colosio. Como Luis Donaldo Colosio estaba opuesto a las ideas del PRI y quería reformar el gobierno de México, esto no le convenia al gobierno y fue así como asesinaron a un gran hombre que demostraba interés de hacer cambios positivos para su patria.

El Gesticulador de Rodolfo Usigli indudablemente representa la decepción y el engaño que frecuentemente ocurre en el sistema político de México. Muchos de los acontecimientos de la novela son semejantes a los que han sucedido en México. El personaje César Rubio es un ejemplo de la estafa que existe entre los políticos del país. Su asesinato se puede comparar con la muerte del candidato presidencial Luis Donaldo Colosio. Hasta la hipocresía del general Navarro, al final de la novela, se puede comparar con éstos, pues sólo viven de la mentira y la hipocresía.

Esta novela a pesar de reflejar la historia de México, a la vez suele enviar un mensaje a sus lectores. A través de sus personajes, *El Gesticulador* nos muestra las situaciones que el país ha enfrentado a causa de individuos corruptivos. Quizá el autor ha creado a César Rubio y el general Navarro para darnos cuenta de que personas como estas si existen en nuestra realidad y no son nomás en novelas. Hasta hoy en día, México no ha podido resolver sus cuestiones políticas y como resultado el país no ha tenido un futuro próspero.

Obras Citadas
Usigli, Rodolfo. 1963. *El Gesticulador*. Prentice-Hall, Inc.

Notas

1. La recolección de los textos fue posible gracias a la participación de Francisco X. Alarcón, director del programa de español para hispanohablantes de la Universidad de California, Davis.

2. Vid Schleppegrell y Colombi 1997 para una descripción más detallada de esta clasificación.

3. El análisis longitudinal de los textos fue llevado a cabo durante el tiempo otorgado por una beca del Davis Humanities Institute de la Universidad de California, Davis en la primavera de 1999.

Referencias

Colombi, M. Cecilia. 1997. Perfil del discurso escrito en textos de hispanohablantes: teoría y práctica. En *La enseñanza del español a hispanohablantes*, ed. M. Cecilia Colombi y Francisco X. Alarcón, 175–189. Boston: Houghton Mifflin.

Cummins, Jim. 1981. Four misconceptions about language proficiency in bilingual education. *NABE* N.3: 31–45.

Cummins, Jim. 1990. Language proficiency, bilingualism, and academic achievement. En *Multicultural classroom*, ed. Patricia A. Richard-Amato y Marguerite Ann Snow, 16–25. New York: Longman.

Cummins, Jim. 1996. *Negotiating identities: Education for empowerment in a diverse society*. Ontario, CA: California Association for Bilingual Education.

Eggins, Suzanne. 1994. *An introduction to systemic functional linguistics*. London: Pinter Publishers.

Elías-Olivares, Lucía. 1995. Discourse strategies of Mexican American Spanish. En *Spanish in four continents: Studies in language contact and bilingualism*, ed. Carmen Silva-Corvalán, 227–240. Washington, DC: Georgetown University Press.

García, MaryEllen. 1995. En los sábados, en la mañana, en veces: A look at en in the Spanish of San Antonio. En *Spanish in four continents: Studies in language contact and bilingualism*. ed. Carmen Silva-Corvalán, 196–213. Washington, DC: Georgetown University Press.

García, Ofelia y Milagro Cuevas. 1995. Spanish ability and use among second-generation Nuyoricans. En *Spanish in four continents: Studies in language contact and bilingualism*, ed. Carmen Silva-Corvalán, 184–195. Washington, DC: Georgetown University Press.

Gutiérrez, Manuel. 1990. Sobre el mantenimiento de las cláusulas subordinadas en el español de Los Angeles. En *Spanish in the United States: Sociolinguistic issues*. ed. John J. Bergen, 31–38. Washington, DC: Georgetown University Press.

Gutiérrez, Manuel. 1995. On the future of the future tense in the Spanish of the Southwest. En *Spanish in four continents: Studies in language contact and bilingualism*. ed. Carmen Silva-Corvalán, 214–226. Washington, DC: Georgetown University Press.

Halliday, M.A.K. 1978. *Language as social semiotic: The social interpretation of language and meaning*. London: Edward Arnold.

Halliday, M.A.K. 1985/89. *Spoken and written language*. Oxford: Oxford University Press.

Halliday, M.A.K. 1993a. On the language of physical science. En *Writing science: Literacy and discoursive power*, ed. M.A.K. Halliday y J.R. Martin, 54–68. London: Falmer Press.

Halliday, M.A.K. 1993b. Some grammatical problems in Scientific English. In *Writing science: Literacy and discoursive power*, ed. M.A.K. Halliday y J.R. Martin, 69–85. London: Falmer Press.

Halliday, M.A.K. 1994 [1985]. *An introduction to functional grammar*. London: Edward Arnold.

Halliday, M.A.K. 1998. Things and relations. In *Reading science: Critical and functional perspectives on discourse of science*, ed. J.R. Martin y R. Veel, 185–235. London: Routledge.

Lipski, John. 1996. Patterns of pronominal evolution in Cuban-American bilinguals. En *Spanish in contact: Issues in bilingualism*, ed. Ana Roca y John B. Jensen, 159–186. Somerville, MA: Cascadilla Press.

Martin, James. 1983. The development of register. En *Developmental issues in discourse*, ed. J. Fine y R.O. Freedle, 1–40. Norwood, NJ.: Ablex Publishing.

Martin, James. 1989. *Factual writing*. Oxford: Oxford University Press.

Martin, James. 1992. *English text: System and structure*. Amsterdam: John Benjamins.

Martin, James. 1993. Genre and literacy: Modeling context in educational linguistics. *Annual Review of Applied Linguistics* 13: 141–172.

Martin, James. 1996. Waves of abstraction: Organizing exposition. *The Journal of TESOL – France* 3.1: 87–105.

Ocampo, Francisco. 1990. El subjuntivo en tres generaciones de hablantes bilingües. En *Spanish in the United States: Sociolinguistic issues*. ed. John J. Bergen, 39–48. Washington, DC: Georgetown University Press.

Ramírez, Arnulfo. 1994. *El español de los Estados Unidos: el lenguaje de los hispanos*. Madrid: Mapfre.

Silva-Corvalán, Carmen. 1994. *Language contact and change: Spanish in Los Angeles*. Oxford: Clarendon Press.

Schleppegrell, Mary y M. Cecilia Colombi. 1997. Text organization by bilingual writers. *Written Communication* 14: 481–503.

Valdés, Guadalupe. 1988. The language situation of Mexican Americans. En *Language diversity*, ed. Sandra Lee McKay y Sau-ling Cynthia Wong, 111–139. San Francisco: Newbury House Publishers.

Valdés, Guadalupe y M. Geoffrion-Vinci. 1998. Chicano Spanish: The problem of the "underdeveloped" code in bilingual repertoires. *The Modern Language Journal* 82.4: 473–501.

Zentella, Ana Celia. 1997. *Growing up bilingual*. Malden, MA: Blackwell.

"Addressing" Business in Puerto Rico: *Tú* vs. *Usted*

Diane Ringer Uber
The College of Wooster

The research project reported in this paper is a study of the forms of address used in Spanish in business environments in metropolitan San Juan, Puerto Rico.[1] We will examine the pronouns of address (*tú* and *usted*), as well as the corresponding verb forms, used to address colleagues, clients, and applicants. The work was carried out in offices, corporations, and stores. In addition, I spent full days with sales representatives and account executives to observe their use of commercial Spanish with buyers and clients. In order to obtain data on the use of forms of address, I have combined the methods of participant observation, notes on overheard speech, recordings of spontaneous speech, notes on discussions with speakers, and the results of a questionnaire. These different methods of data collection complement each other in order to maximize the validity of the results (Schiffrin 1994, Wolfson 1976). My results are compared to results from a larger study also carried out in four other Latin American capitals: Santiago, Chile; Bogotá, Colombia; Caracas, Venezuela; and Mexico City, Mexico.

Commercial language in the Spanish-speaking world is often believed to be characterized by its formality. However, forms of address vary according to the situation. Some regions use a more formal address system (e.g. Bogotá, where *usted* is more common), while other regions use a more familiar system (e.g. the Caribbean, where *tú* is used more frequently). In addition, the power structures which are evident in commercial settings in Latin America may determine the form of address used. Employees may address supervisors with *usted*, whereas supervisors may either reciprocate with *usted* or address employees with *tú*. Employees may use *tú* with their peers in order to express solidarity. This study determines whether the usage of forms of address in San Juan businesses is explainable in terms of the traditional concepts of power and solidarity (Brown and Gilman 1960, Schwenter 1993, Blas Arroyo 1994, Placencia 1997).

 Research on Spanish in the U.S., ed. Ana Roca, 310–318. Somerville, MA: Cascadilla Press.

Brown and Gilman (1960) claim that address forms are always governed by the same two underlying dimensions: solidarity and status (or power). The non-reciprocal power semantic, or asymmetrical status norm, is explained as follows:

> One person may be said to have power over another in the degree that he is able to control the behavior of others. Power is a relationship between at least two persons, and it is nonreciprocal in the sense that both cannot have power in the same area of behavior. The power semantic is similarly nonreciprocal; the superior says T and receives V. (Brown and Gilman 1960: 225)

Within the family, parents would say T and receive V from their children. There were also norms of address for persons of roughly equal power. Between equals, pronominal address was reciprocal; an individual gave and received the same form. Gradually a distinction developed which is sometimes called the T of intimacy and the V of formality. This second dimension is called solidarity or familiarity. Each pronoun has two connotations: T expresses intimacy when it is reciprocal and condescension when it is non-reciprocal; V expresses formality or remoteness when it is reciprocal and deference when it is non-reciprocal (Brown and Gilman 1960: 257–259). Persons of superior status may be solidary (parents, elder siblings) or not solidary (officials one seldom sees). Similarly, persons of inferior status may be solidary (faithful servants) or not solidary (waiters in a strange restaurant). For further details on the norms of power and solidarity, see Brown and Gilman 1960.

1. Methodology

For the project reported here, I spent two weeks in San Juan, Puerto Rico. Friends and colleagues put me in touch with people who work in business. They were told that I teach a course in business Spanish, that I needed to learn more about commercial culture in Latin America, and that I wanted to see practical, everyday occurrences. Thus, I was able to spend several hours observing interactions in workplaces, taking notes, speaking with some employees, and making tape recordings.[2]

For the tape recordings, the recorder was left on during daily interactions in workplaces. Afterwards, totals were noted of the usage of *tú* (T) and of *usted* (U) in situations in which there was variation.[3] If the speakers participating in the situation employed one of the pronouns categorically, the usage was noted without its being counted in the total of occurrences.

The questionnaire was used to record speakers' answers to questions about their address usage. I noted the speaker's age, sex, occupation, nationality, ethnic group, place of birth and residence, and how they were dressed. I asked whether they would use *tú* or *usted* to address a subordinate, the subordinate of a subordinate, their boss, their boss' boss, a colleague, friends, family members, neighbors, professors, and strangers. Then I asked what each of those people would use to address them. I also took notes on usage in different situations of participant observation and overheard speech. The results of the conversations with speakers and of my notes on usage form the basis of the qualitative results of the study. The quantitative results are those tabulated from the tape recordings.

2. Results

This section includes the results of a quantitative analysis of the totals of usage of T and U in the recordings, in addition to a qualitative and interpretative analysis of discussions with speakers, notes from my observations, and the interpretation of the results of a questionnaire.

Let us first examine the results of the recordings, complementing them with qualitative results where available. In addition to noting categorical uses of the forms of address, I performed a quantitative analysis of the uses of T and U in situations in which there was variation. In these cases, I counted only one usage per conversational turn per interlocutor, unless the speaker changed pronoun of address during the same turn with the same interlocutor. For example, if a speaker addressed the same interlocutor for two consecutive minutes using T, without the interlocutor responding or interrupting, it was counted as *one* instance of T. Thus, the results should not be interpreted, for example, as a total of the number of occurrences of the pronoun *tú* and the corresponding second-person verb forms.

2.1. San Juan, Puerto Rico

I spent a day at the offices of a distributor of hardware, plumbing, and small appliances. In addition, I spent one day with a sales representative of the distributor to observe his visits to stores. I recorded 180 minutes in the offices, and 180 minutes with the sales representative. In the offices we note a preference for T, as shown in Table 1:

Table 1. Offices of distributor of hardware, San Juan, Puerto Rico

among themselves and on the telephone			with me		
T	53	89.8%	T	26	41.9%
U	6	10.2%	U	36	58.1%

The employees use T for conversations among themselves and for telephone conversations with clients, including some strangers. The receptionist uses U to answer the telephone, but switches to T during the call even though she may not know the caller. We find a slight preference for U when speaking with me. Some female employees began using U with me but changed to T after a few minutes. For example, the director of the department of accounts payable used U 3 times at first, but after approximately 5 minutes she switched and used T 11 times. As shown in Table 2, the sales representative used U almost exclusively with me, and T almost exclusively with the buyers and owners of hardware stores:

Table 2. Hardware sales representative, San Juan, Puerto Rico

with buyers and owners			with me		
T	79	89.8%	T	3	7.9%
U	9	10.2%	U	35	92.1%

For the employees of this company, we find that the degree of familiarity between individuals determines which form of address a speaker uses.

I spent another day visiting all the departments of a cellular telephone company. I recorded 90 minutes of interactions among employees and with clients in the sales and service department. Table 3 shows the results:

Table 3. Sales dept. of cellular telephone company, San Juan, Puerto Rico

among themselves and with clients			with me		
T	21	87.5%	T	7	58.3%
U	3	12.5%	U	5	41.7%

Quantitative results indicate that there is a preference for T with clients in this department.

I also observed several other departments of the cellular telephone company without recording them. I spent a morning with a customer care operator. She uses U in general with customers calling about problems with their phones. She also uses the affectionate vocatives *mi amor* and *corazón* with U with some women. Some clients used T with her from the beginning, but she continued to use U unless she realized that she knew a caller. If she knows a caller, she switches to T. With co-workers she uses T, and after a few minutes, she began to use T with me also. In the paging division, the operator uses U exclusively because of the anonymity of the callers.

I spent a morning observing sales calls with an executive for corporate accounts. He says that he uses U only with the president of the company, with strangers, and with his father-in-law (whom he also addresses with the respectful *Don* plus first name). He used U with me. He uses T with colleagues and the majority of his clients. With an executive assistant, he used U at first, and later T. I also spent several hours observing an executive for individual accounts, who used T with everyone I observed, including with me. He says that he tries to break through the formality of U in business, although he would not use T with more reserved clients, nor with a bank executive who was not available on the day of our visit.

I spent one day in the offices of a medical supply wholesaler, where I recorded 90 minutes of interactions among employees and by telephone with clients. In Table 4, we see a preference for T, except with me:

Table 4. Medical supply wholesaler, San Juan, Puerto Rico

among themselves and with clients			with me		
T	69	84.1%	T	0	0.0%
U	13	15.9%	U	16	100.0%

The employees use T among themselves, with some supervisors, with clients who are friends, and with some strangers. They use U with other supervisors and with strangers on the telephone. Here we also see a preference for T with more familiar interlocutors. The owner's assistant used U and the affectionate vocative *mi amor* with me on the telephone, although we never met in person. These affectionate vocatives are common in San Juan, and may be used with either T or U.

I also spent a day at a commercial photo developing office, but I did not make recordings there. The office assistant states that she uses T with colleagues and clients of her acquaintance, but that she uses U with older males, whether they are colleagues or supervisors. Her statements are consistent with my observations. Another office assistant, a man of about 60 years, says that he uses U with most people. He used T with me because I am younger, but said that he should use U since I am a professor. In fact, when we later began to discuss my work, he switched to U.

During a day at the office of the National Weather Service, I observed that the receptionist uses U for telephone calls, but T with a colleague. The colleague addresses her with U, but combines it with the affectionate vocative *mija*. The technicians use T among themselves, but addressed me with U.

In a shared taxi from a public stand, all the occupants (a driver in his sixties, an office worker in her thirties, and an elderly woman with a young boy) used T with each other, although it was clear that they were not acquainted. However, they used U with me. They were all dressed casually, while I was wearing a dress with nylon stockings and dress shoes and carrying a briefcase, and had stated my destination as the university.

We can see that in San Juan, T is preferred by many speakers, and that the switch from U to T may occur very rapidly here. T is seldom used with strangers, who would receive U almost exclusively. U is sometimes used to address supervisors or high-level executives, but not exclusively.

2.2 *Summary of results for other cities*

For Santiago, Chile, the quantitative analysis (Uber 1997) indicates that familiarity between individuals is an important factor in the choice of forms of address. Qualitative results also show that solidarity is a factor. The power semantic has not completely disappeared from Santiago business Spanish, although T is used more often to address younger people. The degree of friendship and the age of the speakers appear to be the most important factors. All consultants agree that one would use U with strangers, unless they are much younger, or unless they are friends of friends.

Quantitative analysis (Uber 1997) for Bogotá, Colombia shows variability in forms of address, with a preference for U in some situations (a marble factory, a restaurant, and ceramics and porcelain decorating classes) and a preference for T in others (an employment agency, the cash register at a factory of ceramics and porcelain). Of the five cities studied, Bogotá shows the highest preference for U. Qualitative results for Bogotá are generally consistent with the recorded data, with one exception. Recorded data from a restaurant indicate exclusive U usage among all employees (waiters, cooks, and the owner). However, the qualitative results indicate a considerable amount of T usage by the owner and a younger waiter with each other, with me, and with younger clients and students. Most consultants agree that there is more T usage in Bogotá now than there used to be, especially among young people. My notes also confirm my findings from Uber 1984 and 1985, that U is the most common form of address among family members. Many people use *usted* to indicate their solidarity with family and closest friends. With good friends one may use T or U, or alternate between them, as many of my friends did with me. Those who are younger or more outgoing may use more T, but for many, U is still the more automatic form of address.

Although my quantitative results (Uber 1997) indicate a preference for T at the Caracas, Venezuela real estate agency I visited, U is used with strangers and older people. The head of the sales department uses T with subordinates and members of her department, but is addressed as U by them. In Caracas, it is possible to change from U to T very quickly.

Tape-recorded data (Uber 1997) from four days in the offices and plant of a plastics company near Mexico City, Mexico also show a preference for T among colleagues, while U may be used with supervisors and with strangers. Qualitative data support these findings. Thus, for Mexico City, it appears that T is preferred in business, at least after some degree of familiarity has been established. However, there are still some asymmetrical uses with supervisors.

3. Conclusions

In this paper I have presented the results of a qualitative and quantitative analysis of interactions among employees and with clients in workplaces at a variety of businesses in San Juan, Puerto Rico, with comparisons to results from four other Latin American cities. In most situations, I found a preference for T, with the exception of some companies in Bogotá where U is more prevalent.

The quantitative results from tape recordings indicate that the form of address depends to a great deal on the degree of familiarity among the speakers. Thus we can support the conclusions of Brown and Gilman (1960) and Fairclough (1989), who postulate that solidarity is becoming more important than power in the choice of forms of address as society is becoming more egalitarian, especially among younger people. However, we find some uses of U directed toward the boss or the boss' boss, which indicates that power has not disappeared completely as a semantic determiner of address.

Qualitative results reported here, in agreement with the quantitative results, indicate that power and solidarity are factors in choice of address form. Power may be manifested by differences in age, profession, or perceived position between the speakers involved in a conversational exchange. Solidarity can refer to degree of familiarity or intimacy between speakers.

One universal is that U is always used with strangers. In all tape recordings, speakers use U with people with whom they are not acquainted. Those interviewed also report that they would use U with such people. And this is consistent with my participant observations and notes on usage. Of course, when answering the telephone, until the caller is identified, it must be assumed that it is a stranger. Many receptionists used U on the telephone unless or until they discovered that the caller was an acquaintance. Therefore, it is not true that one can use T with everyone in Puerto Rico.

The form of address used by a speaker does not always affect the form of address received by that speaker. There are cases of asymmetrical usage, in which one person prefers to use T with others, but their interlocutors do not necessarily switch to T. For example, some male speakers began, and continued, to address me as T, even though I addressed males as U while carrying out this research.

Personal style, which cannot be formalized, is also an important factor. More "reserved" people may use and receive more U. For example, of the two account executives of the cellular telephone company, one admits to some U usage, while the other says that he prefers T with most people. However, even the one who prefers T states that he would not use T with "more reserved" clients. My participant observations are consistent with their statements.

Notes

* I would like to thank the Faculty Research Leave Program of The College of Wooster for having granted me an academic year's sabbatical to pursue this research project. In addition, I am grateful to the Henry Luce III Fund for Distinguished Scholarship for a travel grant which enabled me to conduct the fieldwork for this study.

Finally, my deepest gratitude goes to those who so kindly permitted me to visit their places of employment in Latin America to collect data on business Spanish.

1. Previous work on discourse analysis has been conducted in a variety of settings, including formal interviews, conversational interviews (Labov 1972), overheard speech, radio and television broadcasts, teacher-student classroom interactions (Stubbs 1983), legal settings (Conley and O'Barr 1990), and therapeutic settings (Labov and Fanshel 1977). Works of Calvo Ramos (1980), Drew and Heritage, eds. (1993), Firth, ed. (1994), Martín Rojo and Callejo Gallego (1995), and Tannen (1994) have shown the importance of research on language in the workplace. Leeds-Hurwitz (1980); Slobin, Miller, and Porter (1968); and Yamada (1992) have investigated forms of address and discourse in business environments.

Various researchers have studied forms of address, including Bates and Benigni (1975), Braun (1988), Brown and Gilman (1960), Paulston (1984), and Slobin, Miller, and Porter (1968). Some studies of Spanish forms of address are reviewed in my work on *tú* and *usted* in Bogotá (Uber 1984, 1985). More recent work has been carried out by Blas Arroyo (1994) in Spain, Castro-Mitchell (1991) for Honduras, Jaramillo (1990) in New Mexico, Placencia (1997) in Ecuador, Rey (1994) for Colombia, Honduras, and Nicaragua, and Schwenter (1993) on Spain and Mexico.

2. As a participant observer, I used U with my subjects, with the following exceptions: (1) people with whom I had an existing relationship which involved mutual T address; and (2) female subjects who addressed me as T, or switched to T consistently, in which case I would switch to T. If the switch was not consistent, I continued to address them as U. I addressed male subjects as U.

3. I define variation in address as the usage of both T and U by employees of the same department in the same situation, such as speaking with clients, or answering telephone calls. If everyone in a given office used T with everyone else in the office, this was counted as categorical use of one form of address, as were the few conversations where one speaker always used U and the other always used T to address each other in the same situation. Such non-reciprocal usage is uncommon among Puerto Rican speakers.

References

Bates, Elizabeth and Laura Benigni. 1975. Rules of address in Italy: A sociological survey. *Language in Society* 4: 271–288.

Blas Arroyo, José Luis. 1994. De nuevo sobre el poder y la solidaridad: Apuntes para un análisis interaccional de la alternancia *tú/usted. Nueva Revista de Filología Hispánica* 42: 385–414.

Braun, Friederike. 1988. *Terms of address: Problems of patterns and usage in various languages and cultures.* Berlin: Mouton de Gruyter.

Brown, Roger and Albert Gilman. 1960. The pronouns of power and solidarity. In *Style in language*, ed. Thomas A. Sebeok, 253–276. Cambridge, MA: MIT Press.

Calvo Ramos, Luciana. 1980. *Introducción al estudio del lenguaje administrativo.* Madrid: Gredos.

Castro-Mitchell, Amanda. 1991. *Usted* porque no lo conozco o porque lo quiero mucho? The semantic functions of *usted* in Honduran Spanish. Ph.D. dissertation, University of Pittsburgh.

Drew, Paul and John Heritage, eds. 1993. *Talk at work: Interaction in institutional settings.* New York: Cambridge University Press.

Fairclough, Norman. 1989. *Language and power.* London: Longman.

Firth, Alan, ed. 1995. *The discourse of negotiation: Studies of language in the workplace.* Oxford: Pergamon.

Jaramillo, June A. 1990. Domain constraints on the use of *tú* and *usted.* In *Spanish in the United States: Sociolinguistic issues*, ed. John J. Bergen, 14–22. Washington, DC: Georgetown University Press.

Leeds-Hurwitz, Wendy. 1980. The use and analysis of uncommon forms of address: A business example. *Sociolinguistics Working Papers* 80. Austin, TX: Southwest Educational Development Laboratory.

Martín Rojo, Luisa and Javier Callejo Gallego. 1995. Argumentation and inhibition: Sexism in the discourse of Spanish executives. *Pragmatics* 5: 455–484.

Paulston, Christina Bratt. 1984. Pronouns of address in Swedish: Social class semantics and a changing system. In *Language and language use: Readings in sociolinguistics*, ed. John Baugh and Joel Sherzer, 268–291. Englewood Cliffs, NJ: Prentice-Hall.

Placencia, María E. 1997. Address forms in Ecuadorian Spanish. *Hispanic Linguistics* 9: 165–202.

Rey, Alberto. 1994. The usage of *usted* in three societies: Colombia, Honduras, and Nicaragua. *Language Quarterly* 32: 193–204.

Schiffrin, Deborah. 1994. *Approaches to discourse.* Oxford: Blackwell.

Schwenter, Scott A. 1993. Diferenciación dialectal por medio de pronombres: Una comparación del uso de *tú* y *usted* en España y México. *Nueva Revista de Filología Hispánica* 41: 127–149.

Slobin, Dan I., Stephen H. Miller, and Lyman W. Porter. 1968. Forms of address and social relations in a business organization. *Journal of Personality and Social Psychology* 8: 289–293.

Tannen, Deborah. 1994. *Talking from 9 to 5: How women's and men's conversational styles affect who gets heard, who gets credit, and what gets done.* New York: William Morrow.

Uber, Diane Ringer. 1984. The pronouns of address in the Spanish of Bogotá, Colombia. *The SECOL Review* 8: 59–74.

Uber, Diane Ringer. 1985. The dual function of *usted*: Forms of address in Bogotá, Colombia. *Hispania* 68: 388–392.

Uber, Diane Ringer. 1997. The pronouns of address used in business Spanish in five Latin American cities: a quantitative analysis. In *LA CHISPA '97 selected proceedings*, ed. Claire J. Paolini, 383–394. New Orleans, LA: The Eighteenth Louisiana Conference on Hispanic Languages and Literatures, Tulane University.

Wolfson, Nessa. 1976. Speech events and natural speech: Some implications for sociolinguistic methodology. *Language in Society* 5: 189–209.

Yamada, Haru. 1992. *American and Japanese business discourse: A comparison of interactional styles.* Norwood, NJ: Ablex Publishing.

A Hierarchy of Requests in California Spanish: Are Indirectness and Mitigation Polite?

Silvia Arellano
Georgetown University

1. Introduction

Searle (1969, 1979) claims that indirectness and mitigation are associated with the desire to be polite. Under this generalization, indirect requests would be considered more polite than direct ones. Likewise, a request with a mitigating word such as *please* would be considered more polite than a request without mitigation (Brown and Levinson 1978, 1987). However, the expression of politeness varies within and between language communities. For example, in a study with English native speakers and Venezuelan speakers of English, García (1992) found that English native speakers used negative politeness (not imposing, and giving options) when making requests while the non-natives used positive politeness (making the listener feel good). She emphasized the importance of learning the particular politeness strategies of a target culture and language.

Only a limited number of studies have investigated the expression of politeness in Spanish (e.g. Haverkate 1994). The purpose of the present study is to determine whether indirectness and mitigation are associated with politeness in Spanish requests based on the results of a discourse completion task. First, I will develop a hierarchy of requests based on indirectness and mitigation. Then, I will consider the relationship between this hierarchy and politeness based on the request strategies used by a Mexican-American community.

2. Theoretical background

The first part of this section discusses the concept of saving face in research on politeness. The second part will provide the theoretical background for a hierarchy of requests based on the degree of indirectness and the presence or absence of mitigation. Finally, I present my hypotheses for the study.

2.1. Authority and level of imposition

Lakoff (1973), a pioneer in the research of politeness, gives two essential rules for pragmatic competence: be clear and be polite. But why do people care about being polite when they make requests? Polite behavior is based on an imaginary contract between speaker and listener which specifies the rights and obligations of the participants in a conversation (Haverkate 1994). These conversational rules specify what kind of information is allowed to pass between two particular individuals. For example, a psychologist may ask very personal questions, while a teacher may only ask those questions that evaluate academic knowledge. Similar to requests for information, requests for favors will vary from situation to situation. In either case, the function of politeness is to keep social contacts free of conflict (Fraser and Nolen 1981).

Requests can cause conflict if the hearer interprets the request as a violation of his or her freedom of action. Brown and Levinson (1978) claim that each person has a negative face, which is defined as the desire to not have other people impede one's actions. Speakers usually protect their hearer's negative face because it is in their own interest to avoid conflict. This idea of face was adopted from the English folk phrase 'to lose face,' which means to be humiliated or embarrassed (Goffman 1967). The concept of face is abstract and is used in a metaphorical way to describe the individuality of a person in society. Two aspects of a man's (or a woman's) face are his positive and his negative face. In general, indirectness and mitigation are used in requests to protect face.

The degree to which a speaker protects face may be influenced by various factors. One of those factors is the authority relationship between the speaker and the hearer. Haverkate (1979: 70) breaks down authority relationships into three types: (1) the speaker has power over the hearer; (2) no power relation holds between the speaker and the hearer; or (3) the hearer has power over the speaker. In the present study, I examine how authority relationships affect the participants' choices of request strategies. My prediction is that a speaker will be more polite when addressing an authority. If indirectness is associated with politeness, it follows that speakers will choose indirect requests over direct ones when addressing an authority. When the speaker is the authority, the use of direct requests should be more likely.

Speakers will also try to protect face when they think their request will require effort or sacrifice from their hearer. Brown and Levinson (1978) point out that in American culture, asking for some spare change is different from asking for a large sum of money. The second request is a greater imposition on the hearer and would therefore be a greater threat to his negative face. Since this imposition on the hearer may be a source of conflict, the speaker would be more likely to signal respect for the hearer's freedom of action. Therefore, I predict that speakers will choose higher degrees of politeness, which may include the use of indirect structure and mitigation, when they make a request that would be a great imposition on the hearer.

2.2. Indirectness and mitigation

The locutionary meaning of an indirect request does not match its illocutionary meaning. For example, the question *Can you give me a glass of water?* is, on the surface, a question about a person's ability to perform a task. However, it functions as a request. A person may choose to ask a question rather than making a more direct statement, such as *I want a glass of water* or *Give me a glass of water*, because direct speech is perceived as forceful. The question has the same propositional meaning without the same perlocutionary force. "Politeness is the most prominent motivation for indirectness in requests, and certain forms naturally tend to become the conventionally polite ways for making indirect requests," according to Searle (1979: 49). Indirect requests allow the speaker to ask for what he or she wants from the listener in a way that gives the listener the option of ignoring the request without conflict (Goody 1978).

Indirectness can appear in both conventional and non-conventional (such as a hint) forms (Brown and Levinson 1979). Conventionally indirect speech acts can be interpreted on the basis of their functional meaning alone. For example, we know that the question *Can you give me a glass of water?* is intended as a request because English speakers commonly use questions that function as requests. In a study comparing the ratings of English and Hebrew speakers on a scale of indirectness and on a scale of politeness, Blum-Kulka (1987) found that politeness and indirectness were not always associated. Her findings revealed that hints were considered the most indirect by both English and Hebrew speakers. However, they were not the most polite. Conventional indirectness (questions) was rated as the most polite followed by hints by English native speakers. Hebrew native speakers rated hints a bit lower on the politeness scale. That means that English native speakers consider hints polite, but not as polite as conventional indirectness.

Mitigating words may be attached to a request in order to decrease its perlocutionary force. A request can be fully expressed by a head act such as an imperative, question, or hint (Blum-Kulka 1989). Adding mitigation to this basic structure minimizes any negative reaction that the hearer may have towards the request. For this reason, it entails politeness (Fraser 1980). In English, the disclaimer *please* tends to have a mitigating effect. Other examples include tag questions such as *will you*? Similarly to *will you*, some speakers of Spanish use *sí* 'yes' in front of a request as a mitigating word (see Appendix, #2d). Alternatively, some speakers use the negative *no* as a mitigating word (see Appendix, #1e). This would be similar to English *won't you*.

Leech (1983) described negation as a mitigation strategy in Spanish. However, the use of *no* as a mitigating word was not found to have mitigating effects in a study conducted by Koike (1994). Her participants had to answer an oral questionnaire limited to one request in which the speaker had to ask the hearer to get up from a chair. Contrary to her findings, my observations lead me to believe that *no* is a word with mitigating effects in the target community because it is often used in requests that seem polite. Koike's participants and the participants of the present study belong to different social classes and places of origin. It is possible that factors like class or place of origin reflect variation with the use of *no* and other politeness markers. I chose to include negation as a mitigating word, and to allow the participants to decide whether it is a strategy they use.

Another mitigating device is the choice of verb tense. Searle (1969) claims that English questions are more polite when they use the auxiliaries *could* and *would* than when they use the auxiliaries *can* and *will*. *Could* and *would* are the past tense of *can* and *will*, but they also carry a present conditional meaning. Both *can* and *will* can be translated by the Spanish *poder* 'to be able to.' *Poder* is conjugated as *podría* 'could you' in the conditional mood and *puede* 'can you' in the imperative mood.

I developed a hierarchy of six request structures for this project. The structures listed in the hierarchy go from most direct to most indirect (see Table 1). I considered the imperative more direct than questions or hints. Then, I combined imperatives and questions with mitigating words. It did not seem appropriate to combine hints with a mitigation (consider *I am thirsty, please).* I placed the structures with mitigation lower in the hierarchy than the same structures without mitigation. I put questions with the verb in the conditional tense after questions in the indicative tense mode with a disclaimer. Finally, I placed hints, the least direct structure for requests, last in the hierarchy.

Table 1. Hierarchy of requests

<table>
<tr><th colspan="2">Syntactic Structure</th><th>Example</th><th rowspan="7">↓</th></tr>
<tr><td colspan="2">1a. IMPERATIVES</td><td>Give me a glass of water!</td></tr>
<tr><td colspan="2">1b. IMPERATIVES + DISCLAIMER</td><td>Please give me a glass of water.</td></tr>
<tr><td rowspan="3">QUESTIONS</td><td>2a. Indicative</td><td>Can you give me a glass of water?</td></tr>
<tr><td>2b. Indicative + Disclaimer</td><td>Can you please give me a glass of water?</td></tr>
<tr><td>2c. Conditional</td><td>Would you give me a glass of water?</td></tr>
<tr><td colspan="2">3. STATEMENTS (HINTS)</td><td>Oh, I am thirsty.</td></tr>
</table>

In terms of indirectness, a structure with mitigation and without it is equal. To capture this, I have divided the hierarchy in three parts: imperatives (1), questions (2), and hints (3). The imperatives in (1a) and (1b) are more direct than the questions in (2), and the questions are more direct than the hint (3). Within each section, the structures with mitigation were placed below the same structure without mitigation.

2.3. Hypotheses

This study looks at the following research questions:

1. What kind of syntactic structures do people choose when making a request?
2. Does authority affect the level of directness and use of mitigation?
3. Does the type of request affect the level of directness and use of mitigation?
4. Does the gender of the speaker make a difference in the type of structure chosen and use of mitigation?

I expect that participants' choice of a certain type of request will reveal whether they associate indirectness and mitigation with politeness. If one assumes that speakers will select the structures that they consider more polite when addressing an authority or when the request requires higher degrees of imposition on the hearer, the choice of indirectness and/or mitigation for such requests could reflect the politeness strategies of the target community. The independent variables are the authority relationship between the speaker and hearer, and the level of imposition required by the request. If indirectness is associated with politeness, then speakers will be expected to be more indirect when addressing an authority or when the request poses a greater level of imposition. Furthermore, I will control for gender as a separate independent variable that may or may not affect the results.

Not enough empirical studies have dealt with the distribution of syntactic structures in requests and their possible association with authority and the level of imposition. Furthermore, I only found one study on Spanish requests that controlled for gender (García 1993). For these reasons, null hypotheses based on the research questions have been adopted for this study. A note on Hypothesis 1: If the structures were chosen randomly, each structure would have an equal chance of being selected, and therefore the syntactic structures would be equally distributed across the requests.

Hypotheses:

1. There is equal distribution of syntactic structures among requests.
2. Authority does not make a difference in the choice of directness and use of mitigation.
3. Level of imposition does not make a difference in the choice of directness and use of mitigation.
4. There is no difference between males and females in their choice of directness and use of mitigation.

3. Methodology

3.1. Subjects

A questionnaire was distributed to 100 Mexican-American subjects from two farm worker communities in the Central Valley of California. I have lived in the Central Valley for many years and I am very familiar with the linguistic communities in this area. I chose these communities because they are relatively homogeneous, both linguistically and socially. Most of the people in the communities are Mexican-Americans who work in farms, usually picking and packing table grapes. Many adults in this community do not speak English. Business is conducted in Spanish; most local shops employ at least one Spanish speaker. The children attend school and are placed in mainstream or ESL classes.

The subjects were 50 men and 50 women of low socioeconomic status, most of whom were farm workers. The subjects were Spanish monolinguals and Spanish/English bilinguals. Many of the subjects either immigrated to the United States within the last ten years or still travel to Mexico for a small portion of the year. Consequently, the level of contact with Mexican Spanish is very high.

The distribution of subjects by age is as follows:

Table 2. Breakdown of subjects by age

	Women	Men
Teens	14	14
20s	20	18
30s	14	9
Over 40	6	9

The subjects were selected based on convenience. We looked for places where people would be able to take the time to fill out a long questionnaire. Farm workers and other people work during the day and get home by the afternoon. The researchers walked through the streets of the communities in the late afternoon and knocked at about three houses per street. Usually two people per household were asked to fill out the questionnaire. Other sources of subjects were the park and the local clinic. The park was chosen because many men rest there after work. The local clinic was chosen because people, usually women taking children to the doctor, often have to wait long hours for the doctor and therefore have the time to fill out the questionnaire.

3.2. The questionnaire

The questionnaire was a discourse completion task (DCT) with a multiple-choice format. It asked for demographic information about the participant including age, languages spoken at home and outside of home, education in

Mexico and in the U.S., marital status, and occupation. The demographic questions were followed by 18 DCT scenarios which varied in level of authority and of imposition. The scenarios included the three levels of authority relationships described by Haverkate (1979). They were coded as A1, A2, and A3. In A1 the speaker is the authority; in A2 the hearer and speaker are equals, and in A3 the hearer is the authority. We chose examples of each authority relationship based on participant observation and interaction with the community. A teacher was considered an authority because as a whole, this community has great respect for teachers. Spouses, similar age siblings, and friends were considered equals (see Appendix, #3–4). The speaker was assumed to have authority over sons and daughters, younger brothers and sisters, and servants (see Appendix, #2).

We defined a request as a speech act intended to get the hearer to do something or to ask for an object from the hearer. Using this definition, we chose examples of requests with three levels of imposition. R1, the lowest level of imposition, included requests that did not require a sacrifice from the hearer, such as giving a glass of water. The requests in R2 involved medium levels of imposition (see Appendix, #3). This is considered an R2 request because the speaker is requesting something of value to him, but the imposition is not great because the hearer has no need for the object. The requests in the highest level, R3, required a greater degree of imposition and could therefore threaten the hearer's negative face. An example of R3 was a request to borrow the hearer's brand-new car.

Each scenario combined an authority type with a request type, yielding nine different combinations. The questionnaire included two examples of each combination. Subjects were given a scenario in written form and then asked to select the answer that best described how they would make a request in that situation. The following is an example of an A3/R1 situation:

> You are at the unemployment office and have a dry throat due to a cold you are about to catch. The lady serving you has a gallon of water. How would you ask her for a glass?

The subjects were expected to select one of six possible responses in a written questionnaire. Each choices represented one of the structures in the hierarchy. The order of the structures was randomized. There was also a blank line where subjects could write any comments or alternative answers.

3.3. Procedures

A language informant from the community accompanied the researcher and served as a research assistant. We asked the subjects if they would participate in a survey. We told the subjects that the survey was for academic use only and that their identities would be kept anonymous, so they could answer as honestly as possible. We gave them a pencil and the survey on a clipboard. We encouraged them to answer all questions and gave them enough time to do so. The data was collected over a period of two weeks.

The surveys were then individually coded. The structures in the hierarchy were ranked from direct to indirect. The most direct structure, the imperative, was given the value of 1, and the most indirect, the hint, was given the value of 6. The coding system is shown in Table 3. The information was entered into the statistical program SPSS. The data was analyzed by using the General Linear Model statistical approach for overall results. Then, paired T test were used on pairs of variables to find significant differences.

Table 3. Hierarchy of requests

Syntactic Structure		**Example**	
IMPERATIVES		*Give me a glass of water!*	1
IMPERATIVES + DISCLAIMER		*Please give me a glass of water.*	2
QUESTIONS	Indicative	*Can you give me a glass of water?*	3
	Indicative + Disclaimer	*Can you please give me a glass of water?*	4
	Conditional	*Would you give me a glass of water?*	5
STATEMENTS		*Oh, I am thirsty.*	6

4. Results

The main goal of this study was to discover the kind of syntactic structures that were selected by Mexican-Americans. The data was analyzed first with a General Linear Model test in order to gather overall results that would prove or disprove the four hypotheses (see Table 4). Hypothesis 1 predicted equal distribution among the syntactic structures based on subjects' choices. The results showed that there is unequal distribution among the six structures that form the hierarchy for this study, suggesting that Hypothesis 1 should be rejected. The unequal distribution of the structures indicates that there must be other factors affecting the participants' choice. Hypothesis 2 and 3 predicted that authority and the level of imposition were factors that had no effect on choice of request. In fact, our analysis shows that both authority and the level of imposition did play a role on the type of request chosen. Therefore, Hypotheses 2 and 3 were also rejected. Finally, Hypothesis 4 failed to be rejected because the speaker's gender did not seem to play a role in the type of request selected.

Table 4. Overall results

1. There is equal distribution of syntactic structures.
   F (5, 95) =56.52, p< .05 — Hypothesis rejected
2. Authority does not make a difference in the choices of directness and use of mitigation.
   F (2, 98) =11.85, p< .05 — Hypothesis rejected
3. The level of imposition does not make a difference in the choice of directness and use of mitigation.
   F (2, 98) =22.43, p< .05 — Hypothesis rejected
4. There is no difference between males and females in their choices of directness and use of mitigation.
   See Table 8 — Hypothesis not rejected

Subjects did favor certain syntactic structures over others. The General Linear Model tests showed significant differences among the variables within the hierarchy. The first tests show that the choice of syntactic structure was a significant variable (Table 5). Paired T tests show a significant difference between a given structure and the same structure with mitigating words. Structures with mitigating words were selected significantly more often than similar structures without mitigation.

Table 5. Syntactic structures distribution

Overall significance:	F(5,95) =56.52, p< .05	Hypothesis rejected
Paired T Tests:		
Imperative Imperative + D	t(99) = –10.0, p<0.01	
Indicative Q Indicative Q + D	t(99) = –6.5, p<0.01	
Indicative Q Conditional Q	t(99) = –5.6, p<0.01	

Authority also turned out to be a significant factor in the choice of syntactic structures. The General Model test showed overall significance of authority. The paired T test revealed that there was significant difference between choices when the hearer was the authority (Table 6). The structures chosen were considered more indirect and had words with mitigating effects.

Table 6. Three levels of authority

Overall significance:	F(2,98) =11.85, p< .05	Hypothesis rejected
Paired T Tests:		
Speaker = authority Hearer = authority	t(99) = –4.0, p<0.01	
Authority equals Hearer = authority	t(99) = –4.4, p<0.01	

The level of imposition also proved to be a significant factor in the choice of request. Subjects were more direct with low levels of imposition. Table 7 shows the results of a paired T test where there is significant difference between low and medium levels of imposition and between low and high levels of imposition.

Table 7. Three levels of imposition (type of request)

Overall significance:	F(2,98) =22.43, p< .05	Hypothesis rejected
Paired T tests:		
Low level of imposition Medium level of imposition	t(99) = –5.9, p<0.01	
Low level of imposition High level of imposition	t(99) = –5.1, p<0.01	

There was no significant difference between men and women. This supports García's (1993) findings, for she found no significant difference between Peruvian men and women. The choices of men and women were only slightly different. For example, women chose more conditional questions than men. The following table shows the mean distribution of the structures:

Table 8. Mean occurrences of syntactic structures (all 18 questions)

	Imperative +D	Indicative Q+D	Conditional Q	Hint	Indicative Q	Imperative
Total:	4.45	3.99	3.88	2.48	2.12	1.08
(n=100)	(24.7%)	(22.2%)	(21.6%)	(13.8%)	(11.8%)	(6.0%)
Males:	4.66	4.10	3.58	2.74	1.88	1.04
Females:	4.24	3.88	4.18	2.22	2.36	1.12

5. Discussion

The hierarchy for this study was based on the degree of indirectness and the use of mitigation (Table 1). The hierarchy of requests proposed in this study does not match the order given by the participants as based on the frequency of each structure. The order given by the participants places the imperative with *por favor* as the most common structure and the bare imperative as the least frequent one. A careful analysis of the order of frequencies chosen will suggest that although indirectness plays a role on the frequency of the structure, it is obscured by the use of mitigation on any structure (Table 8).

I believe that the mean occurrences on Table 8 can reveal some interesting information. First, there is unequal distribution of syntactic structures across categories (Tables 5 and 8). Those structures without mitigation include imperatives, questions, and hints (structures 1a, 2a, and 3 in Table 1). Of those three structures, hints had the most occurrences, followed by questions and lastly imperatives. Notice that they go from most indirect to most direct. So, it seems that without mitigation, participants do base the frequency of their choices on the level of indirectness.

When mitigation is introduced into the structures, the distribution changes significantly. Indirectness no longer plays an important role; rather, mitigation overpowers indirectness in every structure. The most frequent structures were imperatives with *por favor*, questions with *sí* and *no,* and conditional sentences, all of which include mitigation (structures 1b, 2b, and 2c in Table 1). As shown in Table 8, every structure with mitigation has a greater frequency of occurrence than any structure without mitigation regardless of the level of indirectness. This indicates that even if indirectness is associated with authority and level of imposition, this relationship is obscured by the use of mitigation in structures. The frequencies make it clear that this Mexican-American community uses mitigation as their primary request strategy across scenarios.

The question remains whether higher frequencies are indicative of an association between authority and imposition with indirectness and mitigation. The results of the T-tests (Tables 6 and 7) suggest a significant relationship between the choice of structure and both authority and level of imposition. Participants selected structures with mitigation and/or indirectness in situations when the hearer was the authority, or when there were medium to high levels of imposition.

The association of authority and imposition with indirectness and mitigation is not indicative of their relationship with politeness. In the case of bare imperatives, questions, and hints, we do not know if participants chose hints more often because they consider them more polite. However, as postulated by Haverkate (1979) and Brown and Levinson (1978), speakers tend to be more polite when speaking to an authority and when the request requires higher levels of imposition, suggesting that the association between indirectness and politeness is possible. Similarly, the frequency of mitigation is only indicative of the fact that it is associated with authority and imposition. Its association with politeness is not clear from the results of this study. However, the use of mitigation as a politeness tool is supported in the literature (Fraser 1980, Koike 1994, Leech 1983, Searle 1969), suggesting a possible relationship between the results of the present study and politeness.

6. Conclusion

This Mexican-American community uses mitigation as their primary request strategy across scenarios. For example, the imperative was the least selected structure (6%), but the imperative with mitigation was the most frequent structure. This structure is both clear and polite, thus supporting Lakoff's (1973) rules of pragmatic competence. Questions with mitigation were also selected significantly more frequently than questions with no mitigation. It was concluded earlier that both authority and level of imposition are associated with indirectness and mitigation. It seems reasonable to assume that participants would choose structures that they considered more polite when addressing an authority and with higher levels of imposition.

7. Further research

This study concluded that mitigation had an impact on the structure chosen. Imperatives had the word *por favor*, questions had *sí* and *no* as mitigating words; a second question type had the conditional verb tense. The order of frequency of the above structures can be indicative of a possible impact of the type of mitigation selected in the respondents' choices. In other words, *por favor* was the most frequent followed by *sí* and *no* and the conditional. It is possible that these forms of mitigation have various levels of impact on authority and imposition. This cannot be concluded from this study.

Also, with a written questionnaire, it was only possible for us to find out what responses the speakers perceived as appropriate. People's perceptions of how they express themselves do not always match what they actually say, so we do not know what they would actually say. Another limitation is that a written questionnaire cannot capture other aspects of communication, such as intonation and body language. For example, an imperative could sound very friendly if spoken in the appropriate tone of voice. In further research, real interactions could be audiotaped or videotaped.

Since the association between politeness and indirectness has been challenged, it would be useful to ask speakers to rate the politeness of the structures as Blum-Kulka (1985) did.

A replication of this study with other communities would provide more information on the role that indirectness and mitigation have in politeness in the Mexican community and in other communities. Words with mitigating effects especially require further research that is targeted to specific communities.

Notes

* This study was funded by the Sally Casanova Pre-Doctoral Program. I would like to thank Dr. Juergen Kempff from the Spanish Department of the University of California, Irvine for his guidance during the design and data collection stages. I also thank Dr. Cathy Doughty and Dr. Ru San Chen for their valuable feedback on earlier stages of this project; however, I am responsible for any errors and omissions.
Correspondence concerning this article should be sent to arrellans@georgetown.edu

Appendix

1. Está en la oficina de desempleo y tiene la garganta seca por una gripa que quiere darle. La señora atendiéndolo tiene un garrafón de agua. ¿Cómo le pediría un vaso?
a) ¡Deme un vaso de agua!
b) Ah, cómo tengo sed.
c) ¿Me da un vaso de agua?
d) Deme un vaso de agua, por favor.
e) ¿Sí me da un vaso de agua?
f) ¿Podría darme un vaso de agua?

2. El muchacho que le ayuda piensa ir a ver a su mamá este fin de semana y usted lo necesita para terminar de pintar la casa. ¿Cómo le pediría que no se fuera de su casa?
a) ¿Por qué no te quedas este fin de semana?
b) Quédate este fin de semana, por favor.
c) ¿Te quedarías este fin de semana?
d) ¿No te quedas este fin de semana?
e) No hemos terminado de pintar.
f) Quédate este fin de semana.

3. Su amigo tiene una computadora usada que no quiere y piensa dársela a un sobrinito. Usted quiere la computadora. ¿Qué le diría?
a) ¿No me das la computadora a mí?
b) Te diré que yo necesito mucho una computadora.
c) ¿Me darías la computadora a mí?
d) Dame la computadora a mí.
e) Dame la computadora a mí, por favor.
f) ¿Me das la computadora?

4. Acaba de legar de trabajar con hambre y cansado y su esposa ya está en casa. Ella ya cocinó y usted quiere pedirle que le sirva la comida. ¿Cómo le diría?
a) ¡Sírveme de comer!
b) Sírveme de comer, por favor.
c) Ya me voy a sentar en la mesa.
d) ¿Podrías servirme de comer?
e) ¿No me sirves de comer?
f) ¿Me sirves de comer?

References

Blum-Kulka, Shoshana. 1987. Indirectness and politeness in requests: Same or different? *Journal of Pragmatics* 11: 131–146.

Blum-Kulka, Shoshana, Juliane House, and Gabriele Kasper. 1989. *Cross-cultural pragmatics: Requests and apologies.* NY: Ablex Publishing.

Brown, Penelope and Steven Levinson. 1978. Universals in language usage: Politeness phenomena. In *Questions and politeness: Strategies in social interaction*, ed. Esther N. Goody, 56–289. Cambridge: Cambridge University Press.

Brown, Penelope and Steven Levinson. 1987. *Politeness: Some universals in language usage.* Cambridge: Cambridge University Press.

Fraser, Bruce. 1980. Conversational mitigation. *Journal of Pragmatics* 4: 341–350.

Fraser, Bruce. 1990. Perspectives on politeness. *Journal of Pragmatics* 14: 219–236.

Fraser, Bruce and William Nolen. 1981. The association of deference with linguistic form. *International Journal of the Sociology of Language* 27: 93–109.

García, Carmen. 1992. Responses to a request by native and non-native English speakers: Deference vs. camaraderie. *Multilingua* 11: 387–406.

García, Carmen. 1993. Making a request and responding to it: A case study of Peruvian Spanish speakers. *Journal of Pragmatics* 19: 127–152.

Goffman, Erving. 1967. *Interaction ritual: Essays on face-to-face behavior*. New York: Anchor Books.

Goody, Esther. N. 1978. *Questions and politeness: Question in social interaction.* Cambridge: Cambridge.

Haverkate, Henk. 1979. *Impositive sentences in Spanish: Theory and description in linguistic pragmatics.* New York: North-Holland.

Haverkate, Henk. 1984. *Speech acts, speakers, and hearers: Reference and referential strategies in Spanish.* Amsterdam: John Benjamins.

Haverkate, Henk. 1994. *La cortesía verbal: Estudio pragmalingüístico.* Madrid: Editorial Gredos

Koike, D. A. 1994. Negation in Spanish and English suggestions and requests: Mitigating effects? *Journal of Pragmatics* 21: 513–526.

Lakoff, Robin T. 1993. Review of 'Aspects of Japanese women's language' by Sachiko Ide and Naomi Hanaoka McGloin. *Multilingua* 12: 95–99.

Leech, Geoffrey. 1983. *Principles of pragmatics.* London: Longman.

Searle, John R. 1969. *Speech acts.* Cambridge: Cambridge University Press.

Searle, John R. 1975. Indirect speech acts. In *Syntax and semantics, Vol. 3: Speech acts*, ed. Peter Cole and Jerry L. Morgan, 59–82. New York: Academic Press.

Weizman, Elda. 1993. Interlanguage requestive hints. In *Interlanguage pragmatics*, ed. Gabriele Kasper and Shoshana Blum-Kulka, 123–137. New York: Oxford University Press.

The Multiple Vibrant Liquid in U.S. Spanish

Robert M. Hammond
Purdue University

1. Introduction

The purpose of this study is to compare the actual phonetic realizations of [r̃], a voiced alveolar multiple vibrant, in U.S. Spanish with the requirements of the prescriptive norm. When teaching Spanish dialectology, it seemed that I was always having to apologize to students for the fact that Spanish speakers simply did not produce the phone [r̃] like they were supposed to according to the norms of the Real Academia Española (1992). After listening to a corpus of more than 500 Spanish-speaking subjects recording the reading passage used in this study, I had the general impression that almost none of the subjects produced the phone [r̃]. Under normal conditions, one would expect to find differences between linguistic reality and normative standards. However, in the case of the Spanish segment [r̃], such differences are so great as to be astounding.

A satisfactory account of the role of the voiced alveolar multiple vibrant has long been elusive in Spanish phonology from both theoretical and acquisitional perspectives. In traditional theoretical accounts of Spanish phonology (Navarro Tomás 1977, Stockwell and Bowen 1965, and Dalbor 1969, 1980 among numerous others), [r̃] was accorded phonemic status. This analysis made the rather unsatisfactory claim that the phonemic inventory of Spanish contained two non-lateral liquid phonemes, /r/ and /r̃/, in spite of the fact that these two purported phonemes contrast only in intervocalic environments, e.g., *pero* /pero/ 'but' vs. *perro* /per̃o/ 'dog.' In more recent accounts, Spanish phonologists (Saporta and Contreras 1962, Harris 1983, and Núñez Cedeño 1989 among many others) have generally adopted a more theoretically relevant analysis of non-lateral liquids in Spanish which claims that the Spanish phonological inventory contains only one non-lateral liquid phoneme, /r/, a voiced alveolar flap, and that all surface-level occurrences of [r̃] are derived from the phoneme /r/ by the application of phonological rules. Following this analysis, the lexemes *pero* and *perro* would be represented phonologically as /pero/ and /perro/.

The segment [r̃] presents the learner with highly significant difficulties. In L1 acquisition, children acquiring Spanish have notable difficulties acquiring the prescribed phone [r̃]. Indeed, the present study will make it clear that most never do. Such acquisitional difficulty is readily explained: [r̃] is a highly marked segment, and phonetically, the articulation of [r̃] requires considerable speaker effort, as it involves both extreme muscular tension and the expellation of a large quantity of air at a high expiratory speed across and around the apex of the tongue. While all Romance languages inherited a geminate /rr/ from Vulgar Latin varieties, the segment is so difficult that no other major Romance language has maintained /r̃/ in its phonemic inventory. Spanish-speaking children need so much reinforcement to acquire the phone that they are taught to memorize and recite stretches of discourse which contain numerous occurrences of [r̃] (e.g., *Erre con erre cigarro, erre con erre barril . . .*).

In learning Spanish as a second language, the acquisition of [r̃] is even more difficult. Americans studying Spanish are highly unsuccessful in their attempts to acquire [r̃]. Considering that many native Spanish speakers are unsuccessful at acquiring [r̃], it should not be surprising to discover that Americans studying Spanish as a second language also have a very low rate of [r̃]-acquisition. Even L2 Spanish teachers rarely utilize this sound in their everyday speech in spite of what the classroom text dictates.

This study presents a survey of the available data on the occurrence of [r̃] in American Spanish dialects. It then presents an analysis of auditory data from both American and Iberian Spanish speakers. It concludes that the difficulty experienced in theoretical accounts of [r̃] can be readily explained by the following claim:

- In normal Spanish discourse, the segment [r̃] simply does not occur in the speech of the vast majority of native Spanish speakers.

The study finds that the phone [r̃] occurs systematically in normal Spanish discourse among only a very small number of native speakers. Among all other native speakers, [r̃] occurs only in highly affected discourse.

2. The segment [r̃] in Spanish dialectology

A detailed survey of published studies dealing with the different dialects of the Spanish language reveals a rather strange split between analyses of the Spanish spoken on the Iberian Peninsula and analyses of American Spanish. Studies of different American Spanish speech areas easily number in the hundreds, and probably in the thousands. These analyses consider both horizontal and vertical variables. Some cover entire countries, while others focus on particular regions of each country, including both urban and rural areas. For the small island of Puerto Rico alone, which measures approximately 100 miles long and 35 miles wide, there are more than 100 published dialect studies.

The current status within Peninsular Spanish dialectology, however, is quite different, and an overall analysis of dialect studies on the Iberian Peninsula reveals at least four shortcomings:

- Overall, there are relatively few published studies which describe the different Peninsular Spanish dialects.
- Most dialect studies on Peninsular Spanish analyze the speech of Andalucía and largely ignore other important dialect zones.
- The vast majority of non-Andalusian Peninsular Spanish dialect studies have been done on the speech of rural peasants and very few deal with urban areas.
- Almost all non-Andalusian dialect descriptions done on Peninsular Spanish tend to be either highly prescriptive in nature or highly apologetic when encountering linguistic phenomena, such as *yeísmo*, which run counter to the well-established Real Academia Española (1992) norms.

2.1. The segment [r̃] in Peninsular Spanish dialectology

The impression given by the available published literature on Peninsular Spanish dialects is that in their pronunciation these dialects generally coincide with the linguistic norms established by the Real Academia Española (1924, 1979, 1992). The reader is led to believe, among other things, *lleísmo* predominates, that post-nuclear consonants are rigidly maintained in their standard, prescribed form, and that /rr/ is pronounced as [r̃]. While studies on the Spanish of Andalucía and the Canary Islands suggest that *yeísmo* and final consonant weakening are the norm, most studies still suggest that the prescribed [r̃] is also the norm in these areas. However, recent personal experience in northern and central Spain along with relatively recent publications on Peninsular Spanish (see, for example, Calero Fernández 1993 and Molina Martos 1991) suggest that the Spanish on the Iberian Peninsula is considerably different than earlier studies have suggested and that Peninsular Spanish pronunciation is far from being the linguistic model suggested by the norms of the Real Academia Española.

2.2. The segment [r̃] in American Spanish dialectology

A general survey of where the voiced alveolar multiple vibrant occurs in American Spanish was carried out by consulting three of the most complete recent analyses of American Spanish dialectology: Canfield 1981, Cotton and Sharp 1988, and Lipski 1994. For various reasons, however, none of these texts is a completely reliable source for American Spanish dialects.

Some of the material in Canfield is dated. The book itself is very short – a total of 62 pages to describe the Spanish of 19 Latin American countries. Some countries receive less than one page of coverage, and some of the facts presented are, at least today, wrong. For example, in the extreme southeast of the Dominican Republic, /r̃/ is not usually [R̥] (Canfield 1981: 45–47); and the /r̃/ in Southwest Puerto Rico, unlike the rest of the island, is not always [r̃] (Canfield 1981: 77–78). The observations made by Canfield himself are remarkably accurate, but the information he gleaned from secondary sources is sometimes of dubious value.

The weakest of these three sources is Cotton and Sharp 1988. This text uses secondary sources almost exclusively and many of these are, once again, of questionable value. For example, Cotton and Sharp repeat the well-worn notion that in the Caribbean, open vowel phonemes /ɛ, ɔ/ and the more velar /ɑ/ appear before deleted /s/, in spite of the clear evidence that such a phonemicization does not occur in Cuba (Hammond 1978) or in Puerto Rico (Alemán 1977 and Figueroa 1997). They often combine Latin American countries into areas, e.g., the Andean countries, that cloud the distinctions they are attempting to make. Their exposition is at times internally contradictory. Likewise, many of the characteristics that Cotton and Sharp (1988: 192) present as characteristic of one country or region are found throughout Latin America. For example, *¿Qué horas son?* is not unique to Colombia and Ecuador. It is the standard way of asking the time of day in many areas of Mexico, and it appears in many other dialect areas.

Lipski 1994 is much more complete, accurate, and current. However, this text is not without its problems. Lipski often obscures whether the data he is reporting are his own or from other sources. Also, as can be expected in a volume filled with so much data, some of the information Lipski gleaned from secondary sources is either inaccurate or wrong: for example, the repeated claims of the former presence of *voseo* in Cuba (Lipski 1994: 233); the description of Cuban *(arroz) congrí* as a 'dish made of black beans and rice cooked together' (Lipski 1994: 234), true of most of Cuba, but not of Oriente; the presentation of lists of lexical items as general or typical of one dialect or another, e.g., *matrimonio* as 'dish of red beans and rice' as a lexical item characteristic of Puerto Rican Spanish (Lipski 1994: 336), etc. Finally, Lipski at times presents muddled descriptions which are sometimes self-contradictory or wrong, e.g., "Although Puerto Ricans sometimes joke that *Ramón* 'Raymond' and *jamón* 'ham' become homophones, this rarely occurs" (Lipski 1994: 333). Clearly, these two lexical items are never homophones in Puerto Rican Spanish. The lexeme *Ramón* is pronounced with either a voiceless velar fricative, a voiced or voiceless uvular liquid, or the standard Spanish [r̃], while the initial consonant of *jamón* can only be a voiceless glottal spirant /h/ in Puerto Rico. The description of the phonology and morphology of *fronterizo* Uruguayan Spanish is particularly problematic. For example, Lipski suggests that the Spanish Uruguayan border palatalization of /t/ and /d/ before high front vocoids is due to contact with the Brazilian border area, even though this type of coronal stop palatalization does not occur in Southern Brazilian Portuguese (the Paulista dialect) and is generally limited to areas from Rio de Janeiro northward.

These three sources have divided the 17 Spanish-speaking Latin American countries into a total of 41 dialect areas. They provide specific data concerning the pronunciation of /rr/ a total of 72 times.

Out of 72 reports of how /rr/ is articulated in these 41 dialect areas, the standard Spanish [r̃] is reported only 32 times, or 44.4% of the time. Some other pronunciation is used 55.6% of the time. Since the Real Academia Española (1924, 1979, 1992) and the Spanish textbooks used by both native and second-language learners declare that /rr/ in Spanish is to be pronounced as [r̃], this non-compliance rate of 55.6% is rather astounding. However, as the present study will indicate, [r̃] actually occurs far less frequently than 44.4% of the time in normal Spanish discourse.

Table 1 shows only those Spanish-speaking areas where /rr/ is reported to be pronounced as a voiced alveolar multiple vibrant. The sources sometimes disagree over how /rr/ is pronounced in a specific country or region. For example, Lipski (1994: 308) reports a [r̃] of /rr/ for Paraguay, while Canfield (1981: 24, 71) claims an assibilated [r̃] articulation. If the sources disagree about the pronunciation of /rr/ for a particular region, it is not included in Table 1. However, the sources do not all focus on the same regions. Canfield claims that /rr/ is pronounced as the prescriptive [r̃] in Southwest Puerto Rico, while the other two sources assume that the pronunciation of /rr/ is consistent for all of Puerto Rico. Southwest Puerto Rico is included in the list of regions where the three sources agree that /rr/ is pronounced as [r̃], but the other sources' silence about this region suggests that Canfield's claim may be inaccurate.

The data in Table 1 reveal that Canfield, Cotton and Sharp, and Lipski only agree that the standard Spanish [r̃] occurs in 15 dialect areas, or in slightly less than 37% of the 41 American Spanish dialect zones.

Table 1: Countries and regions where /rr/ is always a voiced alveolar trill

ARGENTINA: Buenos Aires and Southern Litoral	Lipski 1994: 170 Canfield 1981: 24
BOLIVIA: Lowland llanos	Lipski 1994: 190 – "some intrusion of assibilated /rr/ and /r/. . . ." Canfield 1981: 28
CHILE: Coastal Region	Cotton & Sharp 1988: 179
COLOMBIA: Caribbean Coast, Pacific Coast, Amazonian Region	Canfield 1981: 35, 36
COSTA RICA: Guanacaste/Nicoya	Lipski 1994: 223 Canfield 1981: 39, 41
ECUADOR: Coastal Region (includes Esmeraldas, Guayas, Los Ríos, Manabí)	Lipski 1994: 247 Canfield 1981: 50, 51 Cotton & Sharp 1988: 179
ECUADOR: Extreme North-Central (Carchi)	Lipski 1994: 248 Canfield 1981: 50
EL SALVADOR	Canfield 1981: 53
NICARAGUA	Canfield 1981: 66
PERU: Amazonian Lowlands	Lipski 1994: 322
PERU: Lima and Northern Coast	Canfield 1981: 73, 75 Cotton & Sharp 1988: 179
PUERTO RICO: Southwest	Canfield 1981: 77, 78
URUGUAY	Lipski 1994: 337 – generally attributed to characteristics of Porteño Spanish Canfield 1981: 88, 89

3. Auditory analysis of [r̃] in Spanish dialects

To test the validity of the claim that the phone [r̃] rarely occurs, an analysis of the recorded speech of 108 speakers of U.S. Spanish from 17 Spanish dialects was carried out. These subjects represent Latin America, the Canary Islands and Spain, including Andalucía. The subjects were asked to read aloud an approximately two-minute excerpt taken from the Mexico City newspaper *Excelsior*. The oral reading of written material in the presence of a microphone, recording equipment, and an investigator generally unknown to the subject should promote the production of formal pronunciation styles. Therefore, the data-recording process should encourage the production of the more standard or prescriptive [r̃] phone.

There was not a single subject whose regular pronunciation of /rr/ in the oral reading was the prescribed standard Spanish [r̃]. This two-minute reading passage contains a total of seven occurrences of /rr/. These included the Spanish graphemes "rr" and "r" after the phonemes /n, l, s/ and in word-initial environments, all of which are environments where the phone [r̃] is prescribed in Spanish. Only 5 of the 180 subjects (4.63%) successfully produced the prescribed articulation of [r̃] at all. Out of these five subjects, only two produced two occurrences of [r̃] and only one articulated three instances of the phone [r̃]. Therefore, these 108 subjects produced only nine occurrences of [r̃], or 1.19% of the 756 occurrences of /rr/ in the total sample. If these data are typical, and I believe they are, then the prescriptive phone [r̃] in Spanish occurs about as frequent as *lleísmo*, which is also prescribed by the Real Academia Española (1924, 1979, 1992).

It is clear that [r̃] is not the pronunciation adopted by these 108 speakers. Determining what phonetic realization of /rr/ does occur is more difficult, as there are numerous variations. Among the articulations of /rr/ observed are sounds that could be described as a voiceless velar or uvular fricative ([x] or [ʀ̥]), a retroflex [ɹ], a preaspirated flap [hr], a partially devoiced flap [r̥] and a voiced flap [r].

4. Acoustic analysis of [r̃] in Spanish dialects

Acoustic data were used to verify auditory discrimination of the subjects' production. Sound spectrographs were made of randomly selected occurrences of the phoneme /rr/ from four representative subjects. For Subject 1, spectrograms were made of two occurrences of /rr/ because the first occurrence contains a back realization of /rr/, while the second utilizes an anterior articulation. All spectrograms were made using a Kay Computerized Speech Lab (CSL), Model 4300.

Sociolinguistic data for these four representative subjects are shown below in Table 2. All four of these subjects are originally from dialect zones where Canfield, Cotton and Sharp, and Lipski report [r̃] as the normal pronunciation of /rr/.

Table 2: Sociolinguistic data for four representative test subjects

	Gender	Age	Original native dialect area
Subject 1	Male	32 years	San Germán, Puerto Rico
Subject 2	Female	30 years	Lima, Perú
Subject 3	Female	30 years	Santiago, Chile
Subject 4	Male	28 years	Buenos Aires, Argentina

Six spectrograms are displayed in Figures 1–6:

Figure 1. Standard Spanish [r̃]: *cigarro*

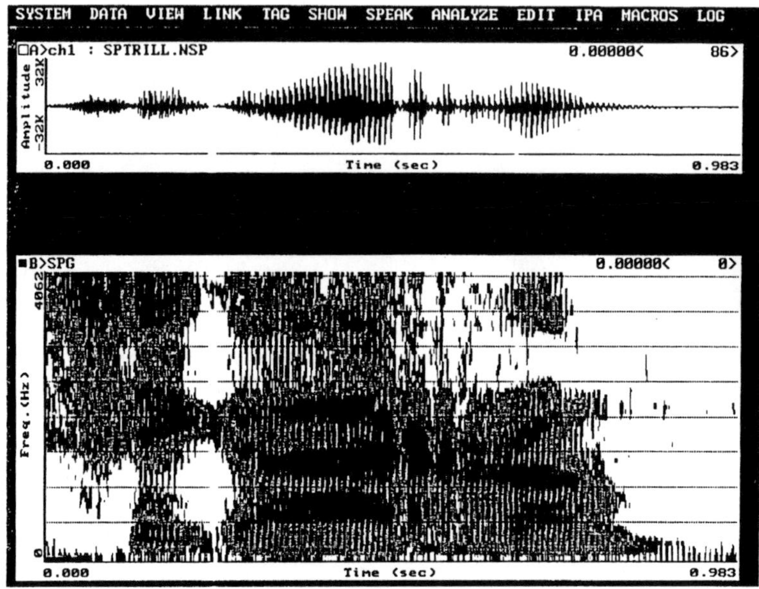

Figure 2. Subject 1: First occurrence of *Ramírez* [x] or [R̥]

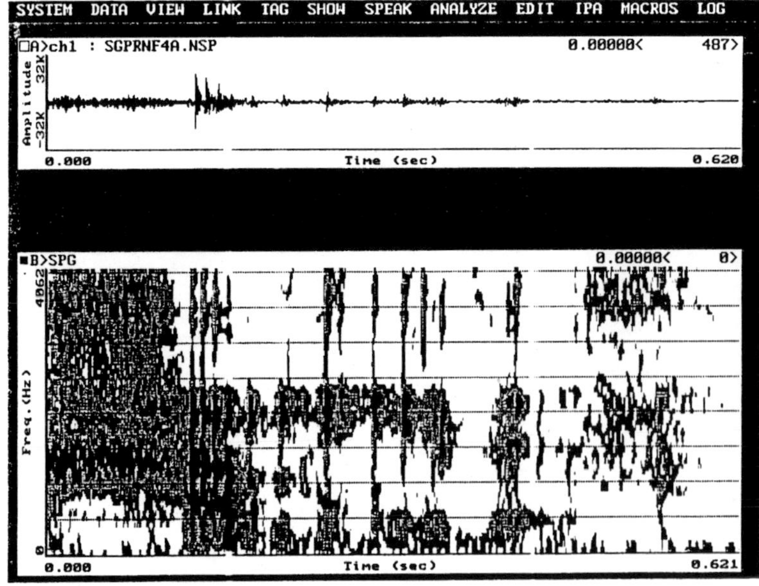

Figure 3. Subject 1: Second occurrence of *Ramírez* [x] or [R̥]

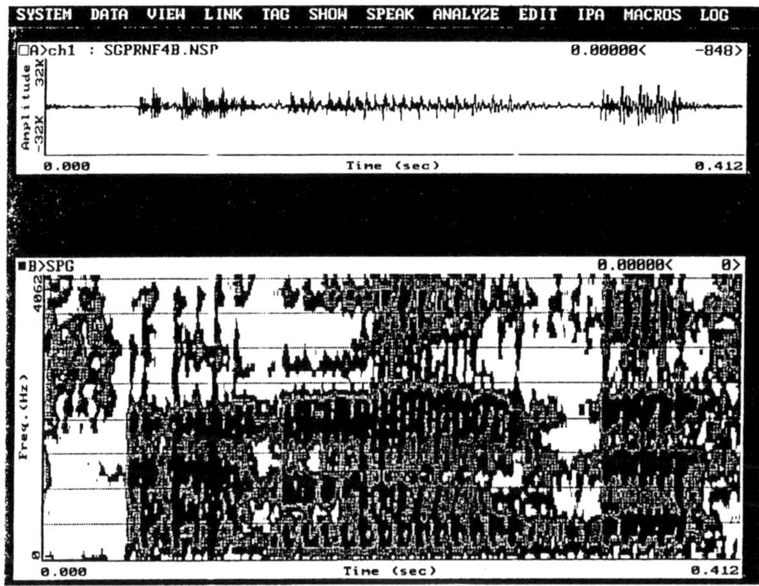

Figure 4. Subject 2: First occurrence of *Ramírez*

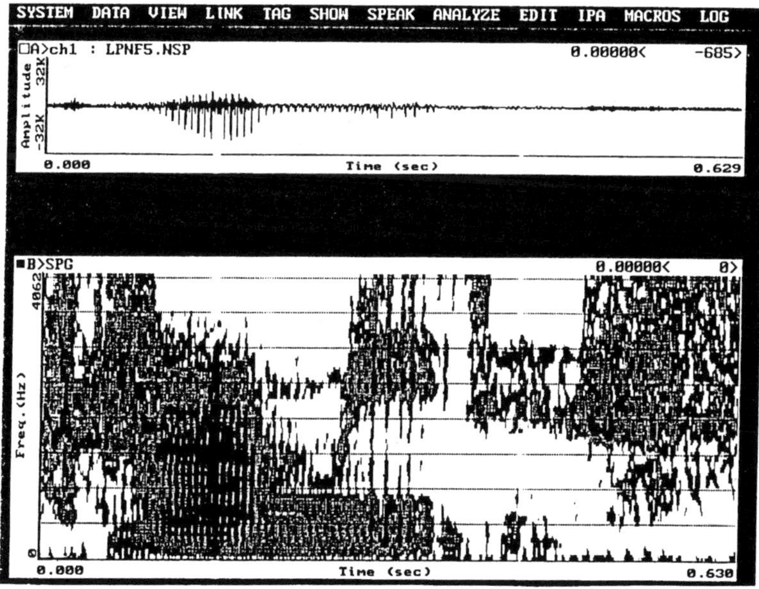

Figure 5. Subject 3: First occurrence of *Ramírez*

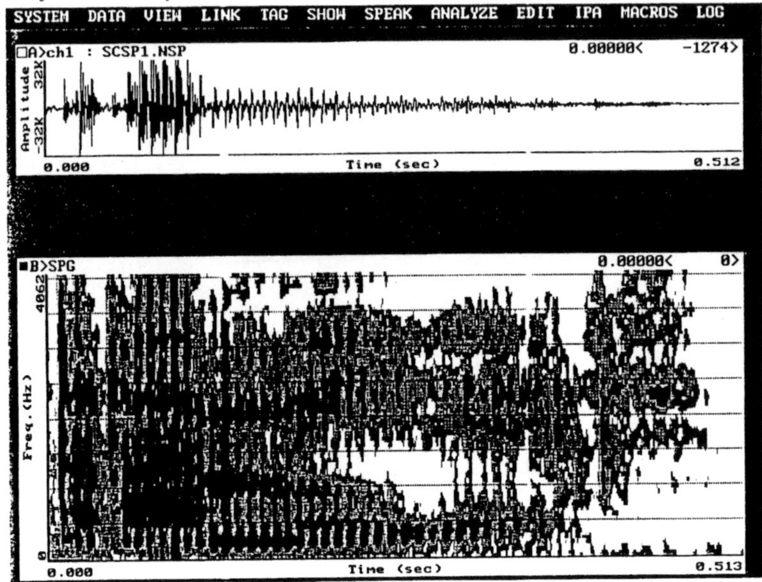

Figure 6. Subject 4: Second occurrence of *Ramírez*

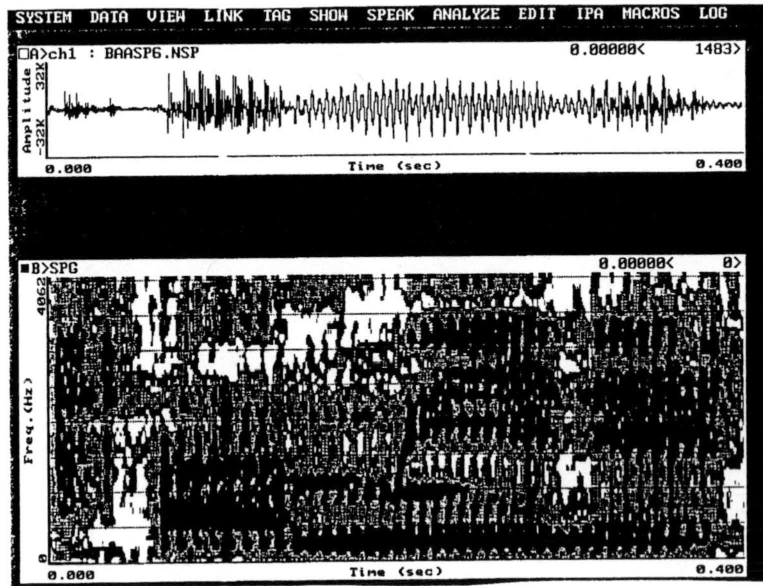

The first of these spectrograms (Figure 1) illustrates, for comparison purposes, a prescriptive, standard Spanish voiced alveolar multiple vibrant [r̃] taken from the lexeme *cigarro* [si.gá.r̃o] from the author's speech. This [r̃] is voiced, contains a clear formant structure and consists of three brief occlusions, the third of which blends into the following vowel /o/. The [r̃] shown in Figure 1 matches the description and spectrogram of a typical, prescribed, standard Spanish [r̃] in Delattre (1965: 98). If occurrences of /rr/ in the recorded passage follow the prescriptive standards, they should all have a formant structure and spectral display similar to that found in Figure 1.

Figure 2 is a spectrogram representing the first occurrence of the lexical item *Ramírez* from Subject 1. The initial consonant of the first segment of this lexeme has the typical spectral characteristics of a largely devoiced fricative. This subject is originally from San Germán, Puerto Rico and on this occasion has articulated the non-anterior /rr/ associated with the relaxed discourse of many Puerto Rican speakers. This is also the typical /rr/ of most lower class speakers of Puerto Rican Spanish. This phonetic realization of /rr/ shows none of the typical spectral structure of the prescriptive Spanish [r̃]. Clearly, the spectrographic data and auditory discrimination are in agreement.

The spectrogram in Figure 3 represents the second occurrence of the lexical item *Ramírez* from Subject 1. The spectral structure of the initial consonant of this word appears to be that of a voiceless approximant and is clearly not that of a prescriptive Spanish [r̃].

Figure 4 displays the spectrogram from the first occurrence of the lexical item *Ramírez* from Subject 2, originally from Lima, Peru, and shows the initial segment of this word to be some type of voiceless fricative.

Figure 5 shows the spectrogram for Subject 3, originally from Santiago, Chile, for the first occurrence of the lexical item *Ramírez*. This /rr/ both sounds like and has the spectral structure of a weakly articulated multiple vibrant. However, this lexeme contains Subject 3's only articulation of /rr/ that approaches the prescriptive Spanish standard [r̃].

Finally, the spectrogram presented in Figure 6 shows the second occurrence of the lexical item *Ramírez* for Subject 4, originally from Buenos Aires, Argentina. Here the initial consonant of this lexical item has the acoustic structure of a voiced spirant.

The acoustic data from these four subjects suggest that in the great majority of the cases these speakers did not produce a standard Spanish [r̃], but rather some type of spirant or sibilant. If we return to Canfield 1981, Cotton and Sharp 1988, and Lipski 1994, we can see that many of their descriptions of the phonetic manifestations of /rr/ are of some type of spirant or sibilant. Often, the non-standard varieties of /rr/ that occur in American Spanish dialects are described as either fricatives produced with the tongue blade in a flat configuration or as sibilants with the blade assuming a concave, rounded configuration.

5. Summary and conclusions

Both the auditory discrimination data and the acoustic data presented here support the claim that the phone [r̃] is generally absent in the normal discourse of the great majority of U.S. Spanish speakers. One additional study (Hammond 1999) also shows that this same phone [r̃] is not present in the normal discourse of the vast majority of all Spanish speakers. If we accept the non-occurrence of [r̃], we can produce a well-motivated theoretical account of /r̃/ in Spanish phonology and potentially eliminate the difficulties encountered with this phone in both L1 and L2 acquisition.

When one analyzes the real surface manifestations of the intervocalic flap [r] in different Spanish dialects, it becomes clear that many dialects have neutralized [r] and [r̃] in intervocalic environments. While such a neutralization may seem problematic, neutralizing phonetic distinctions between pairs of lexical items such as *caro* 'expensive' [ká.ro] and *carro* 'car' [ká.r̃o], a closer examination of the Spanish language reveals that the phone [r̃] does not have a high functional load. While minimal pairs such as *caro*/*carro* do exist in Spanish, one would have a difficult time compiling a list of 20 such minimal pairs of words in common usage in the present-day language. Furthermore, in the great majority of these cases, little potential for semantic confusion really exists because the members of these pairs have different syntactic functions. For example, *caro* is an adjective but *carro* is a noun. In this same vein, even if a phonetic neutralization of [r] and [r̃] did produce numerous cases of semantic ambiguity, this would not be the first such case in Spanish or in other languages. In Caribbean Spanish dialects, the phonemes /r/ and /l/ are frequently neutralized in post-nuclear environments. In the final analysis, languages are structured in a way that captures many redundancies, so apparent neutralizations produced by lexemes in isolation are most often disambiguated in the discourse context.

The usual disclaimers and caveats are in order for an experimental study of this type. First, if the findings of the present study are indeed valid, it must be assumed that the 108 subjects are typical speakers of their dialect areas. Obviously, a larger data base with the same findings would provide further support for the conclusions. Also, one limitation of the present study is that all seven occurrences of /rr/ in the reading passage occur in word-initial position. Since there is no flap/multiple vibrant contrast in this environment, word-initial position may lend itself to greater occurrences of neutralization than intervocalic environments, where the flap and trill do contrast in Spanish. My own experience in analyzing the surface realizations of /rr/ suggest that this is not the case, but it remains a possibility. I have since modified the reading passage so that it now contains several instances of intervocalic /rr/, and a comparison of more recent and on-going recordings with previous recordings will reveal whether there is indeed a systematic difference in the realization of [r̃] in word-initial and intervocalic environments.

Although the Real Academia Española (1992) prescribes [r̃] as the only possible surface variant for the grapheme "r" after "s", "n" and "l", for "r" in word-initial position and for intervocalic "rr", it is clear to me that the vast majority of native Spanish speakers do not utilize this phone in their normal discourse. The data from speakers of U.S. Spanish dialects presented in the present study support this contention.

References

Alemán, Iris. 1977. *Desdoblamiento fonológico en el español de Puerto Rico.* M.A. thesis. Río Piedras: University of Puerto Rico.

Alvar, Manuel. 1972. *Niveles socio-culturales en el habla de Las Palmas de Gran Canaria.* Las Palmas: Ediciones del Excmo. Cabildo Insular de Gran Canaria.

Calero Fernández, María Angeles. 1993. *Estudio sociolingüístico del habla de Toledo: Segmentos fonológicos -/s/ y -/ɟ/.* Lleida, España: Pagès Editors.

Canellada, María Josefa and John Kuhlmann Madsen. 1987. *Pronunciación del español: Lengua hablada y literaria.* Madrid: Editorial Castalia

Canfield, Delos Lincoln. 1962. *La pronunciación del español en América.* Bogotá: Publicaciones del Instituto Caro y Cuervo XVII.

Canfield, Delos Lincoln. 1981. *Spanish pronunciation in the Americas.* Chicago: University of Chicago Press.

Cotton, Eleanor G. and John M. Sharp. 1988. *Spanish in the Americas.* Washington, DC: Georgetown University Press.

Cressey, William W. 1989. A generative sketch of Castilian Spanish pronunciation: A point of reference for the study of American Spanish. In *American Spanish pronunciation: Theoretical and applied perspectives*, ed. Peter C. Bjarkman and Robert M. Hammond, 48–70. Washington, DC: Georgetown University Press.

Dalbor, John B. 1969. *Spanish pronunciation: Theory and practice.* New York: Holt, Rinehart and Winston.

Dalbor, John B. 1980. *Spanish pronunciation: Theory and practice, 2nd edition.* New York: Holt, Rinehart and Winston.

Delattre, Pierre. 1965. *Comparing the phonetic features of English, French, German and Spanish: An interim report.* Philadelphia: Chilton Books.

Esgueva, M. and M. Cantarero. 1981. *El habla de la ciudad de Madrid.* Madrid: Consejo Superior de Investigaciones Científicas Instituto Miguel de Cervantes.

Fernández Sevilla, Julio. 1980. Los fonemas implosivos en español. *Thesaurus* 35.3: 456–505.

Figueroa, Neysa Luz. 1997. *An acoustic and perceptual study of vowels preceding deleted post-nuclear /s/ in Puerto Rican Spanish.* M.A. thesis. West Lafayette: Purdue University.

Flórez, Luis. 1966. Apuntes sobre el español de Madrid, año 1965. *Thesaurus* 31.3: 156–171.

García de Diego, Vicente. 1978. *Dialectología española, 3rd edition.* Madrid: Ediciones Cultura Hispánica del Centro Iberoamericano de Cooperación.

Hammond, Robert M. 1978. An experimental verification of the phonemic status of open and closed vowels in Caribbean Spanish. In *Corrientes actuales en la dialectología del Caribe Hispánico*, ed. Humberto López Morales, 93–143. Río Piedras: University of Puerto Rico Press.

Hammond, Robert M. 1999. On the non-occurrence of the phone [r̄] in the Spanish sound system. In *Advances in Hispanic linguistics*, ed. Javier Gutiérrez-Rexach and Fernando Martínez-Gil, 135–151. Somerville, MA: Cascadilla Press.

Harris, James W. 1983. *Syllable structure and stress in Spanish: A nonlinear analysis.* Cambridge, MA: MIT Press.

Lamíquez, Vidal. 1976. Sociolingüística en un habla urbana: Sevilla. *Revista Española de Lingüística* 6.2: 345–362.

Lapesa, Rafael. 1980. *Historia de la lengua española, 8th edition.* Madrid: Gredos.

Lipski, John M. 1994. *Latin American Spanish.* New York: Longman.

Llorente, Maldonado de Guevara. 1958–59. Importancia para la historia del español de la aspiración y otros rasgos fonéticos del castellano noroccidental. *Revista de Filología Española* 42: 151–167.

Martínez de Campos, Carlos. 1973. Supresión de las consonantes ch y ll. *Boletín de la Real Academia Española* 53: 269–289.

Martínez Martín, Francisco Miguel. 1983. *Fonética y sociolingüística en la ciudad de Burgos.* Madrid: Consejo Superior de Investigaciones Científicas Instituto Miguel de Cervantes.

Molina Martos, Isabel. 1991. *Estudio sociolingüístico de la ciudad de Toledo.* Ph.D. dissertation, Universidad Complutense de Madrid.

Moya Corral, José Antonio. 1979. *La pronunciación del español en Jaén.* Granada: Universidad de Granada.

Narbona Jiménez, Antonio and Ramón Morillo-Velarde Pérez. 1987. *Las hablas andaluzas.* Córdoba: Publicaciones del Monte de Piedad y Caja de Ahorros de Córdoba.

Navarro Tomás, Tomás. 1957. *Manual de pronunciación española.* New York: Hafner.

Navarro Tomás, Tomás. 1966. *Estudios de fonología española.* New York: Las Americas Publishing Company.

Navarro Tomás, Tomás. 1974. (18th edn.) *Manual de pronunciación española.* Madrid: Consejo Superior de Investigaciones Científicas.

Navarro Tomás, Tomás. 1977. (19th ed.) *Manual de pronunciación española.* Madrid: Consejo Superior de Investigaciones Científicas.

Núñez Cedeño, Rafael. 1989. La /r/, único fonema vibrante en español. *Anuario de Lingüística Hispánica* 5: 153–171.

Quilis, Antonio and Joseph A. Fernández. 1969. *Curso de fonética y fonología españolas.* Madrid: Consejo Superior de Investigaciones Científicas.

Real Academia Española. 1924. *Gramática de la lengua española.* Madrid: Perlado, Páez y Cía.

Real Academia Española. 1979. *Esbozo de una nueva grámatica de la lengua española.* Madrid: Espasa-Calpe.

Real Academia Española. 1992. *Diccionario de la lengua española, 21st edition.* Madrid: Espasa Calpe.

Resnick, Melvyn C. 1975. *Phonological variants and dialect identification in Latin American Spanish.* The Hague: Mouton.

Resnick, Melvyn C. 1989. Structuralist theory and the study of pronunciation in American Spanish dialectology. In *American Spanish pronunciation: Theoretical and applied perspectives*, ed. Peter C. Bjarkman and Robert M. Hammond, 9–30. Washington, DC: Georgetown University Press.

Samper Padilla, José Antonio. 1990. *Estudio sociolingüístico del español de Las Palmas de Gran Canaria*. Las Palmas de Gran Canaria: La Caja de Canarias.

Saporta, Sol and Heles Contreras. 1962. *A phonological grammar of Spanish*. Seattle: University of Washington Press.

Stockwell, Robert P. and J. Donald Bowen. 1965. *The sounds of English and Spanish*. Chicago: University of Chicago Press.

Zamora Vicente, Alonso. 1979. *Dialectología española*. Madrid: Gredos.

Zamora Vicente, Alonso. 1986. *Estudios de dialectologia hispánica*. Santiago de Compostela: Universidad de Santiago de Compostela (Verba, Anuario Galego de Filoloxia).

Estar in Mexican-American Spanish: Phonological or Morphological Variability?

MaryEllen Garcia and Michael Tallon
The University of Texas at San Antonio

1. Introduction

Studies of synchronic phonological variability are common in sociolinguistics, often suggesting potential change-in-progress. Perhaps because it is difficult to distinguish phonological and morphological variability, treatments of the latter type of variability are less common. The problem of deciding between the two types of explanations is relevant when considering *estar* 'to be' in many dialects of popular Spanish. The verb has three common stem forms, which in the present tense, third-person singular, are *está*, *'stá,* and *'tá*, all equivalent to "she/he/it is." *Está*, Variant 1 (V1), is considered the canonical form, while *'stá* and *'tá* (V2, V3) are typically considered to be reduced forms. A phonological explanation would mean that phonetic processes continue to operate on the full form to reduce it to the three forms that occur, while a morphological explanation would mean that each form is available to speakers directly in their mental lexicon, bypassing phonological considerations.

The question of whether the variability is due to synchronic phonological processes or is simply current morphological variability – possibly the result of phonological variability that has become fossilized or frozen in time – is of great interest because of claims that linguists make about underlying phonological representations. Some phonologists might propose that all three are generated by rules that operate on /estar/, in which case phonological processes would produce the non-canonical forms. But if the variability has become fossilized in the verb's morphology, each form would be available to speakers without an active phonological derivation process. The single form hypothesis is supported by pedagogues' beliefs that V1 is the single correct form. Consequently, V2 and V3 are considered to be phonologically "corrupted" and nonstandard by teachers and language purists.

In this study we examine naturalistic speech data from 32 San Antonio Mexican-American Spanish speakers to determine the relative importance of social and linguistic factors on the occurrence of the forms of *estar*. Variable rule analysis is employed to consider all three forms independently in terms of the same constraints. The results of this quantitative analysis will be discussed, as will the stylistic considerations for the non-canonical variants in the Spanish of the community.

2. Review of the literature

Most of the studies which note the variability of *estar* tend to be those done in the tradition of dialectology. Dialectologists observe the three verb stems in many popular dialects throughout the Spanish-speaking world: in Chile (Oroz 1966: 72), in Bolivia (Varas 1960: 73), in Argentina (Vidal de Battini 1949: 35), in Spain (Fernández Gonzáles 1959: 43), in Mexico (Cárdenas 1967: 16), in New Mexico (Espinosa 1930: 251), in Texas (Lance 1975: 39), and in Southwest (or Mexican-American) Spanish in general (e.g. Sánchez 1982: 19).

Although the variability is noted in these studies, it is not usually explained. However, Espinosa (1930: 251), in his classic study of New Mexican Spanish, reports that *'stá* and *'tá* were not unusual in the Spanish of Spain in the 15th and 16th centuries. This appears to lend support to the idea of fossilized morphological variability, particularly because this is the period when Spanish was exported to the New World. At least one study has interpreted these long-standing variants as having grammaticalized in popular contemporary dialects (Carrasquel 1997), a conclusion that also appears to support morphological fossilization. Sánchez (1982: 19), on the other hand, attributes V3, *'tá,* to aphaeresis, or "loss of an unaccented vowel in initial position . . .", which is a common synchronic phonological process that operates on other words as well.

In an earlier study based on data from San Antonio, Garcia and Tallon (1994a) considered the variability of *estar* in a larger study that asked whether syllable-final /-s/ was aspirated or deleted. That study considered 2097 tokens of /-s/ for potential deletion. We determined that syllable-final /-s/ deletion was not typical of this dialect, based on a retention rate of 95.8%. Subsequently, 169 tokens of /-s/ in *estar* alone were considered. The results produced the following frequencies for the stem forms: *está* (58.6%), *'stá (20%)*, *'tá* (17.8%), and *e'tá* (3.6%). We concluded that the variable pronunciation of words such as *estar* and *nosotros* (vs. *nohotros*) 'we' was likely due to morphological rather than phonological variation; that is, that the perceived aspiration had been lexicalized to certain forms. The frequency of the non-standard archaic forms, it was suggested, would account for the over-reporting of aspiration of syllable-final (and sometimes even syllable-initial) /s/ in impressionistic studies of Southwest Spanish.

3. Methods

3.1. Nature of the data

Data for the present study were taken from 32 tape-recorded interviews with Mexican-Americans who were raised in South Texas and were living in San Antonio. The sample was equally distributed between men and women (16 each). The interviewees were divided into three age groups: ten were 15–25 years old, thirteen were 26–50 years old, and nine were over 50. The interviewers included the first author and students in Spanish linguistics from The University of Texas at San Antonio, some of whom were relatively inexperienced at doing sociolinguistic interviews. The setting of the interviews varied as well, from the homes of the informants to their places of business or classrooms at the university. Because of the various interviewers and settings, the speech style of the interviews may have differed. In doing the coding, we consulted both the transcripts of the interviews and the tape recordings themselves to determine the variants. A maximum of 45 minutes worth of speech was considered for each informant.

3.2. Coding parameters

The data were coded for the social factors of age and gender and four linguistic factors: the immediately preceding phonetic segment, verb tense, person-number, and whether the form was said once, twice, or more times, called "sequencing." Some parameters which might otherwise have been relevant were excluded on the basis of the pilot study on some of these same data (Garcia and Tallon 1994b). They were: the number of years of Spanish study, the social distance between the interlocutors, the rapidity or pace of speech, the genre of the discourse (e.g., narrative, opinion, etc.), and education.[1]

4. Results

The number of tokens coded in this fashion from the 32 speakers was 1,025. The raw frequencies of the variants and percentages of the total are as follows: V1 *está* with 484 (47.2%), V2 *'stá* with 275 (26.8%), and V3 *'tá* with 266 (25.9%). The canonical form occurs twice as often as the other two forms. These tokens were then submitted for variable rule analysis. The statistical analysis carried out by Varbrul uses probability values or 'weights' ranging from zero to one to estimate the effect of a particular factor on the application of the rule. A value close to .5 neither favors nor disfavors the application of the rule, as this number is equivalent to a chance occurrence. The closer the value is to one, the more it favors the application of that rule. The input probability is the likelihood that the form selected as the application value would occur even if there were no favoring factors associated with it. For the Varbrul analysis of *estar*, one form at a time was chosen as the application value in order to determine the factors that favored each different form. In each analysis the Varbrul program determines which factor groups are relevant for predicting that particular form and which are not. Therefore the factor groups selected for predicting one form may be different from the others. Not all of the analyses will contain the same factor groups in the results, and so each analysis is to be interpreted on its own.

4.1. Full form as application value

A binomial, one level analysis was done with *estar* as the application value as shown in Table 1, Analysis A. The input probability was .460. Speakers aged 15–25 favored the rule slightly (.623). Gender was relevant, with females favoring the full form slightly (.664) and males disfavoring it (.344). As for linguistic factors, the Preceding Segment factor group revealed a glide /y/ to disfavor the full form (.315). Regarding Tense, the preterite most favored the full form (.884) while the imperfect subjunctive favored it least (.282). The values for Sequence indicated that both single repetitions (.308) and multiple repetitions (.260) disfavored the full form.

Table 1. Analysis A: application value = V1 (*está*)

Age group	**15–25**	**.623**
	26–50	.412
	51+	.533
Gender	**Male**	**.344**
	Female	**.664**
Preceding Segment	Preceding audible unstressed V	.581
	Preceding -e	.407
	Preceding stressed V	.413
	Preceding C (not -s)	.585
	Preceding -s	.427
	Preceding y-glide	**.315**
	Pause or initial in breath group	.528
Tense	Present	.510
	Preterite	**.884**
	Imperfect	.462
	Imperfect Subjunctive	**.282**
	Infinitive	.503
Sequence	Single or only one	.514
	Repeated	**.308**
	One of a list	**.260**

4.2. Reduced forms as application values

The reduced forms V2 and V3 were initially grouped together to test whether the same constraints would be selected subsequently when each would be analyzed separately. Analysis B is the result of that grouping, with an input probability of .520. By this analysis, speakers aged 51 and older favor the rule (.705) and speakers aged 15–25 also favor reduction slightly (.656). Gender proved neutral to reduction. Preceding Segment provided interesting results in that both a preceding pause (.195) and a preceding consonant (.145) disfavor reduction; a preceding glide also disfavors it slightly (.315). However, a strong favoring factor is a preceding [-s] (.914), suggesting that phonological factors might, in fact, play a part in favoring the reduced forms. In terms of Tense, only the imperfect subjunctive (.158) and preterite (.334) disfavor reduction. Sequence was relevant; a single repetition (.607) and multiple repetitions both favor reduction (.877).

Table 2. Analysis B: application value = V2 + V3

Age group	**15–25**	**.656**
	26–50	**.354**
	51+	**.705**
Gender	Male	.501
	Female	.499
Preceding Segment	Preceding audible unstressed V	.533
	Preceding -e	.529
	Preceding stressed V	.568
	Preceding C (not -s)	**.145**
	Preceding -s	**.914**
	Preceding y-glide	**.315**
	Pause or initial in breath group	**.195**
Tense	Present	.560
	Preterite	**.334**
	Imperfect	.417
	Imperfect Subjunctive	**.158**
	Infinitive	.540
Sequence	Single or only one	.485
	Repeated	**.607**
	One of a list	**.877**

We must point out now that the grouping of V2 and V3 into a single category called "reduced forms" assumes that the same factors are relevant to the same degree in predicting both forms. This is clearly not our assumption, as one hypothesis that we wanted to test was whether each form was an independent variant. The following sections report the results of separate Goldvarb analyses.

4.3. V2 as application value ('stá)

A one-level binomial analysis was performed with V2 as the application value as shown in Analysis C. The input probability was .229. Interestingly, speakers aged 15–25 favor it only slightly more (.605) than those aged 51 and over, who neither favor nor disfavor it (.528). The group aged 26–50 disfavors it slightly (.425). Again, not much difference was found in male (.519) vs. female (.480) weightings. A preceding [-s] was the greatest favoring phonetic environment (.798). Other phonetic contexts were neutral except for preceding pause (.274) and preceding consonant (.276). Tense produced neutral weights except for preterite (.090), and imperfect subjunctive (.262), which both disfavor V2. As for Sequence, favoring weights were for a single repetition (.682) and multiple repetitions (.833).

Table 3. Analysis C: application value = V2

Age group	15–25	.605
	26–50	.425
	51+	.528
Gender	Male	.519
	Female	.480
Preceding Segment	Preceding audible unstressed V	.484
	Preceding -e	.605
	Preceding stressed V	.580
	Preceding C (not -s)	**.276**
	Preceding -s	**.798**
	Preceding y-glide	.453
	Pause or initial in breath group	**.274**
Tense	Present	.535
	Preterite	**.090**
	Imperfect	.483
	Imperfect Subjunctive	**.262**
	Infinitive	.486
Sequence	Single or only one	.485
	Repeated	**.682**
	One of a list	**.833**

4.4. V3 as application value ('tá)

Finally, we consider the most radical form, V3, as the application value in Analysis D. The input probability was .204. In a dialect that does not aspirate syllable-final [-s], what are the constraints that favor the occurrence of this greatly reduced form? The age group that most favors V3 is the middle group, ages 26–50 (.643), whereas the other groups show neutral weights. In terms of gender, males favor this form (.609) slightly more than females (.385).

Phonetically, a preceding [-s] disfavors the rule (.136), while a preceding [-y] favors it (.739) as does a preceding pause (.675) and a preceding consonant (.611). Another relevant factor group, Tense, indicates that preterite greatly disfavors V3 (.202), while the imperfect subjunctive greatly favors it (.819). The program did not select Sequence as important, so there are no results for this factor group.

Table 4. Analysis D: application value = V3

Age group	15–25	.358
	26–50	**.643**
	51+	.370
Gender	**Male**	**.609**
	Female	**.385**
Preceding Segment	Preceding audible unstressed V	.454
	Preceding -e	.545
	Preceding stressed V	.564
	Preceding C (not -s)	**.611**
	Preceding -s	**.136**
	Preceding y-glide	**.739**
	Pause or initial in breath group	**.675**
Tense	Present	.464
	Preterite	**.202**
	Imperfect	.582
	Imperfect Subjunctive	**.819**
	Infinitive	.430

5. Discussion of results

Before interpreting these results, we should consider the findings of Garcia and Tallon (1994a), which have shown San Antonio Spanish not to be a radical dialect, as discussed by Zamora-Munné and Guitart (1982: 107). In a radical dialect, the phonetic character of a syllable-final allophone is greatly different from its phonemic character, as found in Cuban American and Puerto Rican communities, where phonemic /-s/ can be realized as [s], [h], or [ø]. However, San Antonio Spanish does not aspirate or delete /-s/, so other explanations must be sought for the variability across verb stems. If synchronic phonological processes explained the variability, V2 might be accounted for as the result of collapsing like vowels across word boundaries, such as in *que está* > *que 'stá*. This explanation would be supported by the observation that this dialect routinely reduces sequences of contiguous vowels (cf. Martinez-Gil forthcoming). But a similar explanation would not work for V3, which lacks the entire first syllable.

The three variable rule analyses of *estar* presented here suggest that phonological factors do, in fact, influence the occurrence of the three forms. First, a preceding [–e] results in the elimination of hiatus due to linking of like vowels, followed by a collapse of the two syllabic nuclei into a single one. This environment is shown in Analysis C to favor *'stá* (V2) slightly, but is neutral regarding *'tá* (V3) in Analysis D. It seems reasonable to suggest from this result that there is not a stepwise erosion of the forms in the direction of *'stá>'tá*. Analysis A shows that a preceding pause or consonant are neutral regarding the full form. This goes counter to the expectation that these environments would produce a greater favoring effect for *estar*, particularly in the case of a preceding consonant, which would produce the preferred CV syllable structure of Spanish via linking. This suggests that the full form is simply one possible choice made by the speaker even when there are phonological environments which would seem to favor its selection.

Analysis B, which treats reduced forms as a single phenomenon, has provided a baseline against which to compare the phonological constraints on V2 vs. V3. While this analysis presents a preceding pause as disfavoring reduction (.195), the results from Analyses C and D reveal that it favors V3 (.675) but disfavors V2 (.274). This suggests that V2 is more constrained by phonological environment than V3, *'tá*, which can more readily initiate a breath group. We interpret this to be a sign of lexical independence of *'tá*, the form more structurally different from the canonical form.

More evidence for the independence of V2 from V3 is also suggested by comparing the analyses. While Analysis B shows that a preceding [-s] favors reduction (.914), Analysis C shows that it favors V2 (.798), and Analysis D shows that it disfavors V3 (.136). A preceding [-y] glide seems to disfavor reduction (.315) by Analysis B, Analysis C shows that it is neutral regarding V2 (.453), but Analysis D shows that it favors V3 (.739).[2] From these analyses it appears that V2 and V3 are quite different from each other in terms of phonetic constraints. It is doubtful that a singular phenomenon known as "reduction" is the explanation for the occurrence of the two variants, although the two forms are clearly related morphologically and functionally.

While these variable rule analyses have not proven conclusively that V2 (*'stá*) and V3 (*'tá*) are morphological variants of *está* rather than phonologically derived ones, we believe that this interpretation allows the phonology to retain certain generalizations that would otherwise be violated. For example, deriving V3 (*'tá*) from *está* would require a rule that deleted an entire initial #VC- syllable, which is not a productive process in modern-day Spanish. Such a rule would be very odd, as words with similar initial phonotactic structures such as *estrella* and *espina* do not typically reduce in this dialect to **'trella* and **'pina*. On the other hand, proposing *'stá* (V2) as an underlying form is problematic because it would violate syllabic phonotactic constraints. In the borrowings *esquí* 'ski' and *esmoking* 'smoking jacket,' for example, a vowel must be inserted to prevent an initial #sC- cluster. Analysis C shows that a preceding pause does not favor this variant (.274), which supports our conclusion that this form is not as independent from *estar* as is V3. We state the obvious in saying that V1 and V2 are more closely related phonologically. More phonetic substance is shared between them, and aphaeresis can easily account for the loss of the initial *e-* in *'stá.*

From the evidence that *estar* is disfavored when repeated once (.308) or several times (.260) by Analysis A, we may infer that there is no perception of "agrammaticality" or production error when speakers use the non-canonical forms. Rather, when speakers use one of them, the fact that they intended that variant and not another is reinforced by their repetition of the same form, rather than making a "repair" to a misstatement.

5.1. Stylistic considerations

Although our initial analyses on some of these same data (Garcia and Tallon 1994b) did not reveal interesting results when these data were coded for Style, we now would try to get a greater variety of speech styles and recording situations in which to examine this variability. While the present study succeeded in demonstrating the variability across forms, the type of data collection methods may not have been conducive to finding the true stylistic correlates of V2 and V3. We may have succeeded in obtaining only the most formal type of speech in these interview situations. If so, the results from our analyses reflect how people speak when being observed, as Labov's "Observer's Paradox" (1972) would have predicted. The fact that both V2 and V3 occur in roughly equal percentages (approximately one quarter) of the 1025 tokens, and that the full form V1 accounts for almost half, seems to us to be more than coincidental. That the more formal variant is used twice as much as those considered less formal may reflect an unconscious awareness of its stylistic status as the "proper" form. Interestingly, Analysis D shows that V3, *'tá*, is more characteristic of male speech (.609) than female (.385). As male speech typically is considered less normative, V3 may be the least formal variant. Future research on the stylistic function of this variant is recommended.[3]

6. Conclusions

This study has shown that the preceding phonetic environment is the linguistic factor that best explains the variability across the three forms of *estar*. Unfortunately, no compelling evidence has been presented in these three analyses to allow us to decide between the hypotheses of phonological vs. morphological variability. However, the discussion has suggested that *está* and *'stá* are more phonologically related than *'tá*. The fact that the latter form is favored by a preceding pause, although the same environment does not favor *'stá*, indicates that these two forms may be independent lexically. Explainable historically by fossilization, they are clearly related in form and function; however, we consider each form currently to have its own lexical status. In her discussion of Natural Generative Phonology, (Bybee-)Hooper (1976) suggested that certain historically related forms are related by "via" rules, which apply to forms that are semantically and phonologically similar in the lexicon. These rules would not derive them from a single underlying form. The same type of relationship among the three forms of *estar* can be seen here.[4] Other linguistic constraints, such as Tense, also appear to be linked to one form or another, such as would be characteristic of lexicalized differences. The fact that V3 is favored by male more than female speakers suggests that it may be a marker of male speech. Future research should collect data in a wider range of settings and social contexts so that the effect of social factors on the variants may be studied more rigorously.

Independent support of the interpretation of fossilized morphological variation is the fact that this and other geographically-dispersed popular dialects seem to maintain historical variability (Cárdenas 1975: 4). Current synchronic morphological variability of modern standard forms with so-called archaic forms from the 14th through 16th centuries in Spain is frequently noted in research on popular Spanish. Green (1986: 27), reporting on the Spanish of the Lower Rio Grande Valley in Texas, cites the use of standard/archaic doublets such as *mucho/muncho* 'much,' *vi/vido* 'I saw,' and *así/asina* 'in that way' as being current usage, with the archaic variant imparting affective or emotional meaning (Green 1986: 28). The Spanish of New Mexico / Southern Colorado is most commonly acknowledged to be characterized by "archaisms," representing fossilized forms that were in use in the 16th century when the area was colonized by the Spanish, whether the result of then-current phonological processes or of analogy with other forms.

To conclude, variability between *está*, *'stá*, and *'tá* appears to have been maintained across the centuries in widespread regions, as noted above. That it occurs in many contemporary dialects of popular Spanish which have many other phonological and morphological features in common (cf. Lipski 1994: 148) suggests that the variability may be inherent in what could be considered a global macro-dialect of popular Spanish. First discussed for phonological rules, the unconscious sharing of norms for linguistic variability has been considered an important aspect of speech community membership (Cedergren and Sankoff 1974). Likewise, we suggest that an ability to use all of the variants of *estar* may be a marker of membership in a community of speakers of a global macro dialect of popular Spanish.

Notes

1. We initially coded for the education of the interviewees as one indicator of socio-economic status (SES). Although SES has been proven to be relevant to explaining linguistic variation in monolingual communities, particularly English speakers in North

America, its usefulness for minority communities has been called into question (Garcia 1981, Rickford 1989). While middle-class speakers in monolingual communities may aspire to using prestige forms, following prescriptive norms for the ethnic language may not be as relevant to economic mobility as the linguistic norms for speaking the non-ethnic prestige language. Speaking Spanish in the Southwest, while clearly relevant for purposes of in-group identity, is not crucial for success in the greater employment market, where English is the language of prestige and mobility. In San Antonio, bilingualism is an asset for some jobs, but English-speaking ability is far more important in securing employment. The model that correlates social class and level of language, therefore, may be more appropriate to monolingual rather than bilingual communities.

2. An example of this type of structure is *ay 'tá* 'there it is,' which can be interpreted figuratively as well as literally. Common in the vernacular, it may be a grammaticalized single phrasal unit in popular dialects of Mexican and Mexican-American Spanish.

3. One phrase that strikes the out-group Spanish speaker is the use in San Antonio of the approbative "'*Tá weno*" for the more formal "*Está bien*." It is used pragmatically either as an agreement to do something or to as a discourse marker to wind up a conversation. A San Antonio native comments that he notices its use by younger females, whereas twenty or more years ago it was used primarily by males. It is our impression that a more formal equivalent, "*Está/'stá bueno*" does not occur for these functions.

4. Forms V1 and V2 are more closely related phonologically than *'tá*, as the environment of preceding [-e] neutralizes any phonological contrast between them.

References

Cárdenas, Daniel N. 1967. *El español de Jalisco.* Madrid: Sucesores de Rivadeneyra.

Cárdenas, Daniel N. 1975. Mexican Spanish. In *El lenguaje de los chicanos*, ed. Eduardo Hernández-Chávez, Andrew D. Cohen, and Anthony F. Beltramo, 1–5. Arlington, VA: Center for Applied Linguistics.

Carrasquel, José. 1997. Evidence of further grammaticalization of the Spanish auxiliaries *estar* and *haber.* Paper presented at LASSO Conference, UCLA, California.

Cedergren, Henrietta and David Sankoff. 1974. Variable rules: Performance as a statistical reflection of competence. *Language* 50: 333–355.

Espinosa, Aurelio M. 1930. *Estudios sobre el español de Nuevo Méjico. Parte 1, Fonética.* Buenos Aires: Universidad de Buenos Aires.

Fernández Gonzáles, Angel R. 1959. *El habla y la cultura popular de Oseia de Sajambre.* Oviedo, Asturias: Instituto de Estudios Asturianos.

Garcia, MaryEllen. 1981. *Para-Pa usage in the Spanish of El Paso, Texas.* Ph.D. dissertation, Georgetown University.

Garcia, MaryEllen and Michael Tallon. 1994a. Postnuclear /-s/ in San Antonio Spanish: Nohotros no aspiramos. *The Georgetown Journal of Languages & Linguistics* 3.2–4: 139–162.

Garcia, MaryEllen and Michael Tallon. 1994b. Variability of *estar* in a dialect of Chicano Spanish: *Si 'stá bien decir 'tár o no.* Paper presented at NWAV23, Stanford, Palo Alto, California.

Green, George K. 1986. Archaic forms with a parallel ponderative function in the Spanish of the lower Rio Grande Valley. In *Mexican-American language: Usage, attitudes, maintenance, instruction, and policy*, ed. George K. Green and Jacob L. Ornstein-Galicia, 25–33. Pan American University at Brownsville, Texas.

Hooper, Joan B. 1976. *An introduction to natural generative phonology*. New York: Academic.

Labov, William. 1972. *Sociolinguistic patterns*. Philadelphia: University of Pennsylvania.

Lance, Donald M. 1975. Dialectal and nonstandard forms in Texas Spanish. In *El lenguaje de los chicanos*, ed. Eduardo Hernández-Chávez, Andrew D. Cohen, and Anthony F. Beltramo, 37–51. Arlington, VA: Center for Applied Linguistics.

Lipski, John. 1994. *Latin American Spanish*. New York: Longman.

Martínez-Gil, Fernando. Forthcoming. La estructura prosódica y la especificación vocálica en español: el problema de la sinalefa en ciertas variedades de la lengua coloquial contemporánea. In *Panorama de la fonología española*, ed. Juana Gil. Madrid: Arco Libros.

Oroz, Rodolfo. 1966. *La lengua castellana en Chile*. Santiago: Facultad de filosofía y educación.

Rickford, John. 1987. The haves and have nots: Sociolinguistic surveys and the assessment of speaker competence. *Language in Society* 16.2: 149–178.

Sánchez, Rosaura. 1982. Our linguistic and social context. In *Spanish in the U.S. setting: Sociolinguistic aspects*, ed. Jon Amastae and Lucía Elías-Olivares, 9–46. Cambridge: Cambridge University Press.

Varas Reyes, Victor. 1960. *El castellano popular en Tarija*. Argentina: (No publisher given).

Vidal de Battini, Berta Elena. 1949. *El habla rural de San Luís, Parte I*. BDH, Tomo VII. Buenos Aires: Universidad de Buenos Aires.

Zamora-Munné, Juan C. and Jorge Guitart. 1982. *Dialectología hispanoamericana*. Salamanca: Colegio de España.

Aspectos morfosintácticos del español como lengua materna entre universitarios californianos

Francisco Zabaleta
California Polytechnic State University, San Luis Obispo

1. Introducción

Hace ya varias décadas que se estudia o bien alguna característica del español que se habla en los Estados Unidos, en general, o bien el español de ciertas comunidades hispanas agrupadas por su origen nacional – puertorriqueños, cubanos, mexico-americanos etc. – o bien el de algún estado o territorio de la Unión Americana. Estos estudios han enfocado su atención en diferentes aspectos lingüísticos. Entre ellos cabe citar los relacionados con la descripción de las características morfosintácticas de la variedad en cuestión, o quizá las fonológicas o semánticas. También existen muchos trabajos relacionados con temas sociolingüísticos, como la relación diglósica entre la lengua dominante, el inglés, y la subordinada, el español, y sus consecuencias a nivel educativo, como la educación bilingüe, por ejemplo. Se ha prestado mucha atención también al mantenimiento o pérdida del español entre estas comunidades hispanas debido a su relativo aislamiento o a su contacto con el inglés. Uno de los temas más estudiados es el cambio de código (codeswitching, en inglés), que ha sido y sigue siendo campo fértil para el estudio de aspectos tanto sociolingüísticos como exclusivamente gramaticales, sobre todo sintácticos.

Como parte de esta tradición investigadora, el estudio del español como lengua materna entre estudiantes universitarios de California es un proyecto que se ha llevado a cabo en el Departamento de Español y Portugués de la Universidad de California, en Santa Bárbara.[1] Aunque este proyecto tenía varios módulos y abarcaba diferentes enfoques lingüísticos, el trabajo que aquí se presenta se limita exclusivamente a la descripción de ciertas características, fundamentalmente morfosintácticas, de esta variedad de español.

2. Propósito del estudio

El objetivo fundamental de este trabajo es la descripción de las características sintácticas más sobresalientes de esta variedad de español. El resultado de esta descripción permitirá hacer una comparación de esta variedad lingüística con otras variedades, fundamentalmente con la norma lingüística mexicana, y qué relación tiene con ella. Otro de los objetivos de esta investigación consiste en averiguar si hay mantenimiento o pérdida de la lengua y si, como consecuencia del contacto con el inglés, la variedad presenta características ajenas a otras variedades de español.

3. Características y composición de la muestra

Para la selección de los participantes se exigió que éstos hubieran nacido o vivido en California durante los últimos 15 años y que fueran mayores de 18 años. La selección de los participantes se hizo de forma aleatoria y aunque no se exigió que también hablaran inglés, la ocupación profesional de todos ellos dio como resultado un grupo bastante homogéneo de hablantes bilingües. En el estudio participaron 50 personas, todas ellas residentes en Santa Bárbara o en sus alrededores. Por su ocupación, 32 de ellos eran estudiantes y los demás se dedicaban a algún tipo de trabajo técnico o administrativo. En esta muestra no había trabajadores agrícolas. El promedio de edad de los participantes era de 23,2 años. Por su lugar de nacimiento, 33 de ellos habían nacido en California, 11 habían nacido en México y 6 en otros países de Latinoamérica. De las 17 personas que no habían nacido en California, solamente 6 de ellos fueron considerados inmigrantes, pues el resto vino a este país antes de cumplir los 5 años de edad, y para el propósito de este estudio tiene sentido considerar a estas 11 personas como si hubieran nacido en California. Una vez hecho este ajuste, es decir, la inclusión de los que vinieron a este país antes de los cinco años de edad, los considerados californianos nativos son, por lo tanto, 44. El resto, los otros 6, son inmigrantes con más de 15 años de residencia en California.

En este trabajo se considera *primera generación* a todos aquellos hispanos nacidos en California cuyos padres tienen el español como lengua materna y han nacido fuera de los Estados Unidos. Este grupo se compone de 36 individuos. *Segunda generación,* 8 en total, se refiere a los que han nacido en California y al menos uno de sus padres también ha nacido en California. Ninguno de los miembros de esta muestra es de *tercera generación,* abuelos, padres y participante nacidos en California, o de generaciones posteriores. Los inmigrantes, como se hacía constancia en el párrafo anterior, suman 6 individuos.

Para saber cúal es la lengua dominante de cada individuo se hizo un cálculo aproximado pero bastante fidedigno basado en cuatro parámetros diferentes: (1) La propia evaluación del participante de su facilidad para desenvolverse en inglés y en español en diferentes situaciones y en las cuatro habilidades lingüísticas, es decir, producción oral y escrita y recepción oral y escrita. (2)

Frecuencia de uso de ambas lenguas en diferentes ámbitos sociales. (3) La lengua en que recibieron su educación formal académica, desde el jardín de infancia hasta la universidad. (4) La opinión del investigador después de escuchar las grabaciones del habla de los participantes tanto en inglés como en español. Con base en estos criterios se obtuvo el siguiente resultado: Hablantes cuya lengua dominante es el inglés, 45. Hablantes cuya lengua dominante es el español, 2. Hablantes balanceados cuyo dominio y frecuencia de uso es igual o casi igual en ambas lenguas, 3.

4. Recogida de datos

Cada participante rellenó un cuestionario con información personal y de su comunidad, y además proporcionó información adicional referente a aspectos socioeconómicos y sociolingüísticos. En un laboratorio de lenguas de la universidad todos ellos grabaron su habla mientras participaban en distintas tareas narrativas y de lectura. Además de esto, cada participante rellenó otro cuestionario en el que se le pedía que hiciera varias tareas de reconocimiento, de preferencia, y también juicios de gramaticalidad. Por ejemplo, se les pidió que suplieran algún elemento omitido, que terminaran una oración a medias, que eligieran entre varias posibilidades o que explicaran cierto significado.

Este último cuestionario y la tarea narrativa son los que sirven para la recogida de los datos que se presentan en este trabajo que, como se mencionaba anteriormente, es sólo uno de los componentes del estudio global del español como lengua materna en California.

Por razones históricas y migratorias de sobra conocidas, se ha asumido en este proyecto que el dialecto mexico-americano guarda una íntima relación con el español de México. Por esta razón, el cuestionario que rellenaron los participantes en este estudio contenía aspectos gramaticales ya estudiados en el español de México con el propósito de establecer tanto sus diferencias como sus semejanzas. Es más, en aras de una fácil comparación, algunas de las oraciones que se utilizaron en este proyecto son las mismas que usó Lope Blanch en los estudios denominados *El habla culta de la cuidad de México: Materiales para su estudio,* y *El habla popular de la ciudad de México: Materiales para su estudio.* Lope Blanch (1993) identifica en el español de México media docena de desviaciones de la norma general en el campo de la morfosintaxis. Estas desviaciones, que también se observan con diferentes grados de vitalidad en otros dialectos latinoamericanos, están firmemente establecidas en el habla de todas las capas sociales mexicanas y constituyen, sin duda, la mejor manera de identificar los rasgos morfosintácticos del español mexicano. Por el contrario, las estructuras y relaciones morfosintácticas que siguen la norma del español general, que son, obviamente, la inmensa mayoría, no se han tenido en cuenta en este estudio puesto que su inclusión no hubiera ayudado a distinguir unos dialectos de otros.

5. Análisis de los datos y discusión

Las cláusulas subordinadas constituyen el terreno donde el subjuntivo muestra mayor vitalidad en el español general. Los datos recogidos sobre el modo verbal en cláusulas subordinadas sustantivas indican que nuestros informantes, por lo general, utilizan el modo subjuntivo de forma canónica (tablas 1 a 5). No obstante, los datos muestran desviaciones de la norma, sobre todo en oraciones donde el verbo de la cláusula principal expresa algún proceso sicológico de duda o temor (tablas 2 y 4 respectivamente).

La subordinación que más variación presenta es la de la tabla 5. En esta oración, la mayoría, el 60%, prefirió el indicativo (presente, futuro, y perifrástica con *ir*), mientras que el 40% restante optó por el presente de subjuntivo. En España y en otras zonas se usa casi exclusivamente el modo indicativo, mientras que en México se favorece el uso del subjuntivo en oraciones interrogativas de duda y con verbos de entendimiento como *creer, esperar, suponer* etc. En México se diría: "No sé si ella *tenga* tiempo" o "¿Crees que el presidente Clinton *sea* capaz de hacer eso?" Las preferencias de nuestros informantes parecen indicar una postura intermedia entre el indicativo y el subjuntivo, lo cual les acerca a la norma mexicana aunque, eso sí, sin alcanzar la frecuencia de uso del subjuntivo que es habitual en México.

Tabla 1. Modo verbal. Estoy seguro de que el presidente Clinton . . .

	Cantidad	Porcentaje
Subordinada en indicativo	48	96
Subordinada en subjuntivo	2	4
Totales	50	100

Tabla 2. Modo verbal. Dudo que el presidente Clinton . . .

	Cantidad	Porcentaje
Subordinada en indicativo	13	26
Subordinada en subjuntivo	36	72
Subordinada en infinitivo	1	2
Totales	50	100

Tabla 3. Modo verbal. Quiero que el presidente Clinton . . .

	Cantidad	Porcentaje
Subordinada en indicativo	4	8
Subordinada en subjuntivo	46	92
Totales	50	100

Tabla 4. Modo verbal. Tengo miedo que el presidente Clinton . . .

	Cantidad	Porcentaje
Subordinada en indicativo	11	22
Subordinada en subjuntivo	39	78
Totales	50	100

Tabla 5. Modo verbal. ¿Crees que el presidente Clinton . . . ?

	Cantidad	Porcentaje
Subordinada en indicativo	30	60
Subordinada en subjuntivo	20	40
Totales	50	100

El uso de la preposición *hasta* sin valor de terminación espacial o temporal es muy frecuente en el español de México. Este uso alterna, curiosamente, con su valor canónico que precisamente significa lo contrario, es decir, finalización espacial o temporal. Así pues, estos usos que son incompatibles en un mismo espacio lingüístico, son causa de frecuentes interferencias en la comunicación. Refiriéndose al uso de esta preposición, dice Lope Blanch (1993: 171) que ". . . es el único caso – felizmente – en nuestra lengua en que la innovación lingüística, el cambio sintáctico dialectal, implica un cambio de contenido y engendra total confusión." En la ciudad de México el mexicanismo *hasta* se utiliza con una intensidad cuatro veces mayor en el habla popular que en el habla culta.

Las respuestas de nuestros informantes, (tablas 6 y 7), revelan ciertas diferencias sustanciales con la situación mexicana. En efecto, solamente 3 (el 6%) de nuestros informantes interpretan la oración *Trabaja hasta las 12* con el significado de "a las 12 empieza a trabajar." En cambio en México, esta interpretación la dan el 14,3% de los encuestados. Aun así, más revelador todavía es el resultado de la oración *Abren hasta las 11.* Aquí, nuestros informantes se dividen en dos grandes bandos: El 60% la interpreta como "abren a las 11," mientras que el otro 40% opina que significa lo contrario, es decir, "cierran a las 11." Esta no es la situación que se da en México. Allí, la inmensa mayoría, el 91%, le da la interpretación mexicana, o sea, "abren a las 11"; mientras que la interpretación canónica del español general solamente es apoyada por un 8,5% de los mexicanos. Por otra parte, se observa cierta semejanza en ambas comunidades en el diferente significado que adquiere la preposición *hasta* dependiendo del verbo con el que se utilice. Es decir, si el contenido semántico del verbo implica un proceso durativo o continuado, como en el verbo *trabajar,* la preposición significa "finalización de ese proceso." En efecto, el 94% de nuestros informantes y el 84,5% de los mexicanos lo interpretan así. Este es el uso común en el español estándar. Sin embargo, cuando el contenido semántico del verbo en cuestión implica una acción puntual, que puede identificarse con cierta precisión en el tiempo, como en el caso del verbo *abrir,* la mencionada preposición pierde su valor canónico y pasa a significar lo contrario, es decir, "comienzo de la acción." Esta interpretación "mexicana" no está tan anclada entre nuestros informantes como lo está entre los mexicanos, pues, como se decía anteriormente, representa el 60% (frente al 91% de los mexicanos). Los resultados de nuestro estudio nos llevan a concluir que la norma mexicana de la preposición *hasta* no está arraigada entre los hablantes de California tan profundamente como lo está en México.

Tabla 6. Preposición *hasta*. ¿Qué significa "Trabaja hasta las 12"?

	Cantidad	Porcentaje
A las 12 empieza a trabajar	3	6
A las 12 termina de trabajar	47	94
Totales	50	100

Tabla 7. Preposición *hasta*. ¿Qué significa "Abren hasta las 11"?

	Cantidad	Porcentaje
Abren a las 11	30	60
Cierran a las 11	20	40
Totales	50	100

El pronombre *le* en construcciones del tipo *pásale*, *éntrale*, etc., ha sido identificado en otros estudios como pronombre vacío, pronombre neutro (Kany 1945) y en general se asocian con su uso connotaciones negativas o usos viciosos y defectuosos del idioma. Dice Lope Blanch (1953: 21) que "Es, ciertamente, una voz vacía, una especie de muletilla sin sentido que se ha incrustado en el lenguaje hablado, y tiene uno que resistir constantemente." Este clítico, común en el habla mexicana, carece, efectivamente, de referente sintáctico en la oración o en el discurso. Aun así, su función lingüística es clara e inequívoca, por lo que discrepamos de estos análisis y consideramos que este mal llamado pronombre sí tiene contenido semántico: Es un marcador de afectividad, familiaridad, confianza, y, en algunos casos, respeto. No es, por tanto, ni el pronombre de complemento indirecto, ni una muletilla sin sentido.

En nuestro estudio, (tablas 8, 9, 10, y 11) se observa una innegable correlación entre el nivel de confianza con el interlocutor y el uso del marcador afectivo *le*. Cuando se habla con amigos, la correspondencia entre las formas verbales familiares (tabla 8) y el clítico afectivo (tres de los informantes utilizaron *te* en lugar de *le*) es del 74%. Por el contrario, el uso de este clítico con las formas formales (usted) arroja una frecuencia del 6% solamente. Hay pues una clara tendencia a utilizar el afectivo *le* (o *te*) con las formas *tú* y a evitarlo con las formas *usted*. El marcador afectivo *te* (6%) parece indicar un grado superior de familiaridad o confianza puesto que únicamente se utiliza con formas verbales familiares y entre amigos solamente. En cambio *le* se utiliza tanto con amigos y desconocidos como con las formas familiares y formales, aunque, eso sí, no en todos los casos por igual.

Tabla 8. Recibes a tu mejor amigo en tu casa y dices . . .

	Cantidad	Porcentaje
Pásale	33	66
Pasa	9	18
Pásate	3	6
Pásele	3	6
Pase	2	4
Totales	50	100

Con desconocidos se da la situación inversa (tabla 9). La incidencia simultánea de formas verbales familiares y clítico afectivo es del 4%. Las formas verbales formales y el clítico afectivo ocurren simultáneamente en el 30% de los casos. En este caso, es decir, en el de la interacción entre dos desconocidos, el uso del afectivo *le* con la forma *usted* indica respeto en lugar de confianza o familiaridad y la ausencia del mismo, 64%, apunta hacia un mayor grado de distanciamiento afectivo.

Tabla 9. Recibes a un desconocido en tu casa y dices . . .

	Cantidad	Porcentaje
Pásale	2	4
Pasa	1	2
Pásate	0	0
Pásele	15	30
Pase	32	64
Totales	50	100

La tabla 10 muestra la frecuencia de los niveles de formalidad en la morfología verbal. Con amigos y desconocidos el uso de estos dos niveles es prácticamente opuesto. Las formas familiares ocurren con amigos en el 90% de los casos pero solamente en el 6% con desconocidos. Por otro lado, las formas formales aparecen el 10% de los casos con amigos, mientras que con desconocidos la incidencia es del 94%.

Tabla 10. Niveles de formalidad

	Con amigos		Con desconocidos	
	Cantidad	Porcentaje	Cantidad	Porcentaje
Familiar (tú)	45	90	3	6
Formal (usted)	5	10	47	94
Totales	50	100	50	100

La tabla 11 muestra la relación que hay entre los clíticos afectivos y el nivel de familiaridad entre los interlocutores al usar mandatos con verbos intransitivos. Cuando éstos son amigos, el clítico (*le* o *te*) está presente en un 78% de las ocasiones y cuando son desconocidos aparece en el 34%. Al comparar las tablas 10 y 11 se observa que hay una marcada relación entre el uso de la morfología familiar y el uso de clíticos afectivos. La morfología pronominal y verbal de carácter familiar distingue nítidamente entre interlocutores que se conocen e interlocutores que no, como se puede observar en la tabla 10. Así mismo, la tabla 11 también muestra esa misma relación, en la que la familiaridad va de la mano con el uso del clítico, mientras que el desconocimiento del interlocutor se asocia más con la ausencia del clítico que con su uso. Aun así, las diferencias de familiaridad que establece el clítico afectivo no son tan decididamente marcadas como las de la tabla 10. Sí son, en cualquier caso, reveladoras de una tendencia mayoritaria que constituye un rasgo dialectal característico.

Tabla 11. Uso de clíticos afectivos en mandatos con verbos intransitivos

	Con amigos		Con desconocidos	
	Cantidad	Porcentaje	Cantidad	Porcentaje
le	36	72	17	34
te	3	6	0	0
(sin clítico)	11	22	33	66
Totales	50	100	50	100

Una de las influencias sintácticas que más se achaca al inglés es el abundante uso de oraciones en voz pasiva, prefiriéndolas a la pasiva refleja que es de uso común en el español general (tablas 12 y 13). Nuestros informantes se inclinaron mayoritariamente por el uso tradicional en español, es decir, "la casa se ha vendido" en lugar de "la casa ha sido vendida." Dado que el pretérito perfecto se usa muy poco en la norma mexicana, se volvieron a usar las mismas oraciones, esta vez en pretérito simple. El resultado (tabla 13) arroja una mayor inclinación todavía hacia la pasiva refleja, 90%, en detrimento de la pasiva con el verbo *ser*, que en español se usa relativamente poco y en inglés, en cambio, abunda.

Tabla 12. Voz pasiva. ¿Qué forma prefiere usted?

	Cantidad	Porcentaje
La casa se ha vendido	39	78
La casa ha sido vendida	11	22
Totales	50	100

Tabla 13. Voz pasiva. ¿Qué forma prefiere usted?

	Cantidad	Porcentaje
La casa se vendió	45	90
La casa fue vendida	5	10
Totales	50	100

Una de las innovaciones morfosintácticas más características del español mexicano es la de insertar un morfema de pluralidad {-s} junto al clítico de complemento directo cuando el complemento dativo es plural. En preguntas como "¿Le diste el libro a tus primos/as?" (tablas 14 y 15), la respuesta adecuada en el español estándar es la número uno, "sí, se lo di." Sin embargo, en el español de México, y en el de California, se añade el morfema de pluralidad al pronombre acusativo en casos como éste porque el complemento dativo "a tus primos/as" es plural. Desde un punto de vista morfológico es evidente que esta construcción representa la simbiosis de un morfema léxico {lo} y uno flexivo {-s} ante la falta de transparencia de número del pronombre *se*. Dice Lope Blanch que ". . . esta incorrección no es sólo popular, sino que se ha propagado al lenguaje culto." (1953: 18).

Tabla 14. Concordancia. ¿Le diste el libro a tus primos?

	Cantidad	Porcentaje
Sí, se lo di	6	12
Sí, se los di	44	88
Totales	50	100

Tabla 15. Concordancia. ¿Le diste el libro a tus primas?

	Cantidad	Porcentaje
Sí, se lo di	7	14
Sí, se los di	25	50
Sí, se las di	18	36
Totales	50	100

En la pregunta de la tabla 15 se sustituyó *primos* por *primas* con el propósito de saber si en el trasvase semántico se incluía también el género además del número. Según Lope Blanch (1953: 19) "... la subordinación del pronombre acusativo al género propio de las personas (dativo) es menos frecuente [en México]; sólo se da en el habla vulgar." En nuestro estudio el 36% de los encuestados lo hicieron así, por lo que habrá que convenir que, si las afirmaciones de Lope Blanch son ciertas, el uso californiano se nutre o se asemeja bastante al uso vulgar de México.

El uso del cuantificador adverbial *medio* como adjetivo, es otra de las características morfosintácticas del español de México. Lope Blanch (1953: 57) afirma que "... esta adjetivación no trasciende a las clases cultas." Sin embargo, él mismo (Lope Blanch 1993: 152) opina posteriormente que "Aunque no tan absolutamente generalizada en la norma culta, la adjetivación del adverbio *medio* se produce muy frecuentemente, inclusive entre hablantes instruidos."

Tabla 16. Concordancia. Estos hombres son ...

	Cantidad	Porcentaje
medio tontos	18	36
medios tontos	32	64
Totales	50	100

En nuestro estudio, la concordancia adjetival se establese no sólo en cuanto al número (64% en la tabla 16 y 70% en la 17) sino también en cuanto al género (72% en la tabla 17 y 78% en la 18). No cabe duda que también aquí el uso californiano está más en consonancia con el uso común del habla de las clases populares mexicanas que con el de las clases cultas.

Tabla 17. Concordancia. Estas mujeres son ...

	Cantidad	Porcentaje
medio tontas	14	28
medias tontas	35	70
media tontas	1	2
Totales	50	100

Tabla 18. Concordancia. Esta mujer es ...

	Cantidad	Porcentaje
medio tonta	11	22
media tonta	39	78
Totales	50	100

En muchos países de habla española es frecuente encontrar concordancia gramatical entre verbos impersonales y su complemento directo, convirtiendo a este último en el sujeto de la oración. Ocurre frecuentemente con el verbo *haber* (ver tabla 19) y con verbos que funcionan como auxiliares de *haber,* como *deber, soler, poder* y otros (tabla 20). Esta estructura sintáctica es común en toda América y también en el español de California.

Tabla 19. Concordancia. ¿Qué forma prefiere usted?

	Cantidad	Porcentaje
Hubo muchas fiestas	36	72
Hubieron muchas fiestas	14	28
Totales	50	100

Esta construcción es típica del español popular y semiculto de México (Lope Blanch 1953: 93). Nuestro estudio indica que hay gran variación en esta construcción. En efecto, el fenómeno está muy extendido, aunque la mayoría de nuestros informantes, el 72% en la tabla 19 y el 68% en la 20, sigue prefiriendo la forma canónica del español general.

Tabla 20. Concordancia. ¿Qué forma prefiere usted?

	Cantidad	Porcentaje
Debía haber muchas personas	34	68
Debían haber muchas personas	16	32
Totales	50	100

Una construcción mexicana muy usada es la de utilizar el presente de indicativo en oraciones regidas por la frase adverbial *todavía no,* en lugar del pretérito perfecto, puesto que este último tiempo verbal ha caido en desuso en México casi por completo (Lope Blanch, 1953: 67). Esta construcción está muy extendida entre los hablantes mexicanos de cualquier nivel cultural (Lope Blanch, 1993: 153) y también se da, como vemos en la tabla 21, en el español de California. Su uso, no obstante, no parece estar tan generalizado como en México, pues el presente simple y el pretérito perfecto de indicativo comparten casi al cincuenta por ciento las preferencias de nuestros informantes.

Tabla 21. Tiempo verbal. ¿Qué forma prefiere usted?

	Cantidad	Porcentaje
Todavía no llega el cartero	28	56
Todavía no ha llegado el cartero	22	44
Totales	50	100

Como es sabido, el condicional simple como futuro de un pretérito es una forma en decadencia en el español de México, sobre todo en la lengua hablada. En nuestro estudio se pretendía saber tanto la vitalidad del mismo como sus posibles sustitutos. En la tabla 22 se ofrecen a modo de resumen las formas verbales utilizadas por nuestros informantes en la cláusula subordinada. En primer lugar, con un 40%, aparece alguna forma perifrástica de *ir+infinitivo*, normalmente en imperfecto de indicativo (*iba a . . .*), aunque también aparece en presente (*va a . . .*). A continuación, con el 30%, está el condicional simple; dato que revela una vitalidad de uso que ciertamente va más allá de lo puramente marginal.

Con este mismo uso, es decir, como futuro del pasado, el condicional en México está en vías de extinción. En México, la mayor parte de las veces que se usa lo es en su función modal, no temporal. De esta manera, los dos sustitutos principales del condicional como futuro del pasado son el pretérito imperfecto de indicativo, con el 46,6%, y el futuro perifrástico *ir+infinitivo* con el 28,3% (Moreno de Alba 1978: 104).

Nuestro estudio, en cambio, da unos resultados muy diferentes de la norma mexicana. Como ya se ha mencionado, la forma perifrástica es la sustitución más popular, viniendo a continuación el condicional, seguido del futuro simple, forma esta última que también está en decadencia en el español hablado en México. Es de destacar que la forma preferida en México, el imperfecto de indicativo, solamente recibe aquí un 6% de las preferencias.

Tabla 22. Tiempo verbal. Ayer, Juan me prometió que . . .

	Cantidad	Porcentaje
Perifrástico *ir+inf.* (pres. o pas.)	20	40
Condicional simple	15	30
Futuro simple	6	12
Subjuntivo (pres. o imperf.)	4	8
Imperfecto de indicativo	3	6
Presente de indicativo	2	4
Totales	50	100

En oraciones condicionales con imperfecto de subjuntivo (*Si yo tuviera . . .*) la apódosis va generalmente en condicional, aunque hay mucha variación de unos dialectos a otros. En el español de México esta forma del condicional es muy infrecuente si nos atenemos a lo que dice Lope Blanch (1953: 78–80), "la forma en *-ría* ha caído en el más completo desuso dentro de la lengua hablada. . . . En definitiva; cuando pueden usarse indistintamente las formas en *-ra* y en *-ría*, el español de México se inclina por completo hacia la forma en *-ra*." En oposición a Lope Blanch, Moreno de Alba afirma no haber recogido ninguna muestra de imperfecto de subjuntivo (la forma en *-ra*) en este tipo de construcciones.[2] Y añade que en el español mexicano "no se usa *cantara* en apódosis de cláusulas condicionales con prótasis en pretérito [imperfecto] de subjuntivo sino sólo el pospretérito [condicional]: "Si las penas mataran, me *moriría* en poco tiempo" (Moreno de Alba 1978: 108). En cualquier caso, en el español general, como decimos, lo más frecuente es usar el condicional en apódosis de cláusulas condicionales.

En nuestro estudio hemos recogido diferentes apódosis que completan la oración de la prótasis *Si yo tuviera mucho dinero* . . . y que se ofrecen en la tabla 23. La forma de mayor frecuencia es precisamente el condicional simple (52%), seguida del imperfecto de subjuntivo (24%) y de otras formas que tienen mucha menos frecuencia. Estos resultados parecen indicar que, además de la vigencia del condicional, el imperfecto de subjuntivo sigue utilizándose por un número importante de usuarios, a semejanza del frecuente uso que de él hacían los clásicos de la literatura española en construcciones similares.

Mención especial merecen las formas híbridas de condicional e imperfecto de subjuntivo que hemos recogido, así como las formas no estándar de condicional. Todas ellas suman un 14% de los casos, porcentaje que no puede pasar desapercibido. Las formas híbridas recogidas son *saldiera*, *salidiera*, *saldriera*, y *salidriera*. Estas formas, producidas por cuatro personas diferentes, parecen tener todas ellas los mismos componentes: el radical irregular del condicional o parte de él (*sald*(*r*)) y la desinencia verbal del imperfecto de subjuntivo (-*iera*). Además de éstas, hay otras tres muestras de condicional que no son estándar: *saliría* (2) y *salidría*. Estas formas híbridas y no estándar podrían interpretarse como un signo de decadencia del condicional, como la competencia de dos formas – el condicional simple y el imperfecto de subjuntivo – por el mismo espacio lingüístico, y también como signo de una deficiente escolarización en español. Sea cual sea la explicación, es evidente que estas formas revelan cierta inestabilidad en el sistema verbal en este tipo de cláusulas.

Tabla 23. Tiempo verbal. Si yo tuviera mucho dinero . . .

	Cantidad	Porcentaje
Condicional simple	26	52
Imperfecto de subjuntivo	12	24
Imperfecto de indicativo	4	8
Forma híbrida cond-subj.	4	8
Condicional simple no estándar	3	6
Infinitivo	1	2
Totales	50	100

En la sección narrativa, los participantes tenían que describir el cuento de Caperucita Roja con la ayuda de una serie de dibujos que, en forma gráfica, resumían el cuento. Con esta tarea se pretendía averiguar el grado de interferencia de la lengua inglesa y cualquier otra característica que se saliera de lo habitual. En general todas las narrativas eran perfectamente entendibles. A pesar de ello, se detectaron las siguientes desviaciones de la norma del español general.

- En primer lugar, y quizá sea esto lo que más destaca, se registró el uso de préstamos del inglés. Esta práctica se debe, seguramente, al desconocimiento de determinado vocablo en español, o quizá al hecho de no recordar en ese momento la palabra más adecuada. Ejemplos: ". . . le dijo a un *hunter* que estaba afuera . . .", "a llevarle una jarrita de *chocomilk,*" "lo esta *shuteando,*" "que le llevara una *basqueta* de comida," "en el bosque había una . . . *squirrel.*" El uso de la expresión *okay*, por "de acuerdo" es frecuente, así como el de *bye-bye* por "adiós," etc.

- El uso de conjunciones e interjecciones en inglés como elementos discursivos. Esta práctica es una especie de muletilla en la que el hablante se apoya mientras reagrupa sus pensamientos o se prepara para continuar la narración. Generalmente sucede en momentos de titubeo. Ejemplos: "*So,* . . . ella se fue por el bosque . . .", "*So,* el lobo salió . . .", ". . . y le dice que . . . *well* . . . que . . ."

- Excluyendo los casos de préstamos léxicos y las citadas muletillas, no se produjo ningún caso de alternancia de códigos en elementos sintácticamente productivos, sólo en algunas frases hechas como en ésta: "y vivieron juntos *happily ever after.*"

- También se han registrado algunas extensiones de tipo semántico. Es decir, la atribución de significados de alguna palabra en inglés a la palabra española que originariamente carece de esa cualidad semántica. Por ejemplo, "y se metió en la cama para *pretender* ser la abuela," donde *pretender* se usa con el significado en inglés de "aparentar" y no con su significado propio de "aspirar, desear." En "algo para *traerle* a la abuela" se da un caso similar, en el que el verbo *traer* se usa como se haría en inglés en la lengua coloquial, en lugar de decir "algo para llevarle a la abuela." En fin, en "para visitar *con* ella" se observa el uso de la preposición *con* tal y como se haría en inglés.

- En estas narrativas también se observa un excesivo uso de tiempos progresivos, "la ardilla le *está diciendo* al cazador..," usos no estándar del binomio ser/estar, "el lobo *estaba* muy grande," falta de distinción aspectual entre el pretérito y el imperfecto de indicativo, "fue a decirle que el lobo *estuvo* en la casa," usos poco comunes de la voz pasiva, como en "*estaban salvadas* por el hombre" y "*estuvieron salvadas* las dos," usos atípicos ambos tanto por la construcción pasiva resultativa como por el uso de *estar* en lugar de *ser*. Por último, cabe mencionar así mismo los usos no estándar del modo verbal, en los que se constata la disminución del uso del subjuntivo en construcciones donde el español estándar lo requiere. Por ejemplo, "como si lo *va* a matar," "no cree que *es* la abuelita," "como si él *era* su abuelita," etc.

6. Conclusión

Los datos que se han recogido en este trabajo constituyen una representación fidedigna de esta muestra de 50 personas. Su extrapolación a la población total de California es más aventurada y conlleva ciertos riesgos. El habla de la población rural, por ejemplo, no está representada en este trabajo. Además, la muestra se basa fundamentalmente en el habla de individuos de primera generación, hecho que también impone límites a la hora de hablar del español de California. Sin embargo, no se puede soslayar el hecho de que este grupo social, por sus características socioeconómicas y educativas, representa una de las porciones de la comunidad hispana con más dinamismo, futuro y posibilidad de ascenso social.

En definitiva, tanto mediante los cuestionarios como las narrativas, se ha observado que este dialecto del español contiene elementos gramaticales que lo identifican fundamentalmente como español mexicano. Es, sin embargo, un mexicano especial, pues se asemeja y se diferencia de la norma mexicana. Los datos que se han recogido en este estudio muestran que el español de California que hablan estos universitarios es de extracción netamente popular, pues muchas de las estructuras sintácticas que en México se indentifican como propias del habla popular, son las habituales entre estos hablantes.

A grandes rasgos, puede decirse que internamente el español de California es más conservador, más tradicional, y por lo tanto, menos propenso a la innovación que su pariente mexicano. Así lo atestigua por ejemplo, el mayor uso del imperfecto de subjuntivo (tabla 23), del pretérito perfecto de indicativo (tabla 21) que en México ya se han perdido mientras que en California todavía se conservan.

Paradójicamente, es al mismo tiempo un dialecto abierto a la innovación motivada por causas externas. Estas causas, por todos conocidas, son su permanente contacto con la lengua dominante del país, su situación diglósica subordinada en la que no comparte con el inglés importantes ámbitos de uso, sino que, al contrario, se ve limitado a ámbitos sociales como la familia, los amigos y la vecindad. Esta situación hace que el español reciba un constante influjo de la lengua dominante en todos los módulos de la lengua: tanto en el dominio de la fonética, como en la morfosintaxis, el léxico y la semántica, las innovaciones originadas como consecuencia del contacto con el inglés son innegables.

Noten que digo innovaciones en lugar de corrupciones, pérdidas, incorrecciones o anomalías porque no creo que estemos ante una situación cataclísmica como a veces se pinta. Este dialecto, con todos sus problemas, es vibrante y dinámico. Su estructura gramatical es sólida y perfectamente entendible por los hablantes de los demás dialectos. Muchas de las desviaciones de la norma que observamos en este dialecto, u otras de la misma naturaleza, se dan en todos y cada uno de los dialectos del español. Sin embargo, en situaciones monolingües o allá donde el español es la lengua dominante, los cambios que constantemente operan en la lengua, se ven como el resultado natural de la evolución de la misma. El español de California también evoluciona, pero lo hace de acuerdo a las circunstancias que le son naturales en su entorno geográfico y social.

En cuanto al mantenimiento o pérdida de la lengua, es necesario diferenciar entre el individuo y la colectividad. En lo concerniente al individuo son de sobra conocidos casos de pérdida parcial o incluso total de la lengua. En cuanto al grupo social hispano, visto de forma global, es más difícil y aventurado hablar de pérdida del idioma. Cabría más bien apuntar hacia ciertos cambios, fundamentalmente de carácter léxico, que en esta variedad son más aparentes que en otras.

En cualquier caso, y a pesar de las recientes disposiciones gubernamentales, el mantenimiento y promoción del español de California está prácticamente asegurado. Los constantes movimientos migratorios, el paulatino ascenso social de la comunidad mexicoamericana, y la creciente toma de conciencia del valor que tiene la lengua materna como amalgama y símbolo de indentidad cultural, hacen prever que esta variedad de español discurra por un único camino, el del progreso y la expansión.

Notas

1. Este proyecto contó con la colaboración de seis investigadores del citado departamento. Se llevó a cabo entre los meses de marzo y abril de 1998 y fue dirigido por Jacqueline Toribio.

2. Dice Moreno de Alba (1978: 150): "Es importante aclarar que, aunque no tengo documentados casos de pretérito de subjuntivo [imperfecto] en funciones de apódosis de condicionales con prótasis tácita del tipo: 'No se preocupe; *estuviera* aullando (si le hubiera picado un alacrán),' sí se escuchan en el habla mexicana. Sin embargo, con prótasis expresa 'No le *guardara* rencor si viniera,' 'Si en sus tiempos hubiera habido cine, también a ella le *gustara*,' tampoco documentados en mi material, no me parecen usuales en el español de México."

Referencias

Kany, Charles E. *American-Spanish syntax*. Chicago: University of Chicago Press.

Lope-Blanch, Juan M. 1953. *Observaciones sobre la sintaxis del español hablado en México*. México: Publicaciones del Instituto Hispano Mexicano de Investigaciones Científicas.

Lope-Blanch, Juan M. 1993. *Ensayos sobre el español de América*. México: Universidad Nacional Autónoma de México.

Moreno de Alba, José G. 1978. *Valores de las formas verbales en el español de México*. México: Universidad Nacional Autónoma de México.

Intraethnic Attitudes among Hispanics in a Northern California Community

Susana V. Rivera-Mills
Northern Arizona University

1. Introduction

The field of language attitudes has been extensively researched in the last twenty years. Attitudes toward Spanish by the three Hispanic groups with the largest populations and the longest history of settlement in the United States have received the majority of researchers' attention. Mexican-Americans in the Southwest and elsewhere have been studied by Elías-Olivares (1976), Amastae (1982), Sánchez (1983), and Aguirre (1985). Puerto Ricans in New York City have received attention from researchers such as Pedraza (1987) and Zentella (1981), and Cuban-Americans have been studied by Solé (1982) and García (1988).

As these various studies have shown, the use of Spanish by these groups is often influenced by the attitudes and behavior of both Anglos and Hispanics toward Spanish. The increased immigration of other Latin American groups has also had a strong influence on the use of Spanish and the established attitudes toward various Hispanic groups; however, it is only in the last decade that these newly arrived Latino groups have been studied within a sociolinguistic context.

Among the researchers who have begun to look at the intraethnic attitudes of various Hispanic groups in the United States are Zentella (1981, 1990) and Galindo (1995). Zentella studies this particular topic by looking at lexical variation and attitudes toward the use of specific lexical items among four Hispanic groups in New York: Puerto Ricans, Dominicans, Colombians, and Cubans. Galindo also examines both interethnic and intraethnic attitudes toward Spanish varieties within a Chicano perspective. Although various Hispanic groups are being included in recent studies, sociolinguistic research still lags behind the ever-changing language ideologies of Hispanic groups in the United States.

 Research on Spanish in the U.S., ed. Ana Roca, 377–389. Somerville, MA: Cascadilla Press.

Given the constant changes in the demographics of Hispanics in the United States, there is a need to look beyond the widely studied interethnic attitudes (attitudes between majority and minority groups) and begin to focus on the dynamics of intraethnic attitudes (attitudes within an ethnic group) in order to further explain the issues surrounding the process of language maintenance and shift. It is the purpose of this study to analyze the intraethnic attitudes that exist among Hispanics of diverse nationalities and backgrounds in the northern California community of Fortuna. This paper focuses specifically on the variables of generation and social class, and how these variables are associated with language loyalty and language politics. Furthermore, the different perspectives of recent immigrants versus those of Hispanic residents are discussed as they relate to intraethnic attitudes.

2. Methodology

Numerous sources were consulted (Fishman 1971, 1972, Cohen 1975, Labov 1984, Hurtado 1994) and various sample questionnaires were collected in order to outline the best measures for each of the attitudinal categories addressed in this study. Overall, the topic of study and the theoretical approach that was chosen determined to a great extent the type of instruments that were utilized in the data collection process.

Sociolinguistic interviews were carried out with 50 Hispanics of various nationalities representing three generations of immigration in the United States. Three domains that currently play strong roles in the community served as initial contact points for the recruitment of participants. Other contacts were made using a networking approach from the points of reference, as well as from individual participants. Each interview was conducted in the home of the participant by the same researcher and lasted from two to five hours. During the interview process, participants were allowed to choose the language with which they felt more comfortable. In addition, ethnographic observations such as social class level, interactions with others, and general behavior were noted separately, immediately following the interview.

The attitudinal section of the questionnaire, relevant to the present study, included scalar statements, discrete point questions, and open-ended questions which elicited information about language loyalty and language politics. The section regarding language politics addressed issues that affect Hispanics in California. This section also attempted to measure the level of political awareness and involvement of the participants.

Fortuna is a small town located in the extreme northern part of California in Humboldt County. It is the city with the highest concentration of Hispanics in the county; 6% of its population of 8,788 is Hispanic (1990 U.S. Census). Of the 50 participants interviewed for the present study, 22 are male and 28 are female. The participants have diverse nationalities, with the largest group coming from Mexico (34%), followed closely by those born in the United States (32%), and the third largest group being from El Salvador (22%). Other nationalities represented are those from Peru, Venezuela, Puerto Rico, Colombia, and Chile. The ages of the participants range from 12 to 71 years old. Within this age range, three generations of immigration of Hispanics in the United States are represented, with 16 belonging to the first generation, 24 belonging to the second generation, and 10 belonging to the third generation. Lastly, participants also were divided into three social classes: lower, middle, and upper.[1] Of the total sample, 23 participants belong to the lower class, 15 to the middle class, and 12 form part of the upper class. As is seen in the following section, both of these variables, generation and social class, are strongly associated with the language attitudes of the sample.

3. Findings

3.1. Language loyalty

With respect to language loyalty, participants were asked to respond on a five-point scale to the following two affective statements: (1) It is important for me to maintain my Spanish, and (2) I prefer to speak Spanish more than English. The scale measured the participant's level of agreement with the statements (1 = strongly agree; 5 = strongly disagree). The mean score for statement #1 for the overall sample is quite high: 1.24. However, the mean score for statement #2 fluctuates a bit toward the opposite end of the scale, showing a 2.56 mean. In both cases there seems to be a strong connection to the Spanish language. When these statements are cross-tabulated with the variable of generation, several changes appear.

Table 1. Agreement with "It is important for me to maintain my Spanish"

Generation	SA	NA/ND	MD	n
1st	88%	6%	6%	16
2nd	100%	0%	0%	24
3rd	50%	25%	25%	10

SA = strongly agree, NA/ND = neither agree nor disagree, MD = moderately disagree

As can be seen in Table 1, when comparing the first and the third generations, the level of agreement with statement #1 greatly diminishes. However, an exception is found with the second generation where 100% of the participants strongly agree with the statement. Because the second generation is the first generation to experience linguistic and cultural distance from Spanish, it is possible to hypothesize that they are especially aware of the importance of maintaining their language. When statement #1 is cross-tabulated with the variable of social class, no significant patterns are found. However, the level of agreement with the statement does decrease from 100% in the lower class to

83% in the upper class, showing a higher level of loyalty among lower class participants.

Table 2. Language participants prefer to speak

Generation / Class	English	Spanish	Both	n
1st generation	19%	75%	6%	16
2nd generation	37%	42%	21%	24
3rd generation	40%	30%	30%	10
Lower class	15%	75%	10%	23
Middle class	42%	38%	20%	15
Upper class	43%	36%	21%	12

p=.062

With respect to statement #2, both variables show associations, as can be seen in Table 2. With each subsequent generation, the preference for English increases. The inverse relationship is also true and more dramatic; Spanish preference decreases by 45% from first to third generation. The same is true as we move from the lower to the upper class, with English being preferred by the upper social class. In both cases, the higher the level of acculturation, as indicated by upper social class and later generation in the United States, the lower the loyalty to Spanish.

Interestingly enough, when participants were asked to expand on their responses, a second-generation female offered the following comment:

> I look in the mirror and I can't deny who I am and where I come from. I know some of us try to pretend we can become 'gringos' by dyeing our hair blond and wearing jeans, but I think even those people must know that they can't deny our heritage – se lleva en la sangre.

Notice that in spite of her strong feelings toward her heritage, the majority of her response was in English. Table 3 shows the responses to the question "Who speaks the best Spanish in Fortuna?"

As the data show, there is not a clear loyalty toward a specific variety of Spanish. The largest percentage of this sample did not have an opinion as to who spoke the best Spanish. In many cases, the participants were not aware of which varieties were spoken in the community and yet did not feel that their variety was the best. The second largest percentage of responses were of those who felt that the best Spanish was spoken by educated Hispanics regardless of their nationality. All of the participants who chose this category also included themselves as part of that group.

Table 3. Assessment of language varieties in Fortuna

Best language variety in Fortuna	Percentage
South American	13%
Salvadorans	15%
Puerto Ricans	2%
Castilians	7%
Educated Spanish	26%
All the same	4%
Don't know	33%

n=50, p=.075

Of all of these varieties, the South American response is the most unusual because it is not representative of the South American participants. Most of the participants who felt that South Americans spoke the best Spanish were of Mexican descent, whereas the majority of the South American participants chose educated Spanish as their response. Furthermore, in spite of the fact that the majority of the participants are of Mexican descent, this particular variety of Spanish was not mentioned as one of the best varieties of the community.

These findings are in contrast with studies such as García et al. 1988, in which South American and Central American participants demonstrate a high level of loyalty toward their specific variety of Spanish. However, even in García's study we find Cuban, Dominican, and Puerto Rican participants who reported that their Spanish was not as good as that of their South American friends. In both cases there seems to be an ambivalence in the loyalty to one's own language variety. Additional research needs to be conducted in order to see if this ambivalence is due to social hierarchies, linguistic discrimination, or lack of proficiency on the part of the participants.

Table 4. Assessment of Spanish spoken at home

Spanish spoken at home	Percentage
Better	75%
Same	8%
Different	17%

n=36, p=.053

Table 4 also reveals interesting perspectives with regard to language loyalty. The participants' comparisons of their home Spanish versus that typically spoken in Fortuna show that three fourths of the sample feels that the Spanish they speak at home is better than that spoken in Fortuna. These results seem contradictory to what is shown in Table 3. However, given the fact that many of the participants did not know which different varieties of Spanish were spoken in the community, and most assumed that the recent immigrant Mexican variety of Spanish, a variety which is not valued, was the "typical variety" of the community, the findings in Table 4 are not surprising.

The last question asked about language loyalty was whether a person needs to speak Spanish in order to be Hispanic. The results of this statement are in Table 5.

Table 5. Spanish as it relates to ethnicity

To be Hispanic you must speak Spanish	Percentage
Strongly agree	30%
Moderately agree	20%
Neither agree nor disagree	17%
Moderately disagree	30%
Strongly disagree	3%

n=50, mean=2.55, p=.083

As can be seen, there is much diversity among the responses that the participants reported. Only 30% of the sample strongly agrees with the statement, whereas the same percentage moderately disagrees. Some participants feel very strongly that language and identity are connected and should never be separated, as stated by a female participant:

> Yo no creo que una persona puede decir que es hispana sin hablar español. La lengua es parte de nuestra identidad y si te da vergüenza hablarla o no te preocupas por mantenerla es porque no te importa ni tu cultura ni tu identidad. . . .
>
> 'I don't think that a person can say that he or she is Hispanic without speaking Spanish. Language is part of our identity and if you are embarrassed speaking it, or you are not concerned with maintaining it, it is because you do not care about your culture or your identity. . . .'

On the other hand, other respondents belonging to the second and third generations feel that language had little to do with identity or culture. A second-generation participant made the following statement:

> I think you can be Hispanic without speaking the language. There are many Hispanics in the United States who don't speak Spanish and they still consider themselves Hispanic because they continue to have the cultural values and traditions of our culture. . . .

And a third-generation participant made the following statement:

> I really don't know how to answer you. When you come to the United States, I think you have to adapt and change. Sometimes that means letting go of other things like language.

When cross-tabulating this statement with the variable of generation, a significant (p<=.01) pattern is revealed, as seen in the top half of Table 6.

Table 6. Agreement with "To be Hispanic you must speak Spanish"

Generation / Class	Agree	NA/ND	Disagree	n
1st generation	69%	13%	18%	16
2nd generation	42%	24%	34%	24
3rd generation	0%	0%	100%	10
Lower class	76%	6%	18%	23
Middle class	36%	18%	46%	15
Upper class	24%	33%	43%	12

The level of agreement with this statement significantly decreases with each subsequent generation. A similar pattern occurs with the variable of social class, as seen in the bottom half of Table 6. The lower class has a much higher level of agreement than the middle or upper class. Overall, language loyalty in this community appears to be strongly tied to both generation and social class.

3.2. Language politics

The section on language politics also contains some telling results. This section contained yes/no questions as well as several open-ended questions and scalar statements. The results of the yes/no statements relevant to this study are shown in Table 7.

Table 7. Responses to political questions

Questions	Yes	No	n
Would you become a U.S. citizen?	79%	21%	14
Do you know what Proposition 187 is?	25%	75%	42
Are you familiar with the English Only movement?	54%	46%	42
Do you know what bilingual education is?	85%	15%	44

The majority of the participants are already citizens of the United States. Of those who are not, 79% said they intend to become citizens. Compared to the findings of Hurtado et al. (1992), which showed a low rate of naturalization among Latinos in southern California, the present results indicate a general feeling of contentment and a willingness to become part of this country. When asked about California's Proposition 187, which denies social services and government benefits to illegal immigrants and has now been extended to deny social security benefits and medical benefits to non-citizens, an overwhelming majority of the participants replied that they were not familiar with this initiative. After an initial response was obtained, the proposition was explained and participants were asked if they felt this would have a negative effect on the Hispanic population of California in the future. The responses suggest a general lack of solidarity among Hispanics in the community. As a first-generation participant explains:

> A mí no me preocupa. Yo soy ciudadana y no tengo ningún problema con eso. En realidad comprendo por qué el gobierno hace esto . . . vienen tantos que supongo que tienen que ver como 'manage' sus recursos ¿no?
>
> 'It doesn't worry me. I am a citizen and I don't have a problem with that. In reality, I understand why the government does this . . . so many come that I suppose they have to figure out how to manage their resources. No?'

However, those who were not United States citizens were most aware of the implications of Proposition 187. They did express concern, as stated by the following participant:

> Por eso es que me quiero hacer ciudadana cuanto antes. Es una desgracia porque siento que estoy traicionando a mi país, pero ¿qué se va a hacer?
>
> 'That is why I want to become a citizen as soon as possible. It is a shame because I feel that I am betraying my country, but what can one do?'

These results confirm the observed division between recent immigrants and those who have been in the United States for a longer period of time. Those who have been here and have become United States citizens feel a certain responsibility and loyalty to their new nation, yet others who are also United States citizens simply are not concerned with immigrant issues because these issues do not affect them directly. With respect to English Only, a bare majority were familiar with some aspects of this movement. Of those who were familiar with the movement nearly 50% agree that English should be the official language of the United States, as stated by one participant: "After all, we are living in the United States . . . just like Mexico has Spanish, why shouldn't we have English?" As with Proposition 187, feelings toward English Only also tend to be divided along citizenship lines. Finally, of the various language politics topics, the one that participants were most familiar with was bilingual education. Of the 85% that were familiar with bilingual education programs, only 28% supported them or felt they were a good idea. Others felt they were a waste of time, that they slowed children down, and that traditional English programs were better. Furthermore, participants were also asked if they felt that children in Fortuna would benefit from an English/Spanish bilingual program. Only 15% of the participants felt that this would be beneficial. Others felt that if their children wanted to learn Spanish they could do so at home or at the high school. Most participants felt that the teaching of Spanish is a responsibility that lies in the home and not with the school, in spite of the fact that they are not teaching their children Spanish in the home. Although no significant correlations were found, with each subsequent generation, less and less was known about politics affecting Hispanics, and less support was given to programs that support the teaching of Spanish. However, with respect to social class, it was observed that the lower social class was more concerned with the general anti-Hispanic atmosphere in California than was the upper class. As stated by one participant, when describing her feelings about shopping at the community mall:

> Cada vez que entro en una de esas tiendas, me siento muy incómoda. Siento que me andan siguiendo como si me fuera a robar algo. Yo creo que ellos piensan que todos somos maleantes. . . .
>
> 'Each time that I go into one of those stores, I feel very uncomfortable. I feel that they are following me as if I were going to steal something. I believe that they think that we are all thieves. . . .'

However, it is interesting to note that most of the participants who belong to the lower class are also recent immigrants. Therefore, it is not so much social class that is associated with these attitudes as it is the division between recent immigrants and established residents of the community.

3.3. Intraethnic attitudes

In addition, in order to further investigate intraethnic attitudes, participants were asked the following question: "What adjectives would you use to describe Hispanics in Fortuna?" As you can see from Table 8, the majority of participants used negative descriptors such as *flojos*, *maleducados*, *sin educación*, *ignorantes*, *vividores*, *impermeables*, etc. A few used positive adjectives such as *trabajadores*, culturally strong, family focus, and helpful. Others were more neutral such as *campesinos*, *constantes*, humble, etc. It is interesting to note that the majority of the negative adjectives were expressed in Spanish. Upon further analysis of the data, an obvious tendency arises in which these negative Spanish adjectives are expressed mostly by first-generation participants. These first-generation participants are also ones who have resided in Fortuna for a minimum of 10 years. When expressing their feelings about other Hispanics by using negative descriptions, it is apparent that they are referring to recent Mexican arrivals. These results confirm a lack of solidarity among Hispanics in this community, and a general tension that, although not stated explicitly, seems to be aimed at the recent arrivals of Mexican origin.

Table 8. Types of adjectives used to describe Hispanics in Fortuna

Adjectives	Percentage used
Negative	71%
Positive	18%
Other	11%

p=.051

This lack of solidarity is seen even among those who share the same country of origin. A first-generation male participant expressed this lack of solidarity in the following way:

> me preguntas ¿qué pienso de los hispanos en la comunidad? Déjame decirte lo que pienso con un pequeño cuento: había un hombre ya viejo caminando por la playa y este hombre llevaba dos baldes amarrados a un palo que cargaba entre los hombros. Estaba caminando por la playa cuando un niño lo vió y salió corriendo para donde él. El niño curioso le preguntó que qué llevaba en los baldes, y el viejo le contesto que llevaba cangrejos. El niño se dió cuenta que uno de los baldes estaba tapado y el otro no, entonces le preguntó al viejo que por qué llevaba uno tapado. El viejo le respondió que en el balde que estaba tapado había cangrejos asiáticos y tenía que taparlos porque constantemente se estaban ayudando el uno al otro a salir del balde. El otro balde tenía cangrejos latinos y ése no se tenía que tapar porque cada vez que uno se quería salir, siempre había otro que lo bajaba para pararse en él . . . así que ves, así son los hispanos de Fortuna, nunca vas a ver que se ayuden como lo hacen los orientales. . . .
>
> 'You ask me what I think about the Hispanics in the community. Let me tell you what I think with a short story. There was an old man walking on the beach, and this man was carrying two buckets that were tied to a stick that he carried on

> his shoulders. He was walking on the beach when a boy saw him and ran toward him. The curious boy asked him what he was carrying in the buckets and the old man responded that he was carrying crabs. The boy noticed that one of the buckets was covered while the other one was not, then he asked the old man why one of them was covered. The old man responded that the bucket that was covered had Asian crabs and he had to cover them because they were constantly helping each other to get out of the bucket. The other bucket had Latino crabs and that one did not need to be covered because each time one wanted to get out, there was always another one that pulled it down to step on it . . . so, you see, that is how the Hispanics of Fortuna are, you will never see them helping each other like the Orientals. . . .'

Although a very discouraging story, it paints a clear picture of intraethnic attitudes and tensions in the community. An additional observation is that this tension seems to diminish with each subsequent generation. Although members of the third generation do not have a sense of belonging to a Hispanic community, because of their level of acculturation, they also do not seem to have negative feelings toward each other. Perhaps the tension is greater among members of the first generation because social class is a large part of their cultural ideology.

4. Conclusion

The results of the present study establish clear parameters of social class associated with the participants' overall language ideology. Both the differences in social class and the varied nationalities contribute to the existing intraethnic tensions in this community. Furthermore, all tensions diminish with each subsequent generation as the level of acculturation increases. This, in turn, minimizes solidarity, language loyalty, and the political awareness of issues affecting new immigrants, particularly with third-generation participants.

New Hispanic immigrants continue to arrive in Fortuna, and their impact on the language and attitudes of this community is difficult to predict. Much will depend on their cultural and social backgrounds as well as the willingness of the current group to accept them as part of the community. The present study has established important variables which allow predictions about the issues that new immigrant populations may face. It will be interesting to see if these predictions are borne out.

Notes

1. The variable of social class was determined by the researcher through observation and a combination of variables such as occupation and education. Given the fact that all interviews were conducted in the participants' homes, it was not difficult to assess the participants' social class in broad terms. The three categories were defined in terms of the following rubric:

- Lower class: high school diploma or less, does not own a home, little material assets, unskilled laborer.
- Middle class: some college education, owns a home and a car, some material assets, skilled blue collar worker.
- Upper class: college degree(s), owns a home and cars, substantial material assets, professional.

Generally speaking, assets were defined as furniture, stereos, televisions, and other objects that were displayed in the person's home. Although originally the variable of social class included income, this proved to be a socially inappropriate question. Certain cultural and social sensitivities had to be observed, and these dictated the need to develop a less intrusive instrument to measure social class. It was for this purpose that the above-mentioned rubric was developed.

References

Aguirre, Adalberto. 1985. An experimental study of code alternation. *International Journal of the Sociology of Language* 53: 59–82.

Amastae, John. 1982. Language shift and maintenance in the lower Rio Grande Valley of southern Texas. In *Bilingualism and language contact: Spanish, English, and Native American languages*, ed. F. Barkin, A. Brandt, and J. Ornstein-Galicia, 261–277. New York: Teachers College Press.

Cohen, Andrew. 1975. Assessing language maintenance in Spanish speaking communities in the Southwest. In *El lenguaje de los Chicanos*, ed. E. Hernández-Chávez et al., 202–219. Arlington, VA: Center for Applied Linguistics.

Elías-Olivares, Lucía. 1976. Ways of speaking in a Chicano community: A sociolinguistic approach. Ph.D. dissertation, University of Texas.

Fishman, Joshua. 1972. *The sociology of language*. Rowley, MA: Newbury House Publishers.

Fishman, Joshua. 1971. *Bilingualism in the barrio*. Bloomington, IN: Indiana University Publications.

Galindo, Leticia. 1995. Language attitudes toward Spanish and English varieties: A Chicano perspective. *Hispanic Journal of Behavioral Sciences* 17: 5–17.

García, Ofelia, Isabel Evangelista, Mabel Martínez, Carmen Disla, and Bonifacio Paulino. 1988. Spanish language use and attitudes: A study of two New York City communities. *Language and Society* 17: 475–511.

Hurtado, Aída. 1994. Does similarity breed respect: Interviewer evaluations of Mexican-descent respondents in a bilingual survey. *Public Opinion Quarterly* 58.1: 77–93.

Hurtado, Aída, David Hayes-Bautista, R. Burciaga Valdez, and Anthony Hernández. 1992. *Redefining California: Latino social engagement in a multicultural society*. Los Angeles, CA: UCLA Chicano Studies Research Center.

Labov, William. 1984. Field methods of the project on linguistic change and variation. In *Language in use: Readings in sociolinguistics*, ed. J. Baugh and J. Sherzer, 28–53. Englewood Cliffs, NJ: Prentice Hall.

Pedraza, Pedro. 1987. An ethnographic analysis of language use in the Puerto Rican community of East Harlem, Working Paper #12. New York: Center for Puerto Rican Studies Language Policy Task Force, Hunter College, City University of New York.

Sánchez, Rosaura. 1983. *Chicano discourse*. Houston, TX: Arte Público Press.

Solé, Carlos A. 1982. Language loyalty and language attitudes among Cuban Americans. In *Bilingual education for Hispanic students in the United States*, ed. J. Fishman and G. Keller, 254–268. New York: Teachers College Press.

Zentella, Ana Celia. 1990. El impacto de la realidad socio-económica en las comunidades hispanoparlantes de los Estados Unidos: Reto a la teoría y metodología lingüística. In *Spanish in the United States: Sociolinguistic issues*, ed. J. Bergen, 152–166. Washington, DC: Georgetown University Press.

Zentella, Ana Celia. 1981. Language variety among Puerto Ricans. In *Language in the U.S.A.*, ed. C. Ferguson and S.B. Heath, 218–238. New York: Cambridge University Press.

“Proyecto para formar un ciudadano bilingüe”: política lingüística y el español en Puerto Rico

Luis A. Ortiz-López
Universidad de Puerto Rico

1. Introducción

Las lenguas, como fenómenos vivos que son, deben estudiarse, además de la perspectiva estrictamente lingüística, en relación con la sociedad con la cual conviven, en especial, con las estructuras de poder y los sistemas políticos con los que se relacionan. Los estudios sociolingüísticos han confirmado tal relación al probar cómo interactúan interdependiente o independientemente variables lingüísticas y sociales en los hechos del lenguaje. Las actitudes y las creencias lingüísticas son un buen ejemplo de los vínculos que se establecen entre la lengua y la sociedad. Muchos fenómenos del español en Puerto Rico, entre ellos, el contacto lingüístico y, como consecuencia, la política lingüística, deben abordarse desde una perspectiva sociolingüística.

Hablar de política lingüística es adentrarnos en temas lingüísticos y extralingüísticos muy complejos y polémicos, que van más allá de la investigación y del conocimiento de los sistemas lingüísticos en cuestión, y se extienden a asuntos socio-políticos profundos, como por ejemplo, el papel que desempeñan la nación, los grupos nacionales y étnicos, la migración, así como los procesos de asimilación, aculturación, transculturación, integración, multiculturalismo, que se producen en situaciones de contacto de lenguas. Por lo tanto, una política lingüística requiere una planificación rigurosa y sistemática que considere consciente y deliberadamente los recursos lingüísticos de una sociedad para lograr determinados fines educativos, políticos y económicos (Pousada 1996: 505). La selección de la lengua nacional y oficial en un determinado país, así como su promoción dentro de la sociedad son objetivos fundamentales de esta disciplina.

 Research on Spanish in the U.S., ed. Ana Roca, 390–405. Somerville, MA: Cascadilla Press.

En este trabajo, examinamos desde una perspectiva sociohistórica y lingüística las diferentes políticas idiomáticas que se han puesto en marcha en el escenario sociolingüístico puertorriqueño, a partir del contacto lingüístico español-inglés que se produce en la Isla con la invasión norteamericana en 1898 y que se extiende hasta nuestros días, así como las consecuencias lingüísticas de tal relación política e idiomática. Sobre este tema se han escrito y se escribirán muchas páginas, pues, representa uno de los temas vitales en la definición política de Puerto Rico. Tan reciente como en 1997, al cumplirse casi un siglo de dominio norteamericano en la Isla, y después de múltiples intentos fallidos por convertir en 'bilingües' a los ciudadanos americanos puertorriqueños, el Departamento de Educación de Puerto Rico aprueba y pone en marcha un nuevo proyecto de política lingüística con el objetivo de "formar un ciudadano puertorriqueño bilingüe." Esta nueva propuesta lingüística representa cambios tanto en la enseñanza del vernáculo como en la enseñanza del inglés. Antes de considerar esta nueva política idiomática, trazaremos una mirada restrospectiva a los cien años de convivencia sociolingüística con los norteamericanos.[1]

2. Lengua y enseñanza: cien años de política lingüística en Puerto Rico

Después de cuatro siglos de predominio político y lingüístico español, España cede el territorio de Puerto Rico a los Estados Unidos en 1898 mediante el Tratado de París. Surge, como consecuencia, el cambio de soberanía y la imposición de un nuevo gobierno en la Isla. Este acontecimiento marca la historia de Puerto Rico, la de su lengua y la de la enseñanza del vernáculo. Con la imposición de un gobierno militar (1898–1900), se crea una corte o Tribunal Federal, cuyos procesos jurídicos serían en inglés, y se inicia el proceso de americanización mediante la aprobación de la 'Ley de los Idiomas Oficiales' en 1902 (Meyn 1983, Negrón de Montilla 1977, Rua 1987, Seda Bonilla 1987) y la enseñanza en el idioma inglés, ignorando, por un lado, el valor que representaba el español como instrumento comunicativo para los puertorriqueños y, por otro, despreciando la variedad hispánica que manejaban los puertorriqueños en ese entonces, como se desprende en las siguientes palabras:

> Entre las multitudes puertorriqueñas no parece existir devoción por su idioma ni por ningún ideal nacional, comparable con la devoción que mueve a los franceses, por ejemplo, en el Canada o en las provincias del Rin. Otra consideración importante que no debe pasarse por alto es que la mayor parte del pueblo de esta Isla no habla un español puro. Su lenguaje es un patois casi ininteligible a los nativos de Barcelona y Madrid. No posee literatura alguna y poco valor como un medio intelectual. Existe la posibilidad de que sería casi más fácil educar esta gente fuera de su patois en

> inglés, que lo que sería educarlos en la elegante lengua de Castilla. (Clark, presidente de la Junta Escolar para Puerto Rico, citado en Delgado 1993: 14)

Más tarde, con la aprobación de la Ley Foraker (1900–1917), se instala en la Isla un gobierno civil regido oficialmente por el idioma inglés; aunque, la vida pública, como era de esperarse, transcurría en español. En 1902, por disposición de la Asamblea Legislativa de Puerto Rico, se aprueba la 'Ley de los Idiomas Oficiales,' vigente hasta el 1991, y reestituida a partir del 1993.

La 'Ley de Idiomas Oficiales' de 1902 colocaba, en supuesta igualdad de condiciones legales y oficiales, la lengua nativa, o sea, el español, y la lengua extranjera, el inglés, pero esta última aventajaba a la nativa en los dominios oficiales. Como dice Delgado (1993: 14) 'esta ley crea un falso bilingüismo en la esfera oficial.' Desde el 1905 al 1916, el Comisionado Roland P. Falkner (1904–1907) impone el inglés como lengua de enseñanza en todos los niveles, entre otras razones, debido al fracaso que se observaba en el aprendizaje del inglés y al retraso en la asimilación de los puertorriqueños, objetivos que no parecían rendir frutos, a pesar del cambio en la política lingüística.

En 1917, con la aprobación de una Segunda Carta Orgánica, la Ley Jones, vigente hasta el 1952, se concede la ciudadanía americana a los puertorriqueños y se promueve una carta de derechos. El español comienza a ganar terreno perdido hasta ese entonces al convertirse en el idioma de los procesos legislativos y en la lengua de enseñanza hasta el cuarto grado; más tarde, hasta el octavo, aunque interrumpido, por las insistencias del presidente Roosevelt en formar un país bilingüe. El pobre aprendizaje del inglés y el aumento en la deserción escolar motivó a funcionarios del gobierno de Puerto Rico ha reestituir el español como lengua de enseñanza. En 1946, el comisionado de Educación, Mariano Villaronga, nombrado por el presidente Truman, proclama, mediante legislación local, la enseñanza en español y la enseñanza del inglés como asignatura en las escuelas públicas, proyecto que fue vetado por el presidente Truman ante los temores de que "la cuestión del status político puertorriqueño sería confundida y su solución retardada por la adopción precisamente ahora de una nueva política sobre la lengua" (Babín 1946: 82–90). Durante estos primeros cincuenta años, mientras las autoridades norteamericanas promovían abiertamente el inglés como símbolo de unidad nacional y cultural, los puertorriqueños se aferraban a su español como sello de identidad puertorriqueña.

Con la elección del primer gobernador puertorriqueño, Luis Muñoz Marín, electo en 1948 por el voto directo del pueblo, se abre un nuevo capítulo en la política lingüística de Puerto Rico. A partir del 1949, el comisionado Villaronga convierte el español en la lengua nacional de enseñanza. Las batallas por el idioma que dieron la Cámara de Delegados, la Asociación de Maestros, el Ateneo Puertorriqueño, profesores de español y muchos puertorriqueños parecían rendir frutos. En 1965, el Tribunal Supremo de Puerto Rico falla a favor del uso del español como idioma oficial de la Rama Judicial:

> Es un hecho no sujeto a rectificaciones históricas que el vehículo de expresión, el idioma del pueblo puertorriqueño – parte integral de nuestro origen y nuestra cultura hispánica – ha sido y sigue siendo el idioma español. (Juez Luis Negrón Fernández, citado en Delgado 1993: 15)

Como demuestran estos datos históricos que hemos expuestos sucintamente, la Ley de Idiomas Oficiales parecía ir perdiendo terreno ante la realidad sociolingüística que vivían los puertorriqueños. Las leyes impuestas parecían apartarse de los hechos lingüísticos, pues, el español, independientemente de los dictámenes del gobierno federal, era el medio de comunicación fundamental de la población.

Con la aprobación en 1952 de un nuevo estatus político en Puerto Rico, el Estado Libre Asociado, se estrechan los lazos con los Estados Unidos y se inicia una nueva etapa en la historia política del país. Puerto Rico se convertía, como ha dicho muy recientemente el escritor puertorriqueño Luis Rafael Sánchez, en 'una isla flotante,' cuya población se ha venido moviendo entre dos aguas: la Isla con 3.5 millones de habitantes y la Metrópoli con más de 2.5 millones de puertorriqueños. Ante una fórmula política inconclusa – considerada colonialista por anexionistas e independentistas, y 'lo mejor de dos mundos,' por estadolibristas, o sea, defensores del Estado Libre Asociado – surgen posiciones de rechazo al coloniaje, y aumentan las presiones para que se defina el destino político de la Isla, patrocinadas mayormente por grupos proamericanos e independentistas locales, quienes con el apoyo de congresistas norteamericanos han manifestado, sin frutos concretos, su rechazo al *status quo.*

En el transcurso de este debate histórico, la lengua ha jugado un papel protagónico. En la década del 80, mientras en la Isla surgían varias organizaciones en apoyo al idioma, entre ellas, *Acción Nacional para la Defensa del Vernáculo y Pro Reafirmación del Idioma Español,* en Estados Unidos se aglutinaban las fuerzas conservadoras en favor del *English Only* (Gynan 1987: 183–189). Durante las vistas celebradas en 1989 en el Senado de Estados Unidos sobre el futuro político de Puerto Rico, que presidía el entonces senador Bennett Johnson, el tema del idioma había estado ausente, según algunos, debido a los efectos adversos que podría representar para el apoyo a la estadidad. Así un grupo de puertorriqueños inserta el tema del idioma en la mirilla pública, y sostiene mediante artículos periodísticos que para los puertorriqueños "el español no era negociable bajo ninguna fórmula de status" (Delgado 1993: 14). Las fuerzas en defensa del español continúan recibiendo apoyo civil. Delgado (1990) en una columna titulada "Un solo idioma oficial en el país," sugiere al gobernador de turno, Rafael Hernández Colón, "que inicie de inmediato el proceso legislativo para que derrogue la 'Ley de Idiomas Oficiales' de 1902 (sic)." Desde el 1986 se había estado presentando legislación local sobre ese particular sin éxito alguno. Además, en 1990 se había aprobado la Ley Orgánica del Departamento de Educación de Puerto Rico que aseguraba que "la educación se impartirá en el idioma vernáculo, el español, y se enseñará el inglés como segundo idioma."

Entre 1990 y 1991, los cuerpos legislativos de Puerto Rico celebran vistas en torno al Proyecto de Ley 417, llamado "La Ley del Idioma." El 5 de abril de 1991, el gobernador estadolibrista, Rafael Hernández Colón, proclama, después de casi 90 años, el español como única lengua oficial de Puerto Rico, con cuyo gesto parecía enviar un claro rechazo a la anexión del pueblo puertorriqueño con los Estados Unidos y, a su vez, afirmar la identidad y la cultura puertorriqueña mediante el español. La aprobación de esta ley le mereció al pueblo de Puerto Rico la concesión del *Premio Príncipe de Asturias de las Letras* ese mismo año. La oficialidad del español provocó el rechazo y la indignación de los anexionistas, quienes interpretaron esta nueva ley como un desafío a la relación con los Estados Unidos y, como consecuencia, un impedimento a la estadidad federada. Asimismo, prometieron, que de triunfar en las elecciones de 1992, devolverían al inglés el estado oficial que había tenido desde el 1902. Al año siguiente, las fuerzas anexionistas logran el triunfo electoral y, como primer proyecto de ley, reestituyen la 'Ley de los dos Idiomas Oficiales.' Empero, según esta legislación, la política lingüística en español se mantendría inalterada:[2]

> ninguna disposición en la ley válida la infundamentada especulación de que, al aprobarla, la Asamblea Legislativa estaría dando paso al uso de un lenguaje que no sea español en los procesos judiciales o como vehículo de enseñanza en las escuelas públicas del país. (Martínez 1993: 8)

Con los anexionistas en el poder, se celebra un nuevo plebiscito en 1993, el cual favorece por estrecho margen el Estado Libre Asociado. Ante la 'ausencia de una definición política,' en 1993 los anexionistas recurren a algunos congresistas norteamericanos, encabezados por el representante Don Young, republicano por el estado de Alaska, en busca de apoyo para la estadidad. El idioma vuelve a ser el eje de la discordia durante la discusión de las vistas, cuando el presidente de la Comisión de Reglas y Calendarios de la Cámara de Representantes de Estados Unidos, Gerald Salomon, exigió la cláusula que obligaba, de Puerto Rico convertirse en el estado 51, la oficialización del inglés en la sociedad puertorriqueña, así como la enseñanza en inglés en las escuelas públicas del país, lo que contribuyó a que los defensores de la estadidad retiraran el Proyecto antes de que bajara a votación en el pleno de la Cámara de Representantes (Mulero 1997: 12). A pesar de que el Proyecto no fue considerado por el pleno de la Cámara de Representantes, los promotores del mismo continuaron adelante, y en 1997 la Cámara Baja vuelve a considerar el Proyecto del Congresista Don Young, esta vez se derrota la enmienda idiomática de Salomon, y se da paso a la enmienda de los representantes Burton y Miller, representantes por los estados de Indiana y California respectivamente, la cual defendía la enseñanza del inglés y en inglés, y la aplicación de los mismos requisitos idiomáticos que a los 50 estados de la nación. A pesar de que la Cámara de Representantes de Estados Unidos aprueba el proyecto por el estrecho margen de un voto el 4 de marzo de 1998, el proyecto muere en el Senado Federal ante la inacción de los senadores. Mientras tanto, Manase Mansur, asesor de Don Young, manifestó: "Puerto Rico permanecerá en la transición hacia la estadidad mientras no acepte el idioma inglés" (Mulero 1998: 24).

Ante el fracaso del Proyecto Young, el gobernador de Puerto Rico, Pedro Roselló, insiste en celebrar un plebiscito criollo, basado en las fórmulas de status que había aprobado el Proyecto Young. El 13 de diciembre de 1998, los puertorriqueños acuden a las urnas, y apoyan con el 50.4% de los votos la alternativa 'Ninguna de las Anteriores,' la cual rechazaba las definiciones del Estado Libre Asociado, la Libre Asociación, la Estadidad y la Independencia que habían aprobado los congresistas norteamericanos el 4 de marzo de 1998. La estadidad obtuvo 46.5% del electorado. El tema del idioma, como en todas las campañas plebiscitarias previas, jugó un papel protagónico en la contienda electoral.

Hace unos días, políticos de Puerto Rico han iniciado el diálogo con congresistas y con el Presidente de los Estados Unidos para que avalen una nueva consulta de status para Puerto Rico. Al parecer han encontrado apoyo oficial a esas gestiones. Los estadolibristas anhelan tomar el poder en el 2000, para así asegurar la perpetuidad y el desarrollo del Estado Libre Asociado de Puerto Rico – colonial, en libre asociación con los Estados Unidos o en forma de república asociada – y eliminar del panorama la opción de la estadidad federada para Puerto Rico. El español será clave en ese proceso, por lo que la reestitución de la ley del español como único idioma oficial podría ser revivida.

Las constantes exigencias de los congresistas norteamericanos, entre ellos, Dan Burton, republicano por estado de Indiana, hacia el inglés o, por lo menos hacia un bilingüismo estable (Proyecto Federal HR 4766, Ley Habilitadora del Inglés), ha obligado al Departamento de Educación de Puerto Rico a diseñar una nueva política lingüística bilingüe, que ha dado lugar a la aprobación y puesta en marcha en abril de 1997 del 'Proyecto para Formar un Ciudadano Bilingüe Puertorriqueño,' proyecto que abre un nuevo capítulo en los cien años de política lingüística en la Isla, y el cual, según el Secretario de Educación, intenta convertir en bilingües a los estudiantes puertorriqueños, pero según la Academia Puertorriqueña de la Lengua (1998: 58), el mismo contribuye a "crear un situación artificial en el país: la de considerar a los niños puertorriqueños como extranjeros (inmigrantes o 'de minorías') en su propia tierra."

3. Formar un ciudadano bilingüe: ¿una 'nueva' política lingüística?

El 'Proyecto para Formar un Ciudadano Bilingüe' se propone, según sus gestores, "iniciar un plan integrador multidisciplinario que incluye diversas alternativas de enseñanza conducentes a formar un ciudadano bilingüe" (Fajardo et ali. 1997: VII), mediante el énfasis del inglés en los primeros grados. El niño se iniciará en la lectoescritura en inglés al finalizar el primer grado, y se espera que en tercer grado, sepa leer y escribir con 'propiedad y corrección' en ambos idiomas; a partir del quinto se impartirán en inglés las materias de matemáticas y ciencias naturales, y en el nivel secundario comenzará la inmersión en inglés. Así, según el Secretario de Educación: "el inglés se convierta en parte del ambiente escolar y no meramente en una clase de 50 minutos como es, en estos momentos" (Associated Press 1997: 20), y "la gente se acostumbre a ver el inglés como una forma rutinaria de trabajo y no como simplemente una clase" (Ghigliotty 1997: 36), sin que con ello se viole la legislación aprobada en 1993, pues, según el Secretario ambas lenguas son oficiales. Asimismo, se iniciará un plan de preparación y certificación de maestros de inglés, ya que la enseñanza de esta lengua en el nivel primario ha estado en manos de maestros generalistas que enseñan todas las asignaturas. Auspiciará, además, el intercambio de maestros de Estados Unidos y de Puerto Rico, con miras a fortalecer el contenido idiomático, la metodología y la supervisión de la enseñanza (Fajardo et al. 1997: 2–3).

El Proyecto parte de las siguientes premisas: (1) la existencia en Puerto Rico de una situación claramente bilingüe desde hace varias décadas; (2) las razones sociales, intelectuales, culturales, económicas, y políticas en Puerto Rico demandan y requieren el uso del idioma inglés; (3) el éxito en el mundo del trabajo dependerá de la capacidad de ser bilingüe; (4) . . . [para] los adelantos en la comunicación tecnológica y la globalización que hace que se acorten las distancias entre los pueblos, aprender inglés no es sólo vital para los puertorriqueños, sino para todos los ciudadanos del mundo; (5) el inglés es el vehículo oficial de comunicación internacional; (6) el conocimiento de ambas lenguas tiene un valor incalculable y unas implicaciones muy profundas para que cualquier ciudadano pueda subsistir con éxito; (7) el dominio de un segundo idioma hace que los hablantes desarrollen unas capacidades intelectuales que no desarrollan los monolingües, y (8) el bilingüismo debe ser una meta educativa de todos los pueblos, ya que las experiencias personales y las ventajas de ser bilingüe sobrepasan las ventajas de ser monolingüe.

Como se desprende de estas premisas, es urgente cambiar la política lingüística en torno a la enseñanza del inglés en las escuelas públicas de Puerto Rico vigente desde el 1948, y la cual estipulaba que el inglés sería asignatura obligatoria en todos los niveles de enseñanza, por una propuesta 'bilingue' que incorpore el inglés, además de asignatura, en la lengua de enseñanza de otras disciplinas, entre ellas, matemática y ciencias naturales. Esta 'nueva' política idiomática formaría un ciudadano bilingüe y, a su vez, garantizaría la inteligencia y el éxito de los estudiantes, así como el progreso económico de la sociedad puertorriqueña en general, pues, Fajardo "clama igualdad de oportunidades en la enseñanza de ese idioma para los estudiantes del sistema público versus los que asisten a las escuelas privadas, algunas de las cuales son de inmersión en inglés y cuyos costos son prohibitivos" (Seda 1998a). El Proyecto presupone que de continuar con la política lingüística anterior, estaríamos destinados al fracaso como pueblo. Según documentamos en la primera parte de este trabajo, y como reconoce muy superficialmente este documento, Puerto Rico ha pasado por prolongados períodos de 'enseñanza bilingüe,' cuyos resultados han sido adversos para el aprendizaje del inglés, y según algunos académicos especializados en el tema (Academia Puertorriqueña de la Lengua 1998; Morales 1997), también muy negativos para el español. Las estadísticas que se tienen bajo la política actual tampoco son muy alagadoras, como se desprende de estudios realizados por el College Board (Morales 1998b) y otras encuestas. Según el censo de 1990, sólo 747,480 de 3,219,765 de puertorriqueños de cinco años o más, o sea el 23.2%, respondió hablar con facilidad el inglés. Entonces, nos preguntamos: ¿cuáles han sido las razones que han impedido el éxito del aprendizaje del inglés en nuestro sistema de enseñanza pública durante este siglo?

El Proyecto identifica algunos de los factores – aunque ha descuidado otros de gran peso – que han contribuido al fracaso de la enseñanza del inglés en Puerto Rico, entre ellos: (1) la ausencia de la enseñanza del inglés en su entorno natural; (2) la política de indiferencia hacia la enseñanza del inglés que ha adoptado el Departamento de Educación de Puerto Rico; (3) la falta de continuidad entre un nivel y el otro (por ejemplo entre el elemental y el intermedio); (4) la escasez de adiestramiento y de desarrollo profesional de los maestros; (5) la ausencia de materiales didácticos, entre ellos libros de textos; (6) un bajo nivel de competencia en inglés en los maestros de los grados primarios, muchos de los cuales no poseen certificados de maestros en la materia; (7) la enseñanza deficiente que hace énfasis en la memoria y la repetición sin comprensión; (8) una tendencia metodológica convencional e inadecuada de parte de los maestros de inglés a la hora de impartir la enseñanza, y (9) una preparación universitaria ajena a las necesidades del sistema de educación pública y de los intereses de los alumnos, la cual enfatiza la enseñanza de la gramática y la estructura de la lengua en lugar de la comunicación.

Como se deduce de estos datos, el Proyecto sólo reconoce los factores pedagógicos como adversos al aprendizaje del inglés, que aunque reales, no explican por sí solos la profundidad de un problema de cien años de historia que trasciende las fronteras del salón de clases y soslayan la esencia misma del pueblo puertorriqueño. Como han señalado muchos estudiosos (Meyn 1983, Negrón de Montilla 1977, Resnick 1993, Pausada 1996, Morales 1998a, 1998b), son muchos los factores lingüísticos y extralingüísticos que han contribuido al fracaso de una política lingüística bilingüe en Puerto Rico, entre los que destacan: primero, los hechos históricos, por ejemplo, las huellas que ha dejado la invasión y las prácticas asimilistas por parte de los nortemericanos, muy explícitas durante las primeras décadas del presente siglo, y muy intensas durante estos últimos años; segundo, el debate político y la lucha por mantener la identidad y la idiosincrasia puertorriqueña, primero, ante la posesión del territorio (1898–1952), luego frente a la indefinición política y a la amenaza pregresiva de la anexión pro estadista y del asimilismo de ciertos grupos al mundo estadounidense. Por ejemplo, los datos obtenidos de una encuesta realizada en 1992 por iniciativa del Ateneo Puertorriqueño (en Delgado 1994: 84–85) son reveladores: el 78% de los encuestados hizo hincapié en que era "extremadamente importante mantener la identidad puertorriqueña," frente a 26% que reconoció la importancia de mantener su identidad estadounidense; a pesar de que un 58.4% dijo sentirse "estadounidense," el 91% manifestó sentirse "puertorriqueño primero" y "americano después"; el 90% prefería hablar español en casi todos los dominios posibles, aunque el 59% consideraba la importancia del inglés en Puerto Rico, y el 78% se mostró "muy interesado o interesado en mejorar sus habilidades en inglés"; el 97% prefiere que el gobierno se comunique en español; el 96%, que se legisle en español; el 95%, que sea la lengua de los documentos oficiales, y el 93% no renunciaría al español en caso de Puerto Rico se convirtiese en estado federado.

El tercer factor se relaciona con las repercusiones del idioma mismo (Morales 1998b). Entre muchos puertorriqueños existe el temor generalizado de que el español se convierta en un 'spanglish' o en un español adulterado, actitudes puristas expuestas por muchos intelectuales puertorriqueños y extranjeros (Granda 1968, Gili Gaya 1965, Narváez 1990), quienes, en sus escritos, han despertado un alto grado de conciencia lingüística en el pueblo y, a su vez, han contribuido en la defensa del español frente al inglés.

El cuarto factor es la ausencia de una planificación lingüística rigurosa (Pousada 1996) que dé marcha a un proyecto viable. Como vemos, la realidad sociolingüística de Puerto Rico es sumamente compleja y la intromisión de la política en los asuntos idiomáticos ha hecho más daño que bien.

El Proyecto para Formar un Ciudadano Bilingüe ha recibido fuertes críticas, principalmente de académicos universitarios, entre ellos, la Academia Puertorriqueña de la Lengua, la Faculta de Educación de la Universidad de Puerto Rico,[3] la Asociación de Maestros, la Federación de Maestros, Educadores en Acción, profesores universitarios, organizaciones sindicales, etc. Según los detractores, este proyecto: (1) evidencia una clara preferencia del inglés sobre el español, por razones políticas, "ya que promueve la dicotomía inglés-útil, español-inútil" (Alberty et al. 1997: 13) y "se inclina más a favorecer la enseñanza del inglés al recomendar y dar directrices sobre cómo trabajar con el inglés, pero no en la misma intensidad con el idioma español . . . si realmente es una política para formar un ciudadano bilingüe, tiene que incluir el español"

(Molina, citada en Seda 1998b); (2) representa un regreso a la educación bilingüe similar a la que se impuso en el país desde principios de siglo con objetivos ideológicos asimilistas que "imponen la ideología cultural, social, política y económica de la mayoría" (Silén 1997: 38), como ha ocurrido con el español en el Suroeste de los Estados Unidos (Hernández Chávez 1994, 1998; Bernal-Enríquez 1998, 1999); (3) descuida peligrosamente la lengua materna en los primeros años de educación formal cuando el niño está en proceso de formarse lingüísticamente, y tan necesaria para procesar el aprendizaje de la segunda lengua, como ha señalado la Academia Puertorriqueña de la Lengua (1998: 59): "la lengua materna es el fundamento básico para acceder al conocimiento y para adquirir con éxito la segunda lengua, el inglés"; (4) atenta contra la identidad y la cultura puertorriqueña, ya que "la adquisición de la cultura mediante la lengua vernácula no es una opción política; es un derecho natural del ciudadano que, por sus graves consecuencias, individuales y colectivas, nunca debe olvidarse" (Academica Puertorriqueña de la Lengua 1998: 59); (5) exagera en sus objetivos de 'formar un ciudadano bilingüe,' ya que convertir a una persona en bilingüe requiere "una experiencia de muchas vivencias . . . en una situación real de comunicación que jamás se va a dar en un salón de clases" (Vega, citada en Diálogo, noviembre 1998: 20), por lo tanto, "el proyecto no responde a la necesidad de aprender y manejar el inglés, sino a la necesidad política de presentarnos como asimilados y listos para la anexión. Por eso se recurre a la educacion bilingüe de transición" (Silén 1997: 38), y (6) descuida los adelantos de la planificación lingüística, pues, como identificamos más adelante, el Proyecto no se fundamenta en los principios que rigen una política lingüística sistemática y viable dentro del contexto sociolingüístico puertorriqueño.

Aún no estamos en condiciones para evaluar los resultados de esta nueva política lingüística, pero a juzgar por especialistas en el campo, el proyecto está destinado al fracaso, similar a como ha ocurrido con las propuestas bilingües previas, ya que, una vez más, imperan intereses político-partidistas en los objetivos bilingües, y no se siguen los procedimientos necesarios para lograr una planificación lingüística acertada y de consenso. Como ha señalado Pousada (1996: 506) "In Puerto Rico, language policy has rarely been planned and even less often been evaluated," por lo tanto, antes de encaminar un proyecto de bilingüismo en la Isla, como pretende este Proyecto, es imperativo desarrollar una planificación lingüística profunda.

Una planificación lingüística profunda y sistemática exige el cumplimiento de varias etapas: primero, una investigación objetiva de la realidad socio-lingüística imperante en el país, por ejemplo, se requiere un estudio riguroso de los dominios de ambas lenguas, así como un examen de las actitudes y creencias lingüísticas que manifiestan los hablantes hacia ellas. En Puerto Rico ya contamos con algunos trabajos preliminares sobre ambos aspectos, los cuales documentan un uso del inglés en áreas relacionadas fundamentalmente con el turismo, los negocios y la tecnología (Blau y Dayton 1997), así como actitudes positivas hacia el inglés entre estudiantes (Livoti 1977, Lladó Berríos 1979) y actitudes ambiguas entre adultos, condicionadas por la afiliación política de los encuestados (López Morales 1986, 1988, López Laguerre 1989, Crespo 1991).[4] En segundo lugar, la planificacion requiere una formulación explícita de una política lingüística definida, partiendo de la investigación previa, que decida el papel que desempeñarán las lenguas en cuestión. Por ejemplo, siguiendo la clasificación propuesta por Moag (1982), habría que responder a la interrogante: ¿cuál debe ser la lengua nativa, la lengua básica, la segunda lengua, o lengua extranjera? Blau y Dayton (1997: 143–144), en base a esta clasificación de Moag (1982), defienden que, según los criterios dominios de uso informales, lengua de mayor competencia y grado de aprendizaje informal, Puerto Rico representa una sociedad hispanohablante, con inglés como lengua extranjera (EFL); mientras que, según el porcentaje de la sociedad que maneja el inglés (23.6%), la influencia de los grupos que usan el inglés y el uso de dominios formales, el inglés adquiere una clasificación de segunda lengua. Por lo tanto, ambas investigadoras concurren que:

> To decide what type of English-using society Puerto Rico is, we must consider Moag's assertion that in a society with a single vernacular, English cannot function as a lingua franca and hence cannot have second language status . . . we would conclude that Puerto Rico is an EFL society (English as a foreign language), albeit one in which English plays a significant internal role. (Blau y Dayton 1997: 144)

En tercer lugar, la planificación exige una implantación cuidadosa de la política lingüística, diseñada, siguiendo metodologías basadas en el tipo de lengua que se persigue desarrollar. Si aceptamos la recomendación de Blau y Dayton (1997), entonces, el inglés se enseñaría en Puerto Rico como lengua extranjera, utilizando la metodología adecuada en este caso. En esta etapa, los maestros y los estudiantes serán piezas fundamentales para el éxito. Desafortunadamente, el Proyecto "no solo enfrenta el problema de la enseñanza de maestros especializados en la enseñanza del inglés, sino también el de la gran cantidad de estudiantes con rezago en su aprovechamiento académico" (Seda 1998b), incluyendo el aprendizaje de la lengua materna, el español. Por lo tanto, es fundamental reforzar el español como vernáculo, de manera que el aprendizaje de la segunda lengua se apoye en el dominio lingüístico de la lengua materna.

Finalmente, la planificación requiere una evaluación sistemática que permita examinar tanto el éxito y las dificultades de los procedimientos empleados, como la política lingüística en general.

Ahora bien, cuáles han sido los efectos que el inglés y las diversas políticas lingüísticas han ocasionado al desarrollo del español en Puerto Rico. Sobre este particular hay posturas encontradas, que van desde un efecto alarmante en el español (Navarro Tomás 1948, Gili Gaya 1965, Granda 1968), pasando por "un nivel de interferencia que sobrepasa, con mucho, las expectativas plausibles de una interferencia de tipo general y común a todas las áreas del mundo hispánico" (Morales 1986, 1992), hasta la posición optimista de un español similar al de otras zonas del mundo hispánico no aisladas del contacto económico y cultural con los Estados Unidos (del Rosario 1985, Pérez Salas 1973). Recientemente, Morales (1997, 1998a) ha interpretado muchas de las alternancias modales en el español de Puerto Rico, en lugar de clases de interferencias, como había propuesto en análisis previos, como casos de simplificaciones lingüísticas del tipo de *interlengua,* provocadas por la ausencia de atención de las complejidades metalingüísticas (Bialystok 1991) en el proceso de enseñanza del vernáculo.

Esta interpretación abre una nueva etapa en el estudio del español de Puerto Rico, ya que Morales (1997: 264–266) asocia, a una incompleta competencia del español, algunas variaciones sintácticas o innovaciones del dialecto puertorriqueno, entre las que destaca: (1) la ausencia de algunos usos del subjuntivo (por ejemplo, en oraciones condicionales), sustituidos por el indicativo o el infinitivo; (2) las oraciones adjetivas que funcionan como frases preposicionales (*Y no se veía nada, sólo montones de basura en que su gran altura impedía ver lo que había detrás*); (3) las oraciones adjetivas no restrictivas; (4) ciertos usos del sistema preposicional y del gerundio, entre otros. Según la autora, estos fenómenos son resultado de "universales lingüísticos de temprana adquisición," caracterizados por procesos de simplificación, sobregeneralización y reanálisis, durante la adquisición de la primera y segunda lengua, como ocurre en la dialectalización y la criollización. Por lo tanto, para lograr una competencia en la segunda lengua es necesario, primero, dominar la lengua materna, como demuestran trabajos recientes realizados con niños hispanos bilingües en los Estados Unidos (Hakuta y Díaz 1985, González 1986). Es decir, en lugar de eliminar contextos formales al español, por ejemplo, en la enseñanza, como propone el Proyecto para Formar un Ciudadano Bilingüe, se debe reforzar el vernáculo, enfatizando la enseñanza de estructuras sintácticas complejas y un lenguaje más abstracto, difícil de adquirir mediante el lenguaje informal, y de esta manera se obtendrían mejores resultados en el aprendizaje de la segunda lengua.

No cabe duda que estamos ante una variedad lingüística que manifiesta cambios en marcha, muchos de ellos condicionados por el contacto con el inglés, otros, motivados por fenómenos internos del propio sistema, los cuales deben ser abordados, siguiendo teorías y metodologías rigurosas que pongan a prueba las variables lingüísticas y extralingüísticas que podrían estar contribuyendo a la gramaticalización de fenómenos tales como la *sustitución modal indicativo por subjuntivo*, el *uso extendido del gerundio*, el *manejo de la voz pasiva,* la *ausencia del complementizador que,* el *uso del pronombre indefinido uno,* el *intercambio de ciertas preposiciones*, entre otros. Es imperativo continuar investigando los muchos rostros del español de Puerto Rico que aún carecen de explicaciones satisfactorias. Hay que buscar respuestas a interrogantes como las siguientes: ¿Qué rasgos lingüísticos innovadores del español de Puerto Rico son particulares de este dialecto, y cuáles son compartidos con el resto de la isoglosa hispano-caribeña? Para ello, es necesario ampliar el foco de investigación, más allá de nuestro dialecto, e integrar, mediante el estudio comparativo, tanto de las variedades caribeñas insulares como las que se hablan en la Metrópoli. Luego, habría que identificar los factores lingüísticos y extralingüísticos que condicionan tales innovaciones, y responder a las preguntas: ¿Es el contacto de lenguas inglés-español la variable que provoca los cambios lingüísticos en la zona?; ¿Son los procesos naturales del propio sistema los incitadores de los cambios ya establecidos y de aquellos en progreso, los cuales se agudizan debido al contacto de lenguas?; ¿Es el aprendizaje incompleto de la lengua, como resultado del contacto lingüístico, lo que contribuye a fosilizar o gramaticalizar ciertas estructuras 'imperfectas' en la competencia lingüística de los hablantes?, o ¿Es la combinación de todos estos factores lo que ha condicionado muchos fenómenos de la variedad puertorriqueña? Esperamos por estudios que consideren estas hipótesis de trabajo con miras a responder a tales interrogantes.

4. Recapitulación

A pesar de que en Puerto Rico, por espacio de un siglo, se han impuesto diferentes políticas lingüísticas, no se ha realizado, a nuestro juicio, una planificación lingüística profunda, objetiva y sistemática que tome en cuenta nuestra realidad sociolingüística. Por otro lado, los factores históricos, políticos e idiomáticos, como resultado de los cien años de relación con los Estados Unidos, han sido descuidados en muchos de los intentos de hacernos ciudadanos bilingües, encaminando la enseñanza bilingüe por rutas ideológicas de improvisación, y provocando fracasos tras fracasos. Nuestra situación particular de nación caribeña y latinoamericana, por un lado, y de territorio de Estados Unidos, por otro, exige una política lingüística sensible a los grupos a los que va dirigida, pues, cuando se descuida nuestra realidad sociolingüística de hispanohablantes y nuestro contexto sociohistórico de país invadido, aún indefinido políticamente, imponiendo un bilingüismo basado en el 'derecho,' el 'bien económico,' la 'igualdad,' el 'multiculturalismo,' etc., los resultados lingüísticos seguirán siendo adversos.

Esta realidad parece explicar los fracasos de las políticas lingüísticas impuestas en el sistema de educación pública. Esperamos que en el futuro no muy lejano se consideren estos y muchos otros planteamientos, y se trabaje junto a especialistas en el campo de la lingüística, antes de encaminar proyectos educativos de gran trascendencia para el destino histórico y sociolingüístico de todos los puertorriqueños. Los adelantos de la lingüística, en especial, de la planificación lingüística y de la enseñanza de lenguas extranjeras, son instrumentos indispensables que deben evaluarse a la hora de desarrollar un plan riguroso y sistemático para la enseñanza del español y el inglés en Puerto Rico. Estamos a tiempo para cumplir con ese objetivo que por cien años ha fracasado.

Notas

1. Para una visión pormenorizada sobre este tema, vea Negrón de Montilla 1977, Castro Pereda 1993, Vaquero 1993, Vélez y Schweers 1993, Delgado 1994.

2. El Senado de Puerto Rico estudia en estos días una nueva ley orgánica que regirá el Departamento de Educación de Puerto Rico, la cual, según el senador Fas Alzamora (citado en Dávila 1999: 13) enmendaría lo que ha sido política pública desde 1949, al establecer que las clases podrán darse lo mismo en español que en inglés . . . a pesar de que "Puerto Rico no es un país bilingüe."

3. Vea número monográfico de la revista Pedagogía, vol. 33, año 1999. San Juan: Universidad de Puerto Rico.

4. Sobre el tema de actitudes y creencias lingüísticas realizamos una investigación basada en la Encuesta sobre el Idioma que llevó a cabo Hispania Research Corporation en 1992 bajo el auspicio del Ateneo Puertorriqueño.

Referencias

Academia Puertorriqueña de la Lengua Española. 1998. La enseñanza del español y del inglés en Puerto Rico: Una polémica de cien años. San Juan: Editorial Playor.

Alberti, Carlos, Europa Piñero, Gloria Prosper y Carmelo Santana. 1997. ¿Un ciudadano bilingüe? *Diálogo* (agosto): 13–15.

Associated Press. 1997. A enseñar más en inglés. *El Nuevo Día,* 22 de abril de 1997: 20.

Babín, María T. 1946. Alrededor del lenguaje de Puerto Rico. *Asomante* 2.4: 82–90.

Bernal-Enríquez, Ysaura. 1998. Spanish language loss in La Nueva México. Ponencia presentada en 7th University of New Mexico Conference on Ibero-American Culture and Society: Spanish and Portuguese in Contact with Other Languages and 16th Conference on Spanish in the United States, University of New Mexico, 12–14 de febrero.

Bernal-Enríquez, Ysaura. 1999. Causas socio-históricas de la pérdida del español del suroeste de los Estados Unidos. Ponencia presentada en 17th Conference on Spanish in the United States, Florida International University, 11–13 de marzo.

Bialystok, Ellen. 1991. Metalinguistic dimensions of bilingual language proficiency. En *Language processing in bilingual children*, ed. Ellen Bialystok, 113–140. Cambridge: Cambridge University Press.

Blau, Eileen K. y Elizabeth Dayton. 1997. Puerto Rico as an English-using society. En *Linguistic studies in honor of Bohdan Sciuk*, ed. Robert Hammond y Marguerite G. MacDonald. U.S.: Learning Systems, Inc.

Castro Pereda, Rafael. 1993. *Idioma, historia y nación.* San Juan: Editorial Talleres.

Crespo, Michelle. 1991. Political affiliations vs. Spanish language maintenance, English language shift, and/or bilingualism in Puerto Rico. Tesis de maestría. Universidad de Puerto Rico, Mayagüez.

Dávila, Jesús. 1999. Controversia por el idioma oficial. *El Nuevo Día*, 12 de mayo de 1999: 31.

del Rosario, Rubén. 1985. *Selección de ensayos lingüísticos*. Madrid: Ediciones Partenón.

Delgado, Carmelo. 1990. Un solo idioma oficial en el país. *El Nuevo Día*, 6 de agosto.

Delgado, Carmelo. 1993. La lucha por el idioma (primera parte). *Claridad*, 22–28 de enero de 1993: 14–15.

Delgado, Carmelo. 1994. El debate legislativo sobre las leyes del idioma en Puerto Rico. San Juan: Editorial de la Revista del Colegio de Abogados de Puerto Rico.

Fajardo, Víctor et ali. 1997. *Proyecto para formar un ciudadano bilingüe*. San Juan: Departamento de Educación de Puerto Rico (mecanografiado).

Ghigliotty, Julio. 1997. Refuerza educación la enseñanza del inglés. *El Nuevo Día,* 11 de marzo de 1997: 36.

Gili Gaya, Samuel. 1965. *Nuestra lengua materna*. San Juan: Instituto de Cultura Puertorriqueña.

González, L. 1986. The effects of first language education on the second language and academic achievement of Mexican immigrant elementary school children in the United States. Disertación doctoral, University of Illinois at Urbana-Champaign.

Granda, Germán de. 1968. Transculturación e interferencia lingüística en el Puerto Rico contemporáneo (1898–1968). Río Piedras: Editorial Edil.

Gynan, Shaw. 1987. La nueva política lingüística en los Estados Unidos: Propósitos y motivos. En *Language and language use: Studies in Spanish dedicated to Joseph H. Mattluck*, ed. Terrell A. Morgan, James F. Lee, y Bill VanPatten, 175–193. Lanham, MD: University Press of America.

Hakuta, K. y R. Díaz. 1985. The relationship between degree of bilingualism and cognitive ability: A critical discussion and some new longitudinal data. En *Children's language vol. V*, ed. K. Nelson Hillsdale. New Jersey: Erlbaum.

Hernández Chávez, Eduardo. 1994. La pérdida del español entre los chicanos: Sus raíces sociopolíticas y las consecuencias para la identidad cultural. Ponencia presentada en la 3rd Annual Conference on Ibero-American Culture and Society. University of New Mexico, febrero.

Hernández Chávez, Eduardo. 1998. Los derechos lingüísticos en Nuevo México: El llamado bilingüismo oficial estatal. Ponencia presentada en 17th Conference on Spanish in the United States, Florida International University, 11–13 de marzo.

Livoti, Paul. 1977. Variables associated with attitude toward learning English in public schools of Puerto Rico. Disertación Doctoral. Lehigh University School of Education, Bethlehem, PA.

Lladó Berríos, Nitza. 1979. English as a second language in Puerto Rico: A language attitude study and its pedagogical implications. Disertación doctoral, University of Florida, Gainesville.

López Laguerre, María. 1989. *Bilingüismo en Puerto Rico*. Río Piedras: Universidad de Puerto Rico.

López Morales, Humberto. 1986. Bilingüismo y actitudes lingüísticas: El caso de Puerto Rico. En *Lenguas peninsulares y proyección hispánica*, ed. Manuel Alvar. Madrid: Fundación Friedrich.

López Morales, Humberto. 1988. Bilingüismo y actitudes lingüísticas en Puerto Rico: Breve reseña bibliográfica. En *Studies in Caribbean Spanish dialectology,* ed. Robert M. Hammond y Melvyn C. Resnick, 66–73. Washington, DC: Georgetown University Press.

Martínez, Andrea. 1993. It's official. *El Nuevo Día*, 29 de enero de 1993: 8.

Meyn, Marianne. 1983. *Lenguaje e identidad cultural: Un acercamiento teórico al caso de Puerto Rico.* San Juan: Editorial Edil, Inc.

Moag, Rodney. 1982. English as a foreign, second, native, and basal language: A new taxonomy of English-using societies. En *New Englishes,* ed. John B. Pride, 11–50. Rowley, MA: Newbury House Publishers.

Morales, Amparo. 1986. *Gramáticas en contacto: Análisis sintácticos sobre el español de Puerto Rico.* Madrid: Playor.

Morales, Amparo. 1992. Variación dialectal e influencia lingüística: El español de Puerto Rico. En *Historia y presente del español de América,* ed. C. Hernández. Valladolid: Junta de Castilla y León.

Morales, Amparo. 1997. Bilingüismo y adquisición de la lengua materna: Algunos casos particulares. *Revista de Estudios Hispánicos* 24.1: 255–271.

Morales, Amparo. 1998a. Acerca de la enseñanza bilingüe: Español e inglés en la escuela puertorriqueña. *REALE* 9 (en prensa).

Morales, Amparo. 1998b. Bilingüismo y planificación lingüística en Puerto Rico. En *Actas del Simposio Internacional de Lengua Española* (en prensa). Austin: Texas University.

Mulero, Leonor. 1997. Bajo amenaza el lenguaje. *El Nuevo Día,* 10 de marzo de 1997: 12.

Mulero, Leonor. 1998. A la sombra del inglés la estadidad. *El Nuevo Día*, 3 de diciembre de 1998: 24.

Navarro Tomás, Tomás. 1948. *El español de Puerto Rico: Contribución a la geografía lingüística hispanoamericana.* Río Piedras: Universidad de Puerto Rico.

Narváez, Eliezer. 1990. *Extralingüismo y realia en la lengua de Puerto Rico y en el español de América.* San Juan: Editorial Grafito, Inc.

Negrón de Montilla, Aida. 1977. *La americanización de Puerto Rico y el sistema de instrucción pública 1900–1930.* San Juan: Editorial de la Universidad de Puerto Rico.

Pérez Salas, Paulino. 1973. *Interferencia lingüística del inglés en el español de Puerto Rico.* San Juan: Interamerican University Press.

Pousada, Alicia. 1996. Puerto Rico: On the horns of a language planning dilemma. *TESOL Quarterly* 30.3: 499–510.

Resnick, Melvyn C. 1993. ESL and language planning in Puerto Rican education. *TESOL Quarterly* 27: 259–273.

Rua, Pedro J. 1987. Idioma en Puerto Rico: Hechos y retos. *Diálogo* (noviembre-diciembre): 32–34.

Seda, Marisol. 1998a. No avanza el programa bilingüe. *El Mundo,* 28 de abril de 1998: 3.

Seda, Marisol. 1998b. Grande el rezago académico. *El Mundo*, 28 de abril de 1998: 4.

Seda Bonilla, E. 1987. El bilingüismo. *El Reportero*, 15 de octubre de 1987: 21.

Silén, Juan A. 1997. Bilingüismo y la ideología de la identidad. *Diálogo* (noviembre): 38.

Vaquero, María. 1993. Política y lengua: El español en Puerto Rico. *Voz y Letra* 4.1: 105–128.

Vega, Ana L. 1998. Desde el francés . . . una experiencia para el inglés. *Diálogo* (noviembre): 20.

Vélez, Jorge A. y C. William Schweers. 1993. A U.S. Colony at a linguistics crossroads: The decision to make Spanish the official language of Puerto Rico. *Language Problems and Language Planning* 17.2: 117–140.

Demographic Changes in Florida and Their Importance for Effective Educational Policies and Practices

Thomas D. Boswell
University of Miami

On November 18, 1997 The Miami Herald ran a front page story (Farrell 1997) that summarized the major findings and recommendations of a task force that was organized by the Greater Miami Chamber of Commerce and called "One Community One Goal." Originally established to investigate Miami's high unemployment rate, this committee soon changed its focus when it identified education as the number one quality-of-life problem facing Miami-Dade County.[1] It found that the perception of the educational system of Miami-Dade County as poorly-performing was a major factor discouraging entrepreneurs from locating new businesses in metropolitan Miami. Among the five major recommendations made by the task force were two that directly relate to the topic of both this chapter and this book: (1) Dade County should mandate four years of foreign language study as a high school graduation requirement; and (2) it also should expand English and other language classes for adults and encourage employers to reimburse the cost to employees who take them. How could language become such an important issue in the largest metropolitan area of a state that only five years earlier had passed an "English Only" ordinance?

To answer this question, I have organized this chapter into three sections. The first describes the rapid change that has occurred in the ethnic composition of the state of Florida and Miami-Dade County and demonstrates how this change has been accompanied by explosive growth in their respective school populations. Based on past experiences, it also provides projections for the ethnic compositions of Florida's county school populations forward to the 2006/07 school year. The second section uses 1990 Census data to analyze the relationships between the ability to speak English and the socioeconomic status of persons who speak some language in their homes in addition to, or instead of, English.[2] I argue that, although it is possible to live, work, and die speaking only

 Research on Spanish in the U.S., ed. Ana Roca, 406–431. Somerville, MA: Cascadilla Press.

Spanish in South Florida, it does not make good economic sense to not learn to speak English well. Not knowing English is clearly an economic disadvantage in both Florida and Miami. The third section demonstrates the socioeconomic benefits of knowing a second language in addition to English and, like the "One Community One Goal" task force, argues that greater effort should be made to promote multilingual learning in the state of Florida.

In this chapter, I concentrate on Hispanics because they are the component of Florida's population that has experienced the most dramatic growth during the past half century and the group that has had the greatest impact on the state's limited English proficient population. In addition, Hispanics represent 56% of the state's total foreign-born population and it is the foreign-born who are most likely to have problems speaking English.

Virtually all of Florida's Hispanics who speak a language other than English speak Spanish. For example, 87% of all Hispanics living in Florida in 1990 spoke Spanish in their homes. A mere 12% spoke only English, and 1% spoke a language other than Spanish or English in their homes. The figures for Miami-Dade County were even more dramatic. In Miami, 94% of all Hispanics spoke Spanish in their homes, 5% spoke only English, and 1% spoke a language other than either Spanish or English (U.S. Bureau of the Census 1995).

1. The changing ethnic and racial composition of Florida's population

The purpose of this section is threefold: (1) to show how rapidly the Hispanic population of Florida has increased since 1960; (2) to note that the state's Hispanics are there to stay regardless of how the political situation may change in Cuba; and (3) to suggest that the Hispanic population of Florida is almost certain to continue to increase, based on projections of the racial and ethnic components of Florida's school enrollments forward to the 2006/07 academic school year.

1.1. Recent history of Florida's changing ethnic demography

In 1960 Florida's population was overwhelmingly White; eight out of every ten Florida residents were classified as being non-Hispanic White (Table 1). At the same time, about one out of every six Floridians were Black. The numbers of Hispanics and non-Hispanic Others (mainly Asians) living in the state were so small that they were hardly noticed. By 1990, the state was still largely comprised of non-Hispanic Whites. Although their absolute number had increased by a factor of nearly 2.4, the proportion of the state's total population that was comprised of non-Hispanic Whites had declined to 73%. Similarly, although the number of Blacks living in Florida nearly doubled during the 30-year period represented in Table 1, their proportion of the state's population declined to from 17 to 13%. In other words, despite their impressive absolute increases in population, both the non-Hispanic Whites and Blacks saw their proportional share of Florida's total population decline. The reason for this apparent contradiction between absolute and percentage figures is clearly shown in Table 1. While the White and Black populations registered impressive numerical increases, the state's Hispanic population virtually exploded, increasing by a factor of almost 17. In 1990, 12% of Florida's population was comprised of Hispanics, compared to 9% for the entire United States (U.S. Bureau of the Census 1994: 3, Table A). The University of Florida's Bureau of Economic and Business Research estimated that by 1995 the number of Hispanics living in Florida had increased by 28% to 2,014,642, thereby representing 14% of the state's total population. By 1995 the number of Hispanics equaled that of Blacks, so Hispanics are now tied with Blacks as Florida's largest minority (Morgan 1996).[3]

Table 1. The changing composition of Florida's population, 1960–1990

	1960 [4]		1970	
Groups [5]	Number	Percent	Number	Percent
Non-Hispanic Whites	3,995,588	80.7%	5,339,467	78.6%
Non-Hispanic Blacks	855,361 [6]	17.3%	1,019,287	15.0%
Hispanics	93,118	1.9%	405,036	6.0%
Non-Hispanic Others	7,493	0.2%	25,653	0.4%
Total	4,951,560	100.1%	6,789,443	100.0%
	1980		1990	
	Number	Percent	Number	Percent
Non-Hispanic Whites	7,476,610	76.7%	9,488,696	73.3%
Non-Hispanic Blacks	1,318,630	13.5%	1,703,544	13.2%
Hispanics	858,105	8.8%	1,555,031	12.0%
Non-Hispanic Others	92,979	1.0%	190,655	1.5%
Total	9,746,324	100.0%	12,937,926	100.0%

Note: Percentages do not always total to 100.0 because of rounding.
Sources: U.S. Bureau of the Census 1962: Tables 15 and 40, U.S. Bureau of the Census 1972: Tables 17, 45, and 49, U.S. Bureau of the Census 1982: Tables 59 and 61, U.S. Bureau of the Census 1992.

Migration has long been the primary form of population growth in Florida. More recently, between 1990 and 1996, 79.3% of the state's population increase was attributable to net in-migration and only 20.7% was due to natural increase – the excess of births over deaths (Smith 1997). Beginning in 1960, immigration (first from Cuba and later from other Latin American countries) has contributed in a big way to the in-migration component of Florida's population increase.

However, there is a basic geographic quality that characterizes all migration flows. Migrants do not evenly disperse throughout a given area of destination. Instead, they concentrate in certain locations. For Hispanics living in Florida, the concentration has been in the three metropolitan areas of Miami, Tampa-St. Petersburg, and Orlando (see Figure 1).[7] Of course, the single largest concentration of Florida's Hispanic population by far has been in metropolitan Miami. In fact, 61% of the state's Hispanics lived in this single county in 1990 (U.S. Bureau of the Census 1992).

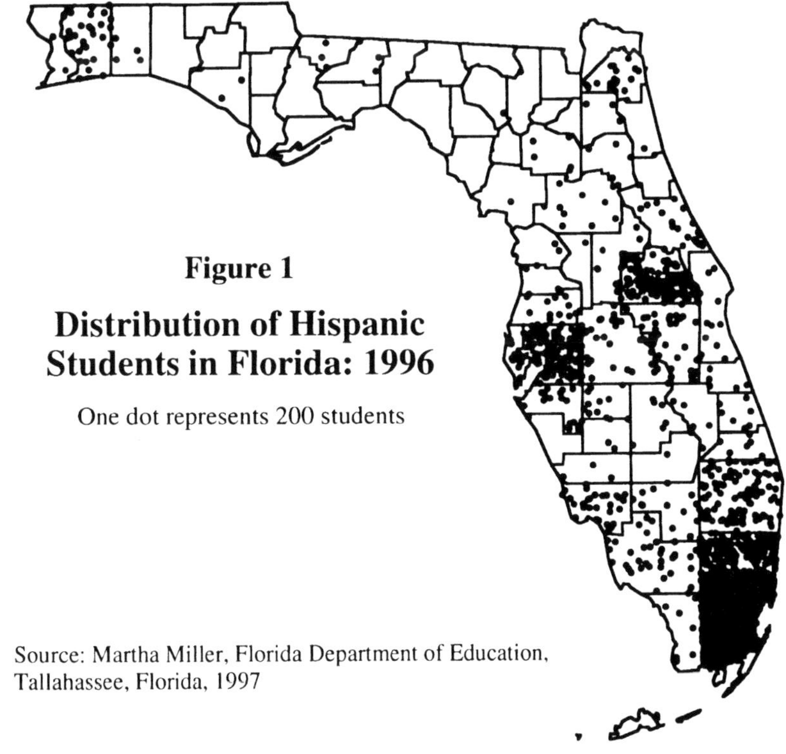

Metropolitan Miami's population composition has been more radically altered by immigration from Cuba and other Latin American countries than the population of the rest of Florida has. In 1960 only about 5% of Miami-Dade County's population was comprised of Hispanics.[8] By 1995, this figure had increased to 56% (Nogle 1996, Morgan 1996). From approximately 50,000 in 1960, Miami-Dade's Hispanic population had increased to about 1.1 million in 1995.

The growth of Florida's and Miami's Hispanic populations has had an enormous impact on both the state and city. One consequence for the state has been its increased trade with Latin America (see Figure 2).

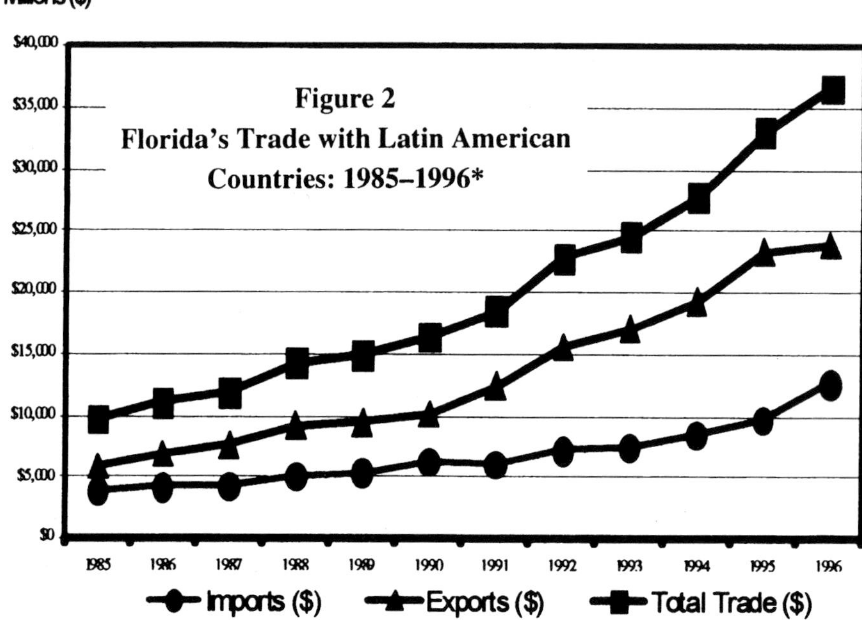

Note: These data include figures for Canada in addition to Latin America. Canada accounted for about 11 percent of Florida's exports to Western Hemisphere countries in 1996.

Source: Enterprise Florida, Florida Hemispheric Partners, Team Florida, 111 Business Forum of the Americas, Orlando, Florida, 1997.

Imports from these countries to Florida increased from less than $4 billion in 1985 to almost $13 billion in 1996. Likewise, exports from Florida to Latin American countries grew in value from about $6 billion to almost $24 billion during the same 11 year period.[9] In 1960, Miami was a metropolitan area of almost one million residents that was heavily dependent upon tourism. The city has been transformed into a metropolitan area of more than two million people with a more diversified economy and a reputation for being a "gateway" to Latin America.[10] Now international trade, finance, and a well-developed Hispanic economic enclave complement tourism to provide a more stable and diversified economy for Greater Miami.

1.2. Will most of Florida's Cubans return to Cuba if the Castro government falls?

Assuming that most Cubans emigrating to Florida were motivated by political dissatisfaction and fear of a government that restricts human rights, it is reasonable to question whether or not most Cuban Americans (who comprised 43.5% of the state's Hispanics and 48% of Miami-Dade County's Hispanics in 1990) would return to their island homeland if a democratic government replaced the current communist one in Cuba. Most researchers believe that this would not be the case. I speculate that only 5% to 15% would return to Cuba under such conditions. Most would not return for at least four reasons.[11] First, Cuba would not be the same as when they left it. More than 40 years of communist governance has changed the cultural, social, and economic structure of the island. Second, Cuba is experiencing a severe housing shortage, so there would be no place for large numbers of returnees to live. Third, most Cuban Americans have adjusted to life in the United States and developed roots here. They have jobs and all their personal resources here, which makes it difficult for them to move back to Cuba. Finally, many now have most of their family and friends living here in the United States, so they no longer have strong family ties that would draw them back to Cuba. Most Cubans are in Florida to stay. It would be a serious mistake to think they will not play as important a role in the educational future of Florida as they do today. Such mistaken thinking would underestimate the relevance of the state's Hispanics to any plans to meet Florida's future educational needs.

1.3. School enrollment projections by racial and ethnic categories

I have used data from the Florida Department of Education (DOE) to provide capital outlay FTE (full-time equivalent) student enrollment projections for all of the state's counties forward to the academic year 2006/07 (Table 2). These projections are broken down separately for non-Hispanic Whites, non-Hispanic Blacks, Hispanics, Asians and Pacific Islanders, and American Indians (including Alaskan Natives). The DOE makes its projections for only the total capital outlay FTE student enrollments, not separately for the ethnic and racial groups shown in Table 2. DOE does count student membership enrollments for each year by race and ethnic affiliation, but it does not project these into the future.[12]

Table 2. Florida capital outlay and populations 1996–2007, by region

Regions	1996 total capital outlay FTEs (estimates by ethnicity)					
	White non-Hisp. FTEs	Black non-Hisp. FTEs	Hispanic FTEs	Asian & Pac. Isl. FTEs	Am. Ind. & Alask. Nat. FTEs	Total FTEs
Panhandle	135637.1	52194.0	3353.7	3582.5	682.6	195450
Crown	206364.5	86427.0	9504.5	5220.5	535.5	308052
East Central	266035.9	82048.5	46997.7	8778.2	1096.7	404957
West Central	366866.7	96408.8	53409.9	8259.6	1158.0	526103
South	255357.0	233209.7	232504.3	12864.9	1543.0	735479
State totals	1231084.1	550167.6	345067.5	38703.2	5018.6	2170041
	1996 total capital outlay FTEs (estimates by ethnicity)					
	% White	% Black	% Hisp.	% Asian & Pac. Isl.	% Am. Ind. & Alask. Nat.	
Panhandle	69.4	26.7	1.7	1.8	0.3	
Crown	67.0	28.1	3.1	1.7	0.2	
East Central	65.7	20.3	11.6	2.2	0.3	
West Central	69.7	18.3	10.2	1.6	0.2	
South	34.7	31.7	31.6	1.7	0.2	
State totals	56.7	25.4	15.9	1.8	0.2	
	Projected capital outlay FTE growth (1996–2006/07)					
	Number White growth	Number Black growth	Number Hisp. growth	# Asian & Pac. Isl. growth	# Am. Ind. & Alask. Nat. growth	Total FTE growth
Panhandle	6360.4	3089.6	759.8	281.7	182.5	10674
Crown	15943.8	11408.5	3522.7	910.2	152.9	31938
East Central	23643.8	16269.4	19783.3	2482.4	406.1	62585
West Central	20115.9	11673.7	14251.6	1434.7	214.1	47690
South	15638.4	48527.6	58713.3	3739.3	525.4	127144
State totals	87841.8	89162.5	92711.9	8763.5	1551.4	280031
	Projected FTE populations for 2006/07					
	Number White non-Hisp.	Number Black non-Hisp.	Number Hisp.	Number Asian & Pac. Isl.	Number Am. Ind. & Alask. Nat.	Total
Panhandle	142104	54372	4725	3928	995	206124
Crown	224369	95825	13062	6021	713	339990
East Central	286252	98699	69539	11571	1481	467542
West Central	387149	107703	68139	9441	1361	573793
South	272457	281556	289947	16592	2071	862623
State totals	1312331	638154	445412	47552	6623	2450072

Table 2 continued. Florida capital outlay and populations 1996–2007, by region

	Projected FTE populations for 2006/07				
	% White	% Black	% Hisp.	% Asian & Pac. Isl.	% Am. Ind. & Alask. Nat.
Panhandle	68.9	26.4	2.3	1.9	0.5
Crown	66.0	28.2	3.8	1.8	0.2
East Central	61.2	21.1	14.9	2.5	0.3
West Central	67.5	18.8	11.9	1.6	0.2
South	31.6	32.8	33.6	1.9	0.2
State totals	53.6	26.0	18.2	1.9	0.3

When making my projections, I used the DOE's counts of student membership enrollments for 1990 and 1996 by racial and ethnic groups.[13] For each county I subtracted the 1990 figures from those for 1996 to obtain the growth that occurred during this six year period. Then I calculated the percentages of this growth that were attributable to each of the five groups shown in Table 2. Next, I used the DOE's count of capital outlay FTE enrollments for 1996 and its projections to the 2006/07 academic year to obtain estimates of the growth that will occur in each county during this period. I made the assumption that the percentages of this projected growth for each of the five groups are the same as they were during the 1990–1996 period. The increase thus projected for each of the five groups was added to its capital outlay enrollment for 1996 to obtain its projected number for the 2006/07 school year.[14]

It is important to remember that these are projections, not predictions. They are based on the assumption that the trends that prevailed during the 1990–1996 period will also prevail during the 1996–2006 period. Of course, we do not know if this will actually be the case in the future. When DOE made their projections for the total capital outlay FTE enrollments for each county they incorporated a decline in fertility into their model and they assumed that the net migration trends that earlier occurred would continue into the future.[15] There is no methodology that will allow for a completely accurate prediction of what will happen with future migration simply because migration is dependent upon unpredictable forces, such as future U.S. immigration policy, political and economic conditions in Latin American countries, and economic circumstances in other parts of the United States.

In 1990, Hispanics represented about 12.4% of the state's students, but by 1996, almost 16% of the state's students were Hispanic, and this proportion is expected to increase to 18% by the academic year 2006. Although their absolute numbers will increase significantly between now and 2006, the percentages of the Florida's students who are non-Hispanic Whites, Blacks, Asians, and American Indians are not likely to change very much.

The ethnic and racial categories of students are distributed among Florida's 67 counties almost identically to the distribution of their respective total populations. Thus, Miami-Dade County has both a large Hispanic population and a large number of Hispanic students. The estimations and projections displayed in Table 2 have been organized by the planning regions used by the Florida Department of Education (Figure 3) to facilitate recognition of general patterns. Four maps (Figures 4–7) also have been produced that show the projected growths in student FTEs among the counties. Figures 4, 5, and 6 show the projected growth patterns of Hispanic, Black, and non-Hispanic White student FTEs respectively. The projected growth patterns of Asians and American Indians have been combined into one map (Figure 7) because there are so few of them living in Florida. Together they comprised only 2.0% of the state's total capital outlay FTEs in 1996, and in the year 2006 their share will probably be about the same (2.2%).

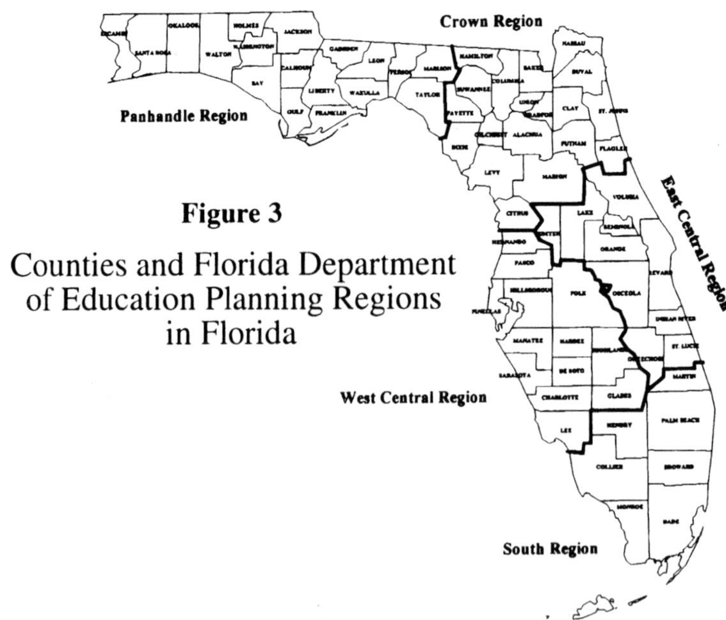

Figure 3

Counties and Florida Department of Education Planning Regions in Florida

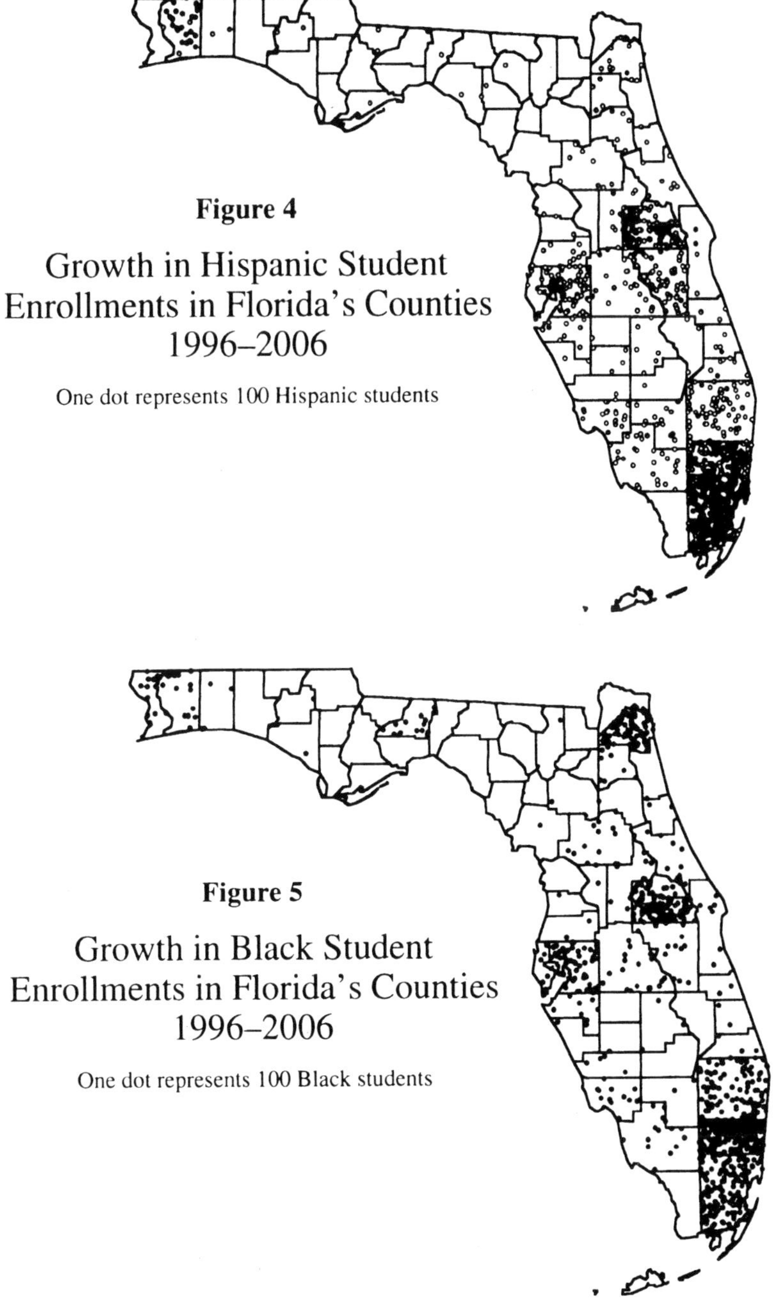

Figure 4

Growth in Hispanic Student Enrollments in Florida's Counties 1996–2006

One dot represents 100 Hispanic students

Figure 5

Growth in Black Student Enrollments in Florida's Counties 1996–2006

One dot represents 100 Black students

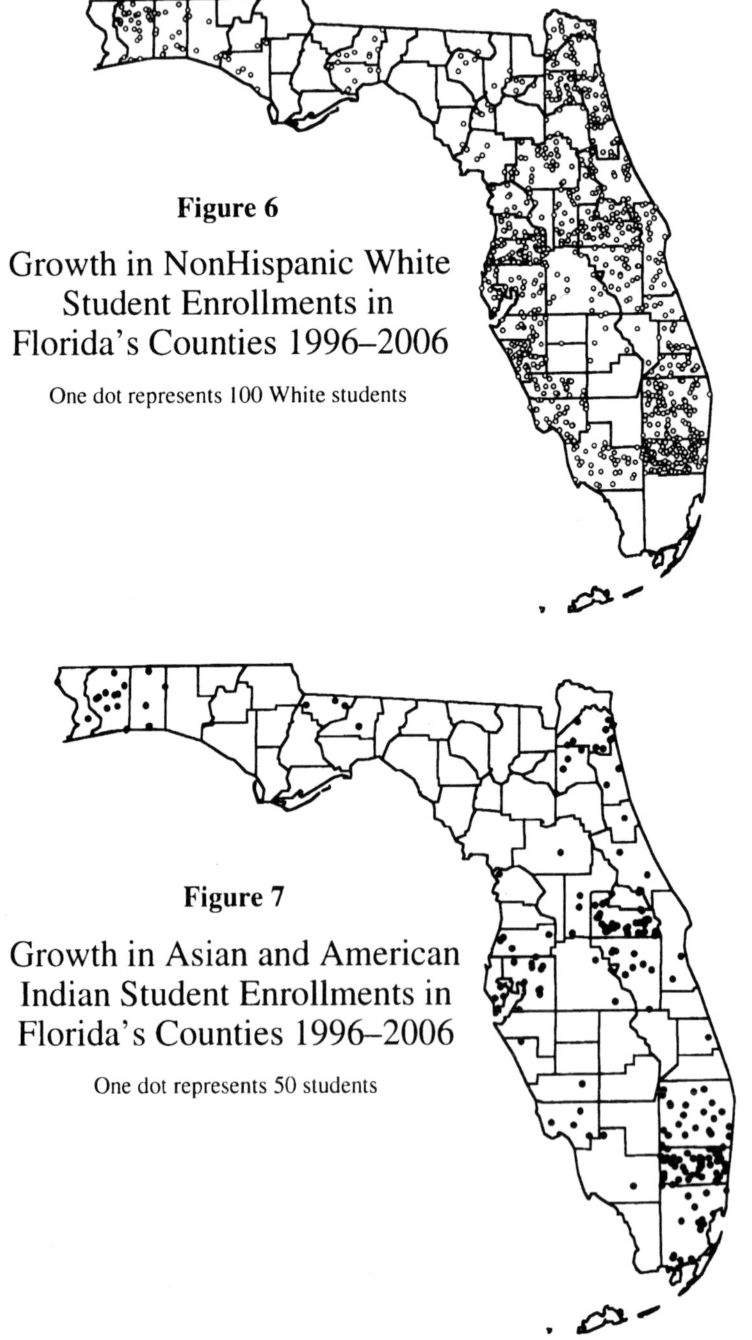

Figure 6

Growth in NonHispanic White Student Enrollments in Florida's Counties 1996–2006

One dot represents 100 White students

Figure 7

Growth in Asian and American Indian Student Enrollments in Florida's Counties 1996–2006

One dot represents 50 students

The numbers in Table 2 and the maps in Figures 4–7 indicate that counties which had the largest number of a particular racial or ethnic group also will most likely experience the largest numeric increases. For example, the largest Hispanic increase in student enrollments (Figure 4) is expected to occur in southeastern Florida (Dade, Broward, and Palm Beach Counties), in metropolitan Orlando (Orange, Seminole, and Osceola Counties), and in the Tampa-St. Petersburg area (Hillsborough and Pinellas Counties), precisely where most of the state's Hispanics were living in 1996 (compare the maps in Figures 1 and 4). Black student enrollments exhibit a growth pattern similar to that of Hispanics, except Jacksonville (Duval County) is added as a significant growth area (Figure 5). In some respects, the projected growth of non-Hispanic Whites shows the most interesting pattern (Figure 6) because of the hollow area that is clearly visible in extreme southern Florida. This is because both Miami-Dade and Monroe Counties are expected to experience declines in the their non-Hispanic White student populations, as has been happening in Miami-Dade County since the 1960s. Much of the growth in the Anglo student population in South Florida has spilled over from Miami-Dade County into neighboring suburban counties like Broward and Collier. The same non-Hispanic White suburbanization process, although less extreme, is occurring in the Orlando, Tampa-St. Petersburg, and Jacksonville metropolitan areas, as well as most other large American metropolitan areas. Asian and American Indian student enrollments will increase most rapidly in the metropolitan areas of South Florida, Orlando, Tampa, and Jacksonville (Figure 7).

2. Ability to speak English and socioeconomic status for Florida's Hispanics who speak another language

I am using data derived from answers to the 15th question on the 1990 U.S. Census of Population questionnaire which asked if the person being counted spoke a language other than English in the home. If the person answered "yes" to this question, he/she was asked what this other language was and then how well he/she speaks English.[16] Data on language spoken at home were recorded for persons 5 years of age or older (U.S. Bureau of the Census 1993: 5–20, B.24–B.25, and E.14). These data come from the one percent 1990 Public Use Microdata Sample (PUMS) CD-ROM for Florida (U.S. Bureau of the Census 1995). When I created the tables used in this section I used individual person weights that take into consideration an individual's socioeconomic characteristics. This is the method recommended by the U.S. Bureau of the Census (1993: 4.1–4.6). All of the crosstabulations used in creating these tables had Chi^2 values that were statistically significant at the .001 level of probability because of the large sizes of the PUMS samples for both the state of Florida and Miami-Dade County.[17]

The figures in Table 3 show clearly that Florida's Hispanics are learning English, contrary to what some people living in South Florida seem to think. Of those born in the U.S. who speak a language other than English in the home, 94% speak English either well or very well. Furthermore, for Hispanic immigrants there is a strong relationship between length of time spent living in the United States and their ability to speak English. The earlier a person immigrated to the U.S. the greater the likelihood that he/she speaks English either well or very well. Two-thirds of all Hispanics living in Florida, who speak some language in their homes in addition to English, speak English either very well or well. For example, among Hispanics who immigrated to the U.S. before 1950, 81% claim to have no problems with English; while among those who arrived more recently during the 1982–1990 period only 52% claim to speak English very well or well.

Table 3. Ability of Hispanics 5 years of age or older living in Florida and Miami-Dade County who speak another language in their homes to speak English, by years of immigration: 1990

Ability to speak English	Year of immigration (percentages)						
	Born in U.S.	1990 to 1980	1979 to 1970	1969 to 1960	1959 to 1950	Before 1950	All non-Hispanic immigrants
State of Florida							
Very well	80.9%	29.4%	39.3%	43.9%	47.6%	48.7%	46.3%
Well	13.4%	23.8%	23.3%	23.1%	30.2%	32.5%	21.8%
Not well	4.8%	25.8%	23.2%	19.5%	18.4%	15.0%	19.0%
Not at all	0.9%	20.9%	14.2%	13.4%	3.8%	3.9%	12.9%
Miami-Dade County							
Very well	84.8%	26.3%	35.3%	41.6%	41.6%	44.7%	41.6%
Well	10.6%	23.1%	22.0%	21.8%	31.3%	35.6%	21.1%
Not well	3.5%	26.4%	25.6%	21.2%	21.6%	16.5%	21.1%
Not at all	1.1%	24.1%	17.0%	15.4%	5.5%	3.2%	16.2%

Note: Percentages do not always total to 100.0% because of rounding.
Source: U.S. Bureau of the Census 1995.

A similar association between years of immigration to the United States and English-speaking abilities are found among Miami-Dade County's Hispanic population (Table 3). Hispanics in South Florida are rapidly learning to speak English, just as they are in the rest of Florida. Almost two-thirds (63%) of Miami-Dade's Hispanic population that speaks Spanish in their homes also claim to speak English either very well or well.

The relationship between ability to speak English and socioeconomic status for Florida's Hispanics who speak another language (Spanish) is clearly demonstrated in Table 4.[18] It is obvious that there is a positive association between English-speaking abilities and socioeconomic achievements. Hispanics who speak English either very well or well have higher incomes, lower poverty rates, higher educational attainments, and better jobs than those who do not. The economic pay-off is particularly apparent when comparing mean incomes. The average Hispanic person who speaks English very well makes about $3,000 more than one who only speaks English well. The differential between Hispanics who speak English very well and those who do not speak it at all is almost $11,000.

Table 4. Ability of Hispanics living in Florida and in Miami-Dade County who speak another language in their homes to speak English by income categories, by socioeconomic characteristics: 1990

Ability to speak English	Socioeconomic characteristics					
	Mean income (16 yrs.+)	% below poverty	% with less than a H.S. ed. (25 yrs.+)	% with a B.A. degree or higher (25 yrs.+)	% working in exec. & admin. occupations	% working in laborer & operator occupations
State of Florida						
Very well	$17,056	14.3%	22.1%	23.6%	23.5%	10.8%
Well	$13,852	16.9%	35.0%	15.1%	15.7%	17.6%
Not well	$9,504	24.3%	59.7%	8.0%	8.0%	28.0%
Not at all	$6,259	32.8%	83.4%	2.5%	4.2%	32.8%
Speak only English	$14,927	16.9%	29.9%	16.4%	19.8%	15.5%
Miami-Dade County						
Very well	$18,105	13.1%	18.2%	26.7%	26.5%	10.2%
Well	$14,477	16.9%	32.4%	16.7%	16.8%	15.9%
Not well	$9,763	23.5%	56.5%	9.5%	9.5%	29.0%
Not at all	$6,147	33.0%	83.4%	2.4%	4.8%	34.8%
Speak only English	$11,261	24.6%	47.9%	9.7%	15.6%	22.4%

Source: U.S. Bureau of the Census 1995.

A lot has recently been written about the enclave economy in Miami that provides an economic support system for Miami-Dade County's Hispanic immigrants.[19] Because it is reasonable to hypothesize that this enclave serves as an advantage for people who speak Spanish in Miami, I produced the lower half of Table 4 to show the condition for Miami-Dade County's Hispanics. I wanted to see if English-speaking abilities have the same relationship to socioeconomic status in metropolitan Miami as they do for the state. My results showed that the data for metropolitan Miami exhibited very similar percentages and trends as those for the state (see also Boswell 1998). It is clear that knowing English either well or very well provides a tremendous advantage over not speaking English well for most Hispanics living both in Florida and in Miami. Thus, there is a strong economic motive for Hispanics living in Florida to learn English, and this is what most are trying to do.

Because I have been focusing on Florida's Hispanics, it is reasonable to ask how the state's non-Hispanics who speak a language other than English compare to Hispanics in terms of their English-speaking abilities. Table 5 provides the answer by demonstrating that the non-Hispanics have fewer problems speaking English. Whereas 32% of the Hispanics speak English either not well or not at all, the comparable figure for non-Hispanics is only 11% in Florida. The data for Miami-Dade County exhibit similar results. While in metropolitan Miami 37% of the Hispanics reported they speak English either not well or not at all, among the non-Hispanics the comparable figure was only 12%. Again, as was the case with the county's Hispanics, there is a clear and positive relationship between length of time in the U.S. and ability to speak English very well.

Table 5. Ability of non-Hispanics 5 years of age or older living in Florida and Miami-Dade County who speak another language in their homes to speak English, by years of immigration: 1990

Ability to speak English	Year of immigration (percentages)						
	Born in U.S.	1990 to 1980	1979 to 1970	1969 to 1960	1959 to 1950	Before 1950	All non-Hispanic immigrants
State of Florida							
Very well	76.7%	47.0%	59.4%	62.9%	63.1%	69.5%	67.1%
Well	15.2%	30.7%	30.2%	28.8%	27.6%	25.3%	21.8%
Not well	7.9%	18.8%	8.8%	6.4%	8.8%	4.1%	9.8%
Not at all	0.2%	3.5%	1.6%	2.0%	0.5%	1.1%	1.2%
Miami-Dade County							
Very well	81.2%	45.0%	55.1%	47.6%	57.0%	74.9%	64.6%
Well	14.0%	30.5%	34.0%	37.1%	28.9%	21.9%	23.4%
Not well	4.3%	19.8%	8.7%	9.6%	11.7%	1.2%	9.6%
Not at all	0.6%	4.7%	2.2%	5.7%	2.3%	2.0%	2.4%

Note: Percentages do not always total to 100.0% because of rounding.
Source: U.S. Bureau of the Census 1995.

Why is it that Florida's Hispanics have more difficulties speaking English than the state's non-Hispanics who also speak something other than English in their homes? The answer lies in the fact that the non-Hispanics speak a wide variety of languages, whereas virtually all the Hispanics speak Spanish, as previously mentioned. Because of the concentration of Hispanics in Florida, and especially in the southern part of the state, it is easier to find someone to speak with in Spanish. Furthermore, the constant infusion of immigrants from Latin American countries ensures that Florida continues to have a large Spanish-speaking population. Immigration is well-known to be a factor that inhibits or slows the processes of assimilation and acculturation.[20]

Table 6 demonstrates that both Florida's and metropolitan Miami's non-Hispanics have the same economic incentives to learn English as do Hispanics. For both the state and county, as abilities to speak English increase, so does socioeconomic status. Better English-speaking abilities are associated with higher mean incomes, lower poverty rates, a smaller percentage who do not complete high school, a higher percentage with college degrees, a higher percentage employed in high-paying white-collar occupations, and a lower proportion employed in blue-collar occupations as laborers and operators.

Table 6. Ability of non-Hispanics living in Florida and in Miami-Dade County who speak another language in their homes, to speak English by socioeconomic characteristics: 1990

Ability to speak English	Socioeconomic characteristics					
	Mean income (16 yrs.+)	% below poverty	% with less than a H.S. ed. (25 yrs.+)	% with a B.A. degree or higher (25 yrs.+)	% working in exec. & admin. occupations	% working in laborer & operator occupations
State of Florida						
Very well	$17,484	13.3%	24.0%	23.7%	27.7%	9.6%
Well	$13,699	19.4%	37.6%	15.4%	18.5%	15.2%
Not well	$11,989	21.8%	49.7%	11.2%	15.0%	16.6%
Not at all	$7,647	28.8%	74.2%	2.9%	21.1%	16.6%
Speak only English	$18,240	10.8%	22.4%	18.9%	24.4%	11.2%
Miami-Dade County						
Very well	$18,526	17.9%	18.8%	32.1%	32.0%	7.4%
Well	$11,970	29.4%	37.6%	20.4%	21.9%	20.4%
Not well	$7,512	38.6%	70.5%	9.7%	7.1%	34.9%
Not at all	$8,138	36.3%	72.5%	NA	31.3%	18.3%
Speak only English	$20,781	14.0%	22.1%	23.6%	28.0%	9.0%

NA = not available. Source: U.S. Bureau of the Census 1995.

3. Socioeconomic benefits of knowing a second language in addition to English

The U.S. Census Bureau does not provide information on the abilities of people to speak a language other than English. People are asked only if they speak a language other than English in their homes. Still, it is possible to determine whether there is an advantage in speaking a second language by comparing the socioeconomic characteristics of Hispanics who speak only English with those who speak another language (Spanish) in addition to English.

Table 4 can be used again, this time to analyze the effects of knowing a second language (Spanish) in addition to English among Hispanics living both in Florida and in greater Miami. I now refer to the two rows in this table that deal with Hispanics who speak only English. It is most appropriate to compare Hispanics in both Florida and Miami-Dade County who speak only English with those who speak English very well. Those who do not speak English very well are burdened with a disadvantage that counteracts the advantages of knowing a second language, which in this case is almost always Spanish.

Table 4 indicates that Hispanics who speak another language in their homes (Spanish) and speak English very well have higher socioeconomic status than those who speak only English in both Florida and Miami-Dade County. Hispanics who speak English very well and speak Spanish have higher incomes, lower poverty rates, higher educational attainment, and better-paying jobs than Hispanics who only speak English. The differential in mean income is especially apparent. In Florida, Hispanics who speak only English have an average income of $14,927; whereas Hispanics who speak English very well and live in a family where Spanish is mainly spoken have a higher average income of $17,056, for a per capita difference of more than $2,000. The difference in Miami-Dade County is even greater, almost $7,000.

Many people visiting Miami remark about the prevalence of spoken Spanish. For example, Joan Didion (1987: 63) has written:

> What was unusual about Spanish in Miami was not that it was so often spoken, but that is was so often heard: in say, Los Angeles, Spanish remained a language only barely registered by the Anglo population, part of the ambient noise, the language spoken by the people who worked in the car wash and came to trim the trees and cleared the tables in restaurants. In Miami Spanish was spoken by the people who ate in the restaurants, the people who owned the cars and the trees, which made on the socioauditory scale, a considerable difference. Exiles who felt isolated or declassed by language in New York or Los Angeles thrived in Miami.

One of the most important reasons that so much Spanish is heard in Miami is that there are economic incentives for knowing Spanish as well as English there. This has been clearly shown in this chapter. However, there are at least three other reasons why Spanish is more frequently heard in Miami than in most other large American cities. First, whereas only about one-third of the Hispanics living in the United States are foreign-born, in Florida the proportion is about two-thirds (68%) and in Miami-Dade County the comparable figure is 79%.[21] Since it is the first generation of immigrants (the foreign-born) who have the greatest difficulty learning English, it is natural that they prefer to speak in Spanish, especially in Miami. Second, Hispanics comprise a majority (about 58%) of the population living in Miami-Dade County, so it is easier to find someone with whom to speak in Spanish in Miami than in most other American cities, where the proportions of the total population that is Hispanic is less.[22] Finally, Hispanics living in Florida and in Miami have higher socioeconomic status, on average, than those living in such states as California, Texas, and New York. Most of Florida's and Miami's Hispanics are solidly members of the middle class. Especially in Miami, Hispanics are empowered both economically and politically. Thus speaking Spanish is not associated with the stigma of poverty and social disaffection in Miami to the same degree that it is in many other large American cities.

The most surprising finding of this chapter is that there is no consistent relationship between knowing a second language, in addition to being able to speak English well, and socioeconomic status among Florida's non-Hispanics.[23] This apparent paradox is demonstrated by the percentages shown in Table 6. For example, Florida's non-Hispanics who speak English very well, and speak another language in their homes, have a lower mean income and a somewhat higher poverty rate when compared to non-Hispanics who speak only English. In contrast, Hispanics who speak English very well and speak another language have a higher percentage who are college graduates and work in higher status jobs in the executive and administrative occupations.[24]

Why is it that Hispanics who speak a second language, in addition to speaking English well, have higher status than other Hispanics who know only English, whereas non-Hispanics who speak a second language do not consistently have higher socioeconomic status than the non-Hispanics who only know English? The answer lies in the greater utility of knowing Spanish in Florida when compared to knowing another foreign language. Because more people speak Spanish in Florida there is a larger domestic market where Spanish is a useful language in business. Perhaps even more importantly, Spanish is also more useful in international trade because of the large amount of business that is transacted between Florida and Latin America, as noted earlier in this chapter.

4. Summary and policy implications

Earlier, I asked how it was possible for language to become such an important issue in Florida and metropolitan Miami. Obviously, the answer is linked to the ethnic change that has taken place in the state and in Miami-Dade County during the relatively brief time since 1960. Today, there are more than 2 million Hispanics living in Florida, but in 1960 there were only about 50,000. By far the majority of Florida's Hispanics speak Spanish as their mother tongue. For most of them, English has been acquired as a second language and they continue speaking Spanish in their homes. Although about two-thirds of the state's Hispanics report that they speak English well or very well, the other three-quarters of a million of them have problems using English. Most of the state's Latin American immigrants will not be returning to their original homelands to live, and all indicators suggest that their numbers in the United States will continue to increase into the foreseeable future. Although the Hispanic population is heavily concentrated in southern Florida, and secondarily in the Orlando and Tampa-St. Petersburg metropolitan areas, Hispanics are diffusing to other regions of the state. It would be going too far to state that what happened to Miami-Dade County is a replica of things to come in Florida's other counties. Still, there can be little doubt that the Hispanic student populations will increase in the vast majority of these other counties.

As more Spanish was spoken in Florida, especially in southern Florida, there was a backlash reaction against it that culminated in 1992, when Florida became the 22nd state to pass a referendum declaring English to be the state's official language. Although language is still an emotional issue, some far-sighted businessmen and women in Miami created the Greater Miami Chamber of Commerce's committee named "One Community One Goal," referred to earlier in this chapter. They had become concerned that South Florida was losing its status as "the gateway to Latin America." It was noted that the number of multinational corporations moving to Miami has declined by 23% from the growth rate five years earlier. Furthermore, the median size of these corporations has declined from 203 employees per firm in 1987 to 65 in 1997. Despite these declines, it is estimated that there are still about 400 multinational firms operating in Miami-Dade County and they employ a labor force of more than 41,000 workers, or roughly 4% of the County's total work force (Fields 1997).

A year earlier, a report was published jointly by the Greater Miami Chamber of Commerce and the Cuban American National Council that called attention to the fact that Miami-Dade County was facing a serious shortage of workers who were fluent enough in Spanish to conduct business with Latin American firms (Fradd 1996). Among other things, this study also reported that the second generation Hispanics (born in the United States by immigrant parents) were not maintaining a level of Spanish language proficiency that would satisfy future labor force demands. In fact, America-born Hispanics preferred conversing in English, rather than the Spanish of their parents. In other words, it was business considerations that changed the mood in metropolitan Miami, at least among some of the city's most influential entrepreneurs, as far as attitudes towards Spanish language proficiency is concerned.

The second and third sections of this study provide evidence in support of the recommendations of the "One Community One Goal" committee as noted on the first page of this chapter. The second presented clear evidence that there is a strong positive association between levels of socioeconomic status and ability to speak English for those Hispanics who live in households where a language other than English is used. This correlation was also found in non-Hispanic households where the language spoken in the home was not either English or Spanish. These results suggest that it simply makes good sense to help people who have difficulties speaking English for at least two reasons: (1) persons who do not speak English well are expensive to the rest of society because they are more likely to be poor, out of work, and pay low taxes; and (2) they are more likely to require public assistance to meet their basic needs and those of their families. The policy implications of this finding are underscored when it is noted that in 1990 there were almost half a million people living in Florida who did not speak English well or did not speak it at all. Of these, 82% were Hispanics.

The third section of this chapter found that Hispanics who know Spanish and can speak English well have an advantage in the labor force that translates into higher incomes, lower poverty rates, higher educational attainment levels, and better jobs than Hispanics who know only English or speak English poorly. This relationship between being able to speak English comfortably and knowing Spanish and high socioeconomic status is consistent for both Florida and Miami-Dade County. However, it was surprising to find that it did not hold true for the state's non-Hispanics, nor was it true for Miami-Dade County's non-Hispanics.

The finding that speaking a language at home, in addition to being able to speak English very well, does not provide the economic payoffs for non-Hispanics that it does for Hispanics is explained by the dominance of Spanish as a second language to English in Florida. Although sometimes Miami is referred to as being a world city, recent evidence suggests that it is more a regional city with a strong focus on Latin America for its international trade. It dominates U.S. trade with Latin America (except for Mexico), but it only provides for 1.5% of U.S. trade with Europe and only 0.5% of trade with East Asia. Of Miami's top ten trading countries, the first nine are in Latin America (Nijman 1996a). The same holds true for Florida's trade: about 64% of the state's exports are directed to Latin American countries.

The finding that Hispanics benefit more than non-Hispanics from knowing two languages emphasizes the importance of Spanish language knowledge in Florida for business. While it is true that languages other than English and Spanish also contribute to Florida's economy, the overwhelming dominance of these two languages suggest that the state's educational policies should focus on them. Spending priorities need to be established for the education budgets. The findings of this study suggest that Florida should focus on teaching English to all residents of the state who do not speak English well or very well and on teaching good communication skills in Spanish to students who choose to study it as a second language or a heritage language.

Notes

1. When I use the term "Miami" in this paper I am referring to metropolitan Miami or greater Miami, which includes all of Miami-Dade County.

2. The 1990 Census of Population in the U.S. did not ask a question regarding what language individuals spoke. Instead, three questions were asked regarding the language most often spoken in their homes. The first of these asked whether or not a language other than English was spoken in the person's home. The second asked what specific language was spoken the most in the home. The third asked how well the person spoke English (U.S. Bureau of the Census 1990: E.14).

3. I have not included these estimates for 1995 in Table 1 because the Bureau of Economic and Business Research (BEBR) figure is for all Blacks. BEBR does not subtract the number of Hispanic Blacks to yield a figure for non-Hispanic Blacks that is comparable to the figures in Table 1. Likewise, the Bureau's figure for Whites does not subtract Hispanic Whites.

4. The figures for 1960 include people who classified themselves as being foreign-born or who indicated they were born to parents at least one of whom was foreign-born. This is what the U.S. Bureau of the Census calls the "foreign stock" population. To estimate the Hispanic foreign stock I added together the figures in the 1960 Census for "Mexican" and "Other America," which did not include Canada, foreign stock (see Table 49 in the 1960 Census source listed below). Because it only includes the first two generations of immigration (the immigrants and their children) it is not strictly comparable with the figures for 1970, 1980, and 1990. The figures for the latter three dates include some members of third and subsequent generations of immigration, as long as the people so classified considered themselves to be of Hispanic origin or descent.

5. The figures for non-Hispanics for 1960, 1970, and 1980 were calculated by subtracting the Hispanic White, Black, and Other populations from the total White, Black, and Other populations, respectively. The U.S. Census Bureau's 1990 Summary Tape File 3A provided separate data for Hispanics and non-Hispanics by racial classes. Data derived from the 1960 Census were not available by race for Hispanics, but figures were published for 1960 Hispanics in Table 45 in the 1970 Census (see sources listed below).

6. The figures for Blacks and non-Hispanic Others for 1960 are rough estimates because the U.S. Census Bureau added together Black Hispanics and Other Hispanics. Under the assumption that the vast majority of these people were Black Hispanics, I treated them as if all were Hispanic Blacks. Thus, my estimate of Black Hispanics is slightly higher than it really was. Because these people were subtracted from the total Black population this means that my estimate of non-Hispanic Blacks is slightly lower than it should be for 1960. Conversely, my estimate of non-Hispanic Others is slightly

higher than it really was because I did not subtract any Hispanic Others from it. This error factor is almost certainly very small because the 1970 Census shows that only 11.1% of the Hispanics counted as being either Black or Other were in the Other category (see Table 49 in the 1970 Census source listed below).

7. I have used Hispanic student enrollments provided by the Florida Department of Education for 1996 to produce the map in Figure 1 because the emphasis in this chapter is on Florida's student population (Miller 1997).

8. For more statistics and information on the changes in Miami-Dade County's population see Boswell 1995.

9. These trade figures are for all countries included within the Summit of the Americas (SOA) consortium of Western Hemisphere countries. As such, they include figures for Canada, as well as most Latin American and Caribbean countries. Of course, Canada is not a Latin American country. In 1996, Canada accounted for 11.3% of all exports from the United States to SOA countries. On the other hand, there are several Caribbean countries that trade with the United States (excluding Cuba) that are not included as SOA countries because they are not politically independent (e.g. Puerto Rico, Guadeloupe, Martinique, and the Netherlands Antilles). They accounted for 1.4% of all U.S. exports in 1996. If we subtract Canada's contribution to U.S. exports (because it is not a Latin American country) and add in the exports to the Caribbean countries that are not included in the SOA consortium (because they are part of Latin America), this would reduce the Latin American export estimate by about 10% (to about $21.6 billion). Comparable figures on U.S. imports are not available from the source I am using to estimate trade with Latin America: Enterprise Florida 1997.

10. For more information regarding Miami's rise to gateway city status see Portes and Stepick 1993, Nijman 1996a, 1996b, 1997.

11. For an elaboration of this argument see Boswell 1985.

12. The Florida Department of Education distinguishes between student memberships and capital outlay FTE enrollments. The numerical difference between these two is not very significant. For the state of Florida the capital outlay FTE figure was 2,450,072 in 1996; whereas, for student memberships it was 2,240,283. However, conceptually these two measures are very different. The student membership numbers are derived from a head count, whereas the capital outlay FTE enrollment represents a count of full-time equivalent enrollments. For example, two half-time students would be counted as two memberships but only one FTE. Conversely, a student who was enrolled full-time and also involved in a special after-school program would be counted as one membership but maybe 1.2 FTE's.

13. When I say 1990 and 1996 I am really referring to the 1990/91 and 1996/97 academic years.

14. When making these projections I encountered problems with counties with small populations and several that registered school enrollment declines between 1960 and 1990, and were expected by DOE to continue to experience declines between 1996 and 2006. Sometimes my projections resulted in negative school enrollments, which is an impossibility. I had to adjust my methodology when making my projections for these few

counties by using anecdotal evidence derived from talking with county officials and Martha Miller (who makes the DOE enrollment projections). There were six counties, all located either in the Panhandle or Crown regions, where these problems were encountered: Franklin, Gadsden, Jefferson, Taylor, Washington, and Dixie.

15. I used an extrapolation method to test the reliability of DOE's projections. The formula used was as follows:

$$P_2 = P_1 e^{rn}$$

Where: P_1 = The population in 1996
P_2 = The population in 2006
e = The mathematical constant 2.718
r = Rate of annual change
n = Number of years between 1996 and 2006 (10)

During the first extrapolation I used an annual growth rate which assumed that exactly the same county growth rates that prevailed during the 1990–1996 period continued during the 1996–2006 period. This yielded a total student capital outlay FTE for the state that was equal to 2,954,505 (compared to the DOE projected value of 2,450,072). Next, I ran the same equation but assumed that each county's population growth rate declined by half of what it was during the 1990–1996 period. This estimate yielded a predicted value of 2,532,074. Both of these extrapolated figures are significantly higher than the DOE projection for the same period. I conclude that if the DOE projections are found to be in error in the future, it will most likely be because they are low.

16. I agree with Fradd (1996: 21), who states:

> While most researchers recognize self-report measures are not as reliable as other less subjective measures of language proficiency, self report, especially of a large cohort, provides a useful picture of respondents' performance in the language (Alejandro Portes & Richard Schaeffler, "Language and the Second Generation," in R. Rumbaut & S. Pedraza (Eds.), *Origins and Destinies: Migration, Race, and Ethnicity in America* (Belmont, CA: Wadsworth, 1995). Large cohorts of data, such as those found in the U.S. Census records offer the most comprehensive information available on national and local language use trends. This, like all other census information, should be considered as an estimate rather than an actual value (L. Hart-Gonzalez & M. Feingold, (1990), "Retention of Spanish in the Home," *International Journal of Social Language*, Vol. 84: 5–34).

17. I calculated the Chi^2 values for these tables using the frequencies of the unweighted figures because this statistical measure is sensitive to sample sizes. Then I created the same crosstabulations using both weighted and unweighted frequencies. The differences in the percentage values between these two tables (weighted and unweighted) were always small (usually less than 2 percentage points). The one percent PUMS sample for the entire state of Florida included 133,399 persons and the five percent PUMS sample for Miami-Dade County included 93,305 persons. The weighted sample sizes,

respectively, were 12,930,156 and 1,933,985, both of which are close to the true 1990 populations of Florida (12,937,926) and Miami-Dade County (1,937,094).

18. Measuring socioeconomic status (SES) is a topic of considerable debate among social scientists. However, most agree that it is a multivariate concept that should include some measures of income levels, educational attainment, and occupational status. I have used one measure of each of these three. I have also used a measure of poverty because of its special importance among Hispanics – the poverty rate for Hispanics is much higher than it is among the U.S. population as a whole: 29.4% for Hispanics in 1997 and 13.7% for the total U.S. population (U.S. Bureau of the Census 1998: 478, Table 759).

19. For more information on Miami's Hispanic enclave economy the reader is referred to Portes 1987, Portes and Bach 1985, Portes and Mozo 1985, Portes and Rumbaut 1990, and Portes and Stepick 1993, particularly pp. 123–149.

20. For more information on the relationship between immigration and assimilation see Jaffe, Cullen, and Boswell 1980.

21. These two figures include Puerto Ricans born in Puerto Rico but living in the United States (U.S. Bureau of the Census 1995).

22. In 1990, 38% of the population living in the Los Angeles-Long Beach Primary Statistical Area was Hispanic, whereas in the New York City Primary Statistical Area it was 22% (U.S. Bureau of the Census 1995).

23. I performed the same analysis for Miami-Dade County's non-Hispanics and found identical results. In Dade County there is no consistent difference between non-Hispanics who speak only English and those who speak English very well and speak another language in their homes.

24. To check the validity of this surprising finding, I computed the age structures for non-Hispanics who know a second language in addition to speaking English very well and for non-Hispanics who speak only English to see if they were significantly different from each other. I found they are very similar. I also recalculated Tables 4 and 6 for persons in the 40–65 year age range, thus standardizing more specifically for age. Once again the results were the same. I therefore concluded that age was not a factor confounding my results.

References

Boswell, Thomas D. 1985. Commentary. In *The Cuban studies project, problems of succession in Cuba*, 99–103. Miami: Graduate School of International Studies, University of Miami.

Boswell, Thomas D. 1995. *The Cubanization and Hispanicization of metropolitan Miami*. Miami: The Cuban American Policy Center, The Cuban American National Council, Inc.

Boswell, Thomas D. 1998. Implications of demographic changes in Florida's public school populations. In *Creating Florida's multilingual global work force*, ed. Sandra Fradd and Okhee Lee, I.1–I.23. Tallahassee: Florida Department of Education.

Didion, Joan. 1987. *Miami*. New York: Pocket Books.

Enterprise Florida. 1997. *Florida hemispheric partners*. Orlando, FL.

Farrell, Jodi Milander. 1997. Business Leaders Urge Improvement for Schools. *The Miami Herald,* November 18: 1A.

Fields, Gregg. 1997. Dade must adapt to salvage global business, study says. *The Miami Herald*, October 29: 1A.

Fradd, Sandra H. 1996. The economic impact of Spanish-language proficiency in metropolitan Miami. Miami: Greater Miami Chamber of Commerce and the Policy Center of the Cuban American National Council.

Jaffe, Abram J., Ruth M. Cullen, and Thomas D. Boswell. 1980. *The changing demography of Spanish Americans*. New York: Academic Press.

Miller, Martha. 1997. Strategy Planning Department, Florida Department of Education, Tallahassee, FL. Personal communication.

Morales, Maria A. 1997. Foreign-born kids find a new path to learning. *The Miami Herald*, August 3: 1A.

Morgan, Curtis. 1996. Hispanic boom is transforming Florida. *The Miami Herald*, August 27: 1A.

Nijman, Jan. 1996a. Breaking the rules: Miami in the urban hierarchy. *Urban Geography* 17: 5–22.

Nijman, Jan. 1996b. Ethnicity, class, and the economic internationalization of Miami. In *Social polarization in post-industrial metropolises*, ed. J. O'Loughlin and J. Friedrichs, 283–300. Chicago: Gruyter-Aldine.

Nijman, Jan. 1997. Globalization to a Latin beat: The Miami growth machine. *Annals of the American Academy of Political and Social Sciences* 551: 163–176.

Nogle, June. 1996. State Hispanic population tops 2 million, UF study finds. Gainesville, FL: Bureau of Economic and Business Research, University of Florida, Gainesville.

Portes, Alejandro. 1987. The social origins of the Cuban enclave economy of Miami. *Sociological Perspectives* 30: 340–372.

Portes, Alejandro and Robert L. Bach. 1985. *Latin journey: Cuban and Mexican immigrants in the United States*. Berkeley: University of California Press.

Portes, Alejandro and Rafael Mozo. 1985. The political adaptation process of immigrants and other refugee minorities in the United States: A preliminary analysis. *International Migration Review* 19: 35–63.

Portes, Alejandro and Ruben G. Rumbaut. 1990. *Immigrant America: A portrait*. Berkeley: University of California Press.

Portes, Alejandro and Alex Stepick. 1993. *City on the edge: The transformation of Miami*. Berkeley: University of California Press.

Smith, Stan. 1997. *Components of population change in Florida, by county, April 1, 1990 to April 1, 1996*. Bureau of Economic and Business Research, University of Florida, Gainesville.

U.S. Bureau of the Census. 1962. *1960 census of population and housing*. Characteristics of the Population. Vol. 1. Washington, DC: U.S. Government Printing Office.

U.S. Bureau of the Census. 1972. *1970 census of population and housing*. Characteristics of the Population. Vol. 1. Part 11, Florida, Washington, DC: U.S. Government Printing Office.

U.S. Bureau of the Census. 1982. *1980 census of population and housing*. Characteristics of the Population, Part 11, Florida, PC80–1–C11, Washington, DC: U.S. Government Printing Office.

U.S. Bureau of the Census. 1992. *1990 census of population and housing, summary tape file 3A*. Washington, DC: Data User Services Division.

U.S. Bureau of the Census. 1993. *1990 census of population and housing, public use microdata samples, technical documentation*. Washington, DC: Economics and Statistics Administration.

U.S. Bureau of the Census. 1994. *County and city data book: 1994*. Washington, DC: U.S. Government Printing Office.

U.S. Bureau of the Census. 1995. *1990 census of population and housing, public use microdata samples, sample B (1%)*. Washington, DC: Data User Services Division.

U.S. Bureau of the Census. 1998. *Statistical Abstract of the United States*, 1998. Washington, DC: U.S. Government Printing Office.

Bilingual Education, the Acquisition of English, and the Retention and Loss of Spanish

Stephen Krashen
University of Southern California

According to many reports in the media, the war between English-only advocates and supporters of bilingual education is a war between rational people who think children should acquire English and irrational fanatics who think children should be prevented from learning English. Articles have proclaimed that bilingual education simply doesn't work, that children in bilingual programs do not learn English. The obvious solution, it is announced, is "immersion." So many immigrants have acquired English successfully, the argument goes, without any special help: Why should today's immigrant children be different? Moreover, it is popularly assumed that immigrants are resisting English language acquisition, and are holding tight onto their first language and culture.

These accusations are not correct. They are, instead, distortions that survive only because of the tendency of some journalists to read only what other journalists write (a phenomenon known as "pack journalism"; see Parenti 1993). When one looks at actual research published in respectable academic journals, the picture is very different. The contrast between media reports and academic reports has been confirmed by McQuillan and Tse (1996), who reported that 87% of academic publications on bilingual education between 1984 and 1994 had conclusions favorable to bilingual education. During this same time span, media reports were only 45% favorable.

I review here what academic research says, focusing on the impact of bilingual education on English language development and on the retention and loss of "heritage languages."

1. Bilingual education and English language development

Before looking at the research, it will be helpful to first discuss how educating children in their first language can help their acquisition of another language. It seems counterintuitive to some people: if we want children to acquire English, why not teach them English?

 Research on Spanish in the U.S., ed. Ana Roca, 432–444. Somerville, MA: Cascadilla Press.

But using and developing the first language can help second language development a great deal. This happens in two ways. When we use the first language to teach subject matter, we give children knowledge, and this knowledge helps make the English children hear and read more comprehensible. A limited-English proficient child who knows her math, for example, thanks to math instruction in her primary language, will understand more in an English-language medium math class than a child without a good background in math. This results in better achievement in math and more English language development.

The second way first language development helps occurs when children develop literacy in their primary language. Literacy developed in the primary language transfers to the second language. The reason literacy transfers is simple: Because we learn to read by reading, by making sense of what is on the page (Smith 1994), it is easier to learn to read in a language we understand. Once we can read in one language, we can read in general.

Subject matter knowledge and literacy, both gained through the primary language, provide indirect but powerful support for English language development and are two of the three components of quality bilingual programs. The third component is direct support for English language development, through English as a Second Language classes and sheltered subject matter teaching, classes in which intermediate level ESL students learn subject matter taught in English in a comprehensible way (Escamilla 1994, Krashen 1996).

1.1. What the research shows

A number of studies have shown that bilingual education is effective, with children in well-designed bilingual programs acquiring academic English as well and often better than children in all-English programs (Willig 1985, Cummins 1989, Krashen 1996, Greene 1997). Willig concluded that the better the experimental design, the more positive were the effects of bilingual education. My conclusion is that when programs have the three components described above (subject matter teaching in the first language, literacy development in the first language, and comprehensible input in English), they succeed especially well (Krashen 1996).

The evidence used against bilingual education is not convincing. One major problem is labeling. Several critics, for example, have claimed that "English immersion" programs in El Paso and McAllen, Texas, were superior to bilingual education (e.g. Rossell and Baker 1996). In each case, however, programs labeled "immersion" were really bilingual education, with a substantial part of the day taught in the primary language. In another study, Gersten (1985) claimed that all-English immersion was better than bilingual education. However, the sample size was very small and the duration of the study was short; also, no description of "bilingual education" was provided. For detailed discussion, see Krashen 1996.

This framework helps answer one of the most frequently stated arguments against bilingual education: how did some immigrants do well in school without it? Here is one case out of the many that have been described in the professional literature (Krashen 1996, 1999a, Ramos and Krashen 1997, Tse 1997). It is particularly interesting because it was published by U.S. English as an argument against bilingual education:

Fernando de la Pena grew up in Mexico and came to the U.S. at age nine, with no knowledge of English. He reports that he learned English quickly, and "by the end of my first school year, I was among the top students" (de la Pena 1991: 19). But de la Pena had de facto bilingual education: Had he stayed in Mexico, he would have been in the fifth grade, but when he came to the U.S., he was put in grade three! His knowledge of subject matter was superior to the other children in the class and he was already literate in Spanish, thanks to his education in Mexico. This helped make the input he heard comprehensible and provided a shortcut to English literacy. Cases like these provide strong support for the principles underlying bilingual education and are confirmed by numerous empirical studies showing that those who have a better education in their primary language excel in English language development (for a review of the research, see Krashen 1996).

1.2. Recent evidence against bilingual education

Some media reports have given the impression that California's Proposition 227 was successful, that children are doing better under all-English programs than they were under bilingual education. I discuss two such reports here.

1.2.1. Did L.A. students "take to immersion"?

Anyone glancing at the headline and opening paragraph of an article appearing in the L.A. Times on January 13, 1999 would get the impression that Proposition 227 was a clear success. The headline proclaimed: "L.A. students take to English immersion" and the first paragraph stated that "teachers are delivering promised reports that their children are learning English more quickly than anticipated."

The rest of the article had a different tone. The reporter conducted (only!) 13 interviews in the Los Angeles Unified School District, and concluded that children were picking up "verbal English at a surprising rate" but also reported that there were concerns that children were falling behind in their studies; many teachers were questioning "whether most of the youngsters have acquired the language skills necessary to comprehend math, reading or history lessons in English." One teacher noted that children were picking up "social English," not academic English, that new concepts still had to be presented in the primary language, and that "we won't have as many readers in our class as we did last year" (under bilingual education). Other teachers said that they had to "water down" core subjects.

This is just what one would expect would happen. Children will pick up conversational language with any kind of program. (No comparison was made with conversational English spoken by children in bilingual programs.) The challenge is to help them develop what Cummins (1989) calls "academic language," the language of school. There were problems in this domain, but apparently the headline writer did not read this far into the article.

1.2.2. The SAT-9 scores

Newspaper articles reported that LEP children in California in certain districts dramatically increased their scores on a standardized test, the SAT-9, after Proposition 227 was implemented. Much of the attention was focused on Oceanside, a district that claimed to have dropped bilingual education completely. But a look at the actual scores shows that not much happened that was noteworthy. In Table 1, I present SAT-9 scores for all LEP children in California for 1998 and 1999, as well as scores for Oceanside. This table reveals two facts of interest: First, Oceanside's SAT-9 scores for both years were very low, compared to state averages. Second, the "dramatic" increase was seen only in grade 2. In other grades, and in California in general, differences between 1998 and 1999 were quite small. There are other questions and concerns as well: we have no idea what kind of a bilingual education program they had, or whether it was set up in agreement with the principles outlined above. In addition, Hakuta (1999) reported that some districts that claimed growth in the SAT-9 did not have bilingual education in 1998 (e.g. Westminster and Cypress), and growth was also seen in districts that kept bilingual education (Vista, Santa Ana, Ocean View).

Table 1. SAT-9 scores for LEP children in California and Oceanside School District

	State of California: LEP		Oceanside	
grade	1998	1999	1998	1999
2	19	23	12	23
3	14	18	9	12
4	15	17	8	10
5	14	16	6	9
6	16	18	9	9
7	12	14	4	5
8	15	17	9	8

In my view, examining SAT-9 scores is an awkward way, at best, to do research. SAT-9 comparisons are very crude – one has no assurance that groups were comparable at the beginning of the year. Last year's scores do not tell us this; among LEP children, those who acquire enough English are recategorized and are no longer LEP the next year. Also, districts differ a great deal in factors that may affect test scores, including whether and how bilingual education is done. Serious research done in a scientifically respectable way (controlled studies) consistently shows that children in quality bilingual programs outperform comparison children in all-second language classes on tests of second language literacy. The results of this kind of research are much more compelling.

Unfortunately, these are not isolated examples. Every case reported so far of the alleged success of "immersion" in California is seriously flawed (Krashen 1999a, 1999b, McQuillan 1998a, Krashen and McQuillan 1999).

1.3. Improving bilingual education

Bilingual education has done well, but it can do much better. The biggest problem, in my view, is the absence of books, in both the first and second language, in the lives of students in these programs. It is now firmly established that reading for meaning, especially free voluntary reading, is the major source of our literacy competence. Those who report that they read more both read better and write better (Krashen 1993), and students who participate in free reading activities in school (e.g. sustained silent reading) show superior literacy development when compared to students who do not (Krashen 1993, Elley 1998). Free reading appears to work for first language, for second language, for children, and for teenagers, and the research has confirmed this in many different countries. Free voluntary reading can help all components of bilingual education: it is a source of comprehensible input in English, a means for developing knowledge and literacy in the first language, and, as we will see later, a way of continuing first language development.

It is also firmly established that those with greater access to books read more; while access is not sufficient to guarantee reading, it is certainly necessary (Krashen 1993, McQuillan 1998b). It is also very clear that many limited English proficient children have little access to books in any language. I present here data on Spanish-speaking children.

The average Hispanic family with limited English proficient children has about 26 books in their home (Ramirez, Yuen, Ramey, and Pasta 1991). This refers to the *total* number of books in the home, including the bible, cookbooks, and dictionaries. This is about one-sixth the U.S. average (Purves and Elley 1994). School is not helping; in fact, school is making things worse. Pucci (1994) investigated school libraries in schools with strong bilingual programs in Southern California and found that books in Spanish were very scarce. Those that were available, while often of high quality, were usually short and for younger children.

Enriching the print environment is not the only recommendation one can make in discussing improvement of bilingual education, but it is a great place to begin. If it is true that learning to read in the primary language is in fact beneficial, children need something to read. My suggestion is a massive book flood in the child's home language as well as in English, a suggestion that is relatively inexpensive to implement.

2. The retention and loss of heritage languages: Are immigrants resisting English?

2.1. Language shift: A powerful force

One of the most consistent findings in the field of sociology of language is the phenomenon of language shift: Heritage languages are usually not maintained and are rarely developed. This fact is nearly unknown to the general public, as well as to many politicians. Robert Dole, for example, felt that immigrants were resisting English, and maintained that we need "the glue of language to help hold us together" (quoted in the Los Angeles Times, October 31, 1995). Newt Gingrich also warned that "immigrants need to make a sharp break with the past" (Los Angeles Times, August 4, 1995).

Here are just a few of the many studies showing that "shift happens": Hudson-Edwards and Bills (1980) examined self-report of ability in Spanish among residents of a section of Albuquerque considered to be a strong Spanish-speaking community. As seen in Table 2, the older generation considered themselves to be better in Spanish than English, but their children rated themselves more highly in English.

Table 2. Self-report of ability in Spanish and English (% claiming "good" or "very good" ability)

Generation	Spanish ability	English ability
Junior	33% (26/80)	81% (69/81)
Senior	85% (74/87)	47% (41/88)

Junior: children of heads of households
Senior: heads of households, spouses, siblings
from Hudson-Edwards and Bills 1980

Portes and Hao (1998) compared English competence to heritage language competence with a sample of eighth and ninth graders of language minority background (n=5,266). All were native-born or had lived in the U.S. at least five years. Self-reported competence in the heritage language was much lower than self-reported competence in English, with only 16% claiming they spoke the heritage language "very well" (Table 3). Even for a group considered by some to be English-resistant, students of Mexican origin, the shift to English was obvious.

Table 3. Self-reported competence in English and in parents' language

	knows English		knows parents' language		prefers
	well	very well	well	very well	English
total	93.6	64.1	44.3	16.1	72.3
Mexican	86.1	43.7	69.1	34.9	44.8

from Portes and Hao 1998

Orellana, Ek, and Hernandez (1999) conducted conversations and interviews with Mexican-American children in bilingual schools in Los Angeles, and observed

> a gradual but marked shift over the middle childhood years toward a preference for English, and a disinclination to use Spanish. When we spoke in English at the start of the year in (a) first-grade classroom, the children called out for Spanish. When we spoke in Spanish in the focus groups with fifth graders, all but the children who arrived in the U.S. within the last year responded in English, and several complained, saying 'Aw, do we have to speak Spanish?' (Orellana, Ek, and Hernandez 1999: 125–126)

2.2. *Why does shift occur?*

The most obvious cause of shift is lack of input in the heritage language. Input/use related variables are clear predictors of heritage language competence.

Some of these input factors may be beyond the control of the subject. A number of studies have confirmed that heritage language competence is related to parental use of the heritage language (HL) (Portes and Hao 1998, Hinton 1999, Kondo 1998, Cho and Krashen 2000). Parental use, however, appears to be necessary but not sufficient. Hinton (1999) reported that in her sample, "many of the families . . . did in fact choose to use the heritage language at home, and yet still found that their children were loosing fluency" (see also Kondo 1998). Not surprisingly, studies also show that those who live in close proximity to other HL speakers maintain it longer (Demos 1988), an effect that appears to be especially predictive of HL maintenance after the first generation (Li 1982). Of course, once the speaker moves away from other HL speakers, competence may diminish (Hinton 1999). Also, those who visit the country of origin more often have higher HL competence (Demos 1988, Kondo 1988, Hinton 1999, Cho and Krashen 2000). Other input factors, such as reading and watching TV (Cho and Krashen 2000), are under the voluntary control of the HL speaker.

Less obvious are affective factors, but they appear to be quite powerful. Tse (1998a) notes that some language minority group members go through a stage in which the desire to integrate into the target culture is so strong that there is apathy toward or even rejection of the heritage culture. Tse refers to this stage as Ethnic Ambivalence or Ethnic Evasion. This stage typically occurs during childhood and adolescence, and may extend into adulthood. Those in this stage have little interest in the heritage language, and may even avoid using it.

> Maria Shao recounted how her knowledge of Chinese was a source of shame. She recalled that when she was in elementary school, 'if I had friends over, I purposely spoke English to my parents. Normally, we only spoke Chinese at home. Because of the presence of a non-Chinese, I used to purposely speak English.' (Tse 1998a: 21)

Those in this stage who did not know the heritage language had no interest in acquiring it:

> David Mura noted these feelings as a child: 'I certainly didn't want to be thought of as Japanese-American. I was American, pure and simple. I was proud I didn't know Japanese, that English was my sole tongue.' (Tse 1998a: 21)

Orellana, Ek, and Hernandez (1999: 124) provide additional examples: Their subject "Andy," an 11-year-old child of Mexican immigrants, "said he didn't like to speak Spanish, because then people thought he was from Mexico. . . ."

For some, this stage gives way to another stage, Ethnic Emergence, in which minority group members get interested in their ethnic heritage. Those in this stage, Tse points out, may be quite motivated to develop their competence in the heritage language.

Another affective factor is a reluctance to use the language because of the negative reactions of other HL speakers. Some imperfect HL speakers (often younger siblings) report that their efforts to speak the heritage language are met with correction and even ridicule by more competent HL speakers, a reaction that discourages the use of the HL, and thus results in less input and even less competence. What is often lacking are late-acquired aspects of language, aspects that typically do not interfere with communication but that indicate politeness or mark social class differences.

In Krashen (1998a) I presented some cases of "language shyness." Subjects confirmed that correction and ridicule discouraged their use of the heritage language. Here is one example:

> I began to realize as I spoke Spanish to my relatives, they would constantly correct my grammar or pronunciation. Of

> course, since I was a fairly young child the mistakes I made were 'cute' to them and they would giggle and correct me. This . . . would annoy me to no end. I wasn't trying to be 'cute'; I was trying to be serious. My relatives would say, 'You would never know that you are the daughter of an Argentine.' Comments like these along with others are what I now believe shut me off to Spanish. . . . (Krashen 1998a: 42)

Sadly, some blamed themselves for not speaking the heritage language better:

> My self-esteem reached an all-time low in college. Several of my peers made well-meaning, but harsh comments upon hearing my Spanish. This was the final blow. It was then I made the decision that I wouldn't speak unless I could speak fluently, grammatically correct, and with a proper native accent. I couldn't even feel comfortable describing myself as bilingual on my resume. I had to add 'limited proficiency' in parentheses to ease my conscience . . . I was ashamed of being Puerto Rican and living in a bilingual home and never learning Spanish . . . the only conclusion I could come to was that it was somehow my fault. . . . (Krashen 1998a: 43)

2.3. Why worry about heritage languages?

There are clear advantages to continuing heritage language development, advantages to the individual and to society. On the individual level, research clearly indicates that those who continue to develop the primary language have certain cognitive advantages over their English-only counterparts (Hakuta 1986), which may be some of the reason why they do somewhat better in school and on the job market (see Krashen 1998b for a review of relevant studies). In addition, better heritage language development means better communication with family members and with other members of the HL community (Wong-Fillmore 1991, Cho, Cho, and Tse 1997, Cho and Krashen 1998). HL development may also help promote a healthy sense of multiculturalism, an acceptance of both the majority and minority cultures, and a resolution of identity conflicts, which Tse (1998a) has termed Ethnic Identity Incorporation. Society also clearly benefits from bilingualism, in terms of business, diplomacy, and national security. Contrary to what some politicians claim, there is no evidence that bilingualism and multiculturalism are the cause of economic or social problems (Fishman 1990).

2.4. Developing the heritage language

If it is worthwhile to develop the HL, how can it be done? The usual solution is formal language classes, either those meant for non-native speakers or specially designed classes ("Spanish for Native Speakers").

Heritage language speakers are in a no-win situation in foreign language classes. If they do well, it is expected. If HL speakers do not do well in foreign language classes, the experience is especially painful. Often, classes focus on conscious learning of grammatical rules that are late acquired. Some HL speakers may not have learned or acquired these items. Non-speakers of the HL who are good at grammar sometimes outperform HL speakers on grammar tests and get higher grades in the language class, even though the non-speaker of the HL may be incapable of communicating the simplest idea in the language while the HL speaker may be quite competent in everyday conversation. Such events could be psychologically devastating, a message to the HL speaker that he or she does not know his or her own language, while an outsider does. Even though the kind of knowledge the outsider has is not genuine, the HL speaker may not understand this, given the authority of the classroom and the value the teacher places on conscious knowledge of grammar.

Some heritage language programs have been successful, particularly those that are integrated into the school day (Tse 1998b). McQuillan (1998c) describes two heritage language classes for university students (Spanish for Native Speakers) that not only succeeded, but provided a foundation for future progress. Both classes included a survey of popular literature as well as self-selected reading. Students showed clear gains in vocabulary and, more importantly, when students in one class were surveyed seven months after the class ended they were reading more in Spanish on their own than a comparison group.

McQuillan's results strongly suggest that providing a print-rich environment is also a strong investment in heritage language development. If heritage language speakers become readers in their primary language, they can continue to develop their primary language whether or not other sources of input are available. Reading is also the perfect method for heritage language speakers who do not want to risk errors in interacting with others: it is the perfect method for the shy language acquirer.

3. Conclusion

If immigrants are dropping their heritage language and embracing English, why do we need bilingual education? When immigrants acquire English informally, the version they acquire is what Cummins (1989) terms "conversational language," the language of everyday interaction. They do not necessarily acquire "academic language," the language of school. Evidence for this is the Los Angeles Times report on the "success" of 227, as reported earlier. Evidence also includes studies such as Romo and Falbo's (1996) investigation of

100 Latino high school students designated as being at risk for dropping out. Romo and Falbo (1996: 9) reported that "almost all students in our sample were comfortable speaking in English . . . yet, almost all students in our sample experienced a skills deficit in reading"; although the students were in the seventh to eleventh grades, their average reading score was sixth grade. In other words, they had acquired conversational but not academic English.

As noted earlier, good bilingual education programs aid in the development of academic English by providing literacy in the first language, which transfers to English, subject matter teaching in the primary language, which provides background knowledge that makes English input more comprehensible, as well as comprehensible subject matter teaching in English. The arguments presented in the second half of this paper indicate that an additional component would be desirable: continuing development of the heritage language.

References

Cho, Grace and Stephen Krashen. 1998. The negative consequences of heritage language loss and why we should care. In *Heritage language development*, ed. Stephen Krashen, Lucy Tse, and Jeff McQuillan, 31–39. Culver City: Language Education Associates.

Cho, Grace and Stephen Krashen. 2000. The role of voluntary factors in heritage language development: How speakers can develop the heritage language on their own. *ITL: Review of Applied Linguistics* 127–128: 127–140.

Cho, Grace, Kyung-Sook Cho, and Lucy Tse. 1997. Why ethnic minorities want to develop their heritage language: The case of Korean-Americans. *Language, Culture and Curriculum* 10.2: 106–112.

Cummins, Jim. 1989. *Empowering minority students*. Ontario, CA: California Association for Bilingual Education.

de la Pena, Fernando. 1991. *Democracy or Babel? The case for official English in the United States*. Washington, DC: U.S. English.

Demos, Vasilikie. 1988. Ethnic mother-tongue maintenance among Greek Orthodox Americans. *International Journal of the Sociology of Language* 69: 59–71.

Elley, Warwick. 1998. *Raising literacy levels in third world countries: A method that works*. Culver City, CA: Language Education Associates.

Escamilla, Kathy. 1994. The sociolinguistic environment of a bilingual school: A case study introduction. *Bilingual Research Journal* 18.1–2: 1–29.

Fishman, Joshua. 1990. Empirical explorations of two popular assumptions: Inter-polity perspective on the relationships between linguistic heterogeneity, civil strife, and per capita gross national product. In *Learning in two languages*, ed. Gary Imhoff, 209–225. New Brunswick, NJ: Transaction Publishers.

Gersten, Russell. 1985. Structured immersion for language minority students: Results of a longitudinal evaluation. *Educational Evaluation and Policy Analysis* 7: 187–196.

Greene, Jay. 1997. A meta-analysis of the Rossell and Baker review of bilingual education research. *Bilingual Research Journal* 21.2–3: 103–122.

Hakuta, Kenji. 1986. *Mirror of language*. New York: Basic Books.

Hakuta, Kenji. 1999. SAT-9 scores and California's Proposition 227. *NABE News* 22.8: 1, 6–7.

Hinton, Leanne. 1999. Involuntary language loss among immigrants: Asian-American linguistic autobiographies. Paper presented at Georgetown Round Table for Languages and Linguistics, Washington, DC, May 1999.

Hudson-Edwards, Alan and Garland Bills. 1980. Intergenerational language shift in an Albuquerque barrio. In *A festschrift for Jacob Ornstein*, ed. Edward Blansitt and Richard Teschner, 139–158. New York: Newbury House.

Kondo, Kimi. 1998. Social-psychological factors affecting language maintenance: Interviews with Shin Nisei university students in Hawaii. *Linguistics and Education* 9.4: 369–408.

Krashen, Stephen. 1993. *The power of reading*. Englewood, CO: Libraries Unlimited.

Krashen, Stephen. 1996. *Under attack: The case against bilingual education*. Culver City, CA: Language Education Associates.

Krashen, Stephen. 1998a. Heritage language development: Some practical arguments. In *Heritage language development*, ed. Stephen Krashen, Lucy Tse, and Jeff McQuillan, 3–13. Culver City: Language Education Associates.

Krashen, Stephen. 1998b. Language shyness and heritage language development. In *Heritage language development*, ed. Stephen Krashen, Lucy Tse, and Jeff McQuillan, 41–49. Culver City: Language Education Associates.

Krashen, Stephen. 1999a. *Condemned without a trial: Bogus arguments against bilingual education*. Portsmouth, NH: Heinemann Publishing Company.

Krashen, Stephen. 1999b. Bilingual education: Arguments for and (bogus) arguments against. Paper presented at the Georgetown Round Table on Languages and Linguistics, Washington, DC, May 1999.

Krashen, Stephen and Jeff McQuillan. 1999. Structured immersion falls short of expectations: An analysis of Clark (1999). *NABE News* 23.1: 13–15.

Li, Wen Lang. 1982. The language shift of Chinese-Americans. *International Journal of the Sociology of Language* 38: 109–124.

McQuillan, Jeff. 1998a. Is 99% failure a "success"? Orange Unified's English immersion program. *The Multilingual Educator* 21.7: 11.

McQuillan, Jeff. 1998b. *The literacy crisis: False claims and real solutions*. Portsmouth, NH: Heinemann Publishing Company.

McQuillan, Jeff. 1998c. The use of self-selected and free voluntary reading in heritage language programs: A review of research. In *Heritage language development*, ed. Stephen Krashen, Lucy Tse, and Jeff McQuillan, 73–87. Culver City: Language Education Associates.

McQuillan, Jeff and Lucy Tse. 1996. Does research really matter? An analysis of media opinion on bilingual education, 1984–1994. *Bilingual Research Journal* 20.1: 1–27.

Orellana, Marjorie Faulstich, Lucila Ek, and Arcelia Hernandez. 1999. Bilingual education in an immigrant community: Proposition 227 in California. *International Journal of Bilingual Education and Bilingualism* 2.2: 114–130.

Parenti, Michael. 1993. *Inventing reality: The politics of the news media*. New York: St. Martins Press.

Portes, Alejandro and Lingxin Hao. 1998. E pluribus unum: Bilingualism and loss of language in the second generation. *Sociology of Education* 71: 269–294.

Pucci, Sandra. 1994. Supporting Spanish language literacy: Latino children and free reading resources in schools. *Bilingual Research Journal* 18.1–2: 67–82.

Purves, Alan and Warwick Elley. 1994. The role of the home and student differences in reading performance. In *The IEA study of reading achievement and instruction in thirty-two school systems*, ed. Warwick Elley, 89–121. Oxford: Pergamon.

Ramirez, J. David, Sandra Yuen, Dena Ramey, and David Pasta. 1991. *Final report: Longitudinal study of an English immersion strategy and an early-exit transitional bilingual education program for language-minority children, volume I.* San Mateo, CA: Aguirre International.

Ramos, Francisco and Stephen Krashen. 1997. Success without bilingual education? Some European cases of de facto bilingual education. *CABE Newsletter* 20.6: 7,19.

Romo, Harriett and Toni Falbo. 1966. *Latino high school graduation: Defying the odds.* Austin: University of Texas Press.

Rossell, Christine and Keith Baker. 1996. The educational effectiveness of bilingual education. *Research in the Teaching of English* 30: 7–74.

Smith, Frank. 1994. *Understanding reading, fifth edition.* Hillsdale, NJ: Erlbaum.

Tse, Lucy. 1997. A bilingual helping hand. *Los Angeles Times*, December 17, 1997.

Tse, Lucy. 1998a. Ethnic identify formation and its implications for heritage language development. In *Heritage language development*, ed. Stephen Krashen, Lucy Tse, and Jeff McQuillan, 15–29. Culver City: Language Education Associates.

Tse, Lucy. 1998b. Affecting affect: The impact of heritage language programs on students attitudes. In *Heritage language development*, ed. Stephen Krashen, Lucy Tse, and Jeff McQuillan, 51–72. Culver City: Language Education Associates.

Willig, Ann. 1985. A meta-analysis of selected studies on the effectiveness of bilingual education. *Review of Educational Research* 55: 269–316.

Wong Fillmore, Lilly. 1991. When learning a second language means losing the first. *Early Childhood Research Quarterly* 6: 323–346.

Index